WHAT TH...
THE JOBB...

"If you are looking for a job...before you go to the newspapers and the help-wanted ads, sten to Bob Adams, editor of *The Metropolitan New York JobBank*."
-**Tom Brokaw**
NBC TELEVISION

"...A superior series of job hunt directories."
-**Cornell University**
Career Center
WHERE TO START

"Help on the job hunt...Anyone who is job-hunting in the New York area can find a lot ? useful ideas in a new paperback called *The Metropolitan New York JobBank*..."
-**Angela Taylor**
THE NEW YORK TIMES

"A timely book for Chicago job hunters follows books from the same publisher that were ell received in New York and Boston...A fine tool for job hunters..."
-**Clarence Petersen**
THE CHICAGO TRIBUNE

"Job hunting is never fun, but this book can ease the ordeal...[*The Los Angeles JobBank*] ill help allay fears, build confidence, and avoid wheel-spinning."
-**Robert W. Ross**
THE LOS ANGELES TIMES

"This well-researched, well-edited job hunter's aid includes most major businesses and stitutional entities in the New York metropolitan area...Highly recommended."
-**Cheryl Gregory-Pindell**
LIBRARY JOURNAL

"Here's the book for your job hunt...Trying to get a job in New York? I would commend a good look through *The Metropolitan New York JobBank*..."
-**Maxwell Norton**
NEW YORK POST

"No longer can jobseekers feel secure about finding employment just through want ads. ith the tough competition in the job market, particularly in the Boston area, they need uch more help. For this reason, *The Boston JobBank* will have a wide and appreciative dience of new graduates, job changers, and people relocating to Boston. It provides a od place to start a search for entry-level professional positions."
-**from a review in**
THE JOURNAL OF
COLLEGE PLACEMENT

What makes the JobBank Series the nation's premier line of employment guides?

With vital employment information on thousands of employers across the nation, the JobBank Series is the most comprehensive and authoritative set of career directories available today.

Each book in the series provides information on **dozens of different industries** in a given city or area, with the primary employer listings providing contact information, telephone numbers, addresses, a thumbnail sketch of the firm's business, and in many cases descriptions of the firm's typical professional job categories, the principal educational backgrounds sought, and the fringe benefits offered.

In addition to the **detailed primary employer listings**, the new 1993 JobBank books--for the first time--also give contact information, telephone numbers, and addresses for hundreds of other large employers as well as for **thousands of smaller and medium-sized employers.**

All of the reference information in the JobBank Series is as up-to-date and accurate as possible. Every year, the entire database is thoroughly researched and verified, first by mail and then by telephone. Bob Adams Inc. publishes **more local JobBank books more often** than any other publisher of career directories.

In addition, the JobBank Series features important information about the local job scene--**forecasts on which industries are the hottest, overviews of local economic trends, and even lists of regional professional associations,** so you can get your job hunt started off right.

Hundreds of discussions with job hunters show they prefer information organized geographically, because most people look for jobs in specific areas. The JobBank Series offers **twenty regional titles,** from Minneapolis to Houston, and from Washington, D.C., to San Francisco. The future employee moving to a particular area can review the local employment data not only for information on the type of industry most common to that region, but also for names of specific employers.

A condensed, but thorough, review of the entire job search process is presented in the chapter **"The Basics of Job Winning",** a feature which has received many compliments from career counselors. In addition, each JobBank directory is completed by a section on **resumes and cover letters** *The New York Times* has acclaimed as "excellent."

The JobBank Series gives job hunters the most comprehensive, most timely, and most accurate career information, organized and indexed to facilitate the job search. An entire career reference library, JobBank books are the consummate employment guides.

Published by Bob Adams, Inc.
260 Center Street, Holbrook MA 02343

The Detroit JobBank and its cover design are trademarks of Bob Adams, Inc.

Brand name products mentioned in the employer listings are proprietary property of the applicable firm, subject to trademark protection, and registered with government offices.

While the publisher has made every reasonable attempt to obtain accurate information and to verify same, occasional errors are inevitable due to the magnitude of the data base. Should you discover an error, please write to the publisher so that corrections may be made in future editions

The appearance of a listing anywhere in this book does not constitute an endorsement from the publisher.

Cover design by Peter Weiss.

ISBN:1-55850-265-3

The Detroit JobBank
4th Edition

Managing Editor
Carter Smith

Associate Editor
Steven Graber

Editorial Assistants
Kenny Brooks
Keith Moore

Top career publications from Bob Adams, Inc:

THE JOBBANK SERIES:

The Atlanta JobBank ($15.95)
The Boston JobBank ($15.95)
The Carolina JobBank ($15.95)
The Chicago JobBank ($15.95)
The Dallas-Ft. Worth JobBank ($15.95)
The Denver JobBank ($15.95)
The Detroit JobBank ($15.95)
The Florida JobBank ($15.95)
The Houston JobBank ($15.95)
The Los Angeles JobBank ($15.95)
The Minneapolis-St. Paul JobBank ($15.95)
The New York JobBank ($15.95)
The Ohio JobBank ($15.95)
The Philadelphia JobBank ($15.95)
The Phoenix JobBank ($15.95)
The San Francisco Bay Area JobBank ($15.95)
The Seattle JobBank ($15.95)
The St. Louis JobBank ($15.95)
The Tennessee JobBank ($15.95)
The Washington DC JobBank ($15.95)

The National JobBank
 (Covers 50 states: $240.00)

The JobBank Guide to Employment Services
 (Covers 50 states: $140.00)

OTHER CAREER TITLES:

America's Fastest Growing Employers ($14.95)
Careers and the College Grad ($9.95)
Careers and the Engineer ($9.95)
Careers and the MBA ($9.95)
Cold Calling Techniques that Really Work ($7.95)

Cover Letters that
 Knock'em Dead ($7.95)
The Elements of Job Hunting ($4.95)
Harvard Guide to Careers in the Mass Media ($7.95)
High Impact Telephone Networking for Job Hunters ($6.95)
How to Become Successfully Self-Employed ($9.95)
How to Get a Job in Education ($6.95)
Job Search Handbook ($6.95)
Knock 'em Dead: The Ultimate Job Seeker's Handbook ($7.95)
The Minority Career Book ($9.95)
Resume Handbook ($5.95)
Resumes that Knock 'em Dead ($7.95)
300 New Ways to Get A Better Job ($7.95)

To order these books or additional copies of this book, send check or money order (including $3.75 for postage) to:

Bob Adams, Inc., 260 Center Street, Holbrook MA 02343

Ordering by credit card?
Just call 1-800/USA-JOBS
(In Massachusetts, call 617/767-8100)

HOW TO USE THIS BOOK

A copy of *The Detroit JobBank* book is one of the most effective tools you can use in your professional job hunt. In this guide, you will find the most up-to-date information available on thousands of businesses throughout Southeastern Michigan. This book will supply you with specific addresses, phone numbers, and personnel contact information--and often much more than that--for companies which employ over 50 people.

Separate yourself from the flock of candidates who rely on help-wanted advertisements as their main job hunting strategy. The method this book offers, direct employer contact, boasts twice the success rate of any other. Exploit it.

Read and use *The Detroit JobBank* to uncover new opportunities. Here's how:

--Read the introductory economic overview in order to gain insights on what the overall trends are for the Detroit economy.

--Map out your job-seeking strategy by reading the "Basics of Job Winning" section. This section gives a condensed version of the most effective job search methods.

--Write a winning resume and learn how to sell yourself most effectively on paper, using the "Resumes and Cover Letters" section.

--Within each industry you will find detailed information on "Primary Detroit Employers." These primary listings give contact information, a telephone number, an address, a thumbnail sketch of the firm, and in many cases, descriptions of the firm's typical professional categories, the educational backgrounds sought, and the fringe benefits offered. Formulate a target list of the potential employers in your field by selecting appropriate companies from the "Primary Detroit Employers" section of each industry. Use the detailed information provided in this section to supplement your own research on the major local employers in your area--so you'll be knowledgeable about each firm before your interview. Then expand your list of target employers by consulting the "Additional large employers" and the "Small to medium sized employers" section within each industry. These listings provide contact information, telephone numbers, and addresses.

--Increase your knowledge of your field, as well as your connections within it, by using our major professional and trade associations.

Whether you are just out of college and starting your first job search, looking for a new position in your current field, or entering an entirely new sector of the job market, *The Detroit JobBank* will give you an idea of the range and diversity of employment possibilities throughout the metropolitan area. Your ultimate success will depend on how rigorously you use the information provided here. This one-of-a-kind employment guide can lead you to a company, and a job, that would otherwise have remained undiscovered. With a willingness to apply yourself, a positive attitude, and the research within these covers, you can attain your career objective.

TABLE OF CONTENTS

Introduction/11
A complete and informative economic overview designed to help you understand all of the forces shaping the Detroit job market.

The Basics of Job Winning/15
A condensed review of the basic elements of a successful job search campaign. Includes advice on developing an effective strategy, time planning, preparing for interviews, interview techniques, etc.

Resumes and Cover Letters/29
Advice on creating a strong resume. Includes sample resumes and cover letters.

Primary Detroit Employers/43
The Detroit JobBank is organized according to industry. Many listings include the address and phone number of each major firm listed, along with a description of the company's basic product lines and services, and, in most cases, a contact name and other relevant hiring information. Also includes thousands of secondary listings providing addresses, numbers, and contact names for smaller and mid-sized firms.

Professional Employment Services /325

Includes the address, phone number, description of each company's services, contact name, and a list of positions commonly filled.

Index/337

An alphabetical index of Detroit's primary employer listings only. Due to space constraints, employers that fall under the headings "Large Employers", or "Small to Medium Sized Employers" are not indexed here.

INTRODUCTION

When most people think of Detroit, they think of cars. Then they think of Japan, and how Detroit auto manufacturers are struggling against foreign competition.

For Southeastern Michigan, the past ten years have been a rough ride. Communities from Detroit to Ann Arbor -- and in dozens of smaller towns -- have been hurt by the ups and downs of the automobile industry. While **General Motors** has invested billions of dollars into the region's economy, the company has been forced to lay off thousands of workers in recent years.

In many respects, Detroit symbolizes America's struggle to remain the world's leading manufacturer. As a region, the struggling industrialized Midwest has been nicknamed "The Rustbelt", with Detroit its unofficial capital. What is happening here? Will 1993 or beyond bring any good news? If one looks solely at the auto industry to rescue the region, then the future remains shaky at best. With strained labor-management relations, the auto industry is often its own worst enemy. For long-term economic improvement, Detroit must broaden its economic base.

On a brighter note, there are signs of improvement for Southeastern Michigan, even within the auto industry. The Big Three are finally beginning to learn to "do it right" in the short-run *and* in the long-run. Many analysts believe that the quality of Detroit's automobiles is the highest it has ever been.

Higher quality has been helping the bottom line, too. After spiraling downward for several years, Detroit's 1992 car and truck production was up 10% by the fall of that year.

This boost in sales has helped other industries as well. Because most of Michigan's raw steel production comes from Southeastern Michigan, increased truck sales helped Detroit's steel output to rise 7% in 1992.

The "Big Three"

General Motors is by far both the largest auto manufacturer and by far largest company in America. Because of the company's immense size, as GM goes, so goes Detroit, and most of Michigan.

GM's troubles, of course, have been well publicized. The company lost more money than all but six companies *made* in the United States in 1991. And in 1992, GM's losses averaged $175 million a month. Even so, GM's sales were 40% higher than their nearest competitor, **Ford Motor** (based in Dearborn). **Chrysler**, in Highland Park, came in a distant third.

Stopping the Bleeding

After the losses of the past couple of years, there were bound to be some changes. The Big Three have not taken their troubles lying down. By the Fall of 1992, Chrysler (helped by their minivan and Jeep) and Ford (helped by their Taurus and Explorer) were both back in the black. Over 90% of all the domestic vans sold in 1992 were built by the Big Three.

Perhaps the best news of all is that the Ford Taurus out-sold the Honda Accord in 1992, making it the best-selling car in America. And while GM is struggling, Ford and Chrysler are filling the gaps -- gaps that were filled primarily by Japanese automakers in the past.

Broadening the Economic Base

In order to spur growth, local leaders have increased their investment in the region. The focus of groups like *The Detroit Economic Growth Corporation* and Detroit's Chamber of Commerce is to decrease dependence on the automotive industry, and to create new jobs.

A Revitalized Waterfront

Another important group has been the *Downriver Metroplex Alliance*. The DMA's aim is to revitalize the heavily industrialized region south of the city, along the Detroit River. Considerable development is taking place in the area, which only 30 years ago was a collection of warehouses, railroad tracks, and coal yards. This revival has attracted national attention. According to the *New York Times*, riverfront property is some of the hottest property in Detroit, and is in demand by developers.

The riverfront's surge of activity has been highlighted by several proposed projects: the *Harbortown Development*, a residential and shopping complex; the *River Place*, a complex of 15 historic buildings clustered on 21 acres of riverfront land; and *Brewery Park*, an office and showroom to be developed by **Stroh Company**, the Detroit brewer.

Real Estate and Construction

According to the Chamber of Commerce, Detroit's office space has been growing continuously since 1980 due to construction in the central business district. Such uncontrolled building has led to one of the highest office space vacancy rates in the nation. While empty office space is not exactly ideal, it does keep rental costs low.

In the residential real estate sector, $1.1 million had been spent in 1992 on residential construction through the fall of that year, marking a one-year increase of 12%. While money spent on nonresidential construction slipped 15% during 1991, the industry gained jobs in 1992, unlike much of the rest of the nation.

Food Products

If the region's economic base is to broaden and diversify, it will depend largely upon the food products, services, and medical sectors -- pockets of strength in Michigan's economy. **Kellogg**, the 12th largest food company in America, is headquartered in a huge, fully-automated plant in Battle Creek. The company made over $600 million in profits during 1991. As the leading producer of dry cereals in the U.S., Kellogg accounts for 40% of all cereals sold in America. **Gerber Products**, based in Fremont, is the largest producer of baby food in the world, and commands the majority of that market.

Health Care

Two Kalamazoo companies are among the most rapidly growing medical products companies in the United States. **Stryker Corporation** develops and manufactures surgical and medical products. **Upjohn Company**, a member of the *Fortune 500*, produces well-known pharmaceutical products like Motrin, Kaopectate, and Rogaine. Upjohn puts a higher percentage of their sales dollars into research than any other drug company. With 8,000 employees, the company is the largest employer in Kalamazoo.

Manufacturing and Retail

According to the Detroit Chamber of Commerce, the average hourly wages of Detroit-area manufacturing workers rose 55 cents during 1991. This wage increase was 50% higher than the nation's average. Manufacturing employment in Grand Rapids is doing well and has grown more than 14% since 1983. According to *Fortune* magazine, Grand Rapids also has favorable labor-management relations.

While the wholesale and retail sector lost 15,000 jobs in the Detroit area in 1991, retail sales jumped 7% to $24.9 million through the first nine months of 1992.

Looking Ahead

In yet another blow to Detroit's inner city, Chrysler is heading for the suburbs. The company is planning to move from Highland Park to Auburn Hills by 1995. Highland Park is an incorporated city located inside Detroit, and the heart of its economy is being ripped out by this move. While Chrysler plans to pay the small city $14 million through the year 2000, Highland Park is already skidding downwards -- unemployment stands at 31%.

General Motors continues to restructure in an attempt to stop its slide. This of course means continued layoffs. Employee relations are strained enough as it is -- the GM assembly plant in Ypsilanti recently won a court battle to remain open, a reprieve welcomed by the more than 2,500 workers with jobs there.

If GM keeps losing its market share during the next year, watch to see Ford and Chrysler continue to gain in response. However, if GM's troubles only mean increased market share for foreign manufacturers, then Detroit will have a very long road back indeed.

THE BASICS OF JOB WINNING: A CONDENSED REVIEW

The best way to obtain a better professional job is to contact the employer directly. Broad-based statistical studies by the Department of Labor show that job seekers find jobs more successfully by contacting employers directly than by using any other method.

However, given the diversity and the increasingly specialized nature of both industries and job tasks, in some situations other job seeking methods may also be successful. Three of the other most commonly used methods are: relying on personal contacts, using employment services, and following up help wanted advertisements. Many professionals have been successful in finding better jobs using one of these methods. However, the Direct Contact method boasts twice the success rate of any other method, and is used successfully by many more professionals. So unless you have specific reasons to believe that another method would work best for you, the Direct Contact method should form the foundation of your job search.

The Objective

With any business task, you must develop a strategy for meeting a goal. This is especially true when it comes to obtaining a better job. First you need to clearly define your objectives.

The first step in beginning your job search is to clearly define your objectives.

Setting your job objectives is better known as career planning (or life planning for those who wish to emphasize the importance of combining the two). Career planning has become a field of study in and of itself. Since many of our readers are probably well-entrenched in their career path, we will touch on career planning only briefly.

If you are thinking of choosing or switching careers, we particularly emphasize two things. First, choose a career where you will enjoy most of the day-to-day tasks. This sounds obvious, but most of us have at one point or another been attracted by a glamour industry or a prestigious sounding job without thinking of the most important consideration: Would we enjoy performing the everyday tasks the position entailed?

The second key consideration is that you are not merely choosing a career, but also a lifestyle. Career counselors indicate that one of the most common problems people encounter in job seeking is that they fail to consider how well-suited they are for a particular position or career. For example, some people, attracted to management consulting by good salaries, early responsibility, and high-level corporate exposure, do not adapt well to the long hours, heavy travel demands, and the constant pressure to produce. So be sure to ask yourself how you might adapt to not only the day-to-day duties and working environment that a specific position entails, but also how you might adapt to the demands of that career or industry choice as a whole.

The Strategy

Assuming that you've established your career objectives, the next step of the job search is to develop a strategy. If you don't take the time to develop a strategy and lay out a plan, you will find yourself going in circles after several weeks of random searching for opportunities that always seem just beyond your reach.

Your strategy can be thought of as having three simple elements:

1. Choosing a method of contacting employers.

2. Allocating your scarce resources. (In most job searches the key scarce resource will be time, but financial considerations will become important in some searches, too.)

3. Evaluating how the selected contact method is working and then considering adopting other methods.

We suggest you consider using the Direct Contact method exclusively. However, we realize it is human nature to avoid putting all your eggs in one basket. So if you prefer to use other methods as well, try to expend at least half your effort on the Direct Contact method, spending the rest on all of the other methods combined. Millions of other jobseekers have already proven that Direct Contact has been twice as effective in obtaining employment, so why not benefit from their effort?

With your strategy in mind, the next step is to work out the details. The most important detail is setting up a schedule. Of course, since job searches aren't something most people do regularly, it may be hard to estimate how long each step will take. Nonetheless, it is important to have a plan so that you can see yourself progressing.

When outlining your job search schedule, have a realistic time frame in mind. If you will be job searching full-time, your search will probably take at least two months. If you can only devote part-time effort, it will probably take four months.

You probably know a few people who seem to spend their whole lives searching for a better job in their spare time. Don't be one of them. Once you begin your job search on a part-time basis, give it your whole-hearted effort. If you don't feel like devoting a lot of energy to job seeking right now, then wait. Focus on enjoying your present position, performing your best on the job, and storing up energy for when you are really ready to begin your job search.

Those of you currently unemployed should remember that job hunting is tough work physically and emotionally. It is also intellectually demanding work that requires you to be at your best. So don't tire yourself out by working on your job campaign around the clock. At the same time, be sure to discipline yourself. The most logical way to manage your time while looking for a job is to keep your regular working hours.

Job hunting is intellectually demanding work that requires you to be at your best. So don't tire yourself out working around the clock.

For those of you who are still employed, job searching will be particularly tiring because it must be done in addition to your regular duties. So don't work yourself to the point where you show up to interviews looking exhausted and start to slip behind at your current job. On the other hand, don't be tempted to quit your current job! The long hours are worth it. Searching for a job while you have one puts you in a position of strength.

If you are searching full-time and have decided to choose several different contact methods, we recommend that you divide up each week allowing some time for each method. For instance, you might devote Mondays to following up newspaper ads because most of them appear in Sunday papers. Then you might devote Tuesdays, and Wednesday mornings to working and developing the personal contacts you have, in addition to trying a few employment services. Then you could devote the rest of the week to the Direct Contact method. This is just one plan that may succeed for you.

By trying several methods at once, job-searching will be more interesting, and you will be able to evaluate how promising each of the methods seems, altering your schedule accordingly. Be very careful in your evaluation, however, and don't judge the success of a particular method just by the sheer number of interviews you obtain. Positions advertised in the newspaper, for instance, are likely to generate many more interviews per opening than positions that are filled without being advertised.

If you are searching part-time and decide to try several different contact methods, we recommend that you try them sequentially. You simply won't have enough time to put a meaningful amount of effort into more than one method at once. So estimate the length of your job search, and then allocate so many weeks or months for each contact method you will use. (We suggest that you try Direct Contact first.)

If you're expected to be in your office during the business day, then you have an additional problem to deal with. How can you work interviews into the business day? And if you work in an open office, how can you even call to set up interviews? As much as possible you should keep up the effort and the appearances on your present job. So maximize your use of the lunch hour, early mornings and late afternoons for calling. If you keep trying you'll be surprised how often you will be able to reach the executive you are trying to contact during your out-of-office hours. Also you can catch people as early as 8 AM and as late as 6 PM on frequent occasions. Jot out a plan each night on how you will be using each minute of your precious lunch break.

Your inability to interview at any time other than lunch just might work to your advantage. If you can, try to set up as many interviews as possible for your lunch hour. This will go a long way to creating a relaxed rapport. (Who isn't happy when eating?) But be sure the interviews don't stray too far from the agenda on hand.

Try calling as early as 8 AM and as late as 6 PM. You'll be surprised how often you will be able to reach the executive you want during these times of the day.

Lunchtime interviews are much easier to obtain if you have substantial career experience. People with less experience will often find no alternative to taking time off for interviews. If you have to take time off, you have to take time off. But try to do this as little as possible. Try to take the whole day off in order to avoid being blatantly obvious about your job search. Try to schedule in two to three interviews for the same day. (It is very difficult to maintain an optimum level of energy at more than three interviews in one day.) Explain to the interviewer why you might have to juggle your interview schedule -- he/she should honor the respect you're showing your current employer by minimizing your days off and will probably appreciate the fact that another prospective employer is interested in you.

We want to stress that if you are searching for a job -- especially part-time -- get out there and do the necessary tasks to the best of your ability and get it over with. Don't let your job search drag on endlessly.

And remember that all schedules are meant to be broken. The purpose of a job search schedule is not to rush you to your goal but to help you map out the road ahead, and then to periodically evaluate how you're progressing.

The Direct Contact Method

Once you have scheduled your time, you are ready to begin your search in earnest. We'll limit discussion here to the Direct Contact method.

The first step in preparing for Direct Contact is to develop a check list for categorizing the types of firms for which you'd like to work. You might categorize firms by product line, size, customer-type (such as industrial or consumer), growth prospects, or, by geographical location. Your list of important criteria might be very short. If it is, good! The shorter it is, the easier it will be to locate the company that is right for you.

Consider where your skills might be in demand, the degree of competition for employment, and the employment outlook at each particular firm.

Next, try to decide at which firms you're most likely to be able to find a job. Try matching your skills with those that a specific job demands. Consider where your skills might be in demand, the degree of competition for employment, and the employment outlook at each particular firm.

Now you'll want to assemble your list of potential employers. Build up your list to at least 100 prospects. Then separate your prospect list into three groups. The first tier of around 25 firms will be your primary target group, the second tier of another 25 firms will be your secondary group, and the remaining names you can keep in reserve.

This book will help you greatly in developing your prospect list. Refer to our primary employers section. You'll notice that employer listings are arranged according to industry, beginning with "Accounting and Auditing", followed by "Advertising, Marketing, and Public Relations", and so on through to "Utilities."

If you know of a firm, but you're unsure of what industry it would be classified under, then refer to the alphabetical employer index at the rear of the book to find the page number that the firm's listing appears on.

After you form your prospect list begin work on your resume. Refer to the sample resumes included in the Resumes and Cover Letters section following this chapter in order to get ideas.

Once your resume is complete, begin researching your first batch of 25 prospective employers. You will want to determine whether you would be happy working at the firms you are researching and also get a better idea of what their employment needs might be. You also need to obtain enough information to sound highly informed about the company during phone conversations and in mail correspondence. But don't go all out on your research yet! At some of these firms you probably will not be able to arrange interviews, so save your big research effort until you start to arrange interviews. Nevertheless, you should plan to spend an average of three to four hours researching each firm. Do your research in batches to save time and energy. Use one resource at a time and find out what you can about each of the 25 firms in the batch. Start with the easiest resources to use (such as this book). Keep organized. Maintain a folder on each firm.

You should plan to spend an average of three or four hours researching each firm.

If you discover something that really disturbs you about the firm (they are about to close their only local office), or if you discover that your chances of getting a job there are practically nil (they have just instituted a hiring freeze), then cross them off your prospect list.

If possible, supplement your research efforts with contacts to individuals who know the firm well. Ideally you should make an informal contact with someone at the particular firm, but often a contact at a direct competitor, or a major supplier or customer will be able to supply you with just as much information. At the very least, try to obtain whatever printed information that the company has available, not just annual reports, but product brochures and any other printed material the firm may have to offer. The company might have printed information about career opportunities.

DEVELOPING YOUR CONTACTS

Some career counselors feel that the best route to a better job is through somebody you already know or through somebody to whom you can be introduced. The counselors recommend that you build your contact base beyond your current acquaintances by asking each one to introduce you, or refer you, to additional people in your field of interest.

The theory goes like this: You might start with 15 personal contacts, each of whom introduces you to three additional people, for a total of 45 additional contacts. Then each of these people introduces you to three additional people, which adds 135 additional contacts. Theoretically, you will soon know every person in the industry.

Of course, developing your personal contacts does not usually work quite as smoothly as the theory suggests because some people will not be able to introduce you to anyone. The further you stray from your initial contact base, the weaker your references may be. So, if you do try developing your own contacts, try to begin with as many people you know personally as you can. Dig into your personal phone book and your holiday greeting card list and locate old classmates from school. Be particularly sure to approach people who perform your personal business such as your lawyer, accountant, banker, doctor, stockbroker, and insurance agent. These people develop a very broad contact base due to the nature of their professions.

Getting The Interview

Now it is time to arrange an interview, time to make the Direct Contact. If you have read many books on job searching you may have noticed that most of these books tell you to avoid the personnel office like the plague. It is said that the personnel office never hires people, they just screen out candidates. Unfortunately, this is often the case, but there are other options available to you. If you can identify the appropriate manager with the authority to hire you, contact that person directly. This will take a lot of time in each case, and often you'll be bounced back to personnel despite your efforts. So we suggest that initially you begin your Direct Contact campaign through personnel offices. If it seems that the firms on your prospect list do little hiring through personnel, you might consider some alternative courses of action. The three obvious means of initiating Direct Contact are:

-Showing up unannounced
-Mail
-Phone calls

Cross out the first one right away. You should never show up to seek a professional position without an appointment. Even if you are somehow lucky enough to obtain an interview, you will appear so unprofessional that you will not be seriously considered.

Mail contact seems to be a good choice if you have not been in the job market for a while. You can take your time to prepare a letter, say exactly what you want, and of course include your resume. Remember that employers receive many resumes every day. Don't be surprised if you do not get a response to your inquiry, so don't spend weeks waiting for responses that may never come. If you do send a cover letter, follow it up (or precede it) with a phone call. This will increase your impact, and because of the initial research you did, will underscore both your familiarity and your interest in the firm.

Always include a cover letter with your resume even if you are not specifically asked to do so.

Another alternative is to make a "Cover Call." Your Cover Call should be just like your cover letter: concise. Your first sentence should interest the employer in you. Then try to subtly mention your familiarity with the firm. Don't be overbearing; keep your introduction to three sentences or less. Be pleasant, self-confident, and relaxed. This will greatly increase the chances of the person at the other end of the line developing the conversation. But don't press. When you are asked to follow up "with something in the mail", don't try to prolong the conversation once it has ended. Don't ask what they want to receive in the mail. Always send your resume and a highly personalized follow-up letter, reminding the addressee of the phone conversation. Always include a cover letter if you are requested to send a resume.

Unless you are in telephone sales, making smooth and relaxed cover calls will probably not come easily. Practice them on your own and then with your friends or relatives.

If you obtain an interview as a result of a telephone conversation, be sure to send a thank you note reiterating the points you made during the conversation. You will appear more professional and increase your impact.

However, unless specifically requested, don't mail your resume once an interview has been arranged. Take it with you to the interview instead.

Preparing For The Interview

Once the interview has been arranged, begin your in-depth research. You should arrive at an interview knowing the company upside down and inside out. You need to know the company's products, types of customers, subsidiaries, the parent company, principal locations, rank in the industry, sales and profit trends, type of ownership, size, current plans, and much more. By this time you have probably narrowed your job search to one industry. If you haven't then be familiar with the trends in the firm's industry, the firm's principal competitors and their relative performance, and the direction that the industry leaders are headed. Dig into every resource you can! Read the company literature, the trade press, the business press, and if the company is public, call your stockbroker (if you have one) and ask for additional information. If possible, speak to someone at the firm before the interview, or if not, speak to someone at a competing firm. The more time you spend, the better. Even if you feel extremely pressed for time, you should set aside at least 12 hours for pre-interview research.

You should arrive at an interview knowing the company upside down and inside out.

If you have been out of the job market for some time, don't be surprised if you find yourself tense during your first few interviews. It will probably happen every time you re-enter the market, not just when you seek your first job after getting out of school.

Tension is natural during an interview, but if you can be relaxed you will have an advantage. Knowing you have done a thorough research job should put you more at ease. Make a list of questions that you think might be asked in an interview. Think out your answers carefully; practice reviewing them with a friend. Tape record your responses to the problem questions. If you feel particularly unsure of your interviewing skills, arrange your first interviews at firms you are not as interested in. (But remember it is common courtesy to seem excited about the possibility of working for any firm at which you interview.) Practice again on your own after these first few interviews. Go over the difficult questions that you were asked.

DON'T BOTHER WITH MASS MAILINGS OR BARRAGES OF PHONE CALLS

Direct Contact does not mean burying every firm within a hundred miles with mail and phone calls. Mass mailings rarely work in the job hunt. This also applies to those letters that are personalized -- but dehumanized -- on an automatic typewriter. Don't waste your time or money on such a project; you will fool no one but yourself.

The worst part of sending out mass mailings or making unplanned phone calls is that you are likely to be remembered as someone with little genuine interest in the firm, who lacks sincerity, and as somebody that nobody wants to hire.

HELP WANTED ADVERTISEMENTS

Only a small fraction of professional job openings are advertised. Yet a majority of job seekers -- and a lot of people not in the job market -- spend a lot of time studying the help wanted ads. As a result, the competition for advertised openings is often very severe.

A moderate-sized Manhattan employer told us about an experience advertising in the help wanted section of a major Sunday newspaper:

It was a disaster. We had over 500 responses from this relatively small ad in just one week. We have only two phone lines in this office and one was totally knocked out. We'll never advertise for professional help again.

If you insist on following up on help wanted ads, then research a firm before you reply to an ad. Preliminary research might help to separate you from all of the other professionals responding to that ad, many of whom will only have a passing interest in the opportunity, and will give you insight about a particular firm to help you determine if it is potentially a good match. That said, your chances of obtaining a job through the want-ads are still much smaller than they are if you use the Direct Contact method.

How important is the proper dress for a job interview? Buying a complete wardrobe of Brooks Brothers pinstripes or Liz Claiborne suits, donning new wing tip shoes or pumps, and having your hair styled every morning is not enough to guarantee you a career position as an investment banker. But on the other hand, if you can't find a clean, conservative suit or a nice skirt and blouse, or won't take the time to wash your hair, then you are just wasting your time by interviewing at all.

The very beginning of the interview is the most important part because it determines the rapport for the rest of it.

Very rarely will the final selection of candidates for a job opening be determined by dress. So don't spend a fortune on a new wardrobe. But be sure that your clothes are adequate. Men applying for any professional position should wear a suit; women should either wear a dress or a suit (but not a pant suit). Your clothes should be at least as formal or slightly more formal and more conservative than the position would suggest.

Top personal grooming is more important than finding the perfect clothes for a job interview. Careful grooming indicates both a sense of thoroughness and self-confidence.

Be sure that your clothes fit well and that they are immaculate. Hair must be neat and clean. Shoes should be newly polished. Women need to avoid excessive jewelry and excessive makeup. Men should be freshly shaven, even if the interview is late in the day.

Be complete. Everyone needs a watch, a pen, and a notepad. Finally, a briefcase or a leather-bound folder (containing extra copies of your resume) will help complete the look of professionalism.

Sometimes the interviewer will be running behind schedule. Don't be upset, be sympathetic. There is often pressure to interview a lot of candidates and to quickly fill a demanding position. So be sure to come to your interview with good reading material to keep yourself occupied. This will help you to relax.

The Interview

The very beginning of the interview is the most important part because it determines the rapport for the rest of it. Those first few moments are especially crucial. Do you smile when you meet? Do you establish enough eye contact, but not too much? Do you walk into the office with a self-assured and confident stride? Do you shake hands firmly? Do you make small talk easily without being garrulous? It is human nature to judge people by that first impression, so make sure it is a good one. But most of all, try to be yourself.

SOME FAVORITE INTERVIEW QUESTIONS

Tell me about yourself...

Why did you leave your last job?

What excites you in your current job?

What are your career goals?

Where would you like to be in 5 years?

What are your greatest strengths?

What are your greatest weaknesses?

Why do you wish to work for this firm?

Where else are you seeking employment?

Why should we hire you?

Often the interviewer will begin, after the small talk, by telling you about the company, the division, the department, or perhaps, the position. Because of your detailed research, the information about the company should be repetitive for you and the interviewer would probably like nothing better than to avoid this regurgitation of the company biography. So if you can do so tactfully, indicate to the interviewer that you are very familiar with the firm. If he or she seems intent on providing you with background information, despite your hints, then acquiesce.

But be sure to remain attentive. If you can manage to generate a brief discussion of the company or the industry at this point, without being forceful, great. It will help to further build rapport, underscore your interests, and increase your impact.

Soon (if it didn't begin that way) the interviewer will begin the questions. This period of the interview falls into one of two categories (or somewhere in between): either a structured interview, where the interviewer has a prescribed set of questions to ask; or an unstructured interview, where the interviewer will ask only leading questions to get you to talk about yourself, your experiences and your goals. Try to sense as quickly as possible which direction the interviewer wishes to proceed. This will make the interviewer feel more relaxed and in control of the situation.

Many of the questions will be similar to the ones that you were expecting and have practiced. Remember to keep attuned to the interviewer and make the length of your answers appropriate to the situation. If you are really unsure as to how detailed a response the interviewer is seeking, then ask.

As the interview progresses, the interviewer will probably mention some of the most important responsibilities of the position. If applicable, draw parallels between your experience and the demands of the position as detailed by the interviewer. Describe your past experience in the same manner that you did on your resume: emphasizing results and achievements and not merely describing activities. If you listen carefully (listening is a very important part of the interviewing process) the interviewer might very well imply the skills needed for the position. Don't exaggerate. Be on the level about your abilities.

Try not to cover too much ground during the first interview. This interview is often the toughest, where many candidates are screened out. If you are interviewing for a very competitive position, you will have to make an impression that will last. Focus on a few of your greatest strengths that are relevant to the position. Develop these points carefully, state them again in other words, and then try to summarize them briefly at the end of the interview.

Often the interviewer will pause towards the end and ask if you have any questions. Particularly in a structured interview, this might be the one chance to really show your knowledge of and interest in the firm. Have a list prepared of specific questions that are of real interest to you. Let your questions subtly show your research and your knowledge of the firm's activities. It is wise to have an extensive list of questions, as several of them may be answered during the interview.

Do not turn your opportunity to ask questions into an interrogation. Avoid bringing your list of questions to the interview.

YOU'RE FIRED!!

You are not the first and will not be the last to go through this traumatic experience. Thousands of professionals are fired every week. Remember, being fired is not a reflection on you as a person. It is usually a reflection of your company's staffing needs and its perception of your recent job performance. Share the fact with your relatives and friends. Being fired is not something of which to be ashamed.

Don't start your job search with a flurry of unplanned activity. Start by choosing a strategy and working out a plan. Now is not the time for major changes in your life. If possible, remain in the same career and in the same geographical location, at least until you have been working again for a while. On the other hand, if the only industry for which you are trained is leaving, or is severely depressed in your area, then you should give prompt consideration to moving or switching careers.

Register for unemployment compensation immediately. A thorough job search could take months. After all, your employers have been contributing to unemployment insurance specifically for you ever since your first job. Don't be surprised to find other professionals collecting unemployment compensation as well. Unemployment compensation is for everybody who is between jobs.

Be prepared for the question, "Why were you fired?", during job interviews. Avoid mentioning you were fired while arranging interviews. Try especially hard not to speak negatively of your past employer and not to sound particularly worried about your status of being temporarily unemployed. But don't spend much time reflecting on why you were fired or how you might have avoided it. Learn from your mistakes and then look ahead. Think positively. And be sure to follow a careful plan during your job search.

Ask questions that you are fairly certain the interviewer can answer (remember how you feel when you cannot answer a question during an interview).

Even if you are unable to determine the salary range beforehand, do not ask about it during the first interview. You can always ask about it later. Above all, don't ask about fringe benefits until you have been offered a position. (Then be sure to get all the details.) You should be able to determine the company's policy on fringe benefits relatively easily before the interview.

Try not to be negative about anything during the interview. (Particularly any past employer or any previous job.) Be cheerful. Everyone likes to work with someone who seems to be happy.

Don't let a tough question throw you off base. If you don't know the answer to a question, say so simply -- do not apologize. Just smile. Nobody can answer every question -- particularly some of the questions that are asked in job interviews.

Before your first interview, you may be able to determine how many interviews there usually are for positions at your level. (Of course it may differ quite a bit even within the different levels of one firm.) Usually you can count on attending at least three or four interviews, although some firms, such as some of the professional partnerships, are well-known to give a minimum of six interviews for all professional positions. While you should be more relaxed as you return for subsequent interviews, the pressure will be on. The more prepared you are, the better.

Depending on what information you are able to obtain, you might want to vary your strategy quite a bit from interview to interview. For instance, if the first interview is a screening interview, then be sure a few of your strengths really stand out. On the other hand, if later interviews are primarily with people who are in a position to veto your hiring, but not to push it forward (and few people are weeded out at these stages), then you should primarily focus on building rapport as opposed to reiterating and developing your key strengths.

If it looks as though your skills and background do not match the position your interviewer was hoping to fill, ask him or her if there is another division or subsidiary that perhaps could profit from your talents.

After The Interview

Write a follow-up letter immediately after the interview, while it is still fresh in the interviewer's mind. Then, if you have not heard from the interviewer within seven days, call to stress your continued interest in the firm, and the position, and request a second interview.

A parting word of advice. Again and again during your job search you will be rejected. You will be rejected when you apply for interviews. You will be rejected after interviews. For every job you finally receive, you will have probably been rejected a multitude of times. Don't let rejections slow you down. Keep reminding yourself that the sooner you go out and get started on your job search, and get those rejections flowing in, the closer you will be to obtaining the job you want.

RESUMES AND COVER LETTERS

RESUMES/OVERVIEW

When filling a position, a recruiter will often have 100 plus applicants, but time to interview only the 5 or 10 most promising ones. So he or she will have to reject most applicants after a brief skimming of their resume.

Unless you have phoned and talked to the recruiter -- which you should do whenever you can -- you will be chosen or rejected for an interview entirely on the basis of your resume and cover letter. So your resume must be outstanding. (But remember -- a resume is no substitute for a job search campaign. YOU must seek a job. Your resume is only one tool.)

RESUME PREPARATION

One page, usually

Unless you have an unusually strong background with many years of experience and a large diversity of outstanding achievements, prepare a one page resume. Recruiters dislike long resumes.

8 1/2 x 11 Size

Recruiters often get resumes in batches of hundreds. If your resume is on small sized paper it is likely to get lost in the pile. If oversized, it is likely to get crumpled at the edges, and won't fit in their files.

Typesetting

Modern photocomposition typesetting gives you the clearest, sharpest image, a wide variety of type styles and effects such as italics, bold facing, and book-like justified margins. Typesetting is the best resume preparation process, but is also the most expensive.

Word Processing

The most flexible way to get your resume typed is on a good quality word processor. With word processing, you can make changes almost instantly because your resume will be stored on a magnetic disk and the computer will do all the re-typing automatically. A word processing service will usually offer you a variety of type styles in both regular and proportional spacing. You can have bold facing for emphasis, justified margins, and clear, sharp copies.

Typing

Household typewriters and office typewriters with nylon or other cloth ribbons are NOT good for typing the resume you will have printed. If you can't get word processing or typesetting, hire a professional who uses a high quality office typewriter with a plastic ribbon (usually called a "carbon ribbon").

Printing

Find the best quality offset printing process available. DO NOT make your copies on an office photocopier. Only the personnel office may see the resume you mail. Everyone else may see only a copy of it. Copies of copies quickly become unreadable. Some professionally maintained, extra-high-quality photocopiers are of adequate quality, if you are in a rush. But top quality offset printing is best.

Proofread your resume

Whether you typed it yourself or had it written, typed, or typeset, mistakes on resumes can be embarrassing, particularly when something obvious such as your name is misspelled. No matter how much you paid someone else to type or write or typeset your resume, YOU lose if there is a mistake. So proofread it as carefully as possible. Get a friend to help you. Read your draft aloud as your friend checks the proof copy. Then have your friend read aloud while you check. Next, read it letter by letter to check spelling and punctuation.

If you are having it typed or typeset by a resume service or a printer, and you can't bring a friend or take the time during the day to proof it, pay for it and take it home. Proof it there and bring it back later to get it corrected and printed.

RESUME FORMAT (See samples)

Basic data

Your name, phone number, and a complete address should be at the top of your resume. (If you are a university student, you should also show your home address and phone number.)

Functional Resume
(Prepared on a Word Processor and Letter-Quality Printer.)

```
                    Michelle Hughes
                 430 Miller's Crossing
                Essex Junction, VT 05452
                     802/555-9354
```

Solid background in plate making, separations, color matching, background definition, printing, mechanicals, color corrections, and supervision of personnel. A highly motivated manager and effective
communicator. Proven ability to:

* Create Commercial Graphics   * Meet Graphic Deadlines
* Produce Embossing Drawings   * Control Quality
* Color Separate   * Resolve Printing Problems
* Analyze Consumer Acceptance   * Expedite Printing Operations

Qualifications

Printing: Black and white and color. Can judge acceptability of color
reproduction by comparing it with original. Can make four or five
color corrections on all media. Have long developed ability to
restyle already reproduced four-color artwork. Can create perfect
tone for black and white match fill-ins for resume cover letters.

Customer Relations: Work with customers to assure specifications are
met and customers are satisfied. Can guide work through entire production process and strike a balance between technical printing capa-
bilities and need for customer approval.

Management: Schedule work to meet deadlines. Direct staff in production procedures. Maintain quality control from inception of project
through final approval for printing.

Specialties: Make silk screen overlays for a multitude of processes.
Velo bind, GBC bind, perfect bind. Have knowledge to prepare post-
ers, flyers, and personalized stationery.

Personnel Supervision: Foster an atmosphere that encourages highly talented artists to balance high level creativity with a maximum of production. Meet or beat production deadlines. Am continually
instructing new employees, apprentices and students in both artistry
and technical operations.

Experience

Professor of Graphic Arts, University of Vermont, Burlington, VT
(1977-present).
Assistant Production Manager, Artsign Digraphics, Burlington, VT
(1981-present) Part time.

Education

Massachusetts Conservatory of Art, PhD 1977
University of Massachusetts, B.A. 1974

Separate your education and work experience

In general, list your experience first. If you have recently graduated, list your education first, unless your experience is more important than your education. (For example, if you have just graduated from a teaching school, have some business experience and are applying for a job in business you would list your business experience first.) If you have two or more years of college, you don't need to list high schools.

Reverse chronological order

To a recruiter your last job and your latest schooling are the most important. So put the last first and list the rest going back in time.

Show dates and locations

Put the dates of your employment and education on the left of the page. Put the names of the companies you worked for and the schools you attended a few spaces to the right of the dates. Put the city and state, or the city and country where you studied or worked to the right of the page.

Avoid sentences and large blocks of type

Your resume will be scanned, not read. Short, concise phrases are much more effective than long-winded sentences. Keep everything easy to find. Avoid paragraphs longer than six lines. Never go ten or more lines in a paragraph. If you have more than six lines of information about one job or school, put it in two or more paragraphs.

RESUME CONTENT

Be factual

In many companies, inaccurate information on a resume or other application material will get you fired as soon as the inaccuracy is discovered. Protect yourself.

Be positive

You are selling your skills and accomplishments in your resume. If you achieved something, say so. Put it in the best possible light. Don't hold back or be modest, no one else will. But don't exaggerate to the point of misrepresentation.

Chronological Resume
(Prepared on a Word Processor and Laser Printer.)

WALLACE R. RECTORIAN
412 Maple Court
Seattle, WA 98404
206/555-6584

EXPERIENCE

1984-present   THE CENTER COMPANY, Seattle, WA
Systems Analyst, design systems for the manufacturing unit. Specifically, physical inventory, program specifications, studies of lease buy decisions, selection of hardware the outside contractors and inside users. Wrote On-Site Computer Terminal Operators Manual. Adapted product mix problems to the LASPSP (Logistical Alternative Product Synthesis Program).

As *Industrial Engineer* from February 1984 to February 1986, computerized system design. Evaluated manufacturing operations operator efficiency productivity index and budget allocations. Analyzed material waste and recommended solutions.

ADDITIONAL EXPERIENCE

1980-1984   *Graduate Research Assistant* at New York State Institute of Technology.

1978-1980   *Graduate Teaching Assistant* at Salem State University.

EDUCATION

1982-1984   NEW YORK STATE INSTITUTE OF TECHNOLOGY, Albany, NY
M.S. in Operations Research. GPA: 3.6. Graduate courses included Advanced Location and Queueing Theories, Forecasting, Inventory and Material Flow Systems, Linear and Nonlinear Determination Models, Engineering Economics and Integer Programming.

1980-1982   M.S. in Information and Computer Sciences. GPA: 3.8
Curriculum included Digital Computer Organization & Programming. Information Structure & Process. Mathematical Logic, Computer Systems, Logic Design and Switching Theory.

1976-1980   SALEM STATE UNIVERSITY, Salem, OR
B.A. in Mathematics. GPA: 3.6.

AFFILIATIONS

Member of the American Institute of Computer Programmers, Association for Computing Machinery and the Operations Research Society of America.

PERSONAL

Married, three dependents, able to relocate.

Be brief

Write down the important (and pertinent) things you have done, but do it in as few words as possible. The shorter your resume is, the more carefully it will be examined.

Work experience

Emphasize continued experience in a particular type of function or continued interest in a particular industry. De-emphasize irrelevant positions. Delete positions that you held for less than four months. (Unless you are a very recent college grad or still in school.)

Stress your results

Elaborate on how you contributed to your past employers. Did you increase sales, reduce costs, improve a product, implement a new program? Were you promoted?

Mention relevant skills and responsibilities

Be specific. Slant your past accomplishments toward the type of position that you hope to obtain. Example: Do you hope to supervise people? Then state how many people, performing what function, you have supervised.

Education

Keep it brief if you have more than two years of career experience. Elaborate more if you have less experience. Mention degrees received and any honors or special awards. Note individual courses or research projects that might be relevant for employers. For instance, if you are a liberal arts major, be sure to mention courses in such areas as: accounting, statistics, computer programming, or mathematics.

Job objective

Leave it out. Even if you are certain of exactly the type of job that you desire, the inclusion of a job objective might eliminate you from consideration for other positions that a recruiter feels are a better match for your qualifications.

Personal data

Keep it very brief. Two lines maximum. A one-word mention of commonly practiced activities such as golf, skiing, sailing, chess, bridge, tennis, etc., can prove to be good way to open up a conversation during an interview. Do not include your age, weight, height, etc.

Chronological Resume
(Prepared on an Office-Quality Typewriter.)

Lorraine Avakian
70 Monback Avenue
Oshkosh, WI 54901
Phone: 414/555-4629

Business Experience

1984-1991 **NATIONAL PACKAGING PRODUCTS,** Princeton, WI

1989-1991 **District Sales Manager.** Improved 28-member sales group from
a company rank in the bottom thirty percent to the top twenty percent. Complete responsibility for personnel, including recruiting,
hiring and training. Developed a comprehensive sales improvement program and advised its implementation in eight additional sales dis-
tricts.

1986-1988 **Marketing Associate.** Responsible for research, analysis, and
presentation of marketing issues related to long-term corporate
strategy. Developed marketing perspective for capital investment opportunities and acquisition candidates, which was instrumental in fi-
nalizing decisions to make two major acquisitions and to construct a
$35 million canning plant.

1984-1986 **Salesperson, Paper Division.** Responsible for a four-county
territory in central Wisconsin. Increased sales from $700,000 to
over $1,050,000 annually in a 15 month period. Developed six new ac-
counts with incremental sales potential of $800,000. Only internal
candidate selected for new marketing program.

AMERICAN PAPER PRODUCTS, INC., Oshkosh, WI
1983-1984 **Sales Trainee.** Completed the intensive six month training
program and was promoted to salesperson status. Received the President's Award for superior performance in the sales training program.

HENDUKKAR SPORTING GOODS, INC., Oshkosh, WI
1983 **Assistant Store Manager.** Supervised six employees on the evening
shift. Handled accounts receivable.

Education
1977-1982 **BELOIT COLLEGE,** Beloit, WI
Received Bachelor of Science Degree in Business Administration in
June 1982. Varsity Volleyball. Financed 50% of educational costs
through part-time and co-op program employment.

Personal Background
Able to relocate; Excellent health; Active in community activities.

SHOULD YOU HIRE A RESUME WRITER?

If you write reasonably well, there are some advantages to writing your resume yourself. To write it well, you will have to review your experience and figure out how to explain your accomplishments in clear, brief phrases. This will help you when you explain your work to interviewers.

If you write your resume, everything in it will be in your own words -- it will sound like you. It will say what you want it to say. And you will be much more familiar with the contents. If you are a good writer, know yourself well, and have a good idea of what parts of your background employers are looking for, you may be able to write your own resume better than anyone else can. If you write your resume yourself, you should have someone who can be objective (preferably not a close relative) review it with you.

When should you have your resume professionally written?

If you have difficulty writing in "resume style" (which is quite unlike normal written language), if you are unsure of which parts of your background you should emphasize, or if you think your resume would make your case better if it did not follow the standard form outlined here or in a book on resumes, then you should have it professionally written.

There are two reasons even some professional resume writers we know have had their resumes written with the help of fellow professionals. First, when they need the help of someone who can be objective about their background, and second, when they want an experienced sounding board to help focus their thoughts.

If you decide to hire a resume writer

The best way to choose a writer is by reputation -- the recommendation of a friend, a personnel director, your school placement officer or someone else knowledgeable in the field.

You should ask, "If I'm not satisfied with what you write, will you go over it with me and change it?"

You should ask, "How long has the person who will write my resume been writing resumes?"

There is no sure relation between price and quality, except that you are unlikely to get a good writer for less than $50 for an uncomplicated resume and you shouldn't have to pay more than $300 unless your experience is very extensive or complicated. There will be additional charges for printing.

Few resume services will give you a firm price over the phone, simply because some people's resumes are too complicated and take too long to do at any predetermined price. Some services will quote you a price that applies to almost all of their customers. Be sure to do some comparative shopping. Obtain a firm price before you engage their services and find out how expensive minor changes will be.

Chronological Resume
(Prepared on a Word Processor and Laser Printer.)

Melvin Winter
43 Aspen Wall Lane
Wheaton, IL 60512
312/555-6923 (home)
312/555-3000 (work)

RELATED EXPERIENCE
1982-Present GREAT LAKES PUBLISHING COMPANY, Chicago, IL
Operations Supervisor (1986-present)
in the Engineering Division of this major trade publishing house, responsible for maintaining on line computerized customer files, title files, accounts receivable, inventory and sales files.

Organize department activities, establish priorities and train personnel. Provide corporate accounting with monthly reports of sales, earned income from journals, samples, inventory levels/value and sales and tax data. Divisional sales average $3 million annually.

Senior Customer Service Representative (1984-1986)
in the Construction Division. Answered customer service inquiries regarding orders and accounts receivable, issued return and shortage credits and expedited special sales orders for direct mail and sales to trade schools.

Customer Service Representative (1982-1983)
in the International Division. Same duties as for construction division except that sales were to retail stores and universities in Europe.

1980-1982 B. DALTON, BOOKSELLER, Salt Lake City, UT
Assistant Manager of this retail branch of a major domestic book seller, maintained all paperback inventories at necessary levels, deposited receipts daily and created window displays.

EDUCATION
1976-1980 UNIVERSITY OF MAINE, Orono, ME
Awarded a degree of Bachelor of Arts in French Literature.

LANGUAGES
Fluent in French. Able to write in French, German and Spanish.

PERSONAL
Willing to travel and relocate, particularly in Europe.

References available upon request.

Chronological Resume
(Prepared on a Word Processor and Laser Printer.)

DAMIEN W. PINCKNEY

U.S. Address: Jamaican Address:
15606 Center Street   Oskarrataan Building, Room 1234
Bottineau, ND 58777   Hedonism II
701/555-9320   Negril, Jamaica
                                       809/555-6634

Experience

1984-present   HEDONISM II, Negril, Jamaica
Resident Engineer for this publicly owned resort with main offices in
Kingston. Responsibilities include:

Maintaining electrical generating and distribution equipment.

Supervising an eight-member staff in maintenance of refrigeration equipment, power and light generators, water purification plant, and general
construction machinery.

1982-1984   NEGRIL BEACH HOTEL, Negril Beach, Jamaica
Resident Engineer for a privately held resort, assigned total responsibility
for facility generating equipment.

Directed maintenance, operation and repair of diesel generating equipment.

1980-1982   Directed overhaul of turbo generating equipment in two Mid-Western localities
and assisted in overhaul of a turbo generating unit in Mexico.

1975-1980   CAPITAL CITY ELECTRIC, Washington, DC
Service Engineer for the power generation service division of this regional
power company, supervised the overhaul, maintenance and repair of large
generators and associated auxiliary equipment.

Education

1972-1975   FRANKLIN INSTITUTE, Baltimore, MD
Awarded a degree of Associate of Engineering. Concentration in Mechanical Power Engineering Technology.

Personal   Willing to travel and relocate.
Interested in sailing, scuba diving, deep sea fishing.

References available upon request.

COVER LETTERS

Always mail a cover letter with your resume. In a cover letter you can show an interest in the company that you can't show in a resume. You can point out one or two skills or accomplishments the company can put to good use.

Make it personal

The more personal you can get, the better. If someone known to the person you are writing has recommended that you contact the company, get permission to include his/her name in the letter. If you have the name of a person to send the letter to, make sure you have the name spelled correctly and address it directly to that person. Be sure to put the person's name and title on both the letter and envelope. This will ensure that your letter will get through to the proper person, even if a new person now occupies this position. But even if you are addressing it to the "Personnel Director" or the "Hiring Partner", send a letter.

Type cover letters in full. Don't try the cheap and easy ways like photocopying the body of your letter and typing in the inside address and salutation. You will give the impression that you are mailing to a multitude of companies and have no particular interest in any one. Have your letters fully typed and signed with a pen.

Phone

Precede or follow your mailing with a phone call.

Bring extra copies of your resume to the interview

If the person interviewing you doesn't have your resume, be prepared. Carry copies of your own. Even if you have already forwarded your resume, be sure to take extra copies to the interview, as someone other than the interviewer(s) might now have the first copy you sent.

General Model for a Cover Letter

Your Address
Date

Contact Person Name
Title
Company
Address

Dear Mr./Ms._____:

Immediately explain why your background makes you the best candidate
for the position that you are applying for. Keep the first paragraph
short and hard-hitting.

Detail what you could contribute to this company. Show how your
qualifications will benefit this firm. Remember to keep this letter
short; few recruiters will read a cover letter longer than half a
page.

Describe your interest in the corporation. Subtly emphasize your
knowledge about this firm (the result of your research effort) and
your familiarity with the industry. It is common courtesy to act extremely eager to work for any company that you interview.

In the closing paragraph you should specifically request an interview. Include your phone number and the hours when you can be
reached. Alternatively, you might prefer to mention that you will
follow up with a phone call (to arrange an interview at a mutually
convenient time within the next several days).

Sincerely,

(signature)

Your full name (typed)

Cover Letter

49 Chinwick Circle
Houston, TX 77031
October 5, 1993

Ms. Ruth Herman-George
V.P./Director of Personnel
Holly Rock Fire Insurance Group
444 Rolling Cloud Lane, Suite 24
Houston, TX 77035

Dear Ms. Herman-George:

I am a career-oriented individual who can successfully provide technical direction and training to pension analysts in connection with FKLE system.

My major and most recent background is directly involved in the administration of pension and profit sharing plans with TRMZ. Furthermore, my extensive experience both as a Group Pension Pre-Scale Underwriter and as a Pension Underwriter involves data processing knowledge and overall pension administration.

A prime function of mine is decision making with reference to group pension business. You specifically seek an idividual who can recommend changes and/or new procedures of plan administration and maintenance plus assistance in development of pension administration kits for use by the field force at Holly Rock. I feel that I possess the ability to fulfill your need dramatically.

I would welcome the practical opportunity to work directly with general agents and plan trustees in qualifying, revising and requalifying pension and profit sharing plans required by TRMZ. You will note in my resume my background in working with others in both an advisory and shirt-sleeve capacity.

I look forward to hearing from you.

Sincerely,

Henry Washington

ACCOUNTING AND AUDITING

Demand for accounting, auditing, and bookkeeping services is on the rise, which will result in higher industry receipts and employment. In times of recession, the accounting industry can actually benefit. Bankruptcies, for example, have more than doubled in the past decade, all of which means more business for accountants.

PLANTE AND MORAN
P.O. Box 307, Southfield MI 48037-0307. 313/352-2500. **Contact:** William J. Bufe, Personnel Director. **Description:** An area company involved in accounting, auditing, and related services. **Employees:** 500. **Common positions:** Accountant. **Educational backgrounds sought:** Accounting. **Special programs:** Internships. **Corporate headquarters:** This location.

Additional small to medium sized employers: 50-249

ACCOUNTING, AUDITING AND BOOKKEEPING
SERVICES

Carolyn Stiles Accounting
761 W Michigan Av, Jackson MI 49201-1913. 517/789-8181. Employs: 50-99.

Deloitte & Touche
101 N Main St 6th Fl, Ann Arbor MI 48104-1400. 313/769-6200. Employs: 50-99.

Ernst & Young
1mich Av Bldg/120 N Wash Ste 1, Lansing MI 48933. 517/487-5000. Employs: 50-99.

Laventhol & Horwath
3000 Prudential Town Ce, Southfield MI 48075. 313/354-6000. Employs: 50-99.

Seidman & Seidman
755 Big Beaver Rd Ste 1700, Troy MI 48084-0178. 313/362-2100. Employs: 50-99.

Bryan Management Services
24943 Ford Rd, Dearborn MI 48128-1036. 313/561-0707. Employs: 50-99.

Costerisan Maner & Ellis CPA
6105 W Saint Joseph Hwy, Lansing MI 48917-4850. 517/323-7500. Employs: 50-99.

Deloitte & Touche
200 Renaissance Ctr, Detroit MI 48243-1209. 313/396-3000. Employs: 100-249.

Control Data
20300 Civic Center Dr, Southfield MI 48076-4105. 313/351-6400. Employs: 100-249.

For more information on career opportunities in accounting and auditing:

Associations

AMERICAN ACCOUNTING ASSOCIATION
5717 Bessie Drive, Sarasota FL 34233. 813/921-7747.

AMERICAN INSTITUTE OF CERTIFIED PUBLIC
ACCOUNTANTS
1211 Avenue of the Americas, New York NY 10036. 212/575-6200.

ASSOCIATION OF GOVERNMENT
ACCOUNTANTS
2000 Mount Vernon Avenue, Alexandria VA 22301. 703/684-6931.

THE EDP AUDITORS FOUNDATION

455 Kehoe Boulevard, Suite 106, Carol Stream IL 60188. 708/682-1200.

INSTITUTE OF INTERNAL AUDITORS
P.O. Box 140099, Orlando FL 32889. 407/830-7600.

INTERNATIONAL CREDIT ASSOCIATION
Education Department, Box 419057, St. Louis MO 63141-1757. 314/991-3030.

INSTITUTE OF MANAGEMENT ACCOUNTING
10 Paragon Drive, Box 433, Montvale NJ 07645. 201/573-9000.

NATIONAL ASSOCIATION OF TAX CONSULTANTS
454 North 13th Street, San Jose CA 92112. 408/298-1458.

NATIONAL ASSOCIATION OF TAX
PRACTITIONERS
720 Association Drive, Appleton WI 54914. 414/749-1040.

NATIONAL SOCIETY OF PUBLIC ACCOUNTANTS
1010 North Fairfax Street, Alexandria VA 22314. 703/549-6400.

Directories

AICPA SURVEYS
American Institute of Certified Public Accountants, 1211 Avenue of the Americas, New York NY 10036. 212/575-6200.

ACCOUNTING FIRMS AND PRACTITIONERS
American Institute of Certified Public Accountants, 1211 Avenue of the Americas, New York NY 10036. 212/575-6200.

Magazines

ACCOUNTING NEWS
Warren, Gorham, and Lamont, Inc., 210 South Street, Boston MA 02111. 617/423-2020.

CPA JOURNAL
200 Park Avenue, New York NY 10166. 212/973-8300.

CPA LETTER
American Institute of Certified Public Accountants, 1211 Avenue of the Americas, New York NY 10036. 212/575-6200.

CORPORATE ACCOUNTING
Warren, Gorham, and Lamont, Inc., 210 South Street, Boston MA 02111. 617/423-2020.

JOURNAL OF ACCOUNTANCY
American Institute of Certified Public Accountants, 1211 Avenue of the Americas, New York NY 10036. 212/575-6200.

MANAGEMENT ACCOUNTING
Institute of Management Accounting, 10 Paragon Drive, Box 433, Montvale NJ 07645. 201/573-9000.

NATIONAL PUBLIC ACCOUNTANT
National Society of Public Accountants, 1010 North Fairfax Street, Alexandria VA 22314. 703/549-6400.

ADVERTISING, MARKETING & PUBLIC RELATIONS

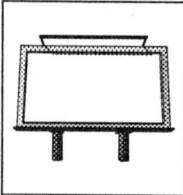

The long recession has put a continued damper on the advertising industry, as client companies put tighter reigns on their advertising budgets. Throughout the past ten years, mergers have played a major role, with advertising giants like Saatchi and Saatchi buying up competitors.

Another trend has been the emergence of in-house agencies, which means that more advertising jobs will be available in addition to the traditional advertising agencies. Overall, however, job prospects remain weak as many companies continue layoffs and job competition grows even fiercer.

CREATIVE UNIVERSAL, INC.

12220 East 13 Mile Road, Warren MI 48093. 313/574-1500. **Contact:** Don Jones, Employment Coordinator. **Description:** A training and marketing communications firm. **Employees:** 350. **Common positions:** Commercial Artist; Draftsperson; Marketing; Public Relations Worker; Reporter/Editor; Technical Writer/Editor. **Educational backgrounds sought:** Art/Design; Communications; Marketing; Instructional Technologist-HRD. **Benefits:** medical, dental, and life insurance; disability coverage; savings plan. **Corporate headquarters:** This location.

DDB NEEDHAM
2600 West Big Beaver, Suite 500, Troy MI 48084. 313/637-3000. **Contact:** Personnel Committee. **Description:** Detroit area office of the national advertising agency handling a variety of corporate accounts.

W.B. DONER AND COMPANY
25900 Northwestern Highway, Southfield MI 48075. 313/354-9700. **Contact:** Carol Cothern, Personnel Director. **Description:** A leading area advertising agency specializing in print and television campaigns. **Employees:** 400.

ANTHONY M. FRANCO INC.
400 Renaissance Center, Suite 600, Detroit MI 48243. 313/567-2300. **Contact:** Karen A. Wise, Human Resources Manager. **Description:** A Detroit public relations firm. **Common positions:** Public Relations Specialist. **Educational backgrounds sought:** Communications; Journalism. **Special programs:** Internships. **Benefits:** medical, dental, and life insurance; disability coverage; profit sharing; savings plan. **Corporate headquarters:** This location. **Other U.S. locations:** New York, NY. **Parent company:** Ross Roy Group. **Operations at this facility:** service.

GANNETT OUTDOOR ADVERTISING/MICHIGAN
88 Custer, Detroit MI 48202. 313/872-6030. **Contact:** Lorraine Whitfield, Personnel Director. **Description:** A Detroit advertising agency which specializes in the design of billboards and billposters. **Employees:** 100.

KUX MANUFACTURING COMPANY
12675 Burt Road, Detroit MI 48223. 313/255-6460. **Contact:** Dick Johnson, Director of Human Resources. **Description:** A Detroit sign and advertising display company. **Employees:** 500.

LINTAS: CAMPBELL-EWALD
30400 Van Dyke Avenue, Warren MI 48093. 313/574-3400. **Contact:** Elena Viviano, Recruiter. **Description:** An advertising agency. **Employees:** 800 people. Major clients include Chevrolet, Princess Cruises, Michigan Bell, and AC Delco. **Common positions:** Account Executive; Art Director; Marketing Specialist; Technical Writer/Editor; Copywriter; Media Planners and Buyers. **Educational backgrounds sought:** Business Administration; Liberal Arts; Marketing. **Benefits:** medical, dental, and life insurance; tuition assistance; disability coverage; savings plan; stock purchase plan. **Corporate headquarters:** This location. **Parent company:** Interpublic Group of Companies, Inc. **Operations at this facility:** administration; service. **Listed on:** New York Stock Exchange. **Other U.S. locations:** New York (Lintas: New York; Lintas: Marketing Communications New York, Inc.) and Los Angeles (Lintas: Campbell-Ewald).

NATIONWIDE ADVERTISING SERVICE INC.
300 Riverplace, Suite 5550, Detroit MI 48207. 313/568-3627. **Contact:** Regional Manager. **Description:** A Detroit advertising agency specializing in help-wanted classifieds for newspapers and other publications.

R.L. POLK & COMPANY
6400 Monroe Boulevard, Taylor MI 48180. 313/292-3200. **Contact:** Patricia Pettit, Personnel Director. **Description:** Primary function at Taylor location is to provide direct marketing services. Very small city directory staff. Marketing Services Division is Taylor Branch. **Common positions:** Computer Programmer; Systems Analyst; Sales Person; Direct Mail Marketing Worker. **Educational backgrounds sought:** Business Administration; Computer Science. **Benefits:** medical, dental, and life insurance; pension plan; tuition assistance; disability coverage; savings plan; vision plan. **Corporate headquarters:** Detroit, MI. **Operations at this facility:** divisional headquarters.

SIMONS MICHELSON ZIEVE ADVERTISING
900 Wilshire Drive, Suite 102, Troy MI 48084-1600. 313/362-4242. **Contact:** Personnel Department. **Description:** A leading Southeastern Michigan advertising agency.

STONE AND SIMONS ADVERTISING INC.
24245 Northwestern Highway, Southfield MI 48075. 313/358-4800. **Contact:** Paula Huttula, Office Manager. **Description:** A leading Southeastern Michigan advertising agency. **Common positions:** Advertising Worker; Commercial Artist; Marketing Specialist; Public Relations Specialist. **Educational backgrounds sought:** Art/Design; Marketing. **Benefits:** medical and life insurance; pension plan; profit sharing. **Corporate headquarters:** This location.

J. WALTER THOMPSON/USA INC.
1 Detroit Center, 500 Woodward, Detroit MI 48226. 313/568-3800. **Contact:** David Janson, Personnel Director. **Description:** The Detroit office of a national advertising and public relations firm.

TRANS-INDUSTRIES INC.
2637 South Adams Road, Rochester Hills MI 48309. 313/852-1990. **Contact:** Mr. Kai Kosanke, Vice President. **Description:** A firm that produces sign and advertising displays. **Employees:** 300.

YOUNG & RUBICAM
200 Renaissance Center, Suite 1000, Detroit MI 48243. 313/446-8600. **Contact:** MaryJo Harris, Human Resources Executive. **Description:** Young & Rubicam, Inc. is involved in commercial communications, advertising, public relations, direct marketing, sales promotion, specialized advertising and design, and corporate identity management. **Common positions:** Advertising Worker; Buyer; Marketing Specialist; Media Planner; Traffic Coordinator. **Educational**

backgrounds sought: Art/Design; Business Administration; Communications; Economics; Liberal Arts; Marketing. **Special programs:** Training programs and internships. **Benefits:** medical insurance; dental insurance; life insurance; tuition assistance; disability coverage; savings plan. **Corporate headquarters:** New York, NY. **Other U.S. locations:** Chicago, San Francisco.

Large employers: 250+

ADVERTISING AGENCIES

D Arcy Masius Benton & Bowles
10 W Long Lk Rd, Bloomfield MI 48304-2746. 313/258-8300. Employs: 500-999.

Ross Roy Group Inc
100 Bloomfield Hills Pkwy, Bloomfield MI 48304-2906. 313/433-6000. Employs: 1000+.

Young & Rubicam Ltd

200 Renaissance Ctr, Detroit MI 48243-1209. 313/446-8600. Employs: 250-499.

DIRECT MAIL ADVERTISING SERVICES

R L Polk & Co
1144 Brewery Park Blvd, Detroit MI 48207. 313/393-0880. Employs: 1000+.

Advo-Systems Inc
12052 Merriman Rd, Livonia MI 48150-1919. 313/425-8190. Employs: 250-499.

Small to medium sized employers: 50-249

ADVERTISING AGENCIES

Berline Group Inc
6735 Telegraph Rd, Bloomfield MI 48301-3141. 313/681-8500. Employs: 50-99.

Bozell Jacobs Kenyon & Eckhardt
30600 Telegraph Rd, Franklin MI 48025-4530. 313/645-6170. Employs: 100-249.

Kolon Bittker & Desmond
100 E Big Beaver Rd, Troy MI 48083-1204. 313/524-2500. Employs: 50-99.

Batten Barton Durstine
26261 Evergreen Rd, Southfield MI 48076-4447. 313/355-7300. Employs: 50-99.

CIMX-Fm 89 X
Detroit-Windsor Tunnel, Detroit MI 48226. 313/961-9811. Employs: 50-99.

Campbell Mithun Esty Advertising
27777 Franklin Rd, Southfield MI 48034-2337. 313/354-5400. Employs: 100-249.

Mars Advertising Co Inc
24209 Northwestern Hwy, Southfield MI 48075-2551. 313/354-9760. Employs: 50-99.

**RADIO, TELEVISION AND PUBLISHERS'
ADVERTISING REPRESENTATIVES**

WMHW 91 Rock Fm
Moore Hall Cmu, Mount Pleasant MI 48858. 517/774-7287. Employs: 50-99.

WJR Division of Capital Cities Abc Inc
21st Flr Fisher Bg, Detroit MI 48202. 313/875-4440. Employs: 50-99.

WILX-TV-Channel 10
500 American Rd, Lansing MI 48911-5978. 517/393-0110. Employs: 50-99.

WKBD TV 50

26905 W 11 Mile Rd, Southfield MI 48034-2292. 313/350-5050. Employs: 50-99.

WGPR-TV 62 & Radio
3140 E Jefferson Ave, Detroit MI 48207-4285. 313/259-8862. Employs: 50-99.

DIRECT MAIL ADVERTISING SERVICES

American Mailers
100 American Way, Detroit MI 48209-2955. 313/842-4000. Employs: 100-249.

Lason Systems
28400 Schoolcraft Rd, Livonia MI 48150-2221. 313/525-4500. Employs: 50-99.

Dun & Bradstreet
1301 W Long Lake Rd, Troy MI 48098-6328. 313/641-3800. Employs: 100-249.

Ancor Inc
31435 Stephenson Hwy, Madison Hts MI 48071-1623. 313/585-3860. Employs: 50-99.

Comprint Inc
525 Avis Dr, Ann Arbor MI 48108-9767. 313/994-1144. Employs: 50-99.

**COMMERCIAL ECONOMIC, SOCIOLOGICAL
AND EDUCATIONAL RESEARCH**

Consumer Pulse Of Detroit
725 S Adams Rd Rm 265, Birmingham MI 48009-6942. 313/540-5330. Employs: 100-249.

Schulz Leasing Co
3024 Commerce Dr, Fort Gratiot MI 48059-3819. 313/385-4432. Employs: 50-99.

PUBLIC RELATIONS SERVICES

P M H Inc
2550 S Telegraph Rd, Bloomfield MI 48302-0950. 313/456-8300. Employs: 100-249.

For more information on career opportunities in advertising, marketing, and public relations:

Associations

ACADEMY OF MARKETING SCIENCE
School of Business Administration, University of Miami, Coral Gables FL 33124. 305/284-6673.

ADVERTISING RESEARCH FOUNDATION
Three East 54th Street, 15th Floor, New York NY 10022. 212/751-5656.

AFFILIATED ADVERTISING AGENCIES INTERNATIONAL
2280 South Xanadu Way, Suite 300
Aurora CO 80014. 303/671-8551.

AMERICAN ADVERTISING FEDERATION
1400 K Street NW, Suite 1000, Washington DC 20005. 202/898-0089.

AMERICAN ASSOCIATION OF ADVERTISING AGENCIES
666 Third Avenue, New York NY 10017. 212/682-2500.

AMERICAN MARKETING ASSOCIATION
250 South Wacker Drive, Suite 200, Chicago IL 60606. 312/648-0536.

BUSINESS-PROFESSIONAL ADVERTISING ASSOCIATION
901 N. Washington Street, Suite 206, Alexandria VA 22314. 703/683-2722.

DIRECT MARKETING ASSOCIATION
1101 17th St. NW, Washington DC 20036. 202/347-1222.

INTERNATIONAL ADVERTISING ASSOCIATION
342 Madison Avenue, Suite 2000, New York NY 10173-0073. 212/557-1133.

INTERNATIONAL MARKETING INSTITUTE
314 Hammond Street, Chestnut Hill MA 02167. 617/552-8690.

LEAGUE OF ADVERTISING AGENCIES
2 South End Avenue #4C, New York NY 10280. 212/945-4991.

MARKETING RESEARCH ASSOCIATION
2189 Silas Deane Highway, Suite #5, Rocky Hill CT 06067. 203/257-4008.

PUBLIC RELATIONS SOCIETY OF AMERICA
33 Irving Place, New York NY 10003. 212/995-2230.

TELEVISION BUREAU OF ADVERTISING
477 Madison Avenue, 10th Floor, New York NY 10022-5892. 212/486-1111.

Directories

AAAA ROSTER AND ORGANIZATION

American Association of Advertising Agencies, 666 Third Avenue, New York NY 10017. 212/682-2500.

DIRECTORY OF MINORITY PUBLIC RELATIONS PROFESSIONALS
Public Relations Society of America, 33 Irving Place, New York NY 10003. 212/995-2230.

O'DWYER'S DIRECTORY OF PUBLIC RELATIONS FIRMS
J. R. O'Dwyer Co., 271 Madison Avenue, New York NY 10016. 212/679-2471.

PUBLIC RELATIONS CONSULTANTS DIRECTORY
American Business Directories, Division of American Business Lists, 5707 South 86th Circle, Omaha NE 68127. 402/331-7169.

PUBLIC RELATIONS JOURNAL REGISTER ISSUE
Public Relations Society of America, 33 Irving Place, New York NY 10003. 212/995-2230.

STANDARD DIRECTORY OF ADVERTISING AGENCIES
National Register Publishing Company, 3004 Glenview Road, Wilmette IL 60091. 708/256-6067.

Magazines

ADVERTISING AGE
Crain Communications, 740 North Rush Street, Chicago IL 60611. 312/649-5316.

ADWEEK
49 E. 21st Street, New York NY 10010. 212/529-5500.

BUSINESS MARKETING
Crain Communications, 740 Rush Street, Chicago IL 60611. 312/649-5260.

JOURNAL OF MARKETING
American Marketing Association, 250 South Wacker Drive, Suite 200, Chicago IL 60606. 312/648-0536.

THE MARKETING NEWS
American Marketing Association, 250 South Wacker Drive, Suite 200, Chicago IL 60606. 312/648-0536.

PR REPORTER
PR Publishing Co., P.O. Box 600, Exeter NH 03833. 603/778-0514.

PUBLIC RELATIONS JOURNAL
Public Relations Society of America, 33 Irving Place, New York NY 10003. 212/995-2230.

PUBLIC RELATIONS NEWS
Phillips Publishing Inc., 7811 Montrose Road, Potomac MD 20854. 301/340-2100.

AEROSPACE

Most analysts believe that while the commercial aerospace industry will continue to be hurt by the recession, the industry is well-poised for solid growth in the long run. Throughout the decade, air traffic is expected to rise rapidly, increasing the demand for new planes. That's good news for jobseekers, especially those with training in aerospace engineering.

ALLIED BENDIX/AEROSPACE DIVISION
375 North Lake Street, Boyne City MI 49712. 616/582-6526. **Contact:** Fred Kugle, Manager/Employee Relations Director. **Description:** Engaged in the manufacture of aircraft and missile systems instruments. Parent company, Allied Signal Corporation, serves a broad spectrum of industries through its more than 40 strategic businesses, which are grouped into three sectors: Aerospace; Automotive; and Engineering Materials and Gas. Allied Signal is one of the nation's largest industrial organizations, and has 115,000 employees in over 30 countries. **Common positions:** Accountant; Computer Programmer; Draftsperson; Electrical Engineer; Industrial Engineer; Mechanical Engineer; Metallurgical Engineer; Personnel & Labor Relations Specialist. **Educational backgrounds sought:** Accounting; Business Administration; Computer Science; Engineering; Finance. **Benefits:** medical insurance; dental insurance; pension plan; life insurance; tuition assistance; disability coverage; savings plan. **Corporate headquarters:** Morristown, NJ. **Operations at this facility:** manufacturing; administration. **Listed on:** New York Stock Exchange.

Large employers: 250+

AIRCRAFT ENGINES AND ENGINE PARTS

Williams International
2280 W Maple Rd, Walled Lake MI 48390. 313/624-5200. Employs: 500-999.

AIRCRAFT PARTS AND AUXILIARY EQUIPMENT

Moeller Manufacturing Co Inc/Aircraft Division
47725 E Michigan Ave, Canton MI 48188-2239. 313/482-8383. Employs: 250-499.

GUIDED MISSILES AND SPACE VEHICLES

Gulfstream Aerospace
Willow Run Airport, Ypsilanti MI 48198. 313/481-1159. Employs: 500-999.

MISC. GUIDED MISSILE AND SPACE VEHICLE PARTS AND AUXILIARY EQUIPMENT

General Motors Corp
3044 W Grand Blvd, Detroit MI 48202-3091. 313/556-5000. Employs: 1000+.

Small to medium sized employers: 50-249

AIRCRAFT

Fun Flights Inc
4995 Bunker Rd, Mason MI 48854-9731. 517/628-3750. Employs: 50-99.

Scale Aircraft

15921 W M-36, Pinckney MI 48169. 313/498-2126. Employs: 50-99.

AIRCRAFT ENGINES AND ENGINE PARTS

Aircraft Precision Products Inc
185 Industrial Pkwy, Ithaca MI 48847. 517/875-4186.
Employs: 100-249.

Aircraft Precision Products Inc
31000 Lahser Rd, Franklin MI 48025-4846. 313/645-9100.
Employs: 50-99.

Equitable Engineering Co
1840 Austin Ave, Troy MI 48083-2204. 313/689-9700.
Employs: 50-99.

Metro Machine Works Inc
11977 Harrison St, Romulus MI 48174-2717. 313/941-4571. Employs: 50-99.

Steel Tool & Engineering Co
22152 Pennsylvania Rd, Taylor MI 48180-5220. 313/285-6262. Employs: 50-99.

MISCELLANEOUS AIRCRAFT PARTS AND AUXILIARY EQUIPMENT

Cade Industries Inc
P O Box 23094, Lansing MI 48909-3094. 517/394-1333.
Employs: 100-249.

M C Aerospace Corp

118 Indianwood Rd, Lake Orion MI 48362-1509. 313/693-8311. Employs: 50-99.

Michigan Dynamics Inc
32400 Ford Rd, Garden City MI 48135-1512. 313/522-4000. Employs: 50-99.

Trigon Tool Corp
10560 Galaxie Ave, Ferndale MI 48220-2134. 313/547-7277. Employs: 50-99.

Uni Boring Co Inc
13420 Wayne Rd, Livonia MI 48150-1246. 313/425-4415.
Employs: 100-249.

MISCELLANEOUS GUIDED MISSILE AND SPACE VEHICLE PARTS AND AUXILIARY EQUIPMENT

Bachan Aerospace
1241 E 11 Mile Rd Ste R, Madison Hts MI 48071-3803.
313/548-2100. Employs: 100-249.

Jet Die
5300 Aurelius Rd, Lansing MI 48911-4116. 517/393-5110.
Employs: 100-249.

Rapp & Sons Inc
3767 11th St, Wyandotte MI 48192-6431. 313/283-1000.
Employs: 50-99.

For more information on career opportunities in aerospace:

Associations

AIR TRANSPORT ASSOCIATION OF AMERICA
1301 Pennsylvania Avenue NW, Suite 1100, Washington DC 20004. 202/626-4000.

AMERICAN INSTITUTE OF AERONAUTICS AND ASTRONAUTICS
555 West 57th Street, New York NY 10019. 212/247-6500.

AVIATION MAINTENANCE FOUNDATION
P.O. Box 2826, Redmond WA 98073. 206/828-3917.

FUTURE AVIATION PROFESSIONALS OF AMERICA
4959 Massachusetts Boulevard, Atlanta GA 30337. 404/997-8097.

NATIONAL AERONAUTIC ASSOCIATION OF USA
1815 North Fort Meyer Drive, Suite 700, Arlington VA 22209. 703/527-0226.

PROFESSIONAL AVIATION MAINTENANCE ASSOCIATION
500 NW Plaza, Suite 809, St. Ann MO 63074. 314/739-2580.

AMUSEMENT, ARTS AND RECREATION

During the past few years, the entertainment industry has been hit by a wave of major buy outs. For jobseekers, the competition is as fierce as in any other industry. The jobs are there but tough to get. Right now, the music industry is in a stronger position than the film industry.

Large employers: 250+

MOTION PICTURE AND VIDEO TAPE PRODUCTION

Sandy Corp
1500 W Big Beaver Rd, Troy MI 48084-3526. 313/649-0800. Employs: 500-999.

MISC. AMUSEMENT AND RECREATION SERVICES

Durant Cady B Natatorium
1401 E Court St, Flint MI 48503-6208. 313/762-0200.
Employs: 500-999.

Small to medium sized employers: 50-249

MOTION PICTURE AND VIDEO TAPE PRODUCTION

General Television
13225 Capitol, Detroit MI 48227. 313/548-2500. Employs: 50-99.

THEATRICAL PRODUCERS (EXCEPT MOTION PICTURE) AND MISCELLANEOUS THEATRICAL SERVICES

Eastern Michigan Univ Thtr
100 College Pl, Ypsilanti MI 48197-2624. 313/487-1221. Employs: 100-249.

BOWLING CENTERS

Great Lakes Realty Corp
28900 Schoolcraft Rd, Livonia MI 48150-2209. 313/425-4870. Employs: 100-249.

Hartfield Lanes & Lounge
3490 W 12 Mile Rd, Berkley MI 48072-1346. 313/543-9337. Employs: 50-99.

MEMBERSHIP SPORTS AND RECREATION CLUBS

Detroit Golf Club
17911 Hamilton Rd, Detroit MI 48203-1708. 313/345-4400. Employs: 50-99.

MISCELLANEOUS AMUSEMENT AND RECREATION SERVICES

Memorial Park
1026 Church St, Flint MI 48502-1051. 313/767-4121. Employs: 50-99.

Palmer Park Renaissance Alliance
900 Merrill Plaisance St, Detroit MI 48203-1776. 313/345-7270. Employs: 50-99.

ARBORETA AND BOTANICAL OR ZOOLOGICAL GARDENS

Detroit Zoological Park
8450 W 10 Mile Rd, Royal Oak MI 48067-3001. 313/398-0900. Employs: 100-249.

For more information on career opportunities in amusement, arts, and recreation:

Associations

ACTOR'S EQUITY ASSOCIATION
165 West 47th Street, New York NY 10036. 212/869-8530.

AFFILIATE ARTISTS
37 West 65th Street, 6th Floor, New York NY 10023. 212/580-2000.

AMERICAN ALLIANCE FOR THEATRE AND EDUCATION
Division of Performing Arts, Virginia Tech, Blacksburg VA 24061-0141. 703/231-5335.

AMERICAN ASSOCIATION OF MUSEUMS
1225 I Street NW, Washington DC 20005. 202/289-1818.

AMERICAN ASSOCIATION OF ZOOLOGICAL PARKS & AQUARIUMS
Oglebay Park, Wheeling WV 26003. 304/242-2160.

AMERICAN COUNCIL FOR THE ARTS
1 E. 53rd Street, New York NY 10022. 212/245-4510.

AMERICAN CRAFTS COUNCIL
72 Spring Street, New York NY 10012. 212/274-0630.

AMERICAN DANCE GUILD
33 West 21st Street, New York NY 10010. 212/627-3790.

AMERICAN FEDERATION OF MUSICIANS
1501 Broadway, Suite 600, New York NY 10036. 212/869-1330.

AMERICAN FEDERATION OF TELEVISION AND RADIO ARTISTS
260 Madison Avenue, New York NY 10016. 212/532-0800.

AMERICAN FILM INSTITUTE
John F. Kennedy Center for the Performing Arts, Washington DC 20566. 202/828-4000.

AMERICAN GUILD OF MUSICAL ARTISTS
1727 Broadway, New York NY 10019-5284. 212/265-3687.

AMERICAN MUSIC CENTER
30 West 26th Street, Suite 1001, New York NY 10010. 212/366-5260.

AMERICAN SOCIETY OF COMPOSERS, AUTHORS, AND PUBLISHERS
1 Lincoln Plaza, New York NY 10023. 212/595-3050.

AMERICAN SYMPHONY ORCHESTRA LEAGUE
777 14th Street NW, Suite 500, Washington DC 20005. 202/628-0099.

ASSOCIATION OF INDEPENDENT VIDEO AND FILMMAKERS
625 Broadway, 9th Floor, New York NY 10012. 212/473-3400.

BUSINESS COMMITTEE FOR THE ARTS
1775 Broadway, Suite 510, New York NY 10019-1942. 212/664-0600.

DANCE THEATER WORKSHOP
219 West 19th Street, New York NY 10011. 212/691-6500.

DANCE USA
777 14th Street NW, Suite 540, Washington DC 20005. 202/628-0144.

INTERNATIONAL SOCIETY OF PERFORMING ARTS ADMINISTRATORS
6065 Pickerel, Rockford MI 49341. 616/874-6200.

NATIONAL ARTISTS' EQUITY ASSOCIATION
P.O. Box 28068, Central Station, Washington DC 20038-8068. 202/628-9633.

NATIONAL DANCE ASSOCIATION
1900 Association Drive, Reston VA 22091. 703/476-3436.

NATIONAL ENDOWMENT FOR THE ARTS
1100 Pennsylvania Avenue NW, Washington DC 20506. 202/682-5400.

NATIONAL FOUNDATION FOR ADVANCEMENT IN THE ARTS
3915 Biscayne Boulevard, Miami FL 33137. 305/573-0490.

NATIONAL ORGANIZATION FOR HUMAN
SERVICE EDUCATION
Fitchburg State College, 160 Pearl Street, Fitchburg MA
01420. 508/345-2151.

NATIONAL RECREATION AND PARK
ASSOCIATION
2775 S. Quincy Street, Suite 300, Arlington VA 22206.
703/820-4940.

PROFESSIONAL ARTS MANAGEMENT
INSTITUTE
408 West 57th Street, New York NY 10019. 212/245-3850.

PRODUCERS GUILD OF AMERICA
400 S. Beverly Drive, Suite 211, Beverly Hills CA 90212.
310/557-0807.

SCREEN ACTORS GUILD
7065 Hollywood Boulevard, Hollywood CA 90028.
213/465-4600.

SOCIETY OF MOTION PICTURE AND
TELEVISION ENGINEERS
595 West Hartsdale Avenue, White Plains NY 10607.
914/761-1100.

THEATRE COMMUNICATIONS GROUP
355 Lexington Avenue, New York NY 10017. 212/697-
5230.

WOMEN'S CAUCUS FOR ART
Moore College of Art, 20th & The Parkway, Philadelphia
PA 19103. 215/854-0922.

Directories

THE ACADEMY PLAYERS DIRECTORIES
The Academy of Motion Picture Arts and Sciences, 8949
Wilshire Boulevard, Beverly Hills CA 90211. 310/247-
3000.

ARTIST'S MARKET
Writer's Digest Books, 1507 Dana Avenue, Cincinnati OH
45207. 513/531-2222.

CREATIVE BLACK BOOK
115 5th Avenue, New York NY 10003. 212/254-1330.

PLAYERS GUIDE
165 West 46th Street, New York NY 10036. 212/869-3570.

ROSS REPORTS TELEVISION
Television Index, Inc., 40-29 27th Street, Long Island City
NY 11101. 718/937-3990.

Magazines

AMERICAN ARTIST
One Astor Place, New York NY 10036. 212/764-7300.

AMERICAN CINEMATOGRAPHER
American Society of Cinematographers, 1782 North
Orange Drive, Los Angeles CA 90028. 213/876-7107.

ART BUSINESS NEWS
Myers Publishing Co., 777 Summer Street, Stamford CT
06901. 203/356-1745.

ART DIRECTION
10 East 39th Street, 6th Floor, New York NY 10016.
212/889-6500.

ARTFORUM
65 Bleecker Street, New York NY 10012. 212/475-4000.

ARTWEEK
12 S. First Street, Suite 520, San Jose CA 95113. 408/279-
2293.

AVISO
American Association of Museums, 1225 I Street NW,
Washington DC 20005. 202/289-1818.

BACK STAGE
330 West 42nd Street, New York NY 10036. 212/947-
0020.

BILLBOARD
Billboard Publications, Inc., 1515 Broadway, New York
NY 10036. 212/764-7300.

CASHBOX
157 West 57th Street, Suite 503, New York NY 10019.
212/586-2640.

CRAFTS REPORT
700 Orange Street, Wilmington DE 19801. 302/656-2209.

DRAMA-LOGUE
P.O. Box 38771, Los Angeles CA 90038. 213/464-5079.

HOLLYWOOD REPORTER
6715 Sunset Boulevard, Hollywood CA 90028. 213/464-
7411.

VARIETY
475 Park Avenue South, New York NY 10016. 212/779-
1100.

WOMEN ARTIST NEWS
300 Riverside Drive, New York NY 10025. 212/666-6990.

APPAREL AND TEXTILES

After employment gains for four straight years in the late 80's, layoffs hit the industry hard as the 90's opened. The worst appears to be over and employment should rise. New jobs will not consist of old-style production line work; automation has changed the industry's make-up, and those with technical and computer backgrounds have a distinct advantage.

ACE WIPING CLOTH COMPANY
7601 Central Avenue, Detroit MI 48210. 313/834-4000. **Contact:** Charlene Swan, Personnel Director. **Description:** Engaged in the manufacture of textile goods including cotton wiping cloths. **Employees:** 650. **Common positions:** Accountant; Administrator; Blue-Collar Worker Supervisor; Customer Service Representative; Financial Analyst; Branch Manager; Department Manager; Management Trainee; Operations/Production Manager; Personnel and Labor Relations Specialist; Purchasing Agent; Quality Control Supervisor; Sales Representative; Transportation and Traffic Specialist. **Educational backgrounds sought:** Accounting; Finance; Liberal Arts; Marketing. **Benefits:** medical, dental, and life insurance; pension plan; disability coverage; profit sharing. **Corporate headquarters:** This location. **Operations at this facility:** regional headquarters; divisional headquarters; manufacturing; administration; service; sales.

BABY BLISS, INC.
227 Spring Street, Middleville MI 49333. 616/795-3341. **Contact:** Personnel. **Description:** Manufactures infants' sleepwear and playwear.

FNT INDUSTRIES, INC.
P.O. Box 157, Menominee MI 49858. 906/863-5531. **Contact:** Personnel. **Description:** Manufactures netting as well as sports bags.

IHLING BROS. EVERARD
2022 Fulford, Kalamazoo MI 49001-4090. 616/381-1340. **Contact:** T.H. Ihling, President. **Description:** Manufactures uniforms and costumes, as well as other consumer products. Direct mail marketing. Retail distributor of office furniture and supplies.

KAUL GLOVE MANUFACTURING COMPANY
1431-41 Brooklyn Avenue, Detroit MI 48226. 313/962-7392. **Contact:** Patrick Feeney, Personnel Department. **Description:** A major Detroit manufacturer of dress and work gloves. **Employees:** 300.

SACKNER PRODUCTS INC.
2700 Patterson Avenue South East, Grand Rapids MI 49546. 616/957-9300. **Contact:** Jennifer Hall, Human Resources Director. **Description:** Manufactures non-woven felts and padding.

WOLVERINE INTERNATIONAL
1400 South Lincoln Street, Bay City MI 48708. 517/893-6541. **Contact:** Personnel Department. **Description:** Manufactures a variety of robes and sleepwear.

Additional large employers: 250+

COATED FABRICS, NOT RUBBERIZED

Ford Motor Co/Plastic Plant
151 Lafayette St, Mount Clemens MI 48043-1557.
313/466-1700. Employs: 250-499.

MEN'S AND BOY'S WORK CLOTHING

Carhartt Inc
P O Box 600, Dearborn MI 48121-0600. 313/271-8460.
Employs: 1000+.

HOUSEFURNISHINGS, EXCEPT CURTAINS AND DRAPES

No-Sag Products
560 Kirts Blvd, Troy MI 48084-4141. 313/244-9450.
Employs: 250-499.

Mitchell Corporation Of Owosso
123 N Chipman St, Owosso MI 48867-2028. 517/725-
2171. Employs: 500-999.

Additional small to medium sized employers: 50-249

BROADWOVEN FABRIC MILLS, MANMADE FIBER AND SILK

Joan Automotive Industries Inc
3221 W Big Beaver Rd Ste 216, Troy MI 48084-2800.
313/649-1550. Employs: 50-99.

Warner Fiberglass Products Inc
6916 Whites Bridge Rd, Belding MI 48809-9242. 616/794-
1130. Employs: 50-99.

LACE AND WARP KNIT FABRIC MILLS

Lace For Less
2300 Lansing Av, Jackson MI 49202-1643. 517/787-8391.
Employs: 50-99.

Lace Gallery
1105 W Ganson St, Jackson MI 49202-4208. 517/784-
4194. Employs: 50-99.

CARPETS AND RUGS

Akro Corporation
503 S Shiawassee St, Corunna MI 48817-1663. 517/743-
6179. Employs: 100-249.

Hagopian & Sons Inc
14000 W 8 Mile Rd, Oak Park MI 48237-3004. 313/399-
2323. Employs: 50-99.

MISCELLANEOUS MEN'S AND BOYS' CLOTHING

Great Lakes Sportswear Ind
11371 E State Fair St, Detroit MI 48234-3239. 313/372-
4500. Employs: 50-99.

Horizon Sportswear Inc
190 Ajax Dr, Madison Hts MI 48071-2424. 313/589-2000.
Employs: 50-99.

Reed Sportswear Manufacturing Co

1652 W Fort, Detroit MI 48216-1915. 313/963-7980.
Employs: 50-99.

DRESS AND WORK GLOVES, EXCEPT KNIT AND ALL-LEATHER

Star Glove Co
18800 Hawthorne, Detroit MI 48203-2178. 313/368-0532.
Employs: 50-99.

CURTAINS AND DRAPERIES

Drapery Boutique
45646 Port St, Plymouth MI 48170-6009. 313/455-4400.
Employs: 100-249.

Parkway Drapery Co Inc
27209 W Warren Ave, Dearborn Hts MI 48127-1804.
313/565-7100. Employs: 50-99.

TEXTILE BAGS

Fairway Products Inc
301 Arch Ave, Hillsdale MI 49242-9975. 517/439-9376.
Employs: 100-249.

CANVAS AND RELATED PRODUCTS

Detroit Cover Co
4892 Grand River Ave, Detroit MI 48208-2257. 313/898-
9202. Employs: 50-99.

The John Johnson Co
1481 14th St, Detroit MI 48216-1806. 313/496-0600.
Employs: 100-249.

PLEATING, DECORATIVE AND NOVELTY STITCHING AND TUCKING FOR THE TRADE

Stahl's Inc
20512 Stephens Dr, St Clair Shrs MI 48080-1083. 313/772-
6161. Employs: 100-249.

AUTOMOTIVE TRIMMINGS, APPAREL FINDINGS AND RELATED PRODUCTS

B C Clothing Co
500 Robbins Dr, Troy MI 48083-4514. 313/585-3160.
Employs: 50-99.

Fair Haven Inds Inc
7445 Mayer Rd, Fair Haven MI 48023. 313/725-2411.
Employs: 100-249.

Renaissance Manufacturing Co
3939 Bellevue St, Detroit MI 48207-1901. 313/924-7200.
Employs: 50-99.

Stripes Plus
3601 Milton Rd, Fort Gratiot MI 48059-4122. 313/982-0387. Employs: 50-99.

LEATHER TANNING AND FINISHING

Willow Winds
2632 Alger Rd, Port Huron MI 48060-2404. 313/987-6217.
Employs: 50-99.

Latorell Interiors
5130 Meijer Dr, Royal Oak MI 48073-1000. 313/288-3642.
Employs: 50-99.

Arrowhead Taxidermy
72 McKinley St, Pontiac MI 48342-2416. 313/332-4787.
Employs: 50-99.

Rima Sunsystems Ltd
1533 N Woodward Ave, Birmingham MI 48009-4861.
313/645-0855. Employs: 50-99.

Trinity Taxidermy
9050 Gale Rd, White Lake MI 48386-1411. 313/666-1004.
Employs: 50-99.

MISCELLANEOUS FOOTWEAR, EXCEPT RUBBER

Yaeger's Shoes
1271 N Telegraph Rd, Monroe MI 48161-3368. 313/241-5090. Employs: 100-249.

MINERAL WOOL

Guardian Fiberglass Inc
1000 E North St, Albion MI 49224-1440. 517/629-9464.
Employs: 100-249.

H L Blachford Inc
1855 Stephenson Hwy, Troy MI 48083-2150. 313/689-7800. Employs: 100-249.

For more information on career opportunities in the apparel and textile industries:

Associations

AFFILIATED DRESS MANUFACTURERS
1440 Broadway, New York NY 10018. 212/398-9797.

AMERICAN APPAREL MANUFACTURERS ASSOCIATION
2500 Wilson Boulevard, Suite 301, Arlington VA 22201.
703/524-1864.

AMERICAN CLOAK AND SUIT MANUFACTURERS ASSOCIATION
450 Seventh Avenue, New York NY 10123. 212/244-7300.

AMERICAN TEXTILE MANUFACTURERS INSTITUTE
1801 K Street NW, Suite 900, Washington DC 20006.
202/862-0500.

CLOTHING MANUFACTURERS ASSOCIATION OF THE USA
1290 Avenue of the Americas, New York NY 10104.
212/757-6664.

COUNCIL OF FASHION DESIGNERS OF AMERICA
1412 Broadway, Suite 1714, New York NY 10018.
212/302-1821.

THE FASHION GROUP
9 Rockefeller Plaza, Suite 1722, New York NY 10020.
212/247-3940.

INTERNATIONAL ASSOCIATION OF CLOTHING DESIGNERS
240 Madison Avenue, New York NY 10016. 212/685-6602.

MEN'S FASHION ASSOCIATION OF AMERICA
240 Madison Avenue, New York NY 10016. 212/683-5665.

NORTHERN TEXTILE ASSOCIATION

230 Congress Street, Boston MA 02110. 617/542-8220.

TEXTILE RESEARCH INSTITUTE
Box 625, Princeton NJ 08540. 609/924-3150.

Directories

AAMA DIRECTORY
American Apparel Manufacturers Association, 2500
Wilson Boulevard, Suite 301, Arlington VA 22201.
703/524-1864.

APPAREL TRADES BOOK
Dun & Bradstreet Inc., 1 Diamond Hill Road, Murray Hill
NJ 07974. 908/665-5000.

FAIRCHILD'S MARKET DIRECTORY OF WOMEN'S AND CHILDREN'S APPAREL
Fairchild Publications, 7 West 34th Street, New York NY
10001. 212/630-4000.

Magazines

AMERICA'S TEXTILES
Billiam Publishing, 211 Century Drive, Suite 208-A,
Greenville SC 29607. 803/242-5300.

APPAREL INDUSTRY MAGAZINE
Shore Communications Inc., 180 Allen Road NE, Suite
300-N, Atlanta GA 30328-4893. 404/252-8831.

BOBBIN
Bobbin Publications, P.O. Box 1986, 1110 Shop Road,
Columbia SC 29202. 803/771-7500.

ACCESSORIES
Business Journals, 50 Day Street, P.O. Box 5550, Norwalk
CT 06856. 203/853-6015.

WOMEN'S WEAR DAILY (WWD)
Fairchild Publications, 7 West 34th Street, New York NY
10001. 212/630-4000.

ARCHITECTURE, CONSTRUCTION AND REAL ESTATE

In the construction industry, home building is expected to stabilize, but commercial real estate construction -- especially office buildings and hotels -- will continue to decline. Home improvement, hospitals, schools, water supply buildings, and public service buildings construction should offer the best opportunities.

ABTCO INC.
3250 West Big Beaver Road, Suite 200, Troy MI 48084. 313/649-3300. **Contact:** Arlene Appleman, Personnel Department. **Description:** Engaged in the research, design, manufacture, and marketing of building products. **Corporate headquarters:** This location. **Common positions:** Accountant; Computer Programmer; Credit Manager; Customer Service Representative; Draftsperson; Chemical Engineer; Electrical Engineer; Mechanical Engineer; Financial Analyst; Forester; Industrial Designer; Management Trainee; Personnel and Labor Relations Specialist; Purchasing Agent; Quality Control Supervisor; Sales Representative; Transportation and Traffic Specialist. **Educational backgrounds sought:** Accounting; Business Administration; Computer Science; Engineering; Finance; Marketing. **Benefits:** medical insurance; dental insurance; pension plan; life insurance; tuition assistance; disability coverage; employee discounts; savings plan.

AUSTIN COMPANY
2300 Austin Parkway, Flint MI 48507. 313/232-9141. **Contact:** Pam Ruhstorfer, Personnel Director. **Description:** A real estate management company.

BARTON-MALOW COMPANY
P.O. Box 5200, Detroit MI 48235. 313/351-4500. **Contact:** Charlotte Barton, Human Resources Director. **Description:** A construction management, program management, and general contract company engaged in the construction of health facilities, commercial, and industrial buildings. **Employees:** 1,200. **Common positions:** Architect; Civil Engineer; Electrical Engineer; Industrial Engineer; Mechanical Engineer. **Educational backgrounds sought:** Engineering. **Benefits:** medical, dental, and life insurance; pension plan; tuition assistance; disability coverage; profit sharing; savings plan. **Corporate headquarters:** This location. **Operations at this facility:** regional headquarters; administration.

BRENCAL CONTRACTORS INC.
6686 East McNichols, Detroit MI 48212. 313/365-4300. **Contact:** Anne Colo, Personnel Director. **Description:** A major Detroit area contracting company which specializes in concrete and industrial construction. **Employees:** 200.

BROAD, VOGT & CONANT, INC.
195 Campbell Road, River Rouge MI 48218. 313/841-8100. **Contact:** Personnel Department. **Description:** A local area company engaged in structural steel erection and industrial engineering. **Employees:** 100.

CAMPBELL MANIX COMPANY INC.
21520 Bridge Street, Smithfield MI 48034. 313/354-5100. **Contact:** Kim Comisso, Personnel. **Description:** A major Detroit contracting company specializing in the design and construction of industrial buildings and warehouses.

JOHN CARLO INC.
21570 Hall Road, Mount Clemens MI 48046. **Contact:** Personnel Department. **Description:** A local area construction company specializing in highway and street construction. **Employees:** 400.

ROBERT CARTER CORPORATION
13305 Capital Avenue, Oak Park MI 48237. 313/547-7000. **Contact:** Wally McKenna, Controller. **Description:** A Detroit area plumbing, pipe fitting, and heating contractor. **Employees:** 300.

CHATEAU ESTATES
19500 Hall Road, Clinton Township MI 48038. 313/286-3600. **Contact:** Marie Rappaport, Personnel. **Description:** An area mobile home park and land development company. **Employees:** 100.

COLDWELL BANKER/SCHWEITZER REAL ESTATE
3555 East 14 Mile Road, Sterling Heights MI 48310. 313/268-1000. **Contact:** Manager of Administrative Office. A major Southeastern Michigan real estate firm specializing in residential properties. **Employees:** 400.

CUNNINGHAM-LIMP COMPANY
5600 Crooks Road, Suite 105, Troy MI 48098. 313/828-4000. **Contact:** Personnel Department. **Description:** A major engineering, architectural, and surveying services company

R.E. DAILEY AND COMPANY
Suite 1600, 2000 Town Center, Southfield MI 48075. 313/352-5800. **Contact:** Personnel Department. **Description:** A major area contracting company engaged in the construction of industrial buildings and warehouses. **Employees:** 200.

DENTON CONSTRUCTION COMPANY
20415 Mack Avenue, Grosse Pointe Woods MI 48236. 313/884-5530. **Contact:** Donald Riddell, Office Manager. **Description:** A major area contracting company specializing in the construction of streets and highways. **Employees:** 400.

DETROIT CONCRETE PRODUCTS
4900 McCarthy Drive, Milford MI 48381. 313/685-9590. **Contact:** Laura Iaquinto, Office Manager. **Description:** A major Detroit company engaged in highway and street construction. **Employees:** 100.

DETROIT-WAYNE JOINT BUILDING AUTHORITY
2 Woodward Avenue, 1316 City County Building, Detroit MI 48226. 313/224-5585. **Contact:** Clifford Sullivan, General Manager. **Description:** A major metropolitan Detroit company of real estate agents, brokers, and managers. **Employees:** 200.

ELLIS/NAEYAERT/GENHEIMER ASSOCIATES, INC.
3290 West Big Beaver Road, Suite 500, Troy MI 48084. 313/649-2000, ext. 126. **Contact:** Carolyn C. Palmer, Human Resources Director. **Description:** Multi-disciplined architectural/engineering firm providing comprehensive planning, design, and problem-solving services to primarily commercial, governmental, industrial, and institutional clients. **Corporate headquarters:** This location. **Common positions:** Architect; Draftsperson; Civil Engineer; Electrical Engineer; Mechanical Engineer; Facility Planner; Structural Engineer; CAD Operator. **Educational backgrounds sought:** Architecture; Engineering. **Benefits:** medical, dental and life insurance; tuition assistance; disability coverage; 401K; flextime work schedule. **Special programs:** Co-op employment. **Revenues (1992):** $8.2 million. **Employees:** 135. **Projected hires for the next 12 months:** 16.

ERICKSON & LINDSTROM
P.O. Box 418, Flint MI 48501. 313/744-4300. **Contact:** Personnel Department. **Description:** A leading area contracting company specializing in the construction of industrial buildings and warehouses. **Employees:** 100.

ALEX J. ETKIN INC.
31440 Northwestern Highway, Suite 150, Farmington Hills MI 48334. 313/737-5800. **Contact:** Personnel Director. **Description:** Engaged in the construction of commercial, educational, retail, and hospital buildings. **Employees:** 200.

GIFFELS ASSOCIATES, INC.
25200 Telegraph Road, Southfield MI 48034. 313/355-4600. **Contact:** Ed Dodge, Human Resources Administrator. **Description:** A leading area engineering, architectural, and surveying firm. **Employees:** 500. **Common positions:** Architect; Draftsperson; Civil Engineer; Electrical Engineer; Industrial Engineer; Mechanical Engineer; Industrial Designer. **Educational backgrounds sought:** Engineering; Architecture. **Benefits:** medical, dental, and

life insurance; tuition assistance; disability coverage; profit sharing; employee discounts; savings plan. **Corporate headquarters:** This location. **Operations at this facility:** administration; service; sales.

JOHN E. GREEN COMPANY
220 Victor Avenue, Highland Park MI 48203. 313/868-2400. **Contact:** Geraldine Lagos, Personnel Director. **Description:** A major area plumbing and heating contracting firm specializing in mechanical and fire protection systems. **Employees:** 200.

HARLAN ELECTRIC COMPANY
24000 Telegraph Road, Southfield MI 48034. 313/353-8660. **Contact:** Glenn Lowenstein, CEO. **Description:** A Southeastern Michigan company providing engineering, architectural, and surveying services. **Employees:** 1,900.

JAY DEE CONTRACTORS INC.
38881 Schoolcraft Road, Livonia MI 48150. 313/591-3400. **Contact:** Thomas D. Ponio, President. **Description:** Underground contractors. **Employees:** 100.

KOENIG FUEL & SUPPLY
500 East 7 Mile Road, Detroit MI 48203. 313/368-1870. **Contact:** Ron Woywood, Controller. **Description:** A leading manufacturer of ready-mix concrete. **Employees:** 100.

McNAMEE, PORTER, AND SEELEY, INC.
3131 South State Street, Ann Arbor MI 48108. 313/665-6000. **Contact:** Personnel Department. **Description:** A leading area engineering, architectural and surveying firm. **Employees:** 200.

THE MILLGARD CORPORATION
12822 Stark Road, Livonia MI 48151. 313/425-8550. **Contact:** Personnel Department. **Description:** A major area contracting firm specializing in foundations for commercial buildings. **Employees:** 300.

PRICE BROTHERS COMPANY
WARREN DIVISION
1955 East 10 Mile Road, Warren MI 48091. 313/759-6700. **Contact:** Bob Proctor, Director of Personnel. **Description:** A leading area manufacturer of concrete products. **Employees:** 100.

PULTE HOME CORPORATION
33 Bloomfield Hills Parkway, Suite 200, Bloomfield Hills MI 48304-2946. 313/644-7300. **Contact:** Personnel Department. **Description:** One of the largest independent publicly-owned homebuilding companies in the United States. Principal business is the construction and sale of moderately priced single-family homes. **Employees:** 1,500. **Listed on:** New York Stock Exchange.

REAUME AND DODDS MANAGEMENT COMPANY
1001 Woodward, Suite 1100, Detroit MI 48226. 313/965-4455. **Contact:** Ms. Gail Yaremchuk, Personnel Director. **Description:** A major Detroit real estate company specializing in the management of office buildings and apartments. **Employees:** 100.

SCHREIBER CORPORATION
2239 Fenkell, Detroit MI 48238. 313/864-4900. **Contact:** Bobby Kirk, Field Superintendent. **Description:** A major Detroit company engaged in roofing and sheet metal work. **Employees:** 200.

SELIGMAN AND ASSOCIATES
1760 South Telegraph Road, Suite 100, Bloomfield Hills MI 48302. 313/334-7300. **Contact:** Donna Sherman, Personnel Department. **Description:** An area real estate brokerage firm specializing in apartment rentals.

SMITH HINCHMAN & GRYLLS ASSOCIATES, INC.
150 West Jefferson Avenue, Suite 100, Detroit MI 48226. 313/983-3600. **Contact:** Personnel Manager. **Description:** A major Detroit-based company engaged in engineering, architecture, and planning. **Employees:** 250. **Common positions:** Architect; Civil Engineer; Electrical Engineer; Industrial Engineer; Mechanical Engineer. **Educational backgrounds sought:** Engineering; Architecture. **Benefits:** medical, dental, and life insurance; tuition assistance; disability coverage; profit sharing. **Corporate headquarters:** This location. **Parent company:** The Smith Group. **Operations at this facility:** service.

STANLEY-CARTER COMPANY
23659 Industrial Park Drive, P.O. Box 116, Farmington Hills MI 48332. 313/478-3100. **Contact:** Tammy Pushies, Personnel. **Description:** A leading area plumbing and heating company.

THOMPSON-McCULLY COMPANY
P.O. Box 787, Belleville MI 48111. 313/397-2050. **Contact:** Joan Wiggins, Personnel. **Description:** An area company engaged in both the manufacture of asphalt and the construction of streets and highways.

TOWNSEND AND BOTTUM INC.
2245 South State Street, Ann Arbor MI 48104. 313/761-3440. **Contact:** Barbara Woolcott, Personnel Department. **Description:** A leading area contracting company involved in heavy construction. **Employees:** 2,500.

TRAYCO INC.
P.O. Box 398, Lapeer MI 48446. 313/664-8501. **Contact:** Anne Ventimaglio-Esser, Human Resource Manager. **Description:** A leading area manufacturer of prefabricated wooden buildings. **Employees:** 100. **Common positions:** Blue-Collar Worker Supervisor; Draftsperson; Mechanical Engineer; Industrial Manager; General Manager; Operations/Production Manager; Personnel and Labor Relations Specialist; Purchasing Agent; Quality Control Supervisor; Sales

Representative. **Educational backgrounds sought:** Business Administration; Engineering; Marketing. **Special programs:** Training programs and internships. **Benefits:** medical, dental, and life insurance; pension plan; disability coverage; profit sharing; employee discounts; savings plan. **Corporate headquarters:** This location. **Parent company:** Masco Corporation. **Operations at this facility:** manufacturing; sales.

Additional large employers: 250+

GENERAL CONTRACTORS - SINGLE FAMILY

S P D D Construction
4660 S Hagadorn Rd Ste 660, East Lansing MI 48823-5371. 517/351-2480. Employs: 250-499.

Rose Edward & Sons
23999 W 10 Mile Rd, Southfield MI 48034-3150. 313/352-0952. Employs: 250-499.

GENERAL CONTRACTORS - NONRESIDENTIAL

The Smith Group Inc
150 W Jefferson, Detroit MI 48226-4429. 313/983-3900. Employs: 250-499.

PLUMBING, HEATING AND AIR CONDITIONING

Glanz & Killian Co
6470 Williamson St, Dearborn MI 48126-2165. 313/584-4700. Employs: 250-499.

ELECTRICAL WORK

Motor City Electric
8140 Walker St, Detroit MI 48202. 313/923-3100. Employs: 500-999.

TERRAZO, TILE, MARBLE AND MOSAIC WORK

New York Carpet World
23840 W 8 Mile Rd, Southfield MI 48034-4237. 313/353-0160. Employs: 250-499.

ROOFING, SIDING AND SHEET METAL WORK

Custom Remodeling Inc
2380 W 11 Mile Rd, Berkley MI 48072-3003. 313/398-5656. Employs: 250-499.

MISC. INSTALLATION OR ERECTION OF BUILDING EQUIPMENT

Commercial Contracting Corp
1743 Maplelawn Dr, Troy MI 48084-4603. 313/643-7600. Employs: 500-999.

READY-MIXED CONCRETE

Holnam Inc
6211 N Ann Arbor Rd Box 122, Dundee MI 48131-9761. 313/529-2411. Employs: 1000+.

BRICK, STONE AND RELATED CONSTRUCTION MATERIALS

Lafarge Corp Great Lakes
4000 Town Ctr, Southfield MI 48075-1410. 313/354-4672. Employs: 50-99.

ROOFING, SIDING AND INSULATION MATERIALS

Cadillac Glass Co Inc
11801 Evernor Hwy, Detroit MI 48214. 313/821-7200. Employs: 50-99.

MISCELLANEOUS CONSTRUCTION MATERIALS

Abitibi Price Corp Building Prod
3250 W Big Beaver Rd Ste 200, Troy MI 48084-2982. 313/649-3300. Employs: 100-249.

Marshall E Campbell Co Inc
2975 Lapeer Rd, Port Huron MI 48060-2558. 313/985-7106. Employs: 50-99.

Star Steel & Building Supply
3855 E Outer Dr, Detroit MI 48234-2936. 313/893-7000. Employs: 100-249.

Asbestos Management Inc-AMI
36700 S Huron Rd, New Boston MI 48164-9513. 313/961-6135. Employs: 100-249.

MORTGAGE BANKERS AND LOAN CORRESPONDENTS

Firemens Fund Mortgage
27555 Farmington Rd, Farmington MI 48334. 313/661-7000. Employs: 500-999.

OPERATORS OF NONRESIDENTIAL BUILDINGS

The Taubman Company Inc
200 E Long Lake Rd Box 200, Bloomfield MI 48303-0200. 313/258-6800. Employs: 1000+.

Albert Kahn Building
7430 2nd Ave, Detroit MI 48202-2739. 313/874-4444. Employs: 250-499.

OPERATORS OF APARTMENT BUILDINGS

Days Hotel Southfield Conevention Center
17017 W 9 Mile Rd, Southfield MI 48075-4501. 313/557-4800. Employs: 250-499.

P M One Ltd
5215 Jolly Cedar Ct, Lansing MI 48911-3747. 517/887-0940. Employs: 250-499.

REAL ESTATE AGENTS AND MANAGERS

Mid America Management Corp
5242 Exchange Dr, Flint MI 48507-2934. 313/230-0720. Employs: 250-499.

Thomson-Brown Realtors
32823 W 12 Mile Rd, Farmington MI 48334-3341. 313/6420703. Employs: 250-499.

AUTOMOBILES AND OTHER MOTOR VEHICLES

Ford Motor Co
235 E Main St, Northville MI 48167-1621. 313/349-0550. Employs: 50-99.

MOTOR VEHICLE SUPPLIES AND NEW PARTS

Allied Accessories
1551 E Lincoln Av, Madison Heights MI 48071-4173.
313/546-2970. Employs: 100-249.

Merrill Engineering Lab
2025 Cheltingham Blvd, Lansing MI 48917-5150. 517/323-
3030. Employs: 50-99.

Nagle Industries Inc
901 W Maple Rd, Clawson MI 48017-1005. 313/280-0333.
Employs: 100-249.

Nippondenso Sales Inc
24777 Denso Dr Box 5133, Southfield MI 48086-5133.
313/352-4440. Employs: 50-99.

Automotive Rep Parts Co Inc
3540 Vinewood St, Detroit MI 48208-2363. 313/897-2990.
Employs: 50-99.

Uni-Bond Brake Inc
1350 Jarvis St, Ferndale MI 48220-2011. 313/547-3870.
Employs: 50-99.

U S Auto Radiator Manufacturing Corp
221 Victor St, Detroit MI 48203-3131. 313/868-0800.
Employs: 100-249.

Cook Automotive Equipment
329 N Lincoln St, Charlotte MI 48813-1330. 313/589-
7815. Employs: 50-99.

Cook Automotive Equip Sales & Svc
426 Sumpter St, Charlotte MI 48813-1120. 517/543-2637.
Employs: 50-99.

Universal Interiors
2300 Legend Woods Dr, Grand Ledge MI 48837-8933.
517/627-3717. Employs: 50-99.

Additional small to medium sized employers: 50-249

GENERAL CONTRACTORS-SINGLE-FAMILY HOUSES

Bond Bilt Construction Co
1940 Northwood Dr, Troy MI 48084-5523. 313/355-5800.
Employs: 50-99.

C J Rogers Inc
G3328 Torrey Rd, Flint MI 48507. 313/767-6060.
Employs: 50-99.

Gator Construction & Design
8100 Radcliffe St, Detroit MI 48210-1814. 313/897-7200.
Employs: 50-99.

Granger Construction Co
6267 Aurelius Rd, Lansing MI 48911-4211. 517/393-1670.
Employs: 100-249.

Holloway Construction Co
29250 S Wixom Rd, Wixom MI 48393-3422. 313/349-
4943. Employs: 100-249.

L & L Construction Co
4195 Willoughby Rd, Holt MI 48842-9743. 517/694-9979.
Employs: 50-99.

Lerner-Linden Inc
28025 Samuel Linden Ct, Novi MI 48377-2431. 313/349-
7800. Employs: 50-99.

Marsh Construction Co
4198 Marsh Trail, Brighton MI 48116. 313/229-9660.
Employs: 50-99.

Pulte Home Corporation
315 S Woodward Ave Ste 110, Royal Oak MI 48067-2488.
313/644-7300. Employs: 50-99.

Shmina Construction Inc
13000 Newburgh Rd, Livonia MI 48150-1093. 313/464-
1600. Employs: 100-249.

Sorensen Gross Constrctn Co
3407 Torrey Rd, Flint MI 48507-3253. 313/767-4821.
Employs: 100-249.

Michigan Deck Builders
464 Joslyn Rd, Lake Orion MI 48362-2223. 313/693-2020.
Employs: 50-99.

GENERAL CONTRACTORS-RESIDENTIAL BUILDINGS, OTHER THAN SINGLE-FAMILY

Amurcon Corporation
26555 Evergreen, Southfield MI 48076-4206. 313/352-
0202. Employs: 100-249.

Burn Hill Country Club
16174 Andover Dr, Fraser MI 48026. 313/791-6285.
Employs: 50-99.

O'Neal Construction Inc
525 W William, Ann Arbor MI 48103-4943. 313/769-0770.
Employs: 50-99.

GENERAL CONTRACTORS-INDUSTRIAL BUILDINGS AND WAREHOUSES

Walbridge Aldinger Co In
35000 Industrial Rd, Livonia MI 48150-1239. 313/591-
6000. Employs: 100-249.

GENERAL CONTRACTORS-NONRESIDENTIAL BUILDINGS, OTHER THAN INDUSTRIAL BUILDINGS AND WAREHOUSES

Turner Construction Co
1800 Fisher Bldg, Detroit MI 48202. 313/871-7070.
Employs: 100-249.

Walbridge Aldinger Co
613 Abbott St, Detroit MI 48226-2522. 313/963-8000.
Employs: 100-249.

HIGHWAY AND STREET CONSTRUCTION, EXCEPT ELEVATED HIGHWAYS

Morrison Co Inc
19366 Allen Rd, Trenton MI 48183-1023. 313/479-2323.
Employs: 50-99.

BRIDGE, TUNNEL AND ELEVATED HIGHWAY CONSTRUCTION

C A Hull Co Inc
8177 Goldie St, Walled Lake MI 48390-4106. 313/363-
3813. Employs: 100-249.

WATER, SEWER, PIPELINE, COMMUNICATIONS AND POWER LINE CONSTRUCTION

Hall Engineering Co
25601 Glendale, Redford MI 48239-2651. 313/255-2800.
Employs: 50-99.

Knight Construction Co
1931 Austin Av, Troy MI 48083-2220. 313/689-4030.
Employs: 100-249.

R L Coolsaet Construction Co
28800 Goddard Rd, Romulus MI 48174-2702. 313/946-9300. Employs: 100-249.

MISCELLANEOUS HEAVY CONSTRUCTION

The Christman Co
408 Kalamazoo Plaza Pl, Lansing MI 48933-1901.
517/482-1488. Employs: 100-249.

Vector Construction Inc
16647 Airport Rd, Lansing MI 48906-9107. 517/321-2351.
Employs: 100-249.

Venderbush Industrial Corp
39200 Groesbeck Hwy, Clinton Twp MI 48036-1538.
313/468-7800. Employs: 50-99.

Ferris Marine Contracting Inc
8145 Medina St, Detroit MI 48209-2736. 313/841-0032.
Employs: 50-99.

PLUMBING, HEATING AND AIR-CONDITIONING

Central Heating Co Inc
24250 W McNichols Rd, Detroit MI 48219-3673. 313/353-8400. Employs: 50-99.

Cramer Dee Inc
1819 S Dort Highway, Flint MI 48503-4363. 313/238-2664. Employs: 100-249.

Fisher & Wright Inc
2421 Branch Rd, Flint MI 48506-2912. 313/736-0110.
Employs: 50-99.

Frank K Blas Plumbing & Heating
5600 W Maple Rd, W Bloomfield MI 48322-3704.
313/737-2220. Employs: 50-99.

Temperature Engineering Corp
6111 Sterling Dr N, Sterling Hts MI 48312-4549. 313/826-8845. Employs: 100-249.

Limbach Co
926 Featherstone St, Pontiac MI 48342-1827. 313/335-4181. Employs: 100-249.

Seaway Mechanical Contr Inc
764 W Jefferson Ave, Trenton MI 48183-1221. 313/282-8300. Employs: 50-99.

The Trane Co
24380 Indoplex Cir, Farmington MI 48335-2524. 313/478-6100. Employs: 50-99.

Bruce Wigle Plumbing & Heating Co
17600 Livernois Ave, Detroit MI 48221-2761. 313/863-7800. Employs: 50-99.

ELECTRICAL WORK

Gray Communications Company
274 Executive Dr, Troy MI 48083-4530. 313/588-9898.
Employs: 100-249.

J I C Electric Inc
6900 Chase Rd, Dearborn MI 48126-1749. 313/582-4700.
Employs: 100-249.

John Miller Electric Co Inc
1100 Combermere St, Troy MI 48083-2702. 313/280-2000.
Employs: 50-99.

Webb Electric O
Webb Dr, Farmingtn Hls MI 48018. 313/553-1246.
Employs: 50-99.

Shaw Electric Co
33200 Schoolcraft Rd, Livonia MI 48150-1643. 313/425-6800. Employs: 50-99.

Smith Bros Electric Inc
13200 Intervale St, Detroit MI 48227-3961. 313/931-1234.
Employs: 50-99.

MASONRY, STONE SETTING AND OTHER STONE WORK

Jones & Simpson Inc
2122 E Hemphill, Burton MI 48529. 313/742-3370.
Employs: 50-99.

Schiffer Mason Contractors
2184 Ne Delhi St, Holt MI 48842-1849. 517/694-2566.
Employs: 100-249.

PLASTERING, DRYWALL, ACOUSTICAL AND INSULATION WORK

Ypsilanti Building Supply
1754 E Michigan Av, Ypsilanti MI 48198-6008. 313/483-4285. Employs: 50-99.

G-Q Of Michigan Inc
44700 Groesbeck Hwy, Clinton Twp MI 48036-1105.
313/469-3404. Employs: 100-249.

CARPENTRY WORK

Architectural Panels Inc
350 S Sanford, Pontiac MI 48342-3448. 313/334-9554.
Employs: 50-99.

MISCELLANEOUS FLOOR LAYING AND OTHER FLOOR WORK

Foster Flooring Corporation
30681 Wixom Rd, Wixom MI 48393-2415. 313/624-6402.
Employs: 50-99.

ROOFING, SIDING AND SHEET METAL WORK

Firebaugh-Reynolds Roofing
45240 Grand River Av, Novi MI 48375-1018. 313/349-6400. Employs: 100-249.

Tremco Incorporated
24445 Hwy 212, Southfield MI 48075. 313/355-5515.
Employs: 50-99.

Single Ply International Inc
29423 6 Mile Rd, Livonia MI 48152-3601. 313/522-1322.
Employs: 50-99.

Mercury Metalcraft Co
29440 Calahan Rd, Roseville MI 48066-1852. 313/779-6800. Employs: 100-249.

S K I Industries Inc
14665 23 Mile, Shelby Twp MI 48315. 313/247-7100.
Employs: 50-99.

CONCRETE WORK

Colasanti Corp
30700 Edison Dr, Roseville MI 48066-1554. 313/371-7570. Employs: 50-99.

G & G Services
23120 Arsenal Rd, Flat Rock MI 48134-9546. 313/782-4380. Employs: 100-249.

STRUCTURAL STEEL ERECTION

Douglas Steel Fabricating Corp
1312 S Waverly Rd, Lansing MI 48917-4259. 517/322-2050. Employs: 100-249.

John Crowley Inc
703 S Airline Dr Se, Jackson MI 49203-1886. 517/782-0491. Employs: 50-99.

Structural Steel Inc
48000 Structural, Harrison Twp MI 48045. 313/949-1900.
Employs: 100-249.

EXCAVATION WORK

Barnhart & Son Construction Inc
6355 Holt Rd, Holt MI 48842-9509. 517/646-6926.
Employs: 50-99.

**MISCELLANEOUS INSTALLATION OR
ERECTION OF BUILDING EQUIPMENT**

Lederman Elevator Co
126 E 3D St Bsmt, Flint MI 48502-1725. 812/2381698.
Employs: 50-99.

NKC Conveyor Installation
14800 Farmington Rd, Livonia MI 48154-5419. 313/525-
3200. Employs: 50-99.

Tim Jones Transportation
6250 H-Row, Waterford MI 48327. 313/666-3234.
Employs: 50-99.

**MISCELLANEOUS SPECIAL TRADE
CONTRACTORS**

D C Byers Company
5715 Rivard St Ste 307, Dearborn MI 48120. 313/875-
0545. Employs: 50-99.

Power Process Piping Inc
45780 Post St Box 8100C, Plymouth MI 48170-6009.
313/479-4000. Employs: 100-249.

William H Kelly Co
43600 Gd River, Novi MI 48375. 313/349-7440. Employs:
50-99.

CEMENT, HYDRAULIC

St Mary's Peerless Cement Co
9333 Dearborn St, Detroit MI 48209-2624. 313/842-4600.
Employs: 100-249.

**CONCRETE PRODUCTS, EXCEPT BLOCK AND
BRICK**

Price Bros Co
8275 White Lake Rd, Clarkston MI 48346. 313/625-5995.
Employs: 50-99.

Shelby Pre-Cast Concrete Products
14660 23 Mile Rd, Shelby Twp MI 48315-3000. 313/247-
9045. Employs: 50-99.

READY-MIXED CONCRETE

Boichot Concrete Corp
1800 Turner St, Lansing MI 48906-4049. 517/482-9066.
Employs: 50-99.

Kurtz Gravel Co
G5300 N Dort Hwy, Flint MI 48505-1833. 313/787-6543.
Employs: 50-99.

**MORTGAGE BANKERS AND LOAN
CORRESPONDENTS**

Banc One Financial Services Inc
20281 Middlebelt Rd, Livonia MI 48152-2001. 313/474-
6420. Employs: 50-99.

Banc One Financial Services Inc
34722 Dequindre Rd, Sterling Hts MI 48310-5287.
313/977-9370. Employs: 50-99.

Comerica Mortgage
280 W Maple Rd, Birmingham MI 48009-3344. 313/645-
8700. Employs: 50-99.

Credit Union One
5601 Eldred St, Detroit MI 48209-2153. 313/849-0080.
Employs: 50-99.

Executive Mortgage Co
18916 Grand River Ave, Detroit MI 48223-2270. 313/838-
6700. Employs: 50-99.

First Federal Of Michigan
16501 W Warren Ave, Detroit MI 48228-3706. 313/581-
8778. Employs: 50-99.

First Federal Of Michigan
14501 Gratiot Ave, Detroit MI 48205-2327. 313/527-3800.
Employs: 50-99.

First Federal Of Michigan
21500 Gd Riv, Detroit MI 48219. 313/533-6100. Employs:
50-99.

Franklin Savings Bank Fsb
26400 W Twelve Mile Rd, Southfield MI 48034-1753.
313/358-4710. Employs: 50-99.

International Mortgage Svc
15311 Joy Rd, Detroit MI 48228-2238. 313/584-8950.
Employs: 50-99.

Lambrecht Co
3300 Penobscot Bg, Detroit MI 48226. 313/964-4522.
Employs: 50-99.

NBD Mortgage Co
16101 Livernois Ave, Detroit MI 48221-3034. 313/345-
3900. Employs: 50-99.

NBD Mortgage Co
18203 Fenkell St, Detroit MI 48223-2312. 313/272-9380.
Employs: 50-99.

NBD Mortgage Co
7400 Gratiot Ave, Detroit MI 48213-2820. 313/923-1145.
Employs: 50-99.

NBD Mortgage Co
13771 Gratiot Ave, Detroit MI 48205-2805. 313/372-5541.
Employs: 50-99.

NBD Mortgage Co
17221 W 8 Mile Rd, Detroit MI 48235-2140. 313/272-
2002. Employs: 50-99.

Security Bank Of Monroe
465 N Telegraph Rd, Monroe MI 48161-3334. 313/241-
6262. Employs: 50-99.

Vacant Live Associates Inc
13800 W 7 Mile Rd, Detroit MI 48235-1715. 313/345-
9640. Employs: 50-99.

OPERATORS OF NONRESIDENTIAL BUILDINGS

Floyd Foren Inc
1413 S Washington Av, Royal Oak MI 48067-3225.
313/547-2277. Employs: 50-99.

Mfrs Bk Lansing Main Ofc Br
101 N Washington Sq 1st Fl, Lansing MI 48933-1604.
517/372-9230. Employs: 100-249.

OPERATORS OF APARTMENT BUILDINGS

Courtyard By Marriott
30190 Van Dyke Ave, Warren MI 48093-2366. 313/751-
5777. Employs: 50-99.

**OPERATORS OF RESIDENTIAL MOBILE HOME
SITES**

Leslie Estates
714 Mill St, Leslie MI 49251-9468. 517/589-8772.
Employs: 50-99.

REAL ESTATE AGENTS AND MANAGERS

Broock Max Inc
1145 W Long Lake Rd Rm 300, Bloomfield MI 48302-1364. 313/646-2200. Employs: 50-99.

Carol Bollo & Associates
8804 Macomb St, Grosse Ile MI 48138-1553. 313/671-1150. Employs: 50-99.

ETS
1328 Gold Smith St, Plymouth MI 48170-1043. 313/453-7900. Employs: 50-99.

F & C Management Co
30295 Embassy Dr, Franklin MI 48025-5021. 313/646-5623. Employs: 50-99.

Merrill Lynch Reloc Mgt Inc
26877 Northwestern Hw, Southfield MI 48034-2141. 313/352-6400. Employs: 50-99.

Triad Corporation
339 E Liberty St 3dfl, Ann Arbor MI 48104-2205. 313/994-4554. Employs: 50-99.

Century 21 East Inc
34204 Van Dyke Ave, Sterling Hts MI 48312-4647. 313/979-1600. Employs: 100-249.

Greenfield Mortgage Co
20031 Carlysle St, Dearborn MI 48124-3803. 313/274-8555. Employs: 50-99.

Roberts Investment Co.
31800 Northwestern Highway, Farmington MI 48334-1667. 313/855-6222. Employs: 100-249.

Saperstein Assoc Corp
30100 Telegraph Rd, Franklin MI 48025-4514. 313/644-8080. Employs: 50-99.

Schostak Brothers & Co Inc
26913 Northwestern Hwy, Southfield MI 48034-4715. 313/262-1000. Employs: 50-99.

Burt Realty Co
12640 Burt Rd, Detroit MI 48223-3315. 313/537-3347. Employs: 50-99.

Prudential Great Lakes Realty
1460 Walton Blvd, Rochester MI 48309-1768. 313/651-8850. Employs: 50-99.

TITLE ABSTRACT OFFICES

First American Title Co
2199 W Jolly Rd Ste 100, Okemos MI 48864-3968. 517/349-7472. Employs: 50-99.

First American Title Ins Co
1221 Beach St, Flint MI 48502-1408. 313/767-3860. Employs: 50-99.

Transamerica Title Ins Co
33762 Schoolcraft Rd, Livonia MI 48150-1506. 313/425-2500. Employs: 50-99.

CEMETERY SUBDIVIDERS AND DEVELOPERS

Christian Memorial Cultural Center
521 E Hamlin Rd, Rochester MI 48307-3516. 313/651-8192. Employs: 50-99.

ARCHITECTURAL SERVICES

Bechtel Corporation
777 Eisenhower Pkwy E 7th Fl, Ann Arbor MI 48108-3258. 313/994-7770. Employs: 100-249.

E David Reitzel Assoc Inc
33765 Tawas Trl, Westland MI 48185-2354. 313/261-1460. Employs: 50-99.

Hobbs & Black Assoc Inc
100 N State St, Ann Arbor MI 48104-1531. 313/663-4189. Employs: 50-99.

University Of Michigan
2000 Bonisteel Dr, Ann Arbor MI 48109-2069. 313/995-0553. Employs: 50-99.

MISC. CONSTRUCTION MATERIALS: WHOLESALE

Wolverine Technology Inc
4 Parklane Bl Ste 600, Dearborn MI 48126-2660. 313/337-7100. Employs: 250-499.

SURVEYING SERVICES

Shepherd Surveying
6326 Robison Ln, Saline MI 48176-9248. 313/429-1284. Employs: 50-99.

MANAGEMENT SERVICES

Clark Construction Co
3225 W St Joseph, Lansing MI 48917-3707. 517/372-0940. Employs: 100-249.

C M Professional
9841 Colby Rd, Greenville MI 48838-9255. 616/754-5440. Employs: 100-249.

Ddg F W McGraw Hill Info Svc
1 Parklane Blvd, Dearborn MI 48126-2402. 313/336-6820. Employs: 50-99.

True Management
9600 Hilton Rd, Brighton MI 48116-7510. 313/229-0447. Employs: 50-99.

True Management Inc
7878 Brighton Rd, Brighton MI 48116-7755. 313/229-7486. Employs: 50-99.

For more information on career opportunities in architecture, construction, and real estate:

Associations

APARTMENT OWNERS AND MANAGERS ASSOCIATION
65 Cherry Plaza, Watertown CT 06795. 203/274-2589.

BUILDING OWNERS AND MANAGERS ASSOCIATION
1521 Ritchie Highway, P.O. Box 9709, Arnold MD 21012. 301/261-2882.

INSTITUTE OF REAL ESTATE MANAGEMENT
430 North Michigan Avenue, Chicago IL 60611. 312/661-1930.

INTERNATIONAL ASSOCIATION OF CORPORATE REAL ESTATE EXECUTIVES
440 Columbia Drive, Suite 100, West Palm Beach FL 33409. 407/683-8111.

INTERNATIONAL REAL ESTATE INSTITUTE
8383 East Evans Road, Scottsdale AZ 85260. 602/998-8267.

NATIONAL ASSOCIATION OF REAL ESTATE INVESTMENT TRUSTS
1129 20th Street NW, Suite 705, Washington DC 20036. 202/785-8717.

NATIONAL ASSOCIATION OF REALTORS
430 North Michigan Avenue, Chicago IL 60611. 312/329-8200.

Magazines

JOURNAL OF PROPERTY MANAGEMENT
Institute of Real Estate Management, 430 North Michigan Avenue, Chicago IL 60611. 312/661-1930.

NATIONAL REAL ESTATE INVESTOR
6255 Barfield, Atlanta GA 30328. 404/256-9800.

REAL ESTATE FORUM
12 West 37th Street, New York NY 10018. 212/563-6460.

REAL ESTATE NEWS
2600 W. Peterson, Suite 100, Chicago IL 60659. 312/465-5151.

AUTOMOTIVE

Industry insiders are counting on a healthier overall economy and the easing of regulatory burdens to revive the long-slumping auto industry. In the meantime, auto manufacturers are slashing costs by reducing production schedules, offering higher price-incentives to buyers, and laying off workers. On a brighter note, sales of American vans and trucks rose during the first half of 1992.

AFM CORPORATION
44650 Merrill Road, Sterling Heights MI 48314. 313/731-6300. **Contact:** Bob Otto, Human Resources Manager. **Description:** Engaged in the manufacture of transmission parts including clutch plates and transmission bands. **Employees:** 300.

ASC INCORPORATED
One Sunroof Center, Southgate MI 48195. 313/246-0248. **Contact:** Marilyn Bannon, Manager, Human Resources. **Description:** International OEM automotive supplier which engineers and develops convertible systems; exterior enhancement programs and sunroofs; interior trim for cars and trucks; and converts imported and domestic sedans to convertibles. **Common positions:** Accountant; Buyer; Draftsperson; Electrical Engineer; Industrial Engineer; Mechanical Engineer; Financial Analyst; Marketing Specialist; Personnel and Labor Relations Specialist; Purchasing Agent; Quality Control Supervisor; Systems Analyst; Product Engineer; RPGIII Programmer/Analyst. **Educational backgrounds sought:** Accounting; Business Administration; Engineering. **Benefits:** medical, dental, and life insurance; pension plan; tuition assistance; disability coverage; profit sharing; employee discounts; savings plan; new car purchase program. **Corporate headquarters:** This location. **Operations at this facility:** research/development; administration; sales. **Employees:** 3,000. **Projected new hires for the next 12 months:** 150.

ACME MANUFACTURING COMPANY
650 West 12 Mile Road, Madison Heights MI 48071. 313/564-6000. **Contact:** Don Carlson, President. **Description:** A manufacturer of automation equipment including polishing, buffing, and grinding machines. **Employees:** over 100.

THE ACME GROUP
5151 Loraine Avenue, Detroit MI 48208. 313/894-7110. **Contact:** Gregg Brumm, Personnel Director. **Description:** Engaged in the wholesale distribution of auto parts, seats and supplies. **Employees:** 100.

ACTIVE INDUSTRIES INC.
81 Drettmann Drive, Elkton MI 48731. 517/375-2201. **Contact:** Personnel. **Description:** Engaged in the manufacture and distribution of automotive stampings. **Employees:** 800. **Common positions:** Accountant; Blue-Collar Worker Supervisor; Computer Programmer; Purchasing Agent; Quality Control Supervisor. **Benefits:** medical insurance; pension plan; life insurance; disability coverage. **Corporate headquarters:** Roseville MI. **Parent company:** Active Tool and Manufacturing. **Operations at this facility:** manufacturing.

ACTIVE TOOL AND MANUFACTURING COMPANY
32901 Gratiot, Roseville MI 48066. 313/294-9220. **Contact:** Richard Laidlaw, Manager of Human Resources. **Description:** Engaged in the manufacture and distribution of automotive stampings. **Employees:** 1,700.

AETNA INDUSTRIES INC.
P.O. Box 3067, Center Line MI 48015. 313/759-2200. **Contact:** Daniel Pierce, Personnel Director. **Description:** Engaged in the manufacture of auto stampings, a heavy-stamping plant.

ALLIED AUTOMOTIVE SECTOR/HEADQUARTERS
20650 Civic Center Drive, P.O. Box 5029, Southfield MI 48086. 313/827-5000. **Contact:** Ms. Gordie Hentgren, Supervisor of Employment. Headquarters for the operating sector engaged in a variety of manufacturing activities. Parent company, Allied Signal Corporation, serves a broad spectrum of industries through its more than 40 strategic businesses, which are grouped into five sectors: Aerospace; Automotive; Chemical; Industrial and Technology; and Oil and Gas. Allied Signal is one of the nation's largest industrial organizations, and has 115,000 employees in over 30 countries. **Corporate headquarters:** Morristown, NJ. **Common positions:** Accountant; Administrator; Financial Analyst; Systems Analyst. **Educational backgrounds sought:** Accounting; Business Administration; Finance. **Special programs:** Internships. **Benefits:** medical insurance; dental insurance; pension plan; life insurance; tuition assistance; disability coverage; profit sharing; savings plan.

ALLIED BENDIX/SAFETY DIVISION
7000 19 Mile Road, Sterling Heights MI 48314. 313/726-3800. **Contact:** Steven Jeffries, Manager of Employee Relations. Engaged in the manufacture of safety restraint products, seat belts, and airbags. **Employees:** 2,100.

AUTOMOTIVE MOULDING COMPANY
1530 Stevens Drive, Warren MI 48089. 313/756-2990. **Contact:** Linda Lentz, Personnel Director. **Description:** Engaged in the manufacture of auto stampings, auto body moulding, and trim work. **Employees:** 800.

AUTOMOTIVE PLASTIC TECHNOLOGY
6600 East 15 Mile Road, Sterling Heights MI 48312. 313/979-5000. **Contact:** Personnel Department. **Description:** Engaged in the manufacture of interior molding for automobiles. **Employees:** 2,500.

BOC BLANC PLANT
10800 South Saginaw, Grand Blanc MI 48439. 313/234-1163. **Contact:** Salaried Employment. **Description:** An area company engaged in the manufacturing of motor vehicles. A division/subsidiary of General Motors. **Employees:** 4,000.

BOC POWER TRAIN/LIVONIA PLANT
12200 Middlebelt, Livonia MI 48150. 313/523-0200. **Contact:** Personnel Department. **Description:** Manufactures motor vehicle engines and components for the General Motors Corporation. **Employees:** 3,000.

BRAUN ENGINEERING COMPANY
19001 Glendale, Detroit MI 48223. 313/270-1763. **Contact:** Human Resource Department. **Description:** Engaged in the manufacture and metal extrusion of vehicle parts. **Employees:** 400.

THE BUDD COMPANY
12141 Charlevoix, Detroit MI 48215. 313/823-9307. **Contact:** Dennis L. Dabney, Senior Human Resources Manager. **Description:** An automotive supplier specializing in body stampings. **Common positions:** Blue-Collar Worker Supervisor; Computer Programmer; Mechanical Engineer; Quality Control Supervisor. **Educational backgrounds sought:** Business Administration; Computer Science; Engineering. **Benefits:** medical, dental, and life insurance; pension plan; tuition assistance; disability coverage; savings plan. **Corporate headquarters:** This location.

CADILLAC GAGE COMPANY
P.O. Box 1027, Warren MI 48090. 313/777-7100. **Contact:** Frank Briggs, Vice President of Human Resources. **Description:** A major area manufacturer of combat vehicles. **Employees:** 700.

G.B. CARPENTER ASSOCIATES
8323 Office Park, Grand Blanc MI 48439. 313/695-1010. **Contact:** Personnel Department. **Description:** An area manufacturer and distributor of vehicle engine parts. **Employees:** 200.

CHIVAS PRODUCTS LIMITED
42555 Merrill, Sterling Heights MI 48314. 313/254-3535. **Contact:** Gary D. Celestini, Corporate Personnel Director. **Description:** Engaged in the manufacture of interior trim for automobiles. **Common positions:** Accountant; Blue-Collar Worker Supervisor; Buyer; Industrial Engineer; Mechanical Engineer; Operations/Production Manager; Personnel and Labor Relations Specialist; Quality Control Supervisor; Sales Representative. **Educational backgrounds sought:** Accounting; Business Administration; Engineering; Marketing. Benefits include: medical, dental, and life insurance; tuition assistance; disability coverage; prescription; 401K; bonus plan. **Corporate headquarters:** This location. **Operations at this facility:** manufacturing; research/development; administration; sales. **Employees:** 450. **Projected new hires for the next 12 months: 15.**

CHRYSLER
MANUFACTURING TECHNICAL CENTER DIVISION
P.O. Box 1318, Detroit MI 48288. 313/369-7506. **Contact:** Human Resources. **Description:** A Detroit area company engaged in the manufacture of auto stampings. **Employees:** 2,000.

CHRYSLER CORPORATION
12000 Chrysler Drive, Highland Park MI 48288-1919. **Contact:** Manager-College Relations and Recruiting. **Description:** Engaged in the manufacture of automobiles and trucks; and automotive, mechanical, electrical, and electronic components systems. Industry classifications: automotive (primary), electrical equipment, electronics, materials, plastics, transportation. Established 1924. **Employees:** 92,000 in the U.S., and 28,000 worldwide. **Common positions:** Accountant; Blue-Collar Worker Supervisor; Buyer; Computer Programmer; Draftsperson; Electrical Engineer; Industrial Engineer; Mechanical Engineer; Metallurgical Engineer; Financial Analyst; Industrial Designer; Management Trainee; Operations/Production Manager; Marketing Specialist; Personnel and Labor Relations Specialist; Public Relations Worker; Purchasing Agent; Quality Control Supervisor; Sales Representative; Systems Analyst; Transportation and Traffic Specialist. **Educational backgrounds sought:** Accounting; Business Administration; Computer Science; Economics; Engineering; Finance; Marketing. **Benefits:** medical, dental, and life insurance; pension plan; tuition assistance; disability coverage; employee discounts; savings plan. **Corporate headquarters:** This location. **Operations at this facility:** manufacturing; research/development; administration; service; sales. **Listed on:** New York Stock Exchange

COLT INDUSTRIES/HOLLEY AUTO DIVISION
11955 East 9 Mile Road, Warren MI 48090-2003. 313/497-4000. **Contact:** John Lowe, Personnel. **Description:** Engaged in the manufacture of automotive components including throttle bodies, fuel injections, and transmission solenoids. **Employees:** 2,200. **Common positions:** Computer Programmer; Electrical Engineer; Industrial Engineer; Mechanical Engineer. **Educational backgrounds sought:** Computer Science; Engineering. **Corporate**

headquarters: New York City, NY. **Parent company:** Colt Industries. **Operations at this facility:** divisional headquarters. **Listed on:** New York Stock Exchange.

CREATIVE INDUSTRIES

12500 East Grand River, Brighton MI 48116. 313/227-1400. **Contact:** Michael S. Pheney, Personnel Manager. **Description:** An area company engaged in the manufacture of custom automotive components like sun roofs. **Employees:** 700. **Common positions:** Accountant; Buyer; Computer Programmer; Mechanical Engineer; Financial Analyst; Industrial Manager; Operations/Production Manager; Personnel and Labor Relations Specialist; Public Relations Specialist; Purchasing Agent; Quality Control Supervisor. **Educational backgrounds sought:** Accounting; Art/Design; Business Administration; Engineering; Finance; Marketing. **Special problems:** Training programs. **Benefits:** medical, dental, and life insurance; tuition assistance; disability coverage; profit sharing; employee discounts; savings plan. **Corporate headquarters:** This location. **Operations at this facility:** regional headquarters; divisional headquarters; manufacturing; research/development; administration; service; sales.

CREATIVE INDUSTRIES GROUP, INC.

275 Rex Blvd., Auburn Hills MI 48326. 313/852-5700. **Contact:** Mary Iwanski, Manager, Recruitment. A metropolitan Detroit company engaged in the engineering, design and manufacturing of motor vehicles. **Common positions:** Draftsperson; Aerospace Engineer; Electrical Engineer; Mechanical Engineer; Shop Personnel. **Educational backgrounds sought:** Art/Design; Computer Science; Engineering; Automotive Design. **Benefits:** medical, dental and life insurance; tuition assistance; disability coverage; employee discounts. **Corporate headquarters:** This location. **Parent company:** Masco. **Employees:** 2,000+. **Projected hires for the next 12 months:** 300+.

THE CROWN GROUP, INC.

2111 Walter Reuther Drive, Warren MI 48091. 313/575-9800. **Contact:** Personnel Representative. **Description:** An automotive manufacturing company specializing in electroplating. **Common positions:** Accountant; Administrator; Computer Programmer; Credit Manager; Industrial Engineer; Department Manager; General Manager; Operations/Production Specialist; Quality Control Supervisor; Sales Representative. **Educational backgrounds sought:** Accounting; Business Administration; Computer Science; Economics; Engineering; Finance; Liberal Arts. **Benefits:** medical and life insurance; tuition assistance; disability coverage; profit sharing. **Corporate headquarters:** This location.

DAVIS TOOL AND ENGINEERING INC.

19250 Plymouth, Detroit MI 48228. 313/835-6000. **Contact:** Ms. Chris Mouton, Personnel. **Description:** A major Detroit manufacturer of auto stampings. **Employees:** 200.

DODGE CITY/WARREN TRUCK DIVISION
21500 Mound Road, Warren MI 48091. 313/497-2500. **Contact:** Fred Castelvetere, Personnel Director. **Description:** A major Detroit manufacturer of motor vehicles. **Employees:** 4,700.

DOUGLAS AND LOMASON COMPANY
24600 Hallwood Court, Farmington Hills MI 48335-1671. 313/478-7800. **Contact:** Nancy Gee, Personnel Director. **Description:** A supplier of bumpers, trim, and complete automobile seats.

DRAW-TITE INC.
40500 Van Born, Canton MI 48188. 313/722-7800. **Contact:** Mary Domeier, Personnel Director. **Description:** Manufacturer of trailer hitches. **Employees:** 400.

DUPONT COMPANY
400 Groesbeck Highway, Mount Clemens MI 48043. 313/468-9269. **Contact:** Martha Jueng, Personnel Assistant. Engaged in research and development for the automotive industry. **Common positions:** Chemist; Lab Technician. **Educational backgrounds sought:** Biology; Chemistry; Physics. **Benefits:** medical, dental, and life insurance; pension plan; tuition assistance; disability coverage; savings plan. **Corporate headquarters:** Wilmington, DE. **Operations at this facility:** manufacturing; research/development; administration. **Employees:** 550.

DURA CONVERTIBLE SYSTEMS
1365 East Beecher Street, P.O. Box 130, Adrian MI 49221. 517/263-7864. **Contact:** William F. Slykas, Industrial Relations Manager. **Description:** Designs and manufactures convertible tops and assembles hydraulic power units and some other miscellaneous auto parts. **Corporate headquarters:** Southfield, MI. **Common positions:** Accountant; Blue-Collar Worker Supervisor; Buyer; Draftsperson; Industrial Engineer; Mechanical Engineer; Department Manager; Operations/Production Manager; Personnel and Labor Relations Specialist; Quality Control Supervisor; Tool Engineer. **Educational backgrounds sought:** Accounting; Business Administration; Engineering; Liberal Arts. **Benefits:** medical and life insurance; pension plan; tuition assistance; disability coverage.

EAGLE PICHER AUTOMOTIVE GROUP
WOLVERINE GASKET DIVISION
2638 Princess Street, Inkster MI 48141. 313/562-6400. **Contact:** Diane Halicki, Personnel/Benefits Specialist. **Description:** Develops, markets, and manufactures automotive components worldwide. **Common positions:** Accountant; Blue-Collar Worker Supervisor; Buyer; Chemist; Computer Programmer; Customer Service Representative; Electrical Engineer; Industrial Engineer; Mechanical Engineer; General Manager; Personnel and Labor Relations Specialist; Purchasing Agent; Quality Control Supervisor; Sales Representative. **Educational backgrounds sought:** Accounting; Business Administration; Chemistry; Engineering; Marketing. **Benefits:** medical and life

insurance; pension plan; tuition assistance; disability coverage; employee discounts; savings plan. **Corporate headquarters:** Cincinnati, OH. **Parent company:** Eagle-Picher Industry, Inc. **Operations at this facility:** divisional headquarters; manufacturing; research/development; sales. **Listed on:** New York Stock Exchange.

FORD MOTOR
BODY AND ASSEMBLY OPERATIONS DIVISION
P.O. Box 1586, Dearborn MI 48121. 313/322-0493. **Contact:** Manager/Personnel. **Description:** Engaged in the manufacture of motor vehicles. **Employees:** 90,000.

FORD MOTOR
ELECTRICAL & FUEL HANDLING DIVISION
P.O. Box 922, Ypsilanti MI 48197. 313/484-8892. **Contact:** William Eaddy, Salaried Personnel and Recruiting. **Description:** EFHD consists of three U.S. manufacturing facilities and two international facilities whose priorities are to design, develop, and manufacture state-of-the-art electromagnetic and fuel systems components for engine and vehicle assembly operations. **Common positions:** Electrical Engineer; Mechanical Engineer; Financial Analyst. **Educational backgrounds sought:** Engineering; Finance. **Special programs:** training programs; internships. **Benefits:** medical, dental and life insurance; pension plan; tuition assistance; disability coverage; profit sharing; employee discounts; savings plan. **Corporate headquarters:** Dearborn, MI. **Other U.S. locations:** Michigan, Indiana. **Operations at this facility:** manufacturing; research/development; administration; sales. **Listed on:** New York Stock Exchange. **Employees:** 5,900. **Projected hires for the next 12 months:** 100.

FORD MOTOR COMPANY
P.O. Box 1899, Room 50, The American Road, Dearborn MI 48121. 313/322-7500. **Contact:** Manager/College Recruiting and Placement. Engaged in the design, development, manufacture, and sale of cars, trucks, tractors, and related components and accessories. Operates facilities in the United States, Canada, and 29 countries worldwide. **Common positions:** Accountant; Buyer; Computer Programmer; Customer Service Representative; Electrical Engineer; Mechanical Engineer; Financial Analyst; Marketing Specialist; Personnel & Labor Relations Specialist; Purchasing Agent; Sales Representative; Systems Analyst. **Educational backgrounds sought:** Accounting; Business Administration; Computer Science; Engineering; Finance; Marketing. **Special programs:** Internships and training programs. **Benefits:** medical, dental, and life insurance; pension plan; tuition assistance; disability coverage; profit sharing; employee discounts; savings plan. **Corporate headquarters:** This location. **Listed on:** New York Stock Exchange.

FORD MOTOR TRACTOR/ROMEO DIVISION
701 East 32 Mile Road, Romeo MI 48065. 313/752-8000. **Contact:** Personnel Department. **Description:** Engaged in the manufacture of industrial trucks and tractors. **Employees:** 900.

FORD MOTOR TRANSMISSION/VAN DYKE DIVISION
41111 Van Dyke, Sterling Heights MI 48314. 313/826-6501. **Contact:** R.S. Frick, Director/Salaried Personnel. **Description:** Engaged in the manufacture of vehicle parts and transmissions. **Common positions:** Accountant; Blue-Collar Worker Supervisor; Chemist; Computer Programmer; Civil Engineer; Electrical Engineer; Industrial Engineer; Mechanical Engineer; Metallurgical Engineer; Financial Analyst; Industrial Manager; Department Manager; General Manager; Management Trainee; Operations/Production Manager; Quality Controller; Systems Analyst. **Educational backgrounds sought:** Business Administration; Computer Science; Engineering; Finance. **Benefits:** medical, dental and life insurance; pension plan; tuition assistance; disability coverage; profit sharing; employee discounts; savings plan. **Corporate headquarters:** Dearborn, MI. **Operations at this facility:** manufacturing. **Listed on:** New York Stock Exchange. **Projected hires for the next 12 months:** 20.

FORD MOTOR VINYL PLANT
151 Lafayette, Mount Clemens MI 48043. 313/466-1700. **Contact:** For information on professional hiring, contact world headquarters at The American Road, Room 467, Dearborn MI 48121. **Description:** A major area manufacturer of coated fabrics. **Employees:** 500.

FORD MOTOR/BODY AND ASSEMBLY DIVISION
50500 Mound Road, Utica MI 48318. 313/826-0005. **Contact:** Personnel Department. **Description:** A major Southeastern Michigan manufacturer of vehicle parts. **Employees:** 2,600.

FORD MOTOR/FORD DIVISION
P.O. Box 43331, Detroit MI 48243. 313/446-4500. **Contact:** Mr. Richard Pamarolli, Personnel Department. **Description:** Engaged in the manufacture of auto and motor vehicles. **Employees:** 1,200.

FORD MOTOR/SALINE PLASTICS DIVISION
7700 Michigan, Saline MI 48176. 313/429-4911. **Contact:** Personnel Department. **Description:** A major Southeastern Michigan manufacturer of vehicle parts. **Employees:** 2,400.

GKN AUTOMOTIVE COMPONENTS/MICHIGAN DIVISION
3300 University Drive, Auburn Hills MI 48326-2362. **Contact:** Personnel Department. **Description:** A leading area company engaged in the manufacture of vehicle parts. **Employees:** 200.

GENERAL MOTORS CORPORATION
AC ROCHESTER DIVISION
4800 South Saginaw Street, P.O. Box 1360, Flint MI 48501-1360. 313/257-7836. **Contact:** David E. Rowe, Supervisor of College Relations. **Description:** Design, development and manufacture of engine management systems. AC Rochester is a leader in the automotive industry in air/fuel management, ignition

and infiltration, fuel handling and control, valve train and exhaust systems. **Other U.S. locations:** Flint, MI; Rochester, NY; Sioux City, IA; Wichita Falls, TX; Grand Rapids, MI; Coopersville, MI; and Milwaukee, WI. **Common positions:** Accountant; Ceramics Engineer; Electrical Engineer; Industrial Engineer; Mechanical Engineer; Metallurgical Engineer. **Educational backgrounds sought:** Accounting; Engineering; Finance. **Special programs:** Training programs and internships. **Benefits:** medical insurance; dental insurance; pension plan; life insurance; tuition assistance; disability coverage; profit sharing; employee discounts. **Corporate headquarters:** This location. **Operations at this facility:** divisional headquarters; manufacturing; research/development; sales. **Listed on:** New York Stock Exchange.

GENERAL MOTORS/
BUICK-OLDSMOBILE-CADILLAC GROUP
30009 Van Dyke, Warren MI 48090-9025. 313/492-8170. **Contact:** Dianne S. Golden, Director of Human Resources Planning. **Description:** Oversees engineering, manufacturing, and assembly operations for the national line of automobiles. Parent company, General Motors, is a major producer of cars, trucks, and buses sold worldwide; the firm has 152 facilities operating in 26 states and 93 cities in the United States and 13 plants in Canada, and also has assembly, manufacturing, distribution, sales or warehousing operations in 37 other countries.

GENERAL MOTORS
CADILLAC LUXURY CAR DIVISION
902 East Hamilton, Flint MI 48550. 313/236-1080. **Contact:** John D. Masserio, Director of Salaried Personnel. **Description:** A major area manufacturer of motor vehicles. **Employees:** 23,000. **Special programs:** Training programs and internships. **Benefits:** medical insurance; dental insurance; pension plan; life insurance; tuition assistance; disability coverage; profit sharing; employee discounts; savings plan. **Corporate headquarters:** Detroit MI. **Operations at this facility:** divisional headquarters; manufacturing; research/development; administration. **Listed on:** New York Stock Exchange.

GENERAL MOTORS/CADILLAC MOTORS DIVISION
2860 Clark Street, Detroit MI 48232. 313/554-6157. **Contact:** John Harless, Personnel Director. **Description:** Engaged in the manufacture of motor vehicles. **Employees:** 7,000.

GENERAL MOTORS/LANSING AUTOMOTIVE
920 Townsend Street, Lansing MI 48921-1036. 517/885-0305. **Contact:** Joyce B. Russaw, Coordinator, Student Programs. **Description:** Primarily engaged in the sale of Oldsmobile passenger cars. Parent company, General Motors, is a major producer of cars, trucks, and buses sold worldwide; the firm has 152 facilities operating in 26 states and 93 cities in the United States and 13 plants in Canada, and also has assembly, manufacturing, distribution, sales or warehousing operations in 37 other countries. **Common positions:** Electrical Engineer; Industrial Engineer; Mechanical Engineer; Metallurgical Engineer;

Industrial Manager. **Educational backgrounds sought:** Business Administration; Computer Science; Engineering; Finance. **Corporate headquarters: Detroit, MI.**

GENERAL MOTORS/POWERTRAIN DIVISION
23500 Mound Road, Warren MI 48091. 313/252-0983. **Contact:** Salaried Personnel. **Description:** A major area manufacturer of vehicle parts. **Employees:** 4,000. **Common positions:** Electrical Engineer; Industrial Engineer; Mechanical Engineer.

GENERAL MOTORS/PROVING GROUNDS
General Motors Road, Milford MI 48380. 313/685-5000. **Contact:** Personnel Department. **Description:** Engaged in the manufacture of motor vehicles. **Employees:** 4,100.

GENERAL MOTORS TECHNICAL CENTER
30200 Mound Road, Warren MI 48090-9010. 313/986-6273. **Contact:** Jann C. Dagg, Manager of Personnel Placement. Research and development in the transportation industry. Subsidiary of General Motors. **Employees:** 6,000. **Common positions:** Electrical Engineer; Mechanical Engineer; Creative Designer. **Educational backgrounds sought:** Art/Design; Engineering. **Special programs:** Training programs; internships. **Corporate headquarters:** Detroit, MI. **Parent company:** General Motors Corporation. **Operations at this facility:** research/development. **Listed on:** New York Stock Exchange.

GENERAL SAFETY CORPORATION
P.O. Box 480, St. Clair Shores MI 48080. 313/777-6530. **Contact:** Richard Reitman, Personnel Director. **Description:** Engaged in the manufacture of vehicle parts. **Employees:** 500.

GOETZE CORPORATION OF AMERICA
1823 Commerce, Muskegon MI 49441. 616/726-5226. **Contact:** Eugene K. Russell, Vice President of Human Resources. **Description:** A manufacturer of automotive sealing systems (piston rings, valve seat inserts, head gaskets, valve guides, exhaust joint sealing rings, piston ring castings, specialized castings, and rubber seals). **Corporate headquarters:** This location. **Operations include:** manufacturing; administration; sales. **Common positions:** Accountant; Administrator; Blue-Collar Worker Supervisor; Buyer; Computer Programmer; Customer Service Representative; Engineer; Industrial Engineer; Mechanical Engineer; Metallurgical Engineer; Financial Analyst; Department Manager; General Manager; Operations/Production Manager; Marketing Specialist; Human Resources Specialist; Purchasing Agent; Quality Control Supervisor; Sales Representative; Systems Analyst; Transportation And Traffic Specialist. **Educational backgrounds sought:** Accounting; Business Administration; Computer Science; Engineering; Marketing; Mathematics. **Benefits:** medical, dental, and life insurance; pension plan; tuition assistance; disability coverage; profit sharing; employee discounts; 401K.

HARVARD INDUSTRIES/TRIM TRENDS, INC.

1271 West Maple Road, Clawson MI 48017. 313/435-4200. **Contact:** Gary Dopirak, Vice President of Human Resources. **Description:** Engaged in the manufacture of auto stampings. **Common positions:** Accountant; Computer Programmer. **Special programs:** Training programs. **Benefits:** medical, dental, and life insurance; pension plan; tuition assistance; disability coverage; savings plan. **Corporate headquarters:** Farmingdale, NJ. **Parent company:** Harvard Industries. **Operations at this facility:** divisional headquarters.

HOWELL INDUSTRIES

17515 West 9 Mile Road, Southfield MI 48075. 313/424-8220. **Contact:** Richard Decker, Personnel Director. **Description:** Engaged in the manufacture of auto stampings. **Employees:** 400.

IVAN DOVERSPIKE COMPANY

9501 Conner, Detroit MI 48213. 313/579-3000. **Contact:** Personnel Department. **Description:** An area company engaged in the manufacture of auto stampings. **Employees:** 500.

JOHNSON CONTROLS, INC.
AUTOMOTIVE SYSTEMS GROUP

49200 Halyard Drive, P.O. Box 8010, Plymouth MI 48170. . **Contact:** Recruiting Department. **Description:** World's largest independent supplier of automotive and light truck seating systems and components. Also, trim supplier. **Common positions:** available for experienced mechanical engineers and experienced computer aided designers (PDGS, CATIA, and Computervision).

KELSEY-HAYES COMPANY

38481 Huron River Drive, Romulus MI 48174. 313/941-2000. **Contact:** Mr. J.W. Goodsir, Director/Management Development. **Description:** Manufacturer of automotive and aerospace components. **Corporate headquarters:** This location. **Listed on:** New York Stock Exchange. **Common positions:** Accountant; Administrator; Buyer; Computer Programmer; Credit Manager; Customer Service Representative; Draftsperson; Industrial Engineer; Mechanical Engineer; Department Manager; General Manager; Management Trainee; Operations/Production Manager; Personnel & Labor Relations Specialist; Purchasing Agent; Quality Control Supervisor; Sales Representative. **Educational backgrounds sought:** Accounting; Business Administration; Engineering; Finance; Liberal Arts; Marketing. **Benefits:** medical, dental, and life insurance; pension plan; tuition assistance; disability coverage; savings plan.

L & L PRODUCTS, INC.

74100 Van Dyke, Romeo MI 48065. 313/752-3591. **Contact:** Greg B. Schankin, Director of Human Resources. **Description:** Engaged in the manufacturing and sale of sealants and adhesives for the automotive industry. **Employees:** 275. **Common positions:** Accountant; Administrator; Blue-Collar Worker Supervisor; Buyer; Chemist; Computer Programmer; Customer Service Representative; Industrial Engineer; Mechanical Engineer; Industrial Manager;

General Manager; Operations/Production Manager; Quality Control Supervisor; Sales Representative. **Educational backgrounds sought:** Accounting; Business Administration; Chemistry; Communications; Computer Science; Engineering; Finance; Marketing. **Special programs:** Training programs. **Benefits:** medical and life insurance; tuition assistance; disability coverage; profit sharing. **Corporate headquarters:** This location. **Operations at this facility:** divisional headquarters; manufacturing; administration; sales.

MACDONALD MOLDING
P.O. Box 604, New Baltimore MI 48047. 313/725-2111. **Contact:** Personnel Manager. Engaged in the manufacture and assembly of plastic automotive products. **Common positions:** Blue-Collar Worker Supervisor; Industrial Engineer; Financial Analyst; Operations/Production Manager; Personnel and Labor Relations Specialist; Quality Control Supervisor; Statistician; Transportation and Traffic Specialist. **Educational backgrounds sought:** Accounting: Business Administration; Finance. **Special programs:** training programs. **Benefits:** medical, dental and life insurance; pension plan; tuition assistance; disability coverage; employee discounts; savings plan; gainsharing plan. **Corporate headquarters:** Troy, MI. **Parent company:** Acustar, Inc. **Operations at this facility:** manufacturing; administration. **Employees:** 250.

MOTOR WHEEL CORPORATION/MICHIGAN DIVISION
717 Norris Street, Ypsilanti MI 48197. 313/481-2120. **Contact:** Personnel Department. **Description:** A leading Ypsilanti manufacturer of vehicle parts. **Employees:** 300.

C.S. OHM MANUFACTURING COMPANY
6640 Sterling Drive South, Sterling Heights MI 48312. 313/939-3000. **Contact:** Larry Wojceichowski, Director of Personnel. **Description:** A leading Southeastern Michigan manufacturer of auto stampings. **Employees:** 500.

PARAMOUNT FABRICATING
13595 Helen, Detroit MI 48212. 313/365-6600. **Contact:** Personnel Department. **Description:** A Detroit area company engaged in the manufacture of auto stampings. **Employees:** 200.

PETERSON AMERICAN CORPORATION
P.O. Box 5059, Southfield MI 48086-5059. 313/353-6400. **Contact:** Personnel Department. **Description:** A Southfield area company engaged in the manufacture of auto stampings. **Employees:** 400.

PRESTIGE STAMPING, INC.
P.O. Box 1086, Warren MI 48090-1086. **Contact:** Mike Solonika, Personnel Manager. **Description:** An area company engaged in the manufacture of auto stampings. **Employees:** 100. **Common positions:** Blue-Collar Worker Supervisor; Blue-Collar Worker. **Special programs:** Training programs. **Benefits:** medical insurance; dental insurance. **Corporate headquarters:** This location. **Operations at this facility:** manufacturing.

PULLMAN INDUSTRIES INC./MICHIGAN

1228 Kirts Boulevard, Suite 500, Troy MI 48084-4831. 313/244-8668. **Contact:** Personnel. **Description:** A company engaged in the manufacture of automotive roll form products, auto and truck door frames, metal stampings, spot and butt weld access. **Common positions:** Sales Representative. **Principle educational backgrounds sought:** Accounting; Engineering; Marketing; Mathematics. **Benefits:** medical insurance; pension plan; life insurance; disability coverage; profit sharing. **Corporate headquarters:** Pullman MI. **Operations at this facility:** sales.

REEF-BAKER CORPORATION

50903 E. Russell Schmidt Blvd, Chesterfield MI 48051. 313/765-8822. **Contact:** Personnel Department. **Description:** A leading area company engaged in the manufacture of vehicle parts. **Employees:** 300.

REGAL STAMPING COMPANY

21601 Hoover Road, Detroit MI 48089. 313/521-0300. **Contact:** Personnel Department. **Description:** A leading area company engaged in the manufacture of auto stampings. **Employees:** 200.

ROCKWELL INTERNATIONAL
AUTOMOTIVE OPERATIONS

2135 West Maple Road, Troy MI 48084. 313/435-1000. **Contact:** Staffing Manager. **Description:** Engaged in the design and development of automotive and truck components. Also develops systems to serve the transportation industry. **Common positions:** Industrial Engineer; Mechanical Engineer; Financial Analyst. **Educational backgrounds sought:** Engineering; Finance. **Benefits:** medical, dental, and life insurance; pension plan; tuition assistance; disability coverage; savings plan. **Corporate headquarters:** Los Angeles, CA. Operations at this facility: divisional headquarters; research/development; administration; service; sales. **Listed on:** New York Stock Exchange.

SAGINAW DETROIT PLANT

1840 Holbrook Street, Detroit MI 48212. 313/974-2561. **Contact:** Tom Sampson, Personnel Director. **Description:** A Detroit manufacturer of vehicle parts. **Employees:** 4,300.

SCHMELZER CORPORATION

5209 Exchange Drive, Flint MI 48507. 313/733-5970. **Contact:** Personnel Director. **Description:** A leading area manufacturer of vehicle parts. **Employees:** 300.

SIMPSON INDUSTRIES INC.

32100 Telegraph Road, Suite 120, Bingham Farms MI 48025-2453. 313/540-6200. **Contact:** Deborah Baluch, Manager/Benefits and Administration. **Description:** An area manufacturer of vehicle parts.

SNOVER STAMPING COMPANY

3279 West Snover, Snover MI 48472. 313/672-9286. **Contact:** Gary Dopirak, Personnel Manager. **Description:** An area company engaged in the manufacture of auto stampings. **Employees:** 200.

T & N INDUSTRIES, INC.

325 E. Eisenhower Parkway, Ann Arbor MI 48108. 313/663-6749. **Contact:** Norma Francis, Human Resources Manager. **Description:** Manufactures engine components, transportation products. **Common positions:** Accountant; Administrator; Advertising Worker; Attorney; Computer Programmer; Customer Service Representative; Financial Analyst; General Manager; Marketing Specialist; Personnel & Labor Relations Specialist; Sales Representative; Systems Analyst. **Educational backgrounds sought:** Accounting; Business Administration; Communications; Computer Science; Finance; Liberal Arts; Marketing. **Benefits:** medical, dental and life insurance; pension and savings plan; tuition assistance; disability coverage; profit sharing; employee discounts. **Corporate headquarters:** This location.

TRW VEHICLE SAFETY SYSTEMS INC.

4505 W. 26 Mile Road, East Building, Washington MI 48094. 313/781-7200. **Contact:** Mr. Ruben Urquidi, Director of Human Relations. **Description:** Produces automotive occupant restraint systems (seat belts and inflatable restraints). Parent company, TRW, is a diversifed technology firm with primary operations in space and defense, information systems, energy markets and automotive equipment for original equipment manufacturers and the replacement market. **Common positions:** Accountant; Computer Programmer; Draftsperson; Mechanical Engineer; Department Manager; Personnel and Labor Relations Specialist; Purchasing Agent. **Educational backgrounds sought:** Accounting; Business Administration; Engineering; Finance; Mathematics. **Benefits:** medical, dental, and life insurance; pension plan; tuition assistance; disability coverage; savings plan. **Corporate headquarters:** Cleveland, OH. **Parent company:** TRW. Operations at this facility: divisional headquarters; research/development. **Listed on:** New York Stock Exchange

U.S. MANUFACTURING CORPORATION

30855 Little Mack Avenue, Roseville MI 48066. 313/293-8744. **Contact:** Human Resources. **Description:** A leading area manufacturer of vehicle parts. **Employees:** 700. **Common positions:** Draftsperson; Industrial Engineer; Mechanical Engineer. **Educational backgrounds sought:** Engineering. **Benefits:** medical, dental, and life insurance; pension plan; tuition assistance; disability coverage. **Corporate headquarters:** This location.

WAGGONER CORPORATION

1400 Rochester Road, Troy MI 48083. 313/588-2121. **Contact:** Patty West, Personnel Director. **Description:** A company engaged in the manufacture of auto stampings. **Employees:** 300.

ZIEBART INTERNATIONAL CORPORATION

P.O. Box 1290, Troy MI 48007-1290. 313/588-4100. **Contact:** J.F. DeSantis, Director of Personnel. **Description:** An area company that runs a network of franchised automotive service locations. **Employees:** 250. **Common positions:** Administrator; Advertising Worker; Chemist; Credit Manager; Customer Service Representative; Chemical Engineer; Personnel and Labor Relations Specialist; Public Relations Worker; Purchasing Agent; Sales Representative. **Educational backgrounds sought:** Business Administration; Chemistry; Liberal Arts; Marketing. **Benefits:** medical, dental, and life insurance; pension plan; tuition assistance; disability coverage; profit sharing; employee discounts; savings plan. **Corporate headquarters:** This location. **Operations at this facility:** administration; service; sales.

Additional large employers: 250+

MOTOR VEHICLES AND PASSENGER CAR BODIES

American Motors Corp
14250 Plymouth Rd, Detroit MI 48227-3042. 313/493-2000. Employs: 500-999.

Buick Oldsmobile Cadillac Div
401 N Verlinden Av, Lansing MI 48915-1246. 517/377-5000. Employs: 1000+.

Chrysler Corp
2101 Conner, Detroit MI 48215-2763. 313/956-7200. Employs: 1000+.

Chrysler Corp/Sterling Asmbly
38111 Van Dyke St, Sterling Hts MI 48312-1138. 313/978-6038. Employs: 1000+.

Ford Motor Co
37625 Michigan Ave, Wayne MI 48184-1070. 313/467-0225. Employs: 1000+.

G M Corp
30009 Van Dyke Ave, Warren MI 48093. 313/492-7128. Employs: 1000+.

G M Corp
4555 Giddings Rd, Lake Orion MI 48359-1713. 313/377-5000. Employs: 1000+.

G M Corp
401 Verlindin St, Lansing MI 48915. 517/885-9063. Employs: 1000+.

G M Corp/Willow Run Assembly
2625 Tyler Rd, Ypsilanti MI 48198-6183. 313/481-4802. Employs: 1000+.

General Motors Truck & Bus Gp
31 Judson St, Pontiac MI 48342. 313/456-5000. Employs: 1000+.

Lear Seating Corp
21557 Telegraph Rd, Southfield MI 48034-4248. 313/746-1500. Employs: 500-999.

Mazda Motor Manufacturing USA Corp
1 Mazda Dr, Flat Rock MI 48134-9401. 313/782-7800. Employs: 1000+.

Pontiac Motor Division
One Pontiac Plaza, Pontiac MI 48340-2952. 313/857-5000. Employs: 1000+.

Saturn Corp
1420 Stephenson Hwy, Troy MI 48083-1189. 313/524-5721. Employs: 500-999.

Spartan Motors Inc
1000 Reynolds Rd, Charlotte MI 48813-2018. 517/543-6400. Employs: 250-499.

Volkswagen Of America Inc
3800 Hamlin Rd, Auburn Hills MI 48326-2829. 313/340-5000. Employs: 500-999.

Concepts Inc Cleaning
2740 Packard St, Ann Arbor MI 48108-3255. 313/677-0040. Employs: 500-999.

Fisher Body Divsn Gen Motors
W Fort & West End, Detroit MI 48209. 313/841-2681. Employs: 500-999.

Stony Creek Collision
3950 Stony Creek, Ann Arbor MI 48103. 313/485-5653. Employs: 500-999.

TRUCK AND BUS BODIES

G M Corp/Truck-Bus Grp
601 Piquette St, Detroit MI 48202-3551. 313/974-3553. Employs: 250-499.

MOTOR VEHICLE PARTS AND ACCESSORIES

Alma Products Co
2000 Michigan Ave, Alma MI 48801-9703. 517/463-1151. Employs: 500-999.

American Bumper & Manufacturing Co Inc
14 N Beardsley Rd, Ionia MI 48846-9734. 616/527-1220. Employs: 500-999.

Automotive Moulding Company
23751 Amber Ave, Warren MI 48089-2647. 313/757-7800. Employs: 250-499.

Baker Electrical Products Inc
2026 S Parker St, Marine City MI 48039-2340. 313/765-4015. Employs: 250-499.

Borg Warner Automotive Corp
3001 W Big Beaver Rd, Troy MI 48084-3101. 317/286-6100. Employs: 1000+.

Camshaft Machine Co
717 Woodworth Rd, Jackson MI 49202-1636. 517/787-2040. Employs: 250-499.

Chrysler Corp/Detroit Axle Plt
6700 Lynch Rd, Detroit MI 48234-4119. 313/252-5427.
Employs: 1000+.

Deco-Grand Inc
4850 Coolidge Hwy, Royal Oak MI 48073-1022. 313/435-0100. Employs: 250-499.

Delco Products Livonia Ope
13000 Eckles Rd, Livonia MI 48150-1068. 313/464-5026.
Employs: 1000+.

Dott Inds Inc
3768 N Main St, Deckerville MI 48427-9797. 313/376-2445. Employs: 250-499.

Eaton Technologies Inc
402 E Haven St, Eaton Rapids MI 48827-1832. 517/663-2161. Employs: 250-499.

Fayette Tubular Products
311 E Elm St, Reading MI 49274-9792. 517/283-2161.
Employs: 250-499.

Federal-Mogul Corp
510 E Grove St, Greenville MI 48838-1718. 616/754-5681.
Employs: 500-999.

Ford Motor Co
39000 Mound Rd, Sterling Hts MI 48310-2733. 313/826-5000. Employs: 1000+.

Ford Motor Co Engine Division
21500 Oakwood Bl, Dearborn MI 48124-4080. 313/323-2700. Employs: 1000+.

Ford Motor Co/Body & Assembly Division
3200 E Elm Ave, Monroe MI 48161-1990. 313/243-4700.
Employs: 1000+.

Ford Motor Co/Transmission Plant
36200 Plymouth Rd, Livonia MI 48150-1442. 313/523-3000. Employs: 1000+.

G M Corp
8435 St Aubin St, Detroit MI 48212-3637. 313/974-3195.
Employs: 1000+.

G M Corp
1840 Holbrook St, Detroit MI 48212-3442. 313/974-2561.
Employs: 1000+.

G M Corp
28400 Plymouth Rd, Livonia MI 48150. 313/523-8201.
Employs: 1000+.

G M Corp
13000 Eckles Rd, Livonia MI 48150-1068. 313/464-5020.
Employs: 1000+.

G M Corp
4425 Purks Dr, Auburn Hills MI 48326-1749. 313/377-6340. Employs: 250-499.

G M Corp
G-1245 E Coldwater Rd, Flint MI 48559. 313/234-4636.
Employs: 1000+.

G M Corp
1300 N Dort Hwy, Flint MI 48556-0001. 313/257-3900.
Employs: 1000+.

G M Corp/Powertrain Div
12200 Middlebelt Rd, Livonia MI 48150-2315. 313/523-0200. Employs: 1000+.

GM Corp/Truck & Bus
G-2238 W Bristol Rd, Flint MI 48553. 313/236-0470.
Employs: 1000+.

GM Rochester Plant

300 N Chevrolet Av, Flint MI 48504-5211. 313/733-1900.
Employs: 1000+.

GM Service Parts Operations
36667 Schoolcraft Rd, Livonia MI 48150-1174. 313/464-5240. Employs: 250-499.

Hillsdale Tool & Manufacturing
135 E South St, Hillsdale MI 49242-1807. 517/439-9381.
Employs: 500-999.

Hydra-Matic Division
Ecorse Rd, Ypsilanti MI 48198. 313/481-5151. Employs:
1000+.

Inland Tool & Manufacturing Inc
400 Renaissance Ctr Ste 2140, Detroit MI 48243-1602.
313/372-1400. Employs: 250-499.

Kelsey-Hayes Co
5300 Livernois Ave, Detroit MI 48210-1700. 313/895-5211. Employs: 250-499.

Kelsey-Hayes Co
9475 Center Rd, Fenton MI 48430-9388. 313/750-1036.
Employs: 250-499.

Kelsey-Hayes Co
1600 Wildwood Ave, Jackson MI 49202-4000. 517/788-9700. Employs: 250-499.

Lear Seating Corp
340 Fenway Dr, Fenton MI 48430-2657. 313/750-1500.
Employs: 250-499.

Michigan Automotive Compressor
2400 N Dearing Rd, Parma MI 49269-9719. 517/531-5500.
Employs: 250-499.

Monroe Auto Equipment Co
International Dr, Monroe MI 48161. 313/243-8000.
Employs: 1000+.

Motor Wheel Corp
4000 Collins Rd, Lansing MI 48910-5883. 517/337-5700.
Employs: 1000+.

Peerless Gear & Machine Co
1120 Tecumseh-Clinton Rd, Clinton MI 49236. 517/456-4144. Employs: 250-499.

Sealed Power Technologies Lp
916 W State St, Saint Johns MI 48879-1404. 517/224-2384. Employs: 250-499.

TRW
902 Lyons Rd, Portland MI 48875-1000. 517/647-4121.
Employs: 250-499.

TRW Inc
34201 Van Dyke Ave, Sterling Hts MI 48312-4648.
313/977-1000. Employs: 500-999.

Van Dresser Westland
1515 Newburg Rd, Westland MI 48185. 313/721-1000.
Employs: 250-499.

TRUCK TRAILERS

Fruehauf Trailer Corp
26999 Central Pk Blvd, Southfield MI 48076-4174.
313/948-1300. Employs: 1000+.

**TOP, BODY AND UPHOLSTERY REPAIR SHOPS
AND PAINT SHOPS**

Buick Motor Div General Motors Corp
902 E Hamilton Av, Flint MI 48505-4785. 313/236-5000.
Employs: 1000+.

Cadillac Motor Car Division Metal Fabricating Operation
10800 Saginaw Rd, Grand Blanc MI 48439-8120. 313/234-1113. Employs: 1000+.

AUTOMOTIVE REPAIR SHOPS, NOT ELSEWHERE CLASSIFIED

PBM Industries Inc
50925 Richard W Blvd, Harrison Twp MI 48045. 313/949-1433. Employs: 250-499.

AUTOMOTIVE SERVICES, EXCEPT REPAIR AND CARWASHES

CDI Transportation Group Inc
28000 Dequindre Rd, Warren MI 48092-2468. 313/578-6000. Employs: 1000+.

Additional small to medium sized employers: 50-249

MOTOR VEHICLES AND PASSENGER CAR BODIES

Ford Motor Co
18751 Oakwood Bl, Dearborn MI 48124-4070. 313/337-7755. Employs: 50-99.

General Motors Design
30100 Mound Rd, Warren MI 48092. 313/556-5000. Employs: 50-99.

Minowitz Manufacturing Co
27941 Groesbeck Hwy, Roseville MI 48066-2756. 313/779-5940. Employs: 100-249.

National Coach Engineering Ltd
2525 Lakeshore Rd, Port Sanilac MI 48469-9714. 313/622-9624. Employs: 50-99.

Novi Manufacturing
25701 Seeley Rd, Novi MI 48375-2058. 313/476-4350. Employs: 50-99.

Synthetex Inc
15850 Wahrman Rd, Romulus MI 48174-3636. 313/941-4300. Employs: 50-99.

T D M World Conversion Ltd
1020 Doris Rd, Auburn Hills MI 48326-2613. 313/377-2288. Employs: 50-99.

Triad Targa Group Inc
570 Executive Dr, Troy MI 48083-4506. 313/588-7423. Employs: 100-249.

TRUCK AND BUS BODIES

Champion Motor Coach
5573 North St, Dryden MI 48428-9794. 313/796-2211. Employs: 50-99.

Champion Motor Coach Inc
275-331 Graham Rd, Imlay City MI 48444-9738. 313/724-0571. Employs: 100-249.

Drake Enterprises Inc
57877 Main St, New Haven MI 48048. 313/749-5128. Employs: 50-99.

Eleven Mile Truck Frame & Axle
1752 E 11 Mile Rd, Madison Hts MI 48071-3814. 313/399-7536. Employs: 50-99.

MOTOR VEHICLE PARTS AND ACCESSORIES

A F M Co
44650 Merrill St, Sterling Hts MI 48314-1451. 313/731-6300. Employs: 100-249.

Acustar Inc
1850 Research Dr, Troy MI 48083-2167. 313/528-6500. Employs: 100-249.

Aeroquip Corp
2345 Petit Ave, Port Huron MI 48060-6429. 313/984-4446. Employs: 100-249.

Aeroquip Corp
19700 Hall Rd, Clinton Twp MI 48038-1478. 313/286-0800. Employs: 100-249.

Aeroquip Corp
44805 Trinity Dr, Clinton Twp MI 48038-1557. 313/463-2341. Employs: 50-99.

Airflow Research & Manufacturing Corp
7565 Haggerty Rd, Belleville MI 48111-1601. 313/397-1660. Employs: 100-249.

Alcolite Products
50350 E Russell, Mount Clemens MI 48043. 313/296-6020. Employs: 100-249.

Automotive Products USA Inc
4000 Pinnacle Corp Ctr, Auburn Hills MI 48326. 313/377-6999. Employs: 100-249.

B & H Manufacturing Co
502 Murray Dr, Tecumseh MI 49286-1835. 517/423-2177. Employs: 50-99.

Baker Manufacturing Inc
5664 N River Rd, Marine City MI 48039. 313/765-8822. Employs: 100-249.

Becker Manufacturing
615 S Delaney Rd, Owosso MI 48867-9114. 517/725-2274. Employs: 50-99.

Bennett Equipment Corp
4647 4th St, Ecorse MI 48229-1042. 313/389-2200. Employs: 100-249.

Black River Manufacturing Inc
2625 20th St, Port Huron MI 48060-6443. 313/982-9812. Employs: 50-99.

Buechler & Sons Inc
27-29 Broadway St, Oxford MI 48371. 313/628-2800. Employs: 50-99.

C M E Corp
2945 Three Leaves Dr, Mount Pleasnt MI 48858. 517/773-0377. Employs: 50-99.

Carpenter Enterprises Limited
3061 W Thomson Rd Box 530, Fenton MI 48430-9705. 313/629-5801. Employs: 100-249.

Curley Machined Products Inc
907 Indl Dr, Tecumseh MI 49286. 517/423-2177. Employs: 50-99.

Cycle Tech Remfrs
1200 Oakman Blvd, Detroit MI 48238-2949. 313/883-8000. Employs: 100-249.

Daisy Parts I I
221 Indl Dr, Hillsdale MI 49242. 517/439-1478. Employs: 100-249.

Dana Corp
5800 Sibley Rd, Chelsea MI 48118-1262. 313/475-8641. Employs: 100-249.

Davidson Interior Trim
210 Dove Rd, Port Huron MI 48060. 313/989-3900.
Employs: 50-99.

Delta USA Corp
1000 Ternes Dr, Monroe MI 48161-5224. 313/241-4882.
Employs: 100-249.

Diversified Svc Technologies
34364 Goddard Rd, Romulus MI 48174-3404. 313/941-
0300. Employs: 100-249.

Dynamic Conversion Inc
210 Industrial Dr, Hillsdale MI 49242-1075. 517/439-1478.
Employs: 50-99.

Electro-Wire Products Inc
1370 E South St, Owosso MI 48867-9764. 517/723-6702.
Employs: 100-249.

Flexon Inc
2615 Wolcott Rd, Ferndale MI 48220-1422. 313/543-6680.
Employs: 100-249.

G K N Automotive Inc
3300 University Dr, Auburn Hills MI 48326-2362.
313/377-1200. Employs: 50-99.

Gel Inc
34000 Autry St, Livonia MI 48150-1323. 313/522-8010.
Employs: 100-249.

Gibraltar Sprocket Co
3592 Military St, Port Huron MI 48060-6639. 313/985-
9511. Employs: 50-99.

Gil-Mar Manufacturing Co
23889 Freeway Pk Dr, Farmington MI 48335-2815.
313/471-2400. Employs: 50-99.

Grant Durban Inc
32329 Milton, Madison Hts MI 48071-5601. 313/588-
5211. Employs: 50-99.

Great Lake Inc
2000 Beard St, Detroit MI 48209-1580. 313/849-0882.
Employs: 50-99.

Hi-Stat Manufacturing Co Inc
2111 W Thompson Rd, Fenton MI 48430-9704. 313/750-
1655. Employs: 50-99.

Huron Manufacturing
2347 Dove Rd, Port Huron MI 48060-6715. 313/985-3355.
Employs: 100-249.

Huron Products Corp
50751 E Russell Schmidt Blvd, Harrison Twp MI 48045.
313/949-5760. Employs: 50-99.

Huron Products Inds
2145 Wadhams Rd, Saint Clair MI 48079-3808. 313/329-
7148. Employs: 50-99.

IMC Plastics Inc
6785 Rochester Dr, Rochester MI 48309. 313/656-0500.
Employs: 100-249.

J P S Automotive Products Corp
2015 Dove Rd, Port Huron MI 48060-6738. 313/985-4666.
Employs: 50-99.

Jacobs Industries Inc
34401 Commerce Rd, Fraser MI 48026-1648. 313/294-
7220. Employs: 50-99.

Johnson Controls Inc
50150 Ryan Rd, Utica MI 48317-1035. 313/254-3210.
Employs: 50-99.

Jubbu Designers Inc

38281 Schoolcraft Rd # D, Livonia MI 48150-5000.
313/451-3300. Employs: 50-99.

Leader Machine Products Inc
6140 Hix Rd, Westland MI 48185-1962. 313/729-1610.
Employs: 50-99.

Lear Seating Corp/Plant 2
36310 Eureka Rd, Romulus MI 48174-3652. 313/942-
5401. Employs: 100-249.

Ligon Bros Manufacturing Co
3776 N Van Dyke Rd, Almont MI 48003-8043. 313/798-
3921. Employs: 50-99.

Lorro Inc
13881 W Chicago St, Detroit MI 48228-2525. 313/931-
1400. Employs: 50-99.

Mariah Inds Inc
13125 E 8 Mile Rd, Warren MI 48089-3276. 313/778-
6271. Employs: 50-99.

May & Scofield Inc
627 S Dearborn St Box 500, Howell MI 48844-0500.
517/546-5820. Employs: 100-249.

Motor Wheel Corp
1600 N Larch St, Lansing MI 48906-4157. 517/487-4200.
Employs: 100-249.

O & S Manufacturing Co
777 W Eight Mile Road, Whitmore Lake MI 48189-9625.
313/449-4401. Employs: 100-249.

O L Anderson Co
12400 Burt Rd, Detroit MI 48228-1045. 313/538-1280.
Employs: 50-99.

Perfection Auto Products Corp
12445 Levan Rd, Livonia MI 48150-1405. 313/591-0111.
Employs: 50-99.

Pivot Manufacturing Co
12685 Stout St, Detroit MI 48223-3344. 313/531-7500.
Employs: 50-99.

Reuland Electric Co
4500 E Grand River Ave, Howell MI 48843-8554.
517/546-4400. Employs: 50-99.

Romeo Rim Inc
74000 Van Dyke, Romeo MI 48065-3208. 313/752-9605.
Employs: 50-99.

Siemens Automotive
2400 Executive Dr, Auburn Hills MI 48326. 313/253-1000.
Employs: 100-249.

Standard Products Co
2401 S Gulley Rd, Dearborn MI 48124-2440. 313/561-
1100. Employs: 50-99.

T R W/Vehicle Safety Systs
61166 Van Dyke, Washington MI 48094. 313/781-0810.
Employs: 100-249.

Takata Inc
2444 Koppy Dr, Auburn Hills MI 48326-2634. 313/373-
8040. Employs: 100-249.

Takata-Fisher Corp
33180 Freeway Dr, St Clair Shrs MI 48082-1005. 313/296-
7660. Employs: 100-249.

Taylor Machine Products Inc
21300 Eureka Rd, Taylor MI 48180-5271. 313/287-3550.
Employs: 50-99.

Tech-Stran Inds Inc
35335 Beattie Dr, Sterling Hts MI 48312-2611. 313/978-
1818. Employs: 50-99.

Tee Jay Inds Inc
34272 Doreka St, Fraser MI 48026-1659. 313/296-5160.
Employs: 100-249.

Teleflex Inc
1179 Maplelawn Dr, Troy MI 48084-5515. 313/643-8190.
Employs: 50-99.

Toyo Seat USA
2155 S Almont Ave, Imlay City MI 48444-9732. 313/724-0300. Employs: 100-249.

Tractech
11445 Stephens Rd, Warren MI 48089-3860. 313/759-3850. Employs: 100-249.

U S Manufacturing Corp
334 Soper Rd, Bad Axe MI 48413. 517/269-9717.
Employs: 100-249.

Walker Manufacturing
929 Anderson Rd, Litchfield MI 49252. 517/542-5511.
Employs: 100-249.

Watson Engineering Inc
12650 Universal Dr, Taylor MI 48180-4070. 313/946-9856. Employs: 50-99.

Webasto Sun Roofs Inc
2700 Product Dr, Rochester MI 48309-3809. 313/853-2270. Employs: 100-249.

TRUCK TRAILERS

Fruehauf Corporation
10900 Harper Av, Detroit MI 48213-3364. 313/267-1000.
Employs: 100-249.

Gates Power Drive Products Inc
1133 W Long Lake Rd, Bloomfield MI 48302-1983.
313/540-4500. Employs: 50-99.

TRUCK RENTAL AND LEASING, WITHOUT DRIVERS

Jerrome-Duncan Inc
8000 Ford Country Lane, Sterling Hts MI 48313-3710.
313/268-7500. Employs: 50-99.

U-Haul Co
13832 Van Dyke St, Detroit MI 48234-3959. 313/365-6000. Employs: 100-249.

McDonald Ofrd Sales Inc
550 7 Mile Rd, Northville MI 48167-1640. 313/349-1400.
Employs: 50-99.

Suburban Rent-It Co
44475 Grand River Ave, Novi MI 48375-1003. 313/348-1530. Employs: 50-99.

PASSENGER CAR RENTAL

Corporate Image
2966 Biddle St, Wyandotte MI 48192-5231. 313/382-4887.
Employs: 50-99.

Fairlane Auto Leasing Inc
1 Parklane Blvd Ste P104, Dearborn MI 48126-2402.
313/336-3744. Employs: 100-249.

George Victor Oldsmobile Inc
G5050 S Saginaw Rd, Flint MI 48505-1676. 313/744-6537.
Employs: 50-99.

Sears Rent A Car
8715 Wickham, Romulus MI 48174-1915. 313/326-5010.
Employs: 50-99.

Avis Ford Inc
29200 Telegraph Rd, Southfield MI 48034-7602. 313/355-7500. Employs: 100-249.

Bill Fox Chevrolet Inc
755 S Rochester Rd, Rochester MI 48307-2739. 313/651-7000. Employs: 50-99.

Hickey Stark West Inc
24760 W 7 Mile Rd, Detroit MI 48219-1602. 313/538-6600. Employs: 100-249.

TOP, BODY AND UPHOLSTERY REPAIR SHOPS AND PAINT SHOPS

Bob Saks Oldsmobile Inc
35300 Gr River, Farmington MI 48335. 313/478-0500.
Employs: 100-249.

Jefferson Chevrolet Co
2130 E Jefferson Ave, Detroit MI 48207-4102. 313/259-1200. Employs: 100-249.

GENERAL AUTOMOTIVE REPAIR SHOPS

John Colone Chrysler Plymouth Dodge
1295 E M-36, Pinckney MI 48169. 313/878-3154.
Employs: 50-99.

AUTOMOBILES AND OTHER MOTOR VEHICLES: WHOLESALE

Volkswagen Of America Inc
888 W Big Beaver, Troy MI 48084-4736. 313/362-6000.
Employs: 500-999.

MOTOR VEHICLE SUPPLIES AND NEW PARTS: WHOLESALE

ASC Inc
One Sunroof Ctr Dr, Southgate MI 48195-3044. 313/285-4911. Employs: 250-499.

Chevrolet Motor Division
30007 Van Dyke Ave, Warren MI 48093. 313/556-5000.
Employs: 1000+.

Flakt Inc
29333 Stephenson Hwy, Madison Heights MI 48071-2307.
313/541-3200. Employs: 250-499.

GMC General Motors Parts
6060 W Bristol Rd, Flint MI 48554. 313/635-5283.
Employs: 1000+.

Pigeon Manufacturing
1245 Chicago Rd, Troy MI 48083-4231. 313/588-8210.
Employs: 250-499.

United Tech Auto Components
2626 20th St, Port Huron MI 48060-6444. 313/987-8500.
Employs: 250-499.

For more information on career opportunities in the automotive industry:

Associations

ASSOCIATION OF INTERNATIONAL AUTOMOBILE MANUFACTURERS

1001 19th Street North, Suite 1200, Arlington VA 22209.
703/525-7788.

AUTOMOTIVE AFFILIATED REPRESENTATIVES
25 Northwest Point Boulevard, Elk Grove Village IL
60007. 708/228-1310.

AUTOMOTIVE ELECTRIC ASSOCIATION
25 Northwest Point Boulevard, Suite 425, Elk Grove
Village IL 60007. 708/228-1310.

AUTOMOTIVE SERVICE ASSOCIATION
1901 Airport Freeway, Suite 100, Bedford TX 76021-0929.
817/283-6205.

AUTOMOTIVE SERVICE INDUSTRY
ASSOCIATION
25 Northwest Point Boulevard, Elk Grove Village IL
60007. 708/228-1310.

MOTOR VEHICLE MANUFACTURERS
ASSOCIATION
7430 2nd Avenue, Suite 300, Detroit MI 48202. 313/872-4311.

NATIONAL AUTOMOTIVE PARTS ASSOCIATION
2999 Circle 75 Parkway, Atlanta GA 30339. 404/956-2200.

NATIONAL INSTITUTE FOR AUTOMOTIVE
SERVICE EXCELLENCE
13505 Dulles Technology Drive, Herndon VA 22071.
703/713-3800.

SOCIETY OF AUTOMOTIVE ENGINEERS

400 Commonwealth Drive, Warrendale PA 15096.
412/776-4841.

Directories

AUTOMOTIVE NEWS MARKET DATA BOOK
Automotive News, 1400 Woodbridge Avenue, Detroit MI
48207. 313/446-6000.

WARD'S AUTOMOTIVE YEARBOOK
Ward's Communications, 28 West Adams Street, Detroit
MI 48226. 313/962-4433.

Magazines

AUTOMOTIVE INDUSTRIES
Chilton Book Co., Chilton Way, Radnor PA 19089.
800/695-1214.

AUTOMOTIVE NEWS
1400 Woodbridge Avenue, Detroit MI 48207. 313/446-6000.

WARD'S AUTO WORLD
Ward's Communications, Inc., 28 West Adams Street,
Detroit MI 48226. 313/962-4433.

WARD'S AUTOMOTIVE REPORTS
Ward's Communications, Inc., 28 West Adams Street,
Detroit MI 48226. 313/962-4433.

BANKING/SAVINGS AND LOAN

Heading into 1993, the banking industry continues to evolve. The industry began the decade with a series of mega-mergers aimed at solidifying its strongest institutions, resulting in a series of major layoffs. Increasingly, banks are facing new competition from mutual funds and other financial services that are not faced with the same regulatory burdens. As a result, short-term job prospects in the banking industry are fairly weak, and the competition is heavy.

CITIZENS TRUST & SAVINGS BANK
433 Phoenix Street, P.O. Box 449, South Haven MI 49090. 616/637-2141. **Contact:** Dorothy Cutshaw, Personnel Manager. **Description:** A full-service banking institution.

CITY BANK
P.O. Box 100, St. Johns MI 48879. 517/224-5880. **Contact:** Personnel Department. **Description:** A full-service banking institution.

COMERICA INCORPORATED
211 West Fort, Detroit MI 48275-2203. **Contact:** Staffing Representative. **Description:** A full-service banking institution with operations in Michigan, Texas, California, Florida, Arizona, Illinois, Ohio, and Indiana. **Common**

positions: Accountant; Attorney; Bank Officer/Manager; Computer Programmer; Credit Manager; Customer Service Representative; Branch Manager; Management Trainee; Operations/Production Manager; Marketing Specialist; Personnel and Labor Relations Specialist; Public Relations Specialist; Systems Analyst; Underwriter. **Educational backgrounds sought:** Accounting; Business Administration; Economics; Finance; Marketing. **Special programs:** Training programs and internships offered. **Benefits:** medical, dental, and life insurance; pension plan; tuition assistance; disability coverage; daycare assistance; employee discounts; 401K. **Corporate headquarters:** This location. **Operations at this facility:** division headquarters; administration; service; sales. **Listed on:** NYSE.

FIRST FEDERAL OF MICHIGAN
1001 Woodward Avenue, Detroit MI 48226-1904. 313/965-1400. **Contact:** Allen Guitar, Employment Manager. **Description:** First Federal of Michigan focuses on originating and investing in single-family residential mortgage loans funded through deposits and borrowings. One of the largest savings and loan associations in the United States and a geographically diverse provider of financial services to major markets in Michigan, Virginia, and South Carolina through a network of 82 offices. **Employees:** 1,400. **Educational backgrounds sought:** Accounting; Business Administration; Computer Science; Economics; Finance; Marketing. **Benefits:** medical, dental, and life insurance; pension plan; tuition assistance; disability coverage; profit sharing; vacations; holidays. **Corporate headquarters:** This location.

FIRST MICHIGAN BANK CORPORATION
101 East Main Street, Box 300, Zeeland MI 49464. 616/396-9000. **Contact:** Personnel. **Description:** A major bank holding company.

FIRST NATIONAL BANK IN MACOMB COUNTY
49 Macomb Place, Mt. Clemens MI 48043. 313/465-2400. **Contact:** Personnel. **Description:** A full-service banking institution.

FIRST OF AMERICA BANK CORPORATION
108 East Michigan Avenue, Kalamazoo MI 49007. 616/376-9000. **Contact:** Employment Manager. **Description:** Corporate headquarters of a multi-bank holding company. **Educational backgrounds sought:** Accounting; Business Administration; Computer Science; Economics; Finance; Marketing. **Special programs:** Training programs and internships. **Benefits:** medical insurance; dental insurance; pension plan; life insurance; tuition assistance; disability coverage. **Corporate headquarters:** This location. **Listed on:** New York Stock Exchange. **Employees:** 13,000.

MANUFACTURERS BANK
211 West Ford Street, 100 Renaissance Center, Detroit MI 48243. 313/222-3806. **Contact:** Personnel. **Description:** A Detroit-based banking institution.

MICHIGAN FINANCIAL CORPORATION
101 West Washington Street, Marquette MI 49855. 906/228-6940. **Contact:** Personnel. **Description:** A major banking corporation.

MICHIGAN NATIONAL BANK
27777 Inkster Road, P.O. Box 9065, Farmington Hills MI 48333-9065. 313/473-3194. **Contact:** Michelle Rowley, Administrator of College Relations. **Description:** A premier financial services corporation with assets of $11 billion. **Employees:** 6,500. **Common positions:** Accountant; Attorney; Financial Analyst; Management Trainee; Operations/Production Specialist; Marketing Specialist; Purchasing Agent. **Educational backgrounds sought:** Accounting; Business Administration; Computer Science; Economics; Finance; Liberal Arts; Marketing. **Special programs:** Training programs offered. **Benefits:** medical, dental, and life insurance; pension plan; tuition assistance; disability coverage; profit sharing; savings plan. **Corporate headquarters:** This location. Operations at this facility: regional headquarters; divisional headquarters; administration. **Listed on:** New York Stock Exchange.

NBD/NATIONAL BANK OF DETROIT
200 Ottawa Avenue North West, Grand Rapids MI 49503. 616/771-7000. **Contact:** Personnel. **Description:** A major full service banking company.

OLD KENT BANK & TRUST COMPANY
One Vandenberg Center, Grand Rapids MI 49503. 616/771-5000. **Contact:** Personnel. **Description:** A full-service banking institution.

OLD KENT BANK-SOUTHEAST
2674 West Jefferson Avenue, Trenton MI 48183. 313/671-2400. **Contact:** Human Resources. **Description:** A full-service banking institution.

SECURITY BANK & TRUST
16333 Trenton Road, Southgate MI 48195. 313/281-5000. **Contact:** Greg Bader, Personnel Director. **Description:** A major Detroit area holding company. **Employees:** 2,000.

SECURITY SAVINGS BANK
301 West Michigan Avenue, Jackson MI 49201. 517/787-9700. **Contact:** Personnel. **Description:** A full-service savings and loan institution.

UNITED BANK OF MICHIGAN
2620 Horizon Drive South East, Grand Rapids MI 49546. 616/957-3941. **Contact:** Personnel. **Description:** A full service banking institution.

Additional large employers: 250+

BANKS, NATIONAL COMMERCIAL

First Of America Bank Cent Br
101 S Washington Sq 1st Fl, Lansing MI 48933-1703.
517/334-1600. Employs: 500-999.

First Of America Bank Southeast Michigan NA
645 Griswold, Detroit MI 48226-4013. 313/596-8000.
Employs: 500-999.

First Of Michigan Corp
100 Renaissance Center, Detroit MI 48243-1002. 313/259-2600. Employs: 250-499.

Manufacturers National Corp
Manufacturers Bank Tower, Detroit MI 48243. 313/222-4000. Employs: 1000+.

Michigan National Corp
4300 W Saginaw Hw, Lansing MI 48917-2112. 517/323-5232. Employs: 500-999.

N B D Ann Arbor
125 S Main St, Ann Arbor MI 48104-1902. 313/995-8111. Employs: 250-499.

NBD Bank N A
611 Woodward Ave, Detroit MI 48226-3408. 313/225-1000. Employs: 1000+.

BANKS, STATE COMMERCIAL

Federal Reserve Bank
160 W Fort St, Detroit MI 48226-3201. 313/961-6880. Employs: 250-499.

First Of America Bank
400 S Main St, Royal Oak MI 48067-2616. 313/691-3850. Employs: 500-999.

Great Lakes Bancorp
401 E Liberty Box 8600, Ann Arbor MI 48104-2268. 313/769-8300. Employs: 250-499.

Macomb Warren Bank
One N Gratiot Ave, Mount Clemens MI 48043-5613. 313/469-6900. Employs: 250-499.

Michigan National Bank
124 W Allegan St, Lansing MI 48933-1701. 517/377-3293. Employs: 1000+.

Security Bank Of Commerce

11300 Joseph Campau Ave, Detroit MI 48212-3039. 313/366-3200. Employs: 250-499.

Society Bank Michigan
100 S Main St, Ann Arbor MI 48104-1903. 313/994-5555. Employs: 250-499.

Sterling Savings Bank
28400 Northwestern Hwy, Southfield MI 48034-1839. 313/355-2400. Employs: 250-499.

SAVINGS INSTITUTIONS, FEDERALLY CHARTERED

Standard Federal Bank
2600 W Big Beaver Rd, Troy MI 48084-3323. 313/643-9600. Employs: 500-999.

SAVINGS INSTITUTIONS, NOT FEDERALLY CHARTERED

Central Holding Co
36800 Gratiot, Mount Clemens MI 48043. 313/792-7000. Employs: 500-999.

OFFICES OF BANK HOLDING COMPANIES

Citizens Banking Corp
One Citizens Banking Center, Flint MI 48502. 313/766-7500. Employs: 1000+.

Comerica Incorporated
211 W Fort St, Detroit MI 48226-3202. 313/222-3300. Employs: 1000+.

Michigan National Corp
29777 Telegraph Rd Ste 2, Southfield MI 48034-1303. 313/626-8200. Employs: 1000+.

Michigan National Corporation
P O Box 9065, Farmington MI 48333-9065. 313/473-3000. Employs: 1000+.

Additional small to medium sized employers: 50-249

BANKS, NATIONAL COMMERCIAL

Ann Arbor Commerce Bank
2930 S State St, Ann Arbor MI 48104-6742. 313/995-3130. Employs: 50-99.

Bank Of Alma-Northtown
7455 N Alger Rd, Alma MI 48801-1071. 517/463-3134. Employs: 50-99.

Bank Of Lenawee
539 S Meridian Rd, Hudson MI 49247-9310. 517/448-7443. Employs: 50-99.

Bank Of Lenawee Waldron Office
102 E Center, Waldron MI 49288. 517/286-6246. Employs: 50-99.

Bank Of Ypsilanti
133 Michigan Ave, Detroit MI 48226-2611. 313/965-7977. Employs: 100-249.

Bank One East Lansing
100 W Grand River Av, East Lansing MI 48823-4325. 517/337-4100. Employs: 100-249.

Bank One Fenton N A
142 S Leroy St, Fenton MI 48430-2601. 313/629-3531. Employs: 50-99.

Bank One Fenton Na
12735 Andersonville Rd, Davisburg MI 48350-2503. 313/634-5700. Employs: 50-99.

Bucker & Associates Inc
17277 W 10 Mile Rd, Southfield MI 48075-2918. 313/423-8230. Employs: 50-99.

C & S Commercial & Savings Bk
3300 Gratiot Blvd, Marysville MI 48040-1490. 313/364-4600. Employs: 50-99.

Capitol National Bank
200 Washington Sq N, Lansing MI 48933-1302. 517/484-5080. Employs: 50-99.

Charter National Bank
2517 Fort St, Wyandotte MI 48192-4433. 313/285-1900. Employs: 50-99.

Chicago-Tokyo Bank Detroit Ofc
1 Woodward Ave, Detroit MI 48226-3402. 313/965-6120. Employs: 100-249.

Citizens Bank
1580 N Leroy St, Fenton MI 48430-2766. 313/750-6777. Employs: 50-99.

Citizens Bank
300 N Saginaw St, Durand MI 48429-1237. 517/288-3725. Employs: 50-99.

Citizens Bank
9484 E Genesee, New Lothrop MI 48460. 313/638-5051. Employs: 50-99.

Citizens Bank Financial Center
3271 E Pontiac Rd, Auburn Hills MI 48326. 313/377-1060.
Employs: 50-99.

Citizens Bank Financial Center
700 E Big Beaver Rd, Troy MI 48083-1407. 313/680-0370.
Employs: 50-99.

Citizens Cml & Svgs Bk Br
2609 W Pierson Rd, Flint MI 48504-6866. 313/766-6950.
Employs: 50-99.

Citizens Cml & Svgs Bk Br
2922 Flushing Rd, Flint MI 48504-4331. 313/766-7964.
Employs: 50-99.

Citizens Cml & Svgs Bk Br
4129 S Saginaw St, Flint MI 48507-2650. 313/766-7805.
Employs: 50-99.

Citizens Cml & Svgs Bk Br
3848 Richfield Rd, Flint MI 48506-2616. 313/766-7724.
Employs: 50-99.

Citizens Cml & Svgs Bk Br
2101 S Chavez Dr, Flint MI 48506. 313/766-7585.
Employs: 50-99.

Citizens Commercial & Svgs Bk
G6452 W Pierson Rd, Flint MI 48504. 313/766-6900.
Employs: 50-99.

City Bank
209 E Grand River Ave, Lansing MI 48906-4329. 517/371-8895. Employs: 50-99.

City Bank & Trust Co National Association
960 N West Av, Jackson MI 49202-3269. 517/788-2858.
Employs: 50-99.

Clinton Bank & Trust Co
2201 E Grand River Av, Lansing MI 48912-3221. 517/372-2024. Employs: 50-99.

Commercial National Bank Drive In Facility
119 W Center St, Alma MI 48801-2205. 517/463-6852.
Employs: 50-99.

Comerica
3736 Pelham Rd, Dearborn MI 48124-3832. 313/277-6676.
Employs: 50-99.

Comerica Bank
20065 Mack, Grosse Pointe MI 48236. 313/884-0161.
Employs: 50-99.

Comerica Bank-Detroit
23400 Michigan Av, Dearborn MI 48124-1915. 313/277-2490. Employs: 50-99.

Comerica Bank-Jackson
1620 W Michigan Av, Jackson MI 49202-4003. 517/788-5143. Employs: 50-99.

Comerica Operations Center
2800 Springport Rd, Jackson MI 49202. 517/787-1632.
Employs: 50-99.

Ctzns Cml & Svgs Bk Dort Hwy
905 S Dort Hwy, Flint MI 48503-2856. 313/766-7624.
Employs: 50-99.

D & N Savings Bank
G3213 N Genesee Rd, Burton MI 48529. 313/736-0440.
Employs: 50-99.

D & N Savings Bank
300 Fenton Sq, Fenton MI 48430-2179. 313/629-2289.
Employs: 50-99.

D & N Savings Bank

1559 E Pierson Rd, Flushing MI 48433-1816. 313/659-4875. Employs: 50-99.

D & N Savings Bank F S B
2401 Davison Rd, Flint MI 48506-3647. 313/232-7455.
Employs: 50-99.

D & N Savings Bk
G4409 Miller Rd, Flint MI 48507. 313/732-6360. Employs: 50-99.

D & N Savings Bk
6120 Fenton Rd, Flint MI 48507-4759. 313/232-3810.
Employs: 50-99.

Dart National Bank
368 S Park St Box 40, Mason MI 48854-1659. 517/676-3661. Employs: 50-99.

Dearborn Bank & Trust
23053 Michigan Av, Dearborn MI 48124-2011. 313/277-7616. Employs: 50-99.

Dearborn Bank & Trust
13550 Ford Rd, Dearborn MI 48126-3207. 313/277-5440.
Employs: 50-99.

Dearborn Bank & Trust Br
15400 N Commerce Dr, Dearborn MI 48120-1221.
313/277-6720. Employs: 50-99.

Detroit Savings Bank
10982 Middlebelt Rd, Livonia MI 48150-3058. 313/522-4551. Employs: 50-99.

Empire Of America Br
32800 Southfield Rd, Franklin MI 48025-3166. 313/644-0440. Employs: 50-99.

Farmer's State Bank
M-52 & M-106, Stockbridge MI 49285. 517/851-8888.
Employs: 50-99.

Farmers State Bank
1402 E Center St, Ithaca MI 48847-1610. 517/875-5080.
Employs: 50-99.

First America Southeast Mi Na
15800 E 8 Mile Rd, Detroit MI 48205-1415. 313/839-9200.
Employs: 100-249.

First America Southeast Mi Na
20055 Ann Arbor Trl, Detroit MI 48228. 313/271-4140.
Employs: 100-249.

First America Southeast Mi Na
4900 E McNichols Rd, Detroit MI 48212-1733. 313/893-8400. Employs: 100-249.

First Federal Of Michigan
23011 Woodward Ave, Ferndale MI 48220-1359. 313/545-3300. Employs: 50-99.

First Federal Of Michigan
55 W Long Lake Rd, Troy MI 48098-4633. 313/689-4263.
Employs: 50-99.

First Federal Savings Lenawee
1300 W Chicago Blvd, Tecumseh MI 49286-1258.
517/423-2640. Employs: 50-99.

First Federal Savings Lenawee
124 E Michigan Ave, Clinton MI 49236-9581. 517/456-7408. Employs: 50-99.

First Federal Savings Lenawee
520 W Adrian St, Blissfield MI 49228-1004. 517/486-4317. Employs: 50-99.

First Federal Savings & Loan Assn
1613 Livernois Rd, Troy MI 48083-1728. 313/362-4210.
Employs: 50-99.

First Federal Savings Bank & Trust
1277 W Square Lake Rd, Bloomfield MI 48302-0845.
313/338-4056. Employs: 50-99.

First Federal Savings Bank & Trust
70 W Tienken Rd, Rochester MI 48306-4348. 313/651-
9500. Employs: 50-99.

First Federal Savings Bank & Trust
7698 Cooley Lake Rd, Waterford MI 48327-4190.
313/363-7163. Employs: 50-99.

First Federal Savings Bank & Trust
2920 E Highland Rd, Highland MI 48356-2810. 313/887-
4141. Employs: 50-99.

First Federal Savings Bank & Trust
69 N Saginaw St, Pontiac MI 48342-2154. 313/338-1300.
Employs: 50-99.

First Federal Savings Bank & Trust
7188 Ortonville Rd, Clarkston MI 48346-1571. 313/625-
2631. Employs: 50-99.

First Federal Savings Bank & Trust
471 S Broadway St, Lake Orion MI 48362-3121. 313/693-
6228. Employs: 50-99.

First Federal Savings Bank & Trust
4104 E 10 Mile Rd, Warren MI 48091-1507. 313/755-
9800. Employs: 50-99.

First Federal Savings Bank & Trust
243 W Congress St, Detroit MI 48226-3205. 313/962-2785.
Employs: 50-99.

First Federal Of Michigan
1510 Woodward, Birmingham MI 48009. 313/647-6700.
Employs: 50-99.

First National Bank
1 E Huron Ave Box 37, Bad Axe MI 48413-1371. 517/269-
9531. Employs: 50-99.

First National Bank Of Bad Axe
119 N Heisterman St, Bad Axe MI 48413-1204. 517/269-
6444. Employs: 50-99.

First Nationwide Bank
75 W Huron St, Pontiac MI 48342-2131. 313/338-7127.
Employs: 50-99.

First Nationwide Bank
16530 E Warren Ave, Detroit MI 48224-2743. 313/885-
6195. Employs: 50-99.

First Nationwide Bank
7707 Michigan Ave, Detroit MI 48210-2217. 313/943-
4813. Employs: 100-249.

First Nationwide Bank
10641 Joy Rd, Detroit MI 48204-3019. 313/933-7664.
Employs: 50-99.

First Nationwide Bank
33408 5 Mile Rd, Livonia MI 48154-2860. 313/427-5350.
Employs: 50-99.

First Nationwide Bank
27270 Cherry Hill Rd, Dearborn Hts MI 48127-3618.
313/943-4820. Employs: 50-99.

First Nationwide Bank
13606 Michigan Av 1stfl, Dearborn MI 48126-3519.
313/943-4426. Employs: 50-99.

First Natl Bk In Mount Clemens
49 Macomb St, Mount Clemens MI 48043-5614. 313/465-
2400. Employs: 100-249.

First Of Amer Bk Ann Arbor Br

115 Washtenaw Pl, Ann Arbor MI 48104-1640. 313/995-
7880. Employs: 100-249.

First Of Amer Bank Livingston
10014 E Gd River, Brighton MI 48116. 313/229-0080.
Employs: 50-99.

First Of America
1880 W Stadium Blvd, Ann Arbor MI 48103-4504.
313/995-7942. Employs: 100-249.

First Of America
7170 Cooley Lake Rd, Waterford MI 48327-4113.
313/363-8348. Employs: 50-99.

First Of America Bank
8025 Clio Rd, Flint MI 48504. 313/686-4420. Employs:
50-99.

First Of America Bank Se Mi
7001 Highland Rd, White Lake MI 48383-2850. 313/887-
3751. Employs: 50-99.

First Of America Bank-Wayne
44520 Michigan Ave, Canton MI 48188-2423. 313/397-
1150. Employs: 50-99.

First Of America Se Mi Na
400 Renaissance Center, Detroit MI 48243. 313/596-8616.
Employs: 100-249.

First Security Sav Bk
536 Perry Rd Ste 7, Grand Blanc MI 48439-1415. 313/694-
5100. Employs: 50-99.

Firts Federal Savings Bank & Trust
4998 Highland Rd, Waterford MI 48328-1146. 313/673-
1278. Employs: 50-99.

First Independence Money Strs
6113 Livernois Ave, Detroit MI 48210-1758. 313/896-
9386. Employs: 100-249.

Genesee Merchants Bank & Trust Co
4930 Clio Rd, Flint MI 48504-1809. 313/766-8366.
Employs: 50-99.

Greater Detroit B I D C O Inc
1101 Washington Blvd, Detroit MI 48226-1903. 313/962-
4326. Employs: 100-249.

Huntington Banks Of Michigan
7 N Gratiot Ave, Mount Clemens MI 48043-5644.
313/466-3283. Employs: 50-99.

Ionia County Natl Bank
302 W Main St, Ionia MI 48846-1618. 616/527-0220.
Employs: 50-99.

Isabella Bank & Trust
1416 E Pickard, Mount Pleasnt MI 48858. 517/773-2129.
Employs: 50-99.

Key State Bank
3015 E Saginaw St, Lansing MI 48912-4709. 517/351-
1111. Employs: 50-99.

Key State Bank
G3501 S Linden Rd, Flint MI 48507. 313/733-6330.
Employs: 50-99.

Litchfield State Savings Bank
900 Hudson Rd, Pittsford MI 49271. 517/523-3476.
Employs: 50-99.

Loan By Phone
102 E Broadway St, Mount Pleasnt MI 48858-2310.
517/772-5626. Employs: 50-99.

Loan Dept
4046 Huron St, North Branch MI 48461-9351. 313/688-
3096. Employs: 50-99.

Madison National Bank
1800 E 12 Mile Rd, Madison Hts MI 48071-2659. 313/548-
2900. Employs: 50-99.

Manufacturer S Bank Lansing Br
5101 N Grand River Av, Lansing MI 48906-2439.
517/886-0233. Employs: 50-99.

Manufacturers Bank Of Lansing
5226 S Cedar St, Lansing MI 48911-3801. 517/394-0733.
Employs: 50-99.

Manufacturers Bank Of Lansing
7016 S Cedar, Holt MI 48842. 517/694-1285. Employs: 50-
99.

Manufacturers Bank Of Lansing
3316 S Logan St, Lansing MI 48910-2944. 517/394-0666.
Employs: 50-99.

Manufacturers National Bank
101 N Main St Box 7940, Ann Arbor MI 48104-1400.
313/930-2450. Employs: 50-99.

Manufacturers Natl Bank
37000 Grand River Ave Ste100, Farmington MI 48335-
2880. 313/474-6400. Employs: 50-99.

Manufactures Bank Mi Mason Ofc
22101 Michigan Av, Dearborn MI 48124-2204. 313/274-
7237. Employs: 50-99.

MFC 1st National Bank & Trust Northgate
6615 Northgate Home Center, Weston MI 49289. 517/786-
5010. Employs: 50-99.

Michigan National Bank
G1160 N Ballenger Hwy, Flint MI 48504-4444. 313/767-
1130. Employs: 50-99.

Michigan National Bank
G3050 W Pasadena Av, Flint MI 48504. 313/733-2720.
Employs: 50-99.

Michigan National Bank
7525 E Saginaw Hwy, Grand Ledge MI 48837-9173.
517/627-3259. Employs: 50-99.

Michigan National Bank
G7606 S Saginaw Rd, Burton MI 48529. 313/695-4410.
Employs: 50-99.

Michigan National Bank
30000 Grand River Ave, Farmington MI 48336-4722.
313/477-3330. Employs: 50-99.

Michigan National Bank
2201 E Hill Rd, Grand Blanc MI 48439-5057. 313/695-
1190. Employs: 50-99.

Michigan National Bank
40950 Garfield Rd, Clinton Twp MI 48038-2536. 313/286-
5811. Employs: 50-99.

Michigan National Bank
1815 Stone St, Port Huron MI 48060-3143. 313/987-1921.
Employs: 50-99.

Michigan National Bank
902 4th St, Port Huron MI 48060. 313/987-1850. Employs:
50-99.

Michigan National Bank
1533 N Woodward Ave, Birmingham MI 48009-4861.
313/433-1800. Employs: 50-99.

Michigan National Bank
28 W Adams Ave, Detroit MI 48226-1617. 313/961-3940.
Employs: 100-249.

Michigan National Bank Br

3080 Washtenaw Rd, Ypsilanti MI 48197-1509. 313/747-
7606. Employs: 50-99.

Michigan National Bank Br
980 N Hunter Blvd, Bloomfield MI 48304. 313/644-0802.
Employs: 50-99.

Michigan National Bank Br
2701 Monroe St, Dearborn MI 48124-3017. 313/563-5000.
Employs: 50-99.

Michigan National Bank S Metro
13020 Warren Av, Dearborn MI 48126-1537. 313/846-
3690. Employs: 50-99.

Midwest Guaranty Bank
33897 5 Mile Rd, Livonia MI 48154-2601. 313/522-0900.
Employs: 100-249.

National Bank Detroit Br 155
18800 Hubbard Dr, Dearborn MI 48126. 313/271-7720.
Employs: 50-99.

National Bank Of Detroit
105 Briarwood Cir, Ann Arbor MI 48108-1601. 313/995-
8100. Employs: 50-99.

National Bank Of Detroit
2801 Union Lake Rd, Commerce Twp MI 48382-3562.
313/360-1900. Employs: 50-99.

National Bank Of Detroit
3166 W Huron, Waterford MI 48328. 313/681-0900.
Employs: 50-99.

National Bank Of Detroit
522 Huron Av, Port Huron MI 48060-3806. 313/985-3223.
Employs: 50-99.

National Bank Of Detroit Br 28
18203 Fenkell St, Detroit MI 48223-2312. 313/837-2233.
Employs: 100-249.

National Bank Of Royal Oak
215 South Center St, Royal Oak MI 48067-3809. 313/399-
5200. Employs: 100-249.

NBD
6211 Cadieux Rd, Detroit MI 48224-2005. 313/886-2000.
Employs: 100-249.

NBD Bank
G5090 E Hill Rd, Grand Blanc MI 48439. 313/766-8410.
Employs: 50-99.

NBD Bank N A
8359 Office Park Dr, Grand Blanc MI 48439-2078.
313/766-4420. Employs: 50-99.

NBD Bank N A
3520 Pine Grove Av, Port Huron MI 48060-1944. 313/982-
6235. Employs: 50-99.

NBD Bank N A
G2413 S Linden Rd, Flint MI 48532. 313/762-5118.
Employs: 50-99.

NBD Commerce Bank
6015 S Pennsylvania Av, Lansing MI 48911-5234.
517/393-6012. Employs: 50-99.

NBD Commerce Bank Br
1749 W Grand River Av, Okemos MI 48864-1803.
517/349-5550. Employs: 50-99.

NBD Genesee Bank
G1232 S Belsay Rd, Burton MI 48529. 313/766-8376.
Employs: 50-99.

NBD Genesee Bank
1320 E Atherton Rd, Flint MI 48507-2820. 313/766-8386.
Employs: 50-99.

NBD Genesee Bank
805 Welch Blvd, Flint MI 48504-5501. 313/766-8245.
Employs: 50-99.

NBD Genesee Bank Br
3430 Richfield Rd, Flint MI 48506-2600. 313/766-8317.
Employs: 50-99.

NBD Genesee Bank Br
1911 N Franklin Av, Flint MI 48506-4413. 313/766-8356.
Employs: 50-99.

NBD Genesee Bank Ofc
3701 Fenton Rd, Flint MI 48507-1554. 313/766-8066.
Employs: 50-99.

NBD Genessee Bank Br
4835 Fenton Rd, Flint MI 48507-3321. 313/766-8346.
Employs: 50-99.

NBD
Griswold St-Buhi Bg, Detroit MI 48226. 313/961-3605.
Employs: 100-249.

NBD
1431 Washington Blvd, Detroit MI 48226-1720. 313/961-
0277. Employs: 100-249.

NBD
7 Mill St, Ecorse MI 48229. 313/838-6440. Employs: 50-
99.

NBD
Dequinder E 8 Mile, Detroit MI 48234. 313/368-2860.
Employs: 100-249.

NBD
5057 Woodward Ave, Detroit MI 48202-4015. 313/833-
1900. Employs: 100-249.

NBD
5622 Michigan Ave, Detroit MI 48210-3037. 313/894-
1960. Employs: 100-249.

NBD
19301 W McNichols Rd, Detroit MI 48219-4029. 313/537-
5277. Employs: 100-249.

NBD
W 7 Mi-Chapel, Detroit MI 48219. 313/255-0880.
Employs: 100-249.

NBD
12840 Dexter Ave, Detroit MI 48238-3325. 313/867-4200.
Employs: 100-249.

NBD
200 Renaissance Ctr, Detroit MI 48243-1209. 313/259-
5008. Employs: 100-249.

NBD
20500 Van Dyke St, Detroit MI 48234-3216. 313/368-
0350. Employs: 100-249.

Oakland Trust Manufacturers Natl Bank
1166 N Woodward Av, Birmingham MI 48009-6739.
313/642-8444. Employs: 50-99.

Old Kent Bank
8393 W Grand River Ave, Brighton MI 48116-2903.
313/227-8750. Employs: 50-99.

Old Kent Bank
1801 W Main St, Owosso MI 48867-1374. 517/725-6291.
Employs: 50-99.

Old Kent Bank and Trust Co
Eastern 754 Franklin Se, Franklin MI 48025. 616/771-
5715. Employs: 50-99.

Old Kent Bank Of St Johns

201 E Walker St, Saint Johns MI 48879-1539. 517/224-
6871. Employs: 50-99.

Old Kent Bank Of St Johns
101 N State St, Pewamo MI 48873-9747. 517/593-2600.
Employs: 50-99.

Peoples Bank Of Port Huron
511 Fort St, Port Huron MI 48060-3922. 313/984-5161.
Employs: 50-99.

Peoples State Bank
105 W Middle St, Williamston MI 48895-1329. 517/655-
3464. Employs: 50-99.

Republic Bank
G3200 Beecher Rd, Flint MI 48532-3613. 313/732-3300.
Employs: 50-99.

Security Bank & Trust
27007 Allen Rd, Trenton MI 48183-4966. 313/675-4455.
Employs: 50-99.

Security Bank & Trust Co Br
23190 Outer Dr, Allen Park MI 48101-3126. 313/562-
5556. Employs: 50-99.

Security Bank Of Commerce
54870 Mound-At 25 Mile Road, Washington MI 48094.
313/781-5591. Employs: 50-99.

Security Bank Of Commerce
45125 Hayes Rd, Shelby Twp MI 48315-6209. 313/731-
7100. Employs: 50-99.

Security Savings Bank
704 S Brown St, Jackson MI 49203-1429. 517/784-3118.
Employs: 50-99.

Society Bank Br
2225 Washtenaw Rd, Ypsilanti MI 48197-1545. 313/485-
9312. Employs: 50-99.

Society National Bank
10 S Gratiot Ave, Mount Clemens MI 48043-7903.
313/465-7360. Employs: 50-99.

Standard Federal Bank
99 W Maple Rd, Birmingham MI 48009-3320. 313/647-
6800. Employs: 50-99.

Standard Federal Bank
1949 E Jefferson Ave, Detroit MI 48207-4111. 313/567-
4600. Employs: 100-249.

State Bank Of Croswell
5200 Peck Rd, Croswell MI 48422-1425. 313/679-3620.
Employs: 50-99.

Sterling Savings Bank
180 Oakland Ave, Birmingham MI 48009-3475. 313/646-
8787. Employs: 50-99.

Texas Commerce Bank Ft Worth
100 Tandy Center Rm 200, Jackson MI 49202. 517/336-
9661. Employs: 50-99.

The Huntington Co
1670 Axtell Rd, Troy MI 48084-4431. 313/362-2613.
Employs: 50-99.

The Madison National Bank
31300 Orchard Lake Rd, Farmington MI 48334-1383.
313/626-6190. Employs: 50-99.

The Miami Valley Bank
24275 Northwestern Hwy, Southfield MI 48075-2530.
313/350-9710. Employs: 50-99.

The State Bank
4043 Grange Hall Rd, Holly MI 48442-1111. 313/750-
8701. Employs: 50-99.

Tri County Bank
4441 Main St, Brown City MI 48416-9701. 313/346-2776.
Employs: 50-99.

Wyandotte Savings Bank
3255 Fort St, Wyandotte MI 48192-5312. 313/284-8800.
Employs: 50-99.

BANKS, STATE COMMERCIAL

Bank Of Alma
311 Woodworth Ave, Alma MI 48801-1826. 517/463-
3131. Employs: 50-99.

Capitol Federal Savings
2119 Hamilton Rd, Okemos MI 48864-1742. 517/374-
3526. Employs: 50-99.

Capitol Federal Savings
6510 S Cedar St, Lansing MI 48911. 517/374-3501.
Employs: 50-99.

Citizens Commercial
G6452 Pierson Rd, Flushing MI 48433. 313/766-6900.
Employs: 50-99.

Citizens Commercial
G3275 Van Slyke, Flint MI 48507-3265. 313/766-7745.
Employs: 50-99.

Citizens Commercial
770 E Genesee St, Mount Morris MI 48458-2026. 313/686-
4970. Employs: 50-99.

Citizens Commercial
5510 Richfield Rd, Flint MI 48506-2243. 313/736-5285.
Employs: 50-99.

Citizens Commercial & Saving
G 4256 E Court St, Burton MI 48509. 313/743-9620.
Employs: 50-99.

Citizens Commercial & Saving
7384 Davison Rd, Davison MI 48423-2012. 313/653-0150.
Employs: 50-99.

Citizens Commercial & Saving
3271 Five Pts Dr, Auburn Hills MI 48326. 313/766-7500.
Employs: 50-99.

City Bank
2017 Lake Lansing Rd, Lansing MI 48912-3660. 517/371-
8885. Employs: 50-99.

City Bank
15431 N East St, Lansing MI 48906-5906. 517/371-8880.
Employs: 50-99.

City Bank & Trust Co
1611 W Morrell, Jackson MI 49203-1442. 517/788-2841.
Employs: 50-99.

City Bank & Trust Co
3323 W Michigan Ave, Jackson MI 49202-1834. 517/788-
2845. Employs: 50-99.

City Bank & Trust Co
4515 Frances St, Jackson MI 49203-5745. 517/788-2875.
Employs: 50-99.

City Bank & Trust Co
1911 E High St, Jackson MI 49203-3413. 517/788-2871.
Employs: 50-99.

Colonial Central Savings
15751 E Nine Mile Rd, East Detroit MI 48021-3906.
313/771-8820. Employs: 50-99.

Colonial Central Savings
28201 Harper Ave, St Clair Shrs MI 48081-1685. 313/774-
8820. Employs: 50-99.

Colonial Central Savings
37020 Garfield, Clinton Twp MI 48036-2050. 313/286-
7480. Employs: 50-99.

Colonial Central Savings
20599 Mack Ave, Grosse Pointe MI 48236. 313/886-8881.
Employs: 50-99.

Comerica Bank
27367 Schoolcraft Rd, Redford MI 48239-3006. 313/537-
1044. Employs: 50-99.

Comerica Bank
4395 Orchard Lake Rd, W Bloomfield MI 48323-1643.
313/626-7001. Employs: 50-99.

Comerica Bank
33140 14 Mile Rd, W Bloomfield MI 48322-3547.
313/626-8202. Employs: 50-99.

Comerica Bank
5680 W Maple Rd, W Bloomfield MI 48322-3713.
313/564-6974. Employs: 50-99.

Comerica Bank
5775 14 Mile Rd, Sterling Hts MI 48310-6538. 313/268-
2400. Employs: 50-99.

Comerica Bank
1915 14 Mile Rd, Sterling Hts MI 48310-5917. 313/536-
7270. Employs: 50-99.

Comerica Bank
13655 15 Mile Rd, Sterling Hts MI 48312-4218. 313/268-
6170. Employs: 50-99.

Comerica Bank
201 S Washington, Oxford MI 48371-4983. 313/222-3300.
Employs: 50-99.

Comerica Bank
41941 Garfield, Clinton Twp MI 48038-1966. 313/228-
0207. Employs: 50-99.

Comerica Bank
27777 Franklin Rd, Southfield MI 48034-2337. 313/355-
1424. Employs: 50-99.

Comerica Bank
25300 Kelly Rd, Roseville MI 48066-4961. 313/771-1521.
Employs: 50-99.

Comerica Bank
28801 Groesbeck Hwy, Roseville MI 48066-2318.
313/773-0860. Employs: 50-99.

Comerica Bank
32455 Gratiot Ave, Roseville MI 48066-1154. 313/294-
6970. Employs: 50-99.

Comerica Bank
27990 Gratiot Ave, Roseville MI 48066-4864. 313/779-
2751. Employs: 50-99.

Comerica Bank
20805 12 Mile Rd, Roseville MI 48066-2244. 313/774-
3050. Employs: 50-99.

Comerica Bank
26500 Gratiot Ave, Roseville MI 48066-3342. 313/777-
1300. Employs: 50-99.

Comerica Bank
29252 Southfield Rd, Southfield MI 48076-1920. 313/559-
4490. Employs: 50-99.

Comerica Bank
42345 Ann Arbor Rd, Plymouth MI 48170-4356. 313/455-
0550. Employs: 50-99.

Comerica Bank
5678 Whitmore Lake Rd, Brighton MI 48116-1942.
313/222-3300. Employs: 50-99.

Comerica Bank
25682 Van Born, Dearborn Hts MI 48127-1145. 313/277-
7660. Employs: 50-99.

Comerica Bank
25745 Ford Rd, Dearborn Hts MI 48127-3025. 313/277-
2626. Employs: 50-99.

Comerica Bank
29370 Plymouth Rd, Livonia MI 48150-2339. 313/421-
0600. Employs: 50-99.

Comerica Bank
31200 Ann Arbor Trl, Westland MI 48185. 313/427-4700.
Employs: 50-99.

Comerica Bank
6870 Wayne Rd, Westland MI 48185. 313/728-3355.
Employs: 50-99.

Comerica Bank
1747 Newburgh Rd, Westland MI 48185. 313/728-5520.
Employs: 50-99.

Comerica Bank
5720 N Sheldon Rd, Canton MI 48187-3112. 313/459-
3911. Employs: 50-99.

Comerica Bank Detroit
1000 E Nine Mile Rd, Ferndale MI 48220-1935. 313/398-
0330. Employs: 50-99.

Comerica Bank Detroit
415 Fisher, Grosse Pointe MI 48230-1602. 313/881-9850.
Employs: 50-99.

Comerica Bank Detroit
5866 Middlebelt, Garden City MI 48135-2458. 313/422-
5630. Employs: 50-99.

Comerica Bank Detroit
35405 Grand River, Farmington MI 48335-3122. 313/442-
9300. Employs: 50-99.

Comerica Bank-Jackson N A
245 W Michigan Ave, Jackson MI 49201-2218. 517/788-
5000. Employs: 100-249.

Community State Bank
7303 Gratiot Rd, Detroit MI 48213-2817. 517/781-2350.
Employs: 100-249.

Dearborn Federal Savings
27115 W Warren, Dearborn Hts MI 48127-1812. 313/278-
5800. Employs: 50-99.

Dearborn Federal Savings
4111 S Telegraph Rd, Dearborn Hts MI 48125-1930.
313/274-1300. Employs: 50-99.

Dearborn Federal Savings
22315 Michigan Ave Box 2009, Dearborn MI 48124-2224.
313/565-3100. Employs: 50-99.

Detroit Savings Bank
511 Woodward Ave, Detroit MI 48226-3406. 313/961-
7600. Employs: 100-249.

Detroit Savings Bank
26800 Ryan Rd, Sterling Hts MI 48310. 313/961-7600.
Employs: 50-99.

Fidelity Bank
17197 N Laurel Park Dr, Livonia MI 48152-2686. 313/953-
0177. Employs: 50-99.

Fidelity Bank

26877 Northwestern Hwy, Southfield MI 48034-2141.
313/356-8810. Employs: 50-99.

Fidelity Bank
400 Galleria Officenter, Southfield MI 48034. 313/353-
1460. Employs: 50-99.

Fidelity Bank
200 Galleria Officentre, Southfield MI 48034. 313/352-
1580. Employs: 50-99.

Fidelity Bank
26911 Northwestern Hwy, Southfield MI 48034-4717.
313/262-1222. Employs: 50-99.

First Independence National Bank
44 Michigan, Detroit MI 48226. 313/256-8200. Employs:
50-99.

First Independence Natl Bank
545 Brush St, Detroit MI 48226-4310. 313/961-1244.
Employs: 100-249.

First Independence Natl Bank
7020 7 Mile At Liverois, Detroit MI 48221-2239. 313/342-
0900. Employs: 100-249.

First Independence Natl Bank
12200 Livernois Ave, Detroit MI 48204-1310. 313/933-
4600. Employs: 100-249.

First Of America Bank
22711 S Chrysler Dr, Hazel Park MI 48030-1706. 313/691-
3884. Employs: 50-99.

First Of America Bank
35207 Groesbeck Hwy, Clinton Twp MI 48035-2514.
313/791-9400. Employs: 50-99.

First Of America Bank
3127 N Woodward Ave, Royal Oak MI 48073-6930.
313/691-3864. Employs: 50-99.

First Of America Bank
2600 W 14 Mile Rd, Royal Oak MI 48073-1711. 313/691-
3924. Employs: 50-99.

First Of America Bank
33523 8 Mile Rd, Livonia MI 48152-4104. 313/478-2061.
Employs: 50-99.

First Of America Bank
20055 Ann Arbor Trail, Dearborn Hts MI 48127-2661.
313/271-4140. Employs: 50-99.

First Of America Bank
33505 Schoolcraft Rd, Livonia MI 48150-1503. 313/422-
8100. Employs: 50-99.

First Of America Bank
15303 S Dixie Hwy, Monroe MI 48161-3774. 313/242-
8600. Employs: 50-99.

First Of America Bank
6230 Orchard Lake Rd, W Bloomfield MI 48322-2392.
313/851-8400. Employs: 50-99.

First Of America Bank
5915 Highland Rd, Waterford MI 48327-1830. 313/674-
0479. Employs: 50-99.

First Of America Bank
11700 E 15 Mile Rd, Sterling Hts MI 48312-5102.
313/268-3010. Employs: 50-99.

First Of America Bank
994 W Huron, Waterford MI 48328-3726. 313/339-5876.
Employs: 50-99.

First Of America Bank
28564 Orchard Lake, Farmington MI 48334-2950.
313/855-1820. Employs: 50-99.

First Of America Bank
5799 Dixie Hwy, Waterford MI 48329-1623. 313/623-1200. Employs: 50-99.

First Of America Bank
584 N Perry St, Pontiac MI 48342-1557. 313/339-5880. Employs: 50-99.

First Of America Bank
955 Woodward Ave, Pontiac MI 48341-2979. 313/339-5883. Employs: 50-99.

First Of America Bank
261 1/2 N Telegraph Rd, Pontiac MI 48341-1936. 313/339-5860. Employs: 50-99.

First Of America Bank
255 N Telegraph Rd, Pontiac MI 48341-1936. 313/339-5855. Employs: 50-99.

First Of America Bank
13401 W 9 Mile Rd, Oak Park MI 48237-2842. 313/691-3904. Employs: 50-99.

First Of America Bank
26500 Greenfield Rd, Oak Park MI 48237-1001. 313/691-3961. Employs: 50-99.

First Of America Bank
21350 Greenfield Rd, Oak Park MI 48237-3005. 313/691-3958. Employs: 50-99.

First Of America Bank
344 N Main, Milford MI 48381-1957. 313/684-1165. Employs: 50-99.

First Of America Bank
1621 Haslett Rd, Haslett MI 48840-8438. 517/334-5262. Employs: 50-99.

First Of America Bank
309 E Grand River, East Lansing MI 48823-4324. 517/334-1600. Employs: 50-99.

First Of America Bank
409 N Mission, Mount Pleasnt MI 48858. 517/772-0942. Employs: 50-99.

First Of America Bank
1419 S Mission, Mount Pleasnt MI 48858. 517/772-0943. Employs: 50-99.

First Of America Bank
1106 W High St, Mount Pleasnt MI 48858-2242. 517/772-0944. Employs: 50-99.

First Of America Bank Livingston
207 N Michigan Ave, Howell MI 48843-1501. 517/546-3410. Employs: 100-249.

Firstbank
4699 E Pickard, Mount Pleasnt MI 48858-2077. 517/773-2335. Employs: 50-99.

FMB Commercial Bank
203 S Lafayette Box 427, Greenville MI 48838-1935. 616/754-7111. Employs: 50-99.

Heritage Federal Savings
4442 Beecher Rd, Flint MI 48532-2611. 313/733-6770. Employs: 50-99.

Heritage Federal Savings
14160 Fenton Rd, Fenton MI 48430-1508. 313/629-8585. Employs: 50-99.

Heritage Federal Savings
220 E Main St, Flushing MI 48433-2026. 313/2330250. Employs: 50-99.

Heritage Federal Savings
127 Hutton St, Northville MI 48167-1657. 313/348-8920. Employs: 50-99.

Heritage Federal Savings
8095 Macomb, Grosse Ile MI 48138-1565. 313/675-8330. Employs: 50-99.

Heritage Federal Savings
28650 Telegraph Rd, Flat Rock MI 48134-1508. 313/782-1411. Employs: 50-99.

Heritage Federal Savings
33111 7 Mile Rd, Livonia MI 48152-1364. 313/477-9340. Employs: 50-99.

Heritage Federal Savings
3805 Oakwood, Melvindale MI 48122-1503. 313/3831312. Employs: 50-99.

Heritage Federal Savings
6634 Allen Rd, Allen Park MI 48101-2004. 313/382-2215. Employs: 50-99.

Heritage Federal Savings
24650 W McNichols, Detroit MI 48219-3671. 313/531-4753. Employs: 100-249.

Heritage Federal Savings
3290 West Rd, Trenton MI 48183-2322. 313/676-2299. Employs: 50-99.

Heritage Federal Savings
22211 West Rd, Trenton MI 48183-3227. 313/676-1144. Employs: 50-99.

Heritage Federal Savings
13628 Eureka, Southgate MI 48195-1333. 313/281-1272. Employs: 50-99.

Heritage Federal Savings
23700 Goddard, Taylor MI 48180-4043. 313/291-3900. Employs: 50-99.

Huntington Banks
27248 Van Dyke Ave, Warren MI 48093-2854. 313/758-3500. Employs: 100-249.

Huntington Banks
10221 W Warren, Dearborn MI 48126-1672. 313/9451117. Employs: 50-99.

Huntington Banks
25719 Grand River, Redford MI 48240-1432. 313/538-4405. Employs: 50-99.

Huntington Banks
37600 W 12 Mile Rd, Farmington MI 48331-3074. 313/553-2600. Employs: 50-99.

Huntington Banks
2229 Metropolitan Pkwy, Sterling Hts MI 48310-4208. 313/795-9300. Employs: 50-99.

Huntington Banks
36291 Harper Ave, Clinton Twp MI 48035-2959. 313/466-7627. Employs: 50-99.

Huntington Banks
39040 Garfield, Clinton Twp MI 48038-2790. 313/466-3370. Employs: 50-99.

Huntington Banks
20650 Hall Rd, Clinton Twp MI 48038-1536. 313/466-3381. Employs: 50-99.

Independent Bank
323 W Main St, Belleville MI 48111-2645. 517/584-3118. Employs: 50-99.

International Bank Detroit
POB 116-A, Detroit MI 48232. 313/225-1000. Employs· 100-249.

Key State Bank
4815 Okemos Rd, Okemos MI 48864-1623. 517/349-1133.
Employs: 50-99.

Liberty State Bank & Trust
9301 Jos Campau Ave, Detroit MI 48212-3433. 313/871-9400. Employs: 100-249.

Manufacturers Bank
4829 Marsh Rd, Okemos MI 48864-1155. 517/349-0090.
Employs: 50-99.

Manufacturers National Bank
20202 Eureka Rd, Taylor MI 48180-5317. 313/282-7743.
Employs: 50-99.

Manufacturers National Bank
360 S Wayne Rd, Westland MI 48185-4381. 313/728-0900.
Employs: 50-99.

Manufacturers National Bank
29049 Joy Rd, Westland MI 48185-5580. 313/425-6550.
Employs: 50-99.

Manufacturers National Bank
7126 N Wayne Rd, Westland MI 48185-2167. 313/728-5000. Employs: 50-99.

Manufacturers National Bank
43443 Joy Rd, Canton MI 48187-2077. 313/454-0045.
Employs: 50-99.

Manufacturers National Bank
18225 Allen Rd, Melvindale MI 48122-1513. 313/386-8400. Employs: 50-99.

Manufacturers National Bank
17111 N Laurel Park Dr, Livonia MI 48152-2647. 313/591-0991. Employs: 50-99.

Manufacturers National Bank
30905 Plymouth Rd, Livonia MI 48150-2103. 313/525-5520. Employs: 50-99.

Manufacturers National Bank
37601 5 Mile Rd, Livonia MI 48154-1543. 313/464-9000.
Employs: 50-99.

Manufacturers National Bank
36450 Goddard Rd, Romulus MI 48174-1280. 313/941-0600. Employs: 50-99.

Manufacturers National Bank
24055 Jefferson, St Clair Shrs MI 48080-1511. 313/773-7480. Employs: 50-99.

Manufacturers National Bank
30200 Harper, St Clair Shrs MI 48082-2611. 313/296-1500. Employs: 50-99.

Manufacturers National Bank
34756 Dequindre, Sterling Hts MI 48310. 313/264-7900.
Employs: 50-99.

Manufacturers National Bank
33390 14 Mile Rd, W Bloomfield MI 48322-3572.
313/737-4998. Employs: 50-99.

Manufacturers National Bank
4430 Orchard Lake Rd, W Bloomfield MI 48323-2953.
313/682-0070. Employs: 50-99.

Manufacturers National Bank
1955 18 Mile Rd, Sterling Hts MI 48314-3701.
313/9399180. Employs: 50-99.

Manufacturers National Bank
24525 Plymouth Rd, Redford MI 48239-1618. 313/537-6129. Employs: 50-99.

Manufacturers National Bank

26095 5 Mile Rd, Redford MI 48239-3235. 313/5359330.
Employs: 50-99.

Manufacturers National Bank
21303 Mack Ave, Grosse Pointe MI 48236-1048. 313/886-7706. Employs: 50-99.

Manufacturers National Bank
19419 Mack Ave, Grosse Pointe MI 48236-2835. 313/881-2344. Employs: 50-99.

Manufacturers National Bank
20200 Mack Ave, Grosse Pointe MI 48236. 313/886-7730.
Employs: 50-99.

Manufacturers National Bank
41660 W 6 Mile Rd, Northville MI 48167-2341. 313/348-0030. Employs: 50-99.

Manufacturers National Bank
24120 Ford Rd At Telegraph, Dearborn Hts MI 48127-3231. 313/274-5500. Employs: 50-99.

Manufacturers National Bank
14048 Woodward Ave, Detroit MI 48203-3629. 313/865-2300. Employs: 100-249.

Michigan National Bank
15010 E Jefferson Ave, Grosse Pointe MI 48230-1323.
313/8216800. Employs: 50-99.

Michigan National Bank
2300 E 8 Mile Rd, Detroit MI 48234-1009. 313/366-3310.
Employs: 100-249.

Michigan National Bank
43059 W 7 Mile Rd, Northville MI 48167-2279. 313/348-0820. Employs: 50-99.

Michigan National Bank
40020 5 Mile, Plymouth MI 48170-2764. 313/420-0077.
Employs: 50-99.

Michigan National Bank
40850 Ann Arbor Rd, Plymouth MI 48170-4447. 313/455-8812. Employs: 50-99.

Michigan National Bank
44421 Ann Arbor Rd, Plymouth MI 48170-3907. 313/453-8460. Employs: 50-99.

Michigan National Bank
8661 W Grand River, Brighton MI 48116-2328. 313/229-4400. Employs: 50-99.

Michigan National Bank
26838 Plymouth At Nathaline, Detroit MI 48279-0001.
313/937-8100. Employs: 100-249.

Michigan National Bank
5054 Dixie Hwy, Detroit MI 48279-0001. 313/674-4693.
Employs: 100-249.

Michigan National Bank
6400 Orchard Lake Rd, W Bloomfield MI 48322-2337.
313/626-5870. Employs: 50-99.

Michigan National Bank
40950 Van Dyke, Sterling Hts MI 48313-3745. 313/268-5800. Employs: 50-99.

Michigan National Bank
3547 Highland Rd, Waterford MI 48328-2324. 313/681-5200. Employs: 50-99.

Michigan National Bank
28177 Orchard Lake, Farmington MI 48334-3738.
313/553-7577. Employs: 50-99.

Michigan National Bank
31215 W 14 Mile Rd, Farmington MI 48334-1402.
313/626-0540. Employs: 50-99.

Michigan National Bank
38200 W 10 Mile Rd, Farmington MI 48335-2806.
313/478-7720. Employs: 50-99.

Michigan National Bank
7606 S Saginaw Rd, Grand Blanc MI 48439-1800.
313/695-4410. Employs: 50-99.

Michigan National Bank
20485 Nunnely Rd, Clinton Twp MI 48036-2446. 313/469-3020. Employs: 50-99.

Michigan National Bank
4101 W Maple At Telegraph, Birmingham MI 48010.
313/851-5000. Employs: 50-99.

Michigan National Bank
3580 W Maple At Lahser Rd, Birmingham MI 48010.
313/644-3886. Employs: 50-99.

Michigan National Bank
275 S Woodward, Birmingham MI 48009-6165. 313/647-7180. Employs: 50-99.

Michigan National Bank
24785 Southfield Rd, Southfield MI 48075-2750. 313/552-7580. Employs: 100-249.

Michigan National Bank
1701 Hamilton Rd, Okemos MI 48864-1810. 517/377-3510. Employs: 50-99.

Michigan National Bank
1390 W Lake Lansing Rd, East Lansing MI 48823-1314.
517/377-3538. Employs: 50-99.

Michigan National Bank
2731 E Grand River Ave, East Lansing MI 48823-4710.
517/377-3541. Employs: 50-99.

Michigan National Bank
4488 W Holt Rd, Holt MI 48842-1673. 517/377-3564.
Employs: 50-99.

Michigan National Bank
G2201 E Hill Rd, Flint MI 48507. 313/695-1190. Employs:
50-99.

Michigan National Bank
573 Dort S Hwy, Flint MI 48503-2848. 313/767-5010.
Employs: 50-99.

Michigan National Bank
519 S Saginaw St, Flint MI 48502-1802. 313/762-5424.
Employs: 50-99.

Mutual Savings Bank
310 E Broadway, Mount Pleasnt MI 48858-2648. 517/772-9405. Employs: 50-99.

Mutual Savings Bank
45001 Ford Rd, Canton MI 48187-2907. 313/981-2020.
Employs: 50-99.

National Bank Of Royal Oak
4710 Rochester Rd, Royal Oak MI 48073-2044. 313/588-0561. Employs: 50-99.

National Bank Of Royal Oak
1821 N Campbell, Royal Oak MI 48073-4237. 313/398-8220. Employs: 50-99.

NBD
3300 Auburn Rd, Auburn Hills MI 48326-3310. 313/852-2500. Employs: 50-99.

NBD Bank
13999 Lakeside Cir, Sterling Hts MI 48313-1319. 313/247-4900. Employs: 50-99.

NBD Bank

6920 Orchard Lake, W Bloomfield MI 48322-3413.
313/855-1005. Employs: 50-99.

NBD Bank
1552 E Pierson Rd, Flushing MI 48433-1817. 313/766-8210. Employs: 50-99.

NBD Bank
124 S Cherry St, Flushing MI 48433-2019. 313/766-8160.
Employs: 50-99.

NBD Bank
7218 N Genesee Rd, Genesee MI 48437. 313/640-2250.
Employs: 50-99.

NBD Bank
900 Joslyn Ave, Pontiac MI 48340-2922. 313/857-5906.
Employs: 50-99.

NBD Bank
1261 Baldwin Ave, Pontiac MI 48340-1911. 313/857-5930.
Employs: 50-99.

NBD Bank
33200 12 Mile Rd, Farmington MI 48334-3309. 313/535-0350. Employs: 50-99.

NBD Bank
4260 Elizabeth Lake Rd, Waterford MI 48328-2912.
313/683-4880. Employs: 50-99.

NBD Bank
28 N Saginaw St, Pontiac MI 48342-2134. 313/857-5800.
Employs: 50-99.

NBD Bank
2886 E Highland Rd, Highland MI 48356-2730. 313/887-3707. Employs: 50-99.

NBD Bank
990 S Lapeer Rd, Oxford MI 48371-5041. 313/628-9781.
Employs: 50-99.

NBD Bank
1600 N Woodward, Birmingham MI 48009-5133. 313/642-1850. Employs: 50-99.

NBD Bank
28660 Northwestern Hwy, Southfield MI 48034. 313/353-8885. Employs: 50-99.

NBD Bank
43101 Garfield Rd, Clinton Twp MI 48038-1113. 313/286-5525. Employs: 50-99.

NBD Bank
45345 Ford Rd, Canton MI 48187-2911. 313/981-1100.
Employs: 50-99.

NBD Bank
35050 Ford Rd, Westland MI 48185-3119. 313/326-1440.
Employs: 50-99.

NBD Bank
31311 Cherry Hill Rd, Westland MI 48185-5073. 313/326-2660. Employs: 50-99.

NBD Bank
7750 N Wayne Rd, Westland MI 48185-2009. 313/425-8605. Employs: 50-99.

NBD Bank
23333 Eureka Rd, Taylor MI 48180-5230. 313/374-8686.
Employs: 50-99.

NBD Bank
7700 Telegraph, Taylor MI 48180-2236. 313/291-5444.
Employs: 50-99.

NBD Bank
20401 Gibralter Rd, Trenton MI 48183-5012. 313/675-5050. Employs: 50-99.

NBD Bank
20920 Allen Rd, Trenton MI 48183-1018. 313/479-1555.
Employs: 50-99.

NBD Bank
685 St Clair Ave, Grosse Pointe MI 48230-1243. 313/884-3408. Employs: 50-99.

NBD Bank
17449 E Jefferson Ave, Grosse Pointe MI 48230-1913.
313/884-3200. Employs: 50-99.

NBD Bank
19616 Kelly Rd, Harper Woods MI 48225-1915. 313/372-1234. Employs: 50-99.

NBD Bank
Eastland Center E 500, Harper Woods MI 48225. 313/371-8000. Employs: 50-99.

NBD Bank
5485 E Huron River Dr, Ypsilanti MI 48197-1011.
313/995-8094. Employs: 50-99.

NBD Bank
2025 Rawsonville Rd, Belleville MI 48111-2219. 313/485-3520. Employs: 50-99.

NBD Bank
23150 Van Born Rd, Dearborn Hts MI 48125-2375.
313/292-1100. Employs: 50-99.

NBD Bank
42901 W 7 Mile Rd, Northville MI 48167-2277. 313/349-7100. Employs: 50-99.

NBD Bank
23210 Ford Rd, Dearborn Hts MI 48127-4006. 313/271-7797. Employs: 50-99.

NBD Bank
24950 W Warren Ave, Dearborn Hts MI 48127-2143.
313/278-9595. Employs: 50-99.

NBD Bank
230 N Telegraph, Dearborn MI 48128-1618. 313/271-7734.
Employs: 50-99.

NBD Bank
37458 6 Mile Rd, Livonia MI 48152-2602. 313/953-0620.
Employs: 50-99.

NBD Bank
27637 Grand River Ave, Livonia MI 48152-2434. 313/474-1345. Employs: 50-99.

NBD Bank
2041 Fort St, Lincoln Park MI 48146-2402. 313/374-3410.
Employs: 50-99.

NBD Bank
14601 Southfield Rd, Allen Park MI 48101-2640. 313/374-3425. Employs: 50-99.

NBD Bank
1749 W Grand River, Okemos MI 48864-1803. 517/487-1020. Employs: 50-99.

NBD Bank
4 W Sanilac, Sandusky MI 48471-1037. 313/648-2110.
Employs: 50-99.

NBD Bank
G3402 Flushing Rd, Flint MI 48504-4216. 313/766-8404.
Employs: 50-99.

NBD Bank
G5312 Corunna Rd, Flint MI 48504. 313/766-8296.
Employs: 50-99.

NBD Bank

4154 Davison Rd, Burton MI 48509-1455. 313/766-8156.
Employs: 50-99.

NBD Bank
3509 S Linden Rd, Flint MI 48507-3011. 313/766-8336.
Employs: 50-99.

Old Kent Bank
7500 E M36 Box 207, Hamburg MI 48139-0207. 313/231-3900. Employs: 50-99.

Old Kent Bank
13880 Middle Gibralter Rd, Rockwood MI 48173-9501.
313/671-2504. Employs: 50-99.

Old Kent Bank
22475 Huron River Dr, Rockwood MI 48173-1123.
313/379-9606. Employs: 50-99.

Old Kent Bank
22000 West Rd, Trenton MI 48183-3226. 313/671-2508.
Employs: 50-99.

Old Kent Bank
17825 Fort St, Wyandotte MI 48192-6600. 313/282-6841.
Employs: 50-99.

Old Kent Bank
140 W Highland, Highland MI 48357-4502. 313/887-4181.
Employs: 50-99.

Old Kent Bank-Southeast
2674 W Jefferson Ave, Trenton MI 48183-2803. 313/671-2400. Employs: 50-99.

Oxford Bank
60 S Washington St, Oxford MI 48371-4972. 313/628-2533. Employs: 50-99.

Republic Bank
G8455 S Saginaw Rd, Grand Blanc MI 48439. 313/694-8222. Employs: 50-99.

Republic Bank
500 N Homer St, Lansing MI 48912-4707. 517/351-4777.
Employs: 50-99.

Republic Bank Central
601 W Grand River, Okemos MI 48864-3110. 517/349-1930. Employs: 50-99.

Republic Bank Se
18720 Mack Ave, Grosse Pointe MI 48236-2923. 313/882-6400. Employs: 50-99.

Security Bank & Trust Co
2140 Rawsonville Rd, Ypsilanti MI 48197. 313/481-0170.
Employs: 50-99.

Security Bank & Trust Co
1601 King Rd, Trenton MI 48183-1248. 313/676-0302.
Employs: 50-99.

Security Bank & Trust Co
2675 W Jefferson Ave, Trenton MI 48183-2802. 313/676-0301. Employs: 50-99.

Security Bank & Trust Co
19076 Allen Rd, Trenton MI 48183-1002. 313/281-5830.
Employs: 50-99.

Security Bank & Trust Co
3701 West Rd, Trenton MI 48183-2251. 313/676-0306.
Employs: 50-99.

Security Bank & Trust Co
2189 West Rd, Trenton MI 48183-3613. 313/676-0304.
Employs: 50-99.

Security Bank & Trust Co
14755 Northline, Southgate MI 48195-2407. 313/281-5824.
Employs: 50-99.

Security Bank & Trust Co
12820 Fort St, Southgate MI 48195-1060. 313/281-5829.
Employs: 50-99.

Security Bank & Trust Co
14951 Dix Toledo Rd, Southgate MI 48195-2507. 313/281-5807. Employs: 50-99.

Security Bank & Trust Co
15055 Allen Rd, Southgate MI 48195-2921. 313/281-5828.
Employs: 50-99.

Security Bank & Trust Co
24121 Goddard Rd, Taylor MI 48180-3909. 313/946-7100.
Employs: 50-99.

Security Bank & Trust Co
25850 Eureka Rd, Taylor MI 48180-4924. 313/946-9010.
Employs: 50-99.

Security Bank & Trust Co
43450 Ford Rd, Canton MI 48187-3121. 313/459-3400.
Employs: 50-99.

Security Bank & Trust Co
4024 W Jefferson, Ecorse MI 48229-1749. 313/281-5000.
Employs: 50-99.

Security Bank & Trust Co
19049 Huron River Dr, New Boston MI 48164-9746.
313/941-3930. Employs: 50-99.

Security Bank & Trust Co
9950 Wayne Rd I-94, Romulus MI 48174-3429. 313/941-4110. Employs: 50-99.

Security Bank & Trust Co
8825 Macomb Rd, Grosse Ile MI 48138-1552. 313/676-0305. Employs: 50-99.

Security Bank Of Commerce
31200 Mound Rd, Warren MI 48092-4734. 313/264-6100.
Employs: 50-99.

Society Bank
5300 Willis Rd, Ypsilanti MI 48197-8922. 313/483-5821.
Employs: 50-99.

Society Bank
117 E Maumee St Box 249, Adrian MI 49221-2703.
517/263-8939. Employs: 100-249.

Standard Federal Bank
55 W 12 Mile Rd, Madison Hts MI 48071-2401. 313/399-7010. Employs: 50-99.

Standard Federal Bank
1406 N Woodward Ave, Royal Oak MI 48067-1080.
313/547-5900. Employs: 50-99.

Standard Federal Bank
134 W Michigan Ave, Jackson MI 49201-1302. 517/787-7200. Employs: 50-99.

Standard Federal Bank
138 W Chicago Blvd, Detroit MI 48202-1413. 514/423-7528. Employs: 100-249.

Standard Federal Bank
17540 Grand River Ave, Detroit MI 48227-1402. 313/838-2950. Employs: 100-249.

Standard Federal Bank
615 Griswold, Detroit MI 48226-3404. 313/965-4774.
Employs: 100-249.

Standard Federal Bank
44101 Ford Rd, Canton MI 48187-3174. 313/981-1685.
Employs: 50-99.

Standard Federal Bank

121 N Wayne Rd, Westland MI 48185-3624. 313/326-8020. Employs: 50-99.

Standard Federal Bank
10700 Pelham Rd, Taylor MI 48180-3827. 313/292-8750.
Employs: 50-99.

Standard Federal Bank
13763 Northline Rd, Southgate MI 48195-1802. 313/283-3336. Employs: 50-99.

Standard Federal Bank
35150 Michigan Ave, Wayne MI 48184-1614. 313/729-4420. Employs: 50-99.

Standard Federal Bank
6071 Middlebelt Rd, Garden City MI 48135-2411.
313/522-6300. Employs: 50-99.

Standard Federal Bank
19700 Mack Ave, Grosse Pointe MI 48236-2502. 313/885-2114. Employs: 50-99.

Standard Federal Bank
25712 Grand River Ave, Redford MI 48240-1431.
313/535-4880. Employs: 50-99.

Standard Federal Bank
25800 Joy Rd, Redford MI 48239-1801. 313/937-2700.
Employs: 50-99.

Standard Federal Bank
32920 W 13 Mile Rd, Farmington MI 48334-1973.
313/855-1444. Employs: 50-99.

Standard Federal Bank
25950 Middlebelt Rd, Farmington MI 48336-1447.
313/477-2110. Employs: 50-99.

Standard Federal Bank
6120 Maple Rd W, W Bloomfield MI 48322-2168.
313/661-5570. Employs: 50-99.

Standard Federal Bank
44100 Schoenherr Rd, Sterling Hts MI 48313-1124.
313/247-3700. Employs: 50-99.

Standard Federal Bank
36909 Schoenherr Rd, Sterling Hts MI 48312-3371.
313/939-4680. Employs: 50-99.

Standard Federal Bank
4320 Orchard Lake Rd, W Bloomfield MI 48323-1646.
313/681-9440. Employs: 50-99.

Standard Federal Bank
39100 Dequindre, Sterling Hts MI 48310-1702. 313/264-3440. Employs: 50-99.

Sterling Savings Bank
2986 Walton Blvd, Waterford MI 48329-2562. 313/674-4901. Employs: 50-99.

Sterling Savings Bank
330 W 14 Mile Rd, Clawson MI 48017-1966. 313/435-2840. Employs: 50-99.

Union Federal Savings
5620 S Pennsylvania, Lansing MI 48911-4014. 517/394-4136. Employs: 50-99.

Union Federal Savings
2801 E Grand River, Lansing MI 48912-4331. 517/372-9334. Employs: 50-99.

Union Federal Savings
2285 W Grand River, Okemos MI 48864-1649. 517/349-3059. Employs: 50-99.

United Savings Bank
32255 Northwestern Hwy, Farmington MI 48334-1566.
313/855-0550. Employs: 50-99.

First Of America Bank
35215 Michigan Ave W Box 804, Wayne MI 48184-1672.
313/721-4151. Employs: 50-99.

Independent Bank
230 W Main St Box 1002, Ionia MI 48846-1617. 616/527-2400. Employs: 100-249.

Isabella Bank & Trust
200 E Broadway Drawer 100, Mount Pleasnt MI 48858-2314. 517/772-9471. Employs: 50-99.

Old Kent Bank
10 S Broad St Box 277, Hillsdale MI 49242-1848.
517/437-4426. Employs: 50-99.

The State Bank
1 Fenton Sq Drawer E, Fenton MI 48430-2146. 313/629-2263. Employs: 50-99.

Commercial & Savings Bank
200 S Riverside Ave Box 28, Saint Clair MI 48079-5330.
313/329-2244. Employs: 100-249.

First Federal Savings Bank
761 W Huron St, Pontiac MI 48341-1529. 313/333-7071.
Employs: 100-249.

Union Federal Savings
121 W Allegan St Box 40710, Lansing MI 48933-1702.
517/485-4385. Employs: 50-99.

SAVINGS INSTITUTIONS, FEDERALLY CHARTERED

Bloomfield Savings F A Br
123 W Michigan Av, Ypsilanti MI 48197-5438. 313/482-7566. Employs: 50-99.

Citizens Federal Savings Bank
3136 Lapeer Rd, Port Huron MI 48060-2550. 313/984-1578. Employs: 50-99.

Comerica Bank-Detroit
20400 W 12 Mile Rd, Southfield MI 48076-5415. 313/358-2017. Employs: 50-99.

D & N Savings Bank
727 S State St, Davison MI 48423-1749. 313/653-5383.
Employs: 50-99.

D & N Savings Bank F S B
4919 Clio Rd, Flint MI 48504-1886. 313/785-0888.
Employs: 50-99.

D & N Savings Bank F S B
1151 N Ballenger Hwy, Flint MI 48504-7535. 313/767-3850. Employs: 50-99.

D & N Savings Bank F S B
3410 S Dort Hwy, Flint MI 48507-2046. 313/743-1000.
Employs: 50-99.

D & N Savings Bank F S B Br
12770 Saginaw Rd, Grand Blanc MI 48439-1831. 313/695-3940. Employs: 50-99.

Empire Of America FSA
24700 Nw Hwy, Southfield MI 48075. 313/354-1300.
Employs: 50-99.

First Federal Of Michigan
324 East St, Rochester MI 48307-2013. 313/652-8300.
Employs: 50-99.

First Nationwide Bank
16 S Washington St, Ypsilanti MI 48197-5426. 313/481-1556. Employs: 50-99.

First Nationwide Bank

23550 Ford Rd, Dearborn Hts MI 48127-2357. 313/943-4824. Employs: 50-99.

Great Lakes Fed Savings Br
201 S Washington Sq, Lansing MI 48933-1807. 517/484-8409. Employs: 50-99.

Guaranty Federal Sav & Ln Assn
17800 Fort St, Wyandotte MI 48192-6634. 313/374-3420.
Employs: 50-99.

Guaranty Federal Savings Bank Br
2410 West Rd, Trenton MI 48183-2402. 313/374-3430.
Employs: 50-99.

Heritage Federal Savings Bank Br
3528 Fort St, Lincoln Park MI 48146-4102. 313/386-4900.
Employs: 50-99.

Heritage Federal Savings Bank Br
957 Dix Av, Lincoln Park MI 48146-1256. 313/383-4502.
Employs: 50-99.

Home Federal Savings & Ln Assn
550 E Warren Ave, Detroit MI 48201-1436. 313/832-3430.
Employs: 100-249.

Interfirst Federal Savings
2250 W Michigan Av, Ypsilanti MI 48197-9049. 313/434-5400. Employs: 50-99.

Interfirst Federal Savings Bank
215 W Michigan Av, Ypsilanti MI 48197-5440. 313/482-5919. Employs: 50-99.

Security Savings Bank
3045 E Michigan Av, Jackson MI 49202-3847. 517/787-0215. Employs: 50-99.

Standard Federal Bank
7957 N Wayne Rd, Westland MI 48185-1109. 313/261-5450. Employs: 50-99.

United Savings Bank
31731 Northwestern Hwy, Farmington MI 48334-1654.
313/855-8913. Employs: 50-99.

United Savings Bank
33505 W 14 Mile Rd, Farmington MI 48331-1596.
313/661-1703. Employs: 50-99.

Yegen Marine
21719 Harper Ave, St Clair Shrs MI 48080-2213. 313/773-5533. Employs: 50-99.

1st Fed Savings & Loan Jackson Br
2680 Airport Rd, Jackson MI 49202-1238. 517/789-7118.
Employs: 50-99.

Home Fed Savings Bank
9108 Woodward, Detroit MI 48202-1612. 313/873-3310.
Employs: 100-249.

Guaranty Fed Savings Bank
23333 Eureka Rd, Taylor MI 48180-5230. 313/374-3300.
Employs: 50-99.

SAVINGS INSTITUTIONS, NOT FEDERALLY CHARTERED

Security Savings Bank
301 West Michigan Ave, Jackson MI 49201-2120.
517/787-9700. Employs: 50-99.

CREDIT UNIONS, FEDERALLY CHARTERED

A & P Farmer Jack Credit Union
3415 Southfield Rd, Allen Park MI 48101-3199. 313/255-4900. Employs: 50-99.

ABD Federal Credit Union
6816 McGraw St, Detroit MI 48210-1628. 313/897-8830.
Employs: 50-99.

Allen Park V A Credit Union
3415 Southfield Rd, Allen Park MI 48101-3199. 313/278-4766. Employs: 50-99.

American One Federal Credit Union
810 W Argyle St, Jackson MI 49202-2056. 517/784-7191.
Employs: 50-99.

American One Federal Credit Union
718 E Michigan Av, Jackson MI 49201-1626. 517/787-6510. Employs: 50-99.

American Postal Workers Union
6193 Miller Rd Bldg B, Swartz Creek MI 48473-1516.
313/635-8033. Employs: 50-99.

Amez United Credit Union
11359 Dexter Ave, Detroit MI 48206-1424. 313/933-1818.
Employs: 50-99.

Assoc Truck Lines Employees
4831 Wyoming Av, Dearborn MI 48126-3722. 313/581-2260. Employs: 50-99.

Associated Financial Services
630 Howard St, Detroit MI 48226-2512. 313/965-2388.
Employs: 50-99.

Auto Body Credit Union
2010 N Larch St, Lansing MI 48906-4113. 517/485-0264.
Employs: 50-99.

Automotive Federal Credit Un
5397 W Michigan Ave, Ypsilanti MI 48197-9005.
313/434-4130. Employs: 50-99.

Birmingham Teachers Credit Union
576 E Lincoln St, Birmingham MI 48009-1757. 313/647-5958. Employs: 50-99.

BSC Health Care Services Credit Union
19850 Harper, Harper Woods MI 48225. 313/884-7882.
Employs: 50-99.

C J Federal Credit Union
11410 Kercheval St, Detroit MI 48214-3307. 313/822-4423. Employs: 50-99.

C S E Credit Union
615 N Main St, Clawson MI 48017-1529. 313/435-0950.
Employs: 50-99.

Cascades Community Fed Crdt Un
108 S Main St, Brooklyn MI 49230-9121. 517/592-3837.
Employs: 50-99.

Cascades Community Fed Crdt Un
1355 Falahee Rd Michigan Cntr, Michigan Ctr MI 49254.
517/764-1600. Employs: 50-99.

Catholic Community Credit Union
3141 Page Av, Jackson MI 49203-2267. 517/787-9146.
Employs: 50-99.

Central Credit Union Of Mi
600 Crescent Rd, East Lansing MI 48823-5762. 517/351-0208. Employs: 50-99.

Chiropractic Federal Crdt Unit
23617 Liberty St, Farmington MI 48335-3530. 313/478-4020. Employs: 50-99.

Co-Op Services Credit Union
269 Oak St, Wyandotte MI 48192-5126. 313/285-0555.
Employs: 50-99.

Communicating Arts Credit Un

630 Howard St, Detroit MI 48226-2512. 313/965-8640.
Employs: 50-99.

Communicating Arts Credit Un
6200 Metro Prkwy, Sterling Hts MI 48312. 313/978-7350.
Employs: 50-99.

Consumers Power Credit Union
516 W Willow St, Lansing MI 48906-4744. 517/372-2400.
Employs: 50-99.

Contrak Credit Union
4104 Schaefer Rd, Dearborn MI 48126-3641. 313/584-2033. Employs: 50-99.

Covenant Credit Union
25835 Southfield Rd, Southfield MI 48075-1827. 313/552-8111. Employs: 50-99.

Craftsman Credit Union
2444 Clark St, Detroit MI 48209-1338. 313/554-9300.
Employs: 50-99.

Credit Union Family Svc Center
25489 Grand River Ave, Redford MI 48240-1426.
313/532-8040. Employs: 50-99.

Credit Union One
9000 15 Mile, Sterling Hts MI 48312. 313/978-7181.
Employs: 50-99.

Credit Union One
642 E 9 Mile Rd, Ferndale MI 48220-1962. 313/542-0390.
Employs: 50-99.

Credit Union One
3355 N Woodward Ave, Royal Oak MI 48073-6934.
313/288-5010. Employs: 50-99.

Crestwood Community Fed Credit Union
23726 Joy Rd, Redford MI 48239-1211. 313/534-7055.
Employs: 50-99.

Crestwood Community Federal Credit Union
23506 Ford Rd, Dearborn Hts MI 48127-2357. 313/274-7310. Employs: 50-99.

Crestwood Community Federal Credit Union
29820 Joy Rd, Livonia MI 48150-3911. 313/427-8184.
Employs: 50-99.

D T I Employees Credit Union
20600 Eureka Rd, Taylor MI 48180-5306. 313/284-4211.
Employs: 50-99.

Dearborn Federal Credit Union Branch Office
400 Town Center Dr Ste 100, Dearborn MI 48126-2737.
313/336-2700. Employs: 50-99.

Dearborn Federal Credit Union
17600 Oakwood Blvd, Dearborn MI 48124-4048. 313/336-3200. Employs: 50-99.

Designing Engineers Credit Un
31010 John R Rd, Madison Hts MI 48071-1908. 313/588-9300. Employs: 50-99.

Detroit Federal Empl Credit Union
17726 W 8 Mile Rd, Southfield MI 48075-4306. 313/569-3999. Employs: 50-99.

Detroit Postal Empl Credit Union
660 Plaza Dr, Detroit MI 48226-1206. 313/963-1795.
Employs: 50-99.

Detroit Teachers Credit Union
770 Puritan St, Detroit MI 48203-2667. 313/345-7200.
Employs: 50-99.

Dort Federal Credit Union
G3116 W Pierson Rd, Flint MI 48504. 313/787-3740.
Employs: 50-99.

Dort Federal Credit Union
1091 W Hill Rd, Flint MI 48507-4731. 313/235-8377.
Employs: 50-99.

Down River Community Federal Credit Union
4320 W Jefferson Av, Ecorse MI 48229-1532. 313/386-2200. Employs: 50-99.

Downriver Community Crdt Un Brkrge
1365 Cass Ave, Detroit MI 48226-1501. 313/964-6666.
Employs: 50-99.

Downriver School Empl Credit Union
14170 Pennsylvania Rd, Southgate MI 48195-2133.
313/284-9410. Employs: 50-99.

Eastern Michigan Univ Credit Union
526 St Johns St, Ypsilanti MI 48197-2484. 313/487-1033.
Employs: 50-99.

El-G A Credit Union
8415 Davison Rd, Davison MI 48423-2100. 313/653-6655.
Employs: 50-99.

El-Ga Credit Union
G-5181 Richfield Rd, Flint MI 48506. 313/736-7224.
Employs: 50-99.

El-Ga Credit Union
G-6238 W Pierson Rd, Flint MI 48506. 313/230-7750.
Employs: 50-99.

El-Ga Credit Union
610 S Dort Hwy, Flint MI 48503-2849. 313/767-6173.
Employs: 50-99.

Electrl Workers Lcl 58 Credit Union
1366 Porter St, Detroit MI 48226-2409. 313/963-6060.
Employs: 50-99.

F M E Federal Credit Union
21103 Gratiot Ave, East Detroit MI 48021-2828. 313/755-8833. Employs: 50-99.

Family Community Credit Union
1149 E Bristol Rd, Burton MI 48529-1128. 313/767-6300.
Employs: 50-99.

Family Credit Union
6250 S Cedar St, Lansing MI 48911-5700. 517/393-5511.
Employs: 50-99.

First Financial Credit Union
300 River Place Dr, Detroit MI 48207-4224. 313/259-5510.
Employs: 50-99.

Flint Area School Employees Cr
1005 W 3D Av, Flint MI 48504-4961. 313/238-9656.
Employs: 50-99.

Flint Municipal Credit Union
606 Stevens St, Flint MI 48502. 313/239-7655. Employs:
50-99.

Flint Service Federal Credit Union
G3311 Van Slyke Rd, Flint MI 48507-3263. 313/767-8370.
Employs: 50-99.

Fr Patrick Kelly K C Fedl Crdt
23663 Park St, Dearborn MI 48124-2547. 313/563-1777.
Employs: 50-99.

Garden City Community Credit Union
6230 Middlebelt Rd, Garden City MI 48135-2409.
313/522-0881. Employs: 50-99.

Good Shepherd Credit Union
4111 Fort St, Lincoln Park MI 48146-4112. 313/386-9220.
Employs: 50-99.

Highland Pk Schl Empl Credit Union

12541 2nd Ave, Detroit MI 48203-3266. 313/869-4466.
Employs: 50-99.

Holbrook Avenue Federal Credit Union
2112 Holbrook St, Detroit MI 48212-3443. 313/872-1277.
Employs: 50-99.

Holy Cross Council Credit Un
6901 Michigan Ave, Detroit MI 48210-2869. 313/842-3993. Employs: 50-99.

Hunt Columbus Federal Credit Union
7080 Garling Dr, Dearborn Hts MI 48127-2655. 313/271-3330. Employs: 50-99.

Immaculate Heart Mary Credit Union
20833 Southfield Rd, Southfield MI 48075-4257. 313/559-9230. Employs: 50-99.

Isabella Community Credit Un
2770 W High St, Mount Pleasnt MI 48858-3067. 517/386-2145. Employs: 50-99.

Jackson Consumers Pwr Emp Fed
1100 Clinton Rd, Jackson MI 49202-2060. 517/784-7101.
Employs: 50-99.

Kemba Credit Union
12701 Middlebelt Rd, Livonia MI 48150-2210. 313/522-3702. Employs: 50-99.

Kent Moore Employees Federal Cr
215 S Dettman Rd, Jackson MI 49203-2204. 517/787-0029.
Employs: 50-99.

Lakeland Catholic Credit Union
4584 W Walton Blvd, Waterford MI 48329-4077. 313/673-0225. Employs: 50-99.

Lansing Bldg Trades Credit Union
1425 Keystone Av, Lansing MI 48911-4039. 517/394-0567. Employs: 50-99.

Loc Federal Credit Union
22981 Farmington Rd, Farmington MI 48336-3915.
313/474-2200. Employs: 50-99.

Local 17 I B E W Credit Union
21700 Greenfield Rd, Oak Park MI 48237-2532. 313/967-4740. Employs: 50-99.

McDonald Dairy Empl Credit Union
507 W Atherton Rd, Flint MI 48507-2404. 313/233-4123.
Employs: 50-99.

Metro North Federal Credit Union
15156 N Holly Rd, Holly MI 48442-1139. 313/634-9061.
Employs: 50-99.

Metro North Federal Credit Un
4594 Pontiac Lake Rd, Waterford MI 48328-2016.
313/674-0491. Employs: 50-99.

Metro Plus Credit Union
2114 N East St, Lansing MI 48906-4103. 517/482-0724.
Employs: 50-99.

Michigan Columbus Federal Credit Union
30419 6 Mile Rd, Livonia MI 48152-3460. 313/425-5080.
Employs: 50-99.

Michigan Federal Credit Union
G1314 E Coldwater Rd, Flint MI 48505. 313/785-3451.
Employs: 50-99.

Michigan Railroaders Credit Union
111 E Ganson St, Jackson MI 49201-1420. 517/784-3198.
Employs: 50-99.

Mid Michigan Federal Credit Un
138 Washington Sq S, Lansing MI 48933-1704. 517/372-5355. Employs: 50-99.

Motor City Co Op Credit Union Br
507 W Atherton Rd, Flint MI 48507-2404. 313/238-8900.
Employs: 50-99.

Motor Parts Fedl Credit Union
14250 Plymouth Rd, Detroit MI 48227-3042. 313/493-2430. Employs: 50-99.

National Steel Federal Credit Union
3815 W Jefferson Ave, Ecorse MI 48229-1701. 313/386-5800. Employs: 50-99.

North Flint Catholic Credit Union
545 W Pierson Rd, Flint MI 48505-3106. 313/785-3447.
Employs: 50-99.

North Oakland Community Credit Union
100 Auburn Ave, Pontiac MI 48342-3005. 313/338-9694.
Employs: 50-99.

Northeast Catholic Credit Un
16012 E 7, Detroit MI 48205. 313/521-4725. Employs: 50-99.

Northwest Airlines Credit Un
9317 Middlebelt Rd, Romulus MI 48174-2510. 313/942-2588. Employs: 50-99.

Northwood Trnsprtn Credit Union
3100 N Woodward Ave, Royal Oak MI 48073-6928.
313/549-3200. Employs: 50-99.

Pac Federal Credit Union
7100 McGraw St, Detroit MI 48210-1938. 313/361-2727.
Employs: 50-99.

Pac Federal Credit Union
11905 Joseph Campau St, Detroit MI 48212-3004.
313/365-1000. Employs: 50-99.

Parda Credit Union
755 Parkdale Rd, Rochester MI 48307-1752. 313/656-1600. Employs: 50-99.

Parda Federal Credit Union
18321 E 8 Mile Rd, East Detroit MI 48021-3231. 313/773-9444. Employs: 50-99.

Parkside Credit Union
36525 Plymouth Rd, Livonia MI 48150-1126. 313/525-0700. Employs: 50-99.

Plymouth Community Federal Credit Union
500 S Harvey St, Plymouth MI 48170-1750. 313/453-2222.
Employs: 50-99.

Plymouth Council Credit Union
150 Fair St, Plymouth MI 48170-1929. 313/455-2020.
Employs: 50-99.

Pon Tel Employees Credit Union
250 N Perry St, Pontiac MI 48342-2345. 313/332-9191.
Employs: 50-99.

Pontiac Municipal Empl Credit Union
144 E Pike St, Pontiac MI 48342-2632. 313/334-0568.
Employs: 50-99.

Poverello Credit Union
2001 W Saginaw St, Lansing MI 48915-1362. 517/484-1937. Employs: 50-99.

PSCU Service Center
39000 7 Mile Rd, Livonia MI 48152-1006. 313/462-4207.
Employs: 50-99.

R M Employees Federal Credit Union
24606 W Warren St, Dearborn Hts MI 48127-2107.
313/278-5565. Employs: 50-99.

Research Federal Credit Union

180 S Milford Rd, Milford MI 48381-2741. 313/685-1583.
Employs: 50-99.

Rochester Schools Credit Union
310 W Tienken Rd, Rochester MI 48306-4406. 313/651-8202. Employs: 50-99.

Royal Oak Community Credit Un
3070 Normandy Rd, Royal Oak MI 48073-2226. 313/549-3838. Employs: 50-99.

Royal Oak Postal Empl Credit Union
500 S Rochester Rd, Clawson MI 48017-2124. 313/585-5415. Employs: 50-99.

Saint Marys Credit Union
726 S Washington Ave, Royal Oak MI 48067-3830.
313/548-6464. Employs: 50-99.

Schmidt S Employees Credit Union
4510 S Pennsylvania Ave, Lansing MI 48910-5610.
517/482-8572. Employs: 50-99.

Security Federal Credit Union Br
G3404 N Linden Rd, Flint MI 48504. 313/732-4880.
Employs: 50-99.

Southgate Community Federal Credit Union
13050 Fort St, Southgate MI 48195-1101. 313/282-3133.
Employs: 50-99.

St Bonaventure Credit Union
1780 Mount Elliott St, Detroit MI 48207-3427. 313/579-0400. Employs: 50-99.

St Gabriel Parish Credit Union
7719 W Vernor Hwy, Detroit MI 48209-1515. 313/841-0720. Employs: 50-99.

St Joh Presby Chrch Credit Union
1961 E Lafayette, Detroit MI 48207. 313/393-1155.
Employs: 50-99.

St Ladislaus Credit Union
2617 Caniff St, Detroit MI 48212-2946. 313/365-7455.
Employs: 50-99.

St Mel's Federal Credit Union
7506 N Inkster Rd, Dearborn Hts MI 48127-1668. 313/562-6045. Employs: 50-99.

St Patrick's Credit Union
9086 Hutchins St, White Lake MI 48386-3331. 313/698-3660. Employs: 50-99.

Sterling Van Dyke Credit Union
39139 Mound Rd, Sterling Hts MI 48310-2737. 313/264-1212. Employs: 50-99.

Suburban Catholic Credit Union
546 N Pontiac Trl, Walled Lake MI 48390-3441. 313/624-3662. Employs: 50-99.

Suburban Catholic Credit Union
31716 Gd River, Farmington MI 48336. 313/474-7100.
Employs: 50-99.

Service Centers Corp
5150 Highland Rd, Waterford MI 48327-1912. 313/673-9770. Employs: 50-99.

Service Centers Corporation
30094 Ford Rd, Garden City MI 48135-2320. 313/422-3530. Employs: 50-99.

Service Centers Corporation
33036 7 Mile Rd, Livonia MI 48152-1358. 313/478-6400.
Employs: 50-99.

Service Centers Corporation
11190 Gratiot Ave, Detroit MI 48213-1334. 313/521-0635.
Employs: 50-99.

Service Centers Corporation
2589 Grand River Ave, Detroit MI 48201-2519. 313/532-8040. Employs: 50-99.

Service Centers Corporation
1419 W 14 Mile Rd, Madison Hts MI 48071-1055. 313/585-6740. Employs: 50-99.

T & C Federal Credit Union
7372 Highland Rd, Waterford MI 48327-1508. 313/666-9744. Employs: 50-99.

T & C Loan Phone Center
939 Woodward Ave, Pontiac MI 48341-2977. 313/338-6260. Employs: 50-99.

T and I Division Credit Union
600 N Main St, Clawson MI 48017-1588. 313/588-6688. Employs: 50-99.

Teacher's Auto Club Inc
12763 Stark Rd, Livonia MI 48150-1551. 313/425-2630. Employs: 50-99.

Teamster Credit Union
2825 Trumbull St, Detroit MI 48216-1270. 313/962-4666. Employs: 50-99.

Trailer Credit Union
26999 Central Park Blvd, Southfield MI 48076-4174. 313/355-1560. Employs: 50-99.

Trenton Federal Credit Union
4550 Division St, Trenton MI 48183-4704. 313/675-3100. Employs: 50-99.

Trenton Governmental Credit Union
2360 W Jefferson Av, Trenton MI 48183-2706. 313/676-8666. Employs: 50-99.

Trenton Resins Credit Union
5100 W Jefferson Ave, Trenton MI 48183-4729. 313/671-2306. Employs: 50-99.

Ukrainian Future Credit Union
3022 Caniff St, Detroit MI 48212-3019. 313/875-9610. Employs: 50-99.

Ukrainian Future Credit Union
4641 Martin St, Detroit MI 48210-2342. 313/843-5411. Employs: 50-99.

V I P Credit Union
37384 Van Dyke Ave, Sterling Hts MI 48312-1830. 313/268-4790. Employs: 50-99.

Vickers & Assocs Federal Credit Union
1333 Anderson Rd, Clawson MI 48017-1045. 313/435-2134. Employs: 50-99.

W Side Auto Employees Federal Cr
G3381 Van Slyke Rd, Flint MI 48507-3263. 313/239-5884. Employs: 50-99.

Wayne Out Cnty Teachers Crdt
9373 Middlebelt Rd, Livonia MI 48150-3060. 313/261-1050. Employs: 50-99.

Wayne Westland Federal Credit Union
37250 Ford Rd, Westland MI 48185-2285. 313/595-6600. Employs: 50-99.

Wyandotte Colum Federal Credit Union
2400 Biddle Av, Wyandotte MI 48192-4652. 313/282-2554. Employs: 50-99.

Wyandotte Federal Crdt Un Mobil
20089 West Rd, Trenton MI 48183-3320. 313/676-7088. Employs: 50-99.

Wyandotte Federal Credit Union

1280 Biddle Av, Wyandotte MI 48192-3433. 313/282-9200. Employs: 50-99.

Ypsilanti Area Federal Credit Union
611 W Cross St, Ypsilanti MI 48197-2501. 313/482-0800. Employs: 50-99.

NONDEPOSIT TRUST FACILITIES

First Of America
33 Bloomfield Hills Pky, Bloomfield MI 48304-2944. 313/433-8800. Employs: 50-99.

MISCELLANEOUS FUNCTIONS RELATED TO DEPOSITORY BANKING

Ace Enterprises
10545 Puritan St, Detroit MI 48238-1018. 313/861-2395. Employs: 50-99.

Clairmount Enterprises
9137 Linwood St, Detroit MI 48206-1958. 313/898-5810. Employs: 50-99.

Dexter Check Cashing No 3
10616 W 7 Mile Rd, Detroit MI 48221-1969. 313/342-4244. Employs: 50-99.

Financial Exchange Co Of Michigan
14205 Gratiot Ave, Detroit MI 48205-2429. 313/372-6750. Employs: 50-99.

Financial Exchange Co Of Michigan
5411 Michigan Ave, Detroit MI 48210-3033. 313/894-1159. Employs: 50-99.

Financial Exchange Co Of Michigan
27313 Michigan Ave, Inkster MI 48141-2335. 313/563-0373. Employs: 50-99.

Maple Lane Investment Co
4801 Conner St, Detroit MI 48215-2030. 313/822-1720. Employs: 50-99.

Midtown Check Cashing
8642 Woodward Ave, Detroit MI 48202-2142. 313/874-5556. Employs: 50-99.

Money Mart Inc
11607 Telegraph Rd, Taylor MI 48180-4028. 313/374-0474. Employs: 50-99.

One Stop Payment Center
1101 Washington Blvd, Detroit MI 48226-1903. 313/963-3737. Employs: 50-99.

United States Chk Cashing Inc
15370 Grand River Ave, Detroit MI 48227-2215. 313/838-2274. Employs: 50-99.

Woodward Currency Exchange
3401 Woodward Ave, Detroit MI 48201-2725. 313/832-4155. Employs: 50-99.

1 Stop Chk Cashing & Pymt Ctr
8296 Woodward Ave, Detroit MI 48202-2532. 313/875-9099. Employs: 50-99.

1 Stop Chk Cashing & Pymt Ctr
13953 Woodward Ave, Detroit MI 48203-3626. 313/868-3200. Employs: 50-99.

1 Stop Check Cashing & Payment Center
20301 W 7 Mile Rd, Detroit MI 48219-3407. 313/532-4242. Employs: 50-99.

Philip F Greco Title Co
111 Cass Ave, Mount Clemens MI 48043-2203. 313/469-0200. Employs: 50-99.

Transamerica Title Ins Co
1 Heritage Dr, Southgate MI 48195-3047. 313/281-0020.
Employs: 50-99.

Foster International
695 John R St, East Lansing MI 48823-3767. 517/351-
8088. Employs: 50-99.

Teleticket
1 Detroit Metro Airpt, Romulus MI 48174. 313/942-4731.
Employs: 50-99.

Chiefs Dly Lottery & Chk
7652 Fenkell St, Detroit MI 48238-1947. 313/863-2144.
Employs: 50-99.

Concession Check Cashing
1201 Woodward Ave, Detroit MI 48226-2006. 313/964-
6652. Employs: 50-99.

Financial Exchange Co Of Michigan
1149 E Grand Blvd, Detroit MI 48207-1930. 313/579-
3764. Employs: 50-99.

Financial Exchange Co Of Michigan
14539 Woodward Ave, Detroit MI 48203-2930. 313/868-
6500. Employs: 50-99.

Financial Exchange Co Of Michigan
4739 Grand River Ave, Detroit MI 48208-2250. 313/894-
3050. Employs: 50-99.

Financial Exchange Co Of Michigan
13243 Livernois Ave, Detroit MI 48238-3162. 313/834-
4790. Employs: 50-99.

General Protection Inc
18986 Schaefer Hwy, Detroit MI 48235-1763. 313/342-
2260. Employs: 50-99.

Henry's Party Store
25551 Van Born Rd, Taylor MI 48180-1259. 313/292-
2010. Employs: 50-99.

K & G Food Mart
2662 W Davison, Detroit MI 48238-3444. 313/865-4028.
Employs: 50-99.

Livernois-Mcgraw Party Store
5545 Livernois Ave, Detroit MI 48210-1703. 313/895-
9820. Employs: 50-99.

Metro Check Cashing
9251 Graves St, Detroit MI 48214. 313/491-2700.
Employs: 50-99.

Minute Stop Food Store

29526 Gratiot Ave, Roseville MI 48066-4113. 313/777-
4423. Employs: 50-99.

Redford Mart
17444 Lahser Rd, Detroit MI 48219-2347. 313/255-0303.
Employs: 50-99.

S S S Party Store
8716 Van Dyke, Detroit MI 48213-2375. 313/922-6166.
Employs: 50-99.

Uncle Pony Market
1253 N Green St, Detroit MI 48209-2271. 313/842-0330.
Employs: 50-99.

Barclays Travelers Cheques
42657 Garfield Rd, Clinton Twp MI 48038-1653. 313/228-
1900. Employs: 50-99.

Manufacturer's Bank
12400 Kelly Rd, Detroit MI 48224-1518. 313/527-8900.
Employs: 50-99.

Manufacturers Bank
19670 Sherwood St, Detroit MI 48234-2923. 313/584-
0590. Employs: 50-99.

Manufacturers Bank
20500 Greenfield Rd, Detroit MI 48235-1854. 313/342-
5800. Employs: 50-99.

Manufacturers National Bank Detroit
14530 Livernois Ave, Detroit MI 48238-2009. 313/342-
3500. Employs: 50-99.

Manufacturers National Bank Detroit
16745 E Warren Ave, Detroit MI 48224-2359. 313/886-
6780. Employs: 50-99.

Manufacturers National Bank Detroit
13233 E Jefferson Ave, Detroit MI 48215-2703. 313/821-
1200. Employs: 50-99.

Manufacturers National Bank Detroit
3031 W Grand Blvd, Detroit MI 48202-3014. 313/872-
5740. Employs: 50-99.

OFFICES OF BANK HOLDING COMPANIES

Cb Financial Corp
One Jackson Sq, Jackson MI 49201. 517/788-2701.
Employs: 100-249.

Cfsb Bancorp Inc
112 E Allegan, Lansing MI 48933-1814. 517/371-2911.
Employs: 100-249.

For more information on career opportunities in the banking/savings and loan industry:

Associations

AMERICAN BANKERS ASSOCIATION
1120 Connecticut Avenue NW, Washington DC 20036.
202/663-5221.

BANK ADMINISTRATION INSTITUTE
1 North Franklin, Chicago IL 60606. 800/323-8552.

BANK MARKETING ASSOCIATION
309 West Washington Street, Chicago IL 60606. 312/782-
1442.

**INDEPENDENT BANKERS ASSOCIATION OF
AMERICA**
One Thomas Circle NW, Suite 950, Washington DC 20005.
202/659-8111.

INSTITUTE OF FINANCIAL EDUCATION
111 East Wacker Drive, 9th Floor, Chicago IL 60601.
312/946-8800.

**NATIONAL COUNCIL OF SAVINGS
INSTITUTIONS**
1101 15th Street NW, Suite 400, Washington DC 20005.
202/857-3100.

**U.S. LEAGUE OF SAVINGS AND LOAN
INSTITUTIONS**
111 East Wacker Drive, Chicago IL 60601. 312/644-3100.

<u>Directories</u>

AMERICAN BANK DIRECTORY
McFadden Business Publications, 6195 Crooked Creek Road, Norcross GA 30092. 404/448-1011.

AMERICAN BANKER DIRECTORY OF U.S. BANKING EXECUTIVES
American Banker, Inc., 1 State Street Plaza, New York NY 10004. 212/943-6700.

AMERICAN BANKER YEARBOOK
American Banker, Inc., 1 State Street Plaza, New York NY 10004. 212/943-6700.

AMERICAN SAVINGS DIRECTORY
McFadden Business Publications, 6195 Crooked Creek Road, Norcross GA 30092. 404/448-1011.

BUSINESS WEEK/TOP 200 BANKING INSTITUTIONS ISSUE
McGraw-Hill, Inc., 1221 Avenue of the Americas, 39th Floor, New York NY 10020. 212/512-4776.

MOODY'S BANK AND FINANCE MANUAL

Moody's Investors Service, Inc., 99 Church Street, New York NY 10007. 212/553-0300.

POLK'S BANK DIRECTORY
R.L. Polk & Co., 2001 Elm Hill Pike, Nashville TN 37210. 615/889-3350.

<u>Magazines</u>

ABA BANKING JOURNAL
American Bankers Association, 1120 Connecticut Avenue NW, Washington DC 20036. 202/663-5221.

BANK ADMINISTRATION
1 North Franklin, Chicago IL 60606. 800/323-8552.

BANKERS MAGAZINE
Warren, Gorham & Lamont, 210 South Street, Boston MA 02111. 617/423-2020.

JOURNAL OF COMMERCIAL BANK LENDING
Robert Morris Associates, 1 Liberty Place, 1650 Market Street, Suite 2300, Philadelphia PA 19103. 215/851-9100.

BOOK AND MAGAZINE PUBLISHING

The continuing recession has hit the book and magazine industries hard. In fact, between 1989 and 1990 alone, over 2,600 book publishing workers lost their jobs. Despite cost containment efforts, most major houses have failed to prevent profits from shrinking further since that time. Higher postal rates and tighter school and library budgets have exacerbated the problem. Gradually, as the economy recovers and disposable income increases, sales in adult trade books should climb.
The expanding 5-14 year-old age group should prompt a rise in sales of juvenile books. These forces should help boost job prospects by about 2,000 new positions annually. In the magazine sector, where much of the revenues are derived from advertising sales, the recession has severely affected bottom lines, and ad pages have declined. An ongoing trend is specialty and niche magazines aimed at increasingly specific audiences.

ARDIS PUBLISHERS
2901 Heatherway, Ann Arbor MI 48104. 313/971-2367. **Contact:** Personnel. **Description:** A book publisher.

BAKER BOOK HOUSE
6030 East Fulton Road, Ada MI 49301. 616/676-9185. **Contact:** Personnel. **Description:** A publisher of religious books.

CHRISTIAN SCHOOLS INTERNATIONAL
3350 East Paris Avenue South East, Grand Rapids MI 49512. 616/957-1070. **Contact:** Personnel. **Description:** A religious book publisher.

CRAIN COMMUNICATIONS INC.

1400 Woodbridge, Detroit MI 48207. 313/446-6000. **Contact:** Kelly Jewett, Personnel. **Description:** Crain is primarily a publishing company producing business, trade, and consumer newspapers and magazines. **Common positions:** Accountant; Computer Programmer; Customer Service Representative; Marketing Specialist; Public Relations Specialist; Reporter/Editor; Sales Representative; Statistician; Systems Analyst; Transportation and Traffic Specialist. **Educational backgrounds sought:** Accounting; Art/Design; Business Administration; Communications; Computer Science; Liberal Arts; Marketing; Journalism. **Special programs:** internships. **Benefits:** medical, dental, and life insurance; pension plan; tuition assistance; disability coverage; profit sharing. **Corporate headquarters:** Chicago, IL. **Operations at this facility:** Sales.

THE DETROITER

600 West Lafayette, Detroit MI 48226. 313/964-4000. **Contact:** Personnel. **Description:** Publishes a business magazine for Greater Detroit.

GALE RESEARCH, INC.

835 Penobscot, Detroit MI 48226. 313/961-2242. **Contact:** Karen Parenteau, Employment Representative. **Description:** A provider of reference information for libraries and businesses worldwide. **Common positions:** Technical Writer/Editor. **Educational backgrounds sought:** Communications; Liberal Arts. **Special programs:** Training programs; internships. **Benefits:** medical, dental and life insurance; pension plan; tuition assistance; disability coverage; profit sharing; savings plan. **Corporate headquarters:** This location. **Parent company:** International Thomson Organization. **Operations at this facility:** research/development; administration; service; sales. **Employees:** 550. **Projected hires for the next 12 months:** 100.

LUDINGTON NEWS COMPANY INC.

1600 East Grand Boulevard, Detroit MI 48211. 313/925-7600. **Contact:** Personnel Department. **Description:** A metropolitan Detroit company engaged in the distribution of a variety of books and magazines. **Employees:** 300.

ZONDERVAN

5300 Patterson South East, Grand Rapids MI 49530. 616/698-6900. **Contact:** Personnel. **Description:** A book publisher.

Additional large employers: 250+

BOOKS: PUBLISHING AND PRINTING

Edwards Brothers Inc
2500 S State St, Ann Arbor MI 48104. 313/769-1000.
Employs: 500-999.

MISCELLANEOUS PUBLISHING

University Microfilms Inc
300 N Zeeb Rd, Ann Arbor MI 48103. 313/761-4700.
Employs: 500-999.

Additional small to medium sized employers: 50-249

PERIODICALS: PUBLISHING OR PUBLISHING
AND PRINTING

Aegis Group Publishers
30400 Van Dyke Ave, Warren MI 48093-2316. 313/574-9100. Employs: 50-99.

Business News Publishing Co
755 W Big Beaver Rd #1000, Troy MI 48084-4903. 313/362-3700. Employs: 50-99.

Contractor Publishing Co
1629 W Lafayette Blvd, Detroit MI 48216-1927. 313/962-3337. Employs: 50-99.

Lintas: Ceco Communications
30400 Van Dyke Ave, Warren MI 48093-2316. 313/575-9400. Employs: 100-249.

Parish Publications Inc
32401 Indl Dr, Madison Hts MI 48071. 313/585-7800. Employs: 100-249.

Quarton Group
2155 Butterfield Rd #200, Troy MI 48084-3452. 313/649-1110. Employs: 50-99.

Scott Advertising & Publishing
30595 8 Mile Rd, Livonia MI 48152-1761. 313/477-6650. Employs: 50-99.

Wheeler Deeler
6837 W Grand River St, Lansing MI 48906-9131. 517/323-9020. Employs: 50-99.

BOOKS: PUBLISHING OR PUBLISHING AND
PRINTING

Rex Publishing Co Inc
24000 Research Dr, Farmington MI 48335-2600. 313/478-9200. Employs: 50-99.

MISCELLANEOUS PUBLISHING

Collier Colortype Inc
661 Plum St, Detroit MI 48201-3353. 313/962-9432. Employs: 50-99.

Copy To Go
1530 Edinborough Rd, Ann Arbor MI 48104-4128. 313/973-6868. Employs: 50-99.

Entertainment Publications Inc
1400 N Woodward Ave, Birmingham MI 48009-5118. 313/637-8400. Employs: 100-249.

GM Photographic
31752 Enterprise Dr, Livonia MI 48150-1960. 313/422-2900. Employs: 100-249.

Realtron Publishing Co
36865 Schoolcraft Rd, Livonia MI 48150-1114. 313/462-2700. Employs: 100-249.

Miles Of Music
7570 Carpenter Rd, Ypsilanti MI 48197-9013. 313/434-5033. Employs: 50-99.

Image Set
1580 Ellsworth, Ann Arbor MI 48108. 313/971-7030. Employs: 50-99.

For more information on career opportunities in book and magazine publishing:

Special Programs

THE NEW YORK UNIVERSITY SUMMER
PUBLISHING PROGRAM
48 Cooper Square, Room 108, New York NY 10003. 212/998-7219.

THE RADCLIFFE PUBLISHING COURSE
77 Brattle Street, Cambridge MA 02138. 617/495-8678.

RICE UNIVERSITY PUBLISHING PROGRAM
Office of Continuing Studies, P.O. Box 1892, Houston TX 77001. 713/520-6022.

UNIVERSITY OF DENVER PUBLISHING
PROGRAM
2199 South University Boulevard, Denver CO 80208. 303/871-2570.

Associations

AMERICAN BOOKSELLERS ASSOCIATION
560 White Plains Road, Tarrytown NY 10591. 914/631-7800.

ASSOCIATION OF AMERICAN PUBLISHERS
220 East 23rd Street, New York NY 10010. 212/689-8920.

MAGAZINE PUBLISHERS ASSOCIATION
575 Lexington Avenue, Suite 540, New York NY 10022. 212/752-0055.

WRITERS GUILD OF AMERICA EAST
555 West 57th Street, Suite 1230, New York NY 10019. 212/767-7800.

WRITERS GUILD OF AMERICA WEST
8955 Beverly Boulevard, Los Angeles CA 90048. 310/550-1000.

BROADCASTING

Across the board, a very tough field to break into - whether it's TV, radio, or cable. Many analysts look to local broadcast outlets for the most job opportunities, and local all-news cable stations are the newest trend on the dial.

BOOTH AMERICAN COMPANY
P.O. Box 888, Detroit MI 48231. 313/965-3360. **Contact:** Personnel. **Description:** The corporate headquarters of a major radio and cable broadcasting company. **Employees:** 400.

WKZO
590 West Maple Street, Kalamazoo MI 49008. 616/345-2101. **Contact:** Personnel. **Description:** A radio broadcasting company.

WXYZ INC.
20777 West 10 Mile Road, Southfield MI 48037. 313/827-7777. **Contact:** Barbara Shivley, Personnel Director. **Description:** A television broadcasting corporation. **Employees:** 300.

Small to medium sized employers: 50-249

RADIO BROADCASTING STATIONS

Federal Enterprises Inc
27700 Northwestern Hw, Southfield MI 48034-4780. 313/352-7560. Employs: 100-249.

Mich Emergency Patrol Inc
1715 Fisher Bg, Detroit MI 48202. 313/875-2555. Employs: 50-99.

W C S X-All Classic Rock
1 Radio Plaza St, Ferndale MI 48220-2140. 313/398-7600. Employs: 50-99.

W I T L
3200 Pinetree Rd, Lansing MI 48911-4228. 517/393-1010. Employs: 50-99.

W J I M Radio
300 N Clippert St Ste 16A, Lansing MI 48912-4637. 517/332-0975. Employs: 50-99.

W J Z Z Radio Station
2994 E Gd Blvd, Detroit MI 48202. 313/871-0590. Employs: 50-99.

TELEVISION BROADCASTING STATIONS

Heritage Broadcasting Group
1500 N Woodward Av Ste 335, Birmingham MI 48009-5127. 313/644-3881. Employs: 50-99.

Petry Tv Inc Regional Ofc
3221 W Big Beaver Rd Ste 102, Troy MI 48084-2859. 313/649-0100. Employs: 50-99.

W F U M-T V-Channel 28
1321 E Court St, Flint MI 48503-2036. 313/762-3028. Employs: 50-99.

W L N S Tv Young Broadcast Inc
2820 E Saginaw St, Lansing MI 48912-4240. 517/372-8282. Employs: 100-249.

W N E M-Tv Five
5409 Gateway Blvd, Flint MI 48507-3992. 313/232-3900. Employs: 50-99.

Black Gospel Network
14951 Wilshire Dr, Detroit MI 48213-1941. 313/526-5305. Employs: 50-99.

Brotherhood Association
151 W Jefferson Ave, Detroit MI 48226-4425. 313/259-9922. Employs: 100-249.

C N B C
2855 Coolidge Hwy, Troy MI 48084-3202. 313/643-9033. Employs: 50-99.

N B C Television Network
2855 Coolidge Hwy, Troy MI 48084-3202. 313/643-8444. Employs: 50-99.

The Discovery Channel
201 W Big Beaver Rd, Troy MI 48084-4152. 313/524-0840. Employs: 50-99.

Tv-22
7605 N Maple Rd, Saline MI 48176-1612. 313/429-3418.
Employs: 50-99.

United Artists Cable-Downriver
21170 Allen Rd, Trenton MI 48183-1602. 313/675-8300.
Employs: 50-99.

United Artists Cable-Downriver
180 Elm St, Trenton MI 48183-2801. 313/675-3200.
Employs: 50-99.

USA Network
2000 Town Center, Southfield MI 48075. 313/353-1200.
Employs: 50-99.

W D Iv-Channel 4
550 W Lafayette Blvd, Detroit MI 48226-3123. 313/222-0444. Employs: 100-249.

W E L M-Tv Cable 11
1070 Trowbridge Rd, East Lansing MI 48823-5220.
517/351-0214. Employs: 50-99.

W E Y I Tv 25
2225 W Willard Rd, Clio MI 48420-8847. 313/687-1000.
Employs: 50-99.

W L A J-T V 53
5815 S Pennsylvania Ave, Lansing MI 48911-5230.
517/394-5300. Employs: 50-99.

W N E M Tv 5
G-2335 S Linden Rd, Flint MI 48532. 313/732-2050.
Employs: 50-99.

CABLE AND OTHER PAY TELEVISION SERVICES

Aichner S Grand Blanc Cable T
G2118 Rollins St, Grand Blanc MI 48439. 313/694-3451.
Employs: 50-99.

Cablevision Ind Dearborn Wayne
15200 Mercantile Dr, Dearborn MI 48120-1207. 313/336-4300. Employs: 50-99.

Continental Cablevision Mi Co
1401 E Miller Rd, Lansing MI 48911-5322. 517/485-8100.
Employs: 100-249.

Fenton Cablevision
112 E Ellen St, Fenton MI 48430-2115. 313/750-9965.
Employs: 50-99.

Mercom Inc
710 N Woodward Ave, Bloomfield MI 48304-2851.
313/647-0850. Employs: 100-249.

Ark-Ken

17421 Telegraph Rd, Detroit MI 48219-3142. 313/592-0390. Employs: 50-99.

Barden Cablevision
12775 Lyndon St, Detroit MI 48227-3960. 313/934-2600.
Employs: 50-99.

Barden Cablevision Inkster Inc
26380 Michigan Ave, Inkster MI 48141-2463. 313/561-5252. Employs: 50-99.

Clear View Cable
13331 Gratiot Ave, Detroit MI 48205-3409. 313/371-8900.
Employs: 50-99.

Comcast Cablevision Macomb
6095 Wall St, Sterling Hts MI 48312-1075. 313/978-8780.
Employs: 50-99.

Continental Cablevision
27800 Franklin Rd, Southfield MI 48034-2363. 313/353-3900. Employs: 50-99.

Continental Cablevision Dearborn
2800 S Gulley Rd, Dearborn Hts MI 48125-1155. 313/277-8750. Employs: 50-99.

Le Com Inc-Detroit
7127 E Davison St, Detroit MI 48212-1924. 313/365-3850.
Employs: 50-99.

MacLean Hunter Cable Tv
29141 Pardo St, Garden City MI 48135-2841. 313/427-4940. Employs: 50-99.

Metrovision Of Livonia
14525 Farmington Rd, Livonia MI 48154-5405. 313/422-3200. Employs: 50-99.

Omnicom Of Michigan
11401 Joseph Campau St, Detroit MI 48212-3040.
313/365-4660. Employs: 50-99.

Public Benefit Corp
614 Vets Meml Bg, Detroit MI 48226. 313/567-2211.
Employs: 50-99.

Vision Cable Communications
6065 Wall St, Sterling Hts MI 48312-1075. 313/268-7150.
Employs: 50-99.

Northcom Inc
35525 Schoolcraft Rd, Livonia MI 48150-1249. 313/522-7155. Employs: 50-99.

Vision Communications-Wtbs
7441 2nd Ave, Detroit MI 48202-2701. 313/873-7200.
Employs: 100-249.

For more information on career opportunities in broadcasting:

Associations

ACADEMY OF TELEVISION ARTS & SCIENCES
5220 Lankershim Boulevard, North Hollywood CA 91601.
818/754-2800.

BROADCAST EDUCATION ASSOCIATION
1771 N Street NW, Washington DC 20036. 202/429-5355.

BROADCAST PROMOTION AND MARKETING EXECUTIVES
6225 Sunset Boulevard, Suite 624, Los Angeles CA 90028.
213/465-3777.

INTERNATIONAL RADIO AND TV SOCIETY
420 Lexington Avenue, Suite 1714, New York NY 10170.
212/867-6650.

INTERNATIONAL TELEVISION ASSOCIATION
6311 North O'Connor Road, LB51, Irving TX 75039.
214/869-1112.

NATIONAL ACADEMY OF TELEVISION ARTS & SCIENCES
111 West 57th Street, Suite 1020, New York NY 10019.
212/586-8424.

NATIONAL ASSOCIATION OF BROADCASTERS
1771 N Street NW, Washington DC 20036. 202/429-5300.

NATIONAL ASSOCIATION OF BUSINESS AND EDUCATIONAL RADIO
1501 Duke Street, Suite 200, Alexandria VA 22314.
703/739-0300.

NATIONAL ASSOCIATION OF PUBLIC
TELEVISION STATIONS
1350 Connecticut Avenue NW, Suite 200
Washington DC 20036. 202/887-1700.

NATIONAL CABLE TELEVISION ASSOCIATION
1724 Massachusetts Avenue NW, Washington DC 20036.
202/755-3550.

TELEVISION BUREAU OF ADVERTISING
477 Madison Avenue, New York NY 10022-5892.
212/486-1111.

WOMEN IN RADIO AND TV, INC.
1101 Connecticut Avenue NW, Suite 700, Washington DC
20036. 202/429-5102.

Magazines

BROADCAST MANAGEMENT/ ENGINEERING
295 Madison Avenue, New York NY 10017. 212/685-
5320.

BROADCASTING
Broadcasting Publications Inc., 1735 DeSales Street NW,
Washington DC 20036. 202/638-1022.

ELECTRONIC MEDIA
Crain Communications, 220 East 42nd Street, New York
NY 10017. 212/210-0100.

TELEVISION RADIO AGE
Television Editorial Corporation, 1270 Avenue of the
Americas, New York NY 10020. 212/757-8400.

CHARITABLE, NON-PROFIT, SOCIAL SERVICES

The outlook for social services workers is better than average. In fact, opportunities for qualified applicants are expected to be excellent, partly due to the rapid turnover in the industry, the growing number of older citizens, and an increased awareness of the needs of the mentally and physically handicapped.

Large employers: 250+

EDUCATIONAL, RELIGIOUS AND CHARITABLE
TRUSTS

Cranbrook Educational Community
380 Lone Pine Rd, Bloomfield MI 48304-3435. 313/645-
3000. Employs: 500-999.

INDIVIDUAL AND FAMILY SOCIAL SERVICES

Lapeer-County Of
1455 Suncrest Dr, Lapeer MI 48446-1151. 313/664-8571.
Employs: 250-499.

JOB TRAINING AND VOCATIONAL
REHABILITATION SERVICES

Community Inds
1057 E Coldwater Rd, Flint MI 48505-1501. 313/785-9332.
Employs: 250-499.

Goodwill Inds/Greater Detroit
3132 Trumbull Ave, Detroit MI 48216-1277. 313/964-
4300. Employs: 500-999.

CHILD DAY CARE SERVICES

Do Re Mi Learning Center Inc
45 Orchard Lane, Bloomfield MI 48304-3455. 313/965-
4171. Employs: 250-499.

Turk Lake Headstart
904 Oak Dr Turk Lake, Greenville MI 48838-9253.
616/754-9315. Employs: 250-499.

BUSINESS ASSOCIATIONS

Society Of Manufacturing Engineers
PO Box 930, Dearborn MI 48121-0930. 313/271-1500.
Employs: 250-499.

LABOR UNIONS AND SIMILAR LABOR
ORGANIZATIONS

United Auto Workers Amer U A W
8000 E Jefferson Ave, Detroit MI 48214-2699. 313/926-
5000. Employs: 500-999.

MISC. MEMBERSHIP ORGANIZATIONS

Siena Heights Endowment Foundation
614 Oakwood Av, Adrian MI 49221-1733. 517/263-0731.
Employs: 250-499.

NONCOMMERCIAL RESEARCH
ORGANIZATIONS

The Edison Institute
20900 Oakwood Blvd, Dearborn MI 48124. 313/271-1620.
Employs: 250-499.

Small to medium sized employers: 50-249

LIBRARIES

Harper Woods Public Library
19601 Harper Ave, Harper Woods MI 48225-2001.
313/343-2575. Employs: 50-99.

Southfield Public Library
26000 Evergreen Rd, Southfield MI 48076-4453. 313/354-9100. Employs: 100-249.

INDIVIDUAL AND FAMILY SOCIAL SERVICES

Leader Dogs For The Blind Inc
1039 S Rochester Rd, Rochester MI 48307-3115. 313/651-9011. Employs: 50-99.

Passages Community Svc
42245 E Ann Arbor Rd, Plymouth MI 48170-4355.
313/459-9420. Employs: 50-99.

Moss Creative Living
871 Starwick Dr, Ann Arbor MI 48105-1285. 313/662-0927. Employs: 50-99.

Metro Detroit Youth Foundation Inc
11000 W McNichols Rd, Detroit MI 48221-2357. 313/863-9394. Employs: 50-99.

St Joseph's Nursing Home Inc
9400 Conant St, Detroit MI 48212-3538. 313/874-4500.
Employs: 100-249.

Work Skills Corporation
69 Enterprise Dr, Ann Arbor MI 48103-9503. 313/663-3553. Employs: 50-99.

**JOB TRAINING AND VOCATIONAL
REHABILITATION SERVICES**

AFL-CIO Job Corps
20314 Grand River Ave, Detroit MI 48219-3342. 313/538-2260. Employs: 50-99.

Buckingham Community Services
3000 Sashabaw Rd, Waterford MI 48329-4040. 313/674-4859. Employs: 100-249.

E B I Breakthru Inc
821 4th Ave, Lake Odessa MI 48849-1001. 616/374-8888.
Employs: 100-249.

Eaton Inter Schools Employment Svc
420 High, Potterville MI 48876. 517/645-7645. Employs: 50-99.

Employment & Training Services
9215 Michigan Ave, Detroit MI 48210-2036. 313/945-5200. Employs: 50-99.

Green Thumb Inc
318 Dolores Dr, Pleasant Lake MI 49272-9762. 517/769-2111. Employs: 50-99.

Growth & Opportunity
525 S Court St, Lapeer MI 48446-2552. 313/664-8504.
Employs: 100-249.

Hillsdale Ofc Employment & Train
154 Lewis St, Hillsdale MI 49242-1102. 517/439-1458.
Employs: 100-249.

Human Investment Corp
877 E 5th Ave, Flint MI 48503-1750. 313/235-6011.
Employs: 50-99.

Job Club
3815 W Fort St, Detroit MI 48216-1652. 313/841-6330.
Employs: 50-99.

Job Connection Inc
1950 Howard Ave, Flint MI 48503-4227. 313/232-5853.
Employs: 50-99.

Jobs Central
711 N Saginaw St, Flint MI 48503-1703. 313/233-5627.
Employs: 50-99.

Key Opportunities Inc
400 N Hillsdale, Hillsdale MI 49242-1068. 517/437-4469.
Employs: 100-249.

Lapeer Team Work Inc
350 N Court St, Lapeer MI 48446-2263. 313/664-2710.
Employs: 100-249.

New Horizons Of Oakland County
117 Turk St, Pontiac MI 48341-3068. 313/338-6176.
Employs: 100-249.

New Horizons Of Oakland County
10445 Dixie Hwy, Davisburg MI 48350-1308. 313/625-0808. Employs: 50-99.

New Horizons Of Oakland County
2124 Franklin Rd, Bloomfield MI 48302-0328. 313/332-2111. Employs: 50-99.

New Horizons Of Oakland County
32021 Howard St, Madison Hts MI 48071-1430. 313/585-9593. Employs: 100-249.

Project Excel
2727 2nd Ave, Detroit MI 48201-2654. 313/965-3147.
Employs: 50-99.

Serco
23400 Michigan Ave, Dearborn MI 48124-1915. 313/278-8367. Employs: 50-99.

Serco
28244 Ford Rd, Garden City MI 48135-2927. 313/522-5627. Employs: 50-99.

Thumb Area Consortium
700 S Main St, Lapeer MI 48446-3077. 313/664-1680.
Employs: 100-249.

Thumb Area Employment & Train
28 Westland Dr, Bad Axe MI 48413-8804. 517/269-2311.
Employs: 50-99.

Thumb Inds Inc
1263 Sand Beach Rd, Bad Axe MI 48413-8817. 517/269-9229. Employs: 100-249.

Greater Detroit Cem Masons Jnt
15101 Wyoming St, Detroit MI 48238-1754. 313/834-2049. Employs: 50-99.

IMI Apprenticeship & Training
1267 W Fort, Detroit MI 48226. 313/965-1175. Employs: 50-99.

Technical Resources Of Detroit
6821 E Ferry St, Detroit MI 48211-3334. 313/925-4600.
Employs: 50-99.

Jewish Vocational Svc
4250 Woodward Ave, Detroit MI 48201-1818. 313/833-8100. Employs: 50-99.

CHILD DAY CARE SERVICES

Canton Crickets
1150 S Canton Center Rd, Canton MI 48188-1608.
313/397-1000. Employs: 100-249.

Dearborn Hts Montessori Ctr
4950 Madison St, Dearborn Hts MI 48125-2364. 313/291-3200. Employs: 50-99.

Little Tots Day Nursery
15115 Farmington Rd, Livonia MI 48154-5413. 313/427-0900. Employs: 50-99.

RESIDENTIAL CARE

Huron View Lodge
355 Huronview Bl, Ann Arbor MI 48103-2949. 313/761-3800. Employs: 50-99.

Pleasant Ridge Manor
2398 Pleasant Ridge, Howell MI 48843-8448. 517/546-1115. Employs: 50-99.

Boulevard Temple Retirement Community
2567 W Grand Blvd, Detroit MI 48208-1235. 313/895-5340. Employs: 50-99.

Cedar Knoll Rest Home Inc
9230 Cedar Knoll Dr, Grass Lake MI 49240-9549. 517/522-8471. Employs: 100-249.

Chandler Hvn Home For Aged Inc
511 E Gd Blvd, Detroit MI 48207. 313/579-2462. Employs: 50-99.

Grace Convalescent Center
18901 Meyers Rd, Detroit MI 48235-1366. 313/864-8481. Employs: 100-249.

Hillsdale County Medical Care
140 Mechanic Rd, Hillsdale MI 49242-1053. 517/439-9341. Employs: 100-249.

Ingleside Convalescent Ctr Inc
9155 Woodward Ave, Detroit MI 48202-1611. 313/872-1420. Employs: 100-249.

Ionia Manor
814 E Lincoln Ave, Ionia MI 48846-1314. 616/527-0080. Employs: 50-99.

Livonia Nursing Center
28910 Plymouth Rd, Livonia MI 48150-2337. 313/522-8970. Employs: 50-99.

Pine Knoll Convalescent Ctr Inc
23600 Northline Rd, Taylor MI 48180-4620. 313/287-8580. Employs: 100-249.

Tender Care Living Ctr 4
28349 Joy Rd, Westland MI 48185-5524. 313/261-9500. Employs: 100-249.

MISCELLANEOUS SOCIAL SERVICES

Burkett's Adult Foster Care
4013 Gratiot Av, Fort Gratiot MI 48059-3919. 313/385-7155. Employs: 50-99.

Adult Well-Being Services
1423 Field St, Detroit MI 48214-2321. 313/924-7860. Employs: 50-99.

League Of Catholic Women
120 Parsons St, Detroit MI 48201-2002. 313/831-1000. Employs: 100-249.

Living Alternatives
8045 Ortonville Rd, Clarkston MI 48348-4457. 313/625-3870. Employs: 100-249.

Residential Systems
7711 Auburn Rd, Utica MI 48317-5220. 313/731-6996. Employs: 100-249.

BUSINESS ASSOCIATIONS

Greater Detroit Chamber Commerce
600 W Lafayette Blvd, Detroit MI 48226-3125. 313/964-4000. Employs: 50-99.

LABOR UNIONS AND SIMILAR LABOR ORGANIZATIONS

UAW GM National Human Resource Center
2630 Featherstone Rd, Auburn Hills MI 48326-2814. 313/377-2400. Employs: 100-249.

CIVIC, SOCIAL AND FRATERNAL ASSOCIATIONS

Detroit Club
712 Cass Ave, Detroit MI 48226-3114. 313/963-8600. Employs: 50-99

North American Benefit Assoc
1338 Military St, Port Huron MI 48060-5423. 313/985-5191. Employs: 50-99.

St Clair County Assn For
1033 26th St, Port Huron MI 48060-4853. 313/364-8380. Employs: 100-249.

RELIGIOUS ORGANIZATIONS

Sacred Heart Parish
302 S Kinney Ave, Mount Pleasnt MI 48858-2707. 517/772-1385. Employs: 50-99.

MISCELLANEOUS MEMBERSHIP ORGANIZATIONS

Citizens For Better Care
416 N Homer St, Lansing MI 48912-4700. 517/482-1297. Employs: 50-99.

Goodwill Industries Mid Mi Inc
501 S Averill Av, Flint MI 48506-4009. 313/762-9968. Employs: 100-249.

Greater Lansing Symphony
230 N Washington Sq Ste 315, Lansing MI 48933-1386. 517/487-5001. Employs: 100-249.

Mi Community Action Agency Assoc
106 W Allegan St Ste 451, Lansing MI 48933-1796. 517/484-1353. Employs: 100-249.

National Sanitation Foundation
3475 Plymouth Rd, Ann Arbor MI 48105-2550. 313/769-8010. Employs: 100-249.

Detroit Tigers Baseball Club
2121 Trumbull St, Detroit MI 48216-1343. 313/962-4000. Employs: 50-99.

NONCOMMERCIAL RESEARCH ORGANIZATIONS

Warde Medical Lab
5025 Venture Dr, Ann Arbor MI 48108-9561. 313/971-0843. Employs: 50-99.

Elizabeth R Harris Foundation
402 S 4th Ave, Ann Arbor MI 48104-2302. 313/663-4991. Employs: 50-99.

Rampant Lion Foundation
611 E William St, Ann Arbor MI 48104-2419. 313/663-7790. Employs: 50-99.

CHEMICAL AND ENVIRONMENTAL

Historically, the chemicals industry has been a cyclical one and is currently on the low end of its cycle. In response, the industry has diversified, imposed tight cost controls, and streamlined operations. Look for a growing number of firms to move into the environmental field. Jobseekers with chemical engineering experience will benefit from the current shortage of workers in the industry.

AKZO COATINGS AMERICA
P.O. Box 7062, Troy MI 48007-7062. 313/637-0400. **Contact:** Personnel Department. **Description:** For information on professional hiring **Contact:** Mary Durham, Personnel Director. **Description:** Engaged in the manufacture and distribution of paint, coatings, and varnishes. **Employees:** 400.

ATOCHEM NORTH AMERICA INCORPORATED
17168 West Jefferson, Riverview MI 48192. 313/246-2080. **Contact:** Personnel Department. **Description:** A Southeastern Michigan manufacturer of industrial inorganic chemicals. **Employees:** 500.

BASF CORPORATION
1609 Biddle Avenue, Wyandotte MI 48192. 313/246-6100. **Contact:** Lorenzo Howard, Human Resources Manager. **Description:** A leading area manufacturer of industrial inorganic chemicals. **Employees:** 800.

BASF CORPORATION
5935 Milford, Detroit MI 48210. 313/361-6500. **Contact:** Gerald Marshall, Personnel Director. **Description:** Engaged in the manufacture of paint and varnish. **Employees:** 200.

BASF/COATINGS AND COLORANTS DIVISION
3301 Bourke Avenue, Detroit MI 48238. 313/861-1000. **Contact:** Human Resources Department. **Description:** Engaged in the manufacture of automotive OEM paint and coatings. **Employees:** 315. **Common positions:** Accountant; Chemist; Chemical Engineer; Production Manager; Personnel and Labor Relations Specialist; Purchasing Agent; Quality Control Supervisor (chemistry background). **Educational backgrounds sought:** Chemistry; Engineering. **Benefits:** medical, dental, and life insurance; pension plan; tuition assistance; disability coverage; employee discounts; savings plan. **Corporate headquarters:** Clifton NJ. **Parent Company:** BASF(West Germany). **Operations at this facility:** manufacturing; research/development. European Stock Exchange.

DETREX CORPORATION
4000 Town Center, Southfield MI 48075. 313/358-5800. **Contact:** Ed Rondeau, Personnel Director. **Description:** A company engaged in the manufacture of industrial inorganic chemicals. **Employees:** 700.

DIVERSEY CORP.
12025 Tech Center Drive, Livonia MI 48150. 313/458-5000. **Contact:** Debra Novitke, Human Resources Representative. **Description:** Part of a worldwide specialty chemical company engaged in the development, manufacturing and marketing of specialty chemicals used in food service, institutional, industrial, food and laundry industries. **Common positions:** Accountant; Biologist; Chemist; Computer Programmer; Credit Manager; Customer Service Representative; Chemical Engineer; Electrical Engineer; Mechanical Engineer; Financial Analyst; Department Manager; Operations/Production Manager; Marketing Specialist; Quality Controller; Sales Representative; Systems Analyst; Transportation and Traffic Specialist. **Educational backgrounds sought:** Accounting; Business Administration; Chemistry; Computer Science; Engineering; Finance; Marketing. **Benefits:** medical, dental and life insurance; pension plan; tuition assistance; disability coverage; savings plan; flexible spending accounts; paid vacations and holidays. **Corporate headquarters:** This location. **Other U.S. locations:** Cincinnati, OH; **Manufacturing facilities:** Stroudsburg, PA; Cinti, OH; City of Ind., CA; Dallas, TX. **Parent Company:** Diversey Corporation, Mississauga, Ontario, Canada. **Operations at this facility:** Administration. **Revenues:** $400 million. **Employees:** 2,900.

EPPERT OIL COMPANY
9100 Freeland Avenue, Detroit MI 48228. 313/273-7374. **Contact:** Ed McDonald, Personnel Director. **Description:** Engaged in the manufacture and distribution of lubricating oil and grease products. **Employees:** 100.

GTE VALENITE
750 Stephenson, Troy MI 48083. 313/589-1000. **Contact:** Marcel Turner, Human Resources Director. **Description:** Manufacturer of pressed and extruded carbide products. **Common positions:** Accountant; Attorney; Blue-Collar Worker Supervisor; Computer Programmer; Credit Manager; Ceramics Engineer; Industrial Engineer; Mechanical Engineer; Metallurgical Engineer; Financial Analyst; Industrial Manager; General Manager; Personnel and Labor Relations Specialist; Purchasing Agent; Quality Controller; Sales Representative. **Educational backgrounds sought:** Business Administration; Computer Science; Finance; Marketing; Materials Science. **Benefits:** medical insurance; dental insurance; pension plan; life insurance; tuition assistance; disability coverage; savings plan; stock options. **Corporate headquarters:** Stamford, CT. **Other U.S. locations:** TX, SC. **Parent company:** GTE. **Operations at this facility:** Administration; Service; Sales. **Listed on:** New York Stock Exchange. **Employees:** 3,500.

GTE VALENITE/WALMET DIVISION
P.O. Box 10, Royal Oak MI 48068. 313/589-6400. **Contact:** Joseph Syler, Human Resources Manager. **Description:** Manufacturer of pressed and extruded carbide products. **Common positions:** Blue-Collar Worker Supervisor; Customer Service Representative; Draftsperson; Metallurgical Engineer; Industrial Manager; General Manager; Sales Representative; Estimator; Data Entry. **Benefits:** medical insurance; dental insurance; pension plan; life insurance; tuition assistance; disability coverage; savings plan.

GUARDSMAN PRODUCTS, INC.
27722 Franklin Road, Southfield MI 48034-2352. 313/350-1600. **Contact:** Craig Conners, Sales and Marketing Manager. **Description:** A Michigan corporation engaged in the manufacture of chemicals, lubricants, coatings, packaging services, and consumer products. **Employees:** 900. **Common positions:** Sales Representative. **Educational backgrounds sought:** Business Administration; Marketing. **Benefits:** medical and life insurance; savings plan. **Corporate headquarters:** Grand Rapids, MI. **Operations at this facility:** sales. **Listed on:** New York Stock Exchange.

HEATBATH/PARK METALLURGICAL
8074 Military Avenue, Detroit MI 48204. 313/895-7215. **Contact:** Pat Trakul, Plant Manager. **Description:** A leading Detroit-based manufacturer of chemicals. **Employees:** 100.

E.F. HOUGHTON AND COMPANY
MICHIGAN DIVISION
2700 East 9 Mile Road, Warrent MI 48091. 313/759-8411. **Contact:** Ed Schmidt, Personnel Director. **Description:** Engaged in the manufacture of lubricated oil and grease products. **Employees:** 200.

METAL WORKING LUBRICANTS
25 Silverdome Industrial Park, Pontiac MI 48342. 313/642-0410. **Contact:** Personnel Department. **Description:** A leading Detroit manufacturer of lubricating oil and grease products. **Employees:** 100.

MOBIL OIL/WOODHAVEN DIVISION
20089 West Road, Woodhaven MI 48183. 313/671-2729. **Contact:** K.F. Goode, Plant Manager. **Description:** A leading area manufacturer of lubricated oil and grease products.

OMI INTERNATIONAL
21441 Hoover Road, Warren MI 48089. 313/497-9100. **Contact:** Elsie Murphy, Employee Relations Manager. **Description:** Engaged in the sale and manufacture of chemicals and surface treatment equipment to a worldwide market. **Corporate headquarters:** This location. **Operations include:** manufacturing; research/development; administration; service; sales. **Common positions:** Accountant; Buyer; Chemist; Computer Programmer; Credit Manager; Customer Service Representative; Draftsperson; Chemical Engineer;

Industrial Engineer; Mechanical Engineer; Industrial Designer; Marketing Specialist; Personnel and Labor Relations Specialist; Purchasing Agent; Quality Control Supervisor; Sales Representative. **Educational backgrounds sought:** Accounting; Chemistry; Computer Science; Engineering; Marketing. **Benefits:** medical, dental, and life insurance; tuition assistance; disability coverage; profit sharing; savings plan; pension plan.

PPG HUGHES PRODUCTS/C&R DIVISION
5875 New King Court, Troy MI 48098. 313/564-5500. **Contact:** Paul Molini, Personnel. **Description:** A Southeastern Michigan manufacturer of adhesive products.

PVS CHEMICALS
10900 Harper Avenue, Detroit MI 48213. 313/921-1200. **Contact:** Don Sosnoski, Director of Personnel. **Description:** A Detroit wholesale distributor of chemicals and allied products. **Employees:** 300.

PARKER & AMCHEM
32100 Stephenson Highway, Madison Heights MI 48071. 313/583-9300. **Contact:** David F. Grandy, Director of Human Resources. **Description:** An area manufacturer of chemical products. Subsidiary of Henkel Corporation (Dusseldorf, Germany. **Common positions:** Accountant; Chemist; Computer Programmer; Credit Manager; Customer Service Representative; Draftsperson; Chemical Engineer; Mechanical Engineer; Branch Manager; Department Manager; General Manager; Operations/Production Manager; Personnel and Labor Relations Specialist; Purchasing Agent; Quality Controller; Sales Representative; Systems Analyst; Transportation and Traffic Specialist; Lab Technician. **Educational backgrounds sought:** Accounting; Chemistry; Finance; Marketing. **Special programs:** internships. **Benefits:** medical insurance; dental insurance; pension plan; life insurance; tuition assistance; disability coverage; profit sharing; 401K plan. **Corporate headquarters:** Gulph Mills, PA. **Operations at this facility:** research and development; administration; service; sales. **Employees:** 650. **Projected number of new hires for the next 12 months:** approximately 30.

RENOSOL CORPORATION
P.O. Box 1424, Ann Arbor MI 48106. 313/429-5418. **Contact:** Bethany Freeland, Personnel. **Description:** Manufactures polyurethane and vinyl products and liquid systems primarily to the automotive industry. **Employees:** 250 in Michigan and South Carolina. **Common positions:** Accountant; Administrator; Chemist; Computer Programmer; Credit Manager; Customer Service Representative; Industrial Manager; Sales Representative. **Educational backgrounds sought:** Accounting; Business Administration; Chemistry; Computer Science; Finance; Marketing. **Benefits:** medical insurance; dental insurance; pension plan; life insurance; tuition assistance; disability coverage; profit sharing; 401K plan. **Other U.S. locations:** Farwell, MI; Bay City, MI; Maudlin, SC. **Operations at this facility:** research and development; administration; sales. **Revenues (1991):** $36 million company wide.

Employees: 40 at this location. **Projected number of new hires for the next 12 months:** 8 at this location.

R.P. SCHERER CORPORATION
2075 West Big Beaver, Troy MI 48084. 313/649-0900. **Contact:** Office Manager. **Description:** A major Southeastern Michigan manufacturer of chemicals. **Employees:** 2,400.

UNITED STATES GYPSUM COMPANY
2 Division Street, River Rouge MI 48218. 313/842-4455. **Contact:** Deborah LeShore, Human Resources Department Manager. **Description:** Engaged in the manufacture of gypsum products. **Employees:** 150. **Common positions:** Civil Engineer; Electrical Engineer; Mechanical Engineer. **Educational backgrounds sought:** Accounting; Engineering; Finance. **Corporate headquarters:** Chicago, IL. **Parent company:** USG Corporation. Operations at this facility: manufacturing.

Additional large employers: 250+

PAINTS, VARNISHES, LACQUERS, ENAMELS AND ALLIED PRODUCTS

Flint Ink Corp
25111 Glendale Ave, Redford MI 48239-2646. 313/538-6800. Employs: 500-999.

ADHESIVES AND SEALANTS

L & L Products Inc
74100 Van Dyke Ave, Romeo MI 48065. 313/752-3591. Employs: 250-499.

MISC. CHEMICALS AND CHEMICAL PREPARATIONS

B A S F Corp
26701 Telegraph Rd, Southfield MI 48034-2442. 313/827-4670. Employs: 250-499.

Diamond Crystal Salt Co
916 S Riverside Av, Saint Clair MI 48079-5335. 313/329-2211. Employs: 500-999.

OMI International Corp
21441 Hoover Rd, Warren MI 48089-3161. 313/497-9100. Employs: 500-999.

Pennwalt Corporation
17168 Jefferson, Wyandotte MI 48192-4270. 313/285-9200. Employs: 250-499.

Additional small to medium sized employers: 50-249

INDUSTRIAL GASES

Liquid Carbonic
4685 Gratiot Rd, Port Huron MI 48060. 313/364-9011. Employs: 50-99.

MISCELLANEOUS INDUSTRIAL INORGANIC CHEMICALS

B A S F Corp/Chemicals Div
13000 Levan Rd, Livonia MI 48150-1240. 313/591-6200. Employs: 50-99.

Great Lakes Chemical Corp
1400 E Michigan St, Adrian MI 49221-3446. 517/265-6138. Employs: 100-249.

Parker Amchem
23343 Sherwood Ave, Warren MI 48091-5362. 313/759-5555. Employs: 50-99.

PAINTS, VARNISHES, LACQUERS, ENAMELS AND ALLIED PRODUCTS

Detroit Quality Brush Manufacturing Co

32165 Schoolcraft Rd, Livonia MI 48150-1810. 313/525-5660. Employs: 50-99.

E I Du Pont De Nemours & Co
1555 James P Cole Blvd, Flint MI 48503-1700. 313/762-9400. Employs: 100-249.

Gage Product Co
625 Wanda St, Ferndale MI 48220-2657. 313/541-3824. Employs: 50-99.

Palmer Paint Products Inc
1291 Rochester Rd, Troy MI 48083-2879. 313/588-4500. Employs: 100-249.

Red Spot Westland Inc
550 S Edwin St, Westland MI 48185-3801. 313/729-7400. Employs: 100-249.

Seibert Oxidermo Inc
6455 Strong, Detroit MI 48211-1861. 313/921-6033. Employs: 50-99.

Standard Detroit Paint Company
8225 Lyndon Ave, Detroit MI 48238-2453. 313/931-3300. Employs: 50-99.

United Paint & Chemical Corp
24671 Telegraph Rd, Southfield MI 48034-3035. 313/353-3035. Employs: 50-99.

CYCLIC ORGANIC CRUDES AND INTERMEDIATES AND ORGANIC DYES AND PIGMENTS

Michigan Chrome & Chemical Co
8615 Grinnell Ave, Detroit MI 48213-1152. 313/267-5200. Employs: 100-249.

MISCELLANEOUS INDUSTRIAL ORGANIC CHEMICALS

Chemcentral Detroit Corp
13395 Huron River Dr, Romulus MI 48174-3631. 313/941-4800. Employs: 50-99.

Michigan Chloride Sls Inc
402 W Jackson Rd, Saint Louis MI 48880-9279. 517/681-5181. Employs: 50-99.

Nutra Sweet Co
30 Buell St, Harbor Beach MI 48441-1116. 517/479-3245. Employs: 100-249.

International Enzymes Marketing Corp
19779 Edshire Ln, Grosse Pointe MI 48236-2714. 313/882-7214. Employs: 100-249.

NITROGENOUS FERTILIZERS

Scott-Hyponex Corp
332 Graham Rd, Imlay City MI 48444-9738. 313/724-2875. Employs: 50-99.

MISCELLANEOUS PESTICIDES AND AGRICULTURAL CHEMICALS

Michigan Peat Co
875 E Sanilac, Sandusky MI 48471-9106. 313/648-2210. Employs: 50-99.

ADHESIVES AND SEALANTS

Adco Products Inc
4401 Page Ave, Michigan Ctr MI 49254-1037. 517/764-0334. Employs: 50-99.

Akzo Coatings Inc
30 Brush St, Pontiac MI 48341-2212. 313/334-7010. Employs: 50-99.

Coat-It Inc
2300 Gainsboro, Ferndale MI 48220-1330. 313/5447606. Employs: 50-99.

E M S Togo Corp
20219 Northline Rd, Taylor MI 48180-4786. 313/374-0700. Employs: 50-99.

Essex Specialty Products Inc
190 Uran, Hillsdale MI 49242-1087. 517/439-9303. Employs: 100-249.

Grow Group Inc
3155 W Big Beaver Rd #200, Troy MI 48084-3010. 313/643-4600. Employs: 50-99.

MISCELLANEOUS CHEMICALS AND CHEMICAL PREPARATIONS

Akzo Chemical Div
9901 Sandcreek Hwy, Weston MI 49289. 517/436-3171. Employs: 50-99.

Allied-Kelite
364 Midland Ave, Detroit MI 48203-3734. 313/883-0100. Employs: 50-99.

Aquatec Chemical International
408 Auburn Ave, Pontiac MI 48342-3208. 313/334-4747. Employs: 100-249.

B A S F Wyandotte Corp
1609 Biddle Av, Wyandotte MI 48192-3729. 313/246-6100. Employs: 100-249.

Benckiser Consumer Products
21702 E Huron River Dr, Rockwood MI 48173-1120. 313/379-9655. Employs: 100-249.

Chem-Trend Incorporated
3205 E Grand River, Howell MI 48843-8552. 517/546-4520. Employs: 100-249.

Difco Labs Inc
17197 N Laurel Pk Dr, Livonia MI 48152-2686. 313/462-8500. Employs: 100-249.

Formax Manufacturing Corp
3178 Bellevue, Detroit MI 48207-2504. 313/921-7030. Employs: 50-99.

H & H Supply Inc
2040 Heiserman Rd, Brighton MI 48116-8969. 313/229-6224. Employs: 50-99.

H B Fuller Automotive Products
13650 E 10 Mile Rd, Warren MI 48089-2110. 313/776-5000. Employs: 100-249.

Magni Group Inc
255 S Woodward Ave #300, Birmingham MI 48009-6178. 313/647-4500. Employs: 50-99.

Olin Corp
35750 Indl Rd, Livonia MI 48150. 313/591-0700. Employs: 50-99.

Quaker Chemical Corp
14301 Birwood St, Detroit MI 48238-2207. 313/931-6910. Employs: 50-99.

Secodyne Inc
3255 Goldner St, Detroit MI 48210-3232. 313/898-9074. Employs: 50-99.

Steelcrete Co
45700 W 12 Mile Rd, Novi MI 48377-2406. 313/349-7600. Employs: 100-249.

For more information on career opportunities in the chemical and environmental industries:

Associations

AMERICAN CHEMICAL SOCIETY
Career Services, 1155 16th Street NW, Washington DC 20036. 202/872-4600.

AMERICAN INSTITUTE OF CHEMICAL ENGINEERING
345 East 47th Street, New York NY 10017. 212/705-7338.

AMERICAN INSTITUTE OF CHEMISTS
7315 Wisconsin Avenue, Bethesda MD 20814. 301/652-2447.

ASSOCIATION OF STATE & INTERSTATE
WATER POLLUTION CONTROL
ADMINISTRATORS
750 First Street NE, Suite 910, Washington DC 20002.
202/898-0905.

CHEMICAL MANUFACTURERS ASSOCIATION
2501 M Street, Washington DC 20037. 202/887-1100.

CHEMICAL MARKETING RESEARCH
ASSOCIATION
60 Bay Street, Staten Island NY 10301. 718/876-8800.

WATER POLLUTION CONTROL FEDERATION
601 Wythe Street, Alexandria VA 22314. 703/684-2400.

Directories

CHEMICAL INDUSTRY DIRECTORY
State Mutual Book and Periodical Service, 521 Fifth
Avenue, New York NY 10175. 212/682-5844.

CHEMICAL INDUSTRY DIRECTORY AND WHO'S
WHO
Taylor & Francis, 1900 Frost Road, Suite 101, Bristol PA
19007. 800/821-8312.

CHEMICALS DIRECTORY
Cahners Publishing, 275 Washington Street, Newton MA
02158. 617/964-3030.

DIRECTORY OF CHEMICAL ENGINEERING
CONSULTANTS
American Institute of Chemical Engineering, 345 East 47th
Street, New York NY 10017. 212/705-7338.

DIRECTORY OF CHEMICAL PRODUCERS
SRI, 333 Ravenswood Avenue, Menlo Park CA 94025.
415/326-6200.

Magazines

CHEMICAL & ENGINEERING NEWS
1155 16th Street NW, Washington DC 20036. 202/872-
4600.

CHEMICAL MARKETING REPORTER
Schnell Publishing Co., 80 Brot Street, 23rd Floor, New
York NY 10004. 212/248-4177.

CHEMICAL PROCESSING
Putnam Publishing Co., 301 East Erie Street, Chicago IL
60611. 312/644-2020.

CHEMICAL WEEK
888 7th Avenue, 26th Floor, New York NY 10106.
212/621-4900.

COLLEGES & UNIVERSITIES/EDUCATION

Job prospects for college faculty will increase at average speed during the 90's. Most openings will result from retirements. The best prospects are in business, engineering, health sciences, physical sciences, and mathematics. Among kindergarten and elementary school teachers, the best opportunities await those with training in special education. Among high school teachers, opportunities will increase rapidly. Increased teacher involvement and higher salaries will attract new applicants.

CENTER FOR CREATIVE STUDIES
COLLEGE OF ART AND DESIGN
201 East Kirby, Detroit MI 48202. 313/872-3118. **Contact:** Janelle Rivers, Personnel Director. **Description:** A major metropolitan Detroit four year college specializing in professional arts programs.

CENTRAL MICHIGAN UNIVERSITY
109 Rowe Hall, Mount Pleasant MI 48859. 517/774-3753. **Contact:** Judy Stovak, Manager/Employment. **Description:** A university of higher education. **Common positions:** Accountant; Administrator; Blue-Collar Worker Supervisor; Buyer; Computer Programmer; Financial Analyst; Food Technologist; Personnel and Labor Relations Specialist; Systems Analyst;

Technical Writer/Editor; Broadcaster; Registered Nurse. **Educational backgrounds sought:** Accounting; Business Administration; Computer Science; Finance; Personnel; Management Information Systems. **Special Programs:** Internships. **Benefits:** medical, dental, and life insurance; pension plan; tuition assistance; disability coverage; savings plan; vision plan. **Corporate headquarters:** this location. **Employees:** 2,300. **Projected hires for the next twelve months:** 40-70.

DAVENPORT COLLEGE OF BUSINESS
415 East Fulton, Grand Rapids MI 49503. 616/451-3511. **Contact:** Personnel Department. **Description:** A major business college.

DETROIT COLLEGE OF BUSINESS
4801 Oakman Boulevard, Dearborn MI 48126. 313/581-4400. **Contact:** Pamela Hodge, Director of Human Resources. **Description:** A leading area undergraduate business college with one, two, and four year programs.

DETROIT COLLEGE OF LAW
130 East Elizabeth Street, Detroit MI 48201. 313/965-0150. **Contact:** Rick Lamenti, Comptroller. **Description:** A private, accredited college with one, two, and four year programs.

FERRIS STATE UNIVERSITY
420 Oaks Street, Big Rapids MI 49307-2000. 616/592-2000. **Contact:** Personnel Department. **Description:** A major state university.

LAWRENCE TECHNOLOGY UNIVERSITY
21000 West Ten Mile, Southfield MI 48075. 313/356-0200. **Contact:** Personnel Department. **Description:** A major university, concentrating in technology.

MARY GROVE COLLEGE
8425 W. McNichols Road, Detroit MI 48221. 313/862-8000. **Contact:** Department of interest. **Description:** A Detroit institution of higher learning which specializes in a 4-year liberal arts program.

MICHIGAN STATE UNIVERSITY
1407 South Harrison Road, 110 Nisbet Building, East Lansing MI 48824. 517/353-3720. **Contact:** Personnel Department. **Description:** A major state university.

MICHIGAN TECH UNIVERSITY
1400 Townsend, Administration Bldg., Houghton MI 49931. 906/487-2280. **Contact:** Sherry Kauppi, Employment Coordinator. **Description:** A major technological university. **Common positions:** Personnel and Labor Relations Specialist; Systems Analyst; Technical Writer/Editor. **Educational backgrounds sought:** Accounting; Biology; Business Administration; Chemistry; Communications; Computer Science; Engineering; Mathematics; Physics. **Benefits:** medical insurance; dental insurance; pension plan; life

insurance; tuition assistance; disability coverage; daycare assistance. **Corporate headquarters:** This location.

NORTHERN MICHIGAN UNIVERSITY
Presque Isle Avenue, Marquette MI 49855. 906/227-1000. **Contact:** Personnel Department. **Description:** A major university.

OAKLAND UNIVERSITY
department of applicant's interest, Rochester MI 48309-4401. 313/370-2100. **Contact:** Personnel. **Description:** An area university.

UNIVERSITY OF DETROIT
P.O. Box 199, Detroit MI 48221-9987. 313/993-1000. **Contact:** Personnel Department. **Description:** A major university.

UNIVERSITY OF MICHIGAN/FLINT
303 East Kearsley, Flint MI 48502-2186. 313/762-3150. **Contact:** Personnel Department. **Description:** Flint location of the major university.

UNIVERSITY OF MICHIGAN
1009 Green Street, 2031 Administrative Services Building, Ann Arbor MI 48109-1432. 313/764-7280. **Contact:** Personnel Department. **Description:** Ann Arbor location of the major university.

WAYNE COUNTY COMMUNITY COLLEGE
801 West Fort Street, Detroit MI 48226. 313/496-2765. **Contact:** Human Resources Department. **Description:** A Detroit-area institution of higher learning offering degrees in a variety of areas. **Common positions:** Accountant; Administrator; Buyer; Computer Programmer; Department Manager; Personnel and Labor Relations Specialist; Systems Analyst; Clerical Worker; Instructor. **Educational backgrounds sought:** Accounting; Business Administration; Marketing. **Benefits:** medical, dental, and life insurance; tuition assistance; disability coverage; optical plan. **Corporate headquarters:** This location.

WAYNE STATE UNIVERSITY
100 Antoinette, Detroit MI 48202. 313/577-2010. **Contact:** Department of interest. **Description:** Nationally ranked research university located in an urban setting, with the mission to serve in the several capacities of teaching, research and community service. **Common positions:** Accountant; Administrator; Architect; Attorney; Biochemist; Biologist; Blue-Collar Worker Supervisor; Buyer; Chemist; Computer Programmer; Economist; Financial Analyst; Department Manager; General Manager; Marketing Specialist; Personnel and Labor Relations Specialist; Public Relations Worker; Purchasing Agent; Systems Analyst. **Educational backgrounds sought:** Accounting; Business Administration; Communications; Computer Science; Economics; Finance; Liberal Arts; Marketing. **Benefits:** medical, dental, and life insurance; pension plan; tuition assistance; disability coverage; employee discounts. **Corporate**

headquarters: This location. **Operations at this facility:** administration; service.

WESTERN MICHIGAN UNIVERSITY

1300 Seibert Administration Building, Kalamazoo MI 49008. 616/387-3626. **Contact:** Sue Rodia, Director, Employment Services. **Description:** A major university. **Common positions:** Accountant; Administrator; Architect; Attorney; Biochemist; Blue-Collar Worker Supervisor; Chemist; Computer Programmer; Counselor; Dietician; Draftsperson; Civil Engineer; Electrical Engineer; Mechanical Engineer; Financial Analyst; Instructor/Teacher; Department Manager; General Manager; Operations/Production Manager; Marketing Specialist; Personnel and Labor Relations Specialist; Physicist; Public Relations Specialist; Purchasing Agent; Reporter/Editor; Systems Analyst; Technical Editor/Writer; Transportation and Traffic Specialist. **Educational backgrounds sought:** Accounting; Art/Design; Biology; Business Administration; Chemistry; Communications; Computer Science; Economics; Engineering; Finance; Liberal Arts; Marketing; Mathematics; Physics. **Benefits:** medical insurance; dental insurance; pension plan; life insurance; tuition assistance; disability coverage; employee discounts. **Corporate headquarters:** this location. **Operations include:** research and development; administration. **Number of employees:** 3,000. **Projected number of new hires for the next 12 months:** 100.

Additional large employers: 250+

ELEMENTARY AND SECONDARY SCHOOLS

Mott Adult High School
1231 E Kearsley St, Flint MI 48503-6114. 313/760-1101.
Employs: 250-499.

Chippewa Valley Schools
19120 Cass Ave, Clinton Twp MI 48038-2301. 313/286-7602. Employs: 250-499.

Croswell Lexington School Dist
5407 Peck Rd, Croswell MI 48422-9108. 313/679-2232.
Employs: 250-499.

Lake Orion Comm School Dist
315 N Lapeer St, Lake Orion MI 48362-3165. 313/693-5410. Employs: 250-499.

COLLEGES, UNIVERSITIES AND PROFESSIONAL SCHOOLS

Detroit College Of Law
130 E Elizabeth St, Detroit MI 48201-3454. 313/965-0150.
Employs: 250-499.

General Motors Institute
1700 W 3rd Av, Flint MI 48504-4832. 313/762-9790.
Employs: 250-499.

Albion College
611 East Porter, Albion MI 49224-1831. 517/692-0215.
Employs: 500-999.

Alma College
614 W Superior, Alma MI 48801-1511. 517/463-7111.
Employs: 500-999.

Detroit College Of Business
3115 Lawndale Ave, Flint MI 48504-2627. 313/239-1443.
Employs: 250-499.

Dietre University
377 Fisher Rd, Grosse Pointe MI 48230-1600. 313/882-5522. Employs: 250-499.

GMI Engineering and Management Institute
1700 West Third Avenue, Flint MI 48504-4832. 313/762-9500. Employs: 250-499.

Hillsdale College
33 East College, Hillsdale MI 49242-1205. 517/437-7341.
Employs: 500-999.

Madonna College
36600 Schoolcraft Road, Livonia MI 48150-1173. 313/591-5000. Employs: 250-499.

Sacred Heart Seminary College
2701 Chicago Boulevard, Detroit MI 48206-1704. 313/883-8500. Employs: 250-499.

Spring Arbor College
106 Main Street, Spring Arbor MI 49283-9701. 517/750-1200. Employs: 500-999.

St Mary's College
Commerce & Orchard Lk Rds, Orchard Lake MI 48033.
313/682-1885. Employs: 250-499.

Univ Of Michigan-Dearborn
4901 Evergreen Road, Dearborn MI 48128-1491. 313/593-5000. Employs: 250-499.

William Tyndale College
35700 W Twelve Mile Road, Farmington MI 48331-3149.
313/553-7200. Employs: 250-499.

JUNIOR COLLEGES AND TECHNICAL INSTITUTES

Oakland Community College
27055 Orchard Lake Rd, Farmington MI 48334. 313/471-7500. Employs: 500-999.

Detroit Inst Of Commerce
4829 Woodward Ave, Detroit MI 48201-1309. 313/832-0200. Employs: 250-499.

Henry Ford Community College
5101 Evergreen Road, Dearborn MI 48128-1495. 313/845-9615. Employs: 250-499.

Highland Park CommunityCollege
Glendale At Third, Detroit MI 48203. 313/252-0475. Employs: 500-999.

Hurley Medical Center School Of Nursing
701 W Eighth Avenue, Flint MI 48503-1261. 313/257-9409. Employs: 250-499.

ITT Tech Inst
1225 E Big Beaver Rd, Troy MI 48083-1905. 313/524-1800. Employs: 250-499.

Jackson Bus Inst
234 S Mechanic St, Jackson MI 49201-2328. 517/789-6123. Employs: 500-999.

Krainz Woods Acad Med Lab Tec
4327 East Seven Mile Road, Detroit MI 48234-2017. 313/366-5204. Employs: 250-499.

Lewis Col Of Bus
17370 Meyers Road, Detroit MI 48235-1423. 313/862-6300. Employs: 250-499.

Mi Paraprof Training
29814 Smith Rd, Romulus MI 48174-2161. 313/721-1777. Employs: 250-499.

Michigan Paraprof Training
21800 Greenfield Road, Oak Park MI 48237-2507. 313/968-2460. Employs: 250-499.

Montcalm Community College
1464 Sidney Road, Sidney MI 48885-9745. 517/328-2111. Employs: 250-499.

New Tribes Bible Inst
1210 E Michigan Ave, Jackson MI 49201-1839. 517/782-9309. Employs: 500-999.

Oakland Community College
2480 Opdyke Rd PO Box 812, Bloomfield MI 48304-2223. 313/540-1500. Employs: 250-499.

Samaritan Health Ctr Rad Sch
5555 Conner, Detroit MI 48213-3405. 313/579-4180. Employs: 250-499.

School Craft College
18600 Haggerty Road, Livonia MI 48152-2696. 313/462-4400. Employs: 1000+.

St Clair City Community College
323 Erie Street, Port Huron MI 48060-3812. 313/984-3881. Employs: 250-499.

United Bible Inst
4805 N Saginaw St, Flint MI 48505-3510. 313/787-2564. Employs: 250-499.

Wayne City Community College
801 Fort Avenue, Detroit MI 48226. 313/496-2500. Employs: 250-499.

BUSINESS AND SECRETARIAL SCHOOLS

Elsa Cooper Institute Ct Rptg
16250 Northland Dr, Southfield MI 48075-5205. 313/552-0061. Employs: 250-499.

Additional small to medium sized employers: 50-249

ELEMENTARY AND SECONDARY SCHOOLS

Adrian Senior High School
785 Riverside Av, Adrian MI 49221-1404. 517/263-2180. Employs: 50-99.

Adult & Community Education Center
1800 E Forest Av, Ypsilanti MI 48198-4119. 313/481-8347. Employs: 50-99.

Bendle East School
G2414 E Hemphill Rd, Burton MI 48529. 313/744-3440. Employs: 50-99.

Benjamin H Sherman Mid School
14470 N Holly Rd, Holly MI 48442-9404. 313/634-8296. Employs: 50-99.

Birmingham Alternative High
1742 Pierce St, Birmingham MI 48009-2056. 313/644-2927. Employs: 50-99.

Bryant Ctr Mott Adult High
201 E Pierson Rd, Flint MI 48505-3380. 313/762-1638. Employs: 50-99.

C W Otto Middle School
500 E Thomas St, Lansing MI 48906-4148. 517/374-4650. Employs: 50-99.

Capitol Alternative Education
1030 S Holmes St, Lansing MI 48912-1950. 517/374-4223. Employs: 50-99.

Carman Ainsworth High School
G1409 W Maple Rd, Flint MI 48507. 313/732-9770. Employs: 50-99.

Carman Ainsworth Senior High
G1300 N Linden Rd, Flint MI 48532. 313/732-1880. Employs: 50-99.

Carman Ainsworth
G1181 W Scottwood Av, Flint MI 48507. 313/238-9641. Employs: 50-99.

Carter Middle School
300 Upland Dr, Clio MI 48420-1265. 313/686-0503. Employs: 50-99.

Central Community High School
601 Crapo St, Flint MI 48503-2057. 313/762-1042. Employs: 50-99.

Central Intermediate School
200 32D St, Port Huron MI 48060-2504. 313/984-6533. Employs: 50-99.

Civic Park School
1402 W Dayton St, Flint MI 48504-2721. 313/762-1441. Employs: 50-99.

Clio High School
1 Mustang Dr, Clio MI 48420-1056. 313/686-4880. Employs: 50-99.

Donald E Johnson Community School
5323 Western Rd, Flint MI 48506-1326. 313/762-1830.
Employs: 50-99.

Dort School
2025 N Saginaw St, Flint MI 48505-3843. 313/762-1450.
Employs: 50-99.

E Jackson Community Schools Supt
1404 N Sutton Rd, Jackson MI 49202-2822. 517/764-2090.
Employs: 50-99.

Eastern High School
222 N Pennsylvania Av, Lansing MI 48912-1515. 517/374-
4200. Employs: 50-99.

Elisabeth Ann Johnson Mem High
G8041 Neff Rd, Mount Morris MI 48458. 313/686-2370.
Employs: 50-99.

Eton Academy
1755 Melton Rd, Birmingham MI 48009-7277. 313/646-
5224. Employs: 50-99.

Everett High School
3900 Stabler St, Lansing MI 48910-4567. 517/374-4400.
Employs: 50-99.

Fenton High School
3200 W Shiawassee St, Fenton MI 48430-1762. 313/629-
4167. Employs: 50-99.

Fiedler Leota Elementary
G6317 Nightingale Dr, Genesee MI 48437. 313/736-7350.
Employs: 50-99.

Flint Remedial Reading Clinic
3313 Miller Rd, Flint MI 48503-4659. 313/239-1711.
Employs: 50-99.

Flint Southwestern Academy
1420 W 12th St, Flint MI 48507-1425. 313/762-1400.
Employs: 50-99.

Flushing Senior High School
5039 Deland Rd, Flushing MI 48433-1307. 313/659-0630.
Employs: 50-99.

Ford Edsel High School
20601 Rotunda Dr, Dearborn MI 48124-3954. 313/582-
2436. Employs: 50-99.

Fordson High School
13800 Ford Rd, Dearborn MI 48126-3209. 313/582-3333.
Employs: 50-99.

Garner Elementary School
10271 Clio Rd, Flint MI 48504. 313/686-1870. Employs:
50-99.

Genesee High School
G7341 N Genesee Rd, Burton MI 48529. 313/640-1450.
Employs: 50-99.

Gladys Dillon Elementary
G1197 E Schumacher Av, Flint MI 48507. 313/239-5666.
Employs: 50-99.

Grand Blanc High School
12500 Holly Rd, Grand Blanc MI 48439-1868. 313/694-
8211. Employs: 50-99.

Grand Ledge High School
225 W Kent St, Grand Ledge MI 48837-1829. 517/627-
5194. Employs: 50-99.

Greenhills School
850 Greenhills Dr, Ann Arbor MI 48105-2720. 313/769-
4010. Employs: 50-99.

Groves Wylie E High School

20500 W Thirteen Mile Rd, Franklin MI 48025-3830.
313/645-0322. Employs: 50-99.

Haas Elementary School
G7347 N Genesee Rd, Burton MI 48529. 313/640-2100.
Employs: 50-99.

Harry C Gardner Jr High School
333 Dahlia Dr, Lansing MI 48911. 517/887-3200.
Employs: 50-99.

Head Start
1036 Jefferson Av, Ypsilanti MI 48197-5293. 313/484-
6680. Employs: 50-99.

Henry R Pattengill Middle School
1017 Jerome St, Lansing MI 48912-1805. 517/374-4463.
Employs: 50-99.

Herbert M Slauson Mid School
1019 W Washington St, Ann Arbor MI 48103-4241.
313/994-2004. Employs: 50-99.

Holly Senior High School
920 E Baird St, Holly MI 48442-1735. 313/634-4451.
Employs: 50-99.

Holmes Community Junior High School
6602 Oxley Dr, Flint MI 48504-1674. 313/762-1620.
Employs: 50-99.

Holt High School
1784 Aurelius Rd, Holt MI 48842-1920. 517/694-2162.
Employs: 50-99.

Holy Rosary Educational Center
G4160 Underhill Dr, Genesee MI 48437. 313/736-7600.
Employs: 50-99.

Huron High School
2727 Fuller Rd, Ann Arbor MI 48105. 313/994-2040.
Employs: 100-249.

J W Sexton High School
102 Mc Pherson Av, Lansing MI 48915-1760. 517/374-
4120. Employs: 50-99.

Jackson Baptist Elementary
801 Halstead Blvd, Jackson MI 49203-2664. 517/784-
6162. Employs: 50-99.

Johnson Head Start Center
5825 Western Rd, Flint MI 48506-1306. 313/762-1878.
Employs: 50-99.

Jonas Sawdon Ninth Grade
220 Lamson St, Grand Ledge MI 48837-1760. 517/627-
6144. Employs: 50-99.

Kate Dowdall Elementary School
G3333 Shillelagh Dr, Genesee MI 48437. 313/736-4280.
Employs: 50-99.

Kinawa Middle School
4006 Okemos Rd, Okemos MI 48864-3213. 517/349-9220.
Employs: 50-99.

Mason High School
1001 S Barnes St, Mason MI 48854-1949. 517/676-9055.
Employs: 50-99.

Mc Grath Elementary School
G5288 Todd St, Flint MI 48507. 313/694-4161. Employs:
50-99.

Monroe Junior High School
503 Washington St, Monroe MI 48161-1309. 313/241-
0772. Employs: 50-99.

Northeast Elementary School
1024 Fleming Av, Jackson MI 49202-2536. 517/789-6151.
Employs: 50-99.

Northern High School
1799 Krafft Rd, Port Huron MI 48060-1532. 313/984-2671.
Employs: 50-99.

Northern High School Board Educ
G3284 Mackin Rd, Flint MI 48504-3285. 313/760-1740.
Employs: 50-99.

Northgate Central Receiving
G5285 Summit St, Flint MI 48505-1328. 313/785-4731.
Employs: 50-99.

Okemos High School
4000 Okemos Rd, Okemos MI 48864-3213. 517/349-4460.
Employs: 50-99.

Owosso High School
765 E North St, Owosso MI 48867-1936. 517/723-8231.
Employs: 50-99.

Parkside Junior High School
2400 4th St, Jackson MI 49203-4573. 517/783-2873.
Employs: 50-99.

Pioneer High School
601 W Stadium Blvd, Ann Arbor MI 48103-5812. 313/994-2126. Employs: 100-249.

Pontiac School District
350 Wide Track Dr E, Pontiac MI 48342-2243. 313/857-8133. Employs: 50-99.

Ralph J Bunche Community School
4121 Martin Luther King Av, Flint MI 48505-3707.
313/762-1700. Employs: 50-99.

Rich Dwight Middle School
2600 Hampden Dr, Lansing MI 48911. 517/374-4850
Employs: 50-99.

River Rouge High School
1411 Coolidge Hwy, River Rouge MI 48218-1117.
313/297-9615. Employs: 50-99.

Roeper Country School
1051 Oakland Av, Birmingham MI 48009-5761. 313/642-1500. Employs: 50-99.

Roeper School For Gifted
2190 Woodward Av, Bloomfield MI 48304-2241. 313/642-1500. Employs: 100-249.

Ruth M Barhitte Elementary
G6080 Roberta St, Burton MI 48529. 313/742-9661.
Employs: 50-99.

Saint Pius X Roman Catholic School
G3139 Hogarth Av, Flint MI 48532-5129. 313/235-8580.
Employs: 50-99.

Seaholm High School
2436 W Lincoln St, Birmingham MI 48009-1876. 313/433-8401. Employs: 50-99.

Sobey Community School
3701 N Averill Av, Flint MI 48506-2511. 313/762-1817.
Employs: 50-99.

The Waverly Middle School
620 Snow Rd, Lansing MI 48917-9564. 517/321-7240.
Employs: 50-99.

Theodore Roosevelt High School
540 Eureka Av, Wyandotte MI 48192-5709. 313/284-3100.
Employs: 50-99.

Willow Run Community Schools
2171 E Michigan Av, Ypsilanti MI 48198-6049. 313/481-8200. Employs: 50-99.

Willow Run High School
235 Spencer La, Ypsilanti MI 48198-4247. 313/482-2827.
Employs: 50-99.

Ypsilanti High School
2095 Packard Rd, Ypsilanti MI 48197-1833. 313/482-8880.
Employs: 100-249.

Catholic Central High School
14200 Breakfast Dr, Redford MI 48239-2909. 313/534-0660. Employs: 50-99.

Powers High School
G-2040 W Carpenter Rd, Flint MI 48505-1028. 313/785-4741. Employs: 50-99.

Lansing Christian Schools
PO Box 25067, Lansing MI 48909-5067. 517/882-5777.
Employs: 50-99.

Hillel Day School
32200 Middlebelt Rd, Farmington MI 48334-1715.
313/851-2394. Employs: 50-99.

Michigan Inst For Child Dev
22930 Chippewa St, Detroit MI 48219-1161. 313/534-2000. Employs: 50-99.

Starr Commonwealth School
13725 Starr Commonwealth Rd, Albion MI 49224-9525.
517/629-5593. Employs: 100-249.

Waterford Community Center
1415 Crescent Lake Rd, Waterford MI 48327-2417.
313/674-4875. Employs: 50-99.

Murray Wright High School
2001 W Warren Ave, Detroit MI 48208-2216. 313/494-2553. Employs: 100-249.

Joy Middle School
4611 Fairview St, Detroit MI 48214-1647. 313/245-3514.
Employs: 50-99.

Lowrey Elem-Jr High School
6601 Jonathan St, Dearborn MI 48126-1864. 313/582-6191. Employs: 50-99.

Vetal Elem-Middle School
14200 Westwood St, Detroit MI 48223-2819. 313/270-0331. Employs: 50-99.

Barbour Magnet Middle School
4209 Seneca St, Detroit MI 48214-4515. 313/245-3474.
Employs: 50-99.

Beaubien Middle School
19701 Wyoming St, Detroit MI 48221-1519. 313/270-0314. Employs: 50-99.

Bedford Junior High School
1623 W Sterns Rd, Temperance MI 48182-1553. 313/847-6736. Employs: 50-99.

Bemis Junior High School
12500 19 Mile Rd, Sterling Hts MI 48313-2682. 313/254-8330. Employs: 50-99.

Boulan Park Middle School
3570 Northfield Pky, Troy MI 48084-1422. 313/643-9404.
Employs: 50-99.

Brake Junior High School
13500 Pine St, Taylor MI 48180-4613. 313/374-1227.
Employs: 50-99.

Brooks Middle School
16101 W Chicago St, Detroit MI 48228-2101. 313/270-0287. Employs: 50-99.

Central Middle School
650 Church St, Plymouth MI 48170-1608. 313/451-6580.
Employs: 50-99.

Cerveny Middle School
15850 Strathmoor St, Detroit MI 48227-2965. 313/270-0520. Employs: 50-99.

Clague Middle School
2616 Nixon Rd, Ann Arbor MI 48105-1420. 313/994-1976. Employs: 50-99.

Cleveland Middle School
13322 Conant St, Detroit MI 48212-2338. 313/252-3206. Employs: 50-99.

Drew Middle School
9600 Wyoming St, Detroit MI 48204-4669. 313/270-0279. Employs: 50-99.

Garden City Junior High School
1851 Radcliff St, Garden City MI 48135-1128. 313/427-8410. Employs: 50-99.

Greenville Middle School
1321 Chase St, Greenville MI 48838-9143. 616/754-0361. Employs: 50-99.

Holt Junior High School
5780 Holt Rd, Holt MI 48842-9696. 517/694-7117. Employs: 50-99.

Jackson Middle School
4180 Marlborough St, Detroit MI 48215-2320. 313/245-3488. Employs: 50-99.

Jefferson Middle School
5102 N Stoney Creek Rd, Monroe MI 48161-9332. 313/289-5565. Employs: 50-99.

Marshall Junior High School
35100 Bayview St, Westland MI 48185-4313. 313/595-2444. Employs: 50-99.

Pierce Middle School
5145 Hatchery Rd, Waterford MI 48329-3435. 313/674-0331. Employs: 50-99.

Pioneer Middle School
46081 Ann Arbor Rd, Plymouth MI 48170-3534. 313/451-6575. Employs: 50-99.

Riverside Middle School
25900 W Warren St, Dearborn Hts MI 48127-2064. 313/274-0140. Employs: 50-99.

Sashabaw Junior High School
5565 Pine Knob Rd, Clarkston MI 48346-3276. 313/674-4169. Employs: 50-99.

Scarlett Middle School
3300 Lorraine St, Ann Arbor MI 48108-1970. 313/994-1994. Employs: 50-99.

Stevenson Junior High School
38501 Palmer Rd, Westland MI 48185-3936. 313/595-2500. Employs: 50-99.

Walled Lake Middle School
615 N Pontiac Trl, Walled Lake MI 48390-3444. 313/960-8550. Employs: 50-99.

West Junior High School
10575 Williams St, Taylor MI 48180-3728. 313/295-5783. Employs: 50-99.

West Middle School
500 Old Perch Rd, Rochester MI 48309-2142. 313/375-9400. Employs: 50-99.

Adams High School
3200 W Tienken Rd, Rochester MI 48306-3734. 313/652-0116. Employs: 50-99.

Algonac Senior High School

5200 Taft Rd, Algonac MI 48001-4701. 313/794-4911. Employs: 50-99.

Athens Senior High School
4333 John Road, Troy MI 48098-3681. 313/524-1200. Employs: 100-249.

Avondale Senior High School
2800 Waukegan St, Auburn Hills MI 48326-3261. 313/852-2850. Employs: 50-99.

Belleville High School
501 W Columbia Ave, Belleville MI 48111-2611. 313/697-9133. Employs: 100-249.

Central Senior High School
2978 S Commerce Rd, Walled Lake MI 48390-1509. 313/960-8600. Employs: 50-99.

Central Senior High School
300 W Huron St, Pontiac MI 48341-1420. 313/857-8400. Employs: 100-249.

Chadsey High School
5335 Martin St, Detroit MI 48210-2327. 313/494-2381. Employs: 50-99.

Chippewa Valley High School
18300 19 Mile Rd, Clinton Twp MI 48038-1204. 313/286-7610. Employs: 100-249.

Clintondale Sr High School
35200 Little Mack Ave, Clinton Twp MI 48035-2634. 313/791-6300. Employs: 50-99.

Cooley High School
15055 Hubbell St, Detroit MI 48227-2943. 313/270-0012. Employs: 100-249.

Cousino Senior High School
30333 Hoover, Warren MI 48093-6532. 313/574-3100. Employs: 50-99.

East Detroit High School
15501 Couzens Ave, East Detroit MI 48021-3911. 313/445-4455. Employs: 100-249.

East Lansing Sr High School
509 Burcham Dr, East Lansing MI 48823-2750. 517/332-2545. Employs: 50-99.

Ferndale Senior High School
881 Pinecrest Dr, Ferndale MI 48220-2310. 313/548-8600. Employs: 100-249.

Fitzgerald Senior High School
23200 Ryan Rd, Warren MI 48091-4551. 313/757-7070. Employs: 50-99.

Garden City High School
6500 Middlebelt Rd, Garden City MI 48135-2129. 313/421-8220. Employs: 50-99.

Harrison Sr High School
29995 W 12 Mile Rd, Farmington MI 48334-3901. 313/489-3499. Employs: 50-99.

Highland Park Community High School
15900 Woodward Ave, Detroit MI 48203-2948. 313/252-0460. Employs: 100-249.

Inkster Senior High School
3250 Middlebelt Rd, Inkster MI 48141-2055. 313/722-6700. Employs: 50-99.

John Glenn Senior High School
36105 Marquette St, Westland MI 48185-3477. 313/595-2300. Employs: 100-249.

Kennedy High School
13505 J F Kennedy Drive, Taylor MI 48180. 313/374-1229. Employs: 50-99.

Kettering High School
6101 Van Dyke, Detroit MI 48213-2451. 313/245-3239.
Employs: 100-249.

Kettering High School
2800 Bender Street, Drayton Plns MI 48330. 313/673-1261. Employs: 50-99.

Kimball Senior High School
1500 Lexington Blvd, Royal Oak MI 48073-2475. 313/435-8500. Employs: 100-249.

L'Anse Creuse High School
38495 Lanse Creuse St, Harrison Twp MI 48045-3483. 313/463-5881. Employs: 50-99.

Lake Orion High School
455 Scripps Road, Lake Orion MI 48360. 313/693-5420. Employs: 50-99.

Lake Shore Senior High School
22980 E 13 Mile Rd, St Clair Shrs MI 48082-2009. 313/296-8240. Employs: 50-99.

Lakeland High School
1630 Bogie Lake Rd, White Lake MI 48383-2728. 313/684-8080. Employs: 50-99.

Lakewood Senior High School
RR 3, Lake Odessa MI 48849-9803. 616/374-8868. Employs: 50-99.

Lapeer East High School
933 S Saginaw St, Lapeer MI 48446-2643. 313/667-2418. Employs: 50-99.

Lincoln Park High School
1701 Champaign Rd, Lincoln Park MI 48146-3237. 313/246-4334. Employs: 100-249.

Lincoln Senior High School
22900 Federal Ave, Warren MI 48089-5308. 313/758-8305. Employs: 50-99.

Melvindale Senior High School
18656 Prospect St, Melvindale MI 48122-1508. 313/382-1911. Employs: 50-99.

Monroe High School
901 Herr Rd, Monroe MI 48161-9702. 313/241-1491. Employs: 50-99.

Mott Senior High School
3131 Twelve Mile Rd, Warren MI 48092-2448. 313/574-3250. Employs: 50-99.

Mount Clemens Sr High School
155 Cass Ave, Mount Clemens MI 48043-2203. 313/469-7070. Employs: 50-99.

North Farmington Sr High School
32900 W 13 Mile Rd, Farmington MI 48334-1904. 313/489-3535. Employs: 100-249.

Northern High School
9026 Woodward Ave, Detroit MI 48202-1823. 313/494-2625. Employs: 50-99.

Northern Senior High School
1051 Arlene Ave, Pontiac MI 48340-2904. 313/857-8460. Employs: 100-249.

Northville Senior High School
775 N Center St, Northville MI 48167-2745. 313/344-8425. Employs: 50-99.

Northwestern High School
2200 W Grand Blvd, Detroit MI 48208-1178. 313/895-1865. Employs: 50-99.

Novi Senior High School
24062 Taft Rd, Novi MI 48375-3022. 313/344-8300. Employs: 50-99.

Oak Park Senior High School
13701 Oak Park Blvd, Oak Park MI 48237-2080. 313/691-8412. Employs: 50-99.

Osborn High School
11600 E 7 Mile Rd, Detroit MI 48205-2112. 313/245-3353. Employs: 100-249.

Pinckney Senior High School
PO Box 9, Pinckney MI 48169-0009. 313/878-3115. Employs: 50-99.

Port Huron High School
2215 Court St, Port Huron MI 48060-4937. 313/984-2611. Employs: 50-99.

Redford Union High School
17711 Kinloch, Redford MI 48240-2246. 313/592-3395. Employs: 50-99.

Rochester Senior High School
180 S Livernois Rd, Rochester MI 48307-1840. 313/651-5590. Employs: 50-99.

Roseville High School
17855 Common Rd, Roseville MI 48066-4651. 313/445-5542. Employs: 50-99.

Salem Senior High School
46181 Joy Rd, Canton MI 48187-1316. 313/451-6600. Employs: 100-249.

Saline Senior High School
7190 N Maple Rd, Saline MI 48176-1601. 313/429-4931. Employs: 50-99.

Southeastern High School
3030 Fairview St, Detroit MI 48214-2205. 313/245-3225. Employs: 50-99.

Southfield High School
24675 Lahser Rd, Southfield MI 48034-3238. 313/423-8544. Employs: 100-249.

Southfield-Lathrup High School
19301 W 12 Mile Rd, Southfield MI 48076-2557. 313/423-8620. Employs: 100-249.

Southwestern High School
6921 W Fort St, Detroit MI 48209-2912. 313/849-4521. Employs: 50-99.

Taylor Center Sr High School
24715 Wick Rd, Taylor MI 48180-3316. 313/295-5700. Employs: 50-99.

Troy Senior High School
3179 Livernois Rd, Troy MI 48083-5029. 313/689-0644. Employs: 100-249.

Truman High School
11211 Beech Daly Rd, Taylor MI 48180-3942. 313/946-6550. Employs: 50-99.

Utica Sr High School
47225 Shelby Rd, Utica MI 48317-3156. 313/254-8300. Employs: 50-99.

Warren Senior High School
5460 Arden, Warren MI 48092-1190. 313/825-2500. Employs: 50-99.

Wayne Memorial Sr High School
3001 4th St, Wayne MI 48184-1358. 313/595-2200. Employs: 50-99.

Western High School
600 Beck Rd, Walled Lake MI 48390-4005. 313/960-8500. Employs: 100-249.

Skill Center
8075 Ritz Ave, Westland MI 48185-1659. 313/523-9388.
Employs: 50-99.

Cass Technical High School
2421 2nd Ave, Detroit MI 48201-2601. 313/494-2605.
Employs: 100-249.

Genesee Area Skill Center
G-5081 Torrey Road, Flint MI 48507. 313/760-1444.
Employs: 50-99.

Oakland Technical Center
5055 Delemere Ave, Royal Oak MI 48073-1004. 313/280-0600. Employs: 50-99.

Academy Of The Sacred Heart
1250 Kensington Rd, Bloomfield MI 48304-3029. 313/646-8900. Employs: 50-99.

Beth Jacob School
14390 West 10 Mile Rd, Oak Park MI 48237-1437.
313/544-9070. Employs: 50-99.

Bethesda Christian School
12900 Frazho Rd, Warren MI 48089-1373. 313/756-6100.
Employs: 50-99.

Fairlane Christian School
24425 Hass St, Dearborn Hts MI 48127-3275. 313/565-9800. Employs: 50-99.

Southfield Christian High School
28650 Lahser Rd, Southfield MI 48034-2020. 313/357-3660. Employs: 50-99.

University Liggett School
1045 Cook Rd, Grosse Pointe MI 48236-2509. 313/884-4444. Employs: 100-249.

Cranbrook Kingswood School
PO Box 801, Bloomfield MI 48303-0801. 313/645-3610.
Employs: 100-249.

Melby Community Ed Center
13900 Masonic Blvd, Warren MI 48093-1417. 313/294-8400. Employs: 50-99.

Franklin Adult Education Ctr
1333 Pine St, Detroit MI 48201-2937. 313/494-2577.
Employs: 50-99.

Center Line Sr High School
26300 Arsenal St, Center Line MI 48015-1632. 313/757-6660. Employs: 50-99.

Field Elementary School
1000 S Haggerty, Canton MI 48188-1308. 313/397-2151.
Employs: 50-99.

Paddock Elementary School
707 Marvin St, Milan MI 48160-1166. 313/439-1525.
Employs: 50-99.

Pleasant Ridge Elementary School
229 Pleasant Ridge Dr, Saline MI 48176-1525. 313/429-4966. Employs: 50-99.

Webster Elementary School
640 W Huron St, Pontiac MI 48341-1520. 313/858-2281.
Employs: 50-99.

Emerson Elem-Middle School
18240 Huntington Rd, Detroit MI 48219-2800. 313/533-3537. Employs: 50-99.

Harding Elem-Middle School
14450 Burt Rd, Detroit MI 48223-2711. 313/533-0920.
Employs: 50-99.

Forsythe Middle School

1655 Newport Rd, Ann Arbor MI 48103-2321. 313/994-1985. Employs: 50-99.

Novi Middle School
25299 Taft Rd, Novi MI 48374-2422. 313/344-8320.
Employs: 50-99.

Birney Middle School
27225 Evergreen Rd, Southfield MI 48076-3263. 313/423-8560. Employs: 50-99.

Davis Jr High School
11311 Plumbrook Rd, Sterling Hts MI 48312-1268.
313/825-2200. Employs: 50-99.

Frost Middle School
14041 Stark Rd, Livonia MI 48154-5409. 313/523-9459.
Employs: 50-99.

Hart Middle School
6500 Sheldon Rd, Rochester MI 48306-4575. 313/651-2930. Employs: 50-99.

Levey Middle School
25300 W 9 Mile Rd, Southfield MI 48034-3906. 313/423-8580. Employs: 50-99.

Lowell Middle School
8400 Hix Rd, Westland MI 48185-1083. 313/451-6503.
Employs: 50-99.

North Middle School
47097 McBride Ave, Belleville MI 48111-1231. 313/697-9171. Employs: 50-99.

Roosevelt Middle School
23261 Scotia St, Oak Park MI 48237-2162. 313/691-8449.
Employs: 50-99.

Tappan Middle School
2251 E Stadium Blvd, Ann Arbor MI 48104-4809.
313/994-2011. Employs: 50-99.

Van Hoosen Middle School
1339 N Adams Rd, Rochester MI 48306-3870. 313/651-7370. Employs: 50-99.

Adams Junior High School
33475 Palmer Rd, Westland MI 48185-4614. 313/595-2377. Employs: 50-99.

Jeannette Jr High School
40400 Gulliver Dr, Sterling Hts MI 48310-1733. 313/825-2210. Employs: 50-99.

Malow Junior High School
6400 25 Mile Rd, Washington MI 48094. 313/781-0400.
Employs: 50-99.

Oakwood Middle School
14825 Nehls Ave, East Detroit MI 48021-2163. 313/445-4600. Employs: 50-99.

South Lyon Middle School
62500 9 Mile Rd, South Lyon MI 48178-1596. 313/437-8176. Employs: 50-99.

Franklin Junior High School
33555 Annapolis St, Wayne MI 48184-2478. 313/595-2400. Employs: 50-99.

Mason Middle School
3835 W Walton Blvd, Waterford MI 48329-4270. 313/674-2281. Employs: 50-99.

Murphy Middle School
23901 Fenkell St, Detroit MI 48223-1431. 313/533-3855.
Employs: 50-99.

Jefferson Senior High School
5707 Williams Rd, Monroe MI 48161-4380. 313/289-5555.
Employs: 50-99.

Lamphere Sr High School
610 W 13 Mile Rd, Madison Hts MI 48071-1858. 313/589-3943. Employs: 50-99.

South Lake Sr High School
21900 E 9 Mile Rd, St Clair Shrs MI 48080-2905. 313/445-4251. Employs: 50-99.

Ionia High School
250 E Tuttle Rd, Ionia MI 48846-9673. 616/527-0600. Employs: 50-99.

Lahser Senior High School
3456 Lahser Rd, Bloomfield MI 48302-1532. 313/338-0311. Employs: 50-99.

Lakeview Senior High School
21100 E 11 Mile Rd, St Clair Shrs MI 48081-1581. 313/445-4045. Employs: 50-99.

Lincoln Senior High School
7425 Willis Rd, Ypsilanti MI 48197-8919. 313/484-7006. Employs: 50-99.

Romeo Senior High School
11091 32 Mile Rd, Romeo MI 48065-4309. 313/752-0300. Employs: 50-99.

Thurston High School
26255 Schoolcraft, Redford MI 48239-2775. 313/535-4000. Employs: 50-99.

Anchor Bay Senior High School
48650 Sugar Bush Rd, New Baltimore MI 48047-2259. 313/949-4510. Employs: 50-99.

Berkley Sr High School
2325 Catalpa Dr, Berkley MI 48072-1851. 313/544-5850. Employs: 50-99.

Charlotte Sr High School
378 State St, Charlotte MI 48813-1704. 517/543-4340. Employs: 50-99.

Clarkston Senior High School
6595 Middle Lake Rd, Clarkston MI 48346-2424. 313/625-0900. Employs: 50-99.

Dearborn Sr High School
19501 Outer Dr, Dearborn MI 48124-1663. 313/582-3152. Employs: 50-99.

Dondero Senior High School
709 N Washington Ave, Royal Oak MI 48067-1735. 313/541-7100. Employs: 50-99.

Farmington Sr High School
32000 Shiawassee St, Farmington MI 48336-3251. 313/489-3455. Employs: 50-99.

Greenville Senior High School
111 N Hillcrest St, Greenville MI 48838-1536. 616/754-3681. Employs: 50-99.

Grosse Pointe N High School
707 Vernier Rd, Grosse Pointe MI 48236-1527. 313/343-2187. Employs: 50-99.

Jackson High School
544 Wildwood Ave, Jackson MI 49201-1013. 517/784-8501. Employs: 50-99.

Kearsley Senior High School
4302 Underhill Dr, Flint MI 48506-1534. 313/736-8000. Employs: 50-99.

L'Anse Creuse North High School
23700 21 Mile Rd, Macomb MI 48042-5105. 313/949-4450. Employs: 50-99.

Lapeer West High School

170 Millville Rd, Lapeer MI 48446-1644. 313/667-2423. Employs: 50-99.

Milford High School
2380 Milford Road, Highland MI 48357. 313/684-8090. Employs: 50-99.

Mount Pleasant Sr High School
1155 S Elizabeth St, Mount Pleasnt MI 48858-3911. 517/773-5500. Employs: 50-99.

Romulus Senior High School
9650 Wayne Rd, Romulus MI 48174-1551. 313/941-2170. Employs: 50-99.

Stevenson Sr High School
39701 Dodge Park Rd, Sterling Hts MI 48313-5131. 313/268-4700. Employs: 50-99.

Warren Woods Tower Sr High School
27900 Bunert Rd, Warren MI 48093-4865. 313/755-8780. Employs: 50-99.

Waverly High School
5027 W Michigan Ave, Lansing MI 48917-3313. 517/323-3831. Employs: 100-249.

West Bloomfield Sr High School
4925 Orchard Lake Rd, W Bloomfield MI 48323-2964. 313/851-6100. Employs: 100-249.

Western High School
1500 Scotten St, Detroit MI 48209-2139. 313/849-4758. Employs: 50-99.

Woodhaven Senior High School
24787 Van Horn Rd, Flat Rock MI 48134-9231. 313/783-3333. Employs: 100-249.

Brighton Senior High School
7878 Brighton Rd, Brighton MI 48116-9701. 313/229-1400. Employs: 50-99.

Central High School
2425 Tuxedo St, Detroit MI 48206-1222. 313/252-3000. Employs: 100-249.

Churchill Sr High School
8900 Newburgh Rd, Livonia MI 48150-3425. 313/523-9200. Employs: 100-249.

Eisenhower Sr High School
6500 25 Mile Rd, Washington MI 48094. 313/781-5571. Employs: 100-249.

Finney High School
17200 Southampton St, Detroit MI 48224-2169. 313/245-3325. Employs: 100-249.

Ford High School
20000 Evergreen Rd, Detroit MI 48219-2006. 313/533-4300. Employs: 100-249.

Franklin Sr High School
31000 Joy Rd, Livonia MI 48150-3916. 313/523-9300. Employs: 100-249.

King High School
3200 E Lafayette St, Detroit MI 48207-3812. 313/494-2553. Employs: 50-99.

Mott High School
1151 Scott Lake Rd, Waterford MI 48328-1526. 313/674-4134. Employs: 50-99.

Mumford High School
17525 Wyoming St, Detroit MI 48221-2414. 313/270-0430. Employs: 100-249.

Redford High School
21431 Grand River Ave, Detroit MI 48219-3801. 313/533-1900. Employs: 100-249.

Sterling Heights High School
12901 Fifteen Mile Rd, Sterling Hts MI 48312-4202.
313/825-2700. Employs: 50-99.

Stevenson Sr High School
33500 6 Mile Rd, Livonia MI 48152-3199. 313/523-9400.
Employs: 100-249.

Torrant Center
1175 W Parnall Rd, Jackson MI 49201-8652. 517/787-
8910. Employs: 50-99.

High Point Center
1735 S Wagner Rd, Ann Arbor MI 48103-9715. 313/994-
8111. Employs: 50-99.

Area Career Center
6800 Browns Lake Rd, Jackson MI 49201-8362. 517/787-
2700. Employs: 100-249.

W D Ford Voc-Tech Center
36455 Marquette St, Westland MI 48185-3235. 313/595-
2106. Employs: 100-249.

Oakland Intermediate Sch District
2100 Pontiac Lake Rd, Waterford MI 48328-2735.
313/858-2121. Employs: 50-99.

New Lothrop Area Schools
9285 Easton Rd, New Lothrop MI 48460-9709. 313/638-
5091. Employs: 100-249.

Blissfield Community School District
630 S Lane St, Blissfield MI 49228-1235. 517/486-2205.
Employs: 50-99.

Clawson City School District
626 Phillips Ave, Clawson MI 48017-1584. 313/435-7500.
Employs: 100-249.

Western School District
1400 S Dearing Rd, Parma MI 49269-9712. 517/531-3321.
Employs: 50-99.

Westwood Community School District
25912 Annapolis St, Inkster MI 48141-3201. 313/565-
1858. Employs: 100-249.

Williamston Comm School District
418 Highland St, Williamston MI 48895-1133. 517/655-
4361. Employs: 100-249.

Charlotte School District
378 State St, Charlotte MI 48813-1704. 517/543-2810.
Employs: 100-249.

Crestwood School District
1501 N Beech Daly Rd, Dearborn Hts MI 48127-3403.
313/278-0903. Employs: 50-99.

Fraser Public School District
33466 Garfield Rd, Fraser MI 48026-1850. 313/293-5100.
Employs: 100-249.

Gibralter School District
33494 W Jefferson, Rockwood MI 48173-9608. 313/379-
5311. Employs: 100-249.

Madison School District
25421 Alger St, Madison Hts MI 48071-3921. 313/399-
7800. Employs: 50-99.

Oak Park School District
13900 Granzon St, Oak Park MI 48237-2756. 313/968-
0310. Employs: 50-99.

West Bloomfield School District
3250 Commerce Rd, W Bloomfield MI 48324-1602.
313/682-3555. Employs: 50-99.

Huron Valley School District

2390 Milford Road, Highland MI 48357. 313/684-8000.
Employs: 50-99.

Royal Oak Public Schools
1123 Lexington Blvd, Royal Oak MI 48073-2438.
313/435-8400. Employs: 50-99.

South Lyon Community Schools
235 W Liberty St, South Lyon MI 48178-1338. 313/437-
8127. Employs: 50-99.

Farmington School District
32500 Shiawassee St, Farmington MI 48336-2338.
313/489-3300. Employs: 50-99.

Rochester Comm School District
501 W University Dr, Rochester MI 48307-1944. 313/651-
6210. Employs: 50-99.

Walled Lake Consol Schools
695 N Pontiac Trl, Walled Lake MI 48390-3444. 313/960-
8300. Employs: 50-99.

Waterford School District
6020 Pontiac Lake Rd, Waterford MI 48327-1847.
313/666-4000. Employs: 50-99.

Flint Community School District
923 E Kearsley St, Flint MI 48503-1974. 313/760-1249.
Employs: 50-99.

Avondale School District
260 S Squirrel Rd, Auburn Hills MI 48326-3255. 313/852-
4411. Employs: 50-99.

Belding Area School District
321 Wilson St, Belding MI 48809-1744. 616/794-1960.
Employs: 50-99.

Bentley Comm School District
1223 S Belsay Rd, Burton MI 48509-1917. 313/742-4990.
Employs: 50-99.

Berkley School District
2211 Oakshire Ave, Berkley MI 48072-1290. 313/544-
5800. Employs: 100-249.

Bloomfield Hills Pub Sch District
4175 Andover Rd, Bloomfield MI 48302-1903. 313/540-
9800. Employs: 50-99.

Carman Ainsworth Comm Schools
G-3475 W Court St, Flint MI 48532-4742. 313/230-3200.
Employs: 50-99.

Chelsea School District
500 Washington St, Chelsea MI 48118-1128. 313/475-
9131. Employs: 50-99.

Columbia School District
11775 Hewitt Rd, Brooklyn MI 49230-8961. 517/592-
6641. Employs: 50-99.

Concord Comm School District
405 S Main St, Concord MI 49237-9737. 517/524-8850.
Employs: 50-99.

Detroit Public School District
5057 Woodward Ave, Detroit MI 48202-4015. 313/494-
1270. Employs: 50-99.

Dexter Comm School District
2615 Baker Rd, Dexter MI 48130-1534. 313/426-4623.
Employs: 50-99.

Ferndale Public School District
725 Pinecrest Dr, Ferndale MI 48220-2356. 313/547-2302.
Employs: 50-99.

Fitzgerald School District
23200 Ryan Rd, Warren MI 48091-4551. 313/757-1750.
Employs: 100-249.

Flat Rock Comm School District
PO Box 130, Flat Rock MI 48134-0130. 313/782-2451.
Employs: 50-99.

Grand Ledge School District
1020 Jenne St, Grand Ledge MI 48837-1807. 517/627-3242. Employs: 100-249.

Greenville Public Schools
516 W Cass St, Greenville MI 48838-1770. 616/754-3686.
Employs: 100-249.

Jackson I S D
6700 Browns Lake Rd, Jackson MI 49201-8362. 517/787-2800. Employs: 50-99.

Lakeview Public Schools
20300 Statler St, St Clair Shrs MI 48081-2181. 313/445-4015. Employs: 50-99.

Lamphere School District
31201 Dorchester Ave, Madison Hts MI 48071-1075.
313/589-1990. Employs: 50-99.

Lincoln Consol School District
8970 Whittaker Rd, Ypsilanti MI 48197-9776. 313/484-7000. Employs: 50-99.

Northville School District
501 W Main St, Northville MI 48167-1528. 313/349-3400.
Employs: 100-249.

Northwest School District
4000 Van Horn Rd, Jackson MI 49201-9403. 517/569-2247. Employs: 50-99.

Novi Community School District
25345 Taft Rd, Novi MI 48374-2423. 313/348-1200.
Employs: 100-249.

Onsted Comm School District
102 W 2nd St, Onsted MI 49265-9435. 517/467-2174.
Employs: 50-99.

Oxford Community Schools
105 Pontiac Rd, Oxford MI 48371-4847. 313/628-2591.
Employs: 50-99.

Pontiac Public School District
350 Wide Track Dr E, Pontiac MI 48342-2243. 313/857-8100. Employs: 50-99.

Southfield Public Schools
24661 Lahser Rd, Southfield MI 48034-3238. 313/746-8500. Employs: 50-99.

COLLEGES, UNIVERSITIES AND PROFESSIONAL SCHOOLS

Riverfront Park
Es N Grand Av, Lansing MI 48933. 517/483-1957.
Employs: 100-249.

Baker Jr College
1020 S Washington St, Owosso MI 48867-4449. 517/723-5251. Employs: 100-249.

Cleary College
2170 Washtenaw Avenue, Ypsilanti MI 48197-1744.
313/483-4400. Employs: 100-249.

Concordia College
4090 Geddes Road, Ann Arbor MI 48105-2750. 313/995-7300. Employs: 100-249.

Davenport Col Lansing

220 E Kalamazoo, Lansing MI 48933-2110. 517/484-2600.
Employs: 100-249.

Detroit College Of Business
27500 Dequindre, Warren MI 48092-3525. 313/581-4400.
Employs: 50-99.

Great Lakes Bible College
P O Box 40060, Lansing MI 48901-7260. 517/321-0242.
Employs: 100-249.

Michigan Christian College
800 West Avon Road, Rochester MI 48307-2704. 313/651-5800. Employs: 50-99.

JUNIOR COLLEGES AND TECHNICAL INSTITUTES

Walsh College Of Account
3838 Livernois Rd, Troy MI 48083-5066. 313/689-8282.
Employs: 50-99.

Ed Inst Of The American Hotel
PO Box 1240/1407 S Harrison R, East Lansing MI 48826-1240. 517/353-5500. Employs: 100-249.

Fashion Sch Of Beauty
49604 Van Dyke, Utica MI 48317-1342. 313/739-1110.
Employs: 50-99.

Jackson Comm College
2111 Emmons Road, Jackson MI 49201-8335. 517/787-0800. Employs: 100-249.

Lansing Comm College
419 N Capitol Avenue, Lansing MI 48933-1207. 517/483-1957. Employs: 100-249.

Macomb Comm College
14500 Twelve Mile Road, Warren MI 48093-3870.
313/445-7999. Employs: 50-99.

St Joseph Mercy Hosp
5301 E Huron Dr PO Box 995, Ann Arbor MI 48106-0995.
313/762-8780. Employs: 100-249.

DATA PROCESSING SCHOOLS

T S I-Training & Support Services
1350 John R Rd, Troy MI 48083-4328. 313/589-7088.
Employs: 100-249.

MISCELLANEOUS VOCATIONAL SCHOOLS

National Education Center
18000 Newburgh Rd, Livonia MI 48152-2695. 313/464-7387. Employs: 50-99.

La Belle Management
405 S Mission, Mount Pleasnt MI 48858. 517/772-2902.
Employs: 100-249.

Machus General Office
725 S Adams Rd, Birmingham MI 48009-6902. 313/642-1560. Employs: 100-249.

Stev-Con Inc
735 Victors Way, Ann Arbor MI 48108-1767. 313/761-7060. Employs: 100-249.

MISCELLANEOUS SCHOOLS AND EDUCATIONAL SERVICES

Agency For Jewish Education
21550 W 12 Mile Rd, Southfield MI 48076-5501. 313/354-1050. Employs: 100-249.

For more information on career opportunities in colleges and universities, and education:

Associations

AMERICAN ASSOCIATION OF SCHOOL ADMINISTRATORS
1801 North Moore Street, Arlington VA 22209. 703/528-0700.

AMERICAN FEDERATION OF TEACHERS
555 New Jersey Avenue NW, Washington DC 20001. 202/879-4400.

ASSOCIATION OF AMERICAN UNIVERSITIES
One Dupont Circle NW, Suite 730, Washington DC 20036. 202/466-5030.

COLLEGE AND UNIVERSITY PERSONNEL ASSOCIATION
1233 20th Street NW, Suite 503, Washington DC 20036. 202/429-0311.

NATIONAL ASSOCIATION OF BIOLOGY TEACHERS
11250 Roger Bacon Drive, #19, Reston VA 22090. 703/471-1134.

NATIONAL ASSOCIATION OF COLLEGE AND UNIVERSITY BUSINESS OFFICERS
1 DuPont Circle, Suite 500, Washington DC 20036. 202/861-2500.

NATIONAL ASSOCIATION OF COLLEGE ADMISSION COUNSELORS
1631 Prince Street, Alexandria VA 22314. 703/836-2222.

NATIONAL SCIENCE TEACHERS ASSOCIATION
1742 Connecticut Avenue NW, Washington DC 20009. 202/328-5800.

Directories

HIGHER EDUCATION DIRECTORY
Council for Advancement and Support of Education, 11 DuPont Circle, Suite 400, Washington DC 20036. 202/328-5900.

Books

ACADEMIC LABOR MARKETS AND CAREERS
Falmer Press, Taylor & Francis, Inc., 1900 Frost Road, Suite 101, Bristol PA 19007. 800/821-8312.

HOW TO GET A JOB IN EDUCATION
Bob Adams, Inc., 260 Center Street, Holbrook MA 02343. 617/787-8100.

COMMUNICATIONS

Revenues in the domestic communications industry are expected to increase as the economy improves. Over the next few years, the globalization of private networks, innovations in broadband and radio technologies, and a steady march toward liberalized regulations will improve the prospects for the industry greatly. The short-term outlook for telecommunications equipment makers is fairly stable, with small 2-3 percent increases expected through the middle of the decade. Unfortunately, employment in the equipment industry continues to decline due to continued mergers, new technology, and improved productivity.

ALNET COMMUNICATIONS, INC.
30300 Telegraph, Suite 350, Bingham Farms MI 48025-4510. 313/647-6920. **Contact:** Joni Nelson, Manager of Human Resources. **Description:** An area long distance communications company. **Common positions:** Accountant; Administrator; Advertising Worker; Attorney; Claim Representative; Computer Programmer; Credit Manager; Customer Service Representative; Financial Analyst; Department Manager; General Manager; Operations/Production Manager; Marketing Specialist; Personnel and Labor Relations Specialist; Public Relations Specialist; Purchasing Agent; Quality Control Supervisor; Sales Representative; Systems Analyst; Technical Writer/Editor. **Educational**

backgrounds sought: Accounting; Business Administration; Communications; Computer Science; Engineering; Finance; Liberal Arts; Marketing. **Special programs:** Training programs and internships. **Benefits:** medical insurance; dental insurance; life insurance; tuition assistance; disability coverage; employee discounts. **Corporate headquarters:** This location. **Parent company:** ALC Communications.

EXECUTONE BUSINESS SYSTEMS
1700 West Big Beaver, Troy MI 48084. 313/649-4454. **Contact:** Human Resources Department. **Description:** A leading area telephone company specializing in the retail sale of telephone systems to businesses. **Employees:** 100.

MICHIGAN BELL TELEPHONE COMPANY
444 Michigan Avenue, Detroit MI 48226. 313/223-9900. **Contact:** Personnel. **Description:** A major Michigan telephone company.

Large employers: 250+

Michigan Bell Communications
2977 Telegraph Rd Ste 1200, Southfield MI 48034.
313/262-6200. Employs: 250-499.

Additional small to medium sized employers: 50-249

TELEPHONE COMMUNICATIONS, EXCEPT RADIOTELEPHONE

CC&S Telco Inc
2 North Plaza, Jackson MI 49202-1412. 517/787-9780.
Employs: 50-99.

General Telephone Co
G7362 Davison Rd, Davison MI 48423. 313/653-9710.
Employs: 100-249.

General Telephone Co Of Mich
2982 W Beecher St, Adrian MI 49221-9769. 517/265-8111.
Employs: 100-249.

General Telephone Co Of Mi
224 W Exchange St, Owosso MI 48867-2818. 517/232-2544. Employs: 100-249.

Michigan Bell Telephone Co
221 N Washington Sq, Lansing MI 48933-1301. 517/377-9022. Employs: 100-249.

Michigan Bell Telephone Co
112 Grand River Av, Port Huron MI 48060-4003. 313/987-2521. Employs: 100-249.

Tele Dial America
12750 Saginaw Rd Ste 204, Grand Blanc MI 48439-1841.
313/695-7902. Employs: 100-249.

Allnet Communication Svc Inc
300 Washington Sq S, Lansing MI 48933-2115. 517/484-4230. Employs: 100-249.

Allnet Communication Services Inc
26877 Northwestern Hwy, Southfield MI 48034-2141.
313/354-7000. Employs: 100-249.

Alltel Mi Engineering

202 N Clinton St, Stockbridge MI 49285-9715. 517/851-8648. Employs: 100-249.

Alltel Michigan Inc
3905 Consear Rd, Lambertville MI 48144-9747. 313/856-1691. Employs: 50-99.

Alltel Michigan Inc
950 S Clinton St, Stockbridge MI 49285-9555. 517/851-6145. Employs: 100-249.

Alternative Telephone Svc
13516 Mansfield St, Detroit MI 48227-1730. 313/838-0220. Employs: 100-249.

American National Communications
26400 Lahser Rd, Southfield MI 48034-2624. 313/358-0007. Employs: 100-249.

American Public Telephone Corp
1551 E Lincoln Ave, Madison Hts MI 48071-4173.
313/258-5115. Employs: 100-249.

AMT Telecommunications
38701 7 Mile Rd, Livonia MI 48152-1058. 313/462-4114.
Employs: 100-249.

Audio Services Inc
100 N Crooks Rd, Clawson MI 48017-2800. 313/435-7766.
Employs: 100-249.

Aventric Technologies Inc
1551 E Lincoln Ave, Royal Oak MI 48067-3401. 313/542-5590. Employs: 100-249.

Cable & Wireless Communications Inc
26500 Northwestern Hwy, Southfield MI 48076-3716.
313/355-0700. Employs: 100-249.

Chelsea Telecommunications Co
14112 N Territorial Rd, Chelsea MI 48118-9501. 313/475-7111. Employs: 100-249.

Comgroup
60549 Mt Vernon Rd, Rochester MI 48306-2041. 313/650-3848. Employs: 100-249.

Communications Development Co
21630 W McNichols Rd, Detroit MI 48219-3209. 313/538-3210. Employs: 100-249.

Communications Resources Inc
27362 Strawberry Ln, Farmington MI 48334-5055. 313/471-3270. Employs: 100-249.

Complete Communications Services
18850 E 9 Mile Rd, East Detroit MI 48021-2030. 313/776-7552. Employs: 100-249.

Detroit Tri County Pay Phone Co
18984 Livernois Ave, Detroit MI 48221-2259. 313/342-1701. Employs: 100-249.

Electronic Systems Svc
3666 Jasper Dr, Sterling Hts MI 48310-2556. 313/826-8787. Employs: 100-249.

Galaxy Electronics
E China Twp, Saint Clair MI 48079. 313/765-3733. Employs: 100-249.

Groesbeck Telecommunications
2127 15 Mi, Sterling Hts MI 48310. 313/979-9260. Employs: 100-249.

Groesbeck Telecommunications
2044 Virginia Ave, Troy MI 48083-2538. 313/528-2822. Employs: 100-249.

Group Long Distance USA Inc
32969 Hamilton Ct, Farmington MI 48334-3351. 313/489-0350. Employs: 100-249.

Lightnet Corp
26911 Northwestern Hwy, Southfield MI 48034-4717. 313/262-1498. Employs: 100-249.

Litel Telecommunications Corp
30200 Telegraph Rd, Franklin MI 48025-4502. 313/258-0707. Employs: 100-249.

Long Distance Of Michigan Inc
8801 Conant St, Detroit MI 48211-1403. 313/873-5500. Employs: 100-249.

Lume Nails
182 Lois Ln, Mount Clemens MI 48043-2243. 313/468-7255. Employs: 100-249.

Mecotel Communication
1658 E 9 Mile Rd, Hazel Park MI 48030-1937. 313/546-1609. Employs: 100-249.

Net Communications Corp
15138 Minock St, Detroit MI 48223-2274. 313/533-7010. Employs: 100-249.

Photophone Of Michigan
3065 Whisper Wood Dr, Ann Arbor MI 48105-3405. 313/663-5522. Employs: 100-249.

Probe Network Design
1700 W Big Beaver Rd, Troy MI 48084-3505. 313/649-6099. Employs: 100-249.

Progressive Communications Tech
1100 S Woodward Ave, Birmingham MI 48009-6739. 313/433-3450. Employs: 100-249.

T L C Telecommunications
12341 Oak St, Carleton MI 48117-9111. 313/654-9317. Employs: 50-99.

Talking Pages Info Systems
17520 W 12 Mile Rd, Southfield MI 48076-1945. 313/557-5830. Employs: 100-249.

Teleamerica
34580 Sims St, Wayne MI 48184-1324. 313/326-3431. Employs: 100-249.

Telecom Management Svc Inc
814 W Grand River Ave, Howell MI 48843-1414. 517/546-5040. Employs: 50-99.

Telecom USA
G-4488 W Bristol Rd, Flint MI 48507. 313/732-7474. Employs: 100-249.

Telegration Inc
288 E Maple Rd, Birmingham MI 48009-6300. 313/644-3190. Employs: 100-249.

Travelers Information Hotline
560 Watkins St, Birmingham MI 48009-1404. 313/642-2677. Employs: 100-249.

TSI Michigan
24701 Halsted Rd, Farmington MI 48335-1612. 313/476-6041. Employs: 100-249.

U S Com Inc
6333 Reynolds Rd, Hanover MI 49241. 517/563-2582. Employs: 50-99.

V V Associates Inc
26100 American Dr, Southfield MI 48034-6179. 313/356-1177. Employs: 100-249.

Wonder Pay Telephone Co
12900 W 7 Mile Rd, Detroit MI 48235-1305. 313/863-2444. Employs: 100-249.

N C N Training Center
24655 Southfield Rd, Southfield MI 48075-2737. 313/552-0047. Employs: 100-249.

National Communications Network Ctr
715 Louisa St, Lansing MI 48911-5144. 517/882-6424. Employs: 100-249.

Philmart Communications Inc Telefund
601 W Davis Rd, Howell MI 48843-8842. 517/548-2770. Employs: 50-99.

Telegration
2820 W Maple Rd, Troy MI 48084-7011. 313/649-1035. Employs: 100-249.

Async Voice Msg Service Detroit
29444 Northwestern Hwy, Southfield MI 48034-1038. 313/351-9393. Employs: 100-249.

Tetcom
723 N Alexander Ave, Royal Oak MI 48067-1945. 313/399-6436. Employs: 100-249.

For more information on career opportunities in communications:

Associations

COMMUNICATIONS WORKERS OF AMERICA
501 3rd Street NW, Washington DC 20001-2797. 202/434-
1100.

UNITED STATES TELEPHONE ASSOCIATION
900 19th Street NW, Suite 800, Washington DC 20006.
202/835-3100.

COMPUTERS

Computer Services: Industry revenues for computer services, systems integration, consulting, and training services have been on the rise. Mergers and acquisitions of computer services firms have been an ongoing trend, and should continue. In the long-term, look for computer services firms to expand overseas, especially into Western Europe. Equipment and Software: The continuing effects of the long national recession have put the equipment and software industries on a bumpy road over the past few years.
Layoffs at major players like IBM, Apple, and Compaq grabbed big headlines. The biggest growth areas for U.S. firms will be in systems design, systems integration, software, and after-sales service. Over the long-term, the computer industry promises to be one of the best bets for jobseekers.

AUTOMATIC DATA PROCESSING
180 Jackson Plaza, Ann Arbor MI 48106-2190. 313/769-6800. **Contact:** Recruitment Specialist. A computer software/data processing firm specializing in software development, sales, and support; remote computing services; and telecommunications. Industry classifications: data processing and software (primary); telecommunications; and telephone. Four divisions of Automatic Data Processing are represented in the Ann Arbor, MI complex: Automotive Claims Services; Dealer Services; Interactive Personnel and Payroll; and Network Services-Division Headquarters. **Common positions:** Computer Programmer; Customer Service Representative; Department Manager; Operations/Production Manager; Systems Analyst; Computer Operator. **Educational backgrounds sought:** Business Administration; Computer Science. **Special programs:** Training programs. **Benefits:** medical, dental, and life insurance; pension plan; tuition assistance; disability coverage; profit sharing; employee discounts; savings plan. **Corporate headquarters:** Roseland, NJ. **Operations at this facility:** divisional headquarters; service. **Listed on:** New York Stock Exchange.

COMPUWARE CORPORATION
31440 Northwestern Highway, Farmington Hills MI 48334-2564. 313/540-0900. **Contact:** Personnel. **Description:** Producers of software.

COMSHARE INC.
3001 South State Street, Ann Arbor MI 48108. 313/994-4800. **Contact:** Kevin McGrath, Personnel Manager. **Description:** A major Southeastern Michigan data processing firm. **Employees:** 800.

KMS ADVANCED PRODUCTS, INC.
P.O. Box 1868, Ann Arbor MI 48106-1868. **Contact:** Personnel. **Description:** KMS is a leading manufacturer of highly rugged microcomputers and communicator systems for U.S./foreign governments and major DoD contractors. **Common positions:** Accountant; Advertising Worker; Buyer; Customer Service Representative; Electrical Engineer; Mechanical Engineer; Financial Analyst; Marketing Specialist; Purchasing Agent; Quality Control Supervisor; Sales Representative; Systems Analyst. **Educational backgrounds sought:** Accounting; Business Administration; Communications; Computer Science; Engineering; Finance; Marketing. **Benefits:** medical, dental, and life insurance; pension plan; tuition assistance; disability coverage; employee discounts; savings plan. **Corporate headquarters:** This location. **Parent company:** KMS Industries, Inc. **Operations at this facility:** manufacturing; research/development; administration; sales. **Listed on:** NASDAQ.

MEDSTAT SYSTEMS INC.
P.O. Box 973, Ann Arbor MI 48106. 313/996-1180. **Contact:** Katy Pek, Human Resources Manager. **Description:** Health care information, software, and consulting firm which designs and builds database systems for use in analyzing health care claims and benefits for large employers; insurance companies; and the research industry. **Common positions:** Computer Programmer; Data Base Administrator; Client Service Consultant and Analyst; Sales Representative. **Educational backgrounds sought:** Business Administration; Communications; Computer Science; Finance; Marketing; Health Care Administration. **Benefits:** medical, dental, and life insurance; disability coverage; profit sharing. **Corporate headquarters:** This location. **Other U.S. locations:** Client Service offices in Boston and San Francisco. **Operations at this facility:** research and development; administration; service; sales. **Employees:** about 300.

SCHLUMBERGER
4251 Plymouth Road, P.O. Box 986, Ann Arbor MI 48106. 313/995-6000. **Contact:** Ellen Smith, Technical Recruiter. **Description:** A computer services firm specializing in computer-aided manufacturing operations and CAD/CAM software. **Corporate headquarters:** This location.

SECUREDATA CORPORATION
1080 West Entrance Drive, P.O. Box 217002, Auburn Hills MI 48321. 313/377-2020. **Contact:** Natalie Gajewski, Personnel Officer. **Description:** A major data processing firm, support bank applications. **Employees:** 200. **Common positions:** Computer Programmer; Operations/Production Manager; Systems Analyst; Computer Operator. **Educational backgrounds sought:** Business Administration; Computer Science. **Benefits:** medical, dental, and life insurance; pension plan; tuition assistance; disability coverage; employee

discounts. **Corporate headquarters:** This location. **Parent company:** Security Bancorp. NASDAQ.

T & B COMPUTING, INC.

1100 Eisenhower Place, Ann Arbor MI 48108. 313/930-3800. **Contact:** Personnel. **Description:** Providers of minicomputer systems and services.

XYCOM, INC.

750 North Maple Road, Saline MI 48176. 313/429-4971. **Contact:** Joyce C. Girdis, Human Resources Manager. **Description:** Engaged in the development, manufacture, and sale of industrial microcomputers. Applications include the regulation and monitoring of continuous batch processes, and the control and monitoring of material handling equipment. **Corporate headquarters:** This location. **Operations include:** manufacturing; research/development; administration. **Common positions:** Accountant; Administrator; Buyer; Computer Programmer; Customer Service Representative; Draftsperson; Electrical Engineer; Industrial Engineer; Mechanical Engineer; Department Manager; Operations/Production Manager; Personnel and Labor Relations Specialist; Purchasing Agent; Marketing Specialist; Sales Representative; Technical Writer/Editor; Software Engineer; Test Engineer; Product Manager; Technician; Applications Engineer. **Educational backgrounds sought:** Computer Science; Engineering; Marketing; Computer Engineering. **Benefits:** medical, dental, and life insurance; pension plan 401(K); tuition assistance; disability coverage; flexible spending account; supplemental life insurance, employee assistance.

Additional large employers: 250+

ELECTRONIC COMPUTER

Unisys Corp
41100 Plymouth Rd, Plymouth MI 48170-1856. 313/451-4000. Employs: 250-499.

COMPUTER PROCESSING AND DATA PREPARATION AND PROCESSING SERVICES

MCN Corporation
500 Griswold St, Detroit MI 48226-3701. 313/256-5500. Employs: 1000+.

Michigan National Corporation
12425 Merriman Rd, Livonia MI 48150-1922. 313/525-8600. Employs: 500-999.

Small to medium sized employers: 50-249

ELECTRONIC COMPUTERS

Applied Dynamics International Inc
3800 Stone School Rd, Ann Arbor MI 48108-2414. 313/973-1300. Employs: 50-99.

Interface Systems Inc
5855 Interface Dr, Ann Arbor MI 48103-9515. 313/769-5900. Employs: 100-249.

Unisys Corp
One Unisys Pl, Detroit MI 48202. 313/972-7000. Employs: 50-99.

COMPUTERS AND COMPUTER PERIPHERAL EQUIPMENT AND SOFTWARE

Amdahl Corp
3000 Town Center, Southfield MI 48075. 313/358-4440. Employs: 50-99.

Burroughs Corporation
14115 Farmington Rd, Livonia MI 48154-5400. 313/523-6100. Employs: 50-99.

Honeywell Inc
17515 W 9 Mile Rd, Southfield MI 48075-4403. 313/424-3500. Employs: 50-99.

Memorex Telex Corporation
23800 W 10 Mile Rd Ste 190, Southfield MI 48034-3163. 313/354-4511. Employs: 100-249.

Rolm Corp
215 Washington Sq S, Lansing MI 48933-1807. 517/482-9812. Employs: 50-99.

World Computer Corporation
985 W Entrance Dr, Auburn Hills MI 48326-2722. 313/377-4840. Employs: 100-249.

COMPUTER PROGRAMMING SERVICES

C Text Inc
1286 Eisenhower Pl, Ann Arbor MI 48108-3248. 313/971-1011. Employs: 50-99.

Dale Computer Company
2467 Science Pk, Okemos MI 48864-2562. 517/349-0200. Employs: 50-99.

Inacomp Computer Ctr Corp Offices
1800 W Maple Rd, Troy MI 48084-7188. 313/649-5580. Employs: 50-99.

Software Services Corp
2850 S Industrial Hwy Ste 300, Ann Arbor MI 48104-7198. 313/971-2300. Employs: 50-99.

Cap Gemini America
5800 Crooks Rd, Troy MI 48098-2848. 313/879-7600. Employs: 50-99.

J M S & Associates
33730 Freedom Rd, Farmington MI 48335-4755. 313/474-1136. Employs: 50-99.

COMPUTER PROCESSING AND DATA PREPARATION AND PROCESSING SERVICES

Allen Bradley Co Comm Div
555 Briarwood Cir, Ann Arbor MI 48108-1609. 313/668-2500. Employs: 100-249.

EDS
Ecorse & Wiard Rd, Ypsilanti MI 48198. 313/481-5471. Employs: 50-99.

Harris Mc Burney Data Proc
180 W Michigan Av Rm 1103, Jackson MI 49201-1313. 517/787-1800. Employs: 100-249.

Horizon View Services Inc
2075 Big Beaver Rd Ste L10, Troy MI 48084-3467. 313/643-6210. Employs: 100-249.

Polack Corporation
1400 Keystone Av, Lansing MI 48911. 517/393-3440. Employs: 50-99.

Cimline Inc
1699 Stutz-Bet Crooks & Clidge, Troy MI 48084. 313/649-0240. Employs: 50-99.

Fisery Galaxy
5600 Crooks Rd, Troy MI 48098-2811. 313/828-1300. Employs: 50-99.

For more information on career opportunities in the computer industry:

Associations

INFORMATION AND TECHNOLOGY ASSOCIATION OF AMERICA
1300 North 17th Street, Suite 300, Arlington VA 22209. 703/522-5055.

ASSOCIATION FOR COMPUTER SCIENCE
P.O. Box 19027, Sacramento CA 95819. 916/421-9149.

ASSOCIATION FOR COMPUTING MACHINERY
1515 Broadway, 17th Floor, New York NY 10036. 212/869-7440.

COMPUTER AND BUSINESS EQUIPMENT MANUFACTURERS ASSOCIATION
1250 Eye Street NW, Suite 200, Washington DC 20005. 202/737-8888.

COMPUTER AND COMMUNICATIONS INDUSTRY ASSOCIATION
666 11th Street NW, Suite 600, Washington DC 20001. 202/783-0070.

COMPUTER SOCIETY OF THE INSTITUTE OF ELECTRICAL & ELECTRONICS ENGINEERS
1730 Massachusetts Avenue NW, Washington DC 20036. 202/371-0101.

COMPUTER-AIDED MANUFACTURING INTERNATIONAL
1250 E. Copeland Road, Suite 500, Arlington TX 76011. 817/860-1654.

IEEE COMPUTER SOCIETY
1730 Massachusetts Avenue NW, Washington DC 20036-1903. 202/371-0101.

INFORMATION INDUSTRY ASSOCIATION
555 New Jersey Avenue NW, Washington DC 20001. 202/639-8260.

SEMICONDUCTOR INDUSTRY ASSOCIATION
4300 Stevens Creek Boulevard, Suite 271, San Jose CA 95129. 408/973-9973.

Directories

INFORMATION INDUSTRY DIRECTORY
Gale Research Inc., 835 Penobscot Building, Detroit MI 48226. 313/961-2242.

Magazines

COMPUTER-AIDED ENGINEERING
Penton Publishing, 1100 Superior Avenue, Cleveland OH 44114. 216/696-7000.

COMPUTERWORLD
CW Communications, P.O. Box 9171, Framingham MA 01701. 508/879-0700.

DATA COMMUNICATIONS
McGraw-Hill, 1221 Avenue of the Americas, New York NY 10020. 212/512-2000.

DATAMATION
275 Washington Street, Newton MA 02158. 617/964-3030.

DESIGN COMPUTING
John Wiley & Sons, 605 Third Avenue, New York NY 10158. 212/850-6645.

IDC REPORT
International Data Corporation, Five Speen Street, Framingham MA 01701. 508/872-8200.

ELECTRICAL AND ELECTRONIC

Electrical component industry shipments are expected to grow at an annual rate of 5-7 percent through the mid-90's. Suppliers will face a constant demand for higher performance products. The increased complexity of packaging and the interconnection of high-performance systems places a premium on compatibility among components. Jobseekers should seek out companies that can anticipate which technologies and product variants will be among industry standards.

ACHESON COLLOIDS COMPANY
P.O. Box 611747, Port Huron MI 48061-1747. 313/984-5581. **Contact:** Bob Thompson, Business Manager. **Description:** A leading Michigan high-tech firm engaged in the production of electrically conductive coatings and dry film lubricants.

CLEO COMMUNICATIONS
3796 Plaza Drive, Ann Arbor MI 48108. 313/662-2002. **Contact:** Jane Gensheimer, Personnel Director. **Description:** Engaged in the manufacture of electrical computing equipment.

CORE INDUSTRIES INC.
500 North Woodward, Bloomfield Hills MI 48034. 313/642-3400. **Contact:** Tony Krull, Personnel Director. **Description:** Engaged in the manufacture of electrical testing and measuring instruments.

DAEDALUS ENTERPRISES INC.
P.O. Box 1869, Ann Arbor MI 48106. 313/769-5649. **Contact:** Vincent Killewald, Controller. **Description:** An area company engaged in the manufacture of optical equipment including infra-red airborne scanning equipment.

DEARBORN GAGE COMPANY
32330 Ford Road, Garden City MI 48135. 313/422-8300. **Contact:** Mario Sciberras, Personnel Director. **Description:** A leading area manufacturer of air gages and electronic gaging equipment. **Employees:** 100.

JABIL CIRCUIT COMPANY
1700 Atlantic Boulevard, Auburn Hills MI 48326. 313/391-5300. **Contact:** Michelle Banganin, Personnel Director. **Description:** A leading area manufacturer of electrical equipment. **Employees:** 400.

LAMB TECHNICON
5663 East 9 Mile Road, Warren MI 48091. 313/497-6000. **Contact:** Steve Renton, Vice President of Personnel. **Description:** Engineering and manufacturing of monitoring and diagnostic systems. **Employees:** 2,200.

MARPOSS CORPORATION
3300 Cross Creek Parkway, Auburn Hills MI 48326. 313/370-0404. **Contact:** Joan Servo, Personnel Manager. **Description:** Engaged in the sales and service of electronic gauging equipment. **Employees:** 200. **Common positions:** Accountant; Electrical Engineer; Mechanical Engineer; Department Manager; General Manager; Sales Representative; Proposal Engineer; Clerical. **Educational backgrounds sought:** Accounting; Engineering. Training programs offered. **Benefits:** medical, dental, and life insurance; pension plan; tuition assistance; disability coverage. **Corporate headquarters:** This location. **Operations at this facility:** administration; service; sales.

ROYALITE COMPANY
54525 S. Dyewood, Flint MI 48502. 313/238-4641. **Contact:** Kate Harris, Operations Manager. **Description:** Wholesale distributors of electrical apparatus and equipment. **Common positions:** Electrical Engineer; Branch Manager; Management Trainee. Educational **backgrounds sought:** Business Administration; Engineering; Marketing. **Special programs:** training programs. **Benefits:** medical and life insurance; tuition assistance; profit sharing; employee discounts. **Corporate headquarters:** This location. **Other U.S. locations: Saginaw, MI; Auburn Hills, MI; Fenton, MI. Operations at this facility:** administration; sales. **Revenues (1991):** $23 million. **Employees:** 83.

STANLEY ELECTRONICS
22700 Heslip, Novi MI 48375. 313/349-3990. **Contact:** Personnel. **Description:** A leading Southeastern Michigan company which manufactures transmitters and receivers for garage door openers. **Employees:** 200.

TRW/TRANSPORTATION ELECTRONICS DIVISION
24175 Research Drive, Farmington Hills MI 48335. 313/478-7210. **Contact:** Drew Fishburn, Manager. **Description:** Produces electronic controls, sensors and displays for passenger cars, trucks and buses, including engines and transmissions. Parent company, TRW, is a diversified technology firm with operations in electronics and space systems, car and truck equipment for both original equipment manufacturers and the replacement market, and a wide variety of industrial and energy components, including aircraft parts, welding systems, and electromechanical assemblies. **Listed on:** New York Stock Exchange. **Corporate headquarters:** Cleveland, OH.

UNITED TECHNOLOGY
AUTOMOTIVE PRODUCTS DIVISION
5200 Auto-Club Drive, Dearborn MI 48126-9982. 313/593-9600. **Contact:** Personnel Department. **Description:** A major Southeastern Michigan manufacturer of electrical engine equipment. **Employees:** 22,000.

Additional large employers: 250+

SWITCHGEAR AND SWITCHBOARD APPARATUS

Mechanical Products Inc
1824 River St, Jackson MI 49202-1755. 517/782-0391.
Employs: 250-499.

MOTORS AND GENERATORS

Ford Motor Co
15303 Commerce Dr S #100, Dearborn MI 48120-1249.
313/337-5070. Employs: 500-999.

Ford Motor Co/ Rawsonville Plant
McKean & Textile Rds, Ypsilanti MI 48197. 313/484-8000. Employs: 1000+.

Magnetek Universal Electric
300 E Main St, Owosso MI 48867-3137. 517/723-7866.
Employs: 1000+.

RELAYS AND INDUSTRIAL CONTROLS

Faraday Inc
805 S Maumee, Tecumseh MI 49286-2053. 517/423-2111.
Employs: 250-499.

HOUSEHOLD REFRIGERATORS AND HOME AND
FARM FREEZERS

Delfield Co
980 S Isabella Rd, Mount Pleasnt MI 48858-9207.
517/773-7981. Employs: 500-999.

Frigidaire Refrigerator Products
635 W Charles St, Greenville MI 48838-1182. 616/754-7131. Employs: 1000+.

HOUSEHOLD VACUUM CLEANERS

Rexair Inc
900 Tower Dr, Troy MI 48098-2837. 313/879-2600.
Employs: 500-999.

MISCELLANEOUS HOUSEHOLD APPLIANCES

Masco Corp
21001 Van Born Rd, Taylor MI 48180-1340. 313/274-7400. Employs: 1000+.

MISC. LIGHTING EQUIPMENT

Federal-Mogul Corporation
P O Box 1966, Detroit MI 48235-0906. 313/354-7700.
Employs: 1000+.

MISC. COMMUNICATIONS EQUIPMENT

Code-Alarm Inc
950 E Whitcomb, Madison Hts MI 48071-5612. 313/583-9595. Employs: 250-499.

Standard Electric Time Corp
225 Patterson St, Tecumseh MI 49286. 517/423-8331.
Employs: 250-499.

ELECTRONIC MACHINERY

Jabil Circuit Co
32275 Mally Rd, Madison Hts MI 48071-5508. 313/589-3500. Employs: 250-499.

MISC. ELECTRONIC COMPONENTS

Lectron Products Inc
1400 S Livernois Rd, Rochester MI 48307-3362. 313/656-0880. Employs: 500-999.

STORAGE BATTERIES

Johnson Controls Inc Battery
951 Aiken St, Owosso MI 48867-3909. 517/723-7831.
Employs: 250-499.

ELECTRICAL EQUIPMENT FOR INTERNAL
COMBUSTION ENGINES

Electro Design Inc
1481 E 8 Mile Rd, Ferndale MI 48220-2627. 313/543-6222. Employs: 250-499.

G M Fanuc Robotics Corp
2000 S Adams Rd, Auburn Hills MI 48326-2800. 313/377-7000. Employs: 500-999.

MISC. ELECTRONIC PARTS AND EQUIPMENT:
WHOLESALE

At & T Info Systems
4660 S Hagadorn Rd, East Lansing MI 48823-5353.
517/332-9606. Employs: 250-499.

Sparton Corporation
2400 E Ganson St, Jackson MI 49202-3772. 517/787-8600.
Employs: 1000+.

GTE Telecom Marketing Corp
327 E Center St, Alma MI 48801-1806. 517/463-0533.
Employs: 250-499.

Additional small to medium sized employers: 50-249

POWER, DISTRIBUTION AND SPECIALTY
TRANSFORMERS

Dongan Electric Manufacturing Co
2987-3001 Franklin St, Detroit MI 48207-4262. 313/567-8500. Employs: 50-99.

Marelco Power Systems Inc
317 Catrell Dr, Howell MI 48843-1703. 517/546-6330.
Employs: 50-99.

MOTORS AND GENERATORS

Electric Apparatus Co
409 N Roosevelt, Howell MI 48843-1869. 517/546-0520.
Employs: 100-249.

Motor Products
201 S Delaney Rd, Owosso MI 48867-9100. 517/725-5151.
Employs: 100-249.

P S I Repair Services
11900 Mayfield, Livonia MI 48150-1710. 313/261-4160.
Employs: 100-249.

Toledo Commutator Co
1101 S Chestnut St, Owosso MI 48867-4082. 517/725-8192. Employs: 100-249.

RELAYS AND INDUSTRIAL CONTROLS

Ann Arbor Computer
1201 E Ellsworth Rd, Ann Arbor MI 48108-2420. 313/973-7875. Employs: 50-99.

Bra-Con/X-Mation Inc
43850 W 10 Mile Rd, Novi MI 48375-3114. 313/348-0200. Employs: 50-99.

Candid Logic Inc
31681 Dequindre Rd, Madison Hts MI 48071-1522. 313/583-9266. Employs: 50-99.

Dynapath Systems Inc
12843 Greenfield Rd, Detroit MI 48227-2163. 313/272-3710. Employs: 100-249.

Hi-Lex Controls Inc
152 Simpson Dr, Litchfield MI 49252. 517/542-2955. Employs: 100-249.

K D S Controls Inc
307 Robbins Dr, Troy MI 48083-4561. 313/588-5095. Employs: 50-99.

K-R Automation Corp
2000 Centerwood Dr, Warren MI 48091-1619. 313/756-3131. Employs: 100-249.

Sensors Inc
6812 S State Rd, Saline MI 48176-9274. 313/429-2100. Employs: 100-249.

Universal Systems
1401 E Stewart Ave, Flint MI 48505-3616. 313/785-7970. Employs: 50-99.

Warrick Controls Inc
4237 Normandy Ct, Royal Oak MI 48073-2264. 313/545-2512. Employs: 50-99.

MISCELLANEOUS ELECTRICAL INDUSTRIAL APPARATUS

Ekstrom Inds Inc
23850 Freeway Pk Dr, Farmington MI 48335-2814. 313/477-0040. Employs: 50-99.

Electro-Matic Products Inc
23409 Indl Pk Ct, Farmington MI 48335. 313/478-1182. Employs: 50-99.

Magnetek Controls
6380 S Brockway, Peck MI 48466-9783. 313/378-5511. Employs: 100-249.

Martin Systems
121 E Allegan St # 15, Lansing MI 48933-1801. 517/372-6677. Employs: 50-99.

Robotron Corp
21300 8 Mile Rd W, Southfield MI 48075-5638. 313/350-1444. Employs: 100-249.

Westinghouse/Engineering Svc
24700 W 11 Mile, Southfield MI 48034-2494. 313/357-7343. Employs: 50-99.

HOUSEHOLD REFRIGERATORS AND HOME AND FARM FREEZERS

Northland Corp
701 Ranney Dr, Greenville MI 48838-1374. 616/754-5601. Employs: 50-99.

Randell Manufacturing Inc
520 S Coldwater Rd, Weidman MI 48893-9609. 517/644-3331. Employs: 100-249.

HOUSEHOLD LAUNDRY EQUIPMENT

Un Ln Div Robert Shaw Controls
1770 Maplelawn Dr, Troy MI 48084-4604. 313/643-0700. Employs: 50-99.

ELECTRIC HOUSEWARES AND FANS

Dan's Fan City
363 N Maple Rd, Ann Arbor MI 48103-2824. 313/663-8986. Employs: 50-99.

Hydreclaim Corp
3145 Copper Ave, Fenton MI 48430-1779. 313/629-6441. Employs: 50-99.

HOUSEHOLD VACUUM CLEANERS

Rexair Inc
3221 W Big Beaver Rd #200, Troy MI 48084-2811. 313/643-7222. Employs: 50-99.

MISCELLANEOUS HOUSEHOLD APPLIANCES

Smith's Creek Manufacturing
314# Wall St, Port Huron MI 48060-5425. 313/982-7550. Employs: 100-249.

CURRENT-CARRYING WIRING DEVICES

Altair Tool & Engineering
50320 E Russell Schmt Bl, Harrison Twp MI 48045. 313/949-1100. Employs: 50-99.

E H I/Elicon
1155 E Whitcomb, Madison Hts MI 48071-1414. 313/583-2710. Employs: 100-249.

Interlock Corp
1770 Marie St, Westland MI 48185-3233. 313/728-2100. Employs: 100-249.

Micro Craft Inc
41107 Jo Dr, Novi MI 48375-1920. 313/476-6510. Employs: 50-99.

Sine Co's Inc
25325 Joy Blvd, Harrison Twp MI 48045-1321. 313/465-6770. Employs: 100-249.

COMMERCIAL, INDUSTRIAL AND INSTITUTIONAL ELECTRIC LIGHTING FIXTURES

Kirlin Co
3401 E Jefferson Ave, Detroit MI 48207-4237. 313/259-6400. Employs: 100-249.

Paramount Inds Inc
304 N Howard St, Croswell MI 48422-1011. 313/767-1300. Employs: 50-99.

VEHICULAR LIGHTING EQUIPMENT

Transmatic Inc
6145 Delfield Indl Dr, Waterford MI 48329. 313/623-2500. Employs: 50-99.

MISCELLANEOUS LIGHTING EQUIPMENT

B & G Lighting Distributors
6013 N Saginaw St, Flint MI 48505-2979. 313/787-4940. Employs: 50-99.

HOUSEHOLD AUDIO AND VIDEO EQUIPMENT

D D & B Studios Inc
401 S Woodward Av Ste 330, Birmingham MI 48009-6621. 313/642-0640. Employs: 50-99.

Kreidler Audio
823 Willow St, Port Huron MI 48060-3633. 313/984-2105. Employs: 50-99.

Mek Mok Records
7100 Trumble Ln, Saint Clair MI 48079-3619. 313/982-4151. Employs: 50-99.

MISCELLANEOUS COMMUNICATIONS EQUIPMENT

Symplex Communications Corp
5 Research Dr, Ann Arbor MI 48103-2974. 313/995-1555. Employs: 50-99.

ELECTRON TUBES

A D M Technology Inc
1626 E Big Beaver Rd, Troy MI 48083-2017. 313/524-2100. Employs: 50-99.

Circuits D M A Inc
32900 Capitol St, Livonia MI 48150-1706. 313/525-0600. Employs: 100-249.

Com 2 Inc
1556 Woodland Dr, Saline MI 48176-1203. 313/429-9027. Employs: 50-99.

Excel Circuits Co
32096 Howard Av, Madison Hts MI 48071-1406. 313/588-5100. Employs: 50-99.

Excel Circuits Co Inc
50 Northpointe Dr, Lake Orion MI 48359-1846. 313/373-0700. Employs: 100-249.

Intertech Devel Co
38831 Allen St, Livonia MI 48154-4768. 313/453-9200. Employs: 50-99.

Philips Display Components Co
1600 Huron Pkwy, Ann Arbor MI 48104-4140. 313/996-9400. Employs: 50-99.

SEMICONDUCTORS AND RELATED DEVICES

Energy Conversion Devices Inc
1675 W Maple Rd, Troy MI 48084-7118. 313/280-1900. Employs: 100-249.

Industrial Products Division
12163 Globe Rd, Livonia MI 48150-1142. 313/591-0101. Employs: 50-99.

United Solar Systems Corp
1100 W Maple Rd, Troy MI 48084-5352. 313/362-4170. Employs: 50-99.

MISCELLANEOUS ELECTRONIC COMPONENTS

Acme Manufacturing Co
650 W 12 Mile Rd, Madison Hts MI 48071-2407. 313/564-6000. Employs: 100-249.

Bay Electronics Inc
20805 Kraft Blvd, Roseville MI 48066-2232. 313/296-0900. Employs: 100-249.

C P M Electronic Inds
29165 Calahan St, Roseville MI 48066-1850. 313/772-2100. Employs: 100-249.

Controlled Power Co
1955 Stephenson Hwy, Troy MI 48083-2134. 313/528-3700. Employs: 100-249.

Detroit Coil Co
2435 Hilton Rd, Ferndale MI 48220-1570. 313/398-5600. Employs: 100-249.

Empire Electronics Inc
629 E Elmwood Ave, Troy MI 48083-2804. 313/585-8130. Employs: 50-99.

I G K Industries

7232 Jackson Rd, Ann Arbor MI 48103-9506. 313/663-6445. Employs: 50-99.

Midwest Microwave Inc
6564 S State Rd, Saline MI 48176-9569. 313/429-4773. Employs: 100-249.

Novatron Corp
6000 Rinke Ave, Warren MI 48091-5350. 313/755-1300. Employs: 50-99.

Pontiac Coil Inc
5385 Perry Dr, Waterford MI 48329-3460. 313/674-0456. Employs: 50-99.

Precise Technology & Elexs Inc
24727 Gibson Rd, Warren MI 48089-4322. 313/758-7100. Employs: 50-99.

Saturn Electronics Inc
2119 Austin St, Rochester MI 48309-3668. 313/852-2120. Employs: 100-249.

Spacevision Satellite
214 E Mill St, Davison MI 48423-1442. 313/653-2572. Employs: 50-99.

Stanley Electronics
22700 Heslip Dr, Novi MI 48375-4143. 313/349-3990. Employs: 100-249.

Technidisc Inc
2250 Meijer Dr, Troy MI 48084-7111. 313/435-7430. Employs: 50-99.

Vultron Inc
620 E Woodworth Rd, Bad Axe MI 48413-1547. 517/269-9748. Employs: 50-99.

STORAGE BATTERIES

Johnson Controls
32661 Edward Av, Madison Hts MI 48071-1448. 313/583-9600. Employs: 100-249.

PRIMARY BATTERIES, DRY AND WET

Farmers Petroleum Coop Inc
7373 West Saginaw Box 30960, Lansing MI 48909-8460. 517/323-7000. Employs: 100-249.

ELECTRICAL EQUIPMENT FOR INTERNAL COMBUSTION ENGINES

Blue Water Manufacturing
227 Indl Pk, Harbor Beach MI 48441. 517/479-6110. Employs: 50-99.

Clements Manufacturing Co
2381 Black River St, Deckerville MI 48427-9302. 313/376-2215. Employs: 50-99.

G T Products
315 S 1st St, Ann Arbor MI 48104-1353. 313/761-7666. Employs: 100-249.

Great Lakes
6880 Maple Valley Rd, Brown City MI 48416-9101. 313/346-3400. Employs: 100-249.

I T T Automotive
3000 University Dr, Auburn Hills MI 48326-2356. 313/340-3000. Employs: 100-249.

Liberty Manufacturing Co Inc
8678 5th St, Minden City MI 48456. 517/864-3160. Employs: 50-99.

Syncro Corp
3321 W Big Beaver Rd, Troy MI 48084-2808. 313/649-6464. Employs: 100-249.

MISCELLANEOUS ELECTRICAL MACHINERY, EQUIPMENT AND SUPPLIES

ABB Graco Robotics Inc
47700 Halyard Dr, Plymouth MI 48170-2453. 313/459-0111. Employs: 100-249.

Allen-Bradley Company
3469 Pierson Pl, Flint MI 48504-6905. 313/733-3560. Employs: 50-99.

Amerace Corp Ind Electrl Products
17199 N Laurel Park Dr, Livonia MI 48152-2679. 313/464-4444. Employs: 50-99.

American Electrical Heater Co
6110 Cass Ave, Detroit MI 48202-3426. 313/875-2505. Employs: 50-99.

Appleton Electric
29551 Greenfield Rd, Southfield MI 48076-2249. 313/559-6336. Employs: 50-99.

Arrow Hart Div Cooper Ind
32304 Gainsborough Dr, Warren MI 48093-6915. 313/978-2811. Employs: 50-99.

Asea Brown Boveri Inc
27950 Orchard Lake Rd, Farmington MI 48334-3758. 313/855-0333. Employs: 50-99.

Automatic Switch
25925 Telegraph Rd, Southfield MI 48034-2501. 313/356-7760. Employs: 50-99.

Burndy Corporation
6150 Bay Ct, Waterford MI 48327-2900. 313/681-1078. Employs: 50-99.

C B Associates Inc
21727 E Valley Woods Dr, Franklin MI 48025-2638. 313/644-7878. Employs: 50-99.

Challenger Electrl Equip Corp
26200 Town Center Dr, Novi MI 48375-1218. 313/347-2300. Employs: 50-99.

Computer Technology Corp
27750 Rainbow Cir, Southfield MI 48076-3250. 313/569-5159. Employs: 50-99.

Creative Dimension
2294 S Industrial Hwy, Ann Arbor MI 48104-6124. 313/482-7262. Employs: 50-99.

Electra Lume Inc
3302 Crooks Rd, Royal Oak MI 48073-2446. 313/435-8770. Employs: 50-99.

Electrical Materials Inc
44262 Phoenix Dr, Sterling Hts MI 48314-1465. 313/254-0770. Employs: 50-99.

Entrelec Div Alsthom International
405 Main St, Fenton MI 48430-2133. 313/629-6459. Employs: 50-99.

Gilreath Manufacturing Inc
3240 W Grand River St, Howell MI 48843-9601. 313/933-4100. Employs: 100-249.

Ideal Industries Inc
1725 Tiverton Rd, Bloomfield MI 48304-2341. 313/645-6777. Employs: 50-99.

Rice Enterprises
11735 Merriman Rd, Livonia MI 48150-1920. 313/458-7050. Employs: 50-99.

Rittal Corporation
46986 Liberty, Wixom MI 48393-3693. 313/669-7133. Employs: 50-99.

Solvay Automotive Inc
2565 W Maple Rd, Troy MI 48084-7114. 313/435-3300. Employs: 50-99.

Square D Co
1960 Research Dr, Troy MI 48083-2163. 313/680-4444. Employs: 50-99.

Stanley Magic Door
2400 E Lincoln St, Birmingham MI 48009-7126. 313/646-1100. Employs: 50-99.

Telemecanique Inc
432 N Saginaw St, Flint MI 48502-2013. 313/239-2226. Employs: 50-99.

United Electric Co
22508 Ivanhoe Ln, Southfield MI 48034-5195. 313/353-6610. Employs: 50-99.

Advance Business Works
13046 Apple Tree Ln, Dewitt MI 48820-9638. 517/669-3984. Employs: 50-99.

Advanced Laser Applications
47808 Galleon Dr, Plymouth MI 48170-2468. 313/451-0140. Employs: 50-99.

Don El Engineering
4629 Platt Rd, Ann Arbor MI 48108-9726. 313/973-0330. Employs: 50-99.

Image Engineering
560 Kirts Blvd, Troy MI 48084-4141. 313/244-8410. Employs: 50-99.

Laser Equipment Sales Inc
2687 Commerce Dr, Rochester MI 48309-3813. 313/852-9329. Employs: 50-99.

Laser Materials Finishing
1460 Laurelhurst Dr, Temperance MI 48182-9239. 313/241-1510. Employs: 50-99.

Laser Mechanisms Inc
5328 Woodland Estates, Bloomfield MI 48302. 313/540-5929. Employs: 50-99.

Laser Mechanisms Inc
24730 Crestview Ct, Farmington MI 48335-1506. 313/474-9480. Employs: 50-99.

Leading Edge Components
1915 Devonshire Rd, Bloomfield MI 48302-0618. 313/332-5840. Employs: 50-99.

Metalase Engineering Inc
51053 Celeste St, Shelby Twp MI 48315-2921. 313/263-6230. Employs: 50-99.

Michigan Laser Recharge
15918 Drysdale St, Southgate MI 48195-2904. 313/282-5990. Employs: 50-99.

Michigan Laser Level & Tran Inc
27200 Beck Rd, Novi MI 48374-1348. 313/344-0770. Employs: 50-99.

Prototech Laser
44455 Reynolds Dr, Clinton Twp MI 48036-1245. 313/465-9944. Employs: 50-99.

Rofin-Senar Inc
45701 Mast St, Plymouth MI 48170-6008. 313/455-5400. Employs: 50-99.

Spectra-Physics Laserplane Inc
40500 Gd River, Novi MI 48375. 313/471-4722. Employs: 50-99.

Superior Finishing Products & Svc
11085 E 9 Mile Rd, Warren MI 48089-2454. 313/757-4636. Employs: 50-99.

Tempro Industries
47808 Galleon Dr, Plymouth MI 48170-2468. 313/451-5900. Employs: 50-99.

United Specialties
1080 Dunleavy Dr, Highland MI 48356-2163. 313/887-5181. Employs: 50-99.

For more information on career opportunities in the electrical and electronic industry:

Associations

AMERICAN ELECTROPLATERS AND SURFACE FINISHERS SOCIETY
12644 Research Parkway, Orlando FL 32826. 407/281-6441.

AMERICAN CERAMIC SOCIETY
735 Ceramic Place, Westerville OH 43081. 614/890-4700.

ELECTROCHEMICAL SOCIETY
10 South Main Street, Pennington NJ 08534-2896. 609/737-1902.

ELECTRONIC INDUSTRIES ASSOCIATION
2001 Pennsylvania Avenue NW, Washington DC 20006. 202/457-4900.

ELECTRONICS TECHNICIANS ASSOCIATION
602 N. Jackson Street, Greencastle IN 46135. 317/653-8262.

INSTITUTE OF ELECTRICAL AND ELECTRONICS ENGINEERS
345 East 47th Street, New York NY 10017. 212/705-7900.

INTERNATIONAL BROTHERHOOD OF ELECTRICAL WORKERS

1125 15th Street NW, Washington DC 20005. 202/833-7000.

INTERNATIONAL SOCIETY OF CERTIFIED ELECTRONICS TECHNICIANS
2708 West Berry, Fort Worth TX 76109. 817/921-9101.

INTERNATIONAL SOCIETY FOR HYBRID MICROELECTRONICS
1861 Wiehle Avenue, Suite 340, Reston VA 22090. 703/471-0066.

NATIONAL ELECTRICAL MANUFACTURERS ASSOCIATION
2101 L Street NW, Suite 300, Washington DC 20037. 202/457-8400.

NATIONAL ELECTRONICS SALES AND SERVICES ASSOCIATION
2708 West Berry, Fort Worth TX 76109. 817/921-9061.

ROBOTICS INTERNATIONAL OF THE SOCIETY OF MANUFACTURING ENGINEERS
P.O. Box 930, One SME Drive, Dearborn MI 48121. 313/271-1500.

ENERGY, MINING AND PETROLEUM

The short-term future for the petroleum industry depends upon the world economy, OPEC production, and world oil prices. U.S. crude and natural gas production is expected to remain flat, while energy use is forecasted to rise 2-3 percent annually for oil and natural gas respectively. Environmental concerns will have a greater effect on the industry.
Jobseekers, especially those with engineering backgrounds, should keep an eye out for the growing emphasis on the development of alternative fuels like methanol, and for growth in hydroelectric, geothermal, and other environmentally sound energy sources.

A & R PIPELINE COMPANY
500 Renaissance Center, Detroit MI 48243. 313/496-0200. **Contact:** Employment and Placement Department. **Description:** Engaged in the production and distribution of natural gas. **Employees:** 10,900.

CONLEE OIL COMPANY

815 South Mill Street, Clio MI 48420. 313/686-5600. **Contact:** Robert Setzer, Personnel Director. **Description:** The corporate office for an oil distribution company, which owns and operates a chain of gasoline service stations. **Employees:** 100.

MICHIGAN CONSOLIDATED (MICH CON) GAS CO.

500 Griswold Street, Detroit MI 48226. 313/256-5663. **Contact:** Suzanne G. Dibble, Manager, Employment and Placement. A major metropolitan Detroit company engaged in the distribution of natural gas. **Employees:** 3,500. **Common positions:** Accountant; Attorney; Buyer; Chemist; Computer Programmer; Customer Service Representative; Chemical Engineer; Civil Engineer; Electrical Engineer; Mechanical Engineer; Metallurgical Engineer; Financial Analyst; Marketing Specialist; Personnel and Labor Relations Specialist; Purchasing Agent; Systems Analyst. **Educational backgrounds sought:** Accounting; Business Administration; Chemistry; Computer Science; Engineering; Finance; Liberal Arts. **Benefits:** medical, dental, and life insurance; pension plan; tuition assistance; disability coverage; employee discounts; savings plan. **Corporate headquarters:** This location. A subsidiary of MCN Corporation. **Operations at this facility:** research/development; administration; service; sales. **Listed on:** New York Stock Exchange.

SOUTHEASTERN MICHIGAN GAS ENTERPRISES

2915 Lapeer Road, Port Huron MI 48061-5026. 313/987-2200. **Contact:** Mrs. Pat McCabe, Human Resources. **Description:** A major regional gas producer and distributor. **Employees:** 300.

Additional large employers: 250+

PETROLEUM REFINING

Marathon Oil Co
1300 S Fort St, Detroit MI 48217-1208. 313/843-9100.
Employs: 250-499.

LUBRICATING OILS AND GREASES

Acheson Colloids Co
1600 Washington Av, Port Huron MI 48060-3456.
313/984-5581. Employs: 250-499.

LIME

Edward C Levy Co
8800 Dix Ave, Detroit MI 48209-1093. 313/843-7200.
Employs: 250-499.

COAL AND OTHER MINERALS AND ORES: WHOLESALE

American Natural Resources Co
One Woodward Ave, Detroit MI 48226-3402. 313/496-0200. Employs: 1000+.

Additional small to medium sized employers: 50-249

CRUDE PETROLEUM AND NATURAL GAS

Lease Management Inc
503 Industrial Ave, Mount Pleasant MI 48858-4639.
517/773-5948. Employs: 100-249.

Muskegon Development Co
1425 S Mission, Mount Pleasant MI 48858. 517/772-4900.
Employs: 50-99.

Oryx Energy Co

700 S Chippewa Rd, Mount Pleasant MI 48858-9426.
517/772-2925. Employs: 50-99.

Petco Petroleum Corp
15240 Howard Rd, Concord MI 49237. 517/524-6170.
Employs: 50-99.

DRILLING OIL AND GAS WELLS

Scott Don Drill Co Inc Warehouse
11131 Concord Rd, Mosherville MI 49258. 517/549-8229.
Employs: 50-99.

OIL AND GAS FIELD EXPLORATION SERVICES

Calhoun Oil & Gas Inc
37000 Grand River Ave, Farmington MI 48335-2868.
313/473-5415. Employs: 50-99.

EMC Gas Transmission Co
535 Griswold St, Detroit MI 48226-3410. 313/963-3195.
Employs: 50-99.

Goran Resources Inc
234 Maryknoll Rd E, Rochester MI 48309-1955. 313/375-1948. Employs: 50-99.

Kudu Corp
16000 W 9 Mile Rd, Southfield MI 48075-4808. 313/443-1610. Employs: 50-99.

Paragon Petroleum Corp
32401 8 Mile Rd, Livonia MI 48152-1340. 313/471-3900.
Employs: 50-99.

MISCELLANEOUS OIL AND GAS FIELD SERVICES

Dale Leasing Co
5115 W Pickard Rd, Mount Pleasant MI 48858-9631.
517/772-0550. Employs: 100-249.

Total Crude Oil Transport Inc
1300 N Fancher St, Mount Pleasant MI 48858-4610.
517/773-9978. Employs: 100-249.

Indril Inc
2113 Enterprise Dr, Mount Pleasant MI 48858-2300.
517/773-6946. Employs: 100-249.

Petroleum Information
6020 N Hagadorn Rd, East Lansing MI 48823-2243.
517/332-4913. Employs: 50-99.

MISCELLANEOUS CRUSHED AND BROKEN STONE

International Mill Service
3398 E Front St, Monroe MI 48161-1970. 313/241-3007.
Employs: 50-99.

Stoneco Inc Division Se Johnson
Scofield Rd, Maybee MI 48159. 313/587-7125. Employs:
50-99.

CONSTRUCTION SAND AND GRAVEL

American Aggregates Corp
42400 Grand River Ave #101, Novi MI 48375-2572.
313/344-2630. Employs: 100-249.

INDUSTRIAL SAND

Sand Products Corp
660 Woodward Ave #1111, Detroit MI 48226-3513.
313/961-2483. Employs: 50-99.

MISCELLANEOUS CLAY, CERAMIC AND REFRACTORY MINERALS

North American Minerals Corp
455 Eisenhower Pkwy E Ste 75, Ann Arbor MI 48108-3321. 313/769-1105. Employs: 50-99.

PETROLEUM REFINING

Donovan & Avery Oil Co Inc
402 North St, Mason MI 48854-1532. 517/676-9611.
Employs: 50-99.

Marathon Fuel Oil Co
2205 Holland St, Birmingham MI 48009-7810. 313/644-9000. Employs: 100-249.

ASPHALT PAVING MIXTURES AND BLOCKS

Cadillac Asphalt Paving Co
27575 Wixom Rd, Novi MI 48374-1127. 313/349-8600.
Employs: 100-249.

Owens Corning Fiberglas
12460 Stocker St, Detroit MI 48217-1409. 313/843-4450.
Employs: 50-99.

Thompson-Mc Cully Co
5905 Belleville Rd, Belleville MI 48111-1119. 313/397-2050. Employs: 100-249.

LUBRICATING OILS AND GREASES

Detrex Corp/Wayne Metalworking
26000 Capitol Ave, Redford MI 48239-2402. 313/937-1900. Employs: 50-99.

Metal Working Lubricants
25 Silverdome Indl Pk, Pontiac MI 48342. 313/332-3500.
Employs: 100-249.

Mich-I-Penn Oil & Grease Co
9100 Freeland St, Detroit MI 48228-2309. 313/838-8000.
Employs: 50-99.

Mobil Oil Corp
20089 West Rd, Trenton MI 48183-3320. 313/671-2700.
Employs: 50-99.

MISCELLANEOUS PRODUCTS OF PETROLEUM AND COAL

Allied Signal Inc
1200 Zug Isl Rd, Detroit MI 48209-2892. 313/842-4400.
Employs: 50-99.

F W Ritter Sons Co
12670 Dixie Hwy, S Rockwood MI 48179-9706. 313/379-9622. Employs: 50-99.

CONCRETE BLOCK AND BRICK

Grand Blanc Cement Products
10709 S Center Rd, Grand Blanc MI 48439-1032. 313/694-7500. Employs: 50-99.

U S Brick Inc Mi Brick Div
3820 Serr Rd, Corunna MI 48817-1146. 517/743-3444.
Employs: 50-99.

GYPSUM PRODUCTS

Binderline Development Inc
33100 Freeway Dr, St Clair Shrs MI 48082-1005. 313/294-1620. Employs: 50-99.

Goldbond Building Products Div National
24901 Northwestern Hwy, Southfield MI 48075-2203.
313/355-1710. Employs: 50-99.

U S Gypsum Co
2 Division St, River Rouge MI 48218-1352. 313/842-4455.
Employs: 100-249.

ABRASIVE PRODUCTS

Ervin Industries Inc
3893 Research Park Dr, Ann Arbor MI 48108-2217.
313/769-4600. Employs: 100-249.

G T E Valenite/Walmet Div
404 E 10 Mile Rd, Pleasant Ridge MI 48069. 313/589-6400. Employs: 100-249.

Inland Diamond Products Co
32051 Howard St, Madison Hts MI 48071-1430. 313/585-2330. Employs: 50-99.

Cadillac Brick Co
10049 E Grand River Ave, Brighton MI 48116. 313/227-0900. Employs: 50-99.

MINERALS AND EARTHS, GROUND OR OTHERWISE TREATED

American Aggregate Corp
13270 Silver Lake Rd, Brighton MI 48116-8516. 313/437-8171. Employs: 50-99.

Fritz Enterprise Inc
23550 Pennsylvania Rd, Taylor MI 48180-5217. 313/283-7272. Employs: 100-249.

NONCLAY REFRACTORIES

Chase Nedrow Industries Inc
150 Landrow Dr, Wixom MI 48393-2057. 313/669-9886. Employs: 50-99.

Sterling Refractories
1147 Rankin St, Troy MI 48083-6006. 313/583-3434. Employs: 50-99.

CRUDE PETROLEUM PIPELINES

Amoco Oil Co Pipeline Mntnc
6701 W Brooklyn Rd, Napoleon MI 49261. 517/536-8659. Employs: 50-99.

ANR Pipeline Co
36555 29 Mi, New Haven MI 48048. 313/749-9244. Employs: 50-99.

Buckeye Pipe Line Co
4861 White Lake Rd, Clarkston MI 48346-2556. 313/625-1770. Employs: 50-99.

Buckeye Pipe Line Co
2185 W Samaria Rd, Temperance MI 48182-9730. 313/856-1858. Employs: 50-99.

Buckeye Pipe Line Co
4476 Treadwell St, Wayne MI 48184-1508. 313/721-8834. Employs: 50-99.

Buckeye Pipe Line Co
4004 W M 21, Owosso MI 48867-9342. 517/723-5437. Employs: 50-99.

Buckeye Pipe Line Company
Allen Rd, Trenton MI 48183. 313/676-9339. Employs: 50-99.

Great Lakes Gas Transmission
10252 E Remus, Mount Pleasant MI 48858. 517/772-4340. Employs: 50-99.

Lakehead Pipeline Co
28 Mile Rd, Albion MI 49224. 517/629-5884. Employs: 50-99.

Lakehead Pipeline Co Inc
9185 Parshallville Rd, Fenton MI 48430-9212. 313/629-1461. Employs: 50-99.

Marathon Pipe Line Co
2185 Samaria Rd, Lambertville MI 48144. 313/856-6800. Employs: 50-99.

Marathon Pipeline Co
131 Morsherville Rd, Jonesville MI 49250. 517/549-8141. Employs: 50-99.

Michigan Gas Storage Co
12201 E Pleasant Lake Rd, Manchester MI 48158-9569. 313/428-8155. Employs: 50-99.

Mid-Valley Pipe Line
2185 Samaria Rd, Samaria MI 48177. 313/856-3932. Employs: 50-99.

Sun Pipe Line Co
4148 Legion Dr, Mason MI 48854-1042. 517/676-4240. Employs: 50-99.

Sun Pipeline Co
2571 Grimes Rd, Stockbridge MI 49285. 517/851-8961. Employs: 50-99.

Total Pipeline Corp
Grimes Rd, Stockbridge MI 49285. 517/851-8075. Employs: 50-99.

Total Pipeline Corp
2691 E Lake Lansing Rd, East Lansing MI 48823-9714. 517/337-9500. Employs: 50-99.

Wolerine Pipe-Line Co
West Rd, Trenton MI 48183. 313/675-7580. Employs: 50-99.

Wolverine Pipe Line Co
4075 S Fletcher Rd, Manchester MI 48158. 313/428-8386. Employs: 50-99.

Wolverine Pipe-Line Co
28420 Wick Rd, Inkster MI 48141. 313/946-9171. Employs: 50-99.

Wolverine Pipeline Co
6011 Wyoming St, Dearborn MI 48126-2335. 313/584-9262. Employs: 50-99.

Wolverine Pipeline Co
1400 Enterprise, Allen Park MI 48101. 313/271-0311. Employs: 50-99.

MISCELLANEOUS PIPELINES

Anchor Pipeline
3716 Gorey Av, Flint MI 48506-4138. 313/742-1369. Employs: 50-99.

Buckeye Pipe Line Co
250 Murphy Dr, Marysville MI 48040. 313/364-6251. Employs: 50-99.

The Buckeye Pipe Line Co
G5388 N Dort Hwy, Flint MI 48505-1833. 313/789-9279. Employs: 50-99.

Total Pipeline Corp
1500 Bridge Av, Alma MI 48801. 517/463-1161. Employs: 100-249.

For more information on career opportunities in the energy, mining, and petroleum industries:

Associations

AMERICAN ASSOCIATION OF PETROLEUM GEOLOGISTS
P.O. Box 979, Tulsa OK 74101. 918/584-2555.

AMERICAN GAS ASSOCIATION
1515 Wilson Boulevard, Arlington VA 22209. 703/841-8400.

AMERICAN GEOLOGICAL INSTITUTE
4220 King Street, Alexandria VA 22302. 703/379-2480.

AMERICAN INSTITUTE OF MINING, METALLURGICAL AND PETROLEUM
345 East 47th Street, New York NY 10017. 212/705-7695.

AMERICAN NUCLEAR SOCIETY
555 North Kensington Avenue, La Grange Park IL 60525.
708/352-6611.

AMERICAN PETROLEUM INSTITUTE
1220 L Street NW, Washington DC 20005. 202/682-8000.

AMERICAN SOCIETY OF TRIBOLOGISTS AND
LUBRICATION ENGINEERS
840 Busse Highway, Park Ridge IL 60068. 708/825-5536.

CLEAN ENERGY RESEARCH INSTITUTE
P.O. Box 248294, Coral Gables FL 33124. 305/284-4666.

GEOLOGICAL SOCIETY OF AMERICA
3300 Penrose Place, P.O. Box 9140, Boulder CO 80301.
303/447-2020.

PETROLEUM EQUIPMENT INSTITUTE
P.O. Box 2380, Tulsa OK 74101. 918/494-9696.

PETROLEUM MARKETERS ASSOCIATION OF
AMERICA
1120 Vermont Avenue NW, Washington DC 20005.
202/331-1198.

SOCIETY OF EXPLORATION GEOPHYSICISTS
P.O. Box 702740, Tulsa OK 74170-2740. 918/493-3516.

Directories

BROWN'S DIRECTORY OF NORTH AMERICAN
AND INTERNATIONAL GAS COMPANIES
Advanstar Communications, 7500 Old Oak Boulevard,
Cleveland OH 44130. 800/225-4569.

NATIONAL PETROLEUM NEWS FACT BOOK
Hunter Publishing Co., 950 Lee Street, Des Plaines IL
60016. 708/296-0770.

OIL AND GAS DIRECTORY
Geophysical Directory, Inc., P.O. Box 130508, Houston
TX 77219. 713/529-8789.

Magazines

AMERICAN GAS MONTHLY
1515 Wilson Boulevard, Arlington VA 22209. 703/841-
8686.

GAS INDUSTRIES AND APPLIANCE MAGAZINES
Gas Industries and Appliance News, Inc., P.O. Box 558,
Park Ridge IL 60068. 312/693-3682.

NATIONAL PETROLEUM NEWS
Hunter Publishing Co., 950 Lee Street, Des Plaines IL
60016. 708/296-0770.

OIL AND GAS JOURNAL
PennWell Publishing Co., 1421 South Sheridan Road,
Tulsa OK 74112. 918/835-3161.

ENGINEERING AND DESIGN

Job prospects for engineers have been good for a number of years, and will continue to improve into the next century. Employers will need more engineers as they increase investment in equipment in order to expand output. In addition, engineers will find work improving the nation's deteriorating infrastructure.

AERO-DETROIT INC./MADISON HEIGHTS
1100 East Mandolin, Madison Heights MI 48071. 313/583-4900. **Contact:** Ms. Chris Maes, Personnel Director. **Description:** A company providing automotive engineering, architectural, and surveying services. **Employees:** 800.

EG&G STRUCTURAL KINEMATICS
950 Maplelawn, Troy MI 48084. 313/643-4622. **Contact:** Dee McHalpine, Human Resources Coordinator. **Description:** An engineering consulting firm. Services include modal analysis, fatigue testing, structural testing, and road simulation lab. **Operations include:** divisional headquarters; service. **Common positions:** Electrical Engineer; Mechanical Engineer; Sales Representative. **Educational backgrounds sought:** Engineering; Mathematics. **Benefits:** medical, dental, and life insurance; tuition assistance; disability coverage;

savings plan. **Corporate headquarters:** Wellesley MA. **Parent company:** EG&G, Inc. **Listed on:** New York Stock Exchange.

EFFICIENT ENGINEERING COMPANY, INC.
130 Town Center Drive, Troy MI 48084. 313/528-2888. **Contact:** Herb Brown, Personnel Manager. **Description:** A mechanical engineering company. **Employees:** 400. **Common positions:** Draftsperson. **Educational backgrounds sought:** Engineering. **Benefits:** medical and life insurance; disability coverage; savings plan. **Corporate headquarters:** This location.

ENGINEERING SERVICE, INC.
21556 Telegraph Road, Southfield MI 48034. 313/357-3800. **Contact:** Human Resources Department. **Description:** A leading Southeastern Automotive and Aerospace Design/Engineering firm specializing in CAD design for powertrain, electrical, and tooling applications. Offers full-service project management with offices in Southfield and Dearborn, Michigan. **Employees:** 200. **Common positions:** Accountant; Draftsperson; Industrial Designer; Sales Representative; Computer Aided Designer. **Educational backgrounds sought:** Art/Design; Drafting; Computer-Aided Design. **Benefits:** medical, dental, and life insurance; tuition assistance; disability coverage; savings plan; prescriptions. **Corporate headquarters:** This location.

KOLTANBAR ENGINEERING
950 West Maple, P.O. Box 3456, Troy MI 48007. 313/362-2400. **Contact:** Personnel Department. **Description:** A major Southeastern Michigan provider of manufacturing engineering, process development and planning services. **Common positions:** Draftsperson; Manufacturing Engineers; Process Engineers. **Educational backgrounds sought:** Engineering. **Special programs:** Internships. **Benefits:** medical insurance; dental insurance; life insurance.

MODERN ENGINEERING
28000 Dequindre, Warren MI 48092. 313/578-6397. **Contact:** Dick Clark, Manager of Recruiting. **Description:** A major engineering firm supplying services to the automotive and aircraft industries. **Employees:** 3000.

PARLIAMENT DESIGN, INC.
1945 Heide, P.O. Box 99009, Troy MI 48099. 313/362-1650. **Contact:** Herbert Kirchoff, Plant Manager. **Description:** Provides engineering services including computer-aided design and manufacturing (CAD/CAM) services as applied to the automotive, aircraft, and machine tool industries. Areas of operation include: dies, tools, gauges, special machines, welding equipment and related automation, and product design. **Common positions:** Computer Programmer; Draftsperson; Engineer; Aerospace Engineer; Electrical Engineer; Industrial Engineer; Mechanical Engineer; Industrial Designer; CAD/CAM Designer; Systems Analyst; Technical Writer/Editor. **Educational backgrounds sought:** Design; Computer Science; Engineering; Mathematics; Computer Graphics. **Benefits:** medical, dental, and life insurance; disability coverage. **Corporate**

headquarters: This location. **Operations at this facility:** regional headquarters; research/development; administration; service.

PIONEER ENGINEERING AND MANUFACTURING
2500 East 9 Mile Road, Warren MI 48091. 313/755-4400. **Contact:** David Archer, Recruiter. **Description:** A Southeastern Michigan company specializing in engineering services. **Employees:** 900.

STELLAR ENGINEERING INC.
5505 13 Mile Road, Warren MI 48092. 313/978-8444. **Contact:** Ken A. Hojancki, Human Resources Department. **Description:** A firm which offers engineering, full service automotive engineering organization specializing in automotive tooling. **Common positions include:** Draftsperson; Electrical Engineer; Industrial Engineer; Mechanical Engineer; Tool Designer; CAD Operator/Designer. **Educational backgrounds sought:** Engineering. **Benefits:** medical, dental, and life insurance; pension plan; disability coverage; savings plan. **Corporate headquarters:** This location. Operations at this facility: administration; sales.

UNIVERSAL SYSTEMS
1401 East Stewart Avenue, Flint MI 48505-3698. 313/785-7970. **Contact:** Rae Deane Middleton, Vice President. **Description:** An area company engaged in industrial control engineering and industrial electrical construction. Company also installs controls throughout the U.S. **Common positions:** Electrical Engineer (Computer Controls background). **Benefits:** medical insurance; dental insurance; pension plan; life insurance; savings plan. **Corporate headquarters:** This location.

Additional small to medium sized employers: 50-249

ENGINEERING SERVICES

Classic Design
665 Elmwood Av, Troy MI 48083-2804. 313/588-2738. Employs: 50-99.

Cleaver Ketko Gorlitz Papa
31333 Southfield Rd, Franklin MI 48025-5473. 313/642-7970. Employs: 50-99.

Coastal Dynamics Inc
703 Wildwood Ln, Ann Arbor MI 48103-9331. 313/668-1992. Employs: 50-99.

Commonwealth Associates Inc
301 Francis St, Jackson MI 49201-2354. 517/783-4590. Employs: 100-249.

Pine Design Engr & Manufacturing Co
1000 Livernois Rd, Troy MI 48083-2710. 313/585-7100. Employs: 100-249.

Riverside Engineering
9193 Riverside Dr, Brighton MI 48116-8239. 313/231-9620. Employs: 50-99.

Special Engineering Svc
10455 Ford Rd, Dearborn MI 48126-3334. 313/846-0200. Employs: 50-99.

Special Engineering Svc Inc
32233 8 Mile Rd, Livonia MI 48152-1372. 313/834-8700. Employs: 100-249.

Triad Service Inc
24775 Gibson Dr, Warren MI 48089-4322. 313/754-4210. Employs: 50-99.

Troy Design Services
17300 W 10 Mile Rd, Southfield MI 48075-2931. 313/557-3700. Employs: 100-249.

Orchard Hiltz & Mc Climent Inc
34935 Schoolcraft Rd, Livonia MI 48150-1322. 313/522-6711. Employs: 50-99.

Hubbell Roth & Clark Inc
555 Hulet Dr, Bloomfield MI 48302-0360. 313/338-9241. Employs: 100-249.

Altair Engineering Inc
3150 Livernois Rd, Troy MI 48083-5028. 313/680-1670. Employs: 50-99.

Bartech Inc
777 E Eisenhower Prkwy, Ann Arbor MI 48108. 313/665-2666. Employs: 50-99.

Craft-Line Inc
24142 John R Rd, Hazel Park MI 48030-1108. 313/542-7274. Employs: 50-99.

Goodell-Grivas Inc
17320 W 8 Mile Rd, Southfield MI 48075-4317. 313/569-0300. Employs: 50-99.

Harley Ellington Pierce Yee
26913 Northwestern Hwy, Southfield MI 48034-4715. 313/262-1500. Employs: 100-249.

Michigan Sci & Engineering Assocs
1315 Packard St, Ann Arbor MI 48104-3815. 313/994-0280. Employs: 50-99.

Miller Design & Engineering Svc
30810 Greenland St, Livonia MI 48154-3230. 313/425-6790. Employs: 50-99.

Packer Engineering Inc
1116 E Big Beaver Rd, Troy MI 48083-1934. 313/689-5870. Employs: 50-99.

The H M S Co
1230 E Big Beaver Rd, Troy MI 48083-1904. 313/689-3232. Employs: 50-99.

For more information on career opportunities in engineering and design:

Associations

AMERICAN ASSOCIATION OF COST ENGINEERS
209 Prairie Avenue, Suite 100, Morgantown WV 26507. 304/296-8444.

AMERICAN ASSOCIATION OF ENGINEERING SOCIETIES
1111 19th Street, Suite 608, Washington DC 20036. 202/296-2237.

AMERICAN CONSULTING ENGINEERS COUNCIL
1015 15th Street NW, Washington DC 20005. 202/347-7474.

AMERICAN INSTITUTE OF ARCHITECTS
1735 New York Ave NW, Washington DC 20006. 202/626-7300.

AMERICAN INSTITUTE OF PLANT ENGINEERS
3975 Erie Avenue, Cincinnati OH 45208. 513/561-6000.

AMERICAN SOCIETY FOR ENGINEERING EDUCATION
11 Dupont Circle NW, Suite 200, Washington DC 20036. 202/293-7080.

AMERICAN SOCIETY OF CIVIL ENGINEERS
345 East 47th Street, New York NY 10017. 212/705-7496.

AMERICAN SOCIETY OF HEATING, REFRIGERATING AND AIR CONDITIONING ENGINEERS
1791 Tullie Circle NE, Atlanta GA 30329. 404/636-8400.

AMERICAN SOCIETY OF LANDSCAPE ARCHITECTS
4401 Connecticut Avenue, Fifth Floor, Washington DC 20008. 202/686-2752.

AMERICAN SOCIETY OF MECHANICAL ENGINEERS
345 East 47th Street, New York NY 10017. 212/705-7722.

AMERICAN SOCIETY OF NAVAL ENGINEERS
1452 Duke Street, Alexandria VA 22314. 703/836-6727.

AMERICAN SOCIETY OF PLUMBING ENGINEERS
3617 Thousand Oaks Boulevard, Suite #210, Westlake CA 91362. 805/495-7120.

AMERICAN SOCIETY OF SAFETY ENGINEERS
1800 East Oakton Street, Des Plaines IL 60018-2187. 312/692-4121.

ILLUMINATING ENGINEERING SOCIETY OF NORTH AMERICA
345 East 47th Street, New York NY 10017. 212/705-7926.

INSTITUTE OF INDUSTRIAL ENGINEERS
25 Technology Park, Norcross GA 30092. 404/449-0460.

NATIONAL ACADEMY OF ENGINEERING
2101 Constitution Avenue NW, Washington DC 20418. 202334-3200.

NATIONAL ACTION COUNCIL FOR MINORITIES IN ENGINEERING
3 West 35th Street, New York NY 10001. 212/279-2626.

NATIONAL ASSOCIATION OF MINORITY ENGINEERING
500 N. Michigan Avenue, Suite 1400, Chicago IL 60611. 312/661-1700.

NATIONAL ENGINEERING CONSORTIUM
303 E. Wacker Drive, Suite 740, Chicago IL 60601. 312/938-3500.

JUNIOR ENGINEERING TECHNICAL SOCIETY
1420 King Street, Suite 405, Alexandria VA 22314. 703/548-JETS.

NATIONAL INSTITUTE OF CERAMIC ENGINEERS
735 Ceramic Place, Westerville OH 43081. 614/890-4700.

NATIONAL SOCIETY OF BLACK ENGINEERS
1454 Duke Street, Alexandria VA 22314. 703/549-2207.

NATIONAL SOCIETY OF PROFESSIONAL ENGINEERS
1420 King Street, Alexandria VA 22314. 703/684-2800.

SOCIETY FOR THE ADVANCEMENT OF MATERIAL AND PROCESS ENGINEERS
1161 Parkview Drive, Covina CA 91724. 818/331-0616.

SOCIETY OF FIRE PROTECTION ENGINEERS
1 Liberty Square, Boston MA 02109. 617/482-0686.

SOCIETY OF MANUFACTURING ENGINEERS
P.O. Box 930, One SME Drive, Dearborn MI 48121. 313/271-1500.

UNITED ENGINEERING TRUSTEES
345 East 47th Street, New York NY 10017. 212/705-7000.

Directories

DIRECTORY OF ENGINEERING SOCIETIES
American Association of Engineering Societies, 1111 19th Street, Suite 608, Washington DC 20036. 202/296-2237.

DIRECTORY OF ENGINEERS IN PRIVATE PRACTICE
National Society of Professional Engineers, 1420 King Street, Alexandria VA 22314. 703/684-2800.

ENCYCLOPEDIA OF PHYSICAL SCIENCES & ENGINEERING INFORMATION SOURCES
Gale Research Inc., 835 Penobscot Building, Detroit MI 48226. 313/961-2242.

FABRICATED AND PRIMARY METALS

For steel manufacturers, the past few years have been a nightmare, with prices falling to ten-year lows. The industry should begin a modest recovery, however, if lower mortgage rates can spur the home construction industry. Foreign companies will become more and more important; look for more joint ventures between the U.S. and overseas firms. Big Steel's toughest competition is now the increasing number of minimills that have spun off from rivals.
Overall, employment prospects are weak, although metallurgical engineering is in demand.

AAR ADVANCED STRUCTURE
12633 Inkster Road, Livonia MI 48150. 313/522-2000. **Contact:** Personnel. **Description:** Engaged in the manufacture of pallets and fabricated structural metal. **Employees:** 900.

ACORN WINDOW SYSTEMS
12620 Westwood Avenue, Detroit MI 48223. 313/272-5700. **Contact:** Human Resources Representative. **Description:** Engaged in the manufacture of metal doors, frames, and windows. **Employees:** 600. **Benefits:** medical insurance; dental insurance; life insurance; tuition assistance; profit sharing. **Corporate headquarters:** This location.

ADVANCE STAMPING COMPANY
12025 Dixie Avenue, Detroit MI 48239. 313/537-3500. **Contact:** Personnel Department. **Description:** A manufacturer and distributor of metal stampings. **Employees:** 200.

ALPHA BOLT COMPANY
1524 East 14 Mile Road, Madison Heights MI 48071. 313/585-6050. **Contact:** Nancy Philypo, Personnel Director. **Description:** Engaged in the manufacture of bolts, nuts, and screws.

AMBASSADOR STEEL COMPANY INC.
1469 East Atwater, Detroit MI 48207. 313/259-6600. **Contact:** Office Manager. **Description:** Detroit area metal service centers and steel warehouses. **Employees:** 50.

ARMADA CORPORATION
600 Buhl Building, Detroit MI 48226. 313/963-3100. **Contact:** Personnel Department. **Description:** Engaged in the rolling, drawing, and extrusion of nonferrous metals as well as the manufacture of heating elements and spark plug wire. **Employees:** 800.

ASSOCIATED SPRING
1445 Barnes Court, Saline MI 48178. 313/429-2022. **Contact:** Tim Welcer, Personnel Director. **Description:** Engaged in the manufacture of metal work. **Employees:** 300.

BARFIELD MANUFACTURING COMPANY
800 Lowell, Ypsilanti MI 48197. 313/483-5070. **Contact:** Yvonne Hambright, Personnel Director. **Description:** An area manufacturer and distributor of bolts, nuts, screws, and nails. **Employees:** 300.

BARRONCAST INC.
P.O. Box 138, Oxford MI 48371. 313/628-4300. **Contact:** Kathy Mann, Personnel Director. **Description:** A leading area steel and casting investment company. **Employees:** 100.

BEAVER PRECISION PRODUCTS
1970 Big Beaver Road, P.O. Box 1199, Troy MI 48099. 313/689-3100. **Contact:** Anne Bayoff, Human Resources Administrator. **Description:** Engaged in the manufacture of ball-bearing screws and splines for aircraft/aerospace and machine tooling industries. **Corporate headquarters:** Toledo OH. **Common positions:** Aerospace Engineer; Industrial Engineer; Mechanical Engineer; Operations/Production Manager; Quality Control Supervisor; Manufacturing Engineer; Process Engineer; Production Supervisor. **Educational background sought:** Engineering. **Benefits:** medical, dental, and life insurance; tuition assistance; pension plan; disability coverage; savings plan.

BORG-WARNER AUTOMOTIVE
6700 18 1/2 Mile Road, Sterling Heights MI 48314. 313/739-6000. **Contact:** Personnel Department. **Description:** A company engaged in the manufacture of fabricated structural metals and a line of torque converters. **Employees:** 200.

CENTRAL FOUNDRY DIVISION/GENERAL MOTORS
77 West Center Street, Saginaw MI 48601-1292. 517/757-5000. **Contact:** Brian McClelland, Director of Personnel. **Description:** Engaged in the production of metal products, including grey iron, malleable iron, and aluminum. Parent company, General Motors, is a producer of cars, trucks, and buses sold worldwide; the firm has 152 facilities operating in 26 states and 93 cities in the

United States and 13 plants in Canada, and also has assembly, manufacturing, distribution, sales, or warehousing operations in 37 other countries.

COMMONWEALTH INDUSTRIES
5900 Commonwealth, Detroit MI 48208. 313/872-7900. **Contact:** Personnel Department. **Description:** A Detroit area company engaged in the heat treatment of metal parts. **Employees:** 100.

COPPER AND BRASS SALES, INC.
17401 Ten Mile Road, East Detroit MI 48021. 313/775-7710. **Contact:** Mary Ellen Goodrow, Manager of Human Resources Department. **Description:** A national chain of non-ferrous metals service centers. **Common positions:** Accountant; Blue-Collar Worker Supervisor; Buyer; Computer Programmer; Credit Manager; Operations/Production Manager; Purchasing Agent; Quality Control Supervisor; Sales Representative; Systems Analyst. **Educational backgrounds sought:** Accounting; Business Administration; Computer Science; Marketing. **Benefits:** medical, dental, and life insurance; tuition assistance; disability coverage; profit sharing; savings plan. **Corporate headquarters:** This location.

COPPER AND BRASS SALES/DETROIT DIVISION
6555 East Davison, Detroit MI 48212. 313/365-7700. **Contact:** Ginger Schrader, Personnel Director. **Description:** A Detroit metal service center which distributes non-ferrous metals. **Employees:** 200.

DALE INDUSTRIES INC.
6455 Kingsley, Dearborn MI 48126. 313/846-9400. **Contact:** Jim Costello, Personnel Director. **Description:** A Detroit company engaged in the manufacture of sheet metal. **Employees:** 100.

DETROIT STOKER COMPANY
1510 East First Street, P.O. Box 732, Monroe MI 48161. 313/241-9500. **Contact:** Al Miller, Personnel Director. **Description:** An area manufacturer of fabricated plate work. **Employees:** 300.

DODGE CITY/WARREN STAMPING DIVISION
P.O. Box 1119, Detroit MI 48091. 313/497-3630. **Contact:** Personnel Department. **Description:** A major Detroit manufacturer and distributor of metal auto stampings. **Employees:** 3,200.

DUNDEE CASTINGS COMPANY
500 Ypsilanti, Dundee MI 48131. 313/529-2455. **Contact:** Patricia Bradley, Personnel Director. **Description:** A manufacturer of aluminum castings; one of Detroit's largest foundries. **Employees:** 100.

G.B. DUPONT COMPANY
500 West Long Lake, Troy MI 48098. 313/879-0200. **Contact:** Personnel Department. **Description:** Engaged in the manufacture of bolts, nuts, screws, and cold heading fasteners for the automobile industry. **Employees:** 300.

EMPIRE STEEL PRODUCTS
2050 Morrissey, Warren MI 48091. 313/756-6600. **Contact:** Sue Meyer, Personnel Director. **Description:** A leading area metal service center which cuts and distributes steel. **Employees:** 100.

EQUIPMENT MANUFACTURING INC.
21550 Hoover, P.O. Box 748, Warren MI 48090. 313/755-6600. **Contact:** Andrew Bobincheck, Personnel Director. **Description:** Engaged in the manufacture of fabricated metal products including material handling racks. **Employees:** 300.

EUGENE WELDING COMPANY
P.O. Box 249, Marysville MI 48040. 313/364-7421. **Contact:** Don Wrench, Personnel Director. **Description:** Engaged in the manufacture of fabricated structural metal products. **Employees:** 200.

FERROUS PROCESSING & TRADING COMPANY
9100 John Kronk, Detroit MI 48210. 313/582-2910. **Contact:** Gary Schier, Controller. **Description:** An area scrap metal processor. **Employees:** 100.

FITZSIMONS MANUFACTURING COMPANY
3775 East Outer Drive, Detroit MI 48234. 313/891-4800. **Contact:** Personnel Director. **Description:** Engaged in the manufacture of fabricated pipe and fittings. **Employees:** 600.

GENERAL DIE CASTING COMPANY
10750 Capital Avenue, Oak Park MI 48237-3104. 313/548-5555. **Contact:** Personnel Department. **Description:** Engaged in the manufacture of brass, bronze, and copper castings. **Employees:** 200.

GENERAL DYNAMICS/LAND SYSTEMS DIVISION
P.O. Box 2072, Warren MI 48090-2072. 313/825-4000. **Contact:** Human Resources/Professional Staffing. **Description:** Manufactures and assembles the MIAI Main Battle Tank for the U.S. Army. A division of General Dynamics Corporation. Products of other General Dynamics divisions include the F-16 aircraft, the Trident nuclear submarine, and the Stinger shoulder-launch missile. Experienced hires only. **Common positions:** Accountant; Buyer; Draftsperson; Electrical Engineer; Industrial Engineer; Mechanical Engineer; Metallurgical Engineer; Financial Analyst; Personnel and Labor Relations Specialist; Systems Analyst; Technical Writer/Editor. **Educational backgrounds sought:** Accounting; Engineering; Finance; Physics. **Benefits:** medical, dental, and life insurance; pension plan; tuition assistance; disability coverage; employee discounts; savings plan. **Corporate headquarters:** St. Louis MO. **Parent**

Company: General Dynamics. **Operations at this facility:** divisional headquarters; research and development.

GREAT LAKES DIVISION OF NATIONAL STEEL
1 Quality Drive, Ecorse MI 48229. 313/297-2406. **Contact:** Gary S. Kadau, Manager/Human Resources Administration. **Description:** An area manufacturer of steel. **Employees:** 4,500. **Common positions:** Accountant; Blue-Collar Worker Supervisor; Buyer; Computer Programmer; Chemical Engineer; Electrical Engineer; Industrial Engineer; Mechanical Engineer; Metallurgical Engineer; Financial Analyst; Management Trainee; Personnel and Labor Relations Specialist; Purchasing Agent; Quality Control Supervisor; Systems Analyst. **Educational backgrounds sought:** Accounting; Business Administration; Computer Science; Engineering; Finance; Liberal Arts. **Benefits:** medical, dental, and life insurance; pension plan; tuition assistance; disability coverage; profit sharing. **Corporate headquarters:** Pittsburgh PA. **Parent company:** NII/NKK. Operations at this facility: divisional headquarters; manufacturing.

HERMES AUTOMOTIVE
2703 23rd Street, Detroit MI 48216. 313/897-6395. **Contact:** Sherry Thomas, Personnel Manager. **Description:** A major Detroit manufacturer of iron and steel forgings. **Employees:** 400.

HOSKINS MANUFACTURING COMPANY
600 Bunl Building, Detroit MI 48226. 313/963-3100. **Contact:** Paul F. Geene, Human Resources Director. **Description:** An area company engaged in the rolling, drawing, and extrusion of nonferrous metals. **Employees:** 366. **Common positions:** Blue-Collar Worker Supervisor; Buyer; Chemist; Claim Representative; Computer Programmer; Customer Service Representative; Metallurgical Engineer; Industrial Manager; Personnel and Labor Relations Specialist; Purchasing Agent; Quality Controller; Sales Representative; Transportation and Traffic Specialist. **Special programs:** training programs. **Benefits:** medical, dental, and life insurance; pension plan; disability coverage. **Corporate headquarters:** This location. **Parent company:** Armada Corporation. **Operations at this facility:** Manufacturing; Research and Development; Administration; Service; Sales. **Revenues (1991):** $50 million. **Projected hires for the next 12 months:** 1-2.

HURON VALLEY STEEL CORPORATION
41000 Huron River, Belleville MI 48111. 313/697-3400. **Contact:** Joe Beaudoin, Director of Health and Safety. **Description:** Engaged in the manufacture of metal products. **Employees:** 200.

INVERNESS CASTINGS GROUP
P.O. Box 160, Bangor MI 49013. 616/427-7901. **Contact:** Tom Maratea, Corporate Human Resources Director. **Description:** Engaged in zinc, magnesium, and aluminum die casting; and the machining, finishing, and electroplating of various metals. **Corporate headquarters:** This location.

Operations at this facility: manufacturing; administration; sales. **Common positions:** Accountant; Administrator; Blue-Collar Worker Supervisor; Computer Programmer; Draftsperson; Electrical Engineer; Industrial Engineer; Mechanical Engineer; Metallurgical Engineer; Department Manager; General Manager; Management Trainee; Operations/Production Manager; Personnel and Labor Relations Specialist; Purchasing Agent. **Educational backgrounds sought:** Accounting; Business Administration; Engineering; Finance. **Special programs:** Training programs; Internships. **Benefits:** medical, dental, and life insurance; tuition assistance; disability coverage; profit sharing; savings plan. **Parent company:** Inverness Castings Group, Inc. **Revenues (1991):** $80 million. **Employees:** 700. **Projected hires for the next 12 months:** 4-6.

JORGENSEN STEEL & ALUMINUM
13200 West 8 Mile Road, Oak Park Drive MI 48237. 313/547-9000. **Contact:** Personnel. **Description:** A Major Detroit area metal service center. **Employees:** 44. **Projected number of new hires for the next 12 months:** 2. **Common positions:** Sales Representative. **Educational backgrounds sought:** Business Administration; Marketing. **Special programs:** training programs. **Benefits:** medical insurance; dental insurance; pension plan; life insurance; tuition assistance; savings plan. **Other U.S. locations:** Ohio, California, Texas, Illinois, Colorado, Minnesota, Washington, Oklahoma, Missouri, New York. **Operations at this facility:** manufacturing; service; sales. **Revenues (1991):** $14 million. **Corporate headquarters:** Brea, California. **Parent company:** Earle M. Jorgensen Co. **Operations at this facility:** manufacturing; service; sales.

KASLE STEEL CORPORATION
4343 Wyoming Avenue, Dearborn MI 48126. 313/943-2500. **Contact:** David Yates, Personnel Director. **Description:** The corporate office for a chain of metal service centers. **Employees:** 400.

KENWAL PRODUCTS CORPORATION
9301 Central Avenue, Detroit MI 48204. 313/933-4362. **Contact:** Personnel Department. **Description:** The corporate office for a chain of metal service centers. **Employees:** 100.

LINCOLN BRASSWORKS INC.
2051 Rosa Parks, Detroit MI 48216. 313/961-9729. **Contact:** Bernadette Helkowski, Personnel Director. **Description:** Engaged in the manufacture of valve and pipe fittings. **Employees:** 300.

MNP CORPORATION
P.O. Box 189002, Utica MI 48318. 313/254-1320. **Contact:** Barbara Lepla, Personnel Director. **Description:** A leading Southeastern Michigan manufacturer of bolts, nuts, and screws. **Employees:** 400.

MACHINING ENTERPRISES
11400 Toepfer, Warren MI 48089. 313/755-3180. **Contact:** Personnel Department. **Description:** A leading area manufacturer of fabricated metal products. **Employees:** 500.

MANUFACTURERS PRODUCTS COMPANY
26020 Sherwood, Warren MI 48091. 313/961-4034. **Contact:** Personnel Department. Description: A leading area manufacturer of metal stampings. **Employees:** 100.

McLOUTH STEEL
AN EMPLOYEE OWNED COMPANY
1650 West Jefferson Avenue, Trenton MI 48183. 313/246-4023. **Contact:** Mr. Gerald Williams, Administrator, Personnel Services. **Description:** A Southeastern Michigan integrated steel mill that produces hot-rolled coils, cold-rolled sheet and strip steel. **Common positions:** Accountant; Blue-Collar Worker Supervisor; Buyer; Computer Programmer; Electrical Engineer; Mechanical Engineer; Metallurgical Engineer; Financial Analyst; Purchasing Agent; Sales Representative; Statistician; Systems Analyst. **Educational backgrounds sought:** Computer Science; Engineering; Marketing. **Benefits:** medical insurance; dental insurance; pension plan; life insurance; tuition assistance; disability coverage; profit sharing; savings plan; ESOP. **Operations at this facility:** manufacturing; administration; service; sales. **Revenues (1991):** $400 million. **Employees:** 1,650. **Projected number of new hires for the next 12 months:** 20.

MICHIGAN RIVET CORPORATION
13201 Stephens Road, Warren MI 48042. 313/754-5100. **Contact:** Ed Manzo, Director of Personnel. **Description:** A company engaged in the manufacture of bolts, nuts, and screws. **Employees:** 400.

MILFORD FABRICATING
19200 Glendale, Detroit MI 48223. 313/272-8400. **Contact:** Ron Kardynski, Director of Personnel. **Description:** A local area company engaged in the manufacture of metal stampings. **Employees:** 400.

MINKIN CHANDLER CORPORATION
13501 Sanders Avenue, Detroit MI 48217. 313/843-5900. **Contact:** Personnel. **Description:** A metropolitan Detroit scrap and waste metal company. **Employees:** 100.

A.B. MYR SHEET METAL INDUSTRIES
39635 Detroit Industrial Freeway, Belleville MI 48111. 313/941-2200. **Contact:** Mr. Stanis, Personnel Director. **Description:** Engaged in the manufacture of sheet metal. **Employees:** 300.

NEW HUDSON CORPORATION
57077 Pontiac Trail, New Hudson MI 48165. 313/437-1701. **Contact:** Lynn Seamark, Personnel Director. **Description:** An area company engaged in the manufacture of metal roll products. **Employees:** 50.

NUMATICS INC.
1450 North Milford, Highland MI 48357-4560. 313/887-4111. **Contact:** Larry Strauss, Personnel Director. **Description:** Engaged in the manufacture of valve and pipe fittings. **Employees:** 400.

PEERLESS STEEL COMPANY
2450 Austin, Troy MI 48083. 313/528-3200. **Contact:** Duane Douglas, Personnel Manager. **Description:** A Southeastern Michigan metal service center which stores and distributes steel. **Employees:** 100.

QUANEX TUBE GROUP
17177 North Laurel Park Drive, Suite 307, Livonia MI 48152. 313/591-2211. **Contact: Contact:** Lois Dershem, Personnel. **Description:** A leading area manufacturer of steel pipe and tubing. **Employees:** 400.

SAMUEL WHITTAR INC.
20001 Sherwood Avenue, Detroit MI 48234. 313/893-5000. **Contact:** Rita Humphry, Personnel Director. **Description:** A major Detroit-based metal fabricating company. **Employees:** 400.

SENNETT STEEL CORPORATION
1200 East 14 Mile Road, Madison Heights MI 48071. 313/585-6040. **Contact:** Mary Sobota, Human Resources. **Description:** A regional service center engaged in the storage and wholesale distribution of steel. **Employees:** 200. **Common positions:** Customer Service Representative; Sales Representative. **Educational backgrounds sought:** Business Administration; Finance; Marketing. **Benefits:** medical insurance; disability coverage; profit sharing. **Corporate headquarters:** This location. **Operations at this facility:** administration; service; sales.

TRW STEERING & SUSPENSION DIV.
34201 Van Dyke Avenue, Sterling Heights MI 48312. 313/977-1103. **Contact:** Richard Nichols, Human Resources Manager. **Description:** Produces steering linkage, suspension ball joints and assemblies; and manual and power rack and pinion steering gears. Parent company, TRW, is a diversified technology firm with operations in electronics and space systems, car and truck equipment for both original equipment manufacturers and the replacement market, and a wide variety of industrial and energy components, including aircraft parts, welding systems, and electromechanical assemblies. **Listed on:** New York Stock Exchange. **Corporate headquarters:** Cleveland, OH.

THETFORD CORPORATION
P.O. Box 1285, Ann Arbor MI 48106. 313/769-6000. **Contact:** Jack Quigley, Personnel Director. **Description:** Engaged in the manufacture of enameled iron. **Employees:** 300.

TRI-MARK METAL CORPORATION
10106 Grinnell, Detroit MI 48213-1192. 313/925-4900. **Contact:** Sylvia Kalinowski, Office Manager. **Description:** A major Detroit company engaged in sheet metal work. **Employees:** 100.

U.S. BROACH & MACHINE COMPANY
P.O. Box 1127, Jackson MI 49204. 517/787-3791. **Contact:** Personnel Department. **Description:** A Detroit-based manufacturer of metal working machinery. **Employees:** 100.

UNISTRUCT DIVERSIFIED PRODUCTS
35660 Clinton Street, Wayne MI 48184. 313/721-4040. **Contact:** Personnel Department. **Description:** A area manufacturer of fabricated structural metal products. **Employees:** 1,100.

VAN PELT CORPORATION
P.O. Box 12579, Detroit MI 48212. 313/365-3600. **Contact:** Ruth Rosteck, Personnel Director. **Description:** A metropolitan Detroit metal service center engaged in the storage and wholesale distribution of steel. **Employees:** 200.

WA-KAY INDUSTRIES INC.
17403 Mount Elliott Avenue, Detroit MI 48212. 313/891-6262. **Contact:** Thomas R. Walton, President. **Description:** Engaged in the manufacture of primary metal products. **Employees:** 100.

WALKER WIRE AND STEEL COMPANY
660 East 10 Mile Road, Ferndale MI 48220. 313/399-4800. **Contact:** Personnel Department. **Description:** An area manufacturer of steel and wire drawing. **Employees:** 100.

WINSTON STEEL PROCESSING
2700 West Warren, Detroit MI 48208. 313/894-3300. **Contact:** Personnel Director. **Description:** A major Detroit metal service center engaged in the distribution of steel.

WOLVERINE BRONZE COMPANY
28178 Hayes Road, Roseville MI 48066. 313/776-8180. **Contact:** Eugene Piesko, Personnel Director. **Description:** An area company engaged in the manufacture of nonferrous foundries. **Employees:** 100.

Additional large employers: 250+

STEEL WORKS, BLAST FURNACES (INCLUDING COKE OVENS), AND ROLLING MILLS

Acme Steel Co
46835 Bettyhill Ln, Plymouth MI 48170-3070. 313/453-7820. Employs: 250-499.

Hilti Steel Ind Div
3001 Miller Rd, Dearborn MI 48120-1455. 313/271-3953. Employs: 250-499.

Macsteel Sales Office
1172 Yorkshire Rd, Grosse Pointe MI 48230-1436. 313/885-7556. Employs: 250-499.

Sawhill Tubular Div Cyclops
31586 Schoolcraft Rd, Livonia MI 48150-1805. 313/261-2900. Employs: 250-499.

ELECTROMETALLURGICAL PRODUCTS, EXCEPT STEEL

Teleflex Inc
266 Indl Dr, Hillsdale MI 49242. 517/439-1541. Employs: 250-499.

STEEL WIREDRAWING AND STEEL NAILS AND SPIKES

Mc Louth Steel
28000 River Rd, Rockwood MI 48173. 313/285-1200. Employs: 250-499.

Steel & Wire Division M N P Corp
44225 Utica Rd, Utica MI 48317-5464. 313/254-9300. Employs: 250-499.

STEEL PIPE AND TUBES

Huron Inc
6554 Lakeshore Rd, Lexington MI 48450-9763. 313/359-5344. Employs: 250-499.

ITT Higbie Manufacturing Co
4th & Water Sts, Rochester MI 48307. 313/650-0990. Employs: 500-999.

Quanex Corp
400 McMunn St, South Lyon MI 48178-1392. 313/486-0100. Employs: 250-499.

GRAY AND DUCTILE IRON FOUNDRIES

CMI International Inc
30333 Southfield Rd, Southfield MI 48076-1352. 313/642-9450. Employs: 500-999.

Margate Ventures Inc
58391 Main Blvd, New Haven MI 48048. 313/749-5111. Employs: 250-499.

GRAY AND DUCTILE IRON FOUNDRIES

Harvard Inds Inc
601 N Albion St, Albion MI 49224-1218. 517/629-2141. Employs: 500-999.

ALUMINUM EXTRUDED PRODUCTS

Fayette Tubular Products Inc
1835 Technology Dr, Troy MI 48083-4244. 313/589-7710. Employs: 500-999.

ROLLING DRAWING AND EXTRUDING OF NONFERROUS METALS, EXCEPT COPPER AND ALUMINUM

Braun Engineering
19001 Glendale St, Detroit MI 48223-3423. 313/270-1700. Employs: 250-499.

Extruded Metals
302 Ashfield St, Belding MI 48809-1524. 616/794-1200. Employs: 250-499.

Metalloy Foundry Co
103 W Main St, Hudson MI 49247-1022. 517/448-2521. Employs: 250-499.

MISC. PRIMARY METAL PRODUCTS

Federal-Mogul Corp
8111 Middlebelt Rd, Romulus MI 48174-2134. 313/326-9550. Employs: 250-499.

ICM/Krebsoge
38701 Seven Mile Rd, Livonia MI 48152-1058. 313/462-3840. Employs: 500-999.

North Star Steel Co
3000 E Front St, Monroe MI 48161-1973. 313/243-2446. Employs: 250-499.

Kent-Moore Tool
1600 Executive Dr, Jackson MI 49203-3469. 517/788-6210. Employs: 250-499.

MISC. HARDWARE

G M Corp
1450 E Beecher St, Adrian MI 49221-3562. 517/265-4222. Employs: 1000+.

Huron Products Corp
30600 Commerce Blvd, New Haven MI 48048. 313/749-9513. Employs: 250-499.

Huron St Clair Inc/Plant 2
1721 Dove Rd, Port Huron MI 48060-3820. 313/987-2670. Employs: 250-499.

I T T Automotive
1 Park Ave, Elsie MI 48831. 517/862-4293. Employs: 250-499.

Mueller Brass Co
2199 Lapeer Av, Port Huron MI 48060-4155. 313/987-7770. Employs: 1000+.

HEATING EQUIPMENT, EXCEPT ELECTRIC AND WARM AIR FURNACES

Brass-Craft Manufacturing Co
100 Galleria Office Ctr, Southfield MI 48034. 313/827-1100. Employs: 500-999.

Lincoln Brass Works Inc
2051 Rosa Parks Blvd, Detroit MI 48216-1556. 313/961-9729. Employs: 250-499.

SHEET METAL WORK

Carefree Aluminum Products Inc
1023 Reynolds Rd, Charlotte MI 48813-2017. 517/543-0430. Employs: 250-499.

Modern Prototype Co
2927 Elliott Ave, Troy MI 48083-4640. 313/585-0120. Employs: 250-499.

Metalink Inc
302 Ashfield St, Belding MI 48809-1524. 313/763-1200. Employs: 500-999.

M & S Manufacturing Co
550 E Main St, Hudson MI 49247-9535. 517/448-2026. Employs: 250-499.

BELTS, NUTS, SCREWS, RIVETS, AND WASHERS

Beaver Precision Products
1970 E Big Beaver Rd, Troy MI 48083-2021. 313/689-3100. Employs: 250-499.

Federal Screw Works
2400 Buhl Building, Detroit MI 48226. 313/963-2323. Employs: 250-499.

Trimas Corp
315 E Eisenhower Pkwy, Ann Arbor MI 48108-3329. 313/747-7025. Employs: 500-999.

IRON AND STEEL FORGINGS

Melling Forging Division
1709 Thompson St, Lansing MI 48906-4160. 517/482-0791. Employs: 250-499.

AUTOMOTIVE STAMPINGS

Aetna Inds
24331 Sherwood Ave, Center Line MI 48015-1060. 313/759-2200. Employs: 500-999.

Chrysler Corp/Sterling Stamp
35777 Van Dyke Rd, Sterling Hts MI 48312-3565. 313/977-4757. Employs: 1000+.

Chrysler Corp/Warren Stamping
22800 Mound Rd, Warren MI 48091-5401. 313/497-3622. Employs: 1000+.

Chrysler Sterling Stamping Plant
35777 Vandyke, Sterling Heights MI 48077. 313/977-4570. Employs: 1000+.

De Couper Inds Inc
21535 Hoover Rd, Warren MI 48089-3159. 313/755-4488. Employs: 250-499.

Ford Motor/Woodhaven Stamping
20900 West Rd, Trenton MI 48183-3352. 313/671-7131. Employs: 1000+.

General Products Delaware Corp
2400 E South St, Jackson MI 49201-8713. 517/764-2730. Employs: 250-499.

Hawthorne Metal Products Co
4336 Coolidge Rd, Royal Oak MI 48073-1640. 313/549-3800. Employs: 250-499.

ITT Hancock
2300 E Ganson St, Jackson MI 49202-3770. 517/784-3161. Employs: 500-999.

Lobdell-Emery Manufacturing Co
1325 E Superior St, Alma MI 48801-2659. 517/463-3151. Employs: 500-999.

Riverside International
24901 Northwestern Hwy Ste 511, Southfield MI 48075-2209. 313/987-2470. Employs: 250-499.

U S Manufacturing Corp
30855 Little Mack Ave, Roseville MI 48066-1758. 313/293-8744. Employs: 500-999.

MISC. METAL STAMPINGS

Active Tool & Manufacturing
32901 Gratiot Ave, Roseville MI 48066-1150. 313/294-9220. Employs: 250-499.

Budd Co/Detroit Stamping Plant
12141 Charlevoix St, Detroit MI 48215-2438. 313/823-9100. Employs: 1000+.

Carron & Co
26700 Princeton Ave, Inkster MI 48141-2310. 313/274-2300. Employs: 250-499.

Davis Tool & Engineering Co
19250 Plymouth Rd, Detroit MI 48228-1341. 313/835-6000. Employs: 250-499.

L & W Engineering Co Inc/Plant 2
6201 Haggerty Rd, Belleville MI 48111-1137. 313/397-2212. Employs: 500-999.

Lear Seating Inc
4600 Nancy St, Detroit MI 48212-1213. 313/893-3000. Employs: 250-499.

Lenawee Stamping Corp
1200 E Chicago Blvd, Tecumseh MI 49286-9674. 517/423-2400. Employs: 250-499.

M P I International
2129 Austin Ave, Rochester MI 48309-3668. 313/853-9010. Employs: 250-499.

R J Tower Corporation
P O Box 670, Greenville MI 48838-0670. 616/754-2211. Employs: 250-499.

Trumark Inc
1820 Sunset Ave, Lansing MI 48917-1811. 517/482-0795. Employs: 250-499.

Waggoner Corp
1400 Rochester Rd, Troy MI 48083-6014. 313/588-2121. Employs: 250-499.

Western Wheel Howell
2440 W Highland Rd, Howell MI 48843-8625. 517/546-3441. Employs: 250-499.

ELECTROPLATING, PLATING, POLISHING, ANODIZING AND COLORING

Crown Group Inc
2111 Walter Reuther Dr, Warren MI 48091-6108. 313/575-9800. Employs: 500-999.

G M Corp
2860 Clark St, Detroit MI 48210. 313/554-6112. Employs: 1000+.

MISC. COATING, ENGRAVING AND ALLIED SERVICES

Chrysler Corp/Parts Div
840 Huron Blvd, Marysville MI 48040-1462. 313/984-7800. Employs: 250-499.

E I Du Pont De Nemours & Co
400 Groesbeck Hwy, Mount Clemens MI 48043-1553. 313/468-9000. Employs: 250-499.

MISC. ORDNANCE AND ACCESSORIES

Cadillac Gage
25760 Groesbeck Hwy, Warren MI 48089-1544. 313/777-7100. Employs: 250-499.

FLUID POWER VALVES AND HOSE FITTINGS

Savair Products Co
33200 Freeway Dr, St Clair Shrs MI 48082-1071. 313/296-7390. Employs: 250-499.

MISC. VALVES AND PIPE FITTINGS

Kelsey-Hayes Co
101 Oak St, Milford MI 48381-1543. 313/685-1573. Employs: 250-499.

Mac Valves Inc
30569 Beck Rd, Wixom MI 48393-2842. 313/624-7700. Employs: 250-499.

CROWNS AND CLOSURE

Warren Div/Emhart Corp
49201 N Gratiot Ave, Clinton Twp MI 48035-4039.
313/949-0440. Employs: 500-999.

FABRICATED PIPE AND PIPE FITTINGS

Acutus Industries Inc
P O Box 506, Pontiac MI 48056. 313/674-4861. Employs:
250-499.

Apollo Industries Inc
34364 Goddard Rd, Romulus MI 48174-3404. 313/941-
0770. Employs: 250-499.

Douglas & Lomason Co
24600 Hallwood Ct, Farmington MI 48335-1603. 313/478-
7800. Employs: 1000+.

Hitachi Magnetics Corp
7800 Neff Rd, Edmore MI 48829-9345. 517/427-5151.
Employs: 500-999.

METAL SERVICE CENTERS AND OFFICES

Copper & Brass Sales Inc
6555 E Davison St, Detroit MI 48212-1455. 313/365-7700.
Employs: 250-499.

Copper & Brass Sales Inc

17401 Ten Mile Rd, East Detroit MI 48021-1256. 313/755-
7710. Employs: 1000+.

Kasle Steel Corp
PO Box 33536, Detroit MI 48232-5536. 313/943-2500.
Employs: 250-499.

Namasco Inc
30360 Edison Dr, Roseville MI 48066-1543. 313/779-
7950. Employs: 250-499.

U S Manufacturing Corp
2401 16th St, Port Huron MI 48060-6402. 313/984-4145.
Employs: 250-499.

Aluminum Product Division Hoover Group
530 W Lovett St, Charlotte MI 48813-1477. 517/543-2010.
Employs: 500-999.

Bundy Corporation
12345 E 9 Mile Rd, Warren MI 48089-2614. 313/758-
4511. Employs: 500-999.

SCRAP AND WASTE MATERIALS

The Oxford Energy Co
330 Town Center Dr, Dearborn MI 48126-2711. 313/436-
9595. Employs: 250-499.

Handleman Co
500 Kirts Blvd, Troy MI 48084-5225. 313/362-4400.
Employs: 1000+.

Additional small to medium sized employers: 50-249:

**STEEL WORKS, BLAST FURNACES (INCLUDING
COKE OVENS), AND ROLLING MILLS**

Allegheny Ludlum Steel
999 Haynes St, Birmingham MI 48009-6775. 313/645-
2840. Employs: 50-99.

American Steel Corp
7170 E McNichols Rd, Detroit MI 48212-2037. 313/365-
7000. Employs: 100-249.

Armco Advanced Materials Corp
5455 Corporate Dr, Troy MI 48098-2620. 313/641-7993.
Employs: 50-99.

Armco Steel Co LP
5455 Corporate Dr, Troy MI 48098-2620. 313/641-7595.
Employs: 50-99.

Bethlehem Steel Corporation
26999 Central Park Blvd, Southfield MI 48076-4174.
313/353-3000. Employs: 50-99.

Bowman Metal Deck
6016 W Maple Rd, W Bloomfield MI 48322-4411.
313/737-5755. Employs: 50-99.

Citisteel USA
3221 Burberry Ct, Saline MI 48176-9011. 313/429-3788.
Employs: 100-249.

Detroit Coke Corp
7819 W Jefferson Ave, Detroit MI 48209-2857. 313/842-
6222. Employs: 100-249.

Federal Forge Inc
2807 S Logan St, Lansing MI 48910-2653. 517/393-5300.
Employs: 100-249.

Flat Rock Metal Inc
26601 W Huron River Dr, Flat Rock MI 48134-1134.
313/782-4454. Employs: 50-99.

Georgetown Unimetal Sales

2145 Crooks Rd, Troy MI 48084-5318. 313/649-1699.
Employs: 50-99.

Global International Inc
8080 Ortonville Rd, Clarkston MI 48348-4456. 313/620-
1821. Employs: 50-99.

Hamilton Specialty Bar Division
5179 Daniel Dr, Brighton MI 48116-9036. 313/227-9770.
Employs: 50-99.

Heidtman Steel Products Inc
12301 Hubbell St, Detroit MI 48227-2777. 313/838-5000.
Employs: 50-99.

Hitachi Metals America
1732 Kilburn Rd N, Rochester MI 48306-3034. 313/477-
2500. Employs: 50-99.

J & L Specialty Products Corp
330 S Livernois Ave, Detroit MI 48209-3071. 313/843-
4800. Employs: 100-249.

Macsteel
3100 Brooklyn Rd, Jackson MI 49203-4809. 517/764-
0311. Employs: 100-249.

North American Forging Tech
2321 Water St, Port Huron MI 48060-2485. 313/984-3254.
Employs: 100-249.

Ovako Steel Inc
3907 Reseda Rd, Waterford MI 48329-2558. 313/674-
0630. Employs: 50-99.

Plymouth Steel Corp
21750 Hoover Rd, Warren MI 48089-2504. 313/755-7620.
Employs: 100-249.

Republic Engineered Steels Inc
457 Pinehurst, W Bloomfield MI 48322. 313/375-2080.
Employs: 50-99.

Republic Engineered Steel
30823 Misty Dr, Farmington MI 48336. 313/474-7010.
Employs: 50-99.

Shane Steel Processing Inc
17495 Malyn Blvd, Fraser MI 48026-1634. 313/296-1990.
Employs: 100-249.

Thompson Steel Co Inc
27840 Groesbeck Hwy, Roseville MI 48066-2757.
313/526-7110. Employs: 50-99.

U S S Kobe Steel Co
171 Douglas Dr, Bloomfield MI 48304-1631. 313/334-
5880. Employs: 50-99.

W S Lantz Corp
19451 Sherwood St, Detroit MI 48234-2820. 313/368-
1400. Employs: 50-99.

Warren Consolidated Ind Inc
2129 Glencoe Hills Dr, Ann Arbor MI 48108-1041.
313/677-0870. Employs: 100-249.

STEEL WIREDRAWING AND STEEL NAILS AND SPIKES

Kirkhof/Flex-Cable
1875 Stephenson Hwy, Troy MI 48083-2150. 313/689-
4666. Employs: 50-99.

COLD-ROLLED STEEL, SHEET, STRIP AND BARS

Almetals Inc
51035 Grand River Ave, Wixom MI 48393-3329. 313/348-
7722. Employs: 50-99.

Alpha and Omega Leasing Inc
1301 Silman St, Ferndale MI 48220-2600. 313/548-7510.
Employs: 50-99.

B & G Drawing
25655 Sherwood Ave, Warren MI 48091-4157. 313/754-
5261. Employs: 50-99.

B R Ellwanger Co Inc
345 W Square Lake Rd, Troy MI 48098-2969. 313/879-
1616. Employs: 50-99.

Bar Processing Corp
255 S Woodward Ave, Birmingham MI 48009-6182.
313/645-6504. Employs: 50-99.

Barry Steel Corp
10255 Lyndon St, Detroit MI 48238-2266. 313/834-8600.
Employs: 50-99.

Barsteel Corp
29119 Van Laan Dr, Warren MI 48092-2237. 313/892-
8000. Employs: 50-99.

Chappell Steel Co Inc
3545 Scotn, Detroit MI 48210-3159. 313/897-6670.
Employs: 100-249.

City Steel Processing Inc
11111 French Rd, Detroit MI 48234-4041. 313/5711000.
Employs: 100-249.

Detroit Strip Div Cyclops
1025 S Oakwood, Detroit MI 48217-1310. 313/297-9800.
Employs: 100-249.

Godwin Steel Processing Co
6660 Mount Elliott St, Detroit MI 48211-2437. 313/925-
0150. Employs: 100-249.

Header Products Inc
11850 Wayne Rd, Romulus MI 48174-1462. 313/941-
2220. Employs: 100-249.

Heidtman Steel Products

19800 Gibraltar, Rockwood MI 48173. 313/675-0770.
Employs: 50-99.

Hercules Drawn Steel Corp
38901 Amrhein Rd, Livonia MI 48150-1042. 313/464-
4454. Employs: 50-99.

Lakeland Steel Co
6450 E McNichols Rd, Detroit MI 48212-2026. 313/891-
6600. Employs: 100-249.

Mark David Steel Co
2500 22nd St, Detroit MI 48216-1076. 313/895-5500.
Employs: 100-249.

National Metal Processing
3105 Beaufait St, Detroit MI 48207-2401. 313/571-4100.
Employs: 50-99.

Parlove & Associates
1005 Troy Ct, Troy MI 48083-2784. 313/583-1145.
Employs: 50-99.

Quality Steel Service Inc
13712 Elmira St, Detroit MI 48227-3021. 313/834-2500.
Employs: 100-249.

R & M Shearing and Processing Inc
4086 Michigan Ave, Detroit MI 48210-3261. 313/896-
4421. Employs: 100-249.

Samuel Son & Co Detroit Inc
12600 Arnold, Redford MI 48239-2637. 313/538-9373.
Employs: 100-249.

Set Steel Inc
6930 Kingsley St, Dearborn MI 48126-1941. 313/945-
9382. Employs: 100-249.

Thyssen Steel
5151 Wesson St, Detroit MI 48210-1777. 313/894-4800.
Employs: 100-249.

Vogue Industries Inc
16150 Hubbell St, Detroit MI 48235-4025. 313/838-8520.
Employs: 100-249.

STEEL PIPE AND TUBES

ITT Igbie Manufacturing Co
E 4th and Water St, Columbus MI 48063. 313/651-5300.
Employs: 100-249.

James Steel & Tube
29774 Stephenson Hwy, Madison Hts MI 48071-2340.
313/547-4200. Employs: 50-99.

W A Kates Co
965 Wanda St, Ferndale MI 48220-2620. 313/398-1600.
Employs: 50-99.

GRAY AND DUCTILE IRON FOUNDRIES

Alloy Investment Castings Corp
3085 Joyce St, Burton MI 48529-1421. 313/742-6550.
Employs: 50-99.

Amcast Industrial Corporation
26400 Lahser Rd, Southfield MI 48034-2624. 313/352-
1213. Employs: 50-99.

Casting & Machining Services
1637 E Grand Blvd, Detroit MI 48211-3143. 313/925-
9408. Employs: 50-99.

Columbus Foundries Inc
1520 N Woodward Av, Bloomfield MI 48304-2860.
313/338-2323. Employs: 50-99.

F S I Inc
2480 N Dixie Hwy, Monroe MI 48161-5213. 313/289-
2260. Employs: 50-99.

Gold Star Industries Inc
37915 Commerce Dr, Sterling Hts MI 48312-1003.
313/795-5025. Employs: 50-99.

Grede Foundries Inc
1637 W Big Beaver Rd, Troy MI 48084-3540. 313/649-1155. Employs: 50-99.

Hydraulic Tubes & Fittings Inc
3578 S Van Dyke Rd, Almont MI 48003-8039. 313/798-8567. Employs: 50-99.

Martin Foundries Co Inc
25401 W Outer Dr, Melvindale MI 48122-1941. 313/383-7500. Employs: 50-99.

Michigan Casting Corp
67780 Van Dyke, Romeo MI 48065. 313/752-5321. Employs: 50-99.

Motor & Machinery Castings Co
7742 W Davison Ave, Detroit MI 48238-3131. 313/933-0800. Employs: 50-99.

Rochester Manufacturing Co
300 South St Box 1940, Rochester MI 48307-2240. 313/652-2600. Employs: 100-249.

Temperform Corp
25425 Trans X Rd, Novi MI 48375-2445. 313/349-5230. Employs: 50-99.

United Foundries
109 Kenwood Rd, Grosse Pointe MI 48236-3608. 313/894-4900. Employs: 50-99.

Wisconsin Centrifugal Inc
9359 Hidden Lake Cir, Dexter MI 48130-9519. 313/426-2050. Employs: 100-249.

East Jordon Ironworks Inc
7300 Grand Ledge Hwy, Sunfield MI 48890-9776. 517/5667211. Employs: 100-249.

MALLEABLE IRON FOUNDRIES

J D Wilson Inc
18881 Sherwood St, Detroit MI 48234-2840. 313/892-1212. Employs: 50-99.

STEEL INVESTMENT FOUNDRIES

Casting Technology Inc
3828 Oakman Blvd, Detroit MI 48204-1119. 313/491-4500. Employs: 100-249.

Edens Investment Casting Inc
800 F W Moore Hwy, Saint Clair MI 48079. 313/329-9310. Employs: 50-99.

R L M Industries Inc
100 Hummer Lake Rd, Oxford MI 48371-2304. 313/628-5103. Employs: 50-99.

Steve The Geppert Co
1382 Forbes Dr, Bloomfield MI 48302-2715. 313/855-2099. Employs: 50-99.

V S X Corp
1750 Stephenson Hwy, Troy MI 48083-2147. 313/680-2400. Employs: 100-249.

MISCELLANEOUS STEEL FOUNDRIES

Advance Casting Technology
500 N Dixie Hwy, Monroe MI 48161-2566. 313/457-9010. Employs: 50-99.

Alpha Technology Corp
251 Mason Rd, Howell MI 48843-2533. 517/546-9700. Employs: 100-249.

Delray Steel Casting Inc
18900 Rialto Av, Melvindale MI 48122-1951. 313/386-7100. Employs: 50-99.

Diecast Corporation
522-24 Hupp Av, Jackson MI 49203. 517/788-6100. Employs: 100-249.

Eutectic Engineering Co
6350 E Davison St, Detroit MI 48212-1497. 313/892-2248. Employs: 50-99.

Sealed Power Corp Die Cast Div
205 N Grover Av, Alma MI 48801-2513. 517/463-6166. Employs: 100-249.

Simpson Industries Jackson
1801 Wildwood Ave, Jackson MI 49202-4044. 517/788-7880. Employs: 100-249.

PRIMARY PRODUCTION OF ALUMINUM

Hydro Aluminum Bohn
1607 E Maumee St, Adrian MI 49221-3585. 517/265-7141. Employs: 100-249.

PRIMARY SMELTING AND REFINING OF NONFERROUS METALS, EXCEPT COPPER AND ALUMINUM

Louis Padnos Iron & Metal Co
1900 W Willow St, Lansing MI 48917-1838. 517/372-6600. Employs: 100-249.

SECONDARY SMELTING AND REFINING OF NONFERROUS METALS

Arco Alloys Corp
1891 Trombly St, Detroit MI 48211-2127. 313/871-2680. Employs: 50-99.

Erwin Robinson Co
12821 Schaefer Hwy, Detroit MI 48227-3558. 313/837-5458. Employs: 100-249.

Sulzer Plasma Technik Inc
1972 Meijer Dr, Troy MI 48084-7143. 313/288-1200. Employs: 50-99.

ROLLING, DRAWING AND EXTRUDING OF COPPER

H & H Tube & Manufacturing Co
4000 Town Center, Southfield MI 48075-1410. 313/355-2500. Employs: 100-249.

Mehra Tube Inc
99 Wolfe Ln, Ortonville MI 48462-9094. 313/627-4972. Employs: 50-99.

ALUMINUM EXTRUDED PRODUCTS

Extruded Aluminum Corp
7200 Indl Dr, Belding MI 48809. 616/794-0300. Employs: 50-99.

Goodrich Manufacturing Co
8267 S State Rd, Goodrich MI 48438-9717. 313/636-2226. Employs: 50-99.

International Extrusions
5800 Venoy Rd, Garden City MI 48135-1655. 313/427-8700. Employs: 50-99.

Molloy Manufacturing
18450 15 Mile Rd, Fraser MI 48026-3460. 313/293-9000. Employs: 100-249.

S & H Fabricating & Engineering Inc
1020 Decker Rd, Walled Lake MI 48390-3218. 313/624-6300. Employs: 100-249.

ROLLING, DRAWING AND EXTRUDING OF NONFERROUS METALS, EXCEPT COPPER AND ALUMINUM

Anco-Tech Inc
2525 S Beech Daly St, Dearborn Hts MI 48125-1148.
313/274-0350. Employs: 50-99.

Grapentin Specialties
2798 S Van Dyke Rd, Imlay City MI 48444-9730.
313/724-0636. Employs: 50-99.

Titanium & Alloys Corp
21601 Hoover Rd, Warren MI 48089-3157. 313/755-1900.
Employs: 50-99.

Allan Miller Metal Sales
22515 Sunnydale St, St Clair Shrs MI 48081-2497.
313/777-9290. Employs: 50-99.

Hirsch Metals Corporation
29100 Northwestern Hwy, Southfield MI 48034-1046.
313/352-3148. Employs: 50-99.

Metal Merchants
737 Laguna Dr, Walled Lake MI 48390-2013. 313/669-2240. Employs: 50-99.

DRAWING AND INSULATING OF NONFERROUS WIRE

Energy Electric Cable Inc
270 Rex Blvd, Auburn Hills MI 48326-2953. 313/853-0500. Employs: 50-99.

Hoskins Manufacturing Co
10776 Hall Rd, Hamburg MI 48139. 313/231-1900.
Employs: 100-249.

Northern Wire & Cable Inc
1902 Northwood Dr, Troy MI 48084-5523. 313/244-8100.
Employs: 100-249.

ALUMINUM DIE-CASTINGS

Hackett Brass Foundry
1200 Lillibridge St, Detroit MI 48214-3227. 313/822-1214.
Employs: 50-99.

NONFERROUS DIE-CASTINGS, EXCEPT ALUMINUM

Cadmet Corp
20801 Ryan Rd, Warren MI 48091-4662. 313/754-6880.
Employs: 100-249.

Decker Manufacturing Corp
703 N Clark, Albion MI 49224-1455. 517/629-3955.
Employs: 100-249.

ALUMINUM FOUNDRIES

General Bearing Corp
30156 8 Mile Rd, Farmington MI 48336-5509. 313/478-1745. Employs: 50-99.

Sevakis Inds Inc
12693 Marlin Rd, Redford MI 48239-2765. 313/535-6740.
Employs: 50-99.

COPPER FOUNDRIES

Michigan Sintered Metals Inc
1525 W King St, Owosso MI 48867-2010. 517/725-5127.
Employs: 50-99.

Micro Mirror Corp
30210 W 8 Mile Rd, Farmington MI 48336-5510. 313/476-6600. Employs: 50-99.

NONFERROUS FOUNDRIES, EXCEPT ALUMINUM AND COPPER

Buckeye Products Corp
410 E Beecher St, Adrian MI 49221-3903. 517/265-8156.
Employs: 50-99.

Dentron Engineering
10044 Maryann, Madison Hts MI 48071. 313/348-5330.
Employs: 50-99.

I T T Lester Industries Inc
7243 Buckthorn St, W Bloomfield MI 48324-2513.
313/363-2700. Employs: 50-99.

Wolverine Die Cast Corp
22550 Nagel St, Warren MI 48089-2552. 313/757-1900.
Employs: 50-99.

METAL HEAT TREATING

Atmosphere Annealing Inc
1801 Bassett St, Lansing MI 48915-1567. 517/482-1374.
Employs: 50-99.

Diamond Heat Treating Co
5660 W Jefferson Ave, Detroit MI 48209-3116. 313/843-6570. Employs: 50-99.

Heat Treating Services Corp
217 Central Ave, Pontiac MI 48341-2924. 313/858-2230.
Employs: 50-99.

Induction Services Inc
24800 Mound Rd, Warren MI 48091-5334. 313/754-1640.
Employs: 50-99.

Industrial Steel Treating Co
613 Carroll St, Jackson MI 49202-3169. 517/787-6312.
Employs: 100-249.

Kee Services
25120 Easy St, Warren MI 48089-4129. 313/777-6377.
Employs: 50-99.

Lindberg Heat Treating Co
2127 W Willow St, Lansing MI 48917-1815. 517/487-4989. Employs: 50-99.

Machine Tool & Gear Inc
308 N Leroy St, Fenton MI 48430-2730. 313/750-9140.
Employs: 50-99.

Michigan Induction Inc
8468 Ronda Dr, Canton MI 48187-2002. 313/459-8514.
Employs: 50-99.

Solder Craft Inc
503 Amelia St, Plymouth MI 48170-1233. 313/453-6570.
Employs: 50-99.

Super Steel Treating Co
6227 Rinke Ave, Warren MI 48091-5355. 313/755-9140.
Employs: 50-99.

MISCELLANEOUS PRIMARY METAL PRODUCTS

Brazeway Incorporated
2711 E Maumee St, Adrian MI 49221-3534. 517/265-2121.
Employs: 100-249.

Commercial Steel Treating Corp
3290 W Big Beaver Rd Ste 315, Troy MI 48084-2910.
313/649-4179. Employs: 50-99.

Ervin Ind Inc Ervin Amasteel
915 Tabor St, Adrian MI 49221-3921. 517/265-6118.
Employs: 100-249.

Flint Steel Co
2610 N Dort Hwy, Flint MI 48506-2900. 313/234-4411.
Employs: 50-99.

Guardian Roll Form Inc
12980 Capital St, Oak Park MI 48237-3114. 313/548-5790.
Employs: 50-99.

L F Industries Lapeer Met Products
2610 N Dort Hwy, Flint MI 48506-2900. 313/238-2669.
Employs: 50-99.

L T C Roll & Engineering Co
23500 John Gorsuch Dr, Clinton Twp MI 48036-1215.
313/465-1023. Employs: 50-99.

Mac Steel
1 Jackson Sq Ste 500, Jackson MI 49201. 517/782-0415.
Employs: 50-99.

Mueller Brass Co
2409 Wills St, Marysville MI 48040-1979. 313/364-3760.
Employs: 50-99.

Roll-Tech
25224 Hoover Rd Apt 204, Warren MI 48089-1122.
313/776-8443. Employs: 50-99.

Wall Colmonoy Corp
30261 Stephenson Hwy, Madison Hts MI 48071-1613.
313/585-6400. Employs: 100-249.

Brico Metals
340 N Main St, Plymouth MI 48170-1249. 313/451-8282.
Employs: 50-99.

Lyon Powdered Metals Inc
381 N Reese St, South Lyon MI 48178-1224. 313/437-
9401. Employs: 50-99.

Sintering Technologies Inc
31500 W 13 Mile Rd, Farmington MI 48334-2164.
313/932-3499. Employs: 50-99.

**HAND AND EDGE TOOLS, EXCEPT MACHINE
TOOLS AND HANDSAWS**

Accu-Tech Tool
25551 Terra Industrial, Harrison Twp MI 48045. 313/949-
2290. Employs: 50-99.

Accurate Tooling & Enterprises
49241 Bayshore St, New Baltimore MI 48047-3452.
313/725-8913. Employs: 50-99.

Anbo Tool & Manufacturing
22791 Macomb Industrial Dr, Mount Clemens MI 48043.
313/465-7610. Employs: 50-99.

ASAP Tooling & Manufacturing Inc
4445 22 Mile Rd, Utica MI 48317-1509. 313/254-1330.
Employs: 50-99.

Dowley Manufacturing Inc
7750 King Rd, Spring Arbor MI 49283-9741. 517/750-
1430. Employs: 50-99.

Exacto Tool Co
50900 Birch Rd, Shelby Twp MI 48315-3205. 313/247-
0040. Employs: 50-99.

Hougen Manufacturing Inc
G-5072 Corunna Rd, Flint MI 48532. 313/732-5840.
Employs: 50-99.

Industrial Machine Products Inc
32 Louck St, Oxford MI 48371-4637. 313/628-3621.
Employs: 50-99.

J P C Precision Bending & Forge
24471 N River Rd, Harrison Twp MI 48045-1918.
313/463-0529. Employs: 50-99.

Kent-Moore Group Headquarters

28635 Mound Rd, Warren MI 48092-5509. 313/574-2332.
Employs: 100-249.

Klein Tools/Jonesville Plant
121 Water St, Jonesville MI 49250-1031. 517/849-9971.
Employs: 100-249.

Rickert Precision Ind Inc
9271 General Dr, Plymouth MI 48170-4625. 313/459-
2040. Employs: 50-99.

Taylor-Mills Manufacturing Inc
200 Industrial Dr, Hillsdale MI 49242-1075. 517/437-3339.
Employs: 50-99.

MISCELLANEOUS HARDWARE

Algonac Cast Products Inc
Stone Rd, Algonac MI 48001. 313/794-9391. Employs: 50-
99.

Dana Corp/Warner Electric Div
801 E Indl Ave, Mount Pleasant MI 48858. 517/773-6921.
Employs: 50-99.

Defiance Vaungarde Inc
1000 Bradley, Owosso MI 48867-2553. 517/725-8127.
Employs: 100-249.

Gladco Equipment Co
15200 Huron Rd, Taylor MI 48180-5270. 313/246-8230.
Employs: 100-249.

Jered Brown Brothers Inc
1300 Coolidge Box 2006, Troy MI 48084-7018. 313/643-
6930. Employs: 100-249.

Oetiker Inc
3305 Wilson St, Marlette MI 48453-1411. 517/635-3621.
Employs: 50-99.

Parker-Hannifin/Hose Products Div
1355 S Cedar St, Holt MI 48842. 517/694-0491. Employs:
50-99.

Penstone Inc
31605 Gossett Dr, Rockwood MI 48173-9700. 313/379-
3160. Employs: 50-99.

Plasta Fiber Inds
6300 Euclid St, Marlette MI 48453-1424. 517/635-7536.
Employs: 100-249.

Precision Hardware Inc
38100 Jay Kay Dr, Romulus MI 48174-4000. 313/326-
7500. Employs: 50-99.

Standard Stampings
27181 Southern Ave, Inkster MI 48141-2336. 313/563-
3580. Employs: 50-99.

Wellington Manufacturing Inc
5593 North St, Dryden MI 48428. 313/796-2244. Employs:
50-99.

PLUMBING FIXTURE FITTINGS AND TRIM

Alsons Corp
42 Union St, Hillsdale MI 49242-1322. 517/439-1411.
Employs: 100-249.

Aqua-Mist Incorporated
1211 S Monroe St, Monroe MI 48161-3933. 313/457-4545.
Employs: 50-99.

Lor-O-Bin
625 State Cir, Ann Arbor MI 48108-1645. 313/995-3600.
Employs: 50-99.

Plastic Trends Inc
6200 26 Mile Rd, Washington MI 48094. 313/781-2700.
Employs: 50-99.

Salem Lawn Sprinklers
G6393 W Carpenter Rd, Flint MI 48504. 313/733-8813.
Employs: 50-99.

HEATING EQUIPMENT, EXCEPT ELECTRIC AND WARM AIR FURNACES

Heat Controller Inc
1900 Wellworth Ave, Jackson MI 49203-3452. 517/787-2100. Employs: 50-99.

FABRICATED STRUCTURAL METAL

Fab-All Prototype
645 Executive Dr, Troy MI 48083-4536. 313/585-6700.
Employs: 50-99.

Ferguson Steel Inc
2935 Howard St, Port Huron MI 48060-4865. 313/985-5178. Employs: 50-99.

J & J Burning & Fabricating
24622 Mound Rd, Warren MI 48091-2036. 313/758-7619.
Employs: 50-99.

Unistrut Diversified Products
35660 Clinton St, Wayne MI 48184-2051. 313/721-4040.
Employs: 100-249.

Vogt Broad & Conant Inc
195 Campbell, River Rouge MI 48218-1001. 313/841-8100. Employs: 50-99.

Vulcan Iron Works Inc
12700 Lyndon St, Detroit MI 48227-3948. 313/491-0810.
Employs: 100-249.

Walcon Corp
24445 Northwestern Hwy, Southfield MI 48075-6501.
313/352-4960. Employs: 100-249.

METAL DOORS, SASHES, FRAMES, MOLDING AND TRIM

Air Conditioning Products Co
2340 W Lafayette Blvd, Detroit MI 48216-1832. 313/496-1000. Employs: 100-249.

Harvard Inds
1999 Wildwood Ave, Jackson MI 49202-4046. 517/782-9421. Employs: 100-249.

International Window Co
15555 Noecker Way, Southgate MI 48195-2272. 313/287-2030. Employs: 50-99.

Modern Window Corp
10161 Capital Ave, Oak Park MI 48237-3103. 313/543-1720. Employs: 50-99.

FABRICATED PLATE WORK (BOILER SHOPS)

Clawson Tank Co
4545 Clawson Tank Dr, Clarkston MI 48346. 313/625-8700. Employs: 100-249.

Gentz Inds Inc
23600 Schoenherr Rd, Warren MI 48089-4272. 313/772-2500. Employs: 100-249.

J & J Burning Co Inc
6227 Rinke Av, Warren MI 48091-5355. 313/539-7675.
Employs: 50-99.

Livernois Engineering Co
25315 Kean St, Dearborn MI 48124-2406. 313/278-0200.
Employs: 100-249.

Parton & Preble Inc
23507 Groesbeck Hwy, Warren MI 48089-4253. 313/773-6000. Employs: 50-99.

Production Tool Supply Inc
3509 Wayland Dr, Jackson MI 49202-1233. 517/787-5300.
Employs: 50-99.

Trayco Inc
693 S Court St, Lapeer MI 48446-2552. 313/664-8501.
Employs: 50-99.

Viatec Process/Storage Systems
500 Reed St Box 99, Belding MI 48809-1532. 616/794-1230. Employs: 50-99.

Wessels Co
1901 Marston, Detroit MI 48211-1315. 313/875-5000.
Employs: 50-99.

Woolf Aircraft Products Inc
6401 Cogswell Rd, Romulus MI 48174-4039. 313/721-5330. Employs: 50-99.

AA Tanks
190 Marston St, Detroit MI 48202-2540. 313/875-5000.
Employs: 50-99.

R P Lilly Enterprises
17220 Hannan Rd, New Boston MI 48164-9558.
313/7534302. Employs: 50-99.

SHEET METAL WORK

A B B Flakt Inc/Alpha Div
1400 Stevenson Hwy, Troy MI 48083. 313/588-0062.
Employs: 100-249.

Adrian Steel Co
906 James St, Adrian MI 49221-3914. 517/265-6194.
Employs: 50-99.

Auto Metal Craft Inc
10230 Capital Ave, Oak Park MI 48237-3104. 313/398-2600. Employs: 50-99.

Detronic Inds Inc
35800 Beattie Dr, Sterling Hts MI 48312-2620. 313/977-5660. Employs: 50-99.

Experi-Metal Inc
6345 Wall St, Sterling Hts MI 48312-1079. 313/977-7800.
Employs: 50-99.

H M White Inc
12855 Burt Rd, Detroit MI 48223-3316. 313/531-8477.
Employs: 50-99.

J L Sherk Co
9100 Central St, Detroit MI 48204-4327. 313/834-8446.
Employs: 50-99.

Midbrook Products Inc
2080 Brooklyn Rd, Jackson MI 49203-4744. 517/787-3481. Employs: 100-249.

Milbrand Co Inc
21200 Schoenherr Rd, Warren MI 48089-5801. 313/776-1400. Employs: 100-249.

Progressive Metal Manufacturing Co
1300 Channing, Ferndale MI 48220-2606. 313/546-2827.
Employs: 50-99.

Prototype Tooling & Manufacturing
18361 Mike C Ct, Fraser MI 48026-1613. 313/296-2330.
Employs: 50-99.

Reed National Air Products Corp
335 Water St, Waldron MI 49288. 517/286-6221. Employs: 50-99.

Temo Inc
20400 Hall Rd, Clinton Twp MI 48038-1480. 313/286-0410. Employs: 50-99.

Ventcon Inc
500 Enterprise Dr, Allen Park MI 48101-3027. 313/336-4000. Employs: 100-249.

Walcon Corp
4375 2nd St, Ecorse MI 48229-1101. 313/382-4000. Employs: 100-249.

Zack Co
4401 Western Rd, Flint MI 48506-1807. 313/736-2040. Employs: 50-99.

ARCHITECTURAL AND ORNAMENTAL METAL WORK

Foremost Manufacturing Co
21000 W 8 Mile Rd, Southfield MI 48075-5639. 313/352-7373. Employs: 50-99.

J C Goss Co
6330 E Jefferson Ave, Detroit MI 48207-4318. 313/259-3520. Employs: 50-99.

MISCELLANEOUS STRUCTURAL METAL WORK

Conveyor Components Co
130 Seltzer Rd, Croswell MI 48422-9180. 313/679-4211. Employs: 50-99.

Hyduke Industries
6200 Miller Rd, Dearborn MI 48126-2310. 313/582-2590. Employs: 50-99.

Tiechon Inds Inc
1712 Thunderbird St, Troy MI 48084-5461. 313/362-1515. Employs: 100-249.

SCREW MACHINE PRODUCTS

A T & G Co Inc
30790 W 8 Mile Rd, Farmington MI 48336-5303. 313/474-6330. Employs: 100-249.

Allan Tool & Machine Co
1822 E Maple Rd, Troy MI 48083-4240. 313/585-2910. Employs: 50-99.

Approved Manufacturing Co Inc
30790 W 8 Mile Rd, Farmington MI 48336-5303. 313/474-9191. Employs: 100-249.

Burns Automatic Co
27947 Groesbeck Hwy, Roseville MI 48066-2756. 313/778-8000. Employs: 50-99.

C S M Manufacturing Corp
24650 N Indl Dr, Farmington MI 48335. 313/471-0700. Employs: 50-99.

Cape Inds Inc
24055 Mound Rd, Warren MI 48091-2039. 313/754-0898. Employs: 50-99.

Concord Manufacturing Co
405 S Michigan St, Concord MI 49237. 517/524-8970. Employs: 50-99.

Condamtic Co Inc
999 Haynes St Ste 340, Birmingham MI 48009-6775. 313/759-3200. Employs: 50-99.

Condor Manufacturing Inc
11800 E 9 Mile Rd, Warren MI 48089-2588. 313/756-9400. Employs: 50-99.

Dawlen Corp
2029 Micor Dr, Jackson MI 49203-3448. 517/787-2200. Employs: 50-99.

Dirksen Screw Products Co Inc

14490 23 Mile Rd, Shelby Twp MI 48315-2916. 313/247-5400. Employs: 50-99.

Grinnell Screw Products Co Inc
22955 Indl Dr W, St Clair Shrs MI 48080. 313/777-2110. Employs: 50-99.

H & L Tool Co Inc
32701 Dequindre Rd, Madison Hts MI 48071-5002. 313/585-7474. Employs: 50-99.

Holt Products Co Inc
1875 Walnut St, Holt MI 48842-1613. 517/699-2111. Employs: 50-99.

Horton Co
2333 E High St, Jackson MI 49203-3421. 517/784-0501. Employs: 50-99.

K & E Screw Products Co
8763 Dexter-Chelsea Rd, Dexter MI 48130-9782. 313/426-3941. Employs: 50-99.

Len Inds Inc
815 Rice St, Leslie MI 49251-9440. 517/589-8241. Employs: 100-249.

M B Fetcher Co
8525 Livernois Ave, Detroit MI 48204-2145. 313/931-2000. Employs: 50-99.

Master Automatic Inc
12355 Wormer, Redford MI 48239-2424. 313/537-1775. Employs: 100-249.

Melling Machine Co
145 W Monroe St, Jackson MI 49202-2358. 517/787-8807. Employs: 50-99.

Piper Inds Inc
15930 Common Rd, Roseville MI 48066-1812. 313/771-5100. Employs: 50-99.

Re-Fab-Co Screw Products Inc
1099 Rochester Rd, Troy MI 48083-6011. 313/588-6265. Employs: 50-99.

Rima Manufacturing Co
3850 Munson Hwy, Hudson MI 49247-9735. 517/448-8921. Employs: 100-249.

Solar Machine Products Co
29350 Northline Rd, Romulus MI 48174-2836. 313/941-3700. Employs: 100-249.

Versatile Manufacturing Co
650 Hathaway St, East China MI 48054-1533. 313/329-4731. Employs: 50-99.

W A Thomas Co
446 Congdon St, Chelsea MI 48118-1206. 313/475-8626. Employs: 50-99.

Yankee Screw Products Co
29866 John R Rd, Madison Hts MI 48071-5408. 313/543-0990. Employs: 50-99.

BOLTS, NUTS, SCREWS, RIVETS AND WASHERS

Cold Heading Co
22155 Hoover Rd, Warren MI 48089-2566. 313/759-6810. Employs: 100-249.

Everlock Inc
31600 Stephenson Hwy, Madison Hts MI 48071-1642. 313/949-4700. Employs: 50-99.

Exemplar Manufacturing Co
800 Lowell St, Ypsilanti MI 48197-2433. 313/483-5070. Employs: 100-249.

Federal Screw Works
425 Congdon St, Chelsea MI 48118-1205. 313/475-1331.
Employs: 100-249.

Fisher Corp
1625 W Maple Rd, Troy MI 48084-7118. 313/280-0808.
Employs: 100-249.

G B Du Pont Co Inc
1194 Roods Lake Rd, Lapeer MI 48446-8366. 313/664-
7741. Employs: 50-99.

Grant Industries
33415 Groesbeck, Fraser MI 48026-4203. 313/293-9200.
Employs: 50-99.

Hi-Vol Products Inc
12955 Inkster Rd, Livonia MI 48150-2216. 313/525-8181.
Employs: 100-249.

Industrial & Auto Fasteners
3200 W 14 Mile Rd, Royal Oak MI 48073-1609. 313/280-
0880. Employs: 100-249.

Kean Manufacturing Corp
7845 Middlebelt Rd, Romulus MI 48174-2132. 313/561-
9087. Employs: 50-99.

Key Manufacturing Group Inc
27777 Franklin Rd #1850, Southfield MI 48034-8240.
313/355-2410. Employs: 100-249.

Maynard Manufacturing Inc
50855 E Russell Schmidt Blvd, Harrison Twp MI 48045.
313/949-0471. Employs: 50-99.

Micro Manufacturing Inc
35507 Groesbeck Hwy, Clinton Twp MI 48035-2520.
313/791-5880. Employs: 50-99.

Mid-State Bolt & Screw Co
2435 S Grand Traverse St, Flint MI 48503-3848. 313/238-
3555. Employs: 50-99.

N S S Industries
9075 General Dr, Plymouth MI 48170-4623. 313/459-
9500. Employs: 50-99.

Peerless Inds
2800 Tyler Rd, Ypsilanti MI 48198-6184. 313/482-3900.
Employs: 100-249.

Prestige Stamping Inc
23513 Groesbeck Hwy, Warren MI 48089-4253. 313/773-
2700. Employs: 100-249.

Progressive Stamping Co Inc
2807 Samoset Rd, Royal Oak MI 48073-1726. 313/549-
8610. Employs: 50-99.

Ring Screw Works
22100 Sherwood Ave, Warren MI 48091-5444. 313/754-
3300. Employs: 100-249.

Ring Screw Works
2480 Owen Rd, Fenton MI 48430-1769. 313/629-5369.
Employs: 50-99.

Sombur Machine & Tool Co Inc
2211 Beard St, Port Huron MI 48060-6424. 313/982-9917.
Employs: 50-99.

Terry Machine Co
5331 Dixie Hwy, Waterford MI 48329-1612. 313/623-
0800. Employs: 50-99.

Uniflow Corp
26600 Heyn Dr, Novi MI 48374-1821. 313/348-9370.
Employs: 50-99.

Vico Products Co Inc

41555 E Ann Arbor Rd, Plymouth MI 48170-4300.
313/453-3777. Employs: 50-99.

Washers Inc
33375 Glendale St, Livonia MI 48150-1615. 313/523-1000.
Employs: 50-99.

Wolverine Nut Co
6556 E McNichols Rd, Detroit MI 48212-2065. 313/365-
7770. Employs: 50-99.

20th Century Machine Co
6070 E 18 Mile Rd, Sterling Hts MI 48314-4202. 313/536-
0260. Employs: 100-249.

IRON AND STEEL FORGINGS

Avon Gear Co
410 South St, Rochester MI 48307-2242. 313/651-1200.
Employs: 50-99.

Bjerke Forgings Inc
20793 Farmington Rd, Farmington MI 48336-5131.
313/471-3322. Employs: 50-99.

Buchanan Metal Forming
2701 University Dr, Auburn Hills MI 48326-2563.
313/373-0303. Employs: 50-99.

Canron Enterprises Corporation
3043 Waterland Dr, Hadley MI 48440. 313/797-5823.
Employs: 50-99.

Cerro Metal Products Co
3320 Paddington Rd, Troy MI 48084-1241. 313/642-8140.
Employs: 50-99.

De-Sta-Co
250 Park St, Troy MI 48083-2772. 313/589-2008.
Employs: 100-249.

Dexter Gear & Spline Co
15111 Keel St, Plymouth MI 48170-6003. 313/454-7320.
Employs: 50-99.

Fairlane Gear Inc
8182 Canton Ctr Rd, Canton MI 48187-1305. 313/459-
2440. Employs: 50-99.

Forging Specialties Inc
12600 Beech Daly, Redford MI 48239-2455. 313/535-
1784. Employs: 50-99.

Forming Technology Co
2727 W 14 Mile Rd, Royal Oak MI 48073-1712. 313/549-
2700. Employs: 100-249.

Hirschvogel Inc
8616 Dann Dr, Brighton MI 48116-8937. 313/229-3090.
Employs: 50-99.

Horizon Forge
2300 Leroy St, Jackson MI 49202-3775. 517/788-7990.
Employs: 50-99.

L M Gear Co
50550 E Russell Schmidt Blvd, Harrison Twp MI 48045.
313/949-6800. Employs: 50-99.

Lanzen Fabricating Inc
30980 Groesbeck Hwy, Roseville MI 48066-1511.
313/771-7070. Employs: 50-99.

Lefere Forge & Machine Co
665 Hupp Ave, Jackson MI 49203-1975. 517/784-7109.
Employs: 50-99.

Letts Drop Forge
2714 W Jefferson Ave, Detroit MI 48216-2034. 313/496-
1970. Employs: 50-99.

Lyon Gear & Machine Inc
4371 Territorial Rd, Rochester MI 48306-1665. 313/651-1751. Employs: 50-99.

M S I Warren Stamping
27027 Groesbeck Hwy, Warren MI 48089-1538. 313/772-1514. Employs: 50-99.

M S P
45 W Oakwood Rd, Oxford MI 48371-1631. 313/628-4150. Employs: 100-249.

Marine City Stamping Co
857 Degurse Ave, Marine City MI 48039-1532. 313/765-4036. Employs: 50-99.

MDWS Products Cold Forgings
2130 Franklin St, Detroit MI 48207-4414. 313/259-8160. Employs: 50-99.

Pontius Enterprises
2800 S Woodward Ave, Bloomfield MI 48304-1674. 313/332-9910. Employs: 50-99.

Reef Gear Manufacturing M S G Inc
50903 E Russell Schmidt Blvd, Harrison Twp MI 48045. 313/949-2520. Employs: 100-249.

Rochester Gear Inc
4483 Orion Rd, Rochester MI 48306-1659. 313/651-5560. Employs: 50-99.

SMB Of America
12290 Cone Dr, Shelby Twp MI 48315-5700. 313/254-3610. Employs: 50-99.

Spring Engineering & Manufacturing Corp
35300 Glendale St, Livonia MI 48150-1243. 313/525-0240. Employs: 50-99.

Steel Inds Inc
12600 Beech Daly Rd, Redford MI 48239-2455. 313/531-1140. Employs: 100-249.

Supreme Tool & Gear Co
19024 Florida Dr, Roseville MI 48066-4106. 313/755-6325. Employs: 50-99.

Timco Manufacturing Co Inc
27544 Groesbeck Hwy, Roseville MI 48066-2759. 313/776-6720. Employs: 100-249.

U S Panax A Corporation
24333 Southfield Rd, Southfield MI 48075-2822. 313/443-5200. Employs: 50-99.

Uniflow 2
26001 Grand River Ave, Lenox MI 48050. 313/348-9451. Employs: 50-99.

NONFERROUS FORGINGS

Brass Forgings Co
2121 Burdette, Ferndale MI 48220-1402. 313/564-6831. Employs: 50-99.

Jet Engineering
5212 Aurelius Rd, Lansing MI 48911-4114. 517/882-4311. Employs: 50-99.

Troy Forge Co
690 W Maple Rd, Troy MI 48084-5437. 313/362-1844. Employs: 50-99.

AUTOMOTIVE STAMPINGS

Arrow Metal Products Corp
1200 Mt Elliott St, Detroit MI 48207-3464. 313/567-6112. Employs: 50-99.

Capac Manufacturing Corp
14850 Downey Rd, Capac MI 48014. 313/395-4326. Employs: 100-249.

Cardell Corp
2849 Product Dr, Rochester MI 48309-3812. 313/853-3360. Employs: 100-249.

Cavalier Manufacturing Co
1300 E 9 Mile Rd, Hazel Park MI 48030-1959. 313/543-2427. Employs: 50-99.

Clover Tool & Manufacturing Co
130 Groesbeck Hwy, Mount Clemens MI 48043-1529. 313/468-0819. Employs: 50-99.

Crescive Die & Tool Inc
905 Woodland Dr, Saline MI 48176-1259. 313/429-9451. Employs: 100-249.

Delwal Corp
44700 Grand River Ave, Novi MI 48375-1008. 313/348-0400. Employs: 100-249.

E G S Metal Systems Inc
6640 Sterling Dr S, Sterling Hts MI 48312-5845. 313/939-3000. Employs: 100-249.

Edgewood Tool & Manufacturing Co
8900 Inkster Rd, Romulus MI 48174-2614. 313/946-1300. Employs: 50-99.

Ford Motor Co Trim
26090 23 Mile Rd, Harrison Twp MI 48045. 313/466-0700. Employs: 100-249.

Hamlin Tool & Machine Co Inc
1671 E Hamlin Rd, Rochester MI 48307-3624. 313/651-6302. Employs: 50-99.

Imerman Industries Inc
12165 Mack Ave, Detroit MI 48215-2226. 313/823-3410. Employs: 100-249.

Johnson Stamping/Fine Blanking
9120 General Dr, Plymouth MI 48170-4624. 313/477-1600. Employs: 50-99.

M & H Industries Inc
32500 Capitol St, Livonia MI 48150-1703. 313/261-7560. Employs: 50-99.

Metalform Inds Inc
10375 Dixie Hwy, Davisburg MI 48350-1305. 313/625-5800. Employs: 50-99.

Paramount Fabricating Inc
13595 Helen St, Detroit MI 48212-2021. 313/365-6600. Employs: 100-249.

Paramount Newport Inc
8144 S Newport Rd, Newport MI 48166-9601. 313/586-2080. Employs: 100-249.

Precision Stamping Co Inc
1244 Grand Oaks Dr, Howell MI 48843-8511. 517/546-5656. Employs: 50-99.

Ralco Inds Inc
2720 Auburn Ct, Auburn Hills MI 48326-3202. 313/853-3200. Employs: 50-99.

Regal Stamping Co
20530 Hoover St, Detroit MI 48205-1064. 313/521-0300. Employs: 100-249.

Republic Die & Tool Co
45000 Van Born Rd, Belleville MI 48111-1152. 313/699-3400. Employs: 100-249.

Sebewaing Inds Inc
888 Clairpointe St, Detroit MI 48215-3221. 313/822-7211. Employs: 100-249.

Snover Stamping Co
3279 W Snover Rd, Snover MI 48472-9728. 313/672-9288.
Employs: 100-249.

Sparton Engrd Products
1201 N 4th Ave, Lake Odessa MI 48849-1301. 616/374-
8863. Employs: 100-249.

St Clair Metal Products
1721 Dove St, Port Huron MI 48060-8007. 313/984-5123.
Employs: 100-249.

Stamping Service Inc
5505 E Davison St, Detroit MI 48212-1236. 313/891-5377.
Employs: 50-99.

Trend Inds Inc
13700 W Buena Vista St, Detroit MI 48227-3115. 313/273-
3434. Employs: 50-99.

Wellington Inds Inc
39555 I-94 S Service Dr, Belleville MI 48111. 313/942-
1060. Employs: 100-249.

Whitehead Manufacturing Co
6100 Ranspach St, Detroit MI 48209-1258. 313/842-7100.
Employs: 50-99.

MISCELLANEOUS METAL STAMPINGS

A W T Metal Specialties Inc
16590 13 Mile Rd, Roseville MI 48066-1501. 313/773-
0900. Employs: 50-99.

B A E Industries Inc
24400 Sherwood Ave, Center Line MI 48015-2023.
313/754-3000. Employs: 100-249.

Bennett Equipment Corp
17225 Sherwood St, Detroit MI 48212-2046. 313/365-
9220. Employs: 50-99.

Brown Corp Of Ionia Inc
314 S Steele St, Ionia MI 48846-2008. 616/527-1600.
Employs: 100-249.

Burkland Inc
6520 S State Rd, Goodrich MI 48438-9761. 313/636-2233.
Employs: 100-249.

C M X Corp
12700 Stephens Rd, Warren MI 48089-4334. 313/756-
7676. Employs: 50-99.

Creative Assembly & Stamping
12500 E 9 Mile Rd, Warren MI 48089-2634. 313/758-
6620. Employs: 100-249.

Danbar Inc
50320 E Russell Schmidt Blvd, Harrison Twp MI 48045.
313/949-2800. Employs: 50-99.

Deckerville Die-Farm Co
2121 Stoutenberg, Deckerville MI 48427. 313/376-2245.
Employs: 50-99.

Dial Machine & Tool Co Inc
3151 W Michigan Ave, Jackson MI 49202-1832. 517/788-
6900. Employs: 50-99.

E & E Manufacturing Co Inc
300/400 Indl Dr, Plymouth MI 48170. 313/451-7600.
Employs: 100-249.

Eltec Corporation
315 W Ann Arbor Rd, Plymouth MI 48170-2223. 313/453-
1515. Employs: 100-249.

Fourslides Inc
1701 E Lincoln Ave, Madison Hts MI 48071-4175.
313/564-5600. Employs: 50-99.

Gilco Inc
15866 Sturgeon St, Roseville MI 48066-1819. 313/779-
5850. Employs: 50-99.

Hatch Stamping Co
635 E Indl Dr, Chelsea MI 48118. 313/475-8628. Employs:
100-249.

Howell Inds Inc
100 Fair St, Lapeer MI 48446. 313/664-8567. Employs:
100-249.

Hy-Form Products Inc
35588 Veronica Dr, Livonia MI 48150-1204. 313/464-
3811. Employs: 100-249.

Iroquois Die & Manufacturing Co
24400 Hoover Rd, Warren MI 48089-1970. 313/756-6920.
Employs: 100-249.

J & R Manufacturing Inc
40730 Production Dr, Harrison Twp MI 48045. 313/468-
8140. Employs: 50-99.

L & W Engineering Co Inc/Plant 1
6771 Haggerty Rd, Belleville MI 48111-5101. 313/397-
8085. Employs: 100-249.

L E Borden Manufacturing Co
15281 12 Mile Rd, Roseville MI 48066-1838. 313/772-
8180. Employs: 50-99.

La Rose Inds Inc
19101 15 Mile Rd, Clinton Twp MI 48035-2508. 313/791-
0040. Employs: 50-99.

Lapeer Metal Products
930 Saginaw, Lapeer MI 48446-2642. 313/664-8588.
Employs: 100-249.

Lattimore & Tessmer Inc
21625 Telegraph Rd, Southfield MI 48034-4214. 313/353-
2121. Employs: 50-99.

Logghe Stamping Co
16711 E 13 Mile Rd, Fraser MI 48026-2555. 313/293-
2250. Employs: 50-99.

M S I Prototype & Engineering
26269 Groesbeck Hwy, Warren MI 48089-4150. 313/773-
0800. Employs: 100-249.

Manchester Stamping Corp
17951 W Austin Rd, Manchester MI 48158-9603. 313/428-
8301. Employs: 50-99.

Maple Roll Leaf Co
62170 Mt Vernon Rd, Romeo MI 48065. 313/964-6658.
Employs: 50-99.

Mc Intosh
39600 Orchard Hill Pl, Novi MI 48375-5331. 313/349-
7900. Employs: 50-99.

Michigan Fine Blanking
8647 Lyndon St, Detroit MI 48238-2353. 313/933-2810.
Employs: 50-99.

Motor City Stamping Inc
47783 N Gratiot Ave, Clinton Twp MI 48035-4039.
313/949-8420. Employs: 50-99.

Nothdurft Tool & Manufacturing
34660 Centaur Dr, Clinton Twp MI 48035-3700. 313/791-
2500. Employs: 50-99.

O D F Industries Inc
24300 Wahl St, Warren MI 48089-2054. 313/755-6672.
Employs: 50-99.

Ogihara America Corp
1480 W McPherson Pk Dr, Howell MI 48843-1936.
517/548-4900. Employs: 100-249.

Opdyke Stamping Inc
700 N Glaspie St, Oxford MI 48371-5136. 313/628-9596.
Employs: 100-249.

Peterson American Corp
21200 Telegraph Rd, Southfield MI 48034-4243. 313/353-
6400. Employs: 100-249.

Production Stamping Inc
28175 Rosso Wrn P, Mount Clemens MI 48043. 313/949-
1114. Employs: 100-249.

Quality Metalcraft Inc
33355 Glendale St, Livonia MI 48150-1615. 313/261-6700.
Employs: 100-249.

Quasar Inds
2687 Commerce Dr, Rochester MI 48309-3813. 313/852-
0300. Employs: 100-249.

Quigley Inds Inc
21547 Telegraph Rd, Southfield MI 48034-4248. 313/352-
8500. Employs: 50-99.

R J Industries Inc
33671 Doreka St, Fraser MI 48026-1610. 313/296-0480.
Employs: 50-99.

S R S Industries Inc
2655 Product Dr, Rochester MI 48309-3808. 313/853-
3400. Employs: 100-249.

Starboard Inds Inc
1092 Centre Rd, Auburn Hills MI 48326-2600. 313/370-
0020. Employs: 50-99.

Superb Manufacturing
1200 Woodland Rd, Detroit MI 48211-1071. 313/867-
3700. Employs: 100-249.

W C Mc Curdy Co
1148 Rochester Rd, Troy MI 48083-2832. 313/585-3122.
Employs: 100-249.

Walbro Automotive Corp
7325 Douglas Rd, Lambertville MI 48144-9403. 313/856-
4151. Employs: 100-249.

Williams Manufacturing Co
29825 Calahan Rd, Roseville MI 48066-1828. 313/755-
0202. Employs: 50-99.

Williams Manufacturing Co
30707 Commerce Blvd, New Haven MI 48048. 313/749-
6800. Employs: 50-99.

Zenith Indl Corp
23361 Quinn Rd, Clinton Twp MI 48035-3732. 313/791-
7030. Employs: 100-249.

Zero Stamping Co Inc
27165 Wick Rd, Taylor MI 48180-3016. 313/946-8055.
Employs: 50-99.

**ELECTROPLATING, PLATING, POLISHING,
ANODIZING AND COLORING**

A R Indl Cleaning/Maintenance
940 Biddle Ave, Wyandotte MI 48192-2909. 313/285-
7767. Employs: 50-99.

Alpha Metal Finishing Co
8155 Huron St, Dexter MI 48130-1026. 313/426-2855.
Employs: 100-249.

American Anodco Inc
28 Beardsley St, Ionia MI 48846-9734. 616/527-3210.
Employs: 50-99.

Apollo Plating Inc
15765 Sturgeon, Roseville MI 48066-1816. 313/777-0070.
Employs: 100-249.

Auto Anodics Inc
2407 16th St, Port Huron MI 48060-6402. 313/984-5600.
Employs: 50-99.

Cadon Plating Co
3715 11th St, Wyandotte MI 48192-6435. 313/282-8100.
Employs: 50-99.

Cathodic Electrocoating Co
100 Mill St, Ecorse MI 48229-1096. 313/388-4644.
Employs: 100-249.

Centri-Spray Corp
39001 Schoolcraft Rd, Livonia MI 48150-1035. 313/464-
0100. Employs: 50-99.

Chrome Craft Corp
318 Midland Ave, Detroit MI 48203-3734. 313/868-2444.
Employs: 50-99.

Commercial Steel Treating Corp
31440 Stephenson Hwy, Madison Hts MI 48071-1621.
313/588-3300. Employs: 100-249.

Deco Plate
395 Demille Rd, Lapeer MI 48446-3055. 313/667-3460.
Employs: 50-99.

Diamond Chrome Plating Inc
604 S Michigan, Howell MI 48843-2605. 517/546-0150.
Employs: 50-99.

Elm Plating Co
1319 S Elm St, Jackson MI 49203-3307. 517/782-8161.
Employs: 50-99.

General Plating Inc
21841 Wyoming St, Oak Park MI 48237-3116. 313/579-
2639. Employs: 50-99.

Heidtman Steel Products Inc
640 Lavoy Rd, Erie MI 48133-9638. 313/848-2915.
Employs: 100-249.

Honhart Mid-Nite Black Co
501 Stephenson Hwy, Troy MI 48083-1134. 313/588-1515.
Employs: 50-99.

Howard Plating Inds Inc
32565 Dequindre Rd, Madison Hts MI 48071-1520.
313/588-9050. Employs: 100-249.

International Hardcoat Inc
14300 Meyers Rd, Detroit MI 48227-3924. 313/834-5000.
Employs: 50-99.

Kolene Corp
12890 Westwood Ave, Detroit MI 48223-3436. 313/273-
9220. Employs: 50-99.

Lamina Inc
14925 W 11 Mile Rd, Oak Park MI 48237-1013. 313/542-
8341. Employs: 100-249.

Modern Hard Chrome Services
12880 E 9 Mile Rd, Warren MI 48089-2641. 313/455-
0330. Employs: 100-249.

Ryan Polishing Corp
10709 Capital Ave, Oak Park MI 48237-3103. 313/548-
6832. Employs: 50-99.

Spartan Metal Finishing Co
5400 E Nevada St, Detroit MI 48234-2404. 313/368-7888.
Employs: 100-249.

Marsh Plating Corp
103 N Grove St, Ypsilanti MI 48198-2906. 313/483-5767.
Employs: 100-249.

Ring Finishing Co
6431 E Palmer St, Detroit MI 48211-3201. 313/924-6611.
Employs: 50-99.

MISCELLANEOUS COATING, ENGRAVING AND ALLIED SERVICES

American Technical Coatings
31774 Enterprise Dr, Livonia MI 48150-1960. 313/421-7300. Employs: 50-99.

Camtron Coatings Co
434 McCormick Dr, Lapeer MI 48446-2518. 313/664-8861. Employs: 100-249.

Crown Enameling Inc
6300 E 7 Mile Rd, Detroit MI 48234-2827. 313/368-2300.
Employs: 50-99.

Curtis Metal Finishing Co
6645 Sims Dr, Sterling Hts MI 48313-3726. 313/939-2850.
Employs: 50-99.

E & V Plastic Plating Inc
13000 Haggerty Rd, Belleville MI 48111-2878. 313/941-3320. Employs: 50-99.

Enamalum Corp
25460 Novi Rd, Novi MI 48375-1642. 313/349-6600.
Employs: 50-99.

Enamelcote Inc
7243 Miller Dr, Warren MI 48092-4728. 313/826-9100.
Employs: 100-249.

Metal-Cote Inc
41300 Production Dr, Harrison Twp MI 48045-1354.
313/469-1275. Employs: 50-99.

Midwest Products Finishing Inc
6194 Section Rd, Ottawa Lake MI 49267-9526. 313/856-5200. Employs: 50-99.

Morton International/Bee Chemical Div
2910 Waterview Dr, Rochester MI 48309-3484. 313/853-3600. Employs: 50-99.

National Galvanizing Inc
1500 Telb Rd, Monroe MI 48161-2572. 313/243-1882.
Employs: 50-99.

Pak-Rite Industries Inc
4270 High St, Ecorse MI 48229-1572. 313/388-6400.
Employs: 100-249.

Powder Cote I I Inc
80 N Rose St, Mount Clemens MI 48043-5405. 313/463-7040. Employs: 100-249.

Rich Powder Coat Inc
8400 Ronda Dr, Canton MI 48187-2002. 313/459-2640.
Employs: 50-99.

Siebert-Oxidermo Inc
16255 Wahrman Rd, Romulus MI 48174-9725. 313/942-0110. Employs: 50-99.

Stahlin Inds Inc
8080 Grand St, Dexter MI 48130-1109. 313/426-8800.
Employs: 50-99.

Stylecraft Products Inc
1219 Beaufait St, Detroit MI 48207-3408. 313/579-2780.
Employs: 50-99.

Surfinco/Plant 1
1100 Indl Ave, Albion MI 49224. 517/629-2106. Employs:
50-99.

Ti-Coating Inc
50500 Corporate Dr, Shelby Twp MI 48315-3102.
313/726-1900. Employs: 50-99.

Vacumet Inc
4662 Puttygut Rd, East China MI 48054-2109. 313/329-2274. Employs: 100-249.

Wolverine Coil Coating Inc
1725 Cicotte St, Lincoln Park MI 48146-1304. 313/382-9380. Employs: 100-249.

Ziebart International Corp
1290 E Maple Rd, Troy MI 48083-2817. 313/588-4100.
Employs: 100-249.

MISCELLANEOUS ORDNANCE AND ACCESSORIES

Allied Chucker & Eng Co
3529 Scheele Dr, Jackson MI 49202-1217. 517/787-1370.
Employs: 100-249.

INDUSTRIAL VALVES

Automatic Valve Corp
41144 Vincenti Ct, Novi MI 48375-1922. 313/474-6700.
Employs: 50-99.

Numatics Inc
360 Thelma St, Sandusky MI 48471-1415. 313/648-9141.
Employs: 100-249.

MISCELLANEOUS VALVES AND PIPE FITTINGS

I C Warco-I Inc
1102 Lapeer Ave, Port Huron MI 48060-4453. 313/982-1833. Employs: 50-99.

United Brass Manufacturers Inc
35030 Goddard Rd, Romulus MI 48174-3408. 313/941-0700. Employs: 50-99.

MISCELLANEOUS FABRICATED WIRE PRODUCTS

Adrian Fabricators Inc
412 W Beecher, Adrian MI 49221-3806. 517/263-4621.
Employs: 100-249.

Airtec Corp
640 E 7 Mile Rd, Detroit MI 48203-2026. 313/892-7800.
Employs: 50-99.

Allor Manufacturing Inc
46350 Grand River Ave, Novi MI 48374-1322. 313/348-2700. Employs: 100-249.

BMC Manufacturing Inc
100 S Mill St, Plymouth MI 48170-1825. 313/453-5400.
Employs: 100-249.

Chelsea Inds Inc
320 N Main, Chelsea MI 48118-1280. 313/475-8611.
Employs: 100-249.

Clark Engineering Co
8109 M-78, Haslett MI 48840-9307. 517/339-8223.
Employs: 50-99.

Greenville Wire Products
1515 Shearer Rd, Greenville MI 48838. 616/754-4954.
Employs: 50-99.

Industrial Strainer Co
695 Amelia St, Plymouth MI 48170-1204. 313/453-8666.
Employs: 100-249.

Junction Manufacturing Co
4000 Rives Eaton Rd, Rives Jct MI 49277-9650. 517/569-2252. Employs: 50-99.

Monroe Manufacturing Inc
330 Detroit Av Ste A, Monroe MI 48161-2597. 313/457-2868. Employs: 50-99.

Prestolite Wire Corp
3529 24th St, Port Huron MI 48060-6879. 313/987-6300. Employs: 50-99.

Production Spring Corp
15890 Sturgeon Ct, Roseville MI 48066-1836. 313/755-8484. Employs: 50-99.

Semmerling Brighton Colorguard
800 Whitney Ave, Brighton MI 48116-1221. 313/227-3036. Employs: 50-99.

Springport Steel Cntnr Corp
111 Willow St Box 98, Springport MI 49284-9500. 517/857-3010. Employs: 50-99.

Ultimate Manufacturers Inc
3515 Old U S Rt 23, Brighton MI 48116-7520. 313/227-6181. Employs: 50-99.

Union Steel Products Inc
509 N Albion St, Albion MI 49224-1278. 517/629-2181. Employs: 100-249.

Xact Products Inc
11530 Brooklyn Rd, Brooklyn MI 49230-9057. 517/592-6626. Employs: 50-99.

FABRICATED PIPE AND PIPE FITTINGS

A & B Tube Benders Inc
13465 E 9 Mile Rd, Warren MI 48089-2658. 313/773-0440. Employs: 50-99.

Bent Tube Inc
9649 W Van Buren Rd, Fowlerville MI 48836-9230. 517/2239151. Employs: 100-249.

Bundy Corp/Tubing Div
200 Arch Ave, Hillsdale MI 49242-1079. 517/439-1577. Employs: 50-99.

Delta Tube & Fabrication
4149 Grange Hall Rd, Holly MI 48442-1113. 313/634-8267. Employs: 100-249.

Fernco Inc
300 S Dayton St, Davison MI 48423-1502. 313/653-9626. Employs: 100-249.

Harding Tube Corp
1132 Ladd Rd, Walled Lake MI 48390-3032. 313/669-4610. Employs: 50-99.

Hi Mill Manufacturing Co
1704 Highland Rd, Highland MI 48031. 313/887-4191. Employs: 50-99.

Hi-Mill Manufacturing Co
1704 Highland Rd, Highland MI 48356-3037. 313/887-4191. Employs: 50-99.

Hoyt Brumm & Link Inc
2305 Hilton Rd, Ferndale MI 48220-1570. 313/548-3355. Employs: 100-249.

Jonesville Products Co Inc
3980 Beck Rd, Jonesville MI 49250-9464. 517/849-9908. Employs: 100-249.

R & B Manufacturing Co
7495 M-36 E, Hamburg MI 48139. 313/231-1300. Employs: 100-249.

Ryken Tube Inc
3160 Dellavo Ct, Walled Lake MI 48390-1606. 313/669-3232. Employs: 50-99.

Spiral Inds Inc
140 W Summit St, Milford MI 48381-1561. 313/685-8753. Employs: 100-249.

Tru-Val Tubing Co
1314 Crescent Lk Rd, Waterford MI 48327-2414. 313/674-3131. Employs: 50-99.

Universal Tube Inc
2777 Product Dr, Rochester MI 48309-3810. 313/853-5100. Employs: 100-249.

Versatube Corp
4755 Rochester Rd, Troy MI 48098-4963. 313/689-7373. Employs: 50-99.

Delta Tube & Fabricating
4030 Grange Hall Rd, Holly MI 48442-1110. 313/629-2841. Employs: 50-99.

Horizon Screw Machine Products
27991 Northline Rd, Romulus MI 48174-2827. 313/941-4600. Employs: 100-249.

Small Tube Products Inc
1818 Court St, Port Huron MI 48060-4933. 313/985-7470. Employs: 50-99.

MISCELLANEOUS FABRICATED METAL PRODUCTS

A A R Advanced Structures
12633 Inkster Rd, Livonia MI 48150-2216. 313/522-2000. Employs: 100-249.

Hofley Manufacturing Co
22534 Groesbeck Hwy, Warren MI 48089-2625. 313/778-5444. Employs: 100-249.

Howell Industries Inc
17515 W Nine Mile Rd, Southfield MI 48075-4403. 313/424-8220. Employs: 100-249.

Hyper Alloys Inc
29153 Groesbeck Hwy, Roseville MI 48066-1921. 313/772-0571. Employs: 50-99.

Tri-Mark Metal Corp
10106 Grinnell Ave, Detroit MI 48213-1142. 313/925-4900. Employs: 50-99.

Triple A Tube Inc
4700 Beck Rd, Jonesville MI 49250-9401. 517/849-9945. Employs: 100-249.

Yukon Manufacturing
900 Anderson Rd, Litchfield MI 49252. 517/542-2935. Employs: 100-249.

For more information on career opportunities in the fabricated and primary metals industries:

Associations

AMERICAN FOUNDRYMEN'S SOCIETY
505 State Street, Des Plaines IL 60016. 708/824-0181.

AMERICAN IRON & STEEL INSTITUTE
1101 17th Street NW, 13th Floor, Washington DC 20036. 202/452-7100.

AMERICAN POWDER METALLURGY INSTITUTE
105 College Road East, Princeton NJ 08540. 609/452-7700.

AMERICAN SOCIETY FOR METALS
9639 Kinsman Road, Materials Park OH 44073-0002.
216/338-5151.

AMERICAN WELDING SOCIETY
P.O. Box 35140, 550 LeJeune Road NW, Miami FL 33135.
305/443-9353.

ASSOCIATION OF IRON AND STEEL ENGINEERS
Three Gateway Center, Suite 2350, Pittsburgh PA 15222.
412/281-6323.

ASSOCIATION OF STEEL DISTRIBUTORS
401 N. Michigan Avenue, Chicago IL 60611. 312/664-6610.

NATIONAL ASSOCIATION OF METAL FINISHERS
401 N. Michigan Avenue, Chicago IL 60611. 312/644-6610.

Directories

DIRECTORY OF STEEL FOUNDRIES IN THE UNITED STATES, CANADA, AND MEXICO
Steel Founder's Society of America, 455 State Street, Des Plaines IL 60016. 708/299-9160.

Magazines

AMERICAN METAL MARKET
Capital Cities ABC, 825 7th Avenue, New York NY 10019. 212/887-8580.

IRON AGE
191 S. Gary, Carol Stream IL 60188. 708/462-2285.

IRON & STEEL ENGINEER
Association of Iron and Steel Engineers, Three Gateway Center, Suite 2350, Pittsburgh PA 15222. 412/281-6323.

MODERN METALS
400 N. Michigan Avenue, Chicago IL 60611. 312/222-2000.

FINANCIAL SERVICES/MANAGEMENT CONSULTING

Since the 1987 crash, the financial services industry has been struggling to redefine itself. In response to the recession, companies have been cutting costs - and jobs - in order to become leaner and more efficient. Jobseekers should look to conservative firms for the most stable career tracks. Tip: Take a close look at mutual funds, one of the few current hot areas.

CHRYSLER FINANCIAL CORP.
27777 Franklin Road, Southfield MI 48034-8266. 313/948-3008. **Contact:** Chuck Moline or Dawn Eaglin, Recruitment and Placement Administrator. **Description:** Non-bank financial services company. **Employees:** 7,000. **Common positions:** Accountant; Actuary; Attorney; Claim Representative; Computer Programmer; Customer Service Representative; Financial Analyst; Operations/Production Manager; Marketing Specialist; Personnel and Labor Relations Specialist; Systems Analyst; Underwriter. **Educational backgrounds sought:** Accounting; Business Administration; Computer Science; Finance. **Special programs:** Limited training programs and internships. **Corporate headquarters:** This location. **Parent company:** Chrysler Corporation.

CITIZENS BANKING CORPORATION
1 Citizens Banking Center, Flint MI 48502. 313/766-7500. **Contact:** Vice-President. **Description:** A Detroit area holding and finance company.

FIRST OF MICHIGAN CORPORATION
100 Renaissance Center, Detroit MI 48243. 313/259-2600. **Contact:** Personnel. **Description:** A major investment banking corporation.

GENERAL MOTORS ACCEPTANCE CORPORATION
3044 West Grand Boulevard, Annex 312, Detroit MI 48202. 313/556-2649. **Contact:** Employment Activity Staff. Conducts leasing and financing for wholesale and retail GM dealers internationally. Parent company, General Motors, is a major producer of cars, trucks, and buses sold worldwide; the firm has 152 facilities operating in 26 states and 93 cities in the United States and 13 plants in Canada, and also has assembly, manufacturing, distribution, sales or warehousing operations in 37 other countries. **Common positions:** Accountant; Financial Analyst; Underwriter. **Educational backgrounds sought:** Accounting; Finance. **Benefits:** medical, dental, and life insurance; tuition assistance; disability coverage; profit sharing; employee discounts. **Corporate headquarters:** This location. **Parent company:** GM. **Operations at this facility:** regional headquarters. **Listed on:** New York Stock Exchange.

HUNTINGTON BANKS OF MICHIGAN
801 West Big Beaver, Troy MI 48007-5823. 313/362-5000. **Contact:** Personnel Department. **Description:** A prominent Southeastern Michigan holding company.

McCULLAGH LEASING
30803 Little Mack Avenue, Roseville MI 48066. 313/296-4200. **Contact:** J.D. Mosley, Director of Human Resources. **Description:** One of the largest vehicle leasing companies in the U.S. and Canada providing fleet financing and related management services to corporate clients. Headquartered in the Detroit area with offices in eleven cities nationwide. **Employees:** 450. **Common positions:** Computer Programmer; Department Manager; Sales Representative; Systems Analyst; Sales Management. **Educational backgrounds sought:** Accounting; Business Administration; Computer Science; Finance (limited); Liberal Arts; Marketing. **Benefits:** medical, dental, and life insurance; pension plan; tuition assistance; disability coverage; employee discounts; savings plan. **Corporate headquarters:** This location. **Parent company:** Bank of New England Corporation. **Operations at this facility:** divisional headquarters; administration; service; sales.

PHM CORPORATION
33 Bloomfield Hills Parkway, Bloomfield Hills MI 48304-2946. 313/647-2750. **Contact:** Personnel Department. **Description:** A major banking and financing firm.

RONEY AND COMPANY
1 Griswold Street, Detroit MI 48226. 313/963-6700, ext. 471. **Contact:** William G. Kokas, Director of Sales Development & Training. A stock brokerage firm. **Corporate headquarters:** This location. **Other U.S. locations:** 27 branch offices located in Michigan, Indiana, and Ohio.

Additional large employers: 250+

SECURITY BROKERS, DEALERS AND FLOTATION COMPANIES

Associated Mariner Fin Group Inc
17199 Laurel Park Dr N, Livonia MI 48152-2679. 313/462-1010. Employs: 250-499.

OFFICES OF MISC. HOLDING COMPANIES

Grand Trunk Corp
1333 Brewery Park Blvd, Detroit MI 48207-2602. 313/396-6000. Employs: 1000+.

M L X Corporation
100 E Big Beaver Rd Ste 804, Troy MI 48083-1257. 313/528-2400. Employs: 250-499.

Southeastern Mi Gas Ent Inc
405 Water St, Port Huron MI 48060-5432. 313/987-2200. Employs: 250-499.

Suburban Communications Corp
36251 Schoolcraft Rd, Livonia MI 48150-1216. 313/591-2300. Employs: 250-499.

PATENT OWNERS AND LESSORS

Tubby's Sub Shops Inc
34500 Doreka, Fraser MI 48026-1661. 313/296-1270. Employs: 500-999.

Additional small to medium sized employers: 50-249

PERSONAL CREDIT INSTITUTIONS

Co-op Services Credit Union
20291 Middlebelt Rd, Livonia MI 48152-2001. 313/477-7767. Employs: 50-99.

Credit Union One
4201 Saint Antoine St, Detroit MI 48201-2194. 313/832-7030. Employs: 50-99.

D A P Enterprise
14500 Piedmont St, Detroit MI 48223-2241. 313/836-9148. Employs: 50-99.

Equitrust Mortgage Corp
38705 7 Mile Rd, Livonia MI 48152-1056. 313/462-5990. Employs: 50-99.

First Nationwide Bank
28999 5 Mile Rd, Livonia MI 48154-3823. 313/261-8020. Employs: 50-99.

Fleet Mortgage Corp
38705 7 Mile Rd, Livonia MI 48152-1056. 313/462-4041. Employs: 50-99.

GMAC
6750 Chicago Rd, Warren MI 48092-2047. 313/978-0880. Employs: 100-249.

Household Realty Corporation
18772 Middlebelt Rd, Livonia MI 48152-3528. 313/476-4960. Employs: 50-99.

Michigan National Bank
300 River Place Dr, Detroit MI 48207-4224. 313/259-6700. Employs: 50-99.

Motor City Co-Op Credit Union
17950 Van Dyke St, Detroit MI 48234-3954. 313/891-2100. Employs: 50-99.

Peoples Bank Of Port Huron
1226 24th St, Port Huron MI 48060-4824. 313/982-9042. Employs: 50-99.

Security Bank Of Commerce
32981 Utica Rd, Fraser MI 48026-3837. 313/293-2700. Employs: 50-99.

State Employees Credit Union
1011 N Harris St, Mount Pleasant MI 48858-1457. 517/772-4055. Employs: 50-99.

The Money Store
17197 N Laurel Park Dr, Livonia MI 48152-2686. 313/462-2399. Employs: 50-99.

Beneficial Finance Co Of Mi
20132 Plymouth Rd, Detroit MI 48228-1238. 313/836-5130. Employs: 50-99.

Calpat
160 W Robinwood St, Detroit MI 48203-1960. 313/892-2522. Employs: 50-99.

Classic Acceptance Corp
10821 W McNichols Rd, Detroit MI 48221-2305. 313/342-2221. Employs: 50-99.

Express Mortgage
3840 E 8 Mile Rd, Detroit MI 48234-1011. 313/369-9515. Employs: 50-99.

First Quality Finance
19852 Haggerty Rd, Livonia MI 48152-1092. 313/591-9230. Employs: 50-99.

Michigan National Bank
37276 6 Mile Rd, Livonia MI 48152-2700. 313/591-0707. Employs: 50-99.

Michigan National Bank
19120 Middlebelt Rd, Livonia MI 48152-2102. 313/476-5730. Employs: 50-99.

Michigan National Bank
34000 7 Mile Rd, Livonia MI 48152-3074. 313/478-0303. Employs: 50-99.

Michigan National Bank
34900 Plymouth Rd, Livonia MI 48150-1423. 313/425-2020. Employs: 50-99.

Michigan National Bank
30055 Plymouth Rd, Livonia MI 48150-2116. 313/425-1100. Employs: 50-99.

Michigan National Bank
34930 Ann Arbor Trl, Livonia MI 48150-3539. 313/525-3890. Employs: 50-99.

Michigan National Bank
15983 Middlebelt Rd, Livonia MI 48154-3311. 313/261-3410. Employs: 50-99.

Michigan National Bank
20000 Van Dykee, Detroit MI 48234. 313/891-8700. Employs: 100-249.

Michigan National Bank
11640 Morang Dr, Detroit MI 48224-1610. 313/527-5000.
Employs: 100-249.

Michigan National Bank
625 Shelby St, Detroit MI 48226-3206. 313/961-6260.
Employs: 100-249.

Michigan National Bank
3044 W Grand Blvd, Detroit MI 48202-3091. 313/875-2226. Employs: 100-249.

Michigan National Bank
15475 Gratiot Ave, Detroit MI 48205-1328. 313/372-0400.
Employs: 100-249.

Michigan National Bank
21370 W McNichols Rd, Detroit MI 48219-3974. 313/531-8400. Employs: 100-249.

Michigan National Bank
28865 Telegraph Rd, Southfield MI 48034-1949. 313/358-4586. Employs: 50-99.

Michigan National Bank
17117 W 9 Mile Rd, Southfield MI 48075-4602. 313/552-7607. Employs: 50-99.

Michigan National Bank
29630 Southfield Rd, Southfield MI 48076-2039. 313/557-5015. Employs: 50-99.

Michigan National Bank
27035 Greenfield Rd, Southfield MI 48076-3610. 313/569-7308. Employs: 50-99.

Michigan National Bank
14460 Livernois Ave, Detroit MI 48238-2056. 313/933-2705. Employs: 100-249.

Michigan National Bank
18550 E Warren Ave, Grosse Pointe MI 48236-2220.
313/343-5670. Employs: 50-99.

Michigan National Bank Detroit
9149 E Jefferson Ave, Detroit MI 48214-2906. 313/822-2944. Employs: 100-249.

Michigan National Bank Detroit
1505 Woodward Ave, Detroit MI 48226-2016. 313/961-1810. Employs: 50-99.

Michigan National Bank Detroit
500 Griswold St, Detroit MI 48226-3701. 313/962-7144.
Employs: 50-99.

Monroe Bank & Trust
102 E Front St, Monroe MI 48161-2117. 313/241-3431.
Employs: 50-99.

RAS Financial Inc
11077 Minden St, Detroit MI 48205-3758. 313/521-0930.
Employs: 50-99.

Sterling Marketing & Investment Co
3840 Miller St, Detroit MI 48211-1551. 313/368-1142.
Employs: 50-99.

Sunbelt National Mortgage Corp
30100 Telegraph Rd, Franklin MI 48025-4514. 313/647-8600. Employs: 100-249.

SHORT-TERM BUSINESS CREDIT INSTITUTIONS, EXCEPT AGRICULTURAL

Business Funding Corp
3105 E Winchester St, Detroit MI 48234. 313/932-0050.
Employs: 100-249.

MISCELLANEOUS BUSINESS CREDIT INSTITUTIONS

Advent Capital
32316 5 Mile Rd, Livonia MI 48154-3100. 313/422-2295.
Employs: 100-249.

Allen Group Leasing Corp
37519 Schoolcraft Rd, Livonia MI 48150-1009. 313/464-8100. Employs: 100-249.

Copelco Leasing
127N S Main, Plymouth MI 48170. 313/459-2290.
Employs: 100-249.

Future Credit & Investment Inc
20258 John R St, Detroit MI 48203-1138. 313/368-8188.
Employs: 100-249.

G C Leasing Systems
10553 Lanark St, Detroit MI 48224-1232. 313/884-5563.
Employs: 100-249.

Jerry's On Site Trailer Svc
5601 Belleville Rd, Canton MI 48188-2407. 313/397-1840.
Employs: 100-249.

L A Grant Inc
3001 Miller Rd, Dearborn MI 48120-1455. 313/593-3110.
Employs: 100-249.

Lease Advisory Corp
924 Millpond Ct, Northville MI 48167-1070. 313/348-4644. Employs: 100-249.

National Equipment Leasing Corp
32900 5 Mile Rd, Livonia MI 48154-3059. 313/422-3300.
Employs: 50-99.

Omnicorp Financial Inc
38705 7 Mile Rd, Livonia MI 48152-1056. 313/591-2323.
Employs: 100-249.

Southeastern Michigan Management Co
34393 Plymouth Rd, Livonia MI 48150-1539. 313/261-8810. Employs: 100-249.

The Palm Isle Financial Corp
17177 N Laurel Park Dr, Livonia MI 48152-2659. 313/462-5930. Employs: 50-99.

SECURITY BROKERS, DEALERS AND FLOTATION COMPANIES

A G Edwards & Sons Inc
1 Parklane Blvd Ste P101, Dearborn MI 48126-2402.
313/336-9200. Employs: 50-99.

C U Brokerage Services Inc
400 Town Center Dr Ste 102, Dearborn MI 48126-2737.
313/336-5960. Employs: 50-99.

Dean Witter Reynolds Inc
Fairlane Town, Dearborn MI 48126. 313/746-4500.
Employs: 50-99.

First Of Michigan Corp Br
23400 Michigan Av Ste 103, Dearborn MI 48124-1988.
313/277-0300. Employs: 50-99.

Kidder Peabody & Co Troy Ofc
3290 W Big Beaver Rd Ste 444, Troy MI 48084-2914.
313/649-5700. Employs: 100-249.

Manley Bennett Mc Donald
100 Renaissance Ct, Detroit MI 48243. 313/446-8300.
Employs: 50-99.

Merrill Lynch
35 N Gratiot Av, Mount Clemens MI 48043-5631.
313/465-7700. Employs: 100-249.

Merrill Lynch
400 Town Center Dr Ste 400, Dearborn MI 48126-2790
313/336-4500. Employs: 50-99.

Merrill Lynch Pierce Fenner
2100 Woodward Av Rm 265, Bloomfield MI 48304-2263.
313/647-3300. Employs: 100-249.

Prudential Bache Securities
400 Renaissance Ct Ste 160, Detroit MI 48243. 313/259-5000. Employs: 50-99.

Smith Hague & Co Inc
539 Penobscot, Detroit MI 48226. 313/963-5535. Employs: 50-99.

T I Investments
22005 Outer Dr, Dearborn MI 48124-3931. 313/562-5005. Employs: 50-99.

A G Edward & Sons Inc
1471 Woodward Ave, Detroit MI 48226-2001. 313/963-3486. Employs: 50-99.

Advantage Investment Svc
16150 Michigan Ave, Dearborn MI 48126-2936. 313/222-7290. Employs: 50-99.

Br Enterprises Pc
35551 Ford Rd, Westland MI 48185-3113. 313/721-6300. Employs: 50-99.

Burke Christensen and Lewis
100 Renaissance Ctr, Detroit MI 48243-1002. 313/567-8600. Employs: 50-99.

Edward D Jones & Co
555 7 Mile Rd, Northville MI 48167-1639. 313/348-9815. Employs: 50-99.

Financial Network Investment Corp
14507 W Warren Ave, Dearborn MI 48126-1364. 313/581-6141. Employs: 50-99.

First Of Michigan Corporation
13219 Eureka Rd, Southgate MI 48195-1309. 313/285-2000. Employs: 50-99.

Frost Financial Group Inc
2228 Ford Ave, Wyandotte MI 48192-2316. 313/246-8572. Employs: 50-99.

Grigsby Brandford Powell Inc
400 Renaissance Center, Detroit MI 48243. 313/567-4590. Employs: 50-99.

Growth Equity Inc
19606 Joy Rd, Detroit MI 48228-2927. 313/836-6900. Employs: 50-99.

Kemper Securities Group
798 Penniman Ave, Plymouth MI 48170-1620. 313/459-6100. Employs: 50-99.

Luther Walker Securities
600 Renaissance Ctr, Detroit MI 48243-1705. 313/393-8380. Employs: 50-99.

M R Beal & Co
600 Renaissance Ctr, Detroit MI 48243-1705. 313/393-4910. Employs: 50-99.

Merrill Lynch Pierce Fenner
200 Renaissance Center, Detroit MI 48243. 313/446-1111. Employs: 50-99.

Michigan Columbus Brkrge Svc
33288 6 Mile Rd, Livonia MI 48152-3266. 313/525-9333. Employs: 50-99.

National Securities Clearing Corp
3153 Penobscot Bg, Detroit MI 48226. 313/963-0155. Employs: 50-99.

Olde Discount

751 Griswold St, Detroit MI 48226-3209. 313/961-6666. Employs: 100-249.

Olde Discount
2210 West Rd, Trenton MI 48183-3616. 313/675-8900. Employs: 50-99.

Olde Discount
706 S Main St, Plymouth MI 48170-2047. 313/451-2500. Employs: 50-99.

Painewebber
38705 7 Mile Rd, Livonia MI 48152-1056. 313/464-3440. Employs: 50-99.

Painewebber
400 Renaissance Center, Detroit MI 48243. 313/567-7600. Employs: 50-99.

Prescott Ball & Turben Division
440 E Congress St, Detroit MI 48226-2917. 313/965-2800. Employs: 50-99.

Robert Fulton & Associates Inc
44644 W Ann Arbor Rd, Plymouth MI 48170-3908. 313/451-5665. Employs: 50-99.

Roney & Co
691 N Squirrel Rd, Auburn Hills MI 48326-2846. 313/373-5780. Employs: 50-99.

Schaeffner & Co
20360 Harper Ave, Harper Woods MI 48225-1643. 313/884-6625. Employs: 50-99.

Shearson Lehman Brothers Inc
600 Renaissance Ctr, Detroit MI 48243-1705. 313/259-8500. Employs: 50-99.

The Olde Building
24323 Ford Rd, Dearborn MI 48128-1129. 313/565-1400. Employs: 50-99.

W Curits & Co
15751 Farmington Rd, Livonia MI 48154-2857. 313/522-6610. Employs: 50-99.

Waterhouse Securities Inc
600 Renaissance Ctr, Detroit MI 48243-1705. 313/259-4100. Employs: 50-99.

Shearson Lehman Brothers Inc
900 Tower Dr, Troy MI 48098-2837. 313/879-1400. Employs: 50-99.

Shearson Lehman Brothers Inc
4000 Town Ctr, Southfield MI 48075-1410. 313/358-5000. Employs: 100-249.

COMMODITY CONTRACTS BROKERS AND DEALERS

Paul Inman Associates Inc
30095 Northwestern Hwy, Farmington MI 48334-3226. 313/626-8300. Employs: 100-249.

SECURITY AND COMMODITY EXCHANGES

First Of Michigan
501 S Saginaw St, Flint MI 48502-1802. 313/767-7460. Employs: 50-99.

First Of Michigan Corp
G5097 Miller Rd Ste A, Flint MI 48507. 313/732-0550. Employs: 50-99.

Neuron Inc
29100 Northwestern Hwy, Southfield MI 48034-1046. 313/355-0369. Employs: 50-99.

INVESTMENT ADVICE

Acquest Realty Advisors Inc
300 E Long Lk Rd Rm 355, Bloomfield MI 48304-2377.
313/645-5130. Employs: 100-249.

AMN Investments
24601 Maplehurst Dr, Clinton Twp MI 48036-1326.
313/776-5200. Employs: 50-99.

Desah Corp
13020 Puritan St, Detroit MI 48227-4022. 313/862-5911.
Employs: 50-99.

Howard & Kinchen Investment Co
21216 W 7 Mile Rd, Detroit MI 48219-1967. 313/532-
0010. Employs: 50-99.

International Investment Advisory
65 Cadillac Sq, Detroit MI 48226-2812. 313/963-0808.
Employs: 50-99.

Jay A Fishman Ltd
400 Renaissance Center, Detroit MI 48243. 313/567-3600.
Employs: 50-99.

Marquette Capital Management Corp
601 W Fort, Detroit MI 48226. 313/964-4225. Employs:
50-99.

Multi Properties Group
10 First National Bg, Detroit MI 48226. 313/965-6906.
Employs: 50-99.

Quality Financial Svc
11000 W McNichols Rd, Detroit MI 48221-2357. 313/864-
3200. Employs: 50-99.

Union Heritage Capital Management
155 W Congress St, Detroit MI 48226-3204. 313/963-8824.
Employs: 50-99.

Venture Investment Inc
16254 Meyers Rd, Detroit MI 48235-4107. 313/862-8443.
Employs: 50-99.

Wilmoco Capital Management
8027 Prairie St, Detroit MI 48204-3428. 313/934-8064.
Employs: 50-99.

Wilson Kemp and Associates
400 Renaissance Ctr Ste 2155, Detroit MI 48243-1699.
313/259-6210. Employs: 50-99.

Capital Financial Planning Group
19500 Middlebelt Rd, Livonia MI 48152-2114. 313/477-
6578. Employs: 50-99.

Consultek Inc
2727 2nd Ave, Detroit MI 48201-2654. 313/965-5692.
Employs: 50-99.

Educators Preferred Corp
18326 Woodward Ave, Detroit MI 48203-1917. 313/867-
6666. Employs: 50-99.

First Financial Corp
1523 E Jefferson Ave, Detroit MI 48207-3126. 313/567-
4111. Employs: 50-99.

Hathaway Associates
1551 Penobscot Building, Detroit MI 48226. 313/963-
1050. Employs: 50-99.

Sherwood Professional Services
4885 Buckingham, Detroit MI 48224. 313/882-3033.
Employs: 50-99.

Taxline Inc
400 Renaissance Ctr, Detroit MI 48243. 313/567-6622.
Employs: 50-99.

The Savings Bond Informer
1003 N Rademacher St, Detroit MI 48209-2244. 313/843-
1910. Employs: 50-99.

MISCELLANEOUS SERVICES ALLIED WITH THE EXCHANGE OF SECURITIES OR COMMODITIES

Mony Financial Services Br
2347 Stonebridge Dr, Flint MI 48532-5407. 313/733-8200.
Employs: 50-99.

MISCELLANEOUS OFFICES OF HOLDING COMPANIES

Security Bancorp Inc
16333 Trenton Rd, Southgate MI 48195-1407. 313/283-
8733. Employs: 100-249.

Sunshine-Fifty Inc
32961 Middlebelt Rd, Farmington MI 48334-1729.
313/626-7220. Employs: 50-99.

Drusilla Farwell Foundation
1708 Ford Bg, Detroit MI 48238. 313/961-6275. Employs:
100-249.

Strabel Enterprises
2200 E 11 Mile Rd, Warren MI 48091-1088. 313/751-
1700. Employs: 100-249.

Woodbridge Holdings
2380 Meijer Dr, Troy MI 48084-7145. 313/288-3233.
Employs: 100-249.

PATENT OWNERS AND LESSORS

Alrose Incorporated
2350 E Stadium Blvd Ste 11, Ann Arbor MI 48104-4891.
313/971-7727. Employs: 50-99.

David J Stanton & Associates
714 W Michigan Av, Jackson MI 49201-1909. 517/784-
4094. Employs: 50-99.

International Pizza Ventures
548 Church St, Ann Arbor MI 48104-2514. 313/761-2316.
Employs: 50-99.

De Novo Corp
45563 Van Dyke Ave, Utica MI 48317-5679. 313/739-
5520. Employs: 50-99.

Franchise Marketing Inc
28145 Greenfield Rd, Southfield MI 48076-7116. 313/443-
1669. Employs: 50-99.

Southland Corp 7 11 Food Ctr
26200 Town Center Dr, Novi MI 48375-1218. 313/344-
0047. Employs: 50-99.

Subway Development Of Central Michigan
542 Winthrop St, Jackson MI 49201-1018. 517/784-1255.
Employs: 50-99.

Subway Development Of Detroit
8838 Riverview, Redford MI 48239-1244. 313/532-1440.
Employs: 50-99.

Wendetroit Ltd
27301 Dequindre Rd, Madison Hts MI 48071-3473.
313/542-8680. Employs: 50-99.

World Franchise Consultants
15919 W 10 Mile Rd, Southfield MI 48075-2035. 313/559-
1415. Employs: 50-99.

UNIT INVESTMENT TRUSTS, FACE-AMOUNT
CERTIFICATE OFFICES AND CLOSED-END
MANAGEMENT INVESTMENT OFFICES

Carpadinga Investments
3425 Riverside Dr, Port Huron MI 48060-1862. 313/982-
5806. Employs: 50-99.

Colonial Investment Services
123 N Ashley St Ste 204, Ann Arbor MI 48104-1317
313/662-7775. Employs: 50-99.

Garner Financial Services
102 Montcalm St, Durand MI 48429-1216. 517/288-3491.
Employs: 50-99.

Index Corporation
315 Eisenhower Pkwy E Ste 316, Ann Arbor MI 48108-
3330. 313/769-0801. Employs: 100-249.

J & F Investments
3182 Stonybrook La, Port Huron MI 48060-1620. 313/982-
6126. Employs: 50-99.

P G M Investments
4030 Aletha La, Port Huron MI 48060-1735. 313/982-
2887. Employs: 50-99.

Real Investment Corp
121 S Barnard St Rm 10, Howell MI 48843-2305. 517/548-
1093. Employs: 50-99.

Realway Investment
G2067 Kingswood Dr, Flint MI 48507. 313/234-0912.
Employs: 50-99.

Retirement Services
301 E Liberty St Ste 580, Ann Arbor MI 48104-2265.
313/769-1258. Employs: 50-99.

Struthers Export Services Corp
301 E Liberty St Ste 580, Ann Arbor MI 48104-2265.
313/747-6766. Employs: 50-99.

Tricorp Securities L T D
339 E Liberty St Ste 300, Ann Arbor MI 48104-2205.
313/994-4790. Employs: 50-99.

Upchurch Corporation
100 Tandy Center 4th Fl, Jackson MI 49202. 517/870-
0300. Employs: 50-99.

Vlasic & Company
710 Woodward Av Rm 100, Bloomfield MI 48304-2852.
313/642-3380. Employs: 50-99.

Yentema Wood & Company
725 S Adams Rd Rm L67, Birmingham MI 48009-6904.
313/642-4142. Employs: 50-99.

MANAGEMENT CONSULTING SERVICES

Market Opinion Research
550 Washington Bl, Detroit MI 48226-4410. 313/963-
2414. Employs: 50-99.

Phillip B Fischer Co
255 E Brown St Ste 110, Birmingham MI 48009-6212.
313/433-3400. Employs: 50-99.

The Steiner Company
130 S 1st St 4th floor, Ann Arbor MI 48104-1304.
313/761-3912. Employs: 50-99.

Q X P Industrial & Pro Service Inc
29448 Oakley St, Livonia MI 48154-3734. 313/422-4888.
Employs: 50-99.

B D N Ind Hygn Consultants Inc
2107 E 14 Mile Rd, Sterling Hts MI 48310-5970. 313/264-
3939. Employs: 100-249.

Automated Marketing Systems Inc
26533 Evergreen Rd, Southfield MI 48076-4301. 313/352-
5900. Employs: 100-249.

Tom Sullivan Inc
25300 W 8 Mile Rd, Southfield MI 48034-3865. 313/353-
6900. Employs: 100-249.

Avenir Inc
5505 Corporate Dr, Troy MI 48098-2619. 313/641-7889.
Employs: 100-249.

MISCELLANEOUS BUSINESS CONSULTING
SERVICES

Cole Financial Services
65 Cadillac Sq, Detroit MI 48226-2812. 313/962-3575.
Employs: 50-99.

For more information on career opportunities in financial services and management consulting:

Associations

AMERICAN FINANCIAL SERVICES
ASSOCIATION
919 18th Street, 3rd Floor, Washington DC 20006.
202/296-5544.

AMERICAN MANAGEMENT ASSOCIATION
Management Information Service, 135 West 50th Street,
New York NY 10020. 212/586-8100.

AMERICAN SOCIETY OF APPRAISERS
P.O. Box 17265, Washington DC 20041. 703/478-2228.

ASSOCIATION OF MANAGEMENT CONSULTING
FIRMS
521 Fifth Avenue, 35th Floor, New York NY 10175.
212/697-9693.

COUNCIL OF CONSULTANT ORGANIZATIONS
521 Fifth Avenue, 35th Floor, New York NY 10175.
212/697-8262.

FEDERATION OF TAX ADMINISTRATORS

444 North Capital Street NW, Washington DC 20001.
202/624-5890.

ASSOCIATION FOR INVESTMENT
MANAGEMENT AND RESEARCH
200 Park Avenue, 18th Floor, New York NY 10166.
212/957-2860.

FINANCIAL EXECUTIVES INSTITUTE
10 Madison Avenue, P.O. Box 1938, Morristown NJ
07962-1938. 201/898-4600.

INSTITUTE OF FINANCIAL EDUCATION
111 East Wacker Drive, Chicago IL 60601. 312/644-3100.

INSTITUTE OF INTERNATIONAL FINANCE
2000 Pennsylvania Ave NW, Washington DC 20006.
202/857-3600.

INSTITUTE OF MANAGEMENT CONSULTANTS
521 Fifth Avenue, 35th Floor, New York NY 10175.
212/697-8262.

NATIONAL ASSOCIATION OF BUSINESS ECONOMISTS
28790 Chagrin Boulevard, Suite 300, Cleveland OH 44122. 216/464-7986.

NATIONAL ASSOCIATION OF CREDIT MANAGEMENT
8815 Centre Park Drive, Suite 200, Columbia MD 21045-2117. 301/740-5560.

NATIONAL ASSOCIATION OF REAL ESTATE INVESTMENT TRUSTS
1129 20th Street NW, Suite 705, Washington DC 20036. 202/785-8717.

NATIONAL COMMERCIAL FINANCE ASSOCIATION
225 West 34th Street, New York NY 10122. 212/594-3490.

TREASURY MANAGEMENT ASSOCIATION
7315 Wisconsin Avenue, Suite 1250-W, Bethesda MD 20814. 301/907-2862.

SECURITIES INDUSTRY ASSOCIATION
120 Broadway, New York NY 10271. 212/608-1500.

PUBLIC SECURITIES ASSOCIATION
40 Broad Street, New York NY 10004. 212/809-7000.

Directories

DIRECTORY OF AMERICAN FINANCIAL INSTITUTIONS
McFadden Business Publications, 6195 Crooked Creek Road, Norcross GA 30092. 404/448-1011.

MOODY'S BANK AND FINANCE MANUAL
Moody's Investor Service, 99 Church Street, New York NY 10007. 212/553-0300.

Magazines

BARRON'S: NATIONAL BUSINESS AND FINANCIAL WEEKLY
Dow Jones & Co., 200 Liberty Street, New York NY 10281. 212/416-2700.

FINANCIAL PLANNING
40 W. 57th Street, 8th Floor, New York NY 10019. 212/765-5311.

INSURANCE TIMES
M & S Communications, 437 Newtonville Avenue, Newton MA 02160. 617/924-8161.

FINANCIAL WORLD
Financial World Partners, 1450 Broadway, New York NY 10001. 212/594-5030.

FUTURES: THE MAGAZINE OF COMMODITIES AND OPTIONS
250 South Wacker Drive, Suite 1150, Chicago IL 60606. 312/977-0999.

INSTITUTIONAL INVESTOR
488 Madison Avenue, New York NY 10022. 212/303-3300.

FOOD AND BEVERAGES: PROCESSING AND DISTRIBUTION

The best bets in the food industry are meats and poultry; processed fruits and vegetables; and soft drinks. One of the worst areas in the food industry is liquor and spirits.

AWREY BAKERIES INC.
12301 Farmington Road, Livonia MI 48150. 313/522-1100. **Contact:** Personnel Department. **Description:** A producer of bread, pies, pastries, and other delicate bakery products. **Employees:** 600.

BRECTEEN COMPANY
50750 East Russell Schmidt, Chesterfield MI 48051. 313/949-2240. **Contact:** Eric Ahrens, Personnel Director. **Description:** A Detroit company engaged in the manufacture of sausage, sausage casings, and prepackaged meat. **Employees:** 200.

COCA-COLA/DETROIT
5981 West Warren, Detroit MI 48210. 313/897-5000. **Contact:** Personnel. **Description:** Engaged in the bottling and canning of soft drinks. **Employees:** 800. Parent company, headquartered in Atlanta, GA, is one of the world's

leading producers of soft drinks; among the world's largest citrus processors; and the third largest wine company in the United States. Send resumes to: 26777 Farmington Hills, Halsted 48331. Company operates nationwide in two primary areas: Soft Drink Sector (Coca-Cola, Tab, Sprite, Fresca, and many others); and Food and Wine Sector (Minute Maid Orange Juice, Hi-C drinks, Presto plastic wraps, Taylor wines, Sterling wines, Great Western sparkling wines, and other products).

DETROIT CITY DAIRY INC.
15004 3rd Avenue, Highland Park MI 48203. 313/868-5511. **Contact:** James Mrowka, Controller. **Description:** Wholesale distributors of dairy and deli products. **Employees:** 200.

DON LEE DISTRIBUTORS INC.
14301 Prospect, Dearborn MI 48126. 313/584-7100. **Contact:** Jay Yule, Personnel Director. **Description:** A leading area wholesale distributor of beer and ale. **Employees:** 300.

EASTERN MARKET BEEF PROCESSING
1825 Scott, Detroit MI 48207. 313/833-2700. **Contact:** Personnel Department. **Description:** A major Detroit area meat packing and beef processing plant. **Employees:** 200.

EVERFRESH BEVERAGES INC.
6600 East Nine Mile Road, Warren MI 48091. 313/755-9500. **Contact:** Michelle Simon, Personnel Manager. **Description:** Engaged in the manufacture of canned fruit and vegetables. **Common positions:** General Labor. **Benefits:** medical, dental and life insurance; pension plan; disability coverage; savings plan. **Corporate headquarters:** Franklin Park, IL. **Operations at this facility:** manufacturing. **Employees:** 100.

FRITO-LAY INC.
1000 Enterprise Drive, Allen Park MI 48101. 313/271-3000, ext. 240. **Contact:** Human Resources. **Description:** Engaged in the manufacture of food preparations. **Employees:** 500. **Common positions:** Maintenance Mechanic; Project Engineer; Maintenance Supervisor; Production Supervisor; Shipping Supervisor; Chemical Engineer; Electrical Engineer; Industrial Engineer; Mechanical Engineer; Quality Control Supervisor. **Principle educational backgrounds sought:** Business Administration; Engineering. **Benefits:** medical, dental, and life insurance; pension plan; tuition assistance; disability coverage; savings plan. **Corporate headquarters:** Allen Park, MI. **Parent company:** Pepsico. **Operations at this facility:** manufacturing. **Listed on:** New York Stock Exchange.

HOBAN FOODS
1599 East Warren Avenue, Detroit MI 48207. 313/831-7900. **Contact:** Personnel Department. **Description:** A Detroit manufacturer of frozen fresh juices. **Employees:** 200.

PAUL INMAN ASSOCIATES INC.
P.O. Box 1600, Farmington Hills MI 48333. 313/626-8300. **Contact:** Cheri Jerue, Personnel Administrator. Engaged in the wholesale distribution of grocery products.

KELLOGG COMPANY
One Kellogg Square, P.O. Box 3599, Battle Creek MI 49016-3599. 616/961-2405. **Contact:** Paul W. Jones, Personnel. **Description:** Kellogg Company, a diversified international company, specializes in the manufacture and marketing of quality convenience foods. **Common positions:** Accountant; Attorney; Chemist; Computer Programmer; Dietician; Agricultural Engineer; Electrical Engineer; Mechanical Engineer; Food Technologist; Statistician; Systems Analyst. **Educational backgrounds sought:** Accounting; Chemistry; Computer Science; Engineering. **Benefits:** medical insurance; dental insurance; pension plan; life insurance; tuition assistance; disability coverage; savings plan. **Corporate headquarters:** this location. **Operations at this facility:** manufacturing; research/development; administration. **Listed on:** New York Stock Exchange.

KOEGEL MEATS INC.
3400 West Bristol Road, Flint MI 48507. 313/238-3685. **Contact:** Jim Lay, Plant Manager. **Description:** A manufacturer of sausage and prepackaged meats. **Employees:** 100.

KOZAK DISTRIBUTORS INC.
8825 Vincent, Hamtramick MI 48211. 313/925-3220. **Contact:** Judith Ross, Human Resources Manager. **Description:** Engaged in the wholesale distribution of beer and ale. **Employees:** 100.

LONDON DAIRY
2136 Pine Grove, Port Huron MI 48060. 313/984-5111. **Contact:** Walt Wypych, Personnel Director. **Description:** An area producer of milk and dairy products. **Employees:** 200.

McDONALD DAIRY COMPANY
P.O. Box 469, Flint MI 48501. 313/232-9193. **Contact:** Elaine Houle, Personnel. **Description:** A Flint dairy company which produces fluid milk and other dairy products. **Employees:** 200.

McINEVRY-MILLER BROTHERS
2001 Brewster Street, Detroit MI 48207. 313/833-4800. **Contact:** Dick Miller, Director of Personnel. **Description:** A leading metropolitan Detroit wholesaler of poultry and poultry products. **Employees:** 100.

MELODY FOODS INCORPORATED
31111 Industrial Road, Livonia MI 48150. 313/525-4000. **Contact:** Terri Moore, Personnel Director. **Description:** A Southeastern Michigan distributor of dairy, ice cream, juice, and snacks. **Employees:** 200.

METRO GROCERY INC.
1331 Holden Avenue, Detroit MI 48202. 313/871-4000. **Contact:** Personnel. **Description:** A leading metropolitan Detroit wholesale distributor of grocery products. **Employees:** 200.

METZ BAKERIES/TAYSTEE DIVISION
5721 Martin, Detroit MI 48210. 313/896-3400. **Contact:** Kim Carter, Personnel Director. **Description:** A major Detroit bakery which specializes in bread products. **Employees:** 500.

MICHIGAN MILK PRODUCTS
41310 Bridge Street, Novi MI 41302. 313/474-6672. **Contact:** Personnel Department. **Description:** A local milk cooperative which markets milk and dairy products for 400 area dairy farmers. **Employees:** 800.

MORLEY CANDY COMPANY
P.O. Box 463237, Mount Clemens MI 48046-3237. 313/468-4300. **Contact:** Bob Kocis, Director of Personnel. **Description:** An area company engaged in the manufacture of candy and confectionery products.

SARA LEE BAKERY
P.O. Box 1009, Traverse City MI 49685. 616/947-2100. **Contact:** Personnel Department. **Description:** A producer of frozen pies. Parent company, Sara Lee Corporation, is a diversified consumer goods company.

SHERWOOD FOODS
18615 Sherwood Avenue, Detroit MI 48234. 313/366-3100. **Contact:** Personnel Department. **Description:** A leading metropolitan Detroit wholesale distributor of meats and meat products.

STROH BREWERY COMPANY
100 River Place, Detroit MI 48207. 313/446-2020. **Contact:** Bob Inskeep, Director of Personnel. **Description:** Engaged in the production of well-known nationally marketed malt beverages. **Employees:** 3,000. **Common positions:** Chemist; Computer Programmer; Electrical Engineer; Industrial Engineer; Mechanical Engineer; Financial Analyst; Food Technologist; Personnel and Labor Relations Specialist; Purchasing Agent; Sales Representative; Systems Analyst. **Educational backgrounds sought:** Accounting; Biology; Business Administration; Chemistry; Computer Science; Economics; Engineering; Finance; Marketing. **Benefits:** medical, dental and life insurance; pension plan; tuition assistance; disability coverage; savings plan. **Corporate headquarters:** This location. **Operations at this facility:** research/development, administration. **Projected hires for the next 12 months:** 25-30.

THORN APPLE VALLEY INC.
18700 West 10 Mile Road, Southfield MI 48075. 313/552-0700. **Contact:** Personnel Department. **Description:** A major Southeastern Michigan meat packaging plant. **Employees:** 2,700.

TRUAN'S CANDIES
13716 Tireman, Detroit MI 48228. 313/584-3400. **Contact:** Mark Truan, President. **Description:** A leading Detroit manufacturer of candy and confectionery products. **Employees:** 100.

TWIN PINE FARM DAIRY
8101 Greenfield, Detroit MI 48228. 313/584-7900. **Contact:** Personnel Department. **Description:** A major metropolitan Detroit producer of dairy products. **Employees:** 200. **Common positions:** Accountant; Administrator; Credit Manager; Branch Manager; Department Manager; General Manager; Management Trainee; Operations/Production Manager; Purchasing Agent; Quality Control Supervisor; Sales Representative. **Educational backgrounds sought:** Accounting; Biology; Business Administration; Computer Science. **Benefits:** medical, dental, and life insurance; pension plan. **Corporate headquarters:** This location. **Parent company:** C.F. Burger Creamery. **Operations at this facility:** manufacturing; research/development; administration; service; sales.

UTICA PACKING COMPANY
7655 Chapoton Street, Utica MI 48318-0182. 313/731-6080. **Contact:** Janet Loncarski, Personnel. **Description:** A company involved in the wholesale trade of meats and meat products. **Employees:** 100.

HIRAM WALKER AND SONS INC.
P.O. Box 33006, Detroit MI 48232. 313/965-6611. **Contact:** David Porter, Manager of Personnel Services. A producer, bottler, and distributor of wine and spirits products. Subsidiary operations throughout the U.S. **Common positions:** Accountant; Administrator; Advertising Worker; Biochemist; Computer Programmer; Food Technologist; Marketing Specialist; Personnel and Labor Relations Specialist; Quality Control Supervisor; Sales Representative; Systems Analyst. **Educational backgrounds sought:** Accounting; Business Administration; Computer Science; Marketing. Training programs available. **Benefits:** medical insurance; dental insurance; pension plan; life insurance; tuition assistance; disability coverage; savings plan. **Corporate headquarters:** This location. **Operations include:** divisional headquarters; administration.

WESLEY'S ICE CREAM
18940 Weaver Avenue, Detroit MI 48228. 313/270-3220. **Contact:** Personnel Department. **Description:** A major metropolitan Detroit company engaged in the production of milk and dairy products. **Employees:** 200.

WOLVERINE PACKING COMPANY
1340 Winder Avenue, Detroit MI 48207. 313/259-7500. **Contact:** Gail Patrick, Personnel Director. **Description:** A major Detroit wholesale distributor of meats and meat products. **Employees:** 100.

Additional large employers: 250+

SAUSAGES AND OTHER PREPARED MEAT PRODUCTS

Hygrade Food Products Corp
38200 Plymouth Rd, Livonia MI 48150-1050. 313/464-2400. Employs: 250-499.

Thorn Apple Valley
3925 Tillman St, Detroit MI 48208-2445. 313/894-6600. Employs: 250-499.

POULTRY SLAUGHTERING

Borg Poultry Farm
10600 S Meridian Rd, Hudson MI 49247-9402. 517/448-7245. Employs: 250-499.

PICKLED FRUITS AND VEGETABLES, VEGETABLE SAUCES AND SEASONINGS, AND SALAD DRESSINGS

Aunt Jane Foods Inc
55 East Sanborn, Croswell MI 48422-1403. 313/679-2555. Employs: 250-499.

Vlasic Foods Inc
26777 Halsted Rd Ste 100, Farmington MI 48331-3541. 313/851-9400. Employs: 500-999.

PREPARED FLOUR MIXES AND DOUGHS

Chelsea Milling Co
201 North St, Chelsea MI 48118-1259. 313/475-1361. Employs: 250-499.

Dawn Food Products Inc
2021 Micor Dr, Jackson MI 49203-3448. 517/789-4400. Employs: 250-499.

BREAD AND OTHER BAKERY PRODUCTS, EXCEPT COOKIES AND CRACKERS

Continental Baking Co
2845 John C Lodge Fw, Detroit MI 48201-2901. 313/963-2330. Employs: 500-999.

Continental Baking Co
1100 Oakman Blvd, Detroit MI 48238-2949. 313/868-5600. Employs: 500-999.

Sanders Country Home Bakery
100 Oakman Blvd, Detroit MI 48203-3052. 313/868-5700. Employs: 250-499.

BEET SUGAR

Michigan Sugar Co
159 S Howard St, Croswell MI 48422-1317. 313/679-2240. Employs: 250-499.

MISC. SHORTENING, TABLE OILS, MARGARINE AND OTHER EDIBLE FATS AND OILS

Van Den Bergh Foods Inc
14401 Dexter Ave, Detroit MI 48238-2633. 313/868-5810. Employs: 250-499.

DISTILLED AND BLENDED LIQUORS

Heublein Inc
2500 Enterprise Dr, Allen Park MI 48101-3528. 313/594-8900. Employs: 250-499.

BOTTLED AND CANNED SOFT DRINKS AND CARBONATED WATERS

Buffalo Don's Artesian Wells
P O Box 2500, Plymouth MI 48170-0907. 313/455-3600. Employs: 250-499.

Faygo Beverages Co
3579 Gratiot Ave, Detroit MI 48207-1829. 313/925-1600. Employs: 250-499.

Pepsi-Cola Co
1555 Mack Ave, Detroit MI 48207-4719. 313/832-0910. Employs: 250-499.

Vernors Inc
4501 Woodward Av, Detroit MI 48201-1821. 313/356-2400. Employs: 250-499.

MISC. FOOD PREPARATIONS

DSLT Inc
1362 River Rd, Saint Clair MI 48079-2803. 313/329-3100. Employs: 250-499.

MISC. STORES

Meijer Incorporated
2474 W Hill Rd, Flint MI 48507-3821. 313/235-2700. Employs: 250-499.

Hop-In Food Stores Inc
2141 S State St, Ann Arbor MI 48104-6105. 313/663-9320. Employs: 1000+.

POULTRY AND POULTRY PRODUCTS: WHOLESALE

Foodland Distributors
12701 Middlebelt Rd, Livonia MI 48150-2210. 313/523-2100. Employs: 250-499.

MISCELLANEOUS GROCERIES AND RELATED PRODUCTS: WHOLESALE

Coca Cola Bottlers Detroit Inc
5981 W Warren Ave, Detroit MI 48210-1116. 313/897-5000. Employs: 500-999.

Spring Arbor Distributors
10885 Textile Rd, Belleville MI 48111-2315. 313/481-0900. Employs: 500-999.

ERB Lumber
12190 Inkster Rd, Redford MI 48239-2521. 313/937-1990. Employs: 250-499.

Tri-City Aggregates Inc
14300 Shields Rd, Holly MI 48442-9731. 313/694-2840. Employs: 250-499.

Additional small to medium sized employers: 50-249

HOGS

Calderone-Curran Ranches I
4749 Willis Rd, Grass Lake MI 49240-9548. 517/522-4095. Employs: 50-99.

MEAT PACKING PLANTS

Family Packing Distributing Co
1445 E Kirby St, Detroit MI 48211-2519. 313/873-3999. Employs: 50-99.

Hygrade Food Products Corp
P O Box 19170, Detroit MI 48219-0170. 313/355-1100. Employs: 100-249.

Michigan Packing Co
2628 Orleans St, Detroit MI 48207-4507. 313/393-3800. Employs: 50-99.

Premium Natural Casing Ltd
5240 Riopelle St, Detroit MI 48211-2525. 313/831-5400. Employs: 50-99.

Wolverine Packing Co
2426 Scotn, Detroit MI 48209. 313/554-0700. Employs: 50-99.

SAUSAGES AND OTHER PREPARED MEAT PRODUCTS

Bob Evans Farms Inc
200 N Wolcott St, Hillsdale MI 49242-1762. 517/437-3349. Employs: 100-249.

Butcher Boy Meats Inc
20643 Stephens St, St Clair Shrs MI 48080-1047. 313/771-9880. Employs: 50-99.

Dearborn Sausage Co Inc
2444 Ferney St, Dearborn MI 48120-1509. 313/842-2375. Employs: 50-99.

Hygrade Food Products Assocs
40 Oak Hollow #355, Southfield MI 48034-7452. 313/355-1100. Employs: 50-99.

POULTRY SLAUGHTERING AND PROCESSING

Herbruck Poultry Ranch Inc
6425 W Grand River Ave, Saranac MI 48881-9611. 616/642-9421. Employs: 100-249.

DRY, CONDENSED AND EVAPORATED DAIRY PRODUCTS

Twin Pines Farm Dairy
8101 Greenfield Rd, Detroit MI 48228-2220. 313/584-7900. Employs: 100-249.

ICE CREAM AND FROZEN DESSERTS

Wesleys Quaker Maid Inc
18940 Weaver St, Detroit MI 48228-1351. 313/270-3200. Employs: 50-99.

FLUID MILK

C F Burger Creamery Co
8101 Greenfield Rd, Detroit MI 48228-2220. 313/584-4040. Employs: 100-249.

Embest Inc
31770 Enterprise Dr, Livonia MI 48150-1960. 313/261-7980. Employs: 100-249.

Jackson All Star Dairy
1401 Daniel Rd, Jackson MI 49202-4016. 517/782-7141. Employs: 100-249.

Melody Foods Inc
30777 Northwestern Hwy #300, Farmington MI 48334-2594. 313/851-6990. Employs: 100-249.

Melody Foods/Lansing Dairy
2224 W Willow St, Lansing MI 48917-1842. 517/485-7263. Employs: 50-99.

Michigan Dairy
29601 Indl Rd, Livonia MI 48150. 313/522-7060. Employs: 100-249.

Michigan Milk Products Assn
26300 Northwestern Hw, Southfield MI 48076-3714. 313/354-9780. Employs: 50-99.

Michigan Milk Producers Assn
431 W Williams St, Ovid MI 48866-9697. 517/834-2221. Employs: 50-99.

Peninsular Products Co
2701 E Michigan Ave, Lansing MI 48912-4014. 517/487-6771. Employs: 100-249.

Quality Dairy Co
1400 S Washington Av, Lansing MI 48910-1655. 517/487-4634. Employs: 50-99.

CANNED FRUITS, VEGETABLES, PRESERVES, JAMS AND JELLIES

Great Lakes Mushroom Inc
23950 Ryan Rd, Warren MI 48091-4556. 313/757-0888. Employs: 50-99.

Pellerito Foods Inc
2000 Mack Ave, Detroit MI 48207-4724. 313/831-3344. Employs: 50-99.

DRIED AND DEHYDRATED FRUITS, VEGETABLES AND SOUP MIXES

Lafayette Deli
142 W Lafayette Blvd, Detroit MI 48226-2609. 313/964-5026. Employs: 50-99.

PICKLED FRUITS AND VEGETABLES, VEGETABLE SAUCES AND SEASONINGS AND SALAD DRESSINGS

G D McDonald & Sons
3151 W Fillmore, Ithaca MI 48847-9606. 517/875-4719. Employs: 50-99.

Green Bay Food Co
502 Marlin St, Eaton Rapids MI 48827-1844. 517/663-2081. Employs: 100-249.

Vlasic Foods Inc
415 S Blacks Corners, Imlay City MI 48444-9761. 313/724-2715. Employs: 100-249.

Carson City Pickle Co
7451 S Garlock Rd, Carson City MI 48811-9563. 517/584-3148. Employs: 50-99.

M & W Tankyards Inc
20 E Harrington Rd, Croswell MI 48422-1217. 313/679-2900. Employs: 50-99.

FROZEN FRUITS, FRUIT JUICES AND VEGETABLES

Frigid Food Products Inc
1599 E Warren Av, Detroit MI 48207-1035. 313/831-7900. Employs: 50-99.

MISCELLANEOUS FROZEN SPECIALTIES

Twin City Foods Inc
1315 Sherman St, Lake Odessa MI 48849-1334. 616/374-8837. Employs: 100-249.

FLOUR AND OTHER GRAIN MILL PRODUCTS

D C A Food Inds
101 E Bacon St, Hillsdale MI 49242-1666. 517/437-3351. Employs: 100-249.

PREPARED FEEDS AND FEED INGREDIENTS FOR ANIMALS AND FOWL, EXCEPT DOGS AND CATS

Darling & Co
3350 Greenfield, Melvindale MI 48122-1280. 313/928-7400. Employs: 50-99.

BREAD AND OTHER BAKERY PRODUCTS, EXCEPT COOKIES AND CRACKERS

Blue Bird Baking Co
15135 Hamilton Ave, Detroit MI 48203-3725. 313/865-3233. Employs: 50-99.

Bunny's Specialties
1980 Connecticut Ave, Marysville MI 48040-1852. 313/364-9682. Employs: 50-99.

Carol's Cake & Candy Supplies
54 S Monroe St, Monroe MI 48161-2238. 313/243-6540. Employs: 50-99.

Continental Baking Co
808 Gratiot Blvd, Marysville MI 48040-1127. 313/364-6741. Employs: 50-99.

Continental Baking Co
3791 Ann Arbor Rd, Jackson MI 49202-2729. 517/764-1050. Employs: 50-99.

Dawn Donuts
4300 W Pierson Rd, Flint MI 48504-1344. 313/733-0760. Employs: 100-249.

Koepplinger's Bakery Inc
15200 W 8 Mile Rd, Oak Park MI 48237-3007. 313/967-2020. Employs: 100-249.

Metropolitan Baking Co Inc
8579 Lumpkin St, Detroit MI 48212-3622. 313/875-7246. Employs: 50-99.

Metz Baking
26800 Schoenherr Rd, Warren MI 48089-5902. 313/772-0055. Employs: 50-99.

Mister Bread Inc
4025 N Dort Hwy, Flint MI 48506-2320. 313/767-3551. Employs: 50-99.

Quality Bakery Products
8100 Radcliffe St, Detroit MI 48210-1814. 313/897-4444. Employs: 100-249.

Schafer Bakeries
2701 S Logan St, Lansing MI 48910-2652. 517/372-3920. Employs: 50-99.

Sugar Bakers
14278 Fenton Rd, Fenton MI 48430-1544. 313/750-6464. Employs: 50-99.

Way Bakeries Inc
2100 Enterprise Dr, Jackson MI 49203-3410. 517/787-6720. Employs: 100-249.

CANE SUGAR, EXCEPT REFINING

Domino Sugar Corporation
29200 Vassar St, Livonia MI 48152-2116. 313/478-2330. Employs: 50-99.

Great Lakes Sugar Co
11993 E US Highway 223, Blissfield MI 49228-9527. 517/486-2815. Employs: 100-249.

Michigan Sugar Co
1310 E Sanilac Rd, Sandusky MI 48471-9107. 313/648-3236. Employs: 50-99.

CANDY AND OTHER CONFECTIONERY PRODUCTS

Minerva Street Chocolates Inc
1053 Olivia Ave, Ann Arbor MI 48104-3928. 313/996-4090. Employs: 50-99.

Pak-A-Snak Nut Factory
1936 Lapeer Av, Port Huron MI 48060-4154. 313/987-8463. Employs: 50-99.

SALTED AND ROASTED NUTS AND SEEDS

Kar Nut Products Co
1525 Wanda Ave, Ferndale MI 48220-2020. 313/541-7870. Employs: 50-99.

MALT BEVERAGES

Detroit Brewery Inc
470 W Canfield St, Detroit MI 48201-1220. 313/831-2739. Employs: 100-249.

Miller Brewing Co
39555 Orchard Hill Pl, Novi MI 48375-5374. 313/347-5858. Employs: 100-249.

WINES, BRANDY AND BRANDY SPIRITS

J Cooper Lewis Co
12400 Strathmoor St, Detroit MI 48227-2758. 313/835-6400. Employs: 100-249.

DISTILLED AND BLENDED LIQUORS

Anchor Auto Purchases
43574 Champlain Ct, Canton MI 48188-1711. 313/397-2670. Employs: 100-249.

Hiram Walker & Sons Inc
32255 Northwestern Hwy, Farmington MI 48334-1566. 313/626-0575. Employs: 100-249.

Seagram House Of
26913 Northwestern Hwy, Southfield MI 48034-4715. 313/262-1375. Employs: 100-249.

BOTTLED AND CANNED SOFT DRINKS AND CARBONATED WATERS

Coca Cola Bottling Co Of Mi
2515 Lapeer Rd, Flint MI 48503-4350. 313/234-4608. Employs: 50-99.

Coca-Cola Bottling Co Of Mi
3256 Iron St, Burton MI 48529-1425. 313/744-2000. Employs: 50-99.

Pepsi-Cola Bottling Group
6200 Taylor Dr, Flint MI 48507-4681. 313/767-0360. Employs: 50-99.

Pepsi-Cola Bottling Group
500 S Averill Av, Flint MI 48506-4010. 313/762-5700. Employs: 100-249.

Pepsi-Cola Co
755 S McPherson Pk Dr, Howell MI 48843-1933. 517/546-5370. Employs: 50-99.

Seven-Up Of Detroit Inc
12201 Beech-Daly Rd, Redford MI 48239-2431. 313/937-3500. Employs: 50-99.

Wolcott Orchards & Cider Mill
G3284 W Coldwater Rd, Flint MI 48504. 313/789-9561. Employs: 50-99.

MISCELLANEOUS FLAVORING EXTRACTS AND FLAVORING SYRUPS

General Spice Inc
17800 Filer St, Detroit MI 48212-1408. 313/366-7600. Employs: 50-99.

POTATO CHIPS, CORN CHIPS AND SIMILAR SNACKS

Better Made Potato Chips
10148 Gratiot Ave, Detroit MI 48213-3211. 313/925-4774. Employs: 100-249.

Better Made Potato Chips
2765 Michigan Rd, Port Huron MI 48060-2445. 313/987-8206. Employs: 50-99.

C & M Food Service
G3239 W Pasadena Av, Flint MI 48504. 313/230-2300. Employs: 50-99.

Cabana Foods Co
14245 Birwood St, Detroit MI 48238-2207. 313/834-0800. Employs: 100-249.

Frito-Lay
475 Cuttle Rd, Marysville MI 48040-1803. 313/364-8001. Employs: 50-99.

Paramount Potato Chip Co Inc
2727 Lippincott Blvd, Flint MI 48507-2021. 313/239-2191. Employs: 50-99.

MACARONI, SPAGHETTI, VERMICELLI AND NOODLES

Leon's Home Made Foods Inc
521 E Saginaw St, Lansing MI 48906-5250. 517/484-7117. Employs: 50-99.

Prince Co Inc
26155 Groesbeck Hwy, Warren MI 48089-4149. 313/772-0900. Employs: 50-99.

MISCELLANEOUS FOOD PREPARATIONS

Indian Summer Inc
700 Kiddville Rd, Belding MI 48809-9594. 616/794-1400. Employs: 100-249.

Wyeth-Ayerst Labs Inc
W North St, Mason MI 48854. 517/676-5445. Employs: 100-249.

CIGARETTES

Lorillard Tobacco Co
24300 Catherine Industrial Dr, Novi MI 48375-2457. 313/349-7350. Employs: 100-249.

GROCERY STORES

A & P Food Store
2400 Fort St, Lincoln Park MI 48146-2496. 313/383-4488. Employs: 50-99.

A & P Food Store
20125 Ann Arbor Trl, Dearborn Hts MI 48127-2661. 313/271-1666. Employs: 50-99.

A & P Food Stores
20900 Gratiot Ave, East Detroit MI 48021-2857. 313/755-8580. Employs: 50-99.

A & P Food Stores
19020 Fort St, Wyandotte MI 48192-6701. 313/479-1700. Employs: 50-99.

A & P Food Stores
14510 2nd Ave, Detroit MI 48203-3773. 313/868-0656. Employs: 100-249.

A & P Food Stores
605 N Cedar St, Imlay City MI 48444-1175. 313/724-6123. Employs: 50-99.

Bazley Farm Market
45550 Van Dyke Ave, Utica MI 48317-5678. 313/731-3313. Employs: 100-249.

Carter's Food Center
512 S Clinton St, Grand Ledge MI 48837-2201. 517/627-2073. Employs: 50-99.

Felpausch Food Center
1406 N Eaton, Albion MI 49224. 517/629-6313. Employs: 50-99.

Food Town Spr Markets Gen Office
20 W Washington St, Clarkston MI 48346-1576. 313/625-0440. Employs: 100-249.

George's Big C Market
702 W Court St, Flint MI 48503-5012. 313/234-5392. Employs: 50-99.

Hollywood Super Market No 3
2670 W Maple Rd, Troy MI 48084-7133. 313/643-6770. Employs: 50-99.

Hutch's Food Center
8025 Spring Arbor Rd, Spring Arbor MI 49283-9733. 517/788-6181. Employs: 50-99.

Jack Farmer Markets
29583 5 Mile Rd, Livonia MI 48154-3709. 313/522-0877. Employs: 100-249.

Jewel Osco
2105 W Michigan Av, Jackson MI 49202-4011. 517/788-6920. Employs: 50-99.

Kroger Company
23001 Michigan Av, Dearborn MI 48124-2011. 313/563-6647. Employs: 100-249.

Kroger Company
2502 Packard Rd, Ann Arbor MI 48104-6802. 313/971-0288. Employs: 100-249.

Kroger Company
2641 Plymouth Rd, Ann Arbor MI 48105-2425. 313/994-4670. Employs: 100-249.

Kroger Company
15265 S Dixie Hwy, Monroe MI 48161-3709. 313/242-1866. Employs: 100-249.

Kroger Company
1093 N Wisner St, Jackson MI 49202-3143. 517/782-8127. Employs: 100-249.

Kroger Company
3176 Mall Ct, Lansing MI 48912-5210. 517/332-2090. Employs: 100-249.

Kroger Company
2495 N Cedar St, Holt MI 48842-2100. 517/694-4119. Employs: 50-99.

Kroger Company
900 S US 27, Saint Johns MI 48879. 517/224-6841. Employs: 50-99.

Kroger Company Br
3222 S Logan St, Lansing MI 48910-2985. 517/882-4823.
Employs: 50-99.

Kroger Company Br
1140 Broadway St, Ann Arbor MI 48105-1808. 313/665-0979. Employs: 100-249.

Kroger Company Br
3021 E Michigan Av, Jackson MI 49202-3847. 517/787-4982. Employs: 50-99.

Leadway Super Market
8960 Van Dyke, Detroit MI 48213-2149. 313/921-7250.
Employs: 50-99.

Matt's Market
3633 S Telegraph Rd, Dearborn MI 48124-3278. 313/278-7410. Employs: 50-99.

Meadowdale Foods Inc
8711 Meadowdale St, Detroit MI 48228-2555. 313/943-3300. Employs: 100-249.

Mister B's Inc
3402 Richfield Rd, Flint MI 48506-2608. 313/736-2870.
Employs: 50-99.

Polly's Market
1101 M-52, Chelsea MI 48118. 313/475-8230. Employs:
50-99.

Riveria Food & Drugs
11292 W Jefferson Av, River Rouge MI 48218-1210.
313/842-2270. Employs: 50-99.

Saturn Food Center
25200 Van Born Rd, Dearborn Heights MI 48125-2010.
313/292-7400. Employs: 50-99.

Stan's Market
33503 5 Mile Rd, Livonia MI 48154-2861. 313/261-6565.
Employs: 50-99.

Stewart's Foodland
110 Woodworth Av, Alma MI 48801-2441. 517/463-4753.
Employs: 100-249.

The Kroger Co
31 E Long Lake Rd, Troy MI 48098-4738. 313/879-1040.
Employs: 100-249.

The Kroger Co
3611 Mich Av, Wayne MI 48184. 313/326-8600. Employs:
50-99.

The Kroger Co
670 Highland Ave, Milford MI 48381-1518. 313/685-1528.
Employs: 100-249.

The Kroger Co
18870 Mack Ave, Grosse Pointe MI 48236-2925. 313/881-8354. Employs: 50-99.

The Kroger Company
2855 Union Lake Rd, Commerce Twp MI 48382-3562.
313/360-1440. Employs: 100-249.

The Kroger Company
3675 W Maple Rd, Bloomfield MI 48301-3376. 313/647-4976. Employs: 50-99.

The Kroger Company

3663 E Grand River Ave, Howell MI 48843-8513.
517/546-4460. Employs: 50-99.

Tomboy Markets
4120 2nd Ave, Detroit MI 48201-1704. 313/833-5566.
Employs: 50-99.

V G's Food Center
3150 Owen Rd, Fenton MI 48430-1757. 313/629-2627.
Employs: 50-99.

V G's Food Center
710 S Mill St, Clio MI 48420-1443. 313/686-9330.
Employs: 50-99.

Walco Foods Inc
3219 Broad St, Dexter MI 48130-1018. 313/426-4119.
Employs: 50-99.

Wyoming Shortstop
5330 Wyoming St, Detroit MI 48210-2048. 313/846-7867.
Employs: 50-99.

A & P Food Stores
2219 W Vienna Rd, Clio MI 48420-1757. 313/686-8939.
Employs: 50-99.

The Kroger Co
35700 Warren Rd, Westland MI 48185-2016. 313/525-9760. Employs: 50-99.

The Kroger Co
5720 N Sheldon Rd, Canton MI 48187-3112. 313/459-2760. Employs: 100-249.

The Kroger Co
1005 E Grand River Ave, Brighton MI 48116-1803.
313/229-9246. Employs: 50-99.

Bath Shoprite
14049 Webster Rd, Bath MI 48808-9747. 517/641-4081.
Employs: 50-99.

West Saginaw Shop Rite
3800 W Saginaw St, Lansing MI 48917-2275. 517/321-4392. Employs: 50-99.

**MEAT AND FISH (SEAFOOD) MARKETS,
INCLUDING FREEZER PROVISIONERS**

Bazley & Junedale Markets Co
1458 W Grand River, Williamston MI 48895. 517/655-2185. Employs: 100-249.

The Kroger Co
23191 Marter Rd, St Clair Shores MI 48080-2735.
313/771-2290. Employs: 100-249.

FRUIT AND VEGETABLE MARKETS

Pesick Brothers Fruit Mkt Inc
5060 Schaefer Rd, Dearborn MI 48126-3221. 313/582-6256. Employs: 50-99.

MISCELLANEOUS FOOD STORES

Westside Deli & Party Store
6541 S Cedar St, Lansing MI 48911-5962. 517/882-6624.
Employs: 100-249.

Vital Foods
22200 Grove St, Detroit MI 48219-3874. 313/533-2448.
Employs: 50-99.

For more information on career opportunities in food and beverage production and distribution:

Associations

ALLIED TRADES OF THE BAKING INDUSTRY
P.O. Box 398, Memphis TN 38101. 800/238-5765.

AMERICAN ASSOCIATION OF CEREAL CHEMISTS
3340 Pilot Knob Road, St. Paul MN 55121. 612/454-7250.

AMERICAN FROZEN FOOD INSTITUTE
1764 Old Meadow Lane, McLean VA 22102. 703/821-0770.

AMERICAN SOCIETY OF AGRICULTURAL ENGINEERS
2950 Niles Road, St. Joseph MI 49085. 616/429-0300.

AMERICAN SOCIETY OF BREWING CHEMISTS
3340 Pilot Knob Road, St. Paul MN 55121. 612/454-7250.

DAIRY AND FOOD INDUSTRIES SUPPLY ASSOCIATION
6245 Executive Boulevard, Rockville MD 20852. 301/984-1444.

DISTILLED SPIRITS COUNCIL OF THE UNITED STATES
1250 I Street NW, Suite 900, Washington DC 20005. 202/628-3544.

MASTER BREWERS ASSOCIATION OF THE AMERICAS
4513 Vernon Boulevard, Madison, WI 53705. 608/231-3446.

NATIONAL AGRICULTURAL CHEMICALS ASSOCIATION
1155 15th Street NW, Suite 900, Washington DC 20005. 202/296-1585.

NATIONAL BEER WHOLESALERS' ASSOCIATION
5205 Leesburg Pike, Suite 1600, Falls Church VA 22041. 703/578-4300.

NATIONAL DAIRY COUNCIL
10255 W. Higgins Road, Suite 900, Rosemont IL 60018. 708/803-2000.

NATIONAL FOOD PROCESSORS ASSOCIATION
1401 New York Avenue NW, Suite 400, Washington DC 20005. 202/639-5900.

NATIONAL SOFT DRINK ASSOCIATION
1101 16th Street NW, Washington DC 20036. 202/463-6732.

UNITED FOOD AND COMMERCIAL WORKERS INTERNATIONAL UNION
1775 K Street NW, Washington DC 20006. 202/223-3111.

Directories

FOOD ENGINEERING'S DIRECTORY OF U.S. FOOD PLANTS
Chilton Book Co., Chilton Way, Radnor PA 19089. 800/695-1214.

THOMAS FOOD INDUSTRY REGISTER
Thomas Publishing Co., One Penn Plaza, New York NY 10019. 212/695-0500.

Magazines

BEVERAGE INDUSTRY
Advanstar Communications, 7500 Old Oak Boulevard, Cleveland OH 44130. 216/243-8100.

BEVERAGE WORLD
150 Great Neck Road, Great Neck NY 11021. 516/829-9210.

FOOD MANAGEMENT
233 North Michigan, Chicago IL 60601. 312/938-2300.

FOOD PROCESSING
301 East Erie, Chicago IL 60611. 312/644-2020.

FROZEN FOOD AGE
Maclean Hunter Media, #4 Stamford Forum, Stamford CT 06901. 203/325-3500.

PREPARED FOODS
Gorman Publishing Co., 8750 West Bryn Mawr, Chicago IL 60631. 312/693-3200.

GENERAL MERCHANDISE: RETAIL AND WHOLESALE

While much of the retail industry has been struggling against low consumer confidence, discount department stores have been booming. This trend holds true for both merchandise and apparel stores, as well as for other broad areas like health and beauty aides. Overall, retailing will continue to grow at a relatively slow pace. Unfortunately for professionals, most new jobs will be entry-level, where there is currently a major labor shortage.

ACO HARDWARE INC.
23333 Commerce Drive, Farmington Hills MI 48335-2764. 313/471-0100. **Contact:** Wes Mewer, Personnel Director. **Description:** Engaged in the retail trade of tools and hardware products.

ADRAY APPLIANCE & PHOTO
20219 Carlysle, Dearborn MI 48124. 313/274-9500. **Contact:** Carl Johnson, Store Manager. **Description:** A wholesale distributor of household appliances. **Employees:** 100.

ART VAN FURNITURE-TECH PLAZA
6500 East 14 Mile Road, Warren MI 48092. 313/939-2100. **Contact:** Personnel Department. **Description:** A wholesale distributor of a varied line of furniture. **Employees:** 1,000.

BUICK MOTOR DIVISION/GENERAL MOTORS
902 East Hamilton Avenue, Flint MI 48550. 313/236-5000. **Contact:** John Masserio, Director of Personnel. **Description:** Primarily engaged in the sale of Buick passenger cars. Parent company, General Motors, is a major producer of cars, trucks, and buses sold worldwide; the firm has 152 facilities operating in 26 states and 93 cities in the United States and 13 plants in Canada, and also has assembly, manufacturing, distribution, sales, or warehousing operations in 37 other countries

CIS CORPORATION
1695 S. Woodward, Suite 206, Bloomfield Hills MI 48302. 313/456-0000. **Contact:** Personnel Department. **Description:** A third party leasing company engaged in the wholesale trade of telephones, and electronic and industrial machinery.

CADILLAC MOTOR CAR DIVISION/
GENERAL MOTORS
2860 Clark Avenue, Detroit MI 48232. 313/554-6112. **Contact:** Human Resources. **Description:** Primarily engaged in the sale of Cadillac passenger cars. Parent company, General Motors, is a major producer of cars, trucks, and buses sold worldwide; the firm has 152 facilities operating in 26 states and 93 cities in the United States and 13 plants in Canada, and also has assembly, manufacturing, distribution, sales, or warehousing operations in 37 other countries

JIM CAUSLEY INC.
38111 Gratiot Avenue, Mount Clemens MI 48036. 313/776-4455. **Contact:** Dan Weis, Treasurer. **Description:** A major area dealer of new and used vehicles. **Employees:** 200.

CHURCH'S LUMBER YARDS
P.O. Box 189005, Utica MI 48318. **Contact:** Tom Erhart, Vice President of Human Resources. **Description:** A retail chain of lumber, hardware, and building material stores. **Common positions:** Accountant; Buyer; Computer Programmer; Credit Manager; Retail Manager; Personnel and Labor Relations Specialist; Sales Representative. **Educational backgrounds sought:** Accounting; Business Administration; Computer Science; Marketing. **Special Programs:** Training programs. **Benefits:** medical, dental, and life insurance; 401K plan; life insurance; tuition assistance; disability coverage; employee discount.

CROWLEY MILNER AND COMPANY
2301 West Lafayette, Detroit MI 48216. 313/962-2400. **Contact:** Jan Rieckhoff, Director of Human Resources. **Description:** A major metropolitan Detroit chain of department stores. **Employees:** 1,600. **Common positions:** Advertising Worker; Computer Programmer; Department Manager; Personnel and Labor Relations Specialist. **Educational backgrounds sought:** Business Administration; Liberal Arts; Marketing; Retail Merchandising. **Benefits:** medical and life insurance; tuition assistance; disability coverage; profit sharing; employee discounts. **Corporate headquarters:** This location. **Operations at this facility:** regional headquarters; administration. **Listed on:** American Stock Exchange.

DETROIT PUMP & MANUFACTURING COMPANY
18943 John R. Street, Detroit MI 48203. 313/893-4242. **Contact:** Personnel Department. **Description:** A metropolitan Detroit distributor of industrial pumps, machinery, and related equipment. **Employees:** 100.

DURAKON INDUSTRIES INC.
2101 North Lapeer Road, Lapeer MI 48446. 313/664-0850. **Contact:** Cindy Coe, Personnel Director. **Description:** A company engaged in the wholesale trade of auto parts and supplies. **Employees:** 600.

ERB LUMBER COMPANY
P.O. Box 3013, Birmingham MI 48012. 313/644-5300. **Contact:** Richard Kramer, Personnel Director. **Description:** A major Detroit company engaged in the retail dealership of lumber and related construction materials.

EVANS-SHERRATT COMPANY
16619 Wyoming, Detroit MI 48221. 313/341-6600. **Contact:** Ole Lyngklip, Personnel Director. **Description:** Engaged in the wholesale trade of professional equipment and supplies. **Employees:** 100.

J.N. FAUVER COMPANY INC.
1500 East Avis Drive, Madison Heights MI 48071. 313/585-5252. **Contact:** Finance Officer. Engaged in the wholesale trade of industrial machinery and equipment. **Employees:** 300.

FOLAND'S
4100 14 Mile Road, Warren MI 48092. 313/264-0110. **Contact:** Personnel. **Description:** A Southeastern Michigan chain of general merchandising stores. **Employees:** 400.

FRANK'S NURSERY & CRAFTS INC.
6501 East Nevada, Detroit MI 48234. 313/366-8400. **Contact:** Tony Fazioli, Human Resource Manager. **Description:** A specialty retailer of nursery, craft, and Christmas items. Over 275 stores in the Midwest, East, and in central and south Florida. A subsidiary of General Host Corporation. **Corporate headquarters:** Detroit, MI. **Operations include:** administration. **Common positions:** Management Trainee. **Educational backgrounds sought:** Business Administration; Marketing. **Benefits:** medical insurance; dental insurance; pension plan; life insurance; tuition assistance; disability coverage; employee discounts; savings plan.

GENERAL MOTORS
3031 West Grand Boulevard, Detroit MI 48202. 313/974-0190. **Contact:** Personnel. **Description:** Sells and markets service parts and equipment to independent aftermarkets, including automotive, agricultural, marine, and other industries. Parent company, General Motors, is a major producer of cars, trucks, and buses sold worldwide; the firm has 152 facilities operating in 26 states and 93 cities in the United States and 13 plants in Canada, and also has assembly, manufacturing, distribution, sales, or warehousing operations in 37 other countries.

HALL INDUSTRIES CORPORATION
P.O. Box 809, Warren MI 48090. 313/558-8090. **Contact:** Personnel Department. **Description:** Engaged in the wholesale trade of industrial supplies. **Employees:** 400.

HANDLEMAN COMPANY
500 Kirts Road, Troy MI 48084. 313/362-4400. **Contact:** Roger Apple, Personnel Director. **Description:** Engaged in the wholesale distribution of prerecorded music, books on tape, and video. **Employees:** 1,500.

HIGHLAND SUPERSTORES INC.
909 North Sheldon Road, Plymouth MI 48170. 313/451-3200. **Contact:** Human Resources. **Description:** Retail electronics and appliances. **Common positions:** Accountant; Administrator; Advertising Worker; Buyer; Claim Representative; Computer Programmer; Credit Manager; Customer Service Representative; Financial Analyst; Department Manager; General Manager; Operations/Production Manager; Sales Representative; Systems Analyst. **Common positions:** Accounting; Business Administration; Communications; Computer Science; Finance; Marketing; Mathematics. **Special programs:** Training programs available. **Benefits:** medical insurance; dental insurance; life insurance; tuition assistance; disability coverage; profit sharing; employee discounts; savings plan. **Corporate headquarters:** This location.

HIT OR MISS, INC.
833 Hunter Boulevard, Birmingham MI 48009. 313/644-4588. **Contact:** Rigo Hernandez, Regional Manager. **Description:** A chain of women's fashion stores; over 550 stores in 35 states. A division of TJX, Inc. For professional hiring information please **Contact:** Staffing and Career Development, 100 Campanelli Parkway, Stoughton, MA 02072. **Common positions:** Buyer; Assistant Buyer; Branch Manager; Store Manager; Assistant Store Manager; Assistant Store Manager-in-Training (for supervisors with no prior retail experience); Sales Associate; Loss Prevention Specialist; Store Detective. **Special programs:** Paid Training; Internships. **Benefits:** medical, dental, and life insurance; tuition assistance; disability coverage; employee discounts; 401K retirement plan; referral bonus program; scholarship program; savings/profit sharing plan; service award program; stock options. **Corporate headquarters:** Stoughton, MA. **Educational backgrounds sought:** College degree or experience in any customer service-based occupation; Art/Design; Business Administration; Liberal Arts. **Operations at this facility:** Sales. **Employees:** 5,000+. **Projected hires for the next 12 months:** Expect to hire several assistant managers-in-training. **Listed on:** New York Stock Exchange.

HOMEMAKER SHOPS INC./LINENS & MORE
25899 West 12 Mile Road, Suite 300, Southfield MI 48034. 313/353-0404. **Contact:** Sidney Freedland, Personnel Department. **Description:** Engaged in retail trade of linens, domestics, and bed and bath supplies. **Employees:** 500.

INVETECH
1400 Howard Street, Detroit MI 48216. Mailed inquiries only. **Contact:** Manager/Human Resources. **Description:** A distributor of bearings, power transmission products, V-belts, hoses, plastics, chains, and sprockets. **Corporate headquarters:** This location. **Operations include:** administration; service; sales. **Common positions:** Accountant; Administrator; Advertising

Worker; Blue-Collar Worker Supervisor; Buyer; Computer Programmer; Credit Manager; Customer Service Representative; Branch Manager; Department Manager; General Manager; Management Trainee; Operations/Production Manager; Marketing Specialist; Personnel and Labor Relations Specialist; Purchasing Agent; Sales Representative; Systems Analyst; Technical Writer/Editor. **Educational backgrounds sought:** Accounting; Business Administration; Computer Science; Engineering; Finance; Liberal Arts; Marketing. **Benefits:** medical, dental, and life insurance; tuition assistance; disability coverage; profit sharing; employee discounts; savings plan.

K-MART ENTERPRISES
3100 West Big Beaver Road, Troy MI 48084. 313/643-1000. **Contact:** Liz Koerber, Personnel Manager. **Description:** Corporate headquarters location for the nationally known chain of discount department stores.

LAPEER COUNTY CO-OP INC.
155 South Saginaw, Lapeer MI 48446. 313/664-2907. **Contact:** Donald Currey, General Manager. **Description:** A Lapeer area company engaged in the wholesale trade of farm products. **Employees:** 100.

MADISON ELECTRIC COMPANY
31855 Van Dyke, Warren MI 48093-1047. 313/825-0200. **Contact:** Ben Rosenthal, Personnel Director. **Description:** A wholesaler of electrical apparatus and equipment. **Employees:** 200.

McNAUGHTON-McKAY ELECTRIC
1357 East Lincoln, Madison Heights MI 48071. **Contact:** Personnel Department. **Description:** Engaged in the wholesale trade of electrical appliances and equipment. **Employees:** 100.

MEYER TREASURE CHEST STORES
20500 Eureka, Suite 200, Taylor MI 48180. 313/283-0900. **Contact:** Mr. Munoz, Director of Personnel. **Description:** A metropolitan Detroit chain of jewelry stores. **Employees:** 300.

MICHIGAN CAT
24800 Novi Road, Novi MI 48375-2897. 313/349-4800. **Contact:** Clair Ritchie, Personnel. **Description:** A major Southeastern Michigan wholesaler of Caterpillar construction and mining equipment. **Employees:** 400.

MID-WEST PAPER PRODUCTS COMPANY
12350 East 9 Mile Road, Warren MI 48089. 313/758-6700. **Contact:** Hiring. A wholesaler of industrial and personal service paper products. **Employees:** 100. **Common positions:** Accountant; Blue-Collar Worker Supervisor; Buyer; Claim Representative; Computer Programmer; Credit Manager; Customer Service Representative; Department Manager; Operations/Production Manager; Purchasing Agent; Sales Representative; Transportation And Traffic Specialist. **Benefits:** medical, dental, and life insurance; tuition assistance; disability

coverage. **Corporate headquarters:** Warrensville, OH. **Parent company:** Superior Container. **Operations at this facility:** divisional headquarters location; sales.

MURRAY'S BARGAIN CENTER
27207 Plymouth Road, Redford MI 48239. 313/937-8360. **Contact:** Barry Pitt, Owner. **Description:** A metropolitan Detroit based chain of auto parts supply stores. **Employees:** 300.

H.J. OLDENKAMP COMPANY
P.O. Box 865, Warren MI 48090. 313/756-0600. **Contact:** John Maher, Director of Personnel. **Description:** Engaged in the wholesale trade of construction materials. **Employees:** 100.

PRODUCTION TOOL SUPPLY
8655 East 8 Mile Road, Warren MI 48089. 313/755-7770. **Contact:** Michael Brenner, Controller. **Description:** Engaged in the wholesale trade of industrial supplies. **Employees:** 200.

R.S. ELECTRONICS INC.
34443 Schoolcraft, Livonia MI 48150. 313/525-1155. **Contact:** Personnel Department. **Description:** One of the largest wholesale distributors of electronic/electrical components, test and measurement instrumentation in the United States. **Common positions:** Buyer; Computer Programmer; Customer Service Representative; Electrical Engineer; Purchasing Agent; Sales Representative. **Educational backgrounds sought:** Accounting; Business Administration; Computer Science; Engineering; Finance; Liberal Arts. **Benefits:** medical, dental and life insurance; tuition assistance; disability coverage; employee discounts; 401 K. **Corporate headquarters:** This location. **Operations at this facility:** administration; sales.

SEAMAN PATRICK PAPER COMPANY
2000 Howard Street, Detroit MI 48216. 313/496-3131. **Contact:** Rick Akkashian, Vice President of Sales. **Description:** A Detroit-based company engaged in the wholesale distribution of printing and writing paper. **Employees:** 200. **Common positions:** Customer Service Representative; Sales Representative. **Educational backgrounds sought:** Accounting; Business Administration; Liberal Arts. **Benefits:** medical insurance; pension plan; life insurance; disability coverage; profit sharing. **Corporate headquarters:** This location. **Operations at this facility:** regional headquarters; divisional headquarters; administration; sales.

SERVICE PARTS OPERATIONS/GENERAL MOTORS
6060 West Bristol Road, M.C. 2200, Flint MI 48554. 313/635-5268. **Contact:** A.L. Marchio, Personnel Director. **Description:** Responsible for supplying, marketing and distributing replacement parts within the corporation and to independent wholesalers and mass merchandisers internationally. Parent company, General Motors, is a major producer of cars, trucks, and buses sold

worldwide; the firm has 152 facilities operating in 26 states and 93 cities in the United States and 13 plants in Canada, and also has assembly, manufacturing, distribution, sales or warehousing operations in 37 other countries.

SHIFRIN-WILLENS INC.
14510 West 8 Mile Road, Oak Park MI 48237. 313/968-1515. **Contact:** Mr. Bernard Pavlosky, Chief Financial Officer. A local area chain of jewelry stores. **Employees:** 300.

SIBLEY'S SHOES INC.
100 Renaissance Center, Suite 2440, Detroit MI 48243. 313/259-1900. **Contact:** Anne Lewis, Director of Personnel. **Description:** Owners and operators of a chain of area shoe stores. **Employees:** 400.

VOLKSWAGEN OF AMERICA
3800 Hamlin Road, Human Resources Room 2d-01, Auburn Hills MI 48326. 313/340-4970. **Contact:** Mike Elbert, Staffing and Personnel Planning Manager. **Description:** Engaged in the wholesale distribution of automobiles. **Employees:** 1,150. **Common positions:** Field Credit Representative; Accountant; Computer Programmer; Financial Analyst; Management Trainee; Marketing Specialist; Parts Representative; District Sales Representative; Service Representative; Systems Analyst. **Educational backgrounds sought:** Automotive Technology; Accounting; Business Administration; Computer Science; Finance; Marketing. **Benefits:** medical, dental, and life insurance; pension plan; tuition assistance; disability coverage; employee discounts; 401 K savings plan; employee company car purchase and lease plan. **Corporate headquarters:** This location. **Parent company:** Volkswagen AG in Wolfsburg, Germany. **Operations at this facility:** divisional headquarters location; information systems; administration; service; sales; parts; technical support.

WEST SIDE DISTRIBUTORS
41839 Michigan Avenue, Canton MI 48187. 313/397-2500. **Contact:** Jackie Nagy, Personnel. **Description:** An area company engaged in the wholesale distribution of auto parts and supplies. **Employees:** 100.

GEORGE C. WETHERBEE AND CO.
2566 East Grand Boulevard, Detroit MI 48211. 313/871-3200. **Contact:** Personnel Department. **Description:** A major metropolitan Detroit-based chain of hardware stores.

WINKELMAN STORES INC.
45000 Helm, Plymouth MI 48170. 313/451-5225. **Contact:** Patricia A. Mann, Employment Rep./College Relations. **Description:** Publicly-owned corporation operating 50 women's apparel specialty stores in Michigan, Ohio, and Illinois. **Employees:** 1,300.

Additional large employers: 250+

**SERVICE ESTABLISHMENT EQUIPMENT AND
SUPPLIES: WHOLESALE**

Banner Linen Svc
2233 Brooklyn St, Detroit MI 48201-2957. 313/963-7200.
Employs: 250-499.

John E Green Co
220 Victor St, Detroit MI 48203-3116. 313/868-2400.
Employs: 500-999.

**RETAIL NURSERIES, LAWN AND GARDEN
SUPPLY STORES**

J C Penney Co
Fairlane Town Center, Dearborn MI 48126. 313/593-3300.
Employs: 250-499.

J C Penney Co Inc
G3341 Genesee Valley Center, Flint MI 48507. 313/733-
7300. Employs: 250-499.

J L Hudson Co
G3341 Genesee Valley Center, Flint MI 48507. 313/732-
3232. Employs: 250-499.

J L Hudson Co
700 Briarwood Cir, Ann Arbor MI 48108. 313/994-3232.
Employs: 250-499.

K-Mart Department Store
G3083 Miller Rd, Flint MI 48507-1353. 313/238-2615.
Employs: 250-499.

Meijer's
2055 W Grand River Av, Okemos MI 48864-1706.
517/349-6800. Employs: 250-499.

Montgomery Ward & Co
5220 W Saginaw St, Lansing MI 48917-1913. 51 /323-
4550. Employs: 250-499.

Saks Fifth Avenue
2901 Somerset Mall, Troy MI 48084-3211. 313/643-9000.
Employs: 250-499.

Sears Roebuck and Co
4460 24th Ave, Fort Gratiot MI 48059-3809. 313/987-
7000. Employs: 250-499.

Sears Roebuck and Co
G3341 Genesee Valley Center, Flint MI 48507. 313/733-
4400. Employs: 250-499.

Target Store
G3515 Miller Rd, Flint MI 48507-1273. 313/230-7310.
Employs: 250-499.

J C Penney Co Inc
Building P Northland Ctr, Southfield MI 48075. 313/557-
6600. Employs: 250-499.

Hudson's
Lakeside Mall, Sterling Heights MI 48313. 313/566-2800.
Employs: 500-999.

Meijer Inc
2750 S State Rd, Ionia MI 48846-9475. 616/527-9200.
Employs: 250-499.

Sears Roebuck and Co
14100 Lakeside Cir, Sterling Heights MI 48313-1322.
313/566-2000. Employs: 250-499.

MISC. GENERAL MERCHANDISE STORES

Meijer Inc
3301 S Creyts Rd, Lansing MI 48917-9533. 517/487-6300.
Employs: 1000+.

AUTO AND HOME SUPPLY STORES

Action Auto Stores Inc
2128 S Dort Hwy, Flint MI 48507-5202. 313/235-5600.
Employs: 250-499.

J P Industries Inc
325 Eisenhower Pkwy E Ste 300, Ann Arbor MI 48108-
3307. 313/663-6749. Employs: 1000+.

AUTO AND HOME SUPPLY STORES

Jacobson's
17030 Kercheval St, Grosse Pointe MI 48230-1540.
313/882-7000. Employs: 250-499.

Jacobson's
37500 6 Mile Rd, Livonia MI 48152-2682. 313/591-7696.
Employs: 250-499.

WOMEN'S ACCESSORY AND SPECIALTY STORES

Jacobson Stores Inc
3333 Sargent Rd, Jackson MI 49201-8847. 517/764-6400.
Employs: 1000+.

**MISCELLANEOUS APPAREL AND ACCESSORY
STORES**

Bernard Wigs Inc
20530 Southfield Fw, Detroit MI 48235. 313/593-3340.
Employs: 250-499.

MISCELLANEOUS HOMEFURNISHINGS STORES

Linens & More
25899 W 12 Mile Rd, Southfield MI 48034-1800. 313/353-
0404. Employs: 250-499.

Mt Clemens Pottery
261 Church St, Mount Clemens MI 48043-2124. 313/468-
7840. Employs: 250-499.

U S Maintenance Corp
21751 Coolidge Hwy, Oak Park MI 48237-3108. 313/399-
0700. Employs: 250-499.

**RADIO, TELEVISION AND CONSUMER
ELECTRONICS STORES**

Fretter Inc
35901 Schoolcraft Rd, Livonia MI 48150-1215. 313/591-
0600. Employs: 1000+.

**COMPUTER AND COMPUTER SOFTWARE
STORES**

IBM Corp
18000 W 9 Mile Rd, Southfield MI 48075-4002. 313/552-
4200. Employs: 500-999.

Compuware Corp
31440 Northwestern Hwy, Farmington MI 48334-2564.
313/737-7300. Employs: 1000+.

DRUG STORES AND PROPRIETARY STORES

Arbor Drugs
3331 W Big Beaver Rd, Troy MI 48084-2804. 313/643-
9420. Employs: 1000+.

Borman's Inc
P O Box 446, Detroit MI 48231-0446. 313/270-1000.
Employs: 1000+.

Perry Drug Stores Inc
5400 Perry Dr P O Box 1957, Pontiac MI 48340. 313/334-
1300. Employs: 1000+.

Perry Drug Stores
685 N East Blvd, Pontiac MI 48341. 313/333-7152.
Employs: 500-999.

JEWELRY STORES

Foland's Inc
29753 Plymouth Rd, Livonia MI 48150-2125. 313/427-2800. Employs: 250-499.

GIFT, NOVELTY AND SOUVENIR SHOPS

Detroit Institute Of Arts
5200 Woodward Ave, Detroit MI 48202-4008. 313/833-7900. Employs: 250-499.

Hudson's
18000 Vernier Rd, Harper Woods MI 48225-1027.
313/245-2200. Employs: 250-499.

Hudson's
500 W 14 Mile Rd, Troy MI 48083-4219. 313/585-3232.
Employs: 250-499.

Pontchartrain Hotel Gift Shop
2 Washington Blvd, Detroit MI 48226-4416. 313/964-3306. Employs: 250-499.

OPTICAL GOODS STORES

D O C Optics Corporation
19800 W Eight Mile Rd, Southfield MI 48075-5730.
313/354-7100. Employs: 250-499.

Montgomery Ward & Co
28800 Dequindre Rd, Warren MI 48092-2466. 313/751-7500. Employs: 250-499.

J C Penney Co Inc
14300 Lakeside Cir, Sterling Heights MI 48313-1326.
313/247-9220. Employs: 250-499.

MISCELLANEOUS RETAIL STORES

Creative Foam Corp
300 Alloy Dr, Fenton MI 48430. 313/629-4149. Employs: 250-499.

D & C Stores
N Clinton St, Stockbridge MI 49285. 517/851-7925.
Employs: 250-499.

Helm Inc
14310 Hamilton, Detroit MI 48203-3776. 313/865-5000.
Employs: 250-499.

Wright & Filippis Inc
4201 Saint Antoine St, Detroit MI 48201-2194. 313/832-5020. Employs: 250-499.

Additional small to medium sized employers: 50-249

OFFICE EQUIPMENT

Mayer-Schairer Co
112 S Main St, Ann Arbor MI 48104-1903. 313/662-3137.
Employs: 50-99.

Office Products Center
3202 E Court St, Flint MI 48506-4023. 313/767-6600.
Employs: 50-99.

Skf Office Products
32625 N Western Hwy, Farmington MI 48024. 313/851-0686. Employs: 50-99.

The Lewis R P Company
G3248 W Bristol Rd, Flint MI 48507. 313/767-5790.
Employs: 50-99.

Unisys Corporation Br
2290 Science Pkwy, Okemos MI 48864-2522. 517/349-2300. Employs: 100-249.

Xerox
5409 Gateway Blvd, Flint MI 48507-3992. 313/257-1100.
Employs: 50-99.

East Kodak Co
32500 Telegraph Rd, Franklin MI 48025-2461. 313/258-0100. Employs: 50-99.

Union Bank
1150 Jordan Lake St, Lake Odessa MI 48849-1212.
616/374-8829. Employs: 50-99.

MISCELLANEOUS COMMERCIAL EQUIPMENT

Comp U Credit
16250 Northland Dr, Southfield MI 48075-5205. 313/557-1088. Employs: 50-99.

Philip Olender & Co
9001 Vincent, Detroit MI 48211-1560. 313/921-3310.
Employs: 50-99.

Turner-Brook Inc

28811 John R Rd, Madison Heights MI 48071-2817.
313/548-3400. Employs: 100-249.

MISCELLANEOUS PROFESSIONAL EQUIPMENT AND SUPPLIES

ITT Hancock Ind
212 S Pine River St, Ithaca MI 48847-1435. 517/875-5108.
Employs: 50-99.

METALS SERVICE CENTERS AND OFFICES

Advance Steel Co
9635 French Rd, Detroit MI 48213-1250. 313/571-6700.
Employs: 50-99.

Alro Steel
1800 W Willow St, Lansing MI 48915-1430. 517/322-2211. Employs: 50-99.

Alro Steel Corp
3100 E High St, Jackson MI 49203-3467. 517/787-5500.
Employs: 100-249.

Ambassador Steel Co
1469 E Atwater, Detroit MI 48207-4015. 313/259-6600.
Employs: 50-99.

Central Steel & Wire Co
13400 Mt Elliott St, Detroit MI 48212-1302. 313/368-5000.
Employs: 50-99.

Commodity Steel & Processing
8701 E 8 Mile Rd, Warren MI 48089-3069. 313/758-1040.
Employs: 50-99.

Contractors Steel Company
36555 Amrhein Rd, Livonia MI 48150-1101. 313/464-4000. Employs: 100-249.

Dundee Slitt Incorporation
14490 Stowell Rd, Dundee MI 48131-9733. 313/529-3131.
Employs: 50-99.

Fairway Noth American Steel Co
18030 Rialto, Melvindale MI 48122-2101. 313/383-7100.
Employs: 50-99.

Howmet Corp Alloy Division Plymouth
41605 E Ann Arbor Rd, Plymouth MI 48170-4304.
313/455-2200. Employs: 100-249.

Jorgensen Steel & Aluminum
13200 W 8 Mile Rd, Oak Park MI 48237-3214. 313/547-
9000. Employs: 50-99.

Joseph T Ryerson & Son Inc
1600 E Euclid St, Detroit MI 48211-1312. 313/874-3311.
Employs: 100-249.

Kenwal Products Corp
9301 Central Ave, Detroit MI 48204-2863. 313/933-4362.
Employs: 100-249.

Lafayette Steel & Processing
3600 N Military St, Detroit MI 48210-2964. 313/894-4552.
Employs: 100-249.

M S T Steel Corp
24417 Groesbeck Hwy, Warren MI 48089-4723. 313/773-
5460. Employs: 50-99.

Meier Metal Servicenters
1471 E 9 Mile Rd, Hazel Park MI 48030-1960. 313/398-
1900. Employs: 50-99.

Peerless Steel Co
2450 Austin Ave, Troy MI 48083-2030. 313/528-3200.
Employs: 50-99.

Pioneer Steel Corp
7447 Intervale St, Detroit MI 48238-2401. 313/933-9400.
Employs: 50-99.

Procoil Corp
5260 S Haggerty Rd, Canton MI 48188-2775. 313/397-
3700. Employs: 50-99.

Rolled Alloys Inc
125 W Sterns Rd, Temperance MI 48182-9509. 313/847-
0561. Employs: 100-249.

Sennett Steel Corp
1200 E 14 Mile Rd, Madison Heights MI 48071-1440.
313/585-6040. Employs: 50-99.

Service Steel
13700 Sherwood Ave, Detroit MI 48212-2038. 313/365-
3600. Employs: 50-99.

Technical Metals Co
18800 Meginnity St, Melvindale MI 48122-1931. 313/388-
1880. Employs: 50-99.

The Worthington Steel Co
1150 S Elm Av, Jackson MI 49203-3306. 517/783-2673.
Employs: 100-249.

United Metal Products Corp
8101 Lyndon St, Detroit MI 48238-2452. 313/933-8750.
Employs: 50-99

Voss Steel Corp
7925 Beech-Daly Rd, Taylor MI 48180-2033. 313/291-
7500. Employs: 100-249.

Winston Steel Products Co
2700 W Warren Ave, Detroit MI 48208-1948. 313/894-
3300. Employs: 50-99.

Prestolite Wire
32871 Middlebelt Rd, Farmington MI 48334-1728.
313/626-1336. Employs: 50-99.

Crucible Service Centers Div Crucible

1201 Piedmont Ave, Troy MI 48083-1947. 313/528-0332.
Employs: 50-99.

Detroit Tubing Mill
12871 Eaton St, Detroit MI 48227-3945. 313/491-8823.
Employs: 50-99.

Kraftube Inc Suby Dyneer Corp
29551 Greenfield Rd, Southfield MI 48076-2249. 313/557-
0610. Employs: 50-99.

Redman Manufacturing Inc
630 Lycaste St, Detroit MI 48214-3470. 313/822-6600.
Employs: 50-99.

Richfield Iron Works
3313 Richfield Rd, Flint MI 48506-2603. 313/736-2110.
Employs: 50-99.

**ELECTRICAL APPARATUS AND EQUIPMENT,
WIRING SUPPLIES AND CONSTRUCTION
MATERIALS**

Allen-Bradley Company
1849 W Maple Rd, Troy MI 48084-7117. 313/280-7000.
Employs: 100-249.

Detroit Ball Bearing Company
300 S Ford Blvd, Ypsilanti MI 48198-6067. 313/482-1124.
Employs: 100-249.

Fife Electric Co
42860 W 9 Mile Rd, Novi MI 48375-4122. 313/344-4100.
Employs: 50-99.

Madison Electric Co
6000 Woodward Ave, Detroit MI 48202-3595. 313/875-
1560. Employs: 100-249.

Royalite Company
101 Burton St, Flint MI 48503-1873. 313/238-4641.
Employs: 50-99.

Atron Inc Of Michigan
405 Edgar St, Lakeview MI 48850-9101. 517/352-7232.
Employs: 100-249.

Magnetek Controls
1080 N Crooks Rd, Clawson MI 48017-1003. 313/435-
0700. Employs: 100-249.

Mc Naught Mc Kay Electric Co
1357 E Lincoln Ave, Madison Heights MI 48071-4134.
313/399-7500. Employs: 100-249.

Michigan Chandelier Co
20855 Telegraph Rd, Southfield MI 48034-4238. 313/353-
0510. Employs: 50-99.

**ELECTRICAL APPLIANCES, TELEVISION AND
RADIO SETS**

Servall Co
228 E Baltimore St, Detroit MI 48202-3204. 313/872-3655.
Employs: 50-99.

**MISCELLANEOUS ELECTRONIC PARTS AND
EQUIPMENT**

Codex Corporation Dist Office
3310 W Big Beaver Rd Ste 122, Troy MI 48084-2807.
313/649-4230. Employs: 50-99.

Commtron Corp
35245 Schoolcraft Rd, Livonia MI 48150-1209. 313/422-
9955. Employs: 50-99.

Jackson Dawson Comm Inc
1 Parklane Blvd Ite 1105E, Dearborn MI 48126-2402.
313/593-0690. Employs: 50-99.

Lucas Cirtek Corp
3027 N Airpark Dr, Flint MI 48507-3471. 313/238-4231.
Employs: 100-249.

Selcom Select Electronic Inc
1233 Chicago Rd, Troy MI 48083-4231. 313/591-7630.
Employs: 50-99.

Talcup Inc
34443 Schoolcraft Ave, Livonia MI 48150-1316. 313/525-1155. Employs: 50-99.

Albin Business Copiers
24288 Indoplex Cir, Farmington MI 48335-2522. 313/478-0005. Employs: 100-249.

Gilson Ayres Inc
600 Stephenson Hwy, Troy MI 48083-1110. 313/583-0300.
Employs: 100-249.

Omnifax
625 E Big Beaver Rd, Troy MI 48083-1426. 313/524-0223.
Employs: 50-99.

Xerox Corporation
6545 Mercantile Way, Lansing MI 48911-5972. 517/394-1010. Employs: 50-99.

Pagenet
25330 Telegraph Rd, Southfield MI 48034-7454. 313/827-3000. Employs: 100-249.

Security Controls Inc
16143 Wyoming St, Detroit MI 48221-2846. 313/342-2600. Employs: 50-99.

Vigilant Security
27215 Southfield Rd, Southfield MI 48076-3406. 313/559-7100. Employs: 50-99.

HARDWARE

General Fasteners Co Inc
11820 Globe St, Livonia MI 48150-1180. 313/591-9500.
Employs: 50-99.

Ladapa Die & Tool Inc
4756 Ann Arbor Rd, Dundee MI 48131-9759. 313/529-2431. Employs: 100-249.

All State Fastener Corp
14495 E 8 Mile Rd, Warren MI 48089-3433. 313/773-5400. Employs: 50-99.

PLUMBING AND HEATING EQUIPMENT AND SUPPLIES (HYDRONICS)

Gage Company
1121 River St, Lansing MI 48912-1031. 517/487-3601.
Employs: 50-99.

W T Andrew Company
15815 Hamilton Ave, Detroit MI 48203-3725. 313/883-2000. Employs: 50-99.

WARM AIR HEATING AND AIR-CONDITIONING EQUIPMENT AND SUPPLIES

Bumler Heating & Specialties
33457 S Gratiot Av, Clinton Twp MI 48035-4040.
313/791-3491. Employs: 100-249.

Uniwash Inc
25365 Leestock, Farmington MI 48336-1562. 313/474-5077. Employs: 50-99.

Strand Div Eppa
12995 Hillview St, Detroit MI 48227-4000. 313/491-6600.
Employs: 100-249.

CONSTRUCTION AND MINING (EXCEPT PETROLEUM) MACHINERY AND EQUIPMENT

Letts Industries Inc
1111 Bellevue Ave, Detroit MI 48207-3647. 313/579-1100.
Employs: 100-249.

FARM AND GARDEN MACHINERY AND EQUIPMENT

Ford New Holland Inc
1333 Coolidge Hwy, Troy MI 48084-7017. 313/637-7000.
Employs: 100-249.

INDUSTRIAL MACHINERY AND EQUIPMENT

American Safety Equipment
1400 Rankin St, Troy MI 48083-4021. 313/583-3110.
Employs: 100-249.

Buryl Hill Inc
755 W Big Beaver Rd Ste 2300, Troy MI 48084-0231.
313/478-1000. Employs: 50-99.

Ontario Die Co Of Am
2735 20th St, Port Huron MI 48060-6452. 313/987-5060.
Employs: 50-99.

Tri Way Controls
6935 Chase Rd, Dearborn MI 48126-1748. 313/584-3900.
Employs: 50-99.

Young Supply Co
888 W Baltimore, Detroit MI 48202-2904. 313/875-3280.
Employs: 100-249.

Superior Coffee and Foods
6125 Grand River Ave, Detroit MI 48208-1121. 313/898-9111. Employs: 50-99.

Hadron Inc
3020 Indianwood Rd, Lake Orion MI 48362-1113.
313/693-6235. Employs: 100-249.

Schrader Machine and Tool Inc
6422 Hanover Rd, Hanover MI 49241-9721. 517/563-8141.
Employs: 50-99.

Carbide Technologies Inc
18101 Malyn Blvd, Fraser MI 48026-3493. 313/296-5200.
Employs: 50-99.

Balance Technology Inc
120 Enterprise Dr, Ann Arbor MI 48103-9503. 313/769-2100. Employs: 50-99.

Durr Automation Inc
10301 Enterprise Dr, Davisburg MI 48350-1312. 313/625-5400. Employs: 50-99.

Florkey's Conveyor Svc
21810 Schmeman Ave, Warren MI 48089-3280. 313/772-1930. Employs: 50-99.

I & H Conveying & Machine Co
11533 Liberty St, Clio MI 48420-1405. 313/686-0910.
Employs: 50-99.

United Industrial Engineering Corp
1934 Heide St, Troy MI 48084-5314. 313/362-4955.
Employs: 50-99.

Graco Inc
24775 Crestview Ct, Farmington MI 48335-1507. 313/471-0500. Employs: 50-99.

Michigan Air Products
4400 Fernlee Ave, Royal Oak MI 48073-1723. 313/549-6222. Employs: 50-99.

A B B Robotics Inc
1350 W Hamlin Rd, Rochester MI 48309-3361. 313/650-0200. Employs: 50-99.

Roberts Sinto Corporation
3001 W Main St, Lansing MI 48917-4352. 517/371-2460.
Employs: 50-99.

The Kroger Co
6625 Dixie Hwy, Clarkston MI 48346-3422. 313/620-8700.
Employs: 100-249.

INDUSTRIAL SUPPLIES

Commercial Wire Rope & Supplies Co
9955 Grand River Ave, Detroit MI 48204-2003. 313/931-6100. Employs: 50-99.

Granco-Clark Inc
7298 Storey Rd, Belding MI 48809-9360. 616/794-2600.
Employs: 50-99.

Michigan Bearing Co
1700 E Avis Dr, Madison Heights MI 48071-1548.
313/588-8500. Employs: 50-99.

Reinz Wisconsin Gasket
30160 Orchard Lake Rd, Farmington MI 48334-2254.
313/851-1308. Employs: 50-99.

The Coon-De Visser Co
1500 N Stephenson Hwy, Madison Heights MI 48071-2302. 313/399-6000. Employs: 50-99.

Elco Industries Inc
31700 W 13 Mile Rd, Farmington MI 48334-2166.
313/851-5300. Employs: 50-99.

Sterling Supply Co
1220 E 9 Mile Rd, Ferndale MI 48220-1937. 313/546-3200. Employs: 50-99.

Grinding Supplies Co
10800 Galaxie, Oak Park MI 48237. 313/542-9000.
Employs: 50-99.

Mid-West Waltham Abrasive Co
510 S Washington St, Owosso MI 48867-3526. 517/725-7161. Employs: 50-99.

Master Pneumatic Detroit Inc
6701 18 Mi, Sterling Heights MI 48314. 313/254-1000.
Employs: 50-99.

Parker Hannifin Corporation
651 Robbins Dr, Troy MI 48083-4564. 313/589-2400.
Employs: 50-99.

Mold-Ex Rubber Co
23847 Industrial Park Dr, Farmington MI 48335-2860.
313/474-0120. Employs: 100-249.

SERVICE ESTABLISHMENT EQUIPMENT AND SUPPLIES

J Levin Sons Co
7610 W Chicago, Detroit MI 48204-2862. 313/834-6920.
Employs: 50-99.

Bockstanz Brothers Co
13045 Hillview St, Detroit MI 48227-3666. 313/491-5900.
Employs: 50-99.

Bio-Serv Corporation
1130 Livernois Rd, Troy MI 48083-2711. 313/588-1005.
Employs: 100-249.

SPORTING AND RECREATIONAL GOODS AND SUPPLIES

Walker International
1901 W Lafayette Blvd, Detroit MI 48216-1826. 313/496-1171. Employs: 50-99.

TOYS AND HOBBY GOODS AND SUPPLIES

Arkin Distributing Co
43100 W 9 Mile Rd, Novi MI 48375-4125. 313/349-9300.
Employs: 50-99.

SCRAP AND WASTE MATERIALS

S L C Recycling Inds Inc
21000 Hoover Rd, Warren MI 48089-3153. 313/759-6600.
Employs: 50-99.

Schlafer Iron & Steel Inc
1950 Medbury St, Detroit MI 48211-2626. 313/925-8200.
Employs: 50-99.

Environmental Management Corp
345 N Groesbeck Hwy, Mount Clemens MI 48043-1544.
313/731-3130. Employs: 100-249.

JEWELRY, WATCHES, PRECIOUS STONES AND PRECIOUS METALS

Investment Rarities Of Mi Inc
2390 E Stadium Blvd, Ann Arbor MI 48104-4811.
313/973-8577. Employs: 50-99.

MISCELLANEOUS DURABLE GOODS

Handleman Co
1291 Rickett Rd, Brighton MI 48116-1832. 313/227-2231.
Employs: 100-249.

STATIONERY AND OFFICE SUPPLIES

Boise Cascade Corp
13301 Stephens Rd, Warren MI 48089-4341. 313/758-5400. Employs: 50-99.

Executone Business Systems
1700 W Big Beaver Rd Ste 100, Troy MI 48084-3542.
313/649-4454. Employs: 50-99.

United Stationers Supply Co
32432 Capitol St, Livonia MI 48150-1703. 313/425-6000.
Employs: 50-99.

INDUSTRIAL AND PERSONAL SERVICE PAPER

Bunzl Detroit
111 Corporate Dr, Auburn Hills MI 48326-2921. 313/334-5900. Employs: 50-99.

Patrick Seaman Paper Co
2000 Howard St, Detroit MI 48216-1822. 313/496-3131.
Employs: 100-249.

Westvaco Corporation
32985 Industrial Rd, Livonia MI 48150-1617. 313/522-0303. Employs: 100-249.

DRUGS, DRUG PROPRIETARIES AND DRUGGISTS' SUNDRIES

B & E Sales Co Inc
200 E Long Lake Rd, Bloomfield MI 48304-2360.
313/836-8780. Employs: 100-249.

Chaffee Corp
21405 Trolley Ind Dr, Taylor MI 48180-1811. 313/292-3700. Employs: 100-249.

McKesson Drug Co
14100 Oakland St, Detroit MI 48203-2909. 313/868-9876.
Employs: 50-99.

GROCERIES, GENERAL LINE

Associated Grocers Of Michigan
4147 Keller Rd, Holt MI 48842-1253. 517/694-3923.
Employs: 100-249.

Bulk Food Warehouse
Macomb Mall, Roseville MI 48066. 313/294-6040.
Employs: 50-99.

Garden Gourmet
41900 Hayes Rd, Clinton Twp MI 48038-1877. 313/228-9090. Employs: 50-99.

Home Foods
22230 Harper Av, St Clair Shores MI 48080-1816.
313/777-0620. Employs: 50-99.

Lipari Food Products
40585 Production Dr, Harrison Twp MI 48045-1346.
313/469-0131. Employs: 50-99.

Northwest Food Co
12301 Conant St, Detroit MI 48212-2341. 313/368-2500.
Employs: 100-249.

Spartan Stores Inc
9075 N Haggerty Rd, Plymouth MI 48170-4630. 313/455-1400. Employs: 50-99.

Arbor Foods Inc
6018 W Maple Rd, W Bloomfield MI 48322-2212.
313/737-4990. Employs: 50-99.

Blaks Distributing
23402 Whitley Dr, Clinton Twp MI 48035-4634. 313/791-6130. Employs: 50-99.

Ingredients Inc
3705 Country Club Dr, St Clair Shores MI 48082-2953.
313/294-9940. Employs: 50-99.

Petty Food Service Brokerage
25150 Chippendale St, Roseville MI 48066-3906. 313/777-1070. Employs: 50-99.

The Pfeister Co
36300 Schoolcraft Rd, Livonia MI 48150-1219. 313/591-1900. Employs: 50-99.

PACKAGED FROZEN FOODS

Lagrasso Brothers Produce
5001 Bellevue St, Detroit MI 48211-3209. 313/579-1455.
Employs: 50-99.

DAIRY PRODUCTS, EXCEPT DRIED OR CANNED

Detroit City Dairy Inc
15004 Third Ave, Detroit MI 48203-3718. 313/868-5511.
Employs: 50-99.

McDonald Dairy Co
P O Box 469, Flint MI 48501-0469. 313/232-9193.
Employs: 100-249.

Melody Foods Inc
31111 Industrial Rd, Livonia MI 48150-2035. 313/525-4000. Employs: 50-99.

FISH AND SEAFOODS

Chicago Beef Co
1939 Adelaide St, Detroit MI 48207-2128. 313/567-0850.
Employs: 50-99.

MEATS AND MEAT PRODUCTS

Cudahy Specialty Foods Co
4401 Stecker St, Dearborn MI 48126-3815. 313/581-0706.
Employs: 50-99.

United Meat & Deli Inc
1526 Division St, Detroit MI 48207-4506. 313/567-0557.
Employs: 50-99.

Wolverine Packing Co

1340 Winder, Detroit MI 48207-2634. 313/568-1900.
Employs: 50-99.

FRESH FRUITS AND VEGETABLES

Badalament Inc
515 10th St, Detroit MI 48216-1951. 313/963-0746.
Employs: 50-99.

Ben B Schwartz & Sons Inc
7201 W Fort St, Detroit MI 48209-2963. 313/841-8300.
Employs: 100-249.

MISCELLANEOUS GROCERIES AND RELATED PRODUCTS

N Leone & Sons Inc
30660 Plymouth Rd, Livonia MI 48150-2123. 313/427-7650. Employs: 50-99.

Ryan Tom Distributing Co Inc
3302 Kent St, Flint MI 48503-4420. 313/767-8720.
Employs: 50-99.

Stark & Co Inc
30301 Northwestern Hwy, Farmington MI 48334-3260.
313/851-5700. Employs: 100-249.

Sullivan & O'Sullivan Inc
G4047 Market Pl, Flint MI 48507. 313/733-7090. Employs:
50-99.

Sygna Network
660 Detroit Av, Monroe MI 48161-2571. 313/241-2890.
Employs: 50-99.

Coca Cola Bottlers Detroit Inc
880 Doris Rd, Auburn Hills MI 48326-2713. 313/373-2653. Employs: 50-99.

Coca Cola Bottlers Detroit Inc
32500 N Avis Dr, Madison Heights MI 48071-1558.
313/585-1248. Employs: 100-249.

Pepsi-Cola Co
960 Featherstone St, Pontiac MI 48342-1827. 313/334-3512. Employs: 50-99.

Pepsi-Cola Co
5505 Corporate Dr, Troy MI 48098-2619. 313/641-7888.
Employs: 100-249.

Lombardi Foodservice
2465 23 Mile Rd, Shelby Twp MI 48316. 313/254-3550.
Employs: 100-249.

PLASTIC MATERIALS AND BASIC FORMS AND SHAPES

Die Electric Plastic Seal
6081 S Logan St, Lansing MI 48911-4607. 517/882-9044.
Employs: 50-99.

Gen Polymers Div Ashland Chemical
12001 Toepfer Rd, Warren MI 48089-3171. 313/755-1100.
Employs: 50-99.

MISCELLANEOUS CHEMICALS AND ALLIED PRODUCTS

Dow Chemical USA
2655 Evergreen Rd, Southfield MI 48076. 313/358-1300.
Employs: 50-99.

PVS Chemicals Inc
11001 Harper Ave, Detroit MI 48213-3319. 313/921-1200.
Employs: 100-249.

Reichhold Chemicals
707 Woodward Heights, Ferndale MI 48220-1430.
313/542-1037. Employs: 100-249.

PPG Industries Inc
961 Division St, Adrian MI 49221-4023. 517/263-7831.
Employs: 50-99.

Chemserve Corp
9505 Copland St, Detroit MI 48209-2642. 313/842-4900.
Employs: 50-99.

PETROLEUM BULK STATIONS AND TERMINALS

Koenig Fuel & Supply Co
500 7 Mile Rd E, Detroit MI 48203-2024. 313/368-1870.
Employs: 100-249.

PETROLEUM AND PETROLEUM PRODUCTS WHOLESALERS, EXCEPT BULK STATIONS AND TERMINALS

Conlee Oil Co Inc
815 S Mill St, Clio MI 48420-1442. 313/686-5600.
Employs: 50-99.

Davison Oil & Gas Co
107 E Mill St, Davison MI 48423-1439. 313/653-2250.
Employs: 50-99.

Lewis Lansing Energy Co
636 W Michigan Av, Lansing MI 48912-1151. 517/485-9481. Employs: 50-99.

Pipeline Oil Sls Formerly Mc
744 E South St, Jackson MI 49203-4403. 517/782-0467.
Employs: 100-249.

Great Plains Gas
7336 W Remus Rd, Mount Pleasant MI 48858-9625.
517/561-2960. Employs: 50-99.

Mooney Oil Corp
4773 W Grand River Ave, Lansing MI 48906-9122.
517/321-0172. Employs: 100-249.

Vesco Oil Corp
16055 W 12 Mile Rd, Southfield MI 48076-2909. 313/557-1600. Employs: 100-249.

Blodgett Oil Co Inc
1219 N Mission, Mount Pleasant MI 48858. 517/773-3792.
Employs: 50-99.

Imlay City Total Inc
2621 Pine Grove Ave, Port Huron MI 48060-2870.
313/985-6141. Employs: 50-99.

BEER AND ALE

Don Lee Distributors Inc
14301 Prospect St, Dearborn MI 48126-3410. 313/584-7100. Employs: 50-99.

Gerry's Distributing Co
1314 Cedar St, Port Huron MI 48060-6119. 313/987-7575.
Employs: 50-99.

Superior Distr Co Lansing Inc
5400 Aurelius Rd, Lansing MI 48911. 517/394-2060.
Employs: 100-249.

Central Distributors Beer Inc
28100 Gorsuch Ave, Romulus MI 48174-2629. 313/946-6200. Employs: 100-249.

Don Lee Distributors Inc
2651 E 10 Mile Rd, Warren MI 48091-3727. 313/757-4900. Employs: 50-99.

Eastown Distributors Co
14400 Oakland St, Detroit MI 48203-2909. 313/867-6900.
Employs: 50-99.

Jack Smith Beverages

3835 Morgan Dr, Ypsilanti MI 48197-9508. 313/434-1440.
Employs: 50-99.

Jack Smith Beverages
2403 E High St, Jackson MI 49203-3421. 517/782-7191.
Employs: 50-99.

Wolpin Co
9350 Freeland St, Detroit MI 48228-2309. 313/933-7150.
Employs: 100-249.

WINE AND DISTILLED ALCOHOLIC BEVERAGES

Kozak Distributors Inc
8825 Vincent St, Detroit MI 48211-1571. 313/925-3220.
Employs: 100-249.

Petitpren Inc
44500 Groesbeck Hwy, Clinton Twp MI 48036-1111.
313/468-1402. Employs: 50-99.

FLOWERS, NURSERY STOCK AND FLORISTS' SUPPLIES

Fashion Fast Co
14900 Michigan Ave, Dearborn MI 48126-2913. 313/581-4818. Employs: 50-99.

TOBACCO AND TOBACCO PRODUCTS

Fontana Bros Inc
3245 Hubbard St, Detroit MI 48210-3237. 313/897-4000.
Employs: 50-99.

Trepco Tyson Larson Sales Co
PO Box 37285, Oak Park MI 48237-0285. 313/546-3661.
Employs: 50-99.

Walker Jf Co Inc
3200 Cooper St, Jackson MI 49201-9502. 517/787-9880.
Employs: 100-249.

PAINTS, VARNISHES AND SUPPLIES

P P G Industries Inc
2155 W Big Beaver Rd, Troy MI 48084-3422. 313/564-5500. Employs: 50-99.

BASF Corp Automotive Oem Coatings
2855 Coolidge Hwy, Troy MI 48084-3202. 313/649-6700.
Employs: 100-249.

Detroit Container Cleaning Ent
1221 W McNichols Rd, Detroit MI 48203-2558. 313/868-8900. Employs: 50-99.

MISCELLANEOUS NONDURABLE GOODS

M & M Nautical Imports
31693 8 Mile Rd, Livonia MI 48152-4217. 313/478-1600.
Employs: 50-99.

Animal Management Svc Inc
130 E 9 Mile Rd, Ferndale MI 48220-1718. 313/398-6533.
Employs: 50-99.

H & H Distributing Inc
5949 Jackson Rd, Ann Arbor MI 48103-9504. 313/662-1931. Employs: 50-99.

Admore Inc
24707 Wood Ct, Macomb MI 48042-5378. 313/949-8200.
Employs: 100-249.

Merchandising Incentive Corp
352 Oliver St, Troy MI 48084-5401. 313/362-5060.
Employs: 50-99.

LUMBER AND OTHER BUILDING MATERIALS DEALERS

Andy Handy Home Improvement Centers
13507 Middlebelt Rd, Livonia MI 48150-2229. 313/261-7500. Employs: 100-249.

Brayer Lumber & Supply
5300 E Nevada St, Detroit MI 48234-2338. 313/368-2100. Employs: 100-249.

Church's Lumber Yards
44865 Utica Rd, Utica MI 48317-5474. 313/731-2000. Employs: 100-249.

ERB Lumber Co Inc
4600 Aurelius Rd, Lansing MI 48910-5803. 517/393-2550. Employs: 50-99.

Fingerle Lumber Co
617 S 5th Av, Ann Arbor MI 48104-2905. 313/663-0581. Employs: 100-249.

James Lumber Co
G5200 Clio Rd, Flint MI 48504-1200. 313/785-7831. Employs: 50-99.

Kmart Corporation
5100 Dixie Hwy, Waterford MI 48329-1713. 313/674-2236. Employs: 50-99.

Michigan Lumber Co
1919 Clifford St, Flint MI 48503-4033. 313/232-4108. Employs: 50-99.

S & M Lumber Co
424 W Main St, Flushing MI 48433-2036. 313/659-5681. Employs: 50-99.

Valley Lumber
211 S Elm St, Owosso MI 48867-2642. 517/723-6751. Employs: 50-99.

Andy Handy Home Improvement Centers
30785 Gratiot Ave, Roseville MI 48066-1712. 313/294-4810. Employs: 100-249.

Glaser's Lumber Co
215 E Elm, Vernon MI 48476. 517/288-2671. Employs: 50-99.

Michigan Timber & Truss Inc
1258 Rochester Rd, Troy MI 48083-2833. 313/588-4040. Employs: 50-99.

National Lumber Co
24595 Groesbeck Hwy, Warren MI 48089-2145. 313/755-8200. Employs: 100-249.

Durable Fence
6250 Sims Dr, Sterling Heights MI 48313-3717. 313/264-6010. Employs: 50-99.

HARDWARE STORES

Northside True Value Hardware
2912 S Wayne Rd, Wayne MI 48184-1217. 313/721-7244. Employs: 50-99.

R John Lumber Co
27036 John R Rd, Madison Heights MI 48071-3326. 313/541-8080. Employs: 50-99.

Weingartz
46061 Van Dyke Ave, Utica MI 48317-5375. 313/731-7240. Employs: 50-99.

RETAIL NURSERIES, LAWN AND GARDEN SUPPLY STORES

Christensens Plant Ctr
38901 Ann Arbor Rd, Livonia MI 48150-3354. 313/464-3797. Employs: 50-99.

Anderson Sales & Service Inc
1645 S Telegraph Rd, Bloomfield MI 48302-0049. 313/858-2300. Employs: 50-99.

Frank's Nursery & Crafts
34900 Groesbeck Hwy, Fraser MI 48026. 313/791-4770. Employs: 50-99.

DEPARTMENT STORES

Bonwit Teller
2701 Somerset Ma, Troy MI 48084. 313/643-8700. Employs: 100-249.

Brands For Less
1156 Paka Pl, Jackson MI 49202-2041. 517/787-9334. Employs: 50-99.

Crowley Milner & Co
23303 Michigan Av, Dearborn MI 48124-2029. 313/278-8000. Employs: 100-249.

D & C Stores Inc
2311 Gratiot Blvd, Marysville MI 48040-1282. 313/364-3399. Employs: 50-99.

Dayton Hudson Dept Store Co
5700 W Saginaw St, Lansing MI 48917-2457. 517/886-4400. Employs: 100-249.

Elder-Beerman
1357 S Main St Unit C10, Adrian MI 49221-4318. 517/263-3313. Employs: 100-249.

Family Dollar
2919 S Cedar St, Lansing MI 48910-3032. 517/394-5446. Employs: 100-249.

Family Dollar
8755 Monroe Plaza, Durand MI 48429-1062. 517/288-2007. Employs: 50-99.

Family Dollar
1425 E Main St, Owosso MI 48867-9048. 517/723-2741. Employs: 50-99.

G C Murphy Co
200 N Washington St, Owosso MI 48867-2821. 517/723-3400. Employs: 50-99.

H C Prange Company
4350 24th Av, Fort Gratiot MI 48059-3850. 313/385-3300. Employs: 50-99.

Hills
100 Frenchtown Mall, Monroe MI 48161. 313/243-9200. Employs: 50-99.

Hills Department Store #151
1370 S Main St, Adrian MI 49221-4307. 517/263-6004. Employs: 100-249.

Hudson's
1982 W Grand River Av, Okemos MI 48864-1756. 517/349-7770. Employs: 100-249.

J C Penney Co
201 S Washington St, Owosso MI 48867-2901. 517/725-2126. Employs: 50-99.

J C Penney Co Inc
G4156 E Court St, Burton MI 48509. 313/743-4550. Employs: 100-249.

J C Penney Co Inc
1680 Wright Av, Alma MI 48801-1022. 517/463-6081. Employs: 50-99.

J C Penney Co Inc
500 Briarwood Cir, Ann Arbor MI 48108. 313/769-7910.
Employs: 100-249.

J C Penney Co Inc
1357 S Main St Unit A1, Adrian MI 49221-4318. 517/263-0551. Employs: 50-99.

J C Penney Co Inc
1860 W Michigan Av, Jackson MI 49202-4007. 517/788-7300. Employs: 100-249.

J C Penney Inc
5304 W Saginaw St, Lansing MI 48917-1915. 517/323-4000. Employs: 50-99.

J C Penney's
650 Frenchtn Sq Mall, Monroe MI 48161. 313/242-9420.
Employs: 50-99.

J C Penney's
1982 W Grand River Av Unit 115, Okemos MI 48864-1756. 517/349-6912. Employs: 100-249.

J L Hudson's
Fairlane Town Center, Dearborn MI 48126. 313/593-3232.
Employs: 100-249.

Jacobson's
255 W Michigan Av, Jackson MI 49201-2218. 517/783-2841. Employs: 100-249.

K Mart Discount Dept Store
1100 W Argyle St, Jackson MI 49202-2059. 517/782-9481.
Employs: 50-99.

K Mart Store 3327
2051 18 Mile Rd, Sterling Heights MI 48314-3703.
313/739-0800. Employs: 50-99.

K Mart 4238
25201 Outer Dr, Melvindale MI 48122-1940. 313/388-3900. Employs: 50-99.

K-Mart
15255 Michigan Av, Dearborn MI 48126-2915. 313/584-2770. Employs: 50-99.

K-Mart
3880 State Rd, Ann Arbor MI 48108-1661. 313/996-1292.
Employs: 50-99.

K-Mart
215 N Maple Rd, Ann Arbor MI 48103-2823. 313/761-8557. Employs: 50-99.

K-Mart
1390 N Leroy St, Fenton MI 48430-2762. 313/629-3743.
Employs: 50-99.

K-Mart
4045 24th Av, Fort Gratiot MI 48059-3801. 313/385-4492.
Employs: 50-99.

K-Mart
2020 W Grand River Av, Okemos MI 48864-1707.
517/349-3760. Employs: 50-99.

K-Mart
2500 E Main St, Corunna MI 48817. 517/743-5602.
Employs: 50-99.

K-Mart
4002 S Dort Hwy, Flint MI 48507-2138. 313/743-2750.
Employs: 50-99.

K-Mart Department Store
4100 W Pierson Rd, Flint MI 48504-1348. 313/785-4721.
Employs: 50-99.

K-Mart Department Store

G6105 N Saginaw St, Mount Morris MI 48458. 313/787-6585. Employs: 50-99.

K-Mart Department Store
G1145 N Belsay Rd, Burton MI 48509. 313/744-4800.
Employs: 50-99.

K-Mart Discount Store
5400 S Cedar St, Lansing MI 48911-3805. 517/393-8770.
Employs: 50-99.

K-Mart Discount Stores
43825 W Oaks Dr, Novi MI 48377-3309. 313/348-3660.
Employs: 50-99.

K-Mart Discount Stores
242 Steele St S, Ionia MI 48846-2006. 616/527-2580.
Employs: 50-99.

K-Mart Plaza
3001 E Michigan Av, Jackson MI 49202-3847. 517/787-3440. Employs: 50-99.

K-Mart Store Br
1290 N Monroe St, Monroe MI 48161-3163. 313/242-5200. Employs: 50-99.

K-Mart Store No 9640
1755 Wright Av, Alma MI 48801-1023. 517/463-3128.
Employs: 50-99.

Kids Mart
2465 W Stadium Blvd, Ann Arbor MI 48103-3809.
313/662-6410. Employs: 100-249.

Kline's Department Store
306 S Main St, Ann Arbor MI 48104-2108. 313/994-4545.
Employs: 100-249.

Kline's Department Store
136-38 E Maumee St, Adrian MI 49221. 517/265-7469.
Employs: 50-99.

Kline's Dept Store
14 E Front St, Monroe MI 48161-2229. 313/241-9211.
Employs: 50-99.

Kresge Stores
1750 Dix Hwy, Lincoln Park MI 48146-1413. 313/382-1947. Employs: 50-99.

Lord & Taylor
300 Briarwood Cir, Ann Arbor MI 48108-1606. 313/665-4500. Employs: 100-249.

Lord & Taylor
Fairlane Town Center, Dearborn MI 48126. 313/336-3100.
Employs: 100-249.

Meijer Incorporated
217 E US Hwy 223, Adrian MI 49221. 517/265-7820.
Employs: 50-99.

Meijer's
5125 W Saginaw St, Lansing MI 48917-2635. 517/321-1302. Employs: 100-249.

Mervyn's
5780 W Saginaw St, Lansing MI 48917-2457. 517/321-6000. Employs: 100-249.

Mervyn's
1982 W Grand River Av Unit 97, Okemos MI 48864-1756.
517/349-7165. Employs: 100-249.

Mervyn's
990 Eisenhower Pkwy W, Ann Arbor MI 48103-6448.
313/996-8800. Employs: 100-249.

Mervyn's
16301 Ford Rd, Dearborn MI 48126-2800. 313/271-5440.
Employs: 100-249.

Monroe Shopping Center
Monroe Shopping Ce, Monroe MI 48161. 313/242-9420.
Employs: 50-99.

Montgomery Ward & Co
1700 W Michigan Av, Jackson MI 49202-4005. 517/787-
3000. Employs: 100-249.

Mulias & Ellias
2725 Fort St, Trenton MI 48183-2624. 313/676-4080.
Employs: 50-99.

Sears Roebuck and Co
1250 Jackson Crossing, Jackson MI 49202-2042. 517/787-
0711. Employs: 100-249.

Sears Roebuck and Co
1357 S Main St Unit E3, Adrian MI 49221-4318. 517/263-
0641. Employs: 100-249.

Sears Roebuck and Co
2100 Southfield Rd, Lincoln Park MI 48146-2250.
313/383-7000. Employs: 50-99.

Target
2000 Waters Rd, Ann Arbor MI 48103-9648. 313/996-
0700. Employs: 100-249.

Target Stores
4890 Marsh Rd, Okemos MI 48864-1123. 517/347-0700.
Employs: 100-249.

Target Stores No 632
4300 24th Av, Fort Gratiot MI 48059-3806. 313/385-5000.
Employs: 50-99.

The Fair Store
4819 Clio Rd, Flint MI 48504-1806. 313/785-3411.
Employs: 100-249.

Value City Department Store
5101 Fenton Rd, Flint MI 48507-3324. 313/767-5500.
Employs: 100-249.

Woolworth Express
4190 Courtland Center, Burton MI 48529. 313/742-6377.
Employs: 100-249.

Woolworth's Express
G3341 Genesee Valley Center, Flint MI 48507. 313/230-
8383. Employs: 100-249.

J C Penney Co Inc
3375 N Woodward Royal, Royal Oak MI 48073. 313/288-
6200. Employs: 100-249.

J C Penney Co Inc
29050 Van Dyke Ave, Warren MI 48093-2301.
313/5734370. Employs: 100-249.

K Mart Corporation
3900 E Outer Dr, Detroit MI 48234-2937. 313/368-1650.
Employs: 100-249.

K Mart Corporation
18211 Plymouth Rd, Detroit MI 48228-1142. 313/272-
4210. Employs: 50-99.

K Mart Corporation
2905 Union Lake Rd, Commerce Twp MI 48382-3565.
313/360-1197. Employs: 100-249.

K Mart Discount Dept Stores
2051 18 Mile, Sterling Heights MI 48314. 313/739-2122.
Employs: 100-249.

K Mart Discount Dept Stores
2000 E 10 Mile Rd, Warren MI 48091-1380. 313/756-
6880. Employs: 50-99.

Kmart Corporation

Kmart Stores
7 S Glenwood Ave, Pontiac MI 48342-2413. 313/338-
4528. Employs: 50-99.

Kmart Stores
100 E Maple Rd, Troy MI 48083-2714. 313/588-9966.
Employs: 50-99.

Montgomery Ward & Co
930 W Holmes Rd, Lansing MI 48910-4476. 517/887-
1111. Employs: 100-249.

Montgomery Ward & Co
44955 Schoenherr Rd, Sterling Heights MI 48313-1141.
313/726-1600. Employs: 100-249.

Montgomery Ward Distribution Center
13112 Oneida Rd, Grand Ledge MI 48837-9704. 517/627-
1161. Employs: 100-249.

Sears Paint & Hardware Store
37676 Van Dyke Ave, Sterling Heights MI 48312-1836.
313/268-6770. Employs: 100-249.

Sears Roebuck and Co
11850 Sears St, Livonia MI 48150-2107. 313/522-3700.
Employs: 100-249.

Sears Roebuck and Co
20425 Plymouth Rd, Detroit MI 48228-1221. 313/835-
9700. Employs: 50-99.

Wal-Mart Discount
1621 E M 21, Owosso MI 48867-9053. 517/723-2552.
Employs: 50-99.

Wal-Mart Discount Pharmacy
1680 Packard Hwy, Charlotte MI 48813-9717. 517/543-
0700. Employs: 100-249.

American Tourister Outlet
T12247 Beyer Rd, Birch Run MI 48415. 517/624-4616.
Employs: 100-249.

American Tourister Outlet
12158 S Beyer Rd, Birch Run MI 48415-9410. 517/624-
4780. Employs: 100-249.

Beezil Factory Outlet Store
14500 Laplaisance St, Monroe MI 48161-3815. 313/242-
5040. Employs: 50-99.

Bugle Boy Factory Outlet
1220 Beyer, Birch Run MI 48415. 517/624-6280. Employs:
100-249.

Cape Isle Knitters
12373 S Beyer Rd, Birch Run MI 48415-9406. 517/624-
5575. Employs: 100-249.

Ducks and Company
1341 Rickett Rd, Brighton MI 48116-1879. 313/227-3573.
Employs: 100-249.

Gant Company Store
12156 S Beyer Rd, Birch Run MI 48415-9409. 517/624-
4252. Employs: 100-249.

Genuine Article
12373 S Beyer Rd, Birch Run MI 48415-9406. 517/624-
4600. Employs: 100-249.

Just My Size
12365 S Beyer Rd, Birch Run MI 48415-9400. 517/624-
4381. Employs: 100-249.

Leather Manor
12245 S Beyer Rd, Birch Run MI 48415-9403. 517/624-
5191. Employs: 100-249.

Leggs Hanes Bali Factory Outlet
12245 S Beyer Rd, Birch Run MI 48415-9403. 517/624-
4488. Employs: 100-249.

Lenox Factory Outlet
Manufacturers Market Place, Birch Run MI 48415.
517/624-6170. Employs: 100-249.

Mikasa Factory Store
12156 S Beyer Rd, Birch Run MI 48415-9409. 517/624-9341. Employs: 100-249.

Newport Sportswear
12373 S Beyer Rd, Birch Run MI 48415-9406. 517/624-5666. Employs: 100-249.

Pfaltzgraff Collector's Center
12247 S Beyer Rd, Birch Run MI 48415-9405. 517/624-4623. Employs: 100-249.

Sassafras Factory Outlet Inc
12156 S Beyer Rd, Birch Run MI 48415-9409. 517/624-6200. Employs: 100-249.

Specials Number 917
12373 S Beyer Rd, Birch Run MI 48415-9406. 517/624-4144. Employs: 100-249.

Swank Factory Stores
Manufacturers Market Place, Birch Run MI 48415.
517/624-9767. Employs: 100-249.

Totes Factory Outlet
12245 S Beyer Rd, Birch Run MI 48415-9403. 517/624-4343. Employs: 100-249.

Vanheusen Factory Store
12245 S Beyer Rd, Birch Run MI 48415-9403. 517/624-5651. Employs: 100-249.

Villeroy & Boch
12154 S Beyer Rd, Birch Run MI 48415-9408. 517/624-4477. Employs: 100-249.

Warehouse Club
1775 E 8 Mile Rd, Hazel Park MI 48030-2606. 313/544-8777. Employs: 50-99.

All For One #632
28572 Telegraph Rd, Southfield MI 48034-7505. 313/357-0120. Employs: 100-249.

Ames Department Store
1040 S Main St, Chelsea MI 48118-1409. 313/475-6941.
Employs: 100-249.

Ames Department Store
2070 S Cedar St, Imlay City MI 48444-9606. 313/724-7788. Employs: 50-99.

Best Products Company
3150 Carpenter Rd, Ypsilanti MI 48197-9611. 313/973-9590. Employs: 100-249.

Big Lots
16100 E 10 Mile Rd, East Detroit MI 48021-1160.
313/776-0210. Employs: 100-249.

Big Lots
388 N Gratiot Ave, Clinton Twp MI 48036-3123. 313/465-3777. Employs: 100-249.

Big Lots
25495 Gr River, Redford MI 48240. 313/531-4100.
Employs: 100-249.

Big Lots
4146 E Blue Grass Rd, Mount Pleasant MI 48858-7914.
517/773-6016. Employs: 50-99.

Big Lots Store 078
3600 S Dort Hwy, Flint MI 48507-2054. 313/744-4830.
Employs: 100-249.

Big Wheel

Big Wheel
1875 W Genesee St, Lapeer MI 48446-1705. 313/664-8797. Employs: 50-99.

Big Wheel
47 N Dawson St, Sandusky MI 48471-1061. 313/648-4020.
Employs: 100-249.

Big Wheel
710 N Cedar, Mason MI 48854. 517/676-6797. Employs:
100-249.

Big Wheel
560 W Highland Rd, Highland MI 48357-4510. 313/887-6220. Employs: 50-99.

Big Wheel
22185 Pontiac Trl, South Lyon MI 48178-1638. 313/437-4156. Employs: 100-249.

Big Wheel Inc
2990 W Carleton Rd, Hillsdale MI 49242-9368. 517/439-4351. Employs: 50-99.

BJ & LC's Isle Of Beauty
12930 Fenkell St, Detroit MI 48227-4067. 313/862-8480.
Employs: 100-249.

Burlington Coat Factory
29720 Southfield Rd, Southfield MI 48076-2088. 313/559-7460. Employs: 100-249.

Burlington Coat Factory Warehouse
22331 Eureka Rd, Taylor MI 48180-6016. 313/374-5506.
Employs: 100-249.

Candy Palace Emporium
4189 Keewahdin Rd, Fort Gratiot MI 48059-3204.
313/385-9220. Employs: 50-99.

Candy Palace Emporium
1035 St Clair River Dr, Algonac MI 48001-1457. 313/794-2330. Employs: 50-99.

Cole's Vision Corp
35151 Gratiot Ave, Clinton Twp MI 48035-2845. 313/792-9185. Employs: 100-249.

Conley's Workshop Apparel
17250 Dexter Trl, Gregory MI 48137-9546. 517/851-7303.
Employs: 100-249.

Consolidated Stores
1575 N Telegraph Rd, Monroe MI 48161-3341. 313/243-3100. Employs: 50-99.

Crowley's
Livonia Mall, Livonia MI 48152. 313/476-6300. Employs:
100-249.

Crowley's
Tel-Twelve Mall, Southfield MI 48034. 313/354-2000.
Employs: 100-249.

Crowley's
32385 Gratiot Ave, Roseville MI 48066-1135. 313/293-7700. Employs: 100-249.

Crowley's
Wildwood Plaza, Westland MI 48185. 313/722-8000.
Employs: 100-249.

Crowley's
Lakeside Mall, Sterling Heights MI 48313. 313/247-1700.
Employs: 100-249.

D & C Stores Inc
2325 S Venoy Rd, Westland MI 48185-4662. 313/728-2030. Employs: 100-249.

D & C Stores Inc
33091 23 Mile, New Baltimore MI 48047. 313/725-3526.
Employs: 100-249.

D & C Stores Incorporated
85 S Elk St, Sandusky MI 48471-1337. 313/648-4595.
Employs: 100-249.

Dancer's
616 S Lapeer Rd, Lake Orion MI 48362-2916. 313/693-9211. Employs: 100-249.

Dancer's Fashions
66078 Van Dyke, Romeo MI 48065. 313/752-4521.
Employs: 100-249.

Dancer's Fashions
66799 Gratiot Ave, Richmond MI 48062-1909. 313/727-7868. Employs: 100-249.

F W Woolworth Co
24235 Harper Ave, St Clair Shores MI 48080-1270.
313/778-0040. Employs: 100-249.

F W Woolworth Co
16890 Schaefer Hwy, Detroit MI 48235-4270. 313/863-0871. Employs: 100-249.

F W Woolworth Co
2300 Eureka, Taylor MI 48180. 313/287-4490. Employs: 50-99.

F W Woolworth Co
20425 Plymouth Rd, Detroit MI 48228-1221. 313/837-8300. Employs: 100-249.

F W Woolworth Co
14383 Gratiot Ave, Detroit MI 48205-2303. 313/526-0780.
Employs: 100-249.

F W Woolworth Co
29801 Plymouth Rd, Livonia MI 48150-2114. 313/525-4430. Employs: 50-99.

F W Woolworth Co
28746 Dequindre Rd, Warren MI 48092-5607. 313/751-3140. Employs: 50-99.

F W Woolworth Express
29542 7 Mile Rd, Livonia MI 48152-1910. 313/477-5444.
Employs: 100-249.

Family Dollar Stores Inc
33 S Glenwood Ave, Pontiac MI 48342-2413. 313/334-4040. Employs: 100-249.

Family Dollar Store Inc
20528 Lahser Rd, Detroit MI 48219-1238. 313/531-8180.
Employs: 100-249.

Family Dollar Store Inc
14800 Mack Ave, Detroit MI 48215-2526. 313/824-0445.
Employs: 100-249.

Family Dollar Stores Inc
9525 Joseph Campau Ham, Detroit MI 48212. 313/972-5223. Employs: 100-249.

Family Dollar Stores Inc
10220 Gratiot Ave, Detroit MI 48213-3211. 313/923-8488.
Employs: 100-249.

Family Dollar Stores Inc
638 W Adrian St, Blissfield MI 49228-1005. 517/486-2215. Employs: 50-99.

Family Dollar Stores Inc
8218 Telegraph Rd, Taylor MI 48180-2229. 313/374-0866.
Employs: 100-249.

Family Dollar Stores Inc
27208 Eureka Rd, Taylor MI 48180-4845. 313/942-1810.
Employs: 100-249.

Family Dollar Stores Inc

1200 Baldwin Ave, Pontiac MI 48340-1906. 313/333-3120.
Employs: 100-249.

Family Dollar Stores Inc
1507 N Eaton Rd, Albion MI 49224-9462. 517/629-5661.
Employs: 50-99.

Family Dollar Stores Inc
417 Michigan St, Algonac MI 48001-1641. 313/794-4700.
Employs: 50-99.

Family Dollar Stores Inc
3418 Main St, Marlette MI 48453-1239. 517/635-3824.
Employs: 100-249.

Family Dollar Stores
14070 Telegraph Rd, Redford MI 48239-2855. 313/255-1420. Employs: 100-249.

Ford & Dancers Warehouse Office
110 S Clinton, Stockbridge MI 49285. 517/851-7335.
Employs: 100-249.

Giant Family Center
1721 S Mission St, Mount Pleasant MI 48858-4418.
517/773-7917. Employs: 100-249.

Gig Wheel
350 Lansing St, Charlotte MI 48813-1653. 517/543-2720.
Employs: 100-249.

Hudson's
Westland Mall, Westland MI 48185. 313/458-5400.
Employs: 100-249.

Hudson's
1921 Beaubien St, Detroit MI 48226. 313/223-1901.
Employs: 100-249.

J C Penney Co Inc
Southland Shopping Center, Taylor MI 48180. 313/287-2020. Employs: 100-249.

J C Penney Co Inc
44 N Howell St, Hillsdale MI 49242-1621. 517/439-9321.
Employs: 50-99.

J C Penney Co Inc
300 S Greenville West Dr, Greenville MI 48838-1592.
616/754-0033. Employs: 100-249.

Jacobson's
901 E Big Beaver Rd, Troy MI 48083-1409. 313/680-9000.
Employs: 100-249.

K Mart Corporation
40855 E Ann Arbor Rd, Plymouth MI 48170-4448.
313/455-5000. Employs: 50-99.

K Mart Corporation
33400 7 Mile Rd, Livonia MI 48152-3099. 313/474-8810.
Employs: 50-99.

K Mart Corporation
21111 Van Born Rd, Taylor MI 48180-1339. 313/278-3510. Employs: 100-249.

K Mart Corporation
2125 S Mission St, Mount Pleasant MI 48858-4426.
517/772-0951. Employs: 50-99.

K Mart Disc Dept Str No 9288
1450 N Eaton, Albion MI 49224. 517/629-5585. Employs: 50-99.

K Mart Discount Department Store
6730 River Rd, Marine City MI 48039-2252. 313/765-3537. Employs: 50-99.

K Mart Discount Dept Stores
8375 W Gd River, Brighton MI 48116. 313/227-2207.
Employs: 100-249.

K Mart Discount Stores
863 S Main St, Lapeer MI 48446-3044. 313/664-0885.
Employs: 100-249.

K Mart Footwear Regional Office
41425 Joy Rd, Plymouth MI 48170-4674. 313/459-7007.
Employs: 100-249.

K-Mart Schiller Div
7601 23 Mi, Shelby Twp MI 48316. 313/739-6077.
Employs: 100-249.

Kmart Corporation
1100 S Rochester Rd, Rochester MI 48307-3114. 313/651-1766. Employs: 50-99.

Kmart Corporation
1025 S Lapeer Rd, Lake Orion MI 48360-1429. 313/693-6252. Employs: 100-249.

Kmart Disc Dept Store No 9709
1658 Lansing Rd, Charlotte MI 48813-8442. 517/543-0733. Employs: 50-99.

Kmart Discount Department Stores
50770 Gratiot, Harrison Twp MI 48045. 313/949-5800.
Employs: 50-99.

Kmart Discount Department Stores
22801 Harper Ave, St Clair Shores MI 48080-1848.
313/779-3300. Employs: 100-249.

Kmart Discount Department Stores
20880 Gratiot Ave, East Detroit MI 48021-2863. 313/778-6350. Employs: 100-249.

Kmart Discount Department Stores
66011 Van Dyke, Romeo MI 48065. 313/752-4558.
Employs: 50-99.

Kohl's Department Store
18000 Vernier Rd, Harper Woods MI 48225-1027.
313/839-5700. Employs: 100-249.

Kohl's Department Stores
32100 Beaconsfield St, Roseville MI 48066-1177. 313/294-2816. Employs: 100-249.

Kohl's Department Stores
21500 Northwestern Hwy, Southfield MI 48075-5018.
313/559-0330. Employs: 100-249.

Kohl's Department Stores
500 John R Rd, Troy MI 48083-4544. 313/585-2400.
Employs: 100-249.

Kohl's Department Stores
415 S Telegraph Rd, Pontiac MI 48341-2372. 313/681-4800. Employs: 100-249.

Kohl's Department Stores
43550 W Oaks Dr, Novi MI 48377-3302. 313/344-4666.
Employs: 100-249.

Kresge Stores
408 S Washington Ave, Royal Oak MI 48067-3824.
313/541-7240. Employs: 100-249.

Kresge Stores
15221 Houston Whittier St, Detroit MI 48205-4128.
313/521-4550. Employs: 100-249.

Liz Ladies Apparel
1427 Woodward Ave, Detroit MI 48226-2001. 313/961-8919. Employs: 100-249.

Lord & Taylor
27650 Novi Rd, Novi MI 48377-3420. 313/348-3400.
Employs: 100-249.

Lord & Taylor

14250 Lakeside Cir, Sterling Heights MI 48313-1324.
313/247-4500. Employs: 100-249.

Mamouth Inc
15401 Grand River Ave, Detroit MI 48227-2214. 313/273-9600. Employs: 100-249.

Marhalls Dept Store
22275 Eureka Rd, Taylor MI 48180-5234. 313/287-9040.
Employs: 100-249.

Marshall Department Store
43500 W Oaks Dr, Novi MI 48377-3302. 313/348-3355.
Employs: 100-249.

Marshall Dept Stores
29708 Southfield Rd, Southfield MI 48076-2088. 313/557-9113. Employs: 50-99.

Marshall's Dept Store
28780 Gratiot Ave, Roseville MI 48066-4256. 313/445-2306. Employs: 100-249.

Marshalls Department Store
34600 Warren Rd, Westland MI 48185-2791. 313/425-9177. Employs: 100-249.

Marshalls Dept Store
350 N Telegraph Rd, Pontiac MI 48341-1055. 313/333-1991. Employs: 100-249.

McCrory
5505 Michigan Ave, Detroit MI 48210-3021. 313/897-7780. Employs: 100-249.

McCrory
286 W Nepessing St, Lapeer MI 48446-2148. 313/664-6302. Employs: 50-99.

McCrory Store No 9745
25465 Gr River, Redford MI 48240. 313/535-6024.
Employs: 100-249.

McCrory Stores
5656 W Vernor Hwy, Detroit MI 48209-2158. 313/554-1844. Employs: 100-249.

Meijer
15055 Hall Rd, Shelby Twp MI 48315-6206. 313/566-0400. Employs: 100-249.

Meijer Inc
1350 Lake Lansing Rd, Lansing MI 48912-3705. 517/332-2444. Employs: 100-249.

Meijer Inc
1015 E Pickard Rd, Mount Pleasant MI 48858-9661.
517/772-4700. Employs: 50-99.

Mervyn's Department Stores
29650 7 Mile Rd, Livonia MI 48152-1910. 313/478-8700.
Employs: 100-249.

Mervyn's Department Stores
28498 Dequindre Rd, Warren MI 48092-5605. 313/573-8888. Employs: 100-249.

Mervyn's Department Stores
26100 Ingersol Dr, Novi MI 48375-1213. 313/347-0112.
Employs: 100-249.

Mervyn's Department Stores
23000 Eureka Rd, Taylor MI 48180-5254. 313/374-8800.
Employs: 100-249.

Mervyn's Universal Mall
28498 Dequindre Rd, Warren MI 48092-5605. 313/573-9210. Employs: 100-249.

Meryn's Department Stores
35555 Warren Rd, Westland MI 48185-6590. 313/721-1444. Employs: 100-249.

Mitzelfeld's
312 S Main St, Rochester MI 48307-2030. 313/651-8171.
Employs: 100-249.

Montgomery Ward & Co
13665 Eureka Rd, Southgate MI 48195-1332. 313/285-4400. Employs: 100-249.

Off The Boulevard
117 N Evans St, Tecumseh MI 49286-1554. 517/423-2455.
Employs: 50-99.

Pace Membership Warehouse
35400 Cowan Rd, Westland MI 48185-2056. 313/425-4955. Employs: 100-249.

Pace Regional Office
20501 Pennsylvania Ave, Wyandotte MI 48192-8445.
313/284-2766. Employs: 100-249.

Sears Roebuck and Co
435 N Telegraph Rd, Waterford MI 48328-3332. 313/682-2018. Employs: 100-249.

Sears Roebuck and Co
1386 Walton Blvd, Rochester MI 48309-1754. 313/652-0001. Employs: 100-249.

Sears Roebuck and Co
34650 Mound Rd, Sterling Heights MI 48310-5759.
313/939-1900. Employs: 100-249.

Shopper's World
14551 Woodward Ave, Detroit MI 48203-2930. 313/868-1400. Employs: 100-249.

Shopper's World
15510 Joy Rd, Detroit MI 48228-2118. 313/272-7280.
Employs: 100-249.

Shoppers World
200 W 9 Mile Rd, Ferndale MI 48220-1759. 313/547-6790.
Employs: 100-249.

Shoppers World
9820 Joseph Campau Ham, Detroit MI 48212. 313/874-0900. Employs: 100-249.

Shoppers World
21675 Coolidge Hwy, Oak Park MI 48237-3128. 313/839-1040. Employs: 100-249.

T J Maxx
9311 Telegraph Rd, Redford MI 48239-1260. 313/534-2170. Employs: 100-249.

T J Maxx
30955 Orchard Lake Rd, Farmington MI 48334-1338.
313/855-6288. Employs: 100-249.

T J Maxx
43175 Crescent Blvd, Novi MI 48375-1206. 313/348-7700.
Employs: 100-249.

T J Maxx
35655 Warren Rd, Westland MI 48185-2015. 313/721-1400. Employs: 100-249.

T J Maxx
30999 5 Mile Rd, Livonia MI 48154-3641. 313/427-5400.
Employs: 100-249.

T J Maxx
26285 Hoover Rd, Warren MI 48089-1133. 313/757-4050.
Employs: 100-249.

T J Maxx Department Store
2711 S Rochester Rd, Rochester MI 48307-4548. 313/852-4550. Employs: 100-249.

T J Maxx Store

13833 Hall Rd, Shelby Twp MI 48315-6102. 313/247-1530. Employs: 100-249.

Target Store
35401 Warren Rd, Westland MI 48185-6590. 313/728-4444. Employs: 100-249.

Target Store
14099 Pardee Rd, Taylor MI 48180-4792. 313/374-0303.
Employs: 100-249.

Target Stores
26650 Ford Rd, Detroit MI 48228. 313/565-0404.
Employs: 100-249.

Target Stores
15901 Ford Rd, Detroit MI 48228. 313/336-5000.
Employs: 100-249.

Target Stores
5609 W Saginaw Hwy, Lansing MI 48917-2456. 517/886-9488. Employs: 100-249.

Target Stores
13221 Hall Rd, Shelby Twp MI 48315-5834. 313/254-7100. Employs: 100-249.

Target Stores
35700 Van Dyke Ave, Sterling Heights MI 48312-3564.
313/795-9960. Employs: 100-249.

Target Stores
2887 S Rochester Rd, Rochester MI 48307-4580. 313/853-1590. Employs: 100-249.

Target Stores
8500 E 8 Mile Rd, Detroit MI 48234-1116. 313/891-4000.
Employs: 100-249.

Target Stores
30020 Grand River Ave, Farmington MI 48336-4722.
313/476-1808. Employs: 100-249.

Target Stores
355 Summit Dr, Pontiac MI 48341. 313/681-1818.
Employs: 100-249.

Target Stores
27300 Dequindre Rd, Warren MI 48092-2870. 313/573-4200. Employs: 100-249.

Target Stores
30007 Plymouth Rd, Livonia MI 48150-2116. 313/522-7011. Employs: 100-249.

Target Stores
32001 R, Madison Heights MI 48071. 313/585-9000.
Employs: 100-249.

Target Stores
3701 Lapeer Rd, Flint MI 48503-4598. 313/744-4040.
Employs: 100-249.

Target Stores-Regional Office
306 S Washington Ave, Royal Oak MI 48067-3845.
313/542-8300. Employs: 100-249.

Tie Rack
14000 Lakeside Cir, Sterling Heights MI 48313-1320.
313/566-0270. Employs: 100-249.

Winkelman's
Macomb Mall Shopping Center, Roseville MI 48066.
313/293-0300. Employs: 100-249.

Woolworth Express
28746 Dequindre Rd, Warren MI 48092-5607. 313/585-4845. Employs: 100-249.

Woolworth Express #2728
21500 Northwestern Hwy, Southfield MI 48075-5018.
313/559-1696. Employs: 100-249.

Woolworth Express #2737
28616 Telegraph Rd, Southfield MI 48034-1934. 313/948-
8180. Employs: 100-249.

VARIETY STORES

K-Mart
27313 Telegraph Rd, Flat Rock MI 48134-1010. 313/782-
0500. Employs: 50-99.

Pace Membership Warehouse Inc
800 E 14 Mile Rd, Madison Heights MI 48071-1400.
313/588-4407. Employs: 100-249.

The Gap
Westland Shopping Ctr, Westland MI 48185. 313/261-
2343. Employs: 50-99.

**MISCELLANEOUS GENERAL MERCHANDISE
STORES**

F W Woolworth Co
200 S Washington Sq, Lansing MI 48933-1808. 517/484-
1519. Employs: 100-249.

Ind Mutual Assoc
901 E 2nd St, Flint MI 48503-1902. 313/234-4633.
Employs: 50-99.

Target Discount Store
500 Edgewood Blvd E, Lansing MI 48911-5901. 517/882-
9084. Employs: 100-249.

Warehouse Club Inc
4000 Enterprise Dr, Allen Park MI 48101-3533. 313/271-
1742. Employs: 50-99.

MOTOR VEHICLE DEALERS (NEW AND USED)

Applegate Chevrolet Co
3637 S Saginaw St, Flint MI 48503-4149. 313/238-7611.
Employs: 100-249.

Bill Wink Chevrolet Co
10700 Ford Rd, Dearborn MI 48126-3337. 313/582-5400.
Employs: 100-249.

Bob Borst Lincoln Mercury Inc
1950 W Maple Rd, Troy MI 48084-7105. 313/643-6600.
Employs: 50-99.

Charnock Oldsmobile Inc
24555 Michigan Av, Dearborn MI 48124-1731. 313/565-
6500. Employs: 50-99.

Dean Sellers Inc
2600 W Maple Rd, Troy MI 48084-7133. 313/643-7500.
Employs: 50-99.

Frank Mc Nally Inc
1415 E Pierson Rd, Flushing MI 48433-1814. 313/659-
5651. Employs: 50-99.

Friendly Ford Inc
1011 S Monroe St, Monroe MI 48161-3930. 313/243-6000.
Employs: 50-99.

Ken Mac Gillivray Buick Co
1200 S Averill Av, Flint MI 48503-2975. 313/744-0100.
Employs: 100-249.

Lee John Oldsmobile-Saab
3120 Washtenaw Rd, Ann Arbor MI 48104-5122. 313/971-
8100. Employs: 50-99.

Mike Savoie Chevrolet Inc
1900 W Maple Rd, Troy MI 48084-7105. 313/643-8000.
Employs: 50-99.

Paul Mc Glone Cadillac Inc

20903 Harper Av, Harper Woods MI 48225-1132.
313/881-6600. Employs: 100-249.

Rampy Cheverolet Nissan Geo
3515 Jackson Rd, Ann Arbor MI 48103-1815. 313/663-
3321. Employs: 50-99.

Ron Slivka Buick
G6201 Saginaw Rd, Grand Blanc MI 48439. 313/694-5600.
Employs: 50-99.

Sawyers Pontiac
1415 Michigan Av, East Lansing MI 48823-4025. 517/332-
5011. Employs: 50-99.

Somerset Pontiac G M C Inc
1850 W Maple Rd, Troy MI 48084-7104. 313/643-8600.
Employs: 50-99.

Story Oldsmobile Nissan Inc
3165 E Michigan Av, Lansing MI 48912-4618. 517/351-
0400. Employs: 50-99.

Suburban Oldsmobile Cadillac
1810 Maplelawn Dr, Troy MI 48084-4616. 313/643-0070.
Employs: 50-99.

Summerfield Chevrolet Co Inc
G5100 Clio Rd, Flint MI 48504-1267. 313/785-4011.
Employs: 100-249.

Tom Gleason Ford Mercedes
G3450 Miller Rd, Flint MI 48507-1238. 313/732-7400.
Employs: 50-99.

Vic Canever Chevrolet-Geo
3000 Owen Rd, Fenton MI 48430-1766. 313/629-3350.
Employs: 50-99.

Village Ford Inc
23535 Michigan Av, Dearborn MI 48124-1917. 313/565-
3900. Employs: 100-249.

Westborn Chrysler-Plymouth Inc
23300 Michigan Av, Dearborn MI 48124-2030. 313/562-
3200. Employs: 50-99.

Williams Auto World
2845 E Saginaw St, Lansing MI 48912-4239. 517/484-
1341. Employs: 50-99.

Wilson-Crissman Cadillac I
1350 N Woodward Av, Birmingham MI 48009-5113.
313/644-1930. Employs: 100-249.

Lochmoor Chrysler Plymouth Alfa
18165 Mack Ave, Detroit MI 48224-1444. 313/886-3000.
Employs: 100-249.

John Rogin Buick-Isuzu
3939 S Wayne Rd, Wayne MI 48184-1623. 313/729-2000.
Employs: 50-99.

George Bente Cadillac Olds Inc
1701 Prestwick Ave, Grosse Pointe MI 48236-1938.
313/259-9000. Employs: 100-249.

Merollis Chevrolet Sales & Svc
21800 Gratiot Ave, East Detroit MI 48021-2224. 313/755-
8300. Employs: 50-99.

Whelan Buff Chevrolet Inc
40445 Van Dyke Ave, Sterling Heights MI 48313-3736.
313/939-7300. Employs: 50-99.

Roseville Chrysler Plymouth Inc
25800 Gratiot Ave, Roseville MI 48066-4416. 313/772-
0800. Employs: 50-99.

Jorgensen Ford
8333 Michigan Ave, Detroit MI 48210-2172. 313/584-
2250. Employs: 100-249.

Russ Ford Milne Inc
43870 Gratiot Ave, Clinton Twp MI 48036-3332. 313/293-7000. Employs: 50-99.

Stuart Evans Linc Merc Garden City
32000 Ford Rd, Garden City MI 48135-1506. 313/425-4300. Employs: 50-99.

Durand Chevy-Geo-Pontiac-Olds
9009 Lansing Rd, Durand MI 48429-1055. 517/288-2657. Employs: 50-99.

Shelton Pontiac Buick Inc
855 S Rochester Rd, Rochester MI 48307-2741. 313/651-5500. Employs: 50-99.

Dick Genthe Chevrolet Inc
15600 Eureka Rd, Southgate MI 48195-2624. 313/283-3400. Employs: 50-99.

Lou Lariche Chevy Subaru Inc
40875 Plymouth Rd, Plymouth MI 48170-4203. 313/453-4600. Employs: 50-99.

Al Long Ford Inc
13711 E 8 Mile Rd, Warren MI 48089-3353. 313/777-2700. Employs: 50-99.

Bill Snethkamp Chrysler
16400 Woodward Ave, Detroit MI 48203-2818. 313/868-3300. Employs: 50-99.

Flannery Motors Inc
5900 Highland Rd, Waterford MI 48327-1829. 313/674-4781. Employs: 50-99.

Holman Red Pontiac-GMC-Toyota
35300 Ford Rd, Westland MI 48185-3173. 313/721-1144. Employs: 100-249.

Mitchell Suzuki
165 N Gratiot Ave, Mount Clemens MI 48043-5717. 313/468-4567. Employs: 50-99.

Roy O'Brien Inc
22201 E 9 Mile Rd, St Clair Shores MI 48080-2910. 313/776-7600. Employs: 100-249.

Tamaroff Buick Honda Isuzu
28585 Telegraph Rd, Southfield MI 48034-7507. 313/353-1300. Employs: 50-99.

Team One Chevrolet Olds Inc
1616 Lansing Rd, Charlotte MI 48813-8442. 517/543-0200. Employs: 50-99.

MOTOR VEHICLE DEALERS (USED ONLY)

Hank Graff Chevrolet
800 N State St, Davison MI 48423-1132. 313/653-4111. Employs: 100-249.

Dalgleish Cadillac-Peugeot
6160 Cass Ave, Detroit MI 48202-3426. 313/875-0300. Employs: 50-99.

Don Foss-Downtown
1301 Leverette St, Detroit MI 48226-1015. 313/961-0221. Employs: 50-99

Don Massey Cadillac Inc
40475 E Ann Arbor Rd, Plymouth MI 48170-4576. 313/453-7500. Employs: 100-249.

Quality Pontiac Ltd
2470 Elizabeth Lake Rd, Waterford MI 48328-3310. 313/681-2600. Employs: 50-99.

AUTO AND HOME SUPPLY STORES

Goodyear Tire & Rubber

100 Galleria Office Ct, Southfield MI 48086. 313/423-5500. Employs: 50-99.

K-Mart Automobile Center
3100 Washtenaw Rd, Ypsilanti MI 48197-1509. 313/434-0300. Employs: 50-99.

Mechanics Warehouse Auto Parts
710 N State St, Davison MI 48423-1130. 313/653-1090. Employs: 50-99.

Northwest Tire & Service
G3453 W Pierson Rd, Flint MI 48504. 313/785-3433. Employs: 50-99.

Paul Automotive Inc
1118 S Main St, Eaton Rapids MI 48827-1736. 517/482-5521. Employs: 50-99.

U S Edscha A
1700 W Big Beaver Rd Ste 225, Troy MI 48084-3524. 313/649-6995. Employs: 50-99.

Mark Chevrolet Inc
33200 Michigan Ave, Wayne MI 48184-1876. 313/722-9100. Employs: 50-99.

Belle Tire Distributors
5705 W Maple Rd, W Bloomfield MI 48322-2270. 313/851-4600. Employs: 50-99.

Dreisbach & Sons Cadillac Co
24600 Grove St, Detroit MI 48219. 313/531-2600. Employs: 50-99.

K Mart Corporation
44444 Ford Rd, Canton MI 48187-2944. 313/459-2144. Employs: 100-249.

Kmart Stores
29101 John R Rd, Madison Heights MI 48071-5403. 313/546-8880. Employs: 50-99.

Rao Wholesale Tire Center
6031 Joy Rd, Detroit MI 48204-2909. 313/895-1200. Employs: 100-249.

Sears Roebuck and Co
435 S Telegraph Rd, Pontiac MI 48341-2372. 313/681-9900. Employs: 100-249.

GASOLINE SERVICE STATIONS

Bay Petroleum Corp
419 Spring St, Lansing MI 48912-1035. 517/485-2285. Employs: 100-249.

By-Lo Oil Company
2797 Wadhams, Port Huron MI 48060. 313/982-1450. Employs: 100-249.

Drakes Refinery Stations Inc
3125 S Logan St, Lansing MI 48910-2939. 517/393-0418. Employs: 50-99.

Van Dyke & 13 Mile Service Station
31004 Van Dyke Ave, Warren MI 48093-1755. 313/977-1920. Employs: 50-99.

RECREATIONAL VEHICLE DEALERS

Terris Industries
29563 Northwestern Hw, Southfield MI 48034-1021. 313/357-4414. Employs: 50-99.

MEN'S AND BOYS' CLOTHING AND ACCESSORY STORES

Milliken's Department Store
4170 E Blue Grass Rd, Mount Pleasant MI 48858-7914. 517/772-2253. Employs: 50-99.

WOMEN'S CLOTHING STORES

Crowley's
Courtland Center, Burton MI 48509. 313/744-1010.
Employs: 100-249.

Crowley's
28300 Dequindre Rd, Warren MI 48092-2401. 313/574-2240. Employs: 100-249.

Crowley's
3031 W Grand Blvd, Detroit MI 48202-3014. 313/874-5100. Employs: 50-99.

Kay Baum Inc
166 E Maple Rd, Birmingham MI 48009-3322. 313/642-9500. Employs: 50-99.

Marianne 1426 Woodward Cor
1426 Woodward Av, Detroit MI 48226-2002. 313/962-7608. Employs: 50-99.

Mason Shops
7135 Bridge Way, W Bloomfield MI 48322-3500. 313/471-5310. Employs: 50-99.

Maurice Distinctive Apparel
300 Washington Sq S, Lansing MI 48933-2115. 517/484-8455. Employs: 100-249.

Motherhood
C17A Ivonia Mall Shopping Ctr, Livonia MI 48152. 313/478-4392. Employs: 50-99.

CHILDREN'S AND INFANTS' WEAR STORES

Mervyn's Department Store
250 N Telegraph Rd, Pontiac MI 48341-1054. 313/332-5800. Employs: 100-249.

Mervyn's Department Store
32399 John R Rd, Madison Heights MI 48071-1324. 313/589-1112. Employs: 100-249.

Mervyn's Department Stores
13361 Hall Rd, Shelby Twp MI 48315-5835. 313/731-9000. Employs: 100-249.

Minerva's-Dunning's
500 Forest Ave, Plymouth MI 48170-1722. 313/453-0080. Employs: 100-249.

FAMILY CLOTHING STORES

Big Wheel
4082 W Vienna Rd, Clio MI 48420-9402. 313/687-4490. Employs: 50-99.

Burlington Coat Factory Warehouse
3301 E Michigan Av, Lansing MI 48912-4619. 517/337-8988. Employs: 100-249.

Dancer's Fashions
2495 N Cedar St, Holt MI 48842-2100. 517/694-1632. Employs: 100-249.

Dancer's Fashions
108 W Maple St, Mason MI 48854-1657. 517/676-9144. Employs: 50-99.

T J Maxx
5833 W Saginaw St, Lansing MI 48917-2460. 517/321-1304. Employs: 100-249.

T J Maxx
2467 W Stadium Blvd, Ann Arbor MI 48103-3809. 313/665-9525. Employs: 50-99.

Van Horn Incorporated
293 N Telegraph Rd, Pontiac MI 48341-1938. 313/643-4676. Employs: 100-249

SHOE STORES

Baker's Shoe Store
23000 Eureka Rd, Taylor MI 48180-5254. 313/287-4940. Employs: 50-99.

Mr B's Shoes Inc
26045 Greenfield Rd, Southfield MI 48076-4703. 313/569-7463. Employs: 50-99.

MISCELLANEOUS APPAREL AND ACCESSORY STORES

Dancer's Inc
566 N Cedar, Mason MI 48854. 517/676-4474. Employs: 100-249.

Broner Glove & Safety Co
359 Robbins Dr, Troy MI 48083-4561. 313/589-1919. Employs: 50-99.

Ideal Glove Manufacturing
985 Stratford Ln, Bloomfield MI 48304-2929. 313/433-3640. Employs: 50-99.

Lion Store
1165 Seba Rd, Waterford MI 48328-2039. 313/338-9667. Employs: 100-249.

The Sweatshirt Company
12373 S Beyer Rd, Birch Run MI 48415-9406. 517/624-4551. Employs: 100-249.

FURNITURE STORES

Estes Furniture Co
101 E Grand River Av, Lansing MI 48906-4848. 517/372-8710. Employs: 50-99.

House Of Denmark
893 S Rochester Rd, Rochester MI 48307-2741. 313/651-9430. Employs: 50-99.

Jacobson's Store For The Home
115 E Grand River Av, East Lansing MI 48823-4322. 517/351-2550. Employs: 100-249.

Star Furniture Company
33500 7 Mile Rd, Livonia MI 48152-3080. 313/582-1728. Employs: 50-99.

FLOOR COVERING STORES

Englander Triangle Inc
1310 Academy, Ferndale MI 48220-2002. 313/398-4950. Employs: 100-249.

Clyde's Carpets
23140 W 8 Mile Rd, Southfield MI 48034-4366. 313/357-3120. Employs: 50-99.

DRAPERY, CURTAIN AND UPHOLSTERY STORES

Amco Manufacturing Corp
545 Industrial Dr, Adrian MI 49221-9755. 517/265-4028. Employs: 100-249.

MISCELLANEOUS HOMEFURNISHINGS STORES

Corning-Evere Factory Outlet
12245 S Beyer Rd, Birch Run MI 48415-9403. 517/624-9339. Employs: 100-249.

Center Electric
14501 W 8 Mile Rd, Detroit MI 48235-1620. 313/342-3200. Employs: 50-99.

Fireplace & Spa Center
23600 Telegraph Rd, Southfield MI 48034-4116. 313/353-0001. Employs: 50-99.

HOUSEHOLD APPLIANCE STORES

Big Georges Home Appliance Mart
2019 W Stadium Blvd, Ann Arbor MI 48103-4557.
313/665-8653. Employs: 50-99.

Radio Distributing Co
27015 Trolley Dr, Taylor MI 48180-1423. 313/295-4500.
Employs: 100-249.

Smith Furniture Co
1050 E Michigan Ave, Ypsilanti MI 48198-5899. 313/483-4500. Employs: 50-99.

Crump TV & Appliance
3465 Auburn Rd, Auburn Hills MI 48326-3313. 313/852-3000. Employs: 50-99.

RADIO, TELEVISION AND CONSUMER ELECTRONICS STORES

Mickey Shorr
825 S Woodward Ave, Royal Oak MI 48067-3044.
313/398-7204. Employs: 50-99.

COMPUTER AND COMPUTER SOFTWARE STORES

Computer Equipment Industry
2868 Fort St, Lincoln Park MI 48146-2424. 313/852-2250.
Employs: 50-99.

O E Systems Inc
3290 W Big Beaver Rd, Troy MI 48084-2903. 313/643-7220. Employs: 50-99.

Tandem Computers
21800 Haggerty Rd, Northville MI 48167-9051. 313/344-0200. Employs: 50-99.

Computer Decisions International Inc
39500 Orchard Hill Pl, Novi MI 48375-5370. 313/347-4600. Employs: 50-99.

MUSICAL INSTRUMENT STORES

Anderson Music Co
650 N Telegraph Rd, Dearborn MI 48128-1620. 313/278-0100. Employs: 50-99.

DRUG STORES AND PROPRIETARY STORES

Foodtown Pharmacy
211 N Telegraph Rd, Monroe MI 48161-3231. 313/241-2046. Employs: 50-99.

State Discount
501 E Grand River Av, East Lansing MI 48823-4404.
517/332-5580. Employs: 50-99.

K Mart
2095 Rawsonville Rd, Belleville MI 48111-2219. 313/487-5502. Employs: 50-99.

K Mart Corporation
165 S Wayne Rd, Westland MI 48185-4301. 313/326-5200.
Employs: 50-99.

Kmart Discount Department Stores
26100 Gratiot Ave, Roseville MI 48066-3389. 313/771-9280. Employs: 50-99.

The Kroger Co
540 S Main St, Lapeer MI 48446-2467. 313/664-9234.
Employs: 50-99.

Wal-Mart Discount Cities
4208 E Blue Grass Rd, Mount Pleasant MI 48858-7914.
517/772-6302. Employs: 50-99.

Arbor Drugs
21790 W 11 Mile Rd, Southfield MI 48076-3718. 313/353-9898. Employs: 50-99.

Kmart Stores
25700 W 8 Mile Rd, Southfield MI 48034-3750. 313/353-8033. Employs: 50-99.

Maple Drug Stores
31505 Joy Rd, Westland MI 48185-1641. 313/427-9100.
Employs: 50-99.

Meijer
4200 Highland Rd, Waterford MI 48328-2137. 313/682-4001. Employs: 100-249.

Meijer
3175 S Rochester Rd, Rochester MI 48307-5042. 313/853-2180. Employs: 100-249.

Meijer Inc
2601 E M 21, Corunna MI 48817-1104. 517/743-3432.
Employs: 50-99.

Meijer Pharmacy
1220 N Lafayette St, Greenville MI 48838-1038. 616/754-3633. Employs: 100-249.

Meijer Pharmacy
36600 Van Dyke Ave, Sterling Heights MI 48312-2766.
313/978-7640. Employs: 50-99.

Meijer Pharmacy
30800 Little Mack Ave, Roseville MI 48066-1759.
313/296-5577. Employs: 100-249.

LIQUOR STORES

Scotch Castle Liquor Land
2867 E 7 Mile Rd, Detroit MI 48234-1502. 313/368-7500.
Employs: 50-99.

Ammex Inc
Corner Of 21st & Porter, Detroit MI 48216. 313/496-0630.
Employs: 50-99.

Village Liquor & Deli
14241 W McNichols Rd, Detroit MI 48235-3913. 313/838-4040. Employs: 50-99.

USED MERCHANDISE STORES

Sears Roebuck & Co Surplus
3600 S Dort Hwy, Flint MI 48507-2054. 313/742-1370.
Employs: 100-249.

Prestige Loan Co
13216 Dexter Ave, Detroit MI 48238-3329. 313/869-0900.
Employs: 50-99.

SPORTING GOODS STORES AND BICYCLE SHOPS

A L Williams & Huletty
G3163 Flushing Rd, Flint MI 48504-4365. 313/239-5400.
Employs: 50-99.

Three Hundred Bowl
100 S Cass Lake Rd, Waterford MI 48328-3523. 313/683-8730. Employs: 50-99.

BOOK STORES

Adrian College Book Store
110 S Madison St, Adrian MI 49221-2518. 517/265-5161.
Employs: 100-249.

STATIONERY STORES

Silver's Inc
16350 Woodward Ave, Detroit MI 48203-2870. 313/883-4410. Employs: 100-249.

JEWELRY STORES

Burlington Coat Factory Jewelry
9321 Telegraph Rd, Redford MI 48239-1260. 313/592-0215. Employs: 100-249.

Burlington Coat Factory Jewelry
2185 S Telegraph Rd, Bloomfield MI 48302-0250. 313/333-7060. Employs: 100-249.

Michels Jewelry & Watch Repair
43119 7 Mile Rd, Northville MI 48167-2279. 313/348-9380. Employs: 50-99.

Service Merchandise Co
13851 Eureka Rd, Southgate MI 48195-1332. 313/281-0160. Employs: 100-249.

HOBBY, TOY, AND GAME SHOPS

Toys 'R US
3725 Washtenaw Rd, Ann Arbor MI 48104-5252. 313/973-2850. Employs: 100-249.

Toys 'R' US
24411 Michigan Av, Dearborn MI 48124-1827. 313/278-2660. Employs: 50-99.

GIFT, NOVELTY AND SOUVENIR SHOPS

Cunningham Drug Stores Inc
1927 Rosa Parks Blvd, Detroit MI 48216-1555. 313/963-7763. Employs: 50-99.

LUGGAGE AND LEATHER GOODS STORES

Tannery West
18900 Michigan Av, Dearborn MI 48126-3901. 313/593-1870. Employs: 50-99.

SEWING, NEEDLEWORK AND PIECE GOODS STORES

Industrial Mutual Assn Flint
6045 Davison Rd, Burton MI 48509-1606. 313/742-2168. Employs: 100-249.

CATALOG AND MAIL-ORDER HOUSES

Mary Maxim Inc
2001 Holland Ave, Port Huron MI 48060-1519. 313/987-2000. Employs: 100-249.

AUTOMATIC MERCHANDISE MACHINE OPERATORS

Variety Food Services
25235 Hoover Rd, Warren MI 48089-1101. 313/756-8100. Employs: 50-99.

DIRECT SELLING ESTABLISHMENTS

Americoffe-Amvend
47451 Avante Dr, Wixom MI 48393-3616. 313/347-2277. Employs: 50-99.

International Consumers Service Inc
603 Vester St, Ferndale MI 48220-1930. 313/543-0255. Employs: 100-249.

FUEL OIL DEALERS

Carl M Schultz Inc
30 N Saginaw St, Lapeer MI 48446-2659. 313/664-8491. Employs: 50-99.

Foster Oil Co
69120 Foster Rd, Richmond MI 48062-5500. 313/727-3315. Employs: 50-99.

Neeb Corp

136 W Huron Ave, Bad Axe MI 48413-1101. 517/269-6481. Employs: 100-249.

LIQUEFIED PETROLEUM GAS (BOTTLED GAS) DEALERS

Skelgas Inc
1301 N Kinney Ave, Mount Pleasant MI 48858-1714. 517/773-3800. Employs: 50-99.

FLORISTS

The Kroger Co
43525 W Oaks Dr, Novi MI 48377-3303. 313/348-2320. Employs: 50-99.

The Kroger Co
13661 Colson St, Dearborn MI 48126-3232. 313/584-0370. Employs: 100-249.

The Kroger Co
270 W Carleton Rd, Hillsdale MI 49242-3052. 517/437-2940. Employs: 50-99.

Post Gardens Greenhouses Inc
21189 Huron River Dr, Rockwood MI 48173-9601. 313/379-9688. Employs: 50-99.

NEWS DEALERS AND NEWSSTANDS

Ludington News Co Inc
1600 E Gd Bl, Detroit MI 48211. 313/925-7600. Employs: 100-249.

OPTICAL GOODS STORES

Richardson Optical
320 S State St, Ann Arbor MI 48104-2412. 313/662-1945. Employs: 50-99.

MISCELLANEOUS RETAIL STORES

Cecille's
850 S Woodward Av, Birmingham MI 48009-6722. 313/642-5855. Employs: 50-99.

Mc Graphics
755 Big Beaver Rd Ste 217, Troy MI 48084-4903. 313/362-4798. Employs: 100-249.

Unitron Industries Inc
3555 Walnut St, Port Huron MI 48060-2172. 313/982-0166. Employs: 50-99.

Security Corporation Of Mi
1505 E 11 Mile Rd, Royal Oak MI 48067-2027. 313/545-6665. Employs: 50-99.

Northwest Blue Print & Supply Co
13450 Farmington Rd, Livonia MI 48150-4207. 313/525-1990. Employs: 50-99.

Earphonics Inc
18121 E 8 Mile Rd, East Detroit MI 48021-3245. 313/773-3300. Employs: 50-99.

Wright & Filippis Inc
2845 Crooks Rd, Rochester MI 48309-3660. 313/739-3020. Employs: 50-99.

Hawthorne Valley
7300 N Merriman Rd, Westland MI 48185-2429. 313/422-3440. Employs: 50-99.

Franco's Limousine Svc
9540 Wayne Rd, Livonia MI 48150-2622. 313/522-6404. Employs: 50-99.

Wine Barrel Of Reford
25303 Plymouth Rd, Redford MI 48239-2020. 313/533-9463. Employs: 50-99.

Norwest Plumbing & Heating Supplies Co
14555 Meyers Rd, Detroit MI 48227-3949. 313/491-9000.
Employs: 50-99.

For more information on career opportunities in general merchandise retailing:

Associations

AMERICAN INTERNATIONAL AUTOMOTIVE
DEALERS ASSOCIATION
99 Canal Center Plaza, Suite 500, Alexandria VA 22314-
1538. 703/519-7800.

INTERNATIONAL ASSOCIATION OF CHAIN
STORES
38100 Moor Place, Alexandria VA 22305. 703/549-4525.

INTERNATIONAL COUNCIL OF SHOPPING
CENTERS
665 Fifth Avenue, New York NY 10022. 212/421-8181.

MENSWEAR RETAILERS OF AMERICA
2011 I Street NW, Suite 300, Washington DC 20006.
202/347-1932.

NATIONAL AUTOMOTIVE DEALERS
ASSOCIATION
8400 Westpark Drive, McLean VA 22102. 703/821-7000.

NATIONAL INDEPENDENT AUTOMOTIVE
DEALERS ASSOCIATION
2521 Brown Boulevard, Suite 100, Arlington TX 76006.
817/640-3838.

NATIONAL RETAIL MERCHANTS ASSOCIATION
100 West 31st Street, New York NY 10001. 212/244-8780.

Directories

AUTOMOTIVE NEWS MARKET DATA BOOK
Automotive News, 1400 Woodbridge Avenue, Detroit MI
48207. 313/446-6000.

GOVERNMENT

Large employers: 250+

Greenfield Village Cs 2
PO Box 1970, Dearborn MI 48121. 313/271-1620.
Employs: 1000+.

EXECUTIVE, LEGISLATIVE AND GENERAL
GOVERNMENT

City Public Schools Dept Trans
1400 W Monroe St, Jackson MI 49202-1902. 517/782-
1794. Employs: 250-499.

Holly Vlg Area Schools Supt
111 College St, Holly MI 48442-1720. 313/634-4431.
Employs: 250-499.

State Prison Of Southern Mich
4000 Cooper St, Jackson MI 49201-9503. 517/788-7560.
Employs: 1000+.

Troy Civil Service Commission
500 W Big Beaver Rd, Troy MI 48084-5254. 313/524-
3300. Employs: 250-499.

U S Environmental Protection Agency
2565 Plymouth Rd, Ann Arbor MI 48105-2425. 313/668-
4200. Employs: 250-499.

Detroit Fire Commissioner's
250 W Larned St, Detroit MI 48226-4409. 313/596-2902.
Employs: 1000+.

Detroit Police Department
1300 Beaubien St, Detroit MI 48226-2308. 313/224-4400.
Employs: 500-999.

Detroit Recreation Athletic
735 Randolph St Rm 1708, Detroit MI 48226-2868.
313/898-6315. Employs: 1000+.

Detroit Transportation Dept
1301 E Warren Ave, Detroit MI 48207-1034. 313/933-
1300. Employs: 500-999.

Michigan Mental Health Dept
951 E Lafayette, Detroit MI 48207. 313/256-9350.
Employs: 250-499.

Michigan Treasury Department
430 W Allegan, Lansing MI 48933. 517/373-3200.
Employs: 1000+.

JUSTICE PUBLIC ORDER AND SAFETY

Michigan Reformatory
Lock Box 500, Ionia MI 48846-0500. 616/527-2500.
Employs: 250-499.

Office Of Community Correction
PO Box 30003, Lansing MI 48909-7503. 517/373-0415.
Employs: 250-499.

Small to medium sized employers: 50-249

UNITED STATES POSTAL SERVICE

Kroger
5866 Middlebelt Rd, Garden City MI 48135. 313/522-
2870. Employs: 50-99.

Meijers Cs 4
3825 Carpenter Rd, Ypsilanti MI 48197. 313/973-7800.
Employs: 100-249.

EXECUTIVE, LEGISLATIVE AND GENERAL GOVERNMENTAL

City Bd Of Educ
3100 Owen Rd, Fenton MI 48430-1754. 313/629-2268.
Employs: 50-99.

City Bd Of Water & Light
123 W Ottawa St, Lansing MI 48933-1601. 517/487-1885.
Employs: 50-99.

City Court Clerk Office
120 E 5th St, Flint MI 48502-1645. 812/766-7364.
Employs: 50-99.

City Supt Of Schools
2603 Charlton Rd, Trenton MI 48183-2446. 313/676-8600.
Employs: 100-249.

Clio Board Of Education
430 N Mill St, Clio MI 48420-1227. 313/686-0500.
Employs: 100-249.

County Clk
208 N Shiawassee St Rm 211, Corunna MI 48817-1447.
517/743-2279. Employs: 100-249.

County Community Mental Hlth Cntr
324 Airport Industrial Dr, Ypsilanti MI 48198-6061.
313/481-1650. Employs: 100-249.

County Medical Care Facility
1715 Lansing Av, Jackson MI 49202-2135. 517/783-2726.
Employs: 100-249.

County Medical Care Facility
200 Sand Creek Hwy, Adrian MI 49221-1255. 517/263-6794. Employs: 100-249.

Delta Twp Waverly School Dist
515 Snow Rd, Lansing MI 48917-9564. 517/321-7265.
Employs: 50-99.

Genesee Intermediate School Dist
2413 W Maple Av, Flint MI 48507-3429. 313/768-4400.
Employs: 50-99.

Swartz Ck Superintendent
8354 Cappy La, Swartz Creek MI 48473-1242. 313/635-4441. Employs: 50-99.

U S Commerce Department
231 W Lafayette Blvd, Detroit MI 48226-2799. 313/226-7742. Employs: 50-99.

U S Veterans Administration
477 Michigan, Detroit MI 48226. 313/964-5110. Employs: 50-99.

Detroit Birth & Death Records
1151 Taylor St, Detroit MI 48202-1732. 313/876-4133.
Employs: 50-99.

Detroit City Council Planning
1340 City County Building, Detroit MI 48226. 313/224-6225. Employs: 100-249.

Detroit Food Inspections
1151 Taylor St, Detroit MI 48202-1732. 313/876-4500.
Employs: 50-99.

Detroit Law Department
2 Woodward Ave, Detroit MI 48226-3403. 313/224-4550.
Employs: 50-99.

Detroit Mayor's Office
2 Woodward Ave # 1126, Detroit MI 48226-3453.
313/224-3400. Employs: 50-99.

Detroit Personnel
316 City County Building, Detroit MI 48226. 313/224-3700. Employs: 50-99.

Detroit Recreation Dist Ofcs
5650 Conner St, Detroit MI 48213-3408. 313/267-7100.
Employs: 50-99.

Detroit Water & Sewerage Dept
735 Randolph St, Detroit MI 48226-2818. 313/224-4800.
Employs: 100-249.

Flint Street Maintenance
1106 S Averill Ave, Flint MI 48503-2906. 313/766-7343.
Employs: 50-99.

Mount Clemens Manager
1 Crocker Blvd, Mount Clemens MI 48043-2537. 313/469-6803. Employs: 100-249.

Eaton Medical Care Facility
530 Beech St, Charlotte MI 48813-1016. 517/543-2940.
Employs: 100-249.

Genesee County Environmental
630 S Saginaw St, Flint MI 48502-1525. 313/257-3603.
Employs: 50-99.

Huron County Med Care Facility
1116 S Van Dyke Rd, Bad Axe MI 48413-9615. 517/269-6425. Employs: 100-249.

Jackson Road Commission
2400 N Elm Ave, Jackson MI 49201-8803. 517/788-4230.
Employs: 100-249.

Sanilac County Medical Care
137 N Elk St, Sandusky MI 48471-1129. 313/648-3017.
Employs: 50-99.

Michigan Employment Sec Comm
401 E 13 Mile Rd, Madison Hts MI 48071-2176. 313/589-1600. Employs: 50-99.

Michigan Indian Affairs
Ottawa Building North Tower, Lansing MI 48933.
517/373-0654. Employs: 100-249.

Michigan Probation Offices
1441 Saint Antoine St, Detroit MI 48226-2302. 313/224-2600. Employs: 50-99.

Michigan Social Services
21885 Dunham Rd, Clinton Twp MI 48036-1030. 313/469-7700. Employs: 50-99.

POLICE DEPARTMENTS

Berkley Police Department
3338 Coolidge Hwy, Berkley MI 48072-1636. 313/541-9000. Employs: 100-249.

HEALTH CARE AND PHARMACEUTICALS

Employment in the health care industry has gone up steadily from 7 million in 1989, to over 9 million just three years later, with an average annual growth rate of 8 percent -- and that doesn't include medical equipment manufacturers or pharmaceutical companies, which are also booming. Health care expenditures are now rising to over $800 billion a year. Various approaches to controlling the cost of health care have been proposed, although Washington has yet to take any specific action. Reforms to the health care system should lead to more efficient and effective services. The hottest areas in this hot industry are HMOs and home health care.

CHILDREN'S HOSPITAL OF MICHIGAN
3901 Beaubien, Detroit MI 48201. 313/745-5364. **Contact:** Human Resources Department. **Description:** One of the nation's largest pediatric hospitals. **Common positions:** Accountant; Administrator; Biologist; Blue-Collar Worker Supervisor; Buyer; Credit Manager; Dietician; Biomedical Engineer; Electrical Engineer; Mechanical Engineer; Financial Analyst; Personnel and Labor Relations Specialist; Public Relations Worker; Registered Nurse; Pharmacist; Medical Records Technician; Respiratory Care Technician; Physical Therapist. **Educational backgrounds sought:** Accounting; Business Administration; Finance; Liberal Arts; Pharmacology; Radiology; Respiratory Care; Physical Therapy; Medical Records. **Benefits:** medical, dental, and life insurance; pension plan; tuition assistance; disability coverage; employee discounts; child care. **Corporate headquarters:** Detroit, MI. **Parent company:** Detroit Medical Center. **Operations at this facility:** Service (Health Care). Non-Profit.

DOC OPTICS CORPORATION
19800 West 8 Mile Road, Southfield MI 48075. 313/354-7100. **Contact:** Personnel Department. **Description:** Engaged in the manufacture of prescription glass and ophthalmic goods. **Employees:** 800.

DETROIT RECEIVING HOSPITAL &
UNIVERSITY HEALTH CENTER
4201 St. Antoinne, Detroit MI 48202. 313/745-3400. **Contact:** S.A. Noerr-Acker, Employment Manager. **Description:** A major metropolitan Detroit level one Trauma Unit hospital; burn and health clinic center. **Special programs:** Training Programs; Internships. **Benefits:** medical, dental and life insurance; tuition assistance; disability coverage; daycare assistance; profit sharing; employee discounts; savings plan; stock options. **Corporate headquarters:** This location. **Parent company:** Detroit Medical Center. **Employees:** 2,000.

DETROIT RIVERVIEW HOSPITAL

7733 E. Jefferson Avenue, Detroit MI 48214-2596. 313/499-4140. **Contact:** Human Resources Representative. **Description:** Detroit Riverview Hospital is a 215 bed community hospital. The Human Resources Department also recruits for corporate business operations positions. **Common positions:** Accountant; Computer Programmer; any health care related position. **Educational backgrounds sought:** Health Care. **Benefits:** Medical, dental, and life insurance; pension plan; tuition assistance; disability coverage; employee discounts; Section 403(b) plan. **Corporate headquarters:** Warren, MI. **Parent company:** Detroit-Macomb Hospital Corporation. **Employees:** 3,000.

GRACE HOSPITAL

6071 West Outer Drive, Detroit MI 48231. 313/966-3300. **Contact:** Personnel Department. **Description:** A metropolitan Detroit medical facility.

HARPER HOSPITAL

3990 John R. Street, Detroit MI 48201. 313/745-8082. **Contact:** Human Resources. **Description:** A major Detroit area hospital specializing in teaching, cardiology, and oncology. **Common positions:** Accountant; Dietician; Industrial Engineer; Financial Analyst; Personnel and Labor Relations Specialist; Registered Nurse; Physical Therapist; Physician's Assistant. **Educational backgrounds sought:** Business Administration; Finance. **Benefits:** medical, dental, and life insurance; pension plan; tuition assistance; employee discounts; vision insurance; child care center on site. **Corporate headquarters:** This location.

HENRY FORD HEALTH SYSTEM

600 Fisher Building, Detroit MI 48202. 313/876-8450. **Contact:** Employment Division. **Description:** A comprehensive health system. Includes a network of health prevention, diagnosis, treatment, research, education, medical equipment, home health and health care financing services.

HOLY CROSS HOSPITAL

4777 East Outer Drive, Detroit MI 48234. 313/369-9100, ext. 2295. **Contact:** Personnel Services. A Northeast Detroit area medical hospital. **Employees:** 900. **Common positions:** Computer Programmer; Dietician; Department Manager; Systems Analyst; Registered Nurse; Physical Therapist. **Educational backgrounds sought:** Health Care. **Special programs:** Training programs. **Benefits:** medical, dental, life, and vision insurance; pension plan; tuition assistance; disability coverage; TSA/savings plan. **Corporate headquarters:** Sylvania, OH.

HUTZEL HOSPITAL

4707 St. Antoine Boulevard, Detroit MI 48201. 313/745-7214. **Contact:** Robert Griswold, Vice President/Human Resources. **Description:** A Detroit area hospital specializing in obstetrics, orthopedics, ophthalmology. **Common positions:** Accounting; Administrator; Buyer; Computer Programmer; Dietician; Biomedical Engineer; Mechanical Engineer; Management Trainee;

Operations/Production Manager; Personnel and Labor Relations Specialist; Sales Representative; Statistician; Systems Analyst; Technical Writer/Editor. **Educational backgrounds sought:** Accounting; Business Administration; Computer Science; Finance; Liberal Arts. **Special programs:** Training programs. **Benefits:** medical, dental and life insurance; tuition assistance; disability coverage; daycare assistance; employee discounts. **Operations at this facility:** service. **Employees:** 2500. **Projected number of new hires for the next 12 months:** 200.

NEW CENTER HOSPITAL
801 Virginia Park, Detroit MI 48202. 313/874-2800. **Contact:** Nell Dixon, Personnel Director. **Description:** A local 125-bed community hospital with psychiatric and medical surgical units. A major emphasis is on dealing with the complications of drug and alcohol abuse.

NORTH DETROIT GENERAL HOSPITAL
3105 Carpenter Avenue, Detroit MI 48212. 313/369-3000. **Contact:** Regina Whiting, Personnel Director. **Description:** A major metropolitan Detroit general medical facility.

NUVISION INC.
P.O. Box 2600, Flint MI 48501. 313/767-0900. **Contact:** Human Resources. **Description:** A manufacturer and retailer of optometric goods.

PARKE DAVIS-ROCHESTER
870 Parkdale Road, Rochester MI 48307. 313/651-9081. **Contact:** Susan Bauerle, Supervisor of Human Resources. **Description:** A major Southeastern Michigan manufacturer of pharmaceutical products. **Employees:** 600.

PARKE-DAVIS, PARMACEUTICAL RESEARCH DIV.
WARNER-LAMBERT CO.
2800 Plymouth Road, Ann Arbor MI 48106-1047. 313/996-7022. **Contact:** Mr. Donald R. Barnett, Vice President, Human Resources. **Description:** Involved in the research and development of pharmaceutical products. **Employees:** 2,000. **Common positions:** Accountant; Administrator; Attorney; Biochemist; Biologist; Blue-Collar Worker Supervisor; Buyer; Chemist; Computer Programmer; Electrical Engineer; Mechanical Engineer; Financial Analyst; Personnel Specialist; Purchasing Agent; Quality Control Supervisor; Systems Analyst; Technical Writer/Editor. **Educational backgrounds sought:** Accounting; Biology; Business Administration; Chemistry; Computer Science; Engineering; Finance. **Special programs:** Training programs; Internships. **Benefits:** medical, dental and life insurance; tuition assistance; disability coverage; child care and elder care assistance; employee discounts; savings plan. **Corporate headquarters:** Morris Plains, NJ. **Parent company:** Warner-Lambert Co. **Operations at this facility:** research/development; administration. **Listed on:** New York Stock Exchange.

RANDOLPH MEDICAL, INC.

31742 Enterprise Drive, Livonia MI 48150. 313/427-4810. **Contact:** Mark Blohm, Vice President. **Description:** A leading area wholesale distributor of medical equipment and supplies. **Employees:** 225. **Common positions:** Accountant; Buyer; Computer Programmer; Credit Manager; Customer Service Representative; Biomedical Engineer; Branch Manager; Department Manager; General Manager; Management Trainee; Operations/Production Manager; Marketing Specialist; Personnel and Labor Relations Specialist; Purchasing Agent; Sales Representative. **Educational backgrounds sought:** Accounting; Business Administration; Communications; Computer Science; Finance; Liberal Arts; Marketing. **Benefits:** medical, dental, and life insurance; pension plan; disability coverage; employee discounts; savings plan. **Corporate headquarters:** This location. **Operations at this facility:** administration.

REHABILITATION INSTITUTE OF MICHIGAN

261 Mack Boulevard, Detroit MI 48201. 313/745-9870. **Contact:** Paulette Griffin, Director, Human Resources Department. **Description:** A Detroit hospital and rehabilitation facility affiliated with Wayne State University and specializing in physical medicine and rehabilitation. **Common positions:** Neurophycologist; Physical Therapist; Physician Assistant. **Educational backgrounds sought:** Health Care. **Special programs:** internships. **Benefits:** medical, dental and life insurance; pension plan; tuition assistance; disability coverage; daycare assistance; savings plan; vision. **Corporate headquarters:** Detroit, MI. **Parent company:** Detroit Medical Center. **Operations at this facility:** service.

SARATOGA COMMUNITY HOSPITAL

15000 Gratiot Avenue, Detroit MI 48205. 313/245-1200. **Contact:** Mr. Wilfred K. Schuelke, Asst. Administrator of Human Resources. **Description:** A major metropolitan Detroit medical facility.

UPJOHN COMPANY

7000 Portage Road, Kalamazoo MI 49001. 616/323-4000. **Contact:** Employment Office. **Description:** A producer of pharmaceuticals, agricultural products, and industrial products. **Employees:** 20,700.

Additional large employers: 250+

PHARMACEUTICAL PREPARATIONS

R P Scherer Corp
2075 W Big Beaver Rd Ste 700, Troy MI 48084-3432. 313/649-0900. Employs: 1000+.

Warner-Lambert
870 Parkdale Rd, Rochester MI 48307-1740. 313/651-9081. Employs: 500-999.

BIOLOGICAL SUBSTANCES, EXCEPT DIAGNOSTICS

Difco Laboratories Inc

P O Box 331058, Detroit MI 48232-7058. 313/462-8500. Employs: 250-499.

ORTHOPEDIC, PROSTHETIC, AND SURGICAL APPLIANCES AND SUPPLIES

Camp International Inc
744 W Michigan Ave, Jackson MI 49201-1909. 517/787-1600. Employs: 500-999.

**ELECTROMEDICAL AND
ELECTROTHEROTHERAPEUTIC APPARATUS**

Sarns Inc
6200 Jackson Rd, Ann Arbor MI 48103-9504. 313/663-
4145. Employs: 250-499.

**OFFICES AND CLINICS OF DOCTORS OF
OSTEOPATHY**

Mi Osteopathic Medical Center
2700 Martin Luther King Jr Blv, Detroit MI 48208-2561.
313/361-8000. Employs: 1000+.

OFFICES AND CLINICS OF OPTOMETRISTS

D Klar Od
27600 Novi Rd, Novi MI 48377-3420. 313/344-0500.
Employs: 250-499.

Montgomery Ward & Co
29501 Plymouth Rd, Livonia MI 48150-2125. 313/427-
1600. Employs: 250-499.

Montgomery Ward & Co
28500 Telegraph Rd, Southfield MI 48034-7505. 313/358-
1200. Employs: 250-499.

Montgomery Ward & Co
35151 Gratiot Ave, Clinton Twp MI 48035-2845. 313/791-
2000. Employs: 250-499.

SKILLED NURSING CARE FACILITIES

Michigan Masonic Home
1200 Wright Av, Alma MI 48801-1133. 517/463-3141.
Employs: 250-499.

**MISC. NURSING AND PERSONAL CARE
FACILITIES**

Fairline Memorial Conval Home
15750 Joy Rd, Detroit MI 48228-2118. 313/273-6850.
Employs: 500-999.

Lynwood Manor
730 Kimole La, Adrian MI 49221-1463. 517/263-6771.
Employs: 1000+.

GENERAL MEDICAL AND SURGICAL HOSPITALS

Ardmore Center
19810 Farmington Rd, Livonia MI 48152-1452. 313/474-
3500. Employs: 500-999.

Barnum Health Center
746 Purdy St, Birmingham MI 48009-1768. 313/258-3790.
Employs: 500-999.

Beyer Hospital
135 S Prospect St, Ypsilanti MI 48198-7914. 313/484-
2200. Employs: 500-999.

Carlyle Center
6902 Chicago Rd, Warren MI 48092-1686. 313/264-8875.
Employs: 250-499.

Genesee Memorial Hospital
702 S Ballenger Hw, Flint MI 48532-3803. 313/239-1481.
Employs: 500-999.

Hawthorn Center
18471 Haggerty Rd, Northville MI 48167-9542. 313/349-
3000. Employs: 500-999.

Lansing General Hospital
2727 S Pennsylvania Av, Lansing MI 48910-3488.
517/372-8220. Employs: 500-999.

Mc Pherson Hospital
620 Byron Rd, Howell MI 48843-1002. 517/546-1410.
Employs: 250-499.

Memorial Hospital Dialysis Center
918 Corunna Av, Owosso MI 48867-3768. 517/725-3144.
Employs: 250-499.

Michigan Health Center
3245 E Jefferson, Detroit MI 48207-4222. 313/259-4141.
Employs: 500-999.

Milton Community Hospital
234 S B Milton Dr, River Rouge MI 48218. 313/388-2000.
Employs: 500-999.

Monsignor Clement Kern Hospital
21230 Dequindre, Warren MI 48091-2279. 313/759-4520.
Employs: 250-499.

Mt Clemens Gen Hospital
1000 Harrington St, Mount Clemens MI 48043-2920.
313/466-8000. Employs: 250-499.

Oakland Gen Hlth Syst
27351 Dequindre, Madison Hts MI 48071-3487. 313/967-
7000. Employs: 250-499.

Occupational Health Services
135 S Prospect St, Ypsilanti MI 48198-7914. 313/484-
2595. Employs: 500-999.

Outer Drive Hospital
33000 Annapolis St, Wayne MI 48184-2404. 313/594-
6000. Employs: 500-999.

Redford Community Hospital
25210 Grand River Av, Redford MI 48240-1403. 313/531-
6200. Employs: 500-999.

Salvation Army William Booth M
2750 Selden St, Detroit MI 48208-2544. 313/496-1500.
Employs: 500-999.

Southfield Rehabilitation Hospital
22401 Foster Winter Dr, Southfield MI 48075-3724.
313/423-1606. Employs: 500-999.

St Joseph Mercy Hospital
1500 E Medical Ctr Dr, Ann Arbor MI 48109-0001.
313/936-4000. Employs: 500-999.

St Josephs Health Network
215 North Ave, Mount Clemens MI 48043-1716. 313/466-
9300. Employs: 250-499.

Wheelock Memorial Hospital
7280 S State Rd, Goodrich MI 48438-9770. 313/636-2221.
Employs: 500-999.

Woodside Medical
3585 Lorena Dr, Waterford MI 48329-4237. 313/338-7144.
Employs: 500-999.

Straith Hospital
23901 Lahser Rd, Southfield MI 48034-6035. 313/357-
3360. Employs: 500-999.

Brighton Hospital
12851 E Grand River Ave, Brighton MI 48116-8506.
313/227-1211. Employs: 250-499.

Duane L Waters Hospital
3855 Cooper St, Jackson MI 49201-9503. 517/783-4769.
Employs: 500-999.

Doctors Hospital
2730 E Jefferson Ave, Detroit MI 48207-4129. 313/259-
3050. Employs: 500-999.

Genesee Mem Hospital
702 S Ballenger Hwy, Flint MI 48532-3803. 313/766-8800.
Employs: 500-999.

Clinton Valley Ctr
140 Elizabeth Lake Rd, Pontiac MI 48341. 313/452-8700.
Employs: 500-999.

Heritage Hospital
24775 Haig Ave, Taylor MI 48180-3321. 313/295-5000.
Employs: 500-999.

Pontiac Gen Hospital
W Huron St, Pontiac MI 48053. 313/857-7200. Employs:
250-499.

Walter P Reuther Psyc Hospital
30901 Palmer Rd, Westland MI 48185-5340. 313/722-
4500. Employs: 500-999.

PSYCHIATRIC HOSPITALS

Northville Reg Psychiatric Hos
41001 7 Mile Rd, Northville MI 48167-2642. 313/349-
1800. Employs: 1000+.

Kikgswood Hospital
10300 W 8 Mile Rd, Ferndale MI 48220-2153. 313/398-
3200. Employs: 500-999.

SPECIALTY HOSPITALS, EXCEPT PSYCHIATRIC

Veterans Adm Med Ctr
Southfield & Outer Dr, Allen Park MI 48101. 313/562-
6000. Employs: 500-999.

MISC. SPECIALTY OUTPATIENT FACILITIES

Central Michigan CommunityHospital
1221 Sourth Dr, Mount Pleasant MI 48858-3234. 517/772-
6700. Employs: 250-499.

Westland Medical Center
2345 Merriman Rd, Westland MI 48185-5375. 313/467-
2300. Employs: 500-999.

Kingswood Hospital
6641 Burns St, Detroit MI 48213-2641. 313/398-3200.
Employs: 500-999.

Michigan Health Care Corp
5435 Woodward Ave, Detroit MI 48202-4009. 313/494-
0400. Employs: 500-999.

Botsford Gen Hospital
28050 Grand River Ave, Farmington MI 48336. 313/471-
8000. Employs: 500-999.

Cottage Hospital
159 Kercheval Ave, Grosse Pointe MI 48236. 313/884-
8600. Employs: 500-999.

Garden City Osteopathic Hospital
6245 N Inkster Rd, Garden City MI 48135-2541. 313/421-
3300. Employs: 250-499.

Grace Hospital
18700 Meyers Rd, Detroit MI 48235-1394. 313/966-3300.
Employs: 500-999.

Henry Ford Hospital
2799 W Grand Blvd, Detroit MI 48202-2608. 313/876-
2600. Employs: 500-999.

Lapeer Reg Hospital

1375 Main N St, Lapeer MI 48446-1369. 313/664-8511.
Employs: 250-499.

William Beaumont Hospital
44201 Dequindre Rd, Troy MI 48098-1117. 313/828-5100.
Employs: 500-999.

**HEALTH AND ALLIED SERVICES, NOT
ELSEWHERE CLASSIFIED**

Pontiac General Hospital
461 W Huron St, Pontiac MI 48341-1601. 313/857-7362.
Employs: 500-999.

Bon Secours Hospital
468 Cadieux Rd, Grosse Pointe MI 48230-1507. 313/343-
1000. Employs: 500-999.

Detroit Macomb Hospital
7733 E Jefferson Ave, Detroit MI 48214-2502. 313/499-
3000. Employs: 500-999.

Veterans Admin Med Ctr
2215 Fuller Rd, Ann Arbor MI 48105-2300. 313/769-7100.
Employs: 500-999.

**DRUGS, DRUG PROPRIETARIES AND
DRUGGISTS SUNDRIES: WHOLESALE**

National Wholesale Drug Co
21405 Trolley Dr, Taylor MI 48180-1811. 313/292-3000.
Employs: 250-499.

**MEDICAL, DENTAL AND HOSPITAL EQUIPMENT
AND SUPPLIES**

Aeromed Company
600 Huron Av, Port Huron MI 48060-3702. 313/982-1360.
Employs: 50-99.

Baxter Hospital Supply Corp
30400 Cypress Rd, Romulus MI 48174-3529. 313/729-
5000. Employs: 50-99.

General Electric Med Systems
39650 Orchard Hill Pl, Novi MI 48375-5331. 313/544-
9100. Employs: 100-249.

Ketchum Distributors
5203 Loraine St, Detroit MI 48208-1925. 313/896-3960.
Employs: 50-99.

Aventric Medical Instruments
1551 E Lincoln Ave, Royal Oak MI 48067-3401. 313/541-
0862. Employs: 100-249.

Fiberoptic Sensor Technologies
501 Avis Dr, Ann Arbor MI 48108-9195. 313/665-6707.
Employs: 50-99.

Test Equipment Distributors
1370 Piedmont Ave, Troy MI 48083-1917. 313/524-1900.
Employs: 50-99.

OPHTHALMIC GOODS

Nuvision Inc
2284 S Ballenger Hwy, Flint MI 48503-3439. 313/767-
0900. Employs: 100-249.

Additional small to medium sized employers: 50-249

MEDICINAL CHEMICALS AND BOTANICAL PRODUCTS

Mallinckrodt Sensor Systems
1230 Eisenhower Pl, Ann Arbor MI 48108-3248. 313/973-7000. Employs: 100-249.

Thistle Hill Herb Farm
3751 North River Rd, Fort Gratiot MI 48059-4146. 313/985-0761. Employs: 50-99.

PHARMACEUTICAL PREPARATIONS

Columbia Laboratories
24400 Capitol, Redford MI 48239-2444. 313/537-4340. Employs: 50-99.

Ferndale Labs Inc
780 W 8 Mile Rd, Ferndale MI 48220-2422. 313/548-0900. Employs: 100-249.

General Nutrition
4350 24th Av Ste 105, Fort Gratiot MI 48059-3851. 313/385-4500. Employs: 100-249.

Herbalife
1062 Michigan Av, Monroe MI 48161-3012. 313/241-9272. Employs: 100-249.

Immuno U S Inc
1200 Parkdale Rd, Rochester MI 48307-1744. 313/652-7872. Employs: 50-99.

P Leiner Nutritional Products
7047 Murthum Ave, Warren MI 48092-3833. 313/939-0220. Employs: 100-249.

Smithkline Beecham
900 Victors Way Ste 200, Ann Arbor MI 48108-1779. 313/679-5333. Employs: 50-99.

Transidyne General
3711 Plaza Dr, Ann Arbor MI 48108-1655. 313/769-1900. Employs: 50-99.

OPTICAL INSTRUMENTS AND LENSES

Kaiser Optical Systems Inc
371 Parkland Plaza, Ann Arbor MI 48103-6202. 313/665-8083. Employs: 50-99.

Speedring Systs Inc
2909 Waterview Dr, Rochester MI 48309-4600. 313/853-2540. Employs: 50-99.

MISCELLANEOUS MEASURING AND CONTROLLING DEVICES

A G Davis Gage & Eng Co
21435 Dequindre Rd Box 39, Hazel Park MI 48030-2350. 313/548-9444. Employs: 100-249.

Beta Tech Inc
16005 Sturgeon, Roseville MI 48066-1818. 313/772-4612. Employs: 100-249.

George Fischer Foundry Systems Inc
407 Hadley St Box 40, Holly MI 48442-1637. 313/634-8251. Employs: 100-249.

H R Krueger Machine Tool Inc
31506 Grand River Ave, Farmington MI 48336-4232. 313/477-8400. Employs: 100-249.

Intelligent Controls Inc
41000 Vincenti Ct, Novi MI 48375-1921. 313/471-5000. Employs: 100-249.

Machine Vision International
325 E Eisenhower, Ann Arbor MI 48108. 313/996-8033. Employs: 50-99.

Maxitrol Co
23555 Telegraph Rd, Southfield MI 48034. 313/4441500. Employs: 100-249.

Schenck Pegasus Corp
2890 John R Rd, Troy MI 48083-2353. 313/689-9000. Employs: 100-249.

William Christensen Co Inc
30 Silverdome Industr Pa, Pontiac MI 48057. 313/858-2200. Employs: 50-99.

William Christensen Co Inc
30 Silverdome Indl Pk, Pontiac MI 48342. 313/858-2200. Employs: 50-99.

SURGICAL AND MEDICAL INSTRUMENTS AND APPARATUS

Eaton Inds Inc
256 S Wagner Rd, Ann Arbor MI 48103-1940. 313/998-1000. Employs: 100-249.

Leeco Diagnostics Inc
24475 W Ten Mile Rd, Southfield MI 48034-2931. 313/353-2620. Employs: 50-99.

Neogen Corporation
620 Lesher Pl, Lansing MI 48912-1509. 517/372-9200. Employs: 50-99.

Precision Instruments Inc
G5304 S Saginaw Rd, Flint MI 48505-1545. 313/695-2080. Employs: 50-99.

ORTHOPEDIC, PROSTHETIC AND SURGICAL APPLIANCES AND SUPPLIES

Clinical Information Syst Inc
738 Airport Blvd Ste 5, Ann Arbor MI 48108-1640. 313/663-9350. Employs: 50-99.

Dental Art Lab Inc
1721 N Grand River Ave, Lansing MI 48906-3904. 517/485-2200. Employs: 50-99.

Home Care Of Dearborn Inc
15201 Century Dr, Dearborn MI 48120-1232. 313/271-8120. Employs: 100-249.

Kellogg Industries Inc
159 W Pearl St, Jackson MI 49201-1310. 517/782-0579. Employs: 100-249.

MacDee Inc
13800 Luick, Chelsea MI 48118-9543. 313/475-9165. Employs: 50-99.

Sherwood Medical
3075 E Grand River, Howell MI 48843-8525. 517/548-2211. Employs: 50-99.

DENTAL EQUIPMENT AND SUPPLIES

Dental Art Laboratories In
3215 Mall Ct, Lansing MI 48912-5211. 517/332-3521. Employs: 50-99.

Kerr Manufacturing Co
28200 Wick Rd, Romulus MI 48174-2623. 313/946-7800.
Employs: 100-249.

Mason Dental Ceramics Inc
P O Box Cn3311, Livonia MI 48151. 313/525-1070.
Employs: 50-99.

**X-RAY APPARATUS AND TUBES AND RELATED
IRRADIATION APPARATUS**

Kms Industries Inc
700 Kms Pl, Ann Arbor MI 48108-1652. 313/769-1100.
Employs: 100-249.

OPHTHALMIC GOODS

Co-Op Optical Co
2424 E 8 Mile Rd, Detroit MI 48234-1010. 313/366-5100.
Employs: 100-249.

Nu Vision Manufacturing & Dstbn Inc
G-4050 Market Pl, Flint MI 48507. 313/230-1366.
Employs: 50-99.

Sterling Vision Shoppes Inc
140 Macomb St, Mount Clemens MI 48043-5651. 313/468-7370. Employs: 50-99.

**OFFICES AND CLINICS OF DOCTORS OF
MEDICINE**

Connection
310 E 3D St, Flint MI 48502-1786. 313/767-3750.
Employs: 50-99.

Monroe Anesthesia Assocs
740 N Macomb St Rm Cl1, Monroe MI 48161-2993.
313/243-1866. Employs: 50-99.

New Medico Neurologic Center
3003 W Grand River Av, Howell MI 48843-8539. 517/546-4210. Employs: 100-249.

OFFICES AND CLINICS OF DENTISTS

Professional Dental Centers
Northland Mall, Southfield MI 48075. 313/552-0166.
Employs: 50-99.

OFFICES AND CLINICS OF CHIROPRACTORS

NW Chiropractic Clinic
G2408 W Carpenter Rd, Flint MI 48505. 313/787-8126.
Employs: 50-99.

OFFICES AND CLINICS OF OPTOMETRISTS

Montgomery Ward & Co
13551 Michigan Ave, Dearborn MI 48126-3510. 313/584-0500. Employs: 100-249.

**MISCELLANEOUS OFFICES AND CLINICS OF
HEALTH PRACTITIONERS**

Renaissance Health Care
20700 Greenfield Rd, Oak Park MI 48237-3016. 313/968-5300. Employs: 50-99.

Rehabilitation Health Center Inc
2008 Hogback Rd, Ann Arbor MI 48105-9751. 313/971-9790. Employs: 50-99.

SKILLED NURSING CARE FACILITIES

A F Bertram C Adult Foster
G2181 E Kenneth St, Flint MI 48507. 313/743-7697.
Employs: 50-99.

A F Dermyer C Home
414 E Maple Av, Adrian MI 49221-2250. 517/263-1896.
Employs: 50-99.

Adrian Health Care Center
130 Sand Creek Hwy, Adrian MI 49221-1228. 517/265-6554. Employs: 50-99.

Balmoral Skilled Nursing Center
5500 Fort St, Trenton MI 48183-4602. 313/675-1600.
Employs: 100-249.

Beach Nursing Home Inc
1215 N Telegraph Rd, Monroe MI 48161-3368. 313/242-4848. Employs: 50-99.

Beecher Manor Inc
192 W Vienna St, Clio MI 48420-1334. 313/687-4330.
Employs: 50-99.

Brae-Burn Incorporated
1312 Woodward Av, Bloomfield MI 48304-3964. 313/644-8015. Employs: 50-99.

Cambridge Nursing Centre S Inc
18200 W Thirteen Mile Rd, Franklin MI 48025-5446.
313/647-6500. Employs: 50-99.

Chateau Gardens Inc
627 Begole St, Flint MI 48503-2400. 313/234-1667.
Employs: 50-99.

Chisholm Smith Care Home
606 2D St, Jackson MI 49203-1767. 517/784-5974.
Employs: 50-99.

Clinton Living Center
311 E Higham St, Saint Johns MI 48879-1511. 517/224-3952. Employs: 50-99.

East Lansing Health Care Cntr
2815 Northwind Dr, East Lansing MI 48823-5011.
517/332-0817. Employs: 100-249.

Elder House
202 W Shiawassee St, Fenton MI 48430-2093. 313/629-6391. Employs: 50-99.

Evangelical Home Port Huron
5635 Lake Shore Rd, Fort Gratiot MI 48059-2817.
313/385-7447. Employs: 50-99.

Evergreen Hills Nursing Center
1045 Ware Ct, Ypsilanti MI 48198-4113. 313/483-5421.
Employs: 50-99.

Fenton Extended Care Center
512 Beach St, Fenton MI 48430-1873. 313/629-4117.
Employs: 50-99.

Fostrian Manor H C R
540 Sunnyside Dr, Flushing MI 48433-1474. 313/659-5695. Employs: 50-99.

G & M Davis Adult Foster Care
122 W Wilkins St, Jackson MI 49203-1806. 517/789-8223.
Employs: 50-99.

Grand Blanc Convalescent Center
8481 Holly Rd, Grand Blanc MI 48439-1812. 313/694-1711. Employs: 50-99.

Greenbrook Manor Inc
481 Village Green La, Monroe MI 48161-3367. 313/242-6282. Employs: 50-99.

Hamilton's Adult Foster Care
321 Griswold St, Jackson MI 49203-4107. 517/782-6132.
Employs: 50-99.

Hammond Rest Home
700 S Adelaide St, Fenton MI 48430-2020. 313/629-9641.
Employs: 50-99.

Hazel I Findlay Country Manor
1101 S Scott Rd, Saint Johns MI 48879-9039. 517/224-8936. Employs: 50-99.

Heritage Manor Convalescent
G3201 Beecher Rd, Flint MI 48532-3657. 313/732-9200. Employs: 50-99.

Highland Home
1948 Cooper St, Jackson MI 49202. 517/782-1900. Employs: 50-99.

Humphrey's Foster Care Home
346 N East St, Fenton MI 48430-2720. 313/629-4294. Employs: 50-99.

Keyes Care Home
905 Maple Av, Jackson MI 49203-3148. 517/787-8386. Employs: 50-99.

Lyons Care Home
707 S Mechanic St, Jackson MI 49203-1848. 517/784-7007. Employs: 50-99.

Maple Senior Ctzns Home S S H
G1383 E Maple Rd, Flint MI 48507. 313/743-3310. Employs: 50-99.

Margaret May Adult Foster Care
216 Division St, Adrian MI 49221-2911. 517/263-7103. Employs: 50-99.

Marian Hall
529 Martin Luther King Av, Flint MI 48502-2002. 313/238-7646. Employs: 50-99.

Marian Manor Med Center
18591 Quarry Rd, Wyandotte MI 48192-4522. 313/282-2100. Employs: 50-99.

Marlin Manor Nursing Home
434 W North St, Jackson MI 49202-3313. 517/787-3250. Employs: 100-249.

Marwood Manor Nursing Home
1300 Beard St, Port Huron MI 48060-6562. 313/982-8591. Employs: 50-99.

Mc Kamie Home
410 E 4th St, Flint MI 48503-2066. 313/238-2177. Employs: 50-99.

Monroe Convalescent Center
120 Maple Blvd, Monroe MI 48161-2502. 313/242-5656. Employs: 50-99.

Powers Adult Foster Care Home
302 1st St, Jackson MI 49201-2105. 517/783-2452. Employs: 50-99.

Provincial House
700 Lakeshire Trail W, Adrian MI 49221-1565. 517/263-0781. Employs: 50-99.

Provincial House West
731 Starkweather Dr, Lansing MI 48917-1128. 517/323-9133. Employs: 50-99.

Riverbend Nursing Home
11941 Belsay Rd, Burton MI 48509. 313/694-1970. Employs: 100-249.

Roselawn Manor
707 Armstrong Rd, Lansing MI 48911-3906. 517/393-5680. Employs: 100-249.

Sanborn-Gratiot Memorial Home
2732 Cherry St, Port Huron MI 48060-2916. 313/985-5631. Employs: 50-99.

Schuman's Nursing Home

3045 Westcott Dr, Port Huron MI 48060-1744. 313/987-5748. Employs: 50-99.

Seville Manor
1406 8th St, Port Huron MI 48060-5804. 313/985-4650. Employs: 50-99.

Snyder's Care Home
412 Cooper St, Jackson MI 49201-1413. 517/782-4605. Employs: 50-99.

Spooner's Foster Care Home
713 Stockton St, Flint MI 48503-2633. 313/238-6456. Employs: 50-99.

The Rivergate Terrace
14141 Pennsylvania Av, Wyandotte MI 48192-7509. 313/284-8000. Employs: 50-99.

Vista Grande Villa
2251 Springport Rd, Jackson MI 49202-1496. 517/787-0222. Employs: 50-99.

Warner's Adult Foster Care
2775 Michigan Rd, Port Huron MI 48060-2445. 313/984-3247. Employs: 50-99.

Weirick Home For Aged
510 State St, Adrian MI 49221-3346. 517/263-2234. Employs: 50-99.

Westgate Manor Nursing Home
1149 W Monroe Rd, Saint Louis MI 48880-9743. 517/681-3852. Employs: 50-99.

Whitehills Health Care Center
1843 N Hagadorn Rd, East Lansing MI 48823-2229. 517/332-5061. Employs: 50-99.

Williams Homes For The Aged
G6384 N Dort Hwy, Mount Morris MI 48458. 313/686-6740. Employs: 50-99.

Willowbrook Manor
G4436 Beecher Rd, Flint MI 48504. 313/733-0290. Employs: 50-99.

Zion Homes Sabbath House
115 W Ridge St, Owosso MI 48867-4434. 517/725-7054. Employs: 100-249.

INTERMEDIATE CARE FACILITIES

Ingham Cty Medical Care Facili
3860 Dobie Rd, Okemos MI 48864-3704. 517/349-1050. Employs: 100-249.

Oak Hill Nursing Home
34225 Grand River Av, Farmington MI 48335-3440. 313/477-7373. Employs: 50-99.

MISCELLANEOUS NURSING AND PERSONAL CARE FACILITIES

A F Blodgett's C Home
714 E Maumee St, Adrian MI 49221-3051. 517/263-3875. Employs: 50-99.

A F C Home
2006 Corunna Av, Owosso MI 48867-3953. 517/725-9263. Employs: 100-249.

A I Joal S
1217 Joal Dr, Flint MI 48532-2646. 313/230-8022. Employs: 50-99.

A-Jay Services
4823 Forrister Rd, Adrian MI 49221-9418. 517/769-0775. Employs: 50-99.

Abbey Convalescent Center
12250 E 12 Mile Rd, Warren MI 48093-3516. 313/751-6200. Employs: 50-99.

Abby-Foster Home Health Care
G2171 Lodge Rd, Flint MI 48532. 313/230-0440. Employs: 50-99.

Adam's House
120 N Adams St, Ypsilanti MI 48197-2622. 313/485-4127. Employs: 50-99.

Adrian Village Hills
1200 Corporate Dr, Adrian MI 49221-8400. 517/263-8199. Employs: 50-99.

Adult Care Center
610 Park St, Fenton MI 48430-2073. 313/629-1818. Employs: 50-99.

Adult Family Care Home
124 Clinton St, Adrian MI 49221-2802. 517/263-4324. Employs: 50-99.

Adult Foster Care
511 W Cass St, Saint Johns MI 48879-1714. 517/224-2827. Employs: 50-99.

Adult Foster Care Home
314 N Chestnut St, Owosso MI 48867-2007. 517/723-2429. Employs: 100-249.

Adult Foster Care Home
226 E Flint Park Blvd, Flint MI 48505-3442. 313/789-1959. Employs: 50-99.

Adult Foster Care Home
1446 Mabel Av, Flint MI 48506-3343. 313/767-4746. Employs: 50-99.

Adult Foster Care Home
G3105 Myrton St, Flint MI 48507. 313/743-1807. Employs: 50-99.

Adult Foster Care Home
228 N River St, Ypsilanti MI 48198-2843. 313/482-2581. Employs: 50-99.

Adult Foster Care Home
518 State St, Adrian MI 49221-3346. 517/263-7564. Employs: 50-99.

Adult Foster Care Home
111 Connecticut Av, Marysville MI 48040-1073. 313/364-8248. Employs: 50-99.

Adult Foster Home
310-12 W Front St, Monroe MI 48161. 313/242-7131. Employs: 50-99.

Adult Group Home
G4181 Weston Dr, Flint MI 48506. 313/736-4964. Employs: 50-99.

Advance Nursing Center Inc
2936 John Daly St, Inkster MI 48141-2421. 313/278-7272. Employs: 50-99.

Agape Center
110 W 7th Ave, Flint MI 48503-1350. 313/238-3360. Employs: 50-99.

Agape Home
7036 N Bray Rd, Mount Morris MI 48458-8988. 313/686-6220. Employs: 50-99.

Alarie Group Home For Children
1214 Mackin Rd, Flint MI 48503-1200. 313/239-4471. Employs: 50-99.

Allen Park Convalescent Home Inc

9150 Allen Rd, Allen Park MI 48101-1436. 313/386-2150. Employs: 100-249.

Alliance International Inc
15600 Ego Ave, East Detroit MI 48021-3658. 313/776-3553. Employs: 50-99.

Alpha & Omega
35949 Goddard Rd, Romulus MI 48174-3805. 313/942-7920. Employs: 50-99.

Alpha Annex Nursing Home
609 E Grand Blvd, Detroit MI 48207-3533. 313/923-8262. Employs: 50-99.

Alpha Manor Nursing Home
440 E Gd Blvd, Detroit MI 48207. 313/579-2900. Employs: 50-99.

Alternative Service Inc
1221 E Cook Rd, Grand Blanc MI 48439-8020. 313/695-3304. Employs: 50-99.

Americare Convalescent Center
19211 Anglin St, Detroit MI 48234-1460. 313/893-9745. Employs: 50-99.

Amicare Hospice Services Inc
2010 Hogback Rd, Ann Arbor MI 48105-9749. 313/677-0614. Employs: 50-99.

Anglin Extended Care Center
19175 Anglin St, Detroit MI 48234-1407. 313/892-3600. Employs: 50-99.

Applewood Nursing Center
18500 Van Horn St, Trenton MI 48183-3803. 313/676-7575. Employs: 50-99.

Arbor Care
1553 Broadway St, Ann Arbor MI 48105-1876. 313/663-4550. Employs: 50-99.

Arbor Care
2169 Independence Blvd, Ann Arbor MI 48104-6438. 313/973-1032. Employs: 50-99.

Arbor Care Foster Center
2139 Georgetown Blvd, Ann Arbor MI 48105-1534. 313/994-1419. Employs: 50-99.

Arbor Manor Care Center
151 2nd St, Spring Arbor MI 49283-9647. 517/750-1900. Employs: 50-99.

Argentine Care Center
9051 Silver Lake Rd, Linden MI 48451-9730. 313/735-9487. Employs: 50-99.

Arnold Home Inc
18520 W 7 Mile Rd, Detroit MI 48219-2963. 313/531-4001. Employs: 100-249.

Autumn Woods Health Care Facility
29800 Hoover Rd, Warren MI 48093-3483. 313/574-3444. Employs: 50-99.

Autumnwood Of Deckerville
3387 Ella, Deckerville MI 48427. 313/376-2145. Employs: 50-99.

Avonside Nursing Home
791 E Gd Bl, Detroit MI 48207. 313/921-1332. Employs: 50-99.

Baptist Children's Home & Family
214 N Mill St, Saint Louis MI 48880-1523. 517/681-2171. Employs: 50-99.

Barnett Manor
1220 W Maple Av, Adrian MI 49221-1314. 517/264-5722. Employs: 50-99.

Bedford Villa Nursing Care Center
16240 W 12 Mile Rd, Southfield MI 48076-2959. 313/557-3333. Employs: 50-99.

Beverly Enterprises
39290 6 Mile Rd, Livonia MI 48152-2656. 313/462-1950. Employs: 50-99.

Birchwood Retreat
622 N 3rd St # 6, Saint Clair MI 48079-4806. 313/385-4384. Employs: 50-99.

Bloomfield Hills Care Center
50 W Square Lake Rd, Bloomfield MI 48302-0461. 313/338-0345. Employs: 50-99.

Blue Water House
3211 Strawberry La, Port Huron MI 48060-1758. 313/982-3967. Employs: 50-99.

Bon Secours Nursing Care Center
26001 Jefferson Ave, St Clair Shrs MI 48081-2309. 313/779-7000. Employs: 50-99.

Bortz Health Care Of Oakland
1255 W Silverbell Rd, Lake Orion MI 48359-1345. 313/391-0900. Employs: 50-99.

Bortz Health Care Of Warren
11700 E 10 Mile Rd, Warren MI 48089-3903. 313/759-5960. Employs: 50-99.

Bortz Health Care W Bloomfield
6470 Alden Dr, W Bloomfield MI 48324-2006. 313/363-4121. Employs: 50-99.

Cadillac Nursing Home
1533 Cadillac Blvd, Detroit MI 48214-3107. 313/823-0435. Employs: 50-99.

Cambridge East Nurse Care Center
31155 Dequindre Rd, Madison Hts MI 48071-1566. 313/585-7010. Employs: 50-99.

Cambridge North Nurse Care Center
535 N Main St, Clawson MI 48017-1526. 313/435-5200. Employs: 100-249.

Cambridge West Nurse Care Center
18633 Beech Daly Rd, Redford MI 48240-1814. 313/255-1010. Employs: 100-249.

Camelot Hall Convalescent Center
35100 Ann Arbor Trl, Livonia MI 48150-3543. 313/522-1444. Employs: 50-99.

Cameron Home A F C Home
121 N Norton St, Corunna MI 48817-1340. 517/743-4568. Employs: 100-249.

Cardinal Care Corporation
627 Begole St, Flint MI 48503-2400. 313/232-1200. Employs: 50-99.

Charlotte's Adult Foster Care
1308 Griswold St, Port Huron MI 48060-5755. 313/985-5766. Employs: 50-99.

Charter House Of Novi
24500 Meadowbrook Rd, Novi MI 48375-2844. 313/477-2000. Employs: 50-99.

Charterhouse Farmington Hills
21017 Middlebelt Rd, Farmington MI 48336-5547. 313/476-8300. Employs: 100-249.

Chelsea Retirement Community
805 W Middle St, Chelsea MI 48118-1315. 313/475-8633. Employs: 100-249.

Cherrywood Nursing & Lvng Center

2372 15 Mi, Sterling Hts MI 48310. 313/978-2280. Employs: 50-99.

Chisholm Adult Foster Care
2519 Division St, Port Huron MI 48060-4770. 313/984-3396. Employs: 50-99.

Christy Lane A F C Home
4448 Cambridge Dr, Port Huron MI 48060-1643. 313/982-9619. Employs: 50-99.

Church Of Christ Care Center
23575 15 Mi, Mount Clemens MI 48043. 313/791-2470. Employs: 50-99.

Clara Barton Ter Convalescent
1801 E Atherton Rd, Flint MI 48507-2107. 313/742-5850. Employs: 100-249.

Clifford Adult Foster Care
2039 Clifford St, Flint MI 48503-4005. 313/233-5687. Employs: 50-99.

Clinton Aire Nursing Care Center
17001 17 Mi, Macomb MI 48044. 313/286-7100. Employs: 50-99.

Cloud Nine Inc
1128 Garfield St, Port Huron MI 48060-2823. 313/987-2225. Employs: 50-99.

Community Living Facility
8 S Summit St, Ypsilanti MI 48197-4706. 313/482-8093. Employs: 50-99.

Connie Lane Adult Foster Care
3862 North River Rd, Fort Gratiot MI 48059-4152. 313/987-7437. Employs: 50-99.

Community Residence Corp
1706 Pauline Blvd, Ann Arbor MI 48103-5208. 313/663-4805. Employs: 50-99.

County Referral Home
430 W 2D St, Flint MI 48503-2623. 812/239-0406. Employs: 50-99.

Crandell Adult Foster Care
235 Douglas St, Jackson MI 49203-4125. 517/784-5493. Employs: 50-99.

City & Country Convalescent Home
406 W Main St, Stockbridge MI 49285-9719. 517/851-7700. Employs: 50-99.

Davis Home
821 Martin Luther King Av, Flint MI 48503-1437. 313/233-5370. Employs: 50-99.

Dearborn Heights Hlth Care Center
26001 Ford Rd, Dearborn Hts MI 48127-2920. 313/274-4600. Employs: 50-99.

Delores Upleger Adult Foster
4775 West Water St, Port Huron MI 48060. 313/985-7956. Employs: 50-99.

Dorvin Conval & Nurse Center Inc
29270 Morlock St, Livonia MI 48152-2044. 313/476-0550. Employs: 50-99.

Durand Convalescent Center
8750 Monroe Plaza, Durand MI 48429-1000. 517/288-3166. Employs: 100-249.

Eastwood Nursing Center
626 E Gd Bl, Detroit MI 48207. 313/923-5816. Employs: 50-99.

Eaton Manor Inc
511 E Shepherd St, Charlotte MI 48813-2223. 517/543-4750. Employs: 50-99.

Edie's Adult Foster Care
4414 Abel Dr, Fort Gratiot MI 48059-3700. 313/385-3659.
Employs: 50-99.

Elegant Manor
363 E Brooks St, Howell MI 48843-2309. 517/546-1938.
Employs: 50-99.

Elmwood Geriatric Village
1881 E Grand Blvd, Detroit MI 48211-3041. 313/922-
1600. Employs: 50-99.

Evangelical Home-Saline
440 Russell St, Saline MI 48176-1135. 313/429-9401.
Employs: 50-99.

F F C Foster Care Home
117 E Franklin St, Jackson MI 49201-2311. 517/784-0007.
Employs: 50-99.

Fair Acres Nursing Home Inc
22600 Armada Ridge Rd, Armada MI 48005-3205.
313/784-5322. Employs: 50-99.

Faith Medical Care Center
4220 Hospital Dr, East China MI 48054. 313/329-4736.
Employs: 50-99.

Farmington Nursing Home
30405 Folsom Rd, Farmington MI 48336-4702. 313/477-
7400. Employs: 50-99.

Farquhar Adult Foster Care
4909 Lapeer Rd, Port Huron MI 48060. 313/982-0412.
Employs: 50-99.

Feltman Adult Foster Care Home
523 S Winter St, Adrian MI 49221-3304. 517/263-2681.
Employs: 50-99.

Ferguson Convalescent Home
239 S Main St, Lapeer MI 48446-2426. 313/664-6611.
Employs: 50-99.

Foster Home Care
1329 10th Av, Port Huron MI 48060. 313/985-6563.
Employs: 50-99.

Four Seasons Health Care Center
1167 E Hopson St, Bad Axe MI 48413-1509. 517/269-
9983. Employs: 50-99.

Franklin Care Center
12950 W Chicago St, Detroit MI 48228-2651. 313/491-
7830. Employs: 50-99.

Franklin Manor Conval Center
26900 Franklin Rd, Southfield MI 48034-5343. 313/352-
7390. Employs: 50-99.

Fraser Villa
33300 Utica Rd, Fraser MI 48026-2017. 313/293-3300.
Employs: 50-99.

Friendship Manor Nursing Home
3950 Beaubien St, Detroit MI 48201-2120. 313/833-7600.
Employs: 50-99.

Fulton Medical Care Center
4735 W Ranger Rd, Perrinton MI 48871-9775. 517/236-
5433. Employs: 50-99.

Gates Group Home
3425 Oxbow Dr, Fort Gratiot MI 48059-4125. 313/984-
5566. Employs: 50-99.

Gates Residence Adult Foster
5930 East Montevista, Fort Gratiot MI 48059-2839.
313/385-9047. Employs: 50-99.

Gatti Community Living Facil

5931 Western Rd, Flint MI 48506-1305. 313/736-0233.
Employs: 50-99.

Getman Family Home
1675 N M-52, Owosso MI 48867-1281. 517/723-6791.
Employs: 100-249.

Golden Age Manor Adult Foster
G5325 Detroit St, Flint MI 48505-1238. 313/789-7363.
Employs: 50-99.

Goss Foster Care
G1050 E Harvard Av, Flint MI 48505. 313/785-7952.
Employs: 50-99.

Goss Foster Care Home
G5199 Alfred St, Flint MI 48505. 313/785-9354. Employs:
50-99.

Grace Haven Inc
1040 Francis St, Jackson MI 49203-3273. 517/782-2980.
Employs: 50-99.

Greenery Health Care Center
4800 Clintonville Rd, Clarkston MI 48346-4206. 313/674-
0903. Employs: 50-99.

Griffin Home For The Aged
1042 N Shiawassee St, Corunna MI 48817-1127. 517/743-
3791. Employs: 100-249.

Griswold Street Home
727 Griswold St, Port Huron MI 48060-5846. 313/984-
2371. Employs: 50-99.

Harmony Home
224 S Scott St, Adrian MI 49221-2535. 517/263-3604.
Employs: 50-99.

Harris Foster Home
901 Division St, Port Huron MI 48060-6208. 313/985-
7837. Employs: 50-99.

Harrison S Riverside E A F C
2613 13th St, Port Huron MI 48060-6579. 313/982-4310.
Employs: 50-99.

Hart Pines Residential Facil
521 E 1st St, Perry MI 48872. 517/625-7350. Employs:
100-249.

Helpful Homes Inc
1920 W Gnd Blvd, Detroit MI 48208. 313/894-9650.
Employs: 50-99.

Henry Ford Continuing Care
19840 Harper, Harper Woods MI 48225. 313/881-9556.
Employs: 50-99.

Henry Ford Continuing Care
25375 Kelly Rd, Roseville MI 48066-4960. 313/773-6022.
Employs: 100-249.

Hope Nursing Care Center
38410 Cherry Hill Rd, Westland MI 48185-3270. 313/326-
1200. Employs: 50-99.

Hotchkiss Adult Foster Care
3017 Fenton Rd, Flint MI 48507-1574. 313/232-8578.
Employs: 50-99.

Howe Adult Foster Care
128 Orchard St, Grand Blanc MI 48439-1339. 313/694-
0603. Employs: 50-99.

Impact Group Home
599 N Range Rd, Marysville MI 48040. 313/364-7738.
Employs: 50-99.

Ionia Area Hospice
117 N Depot St, Ionia MI 48846-1601. 616/527-0681.
Employs: 100-249.

Jewish Home For Aged
26051 Lahser Rd, Southfield MI 48034-2601. 313/352-2336. Employs: 50-99.

Jewish Home For Aged Borman
19100 W 7 Mile Rd, Detroit MI 48219-2758. 313/532-7112. Employs: 100-249.

Kenworthy House Children's Gp
515 W 3D St, Flint MI 48503-2667. 812/233-3972. Employs: 50-99.

Kinglsey House Community Mental Hlth
346 E Kingsley St, Ann Arbor MI 48104-1142. 313/995-0354. Employs: 50-99.

Kith Haven
G1069 N Ballenger Hwy, Flint MI 48504-4431. 313/235-6676. Employs: 50-99.

Kitson
736 E Grand Blanc Rd, Grand Blanc MI 48439-1333. 313/695-1465. Employs: 50-99.

Knisley Foster Care
2680 Robbins Ct, Port Huron MI 48060-2534. 313/984-3399. Employs: 50-99.

La Salle Nursing Home
241111 W Grand Blvd, Detroit MI 48208. 313/897-5144. Employs: 50-99.

La Villa Nursing Center
660 E Grand Blvd, Detroit MI 48207-3513. 313/923-5800. Employs: 50-99.

Lahser Hills Nursing Home
25300 Lahser Rd, Southfield MI 48034-5868. 313/354-3222. Employs: 50-99.

Lake Orion Nursing Center
585 E Flint St, Lake Orion MI 48362-3209. 313/693-0505. Employs: 50-99.

Lake Shore Manor
4849 Lake Shore Rd, Fort Gratiot MI 48059-3540. 313/385-9541. Employs: 50-99.

Lark Adult Foster Care Home
509 Dubie St, Ypsilanti MI 48198-6195. 313/482-0843. Employs: 50-99.

Law-Den Nursing Home Inc
1640 Webb St, Detroit MI 48206-1350. 313/867-1719. Employs: 100-249.

Leffler Foster Care
4452 North River Rd, Fort Gratiot MI 48059-4059. 313/982-8473. Employs: 50-99.

Lewis Adult Foster Care II
431 S Winter St, Adrian MI 49221-3302. 517/265-8241. Employs: 50-99.

Lincoln Care Center
250 Highland St # 401, Detroit MI 48203-3464. 313/834-1204. Employs: 50-99.

Litchfield Nursing Centre
527 Marshall St, Litchfield MI 49252-9703. 517/542-2323. Employs: 50-99.

Lourdes Nursing Home
2300 Watkins Lake Rd, Waterford MI 48328-1439. 313/674-2241. Employs: 50-99.

Madonna Nursing Center
15311 Schaefer Hwy, Detroit MI 48227-3337. 313/835-4775. Employs: 50-99.

Maes Cloud 9 Too
4228 Maes Dr, Port Huron MI 48060-2420. 313/984-8616. Employs: 50-99.

Malone Adult Foster Care Home
2905 Lapeer Rd, Flint MI 48503-4356. 313/239-3506. Employs: 50-99.

Maple Valley Inc
211 W Wallace, Ashley MI 48806. 517/847-2011. Employs: 50-99.

Maria Health Care Center
1277 E Siena Heights Dr, Adrian MI 49221-1755. 517/263-8810. Employs: 50-99.

Marian Place
408 W Front St, Monroe MI 48161-2302. 313/241-2414. Employs: 50-99.

Marshall Home
1531 Cedarwood Dr, Flushing MI 48433-1810. 313/659-7024. Employs: 50-99.

Mary Avenue Care Center
1313 Mary Av, Lansing MI 48910-5206. 517/393-6130. Employs: 50-99.

Marycrest Manor
15475 Middlebelt Rd, Livonia MI 48154-3805. 313/427-9175. Employs: 50-99.

Marydale Center
3147 10th Av, Port Huron MI 48060-2071. 313/985-9683. Employs: 50-99.

Marywood Nursing Care Center
36975 5 Mile Rd, Livonia MI 48154-1871. 313/464-0600. Employs: 50-99.

Mc Annally S Adult Foster Care
304 E Maumee St, Adrian MI 49221-2908. 517/263-3031. Employs: 50-99.

Medicos Health Care Center
22355 W 8 Mile Rd, Detroit MI 48219-1298. 313/255-6450. Employs: 50-99.

Medilodge Of Howell Inc
1333 W Grand River Av, Howell MI 48843-1980. 517/548-1900. Employs: 50-99.

Medilodge Of Richmond
34901 Division Rd, Richmond MI 48062-1559. 313/727-7562. Employs: 100-249.

Medilodge Of Romeo Inc
309 S Bailey St, Romeo MI 48065-5207. 313/752-2581. Employs: 50-99.

Medilodge Of Yale
90 Jean St, Yale MI 48097-2932. 313/387-3226. Employs: 50-99.

Michigan Community Service
6260 Westview Dr, Grand Blanc MI 48439-9748. 313/694-7038. Employs: 50-99.

Moroun Nursing Home
8045 E Jefferson Ave, Detroit MI 48214-2627. 313/821-3525. Employs: 50-99.

Nancy Hamilton Adult Foster
4530 W US Hwy 223, Adrian MI 49221. 517/263-5419. Employs: 50-99.

Nightingale North Nursing Home
14151 15 Mi, Sterling Hts MI 48312. 313/939-0200. Employs: 50-99.

Nightingale Nursing Care Center
11525 E 10 Mile Rd, Warren MI 48089-3802. 313/759-0700. Employs: 50-99.

Northwest Care Center
16181 Hubbell St, Detroit MI 48235-4026. 313/273-8764.
Employs: 100-249.

Oakland Home For Alternative Living
841 Auburn Ave, Pontiac MI 48342-3374. 313/335-7010.
Employs: 50-99.

Odd Fellow & Rebekah Home Michigan
2388 W Michigan Av, Jackson MI 49202-3919. 517/787-
5140. Employs: 50-99.

Omni Convalescent Center
Conner St, Detroit MI 48213-3405. 313/571-5555.
Employs: 50-99.

Orchard Hills
532 Orchard Lake Rd, Pontiac MI 48341-2156. 313/338-
7151. Employs: 100-249.

Orchard Lake Rest Haven
7277 Richardson Rd, W Bloomfield MI 48323-1266.
313/363-7161. Employs: 50-99.

Ovid Convalescent Manor
9480 E M 21, Ovid MI 48866-9628. 517/834-2228.
Employs: 50-99.

Page Foster Care Home
402 W 3D Av, Flint MI 48503-2524. 812/239-8171.
Employs: 50-99.

Pam's Carehome
19272 Norwood St, Detroit MI 48234-1869. 313/369-9554.
Employs: 50-99.

Paragon Non Profit Housing
G5099 Van Slyke Rd, Flint MI 48507. 313/235-6511.
Employs: 50-99.

Park Geriatric Village Inc
111 Ford St, Detroit MI 48203-3622. 313/883-3585.
Employs: 50-99.

Park Nursing Center
12575 Telegraph Rd, Taylor MI 48180-4019. 313/287-
4710. Employs: 50-99.

Pembrook Nursing Center
9146 Woodward Ave, Detroit MI 48202-1612. 313/875-
1263. Employs: 50-99.

Pine River House
1014 Cheesman Rd, Saint Louis MI 48880-9402. 517/681-
3881. Employs: 50-99.

Pleasant Manor Nursing Home
400 S Crapo St, Mount Pleasant MI 48858-2997. 517/773-
5918. Employs: 100-249.

Plymouth Court
105 N Haggerty Rd, Plymouth MI 48170-1801. 313/455-
0510. Employs: 50-99.

Progression House Innovative
1721 10th Av, Port Huron MI 48060-3101. 313/982-3042.
Employs: 50-99.

Qualicare Nursing Center Inc
695 E Gd Bl, Detroit MI 48207. 313/925-6655. Employs:
50-99.

Redford Geriatric Village Inc
22811 W 7 Mile Rd, Detroit MI 48219-1739. 313/534-
1440. Employs: 50-99.

Reese Family Care
595 E Grand Blvd, Detroit MI 48207-3533. 313/922-1510.
Employs: 50-99.

Regenia's Afc Home

210 South St, Ortonville MI 48462-8530. 313/627-2995.
Employs: 50-99.

Rehabatate Systems Of Michigan
1525 E Pierson Rd, Flushing MI 48433-1816. 313/659-
8507. Employs: 50-99.

Rivergate Convalescent Center
14041 Pennsylvania Av, Wyandotte MI 48192-7508.
313/284-7200. Employs: 100-249.

Riverside Adult Foster Care
1821 Riverside Dr, Port Huron MI 48060-3248. 313/984-
3999. Employs: 50-99.

Riverside Manor Adult Foster
2548 Military St, Port Huron MI 48060-6667. 313/982-
8843. Employs: 50-99.

Riverview
1467 Flushing Rd, Flushing MI 48433-2245. 313/659-
6444. Employs: 50-99.

Robinson's Foster Care Home
3829 Pengelly Rd, Flint MI 48507-5412. 313/742-3456.
Employs: 50-99.

Romeo Nursing Center Inc
250 Denby St, Romeo MI 48065-5228. 313/752-3571.
Employs: 50-99.

Rose Of Sharon
312 W Tyrell Av, Saint Louis MI 48880-1442. 517/681-
5435. Employs: 50-99.

Royal Nursing Center
91 Glendale St, Detroit MI 48203-3274. 313/869-7711.
Employs: 50-99.

Saint Joseph Home
1000 E Porter St, Jackson MI 49202-2415. 517/787-3320.
Employs: 50-99.

Shelby Nursing Center
46100 Schoenherr Rd, Shelby Twp MI 48315-5344.
313/566-1100. Employs: 50-99.

Simpson Group Home
3240 Simpson Rd, Fort Gratiot MI 48059-4241. 313/985-
5706. Employs: 50-99.

Sjoquist Shady Mansion
103 W Tyrell Av, Saint Louis MI 48880-1532. 517/681-
5217. Employs: 50-99.

Spring Meadow S Adult Foster
803 E Rolston Rd, Linden MI 48451-9464. 313/735-7379.
Employs: 50-99.

St Anthony Nursing Care Center
31830 Ryan Rd, Warren MI 48092-3767. 313/977-6700.
Employs: 50-99.

St Clair County
3415 28th St # 200, Port Huron MI 48060-6931. 313/325-
1291. Employs: 50-99.

St James Nurse & Physical Rehabilitation
15063 Gratiot Ave, Detroit MI 48205-1332. 313/372-4065.
Employs: 100-249.

St John Bon Secours Sr Community
18300 E Warren Ave, Detroit MI 48224-1343. 313/343-
8000. Employs: 50-99.

St Josephs Mercy Lvng Care
37700 Harper Ave, Clinton Twp MI 48036-3021. 313/468-
0827. Employs: 50-99.

St Jude Convalescent Center
34350 Ann Arbor Trl, Livonia MI 48150-3606. 313/261-
4800. Employs: 50-99.

St Mary's Nursing Home
22601 E 9 Mile Rd, St Clair Shrs MI 48080-1917. 313/772-4300. Employs: 50-99.

Star Manor Of Northville
520 W Main St, Northville MI 48167-1529. 313/349-4290. Employs: 50-99.

Stoneybrook House
3087 Stonybrook La, Port Huron MI 48060-1648. 313/982-6167. Employs: 50-99.

Sunnybrooke Home
105 Delaware St, Detroit MI 48202-2423. 313/871-9676. Employs: 50-99.

Swinson's Adult Foster Care
4745 Fish Rd, Port Huron MI 48060. 313/982-0035. Employs: 50-99.

Synod Residential Servs
3 N Normal St, Ypsilanti MI 48197-2773. 313/484-1435. Employs: 50-99.

Taylor Total Living Center
22950 Northline Rd, Taylor MI 48180-4627. 313/287-9170. Employs: 50-99.

Tendercare Manor Southgate
15400 Trenton Rd, Southgate MI 48195-2027. 313/284-4620. Employs: 50-99.

Tendercare-Mt Pleasant
1524 Portabella Rd, Mount Pleasant MI 48858-4006. 517/772-2967. Employs: 100-249.

The Lutheran Home
1236 S Monroe St, Monroe MI 48161-3934. 313/241-9533. Employs: 50-99.

The Perkins House
1218 W 2D St, Flint MI 48503-5501. 812/239-4543. Employs: 50-99.

Torrey Pines Residence
34720 24 Mile, New Baltimore MI 48047. 313/725-3501. Employs: 50-99.

United Caring Service
119 E Sanilac Rd, Sandusky MI 48471-1147. 313/648-2670. Employs: 50-99.

University Convalescent & Nurse Home
28550 5 Mile Rd, Livonia MI 48154-3878. 313/427-8270. Employs: 100-249.

Venoy Continued Care Center
3999 Venoy Rd, Wayne MI 48184-1872. 313/326-6600. Employs: 50-99.

Vernon Mount Nursing Center Inc
26715 Greenfield Rd, Southfield MI 48076-4717. 313/557-0050. Employs: 50-99.

Veterans For Promotion Civic
304 W Tobias St, Flint MI 48503-3975. 313/233-6922. Employs: 50-99.

Vettraino Management
17097 17 Mile Rd, Macomb MI 48044. 313/263-9600. Employs: 50-99.

W Bloomfield Nurse & Convalescent
6445 W Maple Rd, W Bloomfield MI 48322-2047. 313/661-1600. Employs: 50-99.

West Hickory Haven
3310 W Commerce Rd, Milford MI 48380-3100. 313/685-1400. Employs: 50-99.

West Trail Nursing Home
395 W Ann Arbor Trl, Plymouth MI 48170-1641. 313/453-3983. Employs: 50-99.

Westland Convalescent Center
36137 Warren Rd, Westland MI 48185-2027. 313/728-6100. Employs: 50-99.

Westwood Nursing Home
16588 Schaefer Hwy, Detroit MI 48235-4249. 313/345-5000. Employs: 50-99.

Whitehall Conval Homes Inc
43455 W 10 Mile Rd, Novi MI 48375-3100. 313/349-2200. Employs: 50-99.

Whitemore Lake Care Center Inc
8633 Main St, Whitmore Lake MI 48189-9571. 313/449-4431. Employs: 100-249.

William D Sparks A V Mem Home
3744 E Michigan Av, Jackson MI 49202-2715. 517/764-5220. Employs: 50-99.

Williams Adult Foster Care
307-09 Quarry St, Jackson MI 49201. 517/788-9917. Employs: 50-99.

10th St Semi Independant Gp
2411 10th St, Port Huron MI 48060-6542. 313/987-8282. Employs: 50-99.

Cranbrook Hospice Svc
2555 Crooks Rd, Troy MI 48084-4742. 313/643-8855. Employs: 50-99.

Downriver Hospice Inc
1545 Kingsway Ct, Trenton MI 48183-1931. 313/671-6343. Employs: 50-99.

Eaton Community Hospice
313 Lansing Rd, Charlotte MI 48813. 517/543-5310. Employs: 50-99.

Hospice Of Central Mi Inc
1012 W High St, Mount Pleasant MI 48858-2241. 517/773-6137. Employs: 100-249.

Hspc Sthestrn Ingham County Inc
1075 Jackson, Dansville MI 48819. 517/623-6477. Employs: 50-99.

Lapeer Area Hospice Inc
544 N Main St, Lapeer MI 48446-1923. 313/667-0042. Employs: 50-99.

GENERAL MEDICAL AND SURGICAL HOSPITALS

Albion Community Hospital
809 W Erie St, Albion MI 49224-1523. 517/629-2191. Employs: 100-249.

Catherine McAuley Hlth Center
5361 Mc Auley Dr, Ann Arbor MI 48106. 313/572-5678. Employs: 100-249.

Rivendell Psychiatric Cntr
101 W Townsend Rd, Saint Johns MI 48879-9200. 517/224-1177. Employs: 100-249.

Riverside Osteopathic Hospital
150 Truax St, Trenton MI 48183-2104. 313/676-4200. Employs: 50-99.

Sheridan Community Hospital
301 N Main St, Sheridan MI 48884-9220. 517/291-3261. Employs: 100-249.

Ionia County Mem Hospital
479 Lafayette St, Ionia MI 48846-1834. 616/527-4200. Employs: 50-99.

PSYCHIATRIC HOSPITALS

New Detroit Nursing Center
716 E Grand Blvd, Detroit MI 48207-2528. 313/923-0300.
Employs: 50-99.

Psychiatric Center
35031 23 Mile Rd, New Baltimore MI 48047-3649.
313/725-5777. Employs: 100-249.

SPECIALTY HOSPITALS, EXCEPT PSYCHIATRIC

Tri County Community Hospital
1131 E Howard City, Edmore MI 48829-9737. 517/427-
5116. Employs: 100-249.

MISCELLANEOUS SPECIALTY OUTPATIENT FACILITIES

Detroit Rescue Mission
3535 3rd St, Detroit MI 48201-2203. 313/832-1333.
Employs: 50-99.

Family Svc Detroit & Wayne Co
220 Bagley St, Detroit MI 48226-1408. 313/965-2141.
Employs: 50-99.

Harbor Beach Community Hospital
Broad & 1st Sts, Harbor Beach MI 48441. 517/479-3201.
Employs: 100-249.

MISCELLANEOUS HEALTH AND ALLIED SERVICES

Deckerville Community Hospital
3559 Pine St, Deckerville MI 48427. 313/376-2835.
Employs: 100-249.

Kelsey Memorial Hospital
418 Washington Ave, Lakeview MI 48850. 517/352-7211.
Employs: 100-249.

For more information on career opportunities in health care and pharmaceuticals:

Associations

ACCREDITING BUREAU OF HEALTH EDUCATION SCHOOLS
Oak Manor Office, 29089 US 20 West, Elkhart IN 46514.
219/293-0124.

AMERICAN ACADEMY OF FAMILY PHYSICIANS
8880 Ward Parkway, Kansas City MO 64114. 816/333-
9700.

AMERICAN ACADEMY OF PHYSICIAN ASSISTANTS
950 North Washington Street, Alexandria VA 22314.
703/836-2272.

AMERICAN ASSOCIATION FOR CLINICAL CHEMISTRY
2029 K Street NW, 7th Floor, Washington DC 20006.
202/857-0717.

AMERICAN ASSOCIATION OF BLOOD BANKS
8101 Glenbrook Road, Bethesda MD 20814. 301/907-
6977.

AMERICAN ASSOCIATION OF COLLEGES OF OSTEOPATHIC MEDICINE
6110 Executive Boulevard, Suite 405, Rockville MD
20852. 301/468-2037.

AMERICAN ASSOCIATION OF COLLEGES OF PHARMACY
1426 Prince Street, Alexandria VA 22314. 703/739-2330.

AMERICAN ASSOCIATION OF COLLEGES OF PODIATRIC MEDICINE
1350 Piccard Drive, Suite 322, Rockville MD 20850.
301/990-7400.

AMERICAN ASSOCIATION OF DENTAL SCHOOLS
1625 Massachusetts Avenue NW, Washington DC 20036.
202/667-9433.

AMERICAN ASSOCIATION OF HOMES FOR THE AGED
901 E Street NW, Suite 500, Washington DC 20004.
202/783-2242.

AMERICAN ASSOCIATION OF MEDICAL ASSISTANTS
20 North Wacker Drive, Suite 1575, Chicago IL 60606.
312/899-1500.

AMERICAN ASSOCIATION OF NURSE ANESTHETISTS

216 Higgins Road, Park Ridge IL 60068. 708/692-7050.

AMERICAN ASSOCIATION OF RESPIRATORY CARE
11030 Ables Lane, Dallas TX 75229-4593. 214/243-2272.

AMERICAN CHIROPRACTIC ASSOCIATION
1701 Clarendon Boulevard, Arlington VA 22209. 703/276-
8800.

AMERICAN COLLEGE OF HEALTHCARE ADMINISTRATORS
325 South Patrick Street, Alexandria VA 22314. 703/549-
5822.

AMERICAN COLLEGE OF HEALTHCARE EXECUTIVES
840 North Lake Shore Drive, Chicago IL 60611. 312/943-
0544.

AMERICAN COUNCIL ON PHARMACEUTICAL EDUCATION
311 West Superior Street, Chicago IL 60610. 312/664-
3575.

AMERICAN DENTAL ASSOCIATION
211 East Chicago Avenue, Chicago IL 60611. 312/440-
2500.

AMERICAN DENTAL HYGIENISTS ASSOCIATION
Division of Professional Development, 444 North Michigan
Avenue, Suite 3400, Chicago IL 60611. 312/440-8900.

AMERICAN DIETETIC ASSOCIATION
216 West Jackson Street, Chicago IL 60606. 312/899-0040.

AMERICAN HEALTH CARE ASSOCIATION
1201 L Street NW, Washington DC 20005. 202/842-4444.

AMERICAN HOSPITAL ASSOCIATION
840 North Lake Shore Drive, Chicago IL 60611. 312/280-
6000.

AMERICAN MEDICAL ASSOCIATION
515 North State Street, Chicago IL 60605. 312/464-5000.

AMERICAN HEALTH INFORMATION MANAGEMENT ASSOCIATION
919 North Michigan Avenue, Suite 1400, Chicago IL
60611. 312/787-2672.

AMERICAN MEDICAL TECHNOLOGISTS
Registered Medical Assistants, 710 Higgins Road, Park
Ridge IL 60068. 708/823-5169.

AMERICAN NURSES ASSOCIATION

AMERICAN OCCUPATIONAL THERAPY
ASSOCIATION
1383 Piccard Drive, P.O. Box 1725, Rockville MD 20849-1725. 301/948-9626.

AMERICAN OPTOMETRIC ASSOCIATION
243 North Lindbergh Boulevard, St. Louis MO 63141.
314/991-4100.

AMERICAN PHARMACEUTICAL ASSOCIATION
2215 Constitution Avenue NW, Washington DC 20037.
202/628-4410.

AMERICAN PHYSICAL THERAPY ASSOCIATION
1111 North Fairfax Street, Alexandria VA 22314. 703/684-2782.

AMERICAN SOCIETY FOR BIOCHEMISTRY AND
MOLECULAR BIOLOGY
9650 Rockville Pike, Bethesda MD 20814. 301/530-7145.

AMERICAN SOCIETY OF HOSPITAL
PHARMACISTS
4630 Montgomery Avenue, Bethesda MD 20814. 301/657-3000.

AMERICAN VETERINARY MEDICAL
ASSOCIATION
1931 North Meacham Road, Suite 100, Schaumburg IL
60173-4360. 708/925-8070.

CARDIOVASCULAR CREDENTIALING
INTERNATIONAL
P.O. Box 611, Dayton OH 45419. 513/294-5225.

MEDICAL GROUP MANAGEMENT ASSOCIATION
104 Inverness Terrace E, Englewood CO 80112. 303/799-1111.

NATIONAL ASSOCIATION OF
PHARMACEUTICAL MANUFACTURERS
747 Third Avenue, New York NY 10017. 212/838-3720.

NATIONAL ASSOCIATION OF PRIVATE
PSYCHIATRIC HOSPITALS
1319 F Street NW, Washington DC 20004. 202/393-6700.

NATIONAL HEALTH COUNCIL
1730 M Street NW, Suite 500, Washington DC 20036.
202/785-3910.

NATIONAL MEDICAL ASSOCIATION
1012 Tenth Street NW, Washington DC 20001. 202/347-1895.

NATIONAL PHARMACEUTICAL COUNCIL
1894 Preston White Drive, Reston VA 22091. 703/620-6390.

Directories

BLUE BOOK DIGEST OF HMOs
National Association of Employers on Health Care
Alternatives, P.O. Box 220, Key Biscayne FL 33149.
305/361-2810.

DRUG TOPICS RED BOOK
Medical Economics Co., P.O. Box 1935, Marion OH
43306-4035. 201/358-7200.

ENCYCLOPEDIA OF MEDICAL ORGANIZATIONS
AND AGENCIES
Gale Research Inc., 835 Penobscot Building, Detroit MI
48226. 313/961-2242.

HEALTH ORGANIZATIONS OF THE UNITED
STATES, CANADA, AND THE WORLD
Gale Research Inc., 835 Penobscot Building, Detroit MI
48226. 313/961-2242.

MEDICAL AND HEALTH INFORMATION
DIRECTORY
Gale Research Inc., 835 Penobscot Building, Detroit MI
48226. 313/961-2242.

NATIONAL DIRECTORY OF HEALTH
MAINTENANCE ORGANIZATIONS
Group Health Association of America, 1129 20th Street
NW, Washington DC 20036. 202/778-3200.

Magazines

AMERICAN MEDICAL NEWS
American Medical Association, 515 North State Street,
Chicago IL 60605. 312/464-5000.

CHANGING MEDICAL MARKETS
Theta Corporation, Theta Building, Middlefield CT 06455.
203/349-1054.

DRUG TOPICS
Medical Economics Co., 5 Paragon Drive, Montvale NJ
07645. 201/358-7200.

HEALTH CARE EXECUTIVE
American College of Health Care Executives, 840 North
Lake Shore Drive, Chicago IL 60611. 312/943-0544.

MODERN HEALTHCARE
Crain Communications, 740 North Rush Street, Chicago IL
60611. 312/649-5374.

PHARMACEUTICAL ENGINEERING
International Society of Pharmaceutical Engineers, 3816 W.
Linebaugh Avenue, Suite 412, Tampa FL 33624. 813/960-2105.

HOSPITALITY: HOTELS AND RESTAURANTS

In the restaurant segment, the fastest-growing sector of the market continues to be fast-food-style establishments, although increased public concern has led industry leaders to develop new products and marketing strategies. McDonald's has released its lower-fat "McLean Deluxe", and Kentucky Fried Chicken has changed its name to "KFC" to de-emphasize the word "Fried". The take-out trend, spurred by changing demographics and eating habits, is changing the industry as a whole, not just at the fast-food end.
Managerial prospects are better than average, but the industry is hampered by a shortage of entry-level workers. The hotel industry is tied closely to other segments of the travel industry, which in turn relies on the U.S. economy as a whole. International arrivals are the fastest-growing segment of the travel industry, so hotels in major American international destinations are better positioned. Look for greater specialization within the industry, with specific companies advertising as "budget", "luxury", or "corporate/meeting", for example. Hotels will also need to respond to the growing number of working couples who take shorter vacations together.

A & W RESTAURANTS, INC.
17197 North Laurel Park Drive, Livonia MI 48152. 313/462-0029. **Contact:** Personnel. **Description:** Operators of fast food restaurants.

DEARBORN INN COMPANY
20301 Oakwood Boulevard, Dearborn MI 48124. 313/271-2700. **Contact:** Personnel. **Description:** Operates a hotel corporation.

ELIAS BROTHERS RESTAURANTS
4199 Marcy, Warren MI 48091. 313/759-6000. **Contact:** Human Resources. **Description:** A Southeastern Michigan area chain of restaurants. **Employees:** 2,200.

GALAXIE INN, INC.
22900 Michigan Avenue, Dearborn MI 48124. 313/278-4800. **Contact:** Personnel. **Description:** Operates the Dearborn location of the Holiday Inn.

GRAND HOTEL
2177 Commons Parkway, Okemos MI 48864. 517/349-4600. **Contact:** Eileen Smith, Personnel Assistant. **Description:** Operates a major summer resort hotel. Seasonal hotel openings - mid-May until late October. Write for employment application at firm's winter address listed above. During the summer, write to Grand Hotel, Macinaw Island, MI 49757. EOE.

HOLLY'S, INC.
3033 Orchard Vista Drive, Grand Rapids MI 49546. 616/949-8899. **Contact:** Personnel. **Description:** Operates restaurants and motor inns.

INDIANHEAD MOUNTAIN/BEAR CREEK RESORT & CONFERENCE CENTER
500 Indianhead Road, Wakefield MI 49968. 906/229-5181. **Contact:** Barry Bohlic, Personnel. **Description:** Full-service year-round resort. In the winter, the resort offers skiing with 18 trails, 9 lifts and a 638' vertical drop, 5 bars, 2 cafeterias, 2 restaurants, and can lodge 1200 people. In summer, the resort offers golf, indoor pool and sauna, health and racquet club, group tours, bar and restaurant, lodging, and conference and meeting facilities. **Common positions:** Accountant; Advertising Worker; Computer Programmer; Customer Service Representative; Financial Analyst; Food Technologist; Hotel Manager/Assistant Manager; Department Manager; Marketing Specialist; Personnel and Labor Relations Specialist; Purchasing Agent; Waiters/Waitresses; Bartenders; Housekeepers; Ski School.

SUGAR LOAF RESORT CORPORATION
4500 South Sugar Loaf Mountain Road, Cedar MI 49621-9755. 616/228-5461. **Contact:** Dawn Czerniak, Personnel Director. **Description:** Operators of a resort hotel. **Common positions:** Department Manager; Sales Representative. **Educational backgrounds sought:** Business Administration; Hotel/Motel Management. **Special programs:** internships. **Benefits:** medical insurance; life insurance; employee discounts. **Corporate headquarters:** This location. **Operations at this facility:** service.

TUBBY'S SUB SHOPS, INC.
34500 Doreka Drive, Fraser MI 48026. 313/296-1270. **Contact:** Personnel. **Description:** Operators of restaurants.

Additional large employers: 250+

EATING PLACES

Cottage Inn Pizzeria
546 Packard St, Ann Arbor MI 48104-3005. 313/665-6005. Employs: 250-499.

H & H Restaurants Inc
3017 S Waverly Rd Ste A, Lansing MI 48911-1498. 517/394-6815. Employs: 250-499.

Taco Management Co
7996 Grand River Rd, Brighton MI 48116-9304. 313/229-8012. Employs: 250-499.

Little Caesars Enterprises Nc
2211 Woodward Ave, Detroit MI 48201-3461. 313/893-6000. Employs: 500-999.

HOTELS AND MOTELS

Sheration Southfield Hotel
16400 J L Hudson Dr, Southfield MI 48075-4875. 313/559-6500. Employs: 250-499.

Westin Hotel
Renaissance Center, Detroit MI 48243. 313/568-8000. Employs: 1000+.

Additional small to medium sized employers: 50-249

EATING PLACES

Alban's Restaurant & Deli
188 N Hunter Blvd, Birmingham MI 48009-5700. 313/258-
5788. Employs: 100-249.

Albee Foods Inc
1431 Washington Blvd, Detroit MI 48226-1720. 313/965-
7245. Employs: 100-249.

Bob Evans Restaurant
G3267 Miller Rd, Flint MI 48507-1358. 313/733-5350.
Employs: 50-99.

Bonanza Steak House
6727 S Cedar St, Lansing MI 48911-6904. 517/694-1299.
Employs: 50-99.

C A Muer Corp
1548 Porter St, Detroit MI 48216-1936. 313/965-5555.
Employs: 50-99.

Cruzado Of Allen Park
14887 Southfield Rd, Allen Park MI 48101-2642. 313/386-
1300. Employs: 50-99.

D Dennison's Seafood Tavern
27909 Orchard Lake Rd, Farmington MI 48334-3734.
313/553-7000. Employs: 50-99.

Dough's Body Shop
22061 Woodward Fern, Ferndale MI 48220. 313/398-1940.
Employs: 100-249.

El Azteco
1014 W Saginaw St, Lansing MI 48915-1967. 517/485-
4589. Employs: 100-249.

Elias Brothers Big Boy Restaurant
7050 S Cedar St, Lansing MI 48911-6914. 517/694-4403.
Employs: 50-99.

Elias Brothers Big Boy Restaurant
3425 E Saginaw St, Lansing MI 48912-4717. 517/332-
0815. Employs: 50-99.

Friar Tuck's Inn
3855 E 12 Mile Rd, Warren MI 48092-2564. 313/573-
6300. Employs: 50-99.

Hathaway House
424 W Adrian St, Blissfield MI 49228-1002. 517/486-
2141. Employs: 50-99.

Houlihans
2850 Coolidge Hwy, Troy MI 48084-3212. 313/649-2990.
Employs: 50-99.

K-Mart Eatery
1075 Emerick St, Ypsilanti MI 48198-6310. 313/482-3680.
Employs: 50-99.

Legends
3600 Plymouth Rd, Ann Arbor MI 48105-2660. 313/769-
9800. Employs: 100-249.

Little Caesar's Pizza
1063 S State Rd # 479, Davison MI 48423-1900. 313/653-
3400. Employs: 50-99.

Machus Foxys Restaurant
1254 Walton Blvd, Rochester MI 48307-1857. 313/652-
1177. Employs: 50-99.

Main Street Ventures Inc
343 S Main St S 209-215, Ann Arbor MI 48104-2107.
313/668-6062. Employs: 50-99.

Mc Donald's

337 Maynard St, Ann Arbor MI 48104-2211. 313/995-
2476. Employs: 50-99.

Mc Donald's Family Restaurants
27480 Van Dyke Ave, Warren MI 48093-2804. 313/755-
0290. Employs: 50-99.

McDonald's
3350 Sterns Rd, Lambertville MI 48144-9738. 313/856-
7338. Employs: 50-99.

McDonald's Of Pontiac
810 N Perry St, Pontiac MI 48342-1568. 313/335-5120.
Employs: 50-99.

Mister Taco Drive In Restaurant
3122 S Logan St, Lansing MI 48910-2940. 517/393-4669.
Employs: 50-99.

Mitch's II
6665 Highland Rd, Waterford MI 48327-1611. 313/666-
4440. Employs: 50-99.

Montrys Pizza Sub Shop
3105 S Logan St, Lansing MI 48910-2939. 517/394-4800.
Employs: 50-99.

Muers Oyster House Inc
2000 Gratiot Ave, Detroit MI 48207-2708. 313/567-1088.
Employs: 100-249.

Old Woodward Grill
555 S Woodward, Birmingham MI 48009. 313/642-9400.
Employs: 50-99.

Peabody's Restaurant & Bar
154 S Hunter Blvd, Birmingham MI 48009-6335. 313/644-
5222. Employs: 50-99.

Pizza Sam
104 E Superior St, Alma MI 48801-1817. 517/463-3881.
Employs: 50-99.

Ram's Horn Of Westland
8590 N Middlebelt Rd, Westland MI 48185-1811. 313/261-
0553. Employs: 50-99.

Ramon's Restaurant & Lounge
1146 S Washington Av, Lansing MI 48910-1660. 517/372-
3010. Employs: 50-99.

Red Lobster Inns Of America
2400 Shirley Dr, Jackson MI 49202-1524. 517/787-7820.
Employs: 50-99.

Red Lobster Restaurants
6850 N Telegraph Rd, Dearborn Hts MI 48127-2206.
313/562-4605. Employs: 50-99.

Steak and Ale Restaurants
24666 Northwestern Hwy, Southfield MI 48075-2301.
313/353-7448. Employs: 50-99.

Sweet Lorraines Cafe Southfield
29101 Greenfield Rd, Southfield MI 48076-5831. 313/559-
5985. Employs: 100-249.

The Brewery
39950 Hayes Rd, Clinton Twp MI 48038-2639. 313/286-
3020. Employs: 50-99.

The Chambertin
22900 Michigan Av, Dearborn MI 48124-2033. 313/278-
6900. Employs: 100-249.

The Pub
G2207 W Bristol Rd, Flint MI 48507. 313/239-4681.
Employs: 50-99.

The Wheel Inn
1825 S US 27, Saint Johns MI 48879. 517/224-4263.
Employs: 50-99.

Thomas Edison Inns Inc
500 N Riverside, Saint Clair MI 48079-5414. 313/329-2222. Employs: 100-249.

Traffic Jam & Snug Restaurant
511 W Canfield St, Detroit MI 48201-1219. 313/831-9470.
Employs: 50-99.

Vanderbilt Room
610 Hilton Blvd, Ann Arbor MI 48108-1620. 313/761-7800. Employs: 50-99.

Whitey's Restaurant
109 N State St, Davison MI 48423-1303. 313/653-6666.
Employs: 50-99.

Big Boy Restaurants
800 N Pontiac Trl, Walled Lake MI 48390-3232. 313/624-2323. Employs: 50-99.

Big Boy Restaurants
4199 Marcy St, Warren MI 48091-1733. 313/759-6000.
Employs: 100-249.

Kroger Co
4080 E Blue Grass Rd, Mount Pleasant MI 48858-7914.
517/773-3943. Employs: 50-99.

The Kroger Co
43680 Van Dyke Ave, Sterling Hts MI 48314-2437.
313/731-1625. Employs: 50-99.

The Kroger Co
26150 Gratiot Ave, Roseville MI 48066-3389. 313/774-6667. Employs: 100-249.

Buscemi's The Original Inc
30360 Gratiot Ave, Roseville MI 48066-1765. 313/294-4477. Employs: 50-99.

Pasquales Restaurant & Pza
3815 N Woodward Ave, Royal Oak MI 48073-6445.
313/549-4002. Employs: 50-99.

Penna's Restaurant & Lounge
27900 Hoover Rd, Warren MI 48093-7715. 313/751-6130.
Employs: 50-99.

Tin Lizzie Restaurant
10915 Belleville Rd, Belleville MI 48111-1386. 313/697-6888. Employs: 50-99.

McDonald's Hamburgers
4819 Rochester Rd, Troy MI 48098-4962. 313/524-2437.
Employs: 100-249.

McDonald's Hamburgers
11525 Dexter Ave, Detroit MI 48206-1437. 313/834-9422.
Employs: 100-249.

Bennigan's
30700 Van Dyke Ave, Warren MI 48093-2162. 313/573-8230. Employs: 100-249.

Friday's
3150 Crooks Rd, Troy MI 48084. 313/362-3113. Employs:
50-99.

Red Lobster Restaurants
101 W 12 Mile Rd, Madison Hts MI 48071-2418. 313/542-1140. Employs: 100-249.

Van Dyke Park Htl & Cnfrnc Center
31800 Van Dyke Ave, Warren MI 48093-7942. 313/939-2860. Employs: 100-249.

Young's Barbeque

5900 Mount Elliott St, Detroit MI 48211-3142. 313/571-2113. Employs: 50-99.

DRINKING PLACES (ALCOHOLIC BEVERAGES)

Alibi Inc
1 Energy Place, Mount Pleasant MI 48858. 517/772-2931.
Employs: 100-249.

City Limits
2900 Jackson Av, Ann Arbor MI 48103-2012. 313/665-4444. Employs: 100-249.

Gibson Lounge
12918 Puritan St, Detroit MI 48227-4020. 313/864-8480.
Employs: 50-99.

Teilgate's Lounge
26555 Telegraph Rd, Southfield MI 48034-5318. 313/353-7700. Employs: 50-99.

Mustang Inn
3400 Wyoming St, Dearborn MI 48120-1414. 313/841-4655. Employs: 50-99.

HOTELS AND MOTELS

Campus Inn
615 E Huron St, Ann Arbor MI 48104-1524. 313/769-2200. Employs: 50-99.

Central Michigan Inns Inc
5665 E Pickard St, Mount Pleasant MI 48858-5013.
517/773-9466. Employs: 100-249.

Courtyard By Marriott
5200 Mercury Dr, Dearborn MI 48126-2851. 313/271-1400. Employs: 50-99.

Holiday Inn
30375 Plymouth Rd, Livonia MI 48150-2116. 313/261-6800. Employs: 50-99.

Holiday Inn
1 W 9 Mile Rd, Hazel Park MI 48030-1701. 313/399-5800.
Employs: 50-99.

Holiday Inn Of Dearborn
22900 Michigan Av, Dearborn MI 48124-2033. 313/278-4800. Employs: 100-249.

Holiday Inn Of Jackson
2000 Holiday Inn Dr, Jackson MI 49202-1405. 517/783-2681. Employs: 100-249.

Holiday Inn Of Monroe
1225 N Dixie Hwy, Monroe MI 48161-5202. 313/242-6000. Employs: 100-249.

Hospice For Communities
135 S Leroy St, Fenton MI 48430-2637. 313/750-0280.
Employs: 50-99.

Howard Johnson S Motor Lodge E
932 S Center Rd, Flint MI 48503-4511. 313/744-0200.
Employs: 50-99.

Howell Park Inn
125 Holiday La, Howell MI 48843-2517. 517/546-6800.
Employs: 50-99.

Hyatt Regency Hotel
200 S Saginaw St, Flint MI 48502-2012. 313/239-1234.
Employs: 100-249.

Portside Inn
3455 Biddle Av, Wyandotte MI 48192-6222. 313/281-6700. Employs: 50-99.

Quality Inn
3121 E Grand River Av, Lansing MI 48912-4726. 517/351-1440. Employs: 50-99.

Ramada Inn
G4300 W Pierson Rd, Flint MI 48504. 313/732-0400.
Employs: 50-99.

Sheraton Inn-Lansing
925 S Creyts Dr, Lansing MI 48917-9222. 517/323-7100.
Employs: 100-249.

Somerset Inn
2601 W Big Beaver Rd, Troy MI 48084-3312. 313/643-
7800. Employs: 100-249.

Weber's Inn
3050 Jackson Av, Ann Arbor MI 48103-1907. 313/769-
2500. Employs: 50-99.

Clarkston Motel Motor Inn
6853 Dixie Hwy, Clarkston MI 48346-2007. 313/625-1522.
Employs: 50-99.

Georgian Inn
31327 Gratiot Ave, Roseville MI 48066-4556. 313/294-
0400. Employs: 100-249.

Courtyard By Marriott Sls Ofc
17200 N Laurel Pr Dr, Livonia MI 48152. 313/462-2266.
Employs: 50-99.

Days Hotel Warren
30000 Van Dyke Ave, Warren MI 48093-2307. 313/573-
7600. Employs: 50-99.

Holiday Inn
20777 Eureka Rd, Taylor MI 48180-5314. 313/283-2200.
Employs: 50-99.

Hotel St Regis
3071 W Gd Bl, Detroit MI 48202. 313/873-3000. Employs:
100-249.

Ramada Inn
8270 Wickham St, Romulus MI 48174-1961. 313/729-
6300. Employs: 100-249.

Rodeway Inn Detroit Metro
8230 Merriman Rd, Romulus MI 48174-1917. 313/729-
7600. Employs: 50-99.

Hilton-Detroit Airport
31500 Wick Rd, Romulus MI 48174-1916. 313/292-3400.
Employs: 100-249.

Holiday Inn
5665 W Pickard Rd, Mount Pleasant MI 48858-9631.
517/772-2905. Employs: 100-249.

Courtyard By Marriott
27027 Northwestern Hwy, Southfield MI 48034-6235.
313/358-1222. Employs: 50-99.

Residnce Inn By Marriott Madison
2600 Livernois Rd, Troy MI 48083-1227. 313/689-6856.
Employs: 50-99.

**ORGANIZATION HOTELS AND LODGING
HOUSES ON MEMBERSHIP BASIS**

Alpha Gamma Delta
605 S Main St, Mount Pleasant MI 48858-3140. 517/772-
9807. Employs: 50-99.

For more information on career opportunities in hospitality - hotels and restaurants:

Associations

AMERICAN HOTEL AND MOTEL ASSOCIATION
1201 New York Avenue NW, Washington DC 20005-3931
202/289-3100

**COUNCIL ON HOTEL, RESTAURANT AND
INSTITUTIONAL EDUCATION**
1200 17th Street NW, Washington DC 20036. 202/331-
5990.

**THE EDUCATIONAL FOUNDATION OF THE
NATIONAL RESTAURANT ASSOCIATION**
250 South Wacker Drive, 14th Floor, Chicago IL 60606.
312/715-1010.

**HOSPITALITY SALES AND MARKETING
ASSOCIATION INTERNATIONAL**
1300 L Street NW, Suite 800, Washington DC 20005.
202/789-0089.

NATIONAL RESTAURANT ASSOCIATION
1200 17th Street NW, Washington DC 20036. 202/331-
5900.

Directories

**DIRECTORY OF CHAIN RESTAURANT
OPERATORS**
Business Guides, Inc., Lebhar-Friedman, Inc., 3922
Coconut Palm Drive, Tampa FL 33619-8321. 813/664-
6700.

**DIRECTORY OF HIGH-VOLUME INDEPENDENT
RESTAURANTS**
Lebhar-Friedman, Inc., 3922 Coconut Palm Drive, Tampa
FL 33619-8321. 813/664-6700.

Magazines

**CORNELL HOTEL AND RESTAURANT
ADMINISTRATION QUARTERLY**
Cornell University School of Hotel Administration, 327
Statler Hall, Ithaca NY 14853. 607/255-2093.

HOTEL AND MOTEL MANAGEMENT
120 West 2nd Street, Duluth MN 55802. 218/723-9440.

INNKEEPING WORLD
Box 84108, Seattle WA 98124. 206/362-7125.

NATION'S RESTAURANT NEWS
425 Park Avenue, New York NY 10022. 212/756-5200.

INSURANCE

The fastest-growing segment of the insurance industry will be in annuities. Premiums of property-casualty insurers should increase by about five percent, according to the Bureau of Labor Statistics. Competition and mergers will increase, while life insurance companies are expected to experience further problems. The industry as a whole has been trimming back through layoffs, although the worst may be over.

AAA MICHIGAN
1 Auto Club Drive, Dearborn MI 48126. 313/336-1600, Jobline. **Contact:** Maureen Farquhar, Professional/Technical Recruiter. **Description:** Provides a variety of insurance protection, travel services, and modern motoring services for 1.5 million members. **Employees:** 4,700. **Common positions:** Actuary.

ACCIDENT FUND OF MICHIGAN
232 South Capitol Avenue, Box 40790, Lansing MI 48901. 517/342-4200. **Contact:** Personnel. **Description:** A workers' compensation insurance company. **Common positions:** Accountant; Actuary; Attorney; Claim Representative; Computer Programmer; Marketing Specialist; Personnel and Labor Relations Specialist; Purchasing Agent; Systems Analyst; Underwriter. **Educational backgrounds sought:** Business Administration; Computer Science; Liberal Arts; Marketing; Insurance. **Special programs:** Training programs and internships. **Benefits:** medical insurance; dental insurance; pension plan; life insurance; tuition assistance; disability coverage. **Corporate headquarters:** this location.

ALEXANDER HAMILTON LIFE INSURANCE
33045 Hamilton Boulevard, Farmington Hills MI 48334. 313/553-2000. **Contact:** John Szutarski, Vice President of Human Resources. **Description:** An area life insurance company. **Common positions:** Accountant; Actuary; Administrator; Attorney; Claim Representative; Computer Programmer; Customer Service Representative; Financial Analyst; Instructor/Trainer/Teacher; Department Manager; Marketing Specialist; Systems Analyst; Underwriter. **Educational backgrounds sought:** Accounting; Business Administration; Communications; Computer Science; Finance; Marketing; Mathematics. **Special programs:** Training programs offered. **Benefits:** medical, dental, and life insurance; pension plan; tuition assistance; disability coverage; profit sharing; employee discounts. **Corporate headquarters:** This location. **Parent company:** Household International. **Listed on:** New York Stock Exchange. **Revenues (1991):** $250 million. **Employees:** 650. **Projected hires for the next 12 months:** 8.

BLUE CROSS AND BLUE SHIELD
600 Lafayette East, Detroit MI 48226. 313/225-8000. **Contact:** Personnel Department. **Description:** A Detroit company that deals primarily with accident insurance, health insurance, and medical service plans. **Employees:** 8,000.

FACTORY MUTUAL
ENGINEERING AND RESEARCH
30150 Telegraph Road, Suite 141, Bingham Hills MI 48025-4250. 313/540-0500. **Contact:** Mike Dekamp, Office Manager. **Description:** A loss-prevention service organization maintained by the Factory Mutual System (Norwood, MA). District offices are located throughout the United States and Canada. Loss Prevention Consultants, also known as field engineers, inspect insured properties on a periodic basis to help pinpoint hazards or conditions that could cause fires or explosions, or result in damage to property or lost production.

FIRST AMERICAN TITLE
1650 West Big Beaver, Troy MI 48084. 313/643-4000. **Contact:** Jim Austin, Training Director. **Description:** An insurance company specializing in title abstracts. **Employees:** 100.

JACKSON NATIONAL LIFE INSURANCE COMPANY
5901 Executive Drive, Lansing MI 48911. 517/394-3400. **Contact:** Personnel. **Description:** A major life insurance company.

MEADOWBROOK, INC.
26600 Telegraph Road, Southfield MI 48034. 313/358-1100. **Contact:** Personnel. **Description:** A major insurance broker.

Additional large employers: 250+

LIFE INSURANCE

American Community Mutual Insurance Co
39201 Seven Mile Rd, Livonia MI 48152-1094. 313/591-9000. Employs: 500-999.

HOSPITAL AND MEDICAL SERVICE PLANS

Sheldon W Berry Associates
14700 Farmington Rd, Livonia MI 48154-5434. 313/421-6680. Employs: 500-999.

FIRE, MARINE AND CASUALTY INSURANCE

Citizens Insurance Co Amer
645 W Grand River Ave, Howell MI 48843-2151. 517/546-2160. Employs: 1000+.

Michigan Mutual Insurance Co
28 W Adams Ave, Detroit MI 48226-1617. 313/965-8600. Employs: 500-999.

SURETY INSURANCE

Ford Holdings Inc
The American Road, Dearborn MI 48121. 313/322-3000. Employs: 1000+.

PENSION, HEALTH AND WELFARE FUNDS

Coopers & Lybrand
400 Renaissance Center, Detroit MI 48243. 313/446-7100. Employs: 250-499.

INSURANCE AGENTS, BROKERS AND SERVICE

Accident Fund Of Michigan
232 S Capitol Av, Lansing MI 48933. 517/3924200. Employs: 250-499.

Auto Owners Insurance Co
6101 Anacapri Blvd, Lansing MI 48917-3968. 517/323-1200. Employs: 500-999.

C N A Insurance
30200 Telegraph Rd, Franklin MI 48025-4502. 313/645-6940. Employs: 250-499.

John Hancock Mutual Life Insurance Co
3200 Greenfield Rd, Dearborn MI 48120-1240. 313/584-1900. Employs: 250-499.

Michigan Millers Mutual Insurance Co
2425 E Grand River Ave, Lansing MI 48912-3225.
517/482-6211. Employs: 250-499.

Delta Dental Plan Of Michigan
34505 W 12 Mile Rd, Farmington MI 48331-3258.
313/489-2000. Employs: 250-499.

The Travelers Companies
26555 Evergreen Rd, Southfield MI 48076-4206. 313/423-2025. Employs: 250-499.

Additional small to medium sized employers: 50-249

HOSPITAL AND MEDICAL SERVICE PLANS

Blue Cross & Blue Shield
1500 Abbott Rd, East Lansing MI 48823-1956. 517/699-3200. Employs: 100-249.

Al Garcia Clu Chfc
4166 Cherrywood Ln, Troy MI 48098-4237. 313/637-2920. Employs: 50-99.

Alliance Health Insurance
490 Maplehill Rd, Rochester MI 48306-4316. 313/650-3535. Employs: 50-99.

Ancona & Associates
11 W 14 Mile Rd, Clawson MI 48017-3104. 313/435-6900. Employs: 50-99.

Associated Benefits
28840 Southfield Rd, Southfield MI 48076-2730. 313/569-4543. Employs: 50-99.

Birmingham Benefits Group Inc
30800 Telegraph Rd, Franklin MI 48025-4542. 313/644-4815. Employs: 50-99.

Capital Insurance Group
21800 W 10 Mile Rd, Southfield MI 48075-1026. 313/354-6110. Employs: 50-99.

Flagship Insurance Agency Inc
2875 Northwind Dr, East Lansing MI 48823-5035.
517/336-9040. Employs: 100-249.

Harold Moldenhauer & Assocs
14500 Lakeside Cir, Sterling Hts MI 48313-1330. 313/773-0010. Employs: 50-99.

Western Life Insurance Co
2855 Coolidge Hwy, Troy MI 48084-3202. 313/643-8848. Employs: 50-99.

FIRE, MARINE AND CASUALTY INSURANCE

Michigan State Accident Fu
232 S Capitol Av, Lansing MI 48933-1504. 517/485-7193. Employs: 100-249.

SURETY INSURANCE

Prime Underwriters Inc
24539 Grove St, Detroit MI 48219. 313/255-5400.
Employs: 50-99.

Surety Guaranty Group Inc
1401 Beaubien St, Detroit MI 48226-2309. 313/961-0301. Employs: 50-99.

PENSION, HEALTH AND WELFARE FUNDS

MacCabees Life Insurance Co
25800 Northwestern Hwy, Southfield MI 48075-8401.
313/357-4800. Employs: 100-249.

Buck Consultants
100 Renaissance Center, Detroit MI 48243-1002. 313/567-2120. Employs: 50-99.

Monroe and Associates
19454 James Couzens Fwy, Detroit MI 48235-1905.
313/864-3758. Employs: 50-99.

TPF&C
200 Renaissance Center, Detroit MI 48243-1209. 313/567-6616. Employs: 50-99.

MISCELLANEOUS INSURANCE CARRIERS

Greater Detroit A L U
3331 W Big Beaver Rd Ste 104, Troy MI 48084-2824.
313/643-9313. Employs: 50-99.

Continuous Auto Protection
35200 Grand River Ave, Farmington MI 48335-3212.
313/474-4470. Employs: 50-99.

Member's Warranty
16118 Silver Shore, Fenton MI 48430. 313/629-0400.
Employs: 100-249.

INSURANCE AGENTS, BROKERS AND SERVICE

Allstate Insurance Co
7200 W Saginaw St, Lansing MI 48917-1121. 517/323-7030. Employs: 50-99.

Great American Insurance Co
280 S Woodward Av, Birmingham MI 48009-6163.
313/642-0500. Employs: 50-99.

Health Care Life Insurance
4300 S Saginaw St, Flint MI 48507-2646. 313/236-0430.
Employs: 100-249.

Health Plus Of Michigan
2050 S Linden Rd, Flint MI 48532-4161. 313/230-2000.
Employs: 100-249.

I M I Firms Insurance Accounting Inc
3322 W Michigan Av, Lansing MI 48917-3749. 517/484-6800. Employs: 50-99 ·

Provident Life & Accident Insurance
1048 Pierpont Dr Ste 3, Lansing MI 48911-5976. 517/882-6409. Employs: 50-99.

Prudential Insurance Co America
23400 Michigan Av Ste 505, Dearborn MI 48124-1991.
313/563-8487. Employs: 50-99.

Blue Care
27000 W 11 Mile Rd, Southfield MI 48034-2293. 313/354-7650. Employs: 100-249.

Fireman's Fund Insurance Co
10 Oak Hollow St, Southfield MI 48034-7405. 313/351-7300. Employs: 50-99.

Prudential Insurance Co America
5215 Highland Rd, Waterford MI 48327-1916. 313/674-4701. Employs: 50-99.

Aetna
400 Renaissance Center, Detroit MI 48243. 313/259-8600.
Employs: 50-99.

For more information on career opportunities in insurance:

Associations

ALLIANCE OF AMERICAN INSURERS
1501 Woodfield Road, Suite 400 West, Schaumburg IL
60173-4980. 708/330-8500.

AMERICAN COUNCIL OF LIFE INSURANCE
1001 Pennsylvania Avenue NW, 5th Floor South,
Washington DC 20004-2599. 202/624-2000.

AMERICAN INSURANCE ASSOCIATION
1130 Connecticut Avenue NW, Suite 1000, Washington
DC 20036. 202/828-7100.

**HEALTH INSURANCE ASSOCIATION OF
AMERICA**
1025 Connecticut Avenue NW, Suite 1200, Washington
DC 20036-3998. 202/223-7780.

INSURANCE INFORMATION INSTITUTE
110 William Street, New York NY 10038. 212/669-9200.

**LIFE INSURANCE RESEARCH AND MARKETING
ASSOCIATION**
8 Farm Springs Road, Farmington CT 06032. 203/677-
0033.

**NATIONAL ASSOCIATION OF LIFE
UNDERWRITERS**
1922 F Street NW, Washington DC 20006-4387. 202/331-
6000.

SOCIETY OF ACTUARIES
475 North Martingale Road, Suite 800, Schaumburg IL
60173-2227. 708/706-3500.

Directories

INSURANCE ALMANAC
Underwriter Printing and Publishing Co., 50 East Palisade
Avenue, Englewood NJ 07631. 201/569-8808.

INSURANCE MARKET PLACE
Rough Notes Company, Inc., P.O. Box 564, Indianapolis
IN 46206. 317/634-1541.

INSURANCE PHONE BOOK AND DIRECTORY
121 Chanlon Road, New Providence NJ 07974. 800/521-
8110.

Magazines

BEST'S REVIEW
A. M. Best Co., A. M. Best Road, Oldwick NJ 08858.
908/439-2200.

INSURANCE JOURNAL
80 Southlake Avenue, Suite 550, Pasadena CA 91101.
818/793-7717.

INSURANCE REVIEW
Journal of Commerce, 2 World Trade Center, 27th Floor,
New York NY 10048. 212/837-7000.

LEGAL SERVICES

The legal profession is undergoing a major adjustment, largely due to the rapid rise in the number of lawyers over the past two decades. In the 70's the number of lawyers doubled, and in the 80's the number rose by another 48 percent. Meanwhile, a decline in civil litigation, coupled with the recent economic downturn, has led to a "produce or perish" climate. Law schools are reporting a 10-20 percent decline in placements, and firms are laying off associates, freezing rates, and firing unproductive partners.
Graduates of prestigious law schools and those who rank high in their classes will have the best opportunities.

ACEVEDO AND BAGGOTT

953 Penobscot Building, Detroit MI 48226. 313/962-3811. **Contact:** Ms. Nancy Baggott, Partner. **Description:** A metropolitan Detroit law firm specializing in divorce cases.

ANDARY AND ANDARY
148 South Gratiot, Detroit MI 48043. 313/463-5000. **Contact:** James Andary, Attorney. **Description:** A leading metropolitan Detroit law firm engaged in general practice law.

BARRIS, SOTT, DENN, AND DRIKER
211 West Fort Street, 15th floor, Detroit MI 48226-3281. 313/965-9725. **Contact:** Janet Iberra, Personnel Director. **Description:** A leading Detroit area law firm specializing in corporate law.

BERMAN, BRAND, AND GOODMAN
22305 Woodward, Ferndale MI 48220. 313/548-6000. **Contact:** Personnel Department. **Description:** A law firm engaged in the practice of all types of law and litigation.

BERRY, MOORMAN, KING, COOK, AND HUDSON
600 Woodbridge Place, Detroit MI 48226. 313/567-1000. **Contact:** Personnel Director. **Description:** A leading area law firm specializing in corporate, taxation, securities regulations, estate planning, and labor law.

BODMAN, LONGLEY, AND DAHLING
100 Renaissance Center, 34th Floor, Detroit MI 48243. 313/259-7777. **Contact:** Personnel Department. **Description:** A Detroit law firm specializing in corporate law.

BUESSER, BUESSER, BLANK,
LYNCH, FRYHOFF, GRAHAM
4190 Telegraph Road, Bloomfield Hills MI 48302. 313/259-5220. **Contact:** Personnel Department. **Description:** Main office located at 4190 Telegraph Road, Suite 201, Bloomfield Hills MI 49013. A major Detroit law firm specializing in malpractice and family law.

BUTZEL LONG
150 West Jefferson, Suite 900, Detroit MI 48226. 313/963-8142. **Contact:** Linda Moore, Personnel Director. **Description:** A major Detroit law firm specializing in corporate law.

CAMPBELL, O'BRIEN, AND MISTELE P.C.
850 Stephenson Highway, Suite 410, Troy MI 48083. 313/965-1752. **Contact:** Henry Mistele, Attorney. **Description:** A major metropolitan Detroit law firm specializing in divorce and civil law practice.

PAUL F. CARRIER AND ASSOC. P.C.
20600 Eureka Road, Suite 321, Taylor MI 48180. 313/285-7011. **Contact:** Paul Carrier, President. **Description:** A leading area law firm engaged in general practice litigation.

COOK AND GOETZ
1400 Woodward, Suite 101, Bloomfield Hills MI 48304. 313/642-4585. **Contact:** John Cook, Personnel Director. **Description:** A leading area general practice law firm.

DENNISON MAXWELL
1750 South Telegraph, Suite 301, Bloomfield Hills MI 48302-0179. 313/253-1100. **Contact:** William Hanson, Director of Personnel. **Description:** Law firm specializing in corporate law.

DIETRICH AND CASSAVAUGH
615 Griswold/Ford Building, Suite 1620, Detroit MI 48226. 313/961-9139. **Contact:** Personnel Department. **Description:** One of metropolitan Detroit's leading general law practitioners.

DYKEMA, GOSSETT, SPENCER, & GORDON
400 Renaissance L-2, Detroit MI 48244. 313/568-6800. **Contact:** Jo Hufford, Personnel Director. **Description:** A leading metropolitan Detroit law firm specializing in corporate law. **Employees:** 600.

EAMES WILCOX MASTEJ BRYANT SWIFT & RIDDELL
1400 Buhl Building, Detroit MI 48226. 313/963-3750. **Contact:** Personnel Department. **Description:** A leading metropolitan Detroit law firm engaged in general practice law.

ERNSTEIN & ERNSTEIN, P.C.
30600 Telegraph Road, Bingham Farms MI 48025. 313/358-5353. **Contact:** Personnel Department. **Description:** A Detroit law firm.

FIEGER & FIEGER & SCHWARTZ, P.C.
19390 West 10 Mile Road, Southfield MI 48075. 313/355-5555. **Contact:** Julie Mareski, Office Manager. **Description:** A leading area law firm specializing in medical malpractice and complex litigation. **Common positions:** Attorney. **Educational backgrounds sought:** Liberal Arts; Law; Paralegal. **Benefits:** medical and life insurance. **Corporate headquarters:** This location. Operations at this facility: service.

FOSTER MEADOWS AND BALLARD PC
3200 Penobscot Building, Corner of Fort, Detroit MI 48226. 313/961-3234. **Contact:** John Foster, Senior Partner. **Description:** A Detroit area law firm specializing in admiralty law.

GARRATT & EVANS, P.C.
300 East Long Lake Road, Suite 375, Bloomfield Hills MI 48304. 313/645-1450. **Contact:** Personnel Director. **Description:** A leading Southeastern Michigan general practice law firm.

GORDON, CUTLER & HOFFMAN
18411 West 12 Mile Road, Southfield MI 48076. 313/443-1500. **Contact:** Arnold Gordon, Managing Partner. **Description:** A Detroit area law firm dealing primarily with personal injury litigation.

GREENSPON SCHEFF AND WASHINGTON
One Kennedy Square, Suite 2137, Detroit MI 48226. 313/963-1921. **Contact:** Personnel Department. **Description:** A Detroit general practice law firm.

HONIGMAN, MILLER, SCHWARTZ & COHN
2290 1st National Building, 660 Woodward Avenue, Detroit MI 48226. 313/256-7800. **Contact:** Judy Jonya, Personnel Manager. **Description:** A metropolitan Detroit general practice law firm. **Employees:** 400.

KELLER, THOMA, DUBAY & KATZ PC
440 East Congress, 5th floor, Detroit MI 48226. 313/965-7610. **Contact:** Susan Korpas, Personnel Director. **Description:** A Detroit law firm specializing in corporate law.

KOTZ & SANGSTER PC
100 Renaissance Center, Suite 1855, Detroit MI 48243. 313/259-8300. **Contact:** Hiring Partner. A Detroit legal services firm specializing in corporate law.

LOPATIN, MILLER, FREEDMAN, BLUESTONE,
ERLICH, ROSEN & BARTNICK
1301 East Jefferson Avenue, Detroit MI 48207. 313/259-7800. **Contact:** Sydney Cohen, Personnel Manager. **Description:** A leading metropolitan Detroit law firm specializing in personal injury cases. **Common positions:** Attorney. **Corporate headquarters:** This location.

LEONARD D. McMAHON
405 Rivard, Detroit MI 48207. 313/393-2005. **Contact:** Jean Suanders, Personnel Manager. **Description:** A Detroit law firm that deals primarily in personal injury law. **Common positions:** Legal Secretary; Receptionist; File Clerk; (personal injury experience). **Educational backgrounds sought:** Business School; Word Processing. **Benefits:** medical insurance; parking. **Corporate headquarters:** This location.

PRATHER AND FOLEY
645 Griswold Street, Suite 3800, Detroit MI 48226. 313/962-7722. **Contact:** Personnel Department. **Description:** A Detroit legal services firm specializing in family law.

ROTH AND DEAN
3000 Town Center, Suite 450, Southfield MI 48075. 313/358-0100. **Contact:** Leslie Schafer, Personnel Director. **Description:** A leading area law firm specializing in personal injury law.

SEAVITT WESTCOTT & STOWE
29777 Telegraph Road, Suite 2650, Southfield MI 48034-7652. 313/357-3430.
Contact: Robert Stowe, Partner. A leading Southeastern Michigan law firm specializing in insurance defense cases.

TEMROWSKI & TEMROWSKI
45109 Van Dyke Avenue, Utica MI 48317. 313/254-5566. **Contact:** Personnel Department. **Description:** A leading metropolitan Detroit law firm specializing in personal injury law.

ZEFF & ZEFF
607 Shelby, Suite 200, Detroit MI 48226. 313/962-3825. **Contact:** Personnel. **Description:** A leading metropolitan Detroit law firm engaged in all aspects of general practice law.

Additional large employers: 250+

LEGAL SERVICES

Miro Miro & Weiner
500 Woodward Av Rm 200, Bloomfield MI 48304-2963. 313/646-2400. Employs: 500-999.

Dickinson Wright Moon Van
800 First National Bg, Detroit MI 48226. 313/223-3500. Employs: 250-499.

Miller Canfield Paddock & Stn
150 W Jefferson Ave, Detroit MI 48226-4429. 313/963-6420. Employs: 500-999.

Small to medium sized employers: 50-249

LEGAL SERVICES

Dickinson Wright Moon Van
525 Woodward Av Rm 2000, Bloomfield MI 48304-2970. 313/646-4300. Employs: 50-99.

Butzel Keidan Simon Myers
2490 1st National Bg, Detroit MI 48226. 313/961-7900. Employs: 50-99.

Kitch Saurbier Drutchas Wagner
1 Woodward Ave, Detroit MI 48226-3402. 313/965-7900. Employs: 100-249.

Kohl Secrest Wardle Lynch
30903 Northwestern Hwy, Farmington MI 48334-2556. 313/851-9500. Employs: 50-99.

Reid & Reid
200 Washington Sq N, Lansing MI 48933-1302. 517/487-6566. Employs: 100-249.

Terence K Jolly
2555 Crooks Rd, Troy MI 48084-4742. 313/643-7900. Employs: 50-99.

For more information on career opportunities in legal services:

Associations

AMERICAN BAR ASSOCIATION
North Lake Shore Drive, Chicago IL 60611. 312/988-5000.

FEDERAL BAR ASSOCIATION
1815 H. Street NW, Suite 408, Washington DC 20006. 202/638-0252.

NATIONAL ASSOCIATION FOR LAW PLACEMENT
1666 Connecticut Avenue, Suite 450, Washington DC 20009. 202/667-1666.

NATIONAL ASSOCIATION OF LEGAL ASSISTANTS
1601 South Main Street, Suite 300, Tulsa OK 74119. 918/587-6828.

NATIONAL FEDERATION OF PARALEGAL ASSOCIATIONS
P.O. Box 33108, Kansas City MO 64114-0108. 816/941-4000.

NATIONAL PARALEGAL ASSOCIATION
P.O. Box 629, 6186 Honey Hollow Road, Doylestown PA 18901. 215/297-8333.

MANUFACTURING: CONSUMER   MISCELLANEOUS

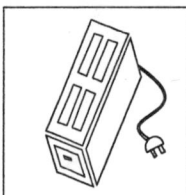

Because the consumer products industry is so diversified, industry outlooks depend more on specific product categories. Here's a sampling: Soaps and Detergents: One of the biggest trends in this category has been to move away from the environmentally damaging phosphates used in detergents. In fact, about 40 percent of the nation has banned phosphates altogether, instead using natural soaps made of tallow and tropical oils. Overall, employment in this area will be increasing. Household Products: The short-term prognosis depends on consumer confidence.
Although disposable incomes have risen slightly, many consumers are replenishing savings and paying off debts instead of buying expensive new items. A recovery in housing and the aging baby-boom generation should contribute to the long-term health of this segment.

AMERICAN TAPE COMPANY
317 Kendall Avenue, Marysville MI 48040. 313/364-9000. **Contact:** Bruce Weinberg, Personnel Director. **Description:** A manufacturer and distributor of masking tape, reinforced tape, and fiberglass tape. **Employees:** 400.

THE KOREX COMPANY
P.O. Box 175, 50000 West Pontiac Trail, Wixom MI 48393. 313/624-0000. **Contact:** Human Resources Department. **Description:** A company engaged in the manufacture and distribution of soaps and detergents. **Employees:** 100.

SILVER'S, INC.
151 West Fort Street, Detroit MI 48226. 313/963-0000. **Contact:** Tom Howe, Director of Human Resources. **Description:** A metropolitan Detroit corporation engaged in corporate and retail sale of office products and office furniture. **Employees:** 275. **Common positions:** Accountant; Administrator; Buyer; Customer Service Representative; Sales Representative; Retail Sales. **Educational backgrounds sought:** Accounting; Art/Design; Business Administration; Communications; Finance; Liberal Arts; Marketing. **Benefits:** medical, dental, and life insurance; employee discounts; savings plan. **Corporate headquarters:** This location. **Operations at this facility:** administration; sales.

STANLEY DOOR SYSTEMS
1225 East Maple Road, Troy MI 48083. 313/528-1400. **Contact:** Roland Bourassa, Personnel Manager. **Description:** Stanley Door Systems, a division of The Stanley Works, is a manufacturer and distributor of residential entry and

garage doors, garage door openers, gate openers, radio controls and security systems. **Common positions:** Accountant; Computer Programmer; Operations/Production Manager; Personnel and Labor Relations Specialist; Quality Controller; Sales Representative; Systems Analyst. **Educational backgrounds sought:** Accounting; Business Administration; Computer Science; Liberal Arts; Marketing. Training programs and internships offered. **Benefits:** Medical insurance; dental insurance; pension plan; life insurance; tuition assistance; disability coverage; profit sharing; employee discounts; savings plan. **Corporate headquarters:** New Britain, CT. Operations at this facility: manufacturing; research and development; administration; service; sales. **Listed on:** New York Stock Exchange. **Revenues (1991):** $2 billion.

Additional large employers: 250+

WOOD HOUSEHOLD FURNITURE, UPHOLSTERED

La-Z-Boy Chair Co
1284 N Telegraph, Monroe MI 48161-3390. 313/242-1444.
Employs: 1000+.

METAL HOUSEHOLD FURNITURE

Michigan State Inds
4000 Cooper St, Lansing MI 48909. 517/373-4277.
Employs: 500-999.

SOAP AND OTHER DETERGENTS, EXCEPT DIAGNOSTIC SUBSTANCES

Diversey Corp
1532 Biddle Ave, Wyandotte MI 48192-3707. 313/281-0930. Employs: 500-999.

GAMES, TOYS AND CHILDREN'S VEHICLES, EXCEPT DOLLS AND BICYCLES

Lionel Trains Inc
26750 23 Mile Rd, Harrison Twp MI 48045. 313/949-4100.
Employs: 500-999.

MISC. SPORTING AND ATHLETIC GOODS

American Plastic Toys Inc
799 Ladd Rd, Walled Lake MI 48390-3025. 313/624-4881.
Employs: 250-499.

SIGNS AND ADVERTISING SPECIALTIES

Trans-Industries Inc

2637 N Adams Rd, Rochester MI 48309-3101. 313/852-1990. Employs: 250-499.

MISC. MANUFACTURING INDUSTRIES

Mid-Michigan Industries Inc
2374 Parkway Dr, Mount Pleasant MI 48858-1163.
517/773-6918. Employs: 250-499.

Modern Engineering Svc
28000 Dequindre Rd, Warren MI 48092-2468. 313/574-9600. Employs: 1000+.

FURNITURE

Carson Business Interiors
2935 Northwestern Hwy Ste 300, Southfield MI 48034.
313/356-6550. Employs: 50-99.

International Foam & Trim
1040 Hurst Rd, Jackson MI 49201-8905. 517/750-9011.
Employs: 50-99.

HOMEFURNISHINGS

Jack Gell Textile Co
5700 Federal St, Detroit MI 48209-1219. 313/554-2000.
Employs: 50-99.

Meskin & Davis Inc
14400 Woodrow Wilson St, Detroit MI 48238-1508.
313/869-4006. Employs: 50-99.

Marathon Services Inc
3433 E Warren Ave, Detroit MI 48207-1258. 313/921-2727. Employs: 50-99.

Additional small to medium sized employers: 50-249

WOOD HOUSEHOLD FURNITURE, EXCEPT UPHOLSTERED

Delmer Inds
4739 18th St, Detroit MI 48208-2103. 313/361-1321.
Employs: 50-99.

James Brandt Co
401 N Cochran St, Charlotte MI 48813-1125. 517/543-5330. Employs: 50-99.

Little Lake Inds
7565 Academy Rd, Cedar Lake MI 48812. 517/427-5057.
Employs: 50-99.

MATTRESSES, FOUNDATIONS AND CONVERTIBLE BEDS

Comfort Mattress Inc
30450 Little Mack Ave, Roseville MI 48066-1707.
313/293-4000. Employs: 50-99.

Sealy Mattress Of Mi
21450 Trolley Indl Dr, Taylor MI 48180. 313/292-0700.
Employs: 100-249.

MISCELLANEOUS HOUSEHOLD FURNITURE

H L F Furniture Inc
44001 Van Born Rd, Belleville MI 48111-1149. 313/697-3000. Employs: 50-99.

PUBLIC BUILDING AND RELATED FURNITURE

Charlotte Co Inc
815 Front St Box 417, Belding MI 48809-2235. 616/794-1700. Employs: 100-249.

Johnson Controls Inc
126 N Groesbeck Hwy, Mount Clemens MI 48043-5428. 313/469-4545. Employs: 100-249.

Michigan Seat Co
2313 Brooklyn Rd, Jackson MI 49203-4749. 517/787-3650. Employs: 100-249.

WOOD OFFICE AND STORE FIXTURES, PARTITIONS, SHELVING AND LOCKERS

Detroit Partition Co
14236 Birwood St, Detroit MI 48238-2208. 313/933-5900. Employs: 50-99.

Equipment Manufacturing Co
21550 Hoover Rd, Warren MI 48089-3160. 313/332-5758. Employs: 100-249.

Ferrante Manufacturing Co
6626 Gratiot Ave, Detroit MI 48207-1912. 313/571-1111. Employs: 50-99.

Unique Custom Store Fixtures
60 Baldwin Rd, Pontiac MI 48342-1275. 313/253-9800. Employs: 50-99.

OFFICE AND STORE FIXTURES, PARTITIONS, SHELVING AND LOCKERS, EXCEPT WOOD

Admiral Inds Inc
155 S Waterman St, Detroit MI 48209-3065. 313/842-6363. Employs: 50-99.

Draco
5225 Williams Lake Rd, Waterford MI 48329-3557. 313/674-4626. Employs: 100-249.

H James Industries Inc
424 S Chicago St, Litchfield MI 49252-9744. 517/542-2316. Employs: 50-99.

Marketing Displays Inc
38271 W 12 Mile Rd, Farmington MI 48331-3041. 313/553-1900. Employs: 100-249.

Mid-West Wire Products Inc
800 Woodward Heights Blvd, Ferndale MI 48220-1431. 313/399-5100. Employs: 50-99.

Banning Associates
1154 N Macomb St, Monroe MI 48161-3145. 313/241-3364. Employs: 50-99.

DRAPERY HARDWARE AND WINDOW BLINDS AND SHADES

House Of Blinds & More Inc
23000 W 8 Mile Rd, Southfield MI 48034-4394. 313/357-4710. Employs: 50-99.

Shady Inds Inc
2240 Greer Blvd, Keego Harbor MI 48320-1469. 313/681-3131. Employs: 100-249.

MISCELLANEOUS FURNITURE AND FIXTURES

Lee L Woodard Inc
317 S Elm St, Owosso MI 48867-2673. 517/723-7881. Employs: 100-249.

Michigan Tube Swagers Inc
1244 W Dean Rd, Temperance MI 48182-9220. 313/847-3875. Employs: 100-249.

SOAP AND OTHER DETERGENTS, EXCEPT SPECIALTY CLEANERS

R & D Distributors
3520 Fenton Rd, Flint MI 48507-1567. 313/767-2235. Employs: 50-99.

Sweeping Beauty Inc
208 E Caroline St, Fenton MI 48430-2106. 313/750-0569. Employs: 50-99.

The Drackett Products Co
2100 Woodward Av Rm 150, Bloomfield MI 48304-2262. 313/258-0333. Employs: 50-99.

SPECIALTY CLEANING, POLISHING AND SANITATION PREPARATIONS

Oakite Products Inc
13177 Huron River Dr, Romulus MI 48174-3631. 313/941-3800. Employs: 50-99.

PERFUMES, COSMETICS AND OTHER TOILET PREPARATIONS

Fragrance World-Perfumania
14750 La Plaisance St Ste H150, Monroe MI 48161. 313/457-3550. Employs: 50-99.

J Scherer Stephen Inc
2850 Commerce Dr, Rochester MI 48309-3816. 313/852-8500. Employs: 50-99.

GAMES, TOYS AND CHILDREN'S VEHICLES, EXCEPT DOLLS AND BICYCLES

Timeline Limited
2032 Congress St Ste 1W, Ypsilanti MI 48197-4414. 313/483-3939. Employs: 50-99.

MISCELLANEOUS SPORTING AND ATHLETIC GOODS

Focus Golf Systs Inc
35005 Automation Dr, Clinton Twp MI 48035-3117. 313/792-6080. Employs: 50-99.

Quality Inds Inc
215 W Mechanic St, Hillsdale MI 49242. 517/439-1591. Employs: 50-99.

School-Tech Inc
745 State Circle, Ann Arbor MI 48108-3024. 313/761-5175. Employs: 50-99.

Snapper Inc
130 N Larch St, Lansing MI 48912-1244. 517/372-0115. Employs: 50-99.

MARKING DEVICES

Volk Corp
23936 Indl Pk Dr, Farmington MI 48335. 313/477-6700. Employs: 50-99.

BROOMS AND BRUSHES

Fuller Brush Sales
706 4th St, Jackson MI 49203-1642. 517/784-3393. Employs: 50-99.

Helmac Products Corp
528 Kelso St, Flint MI 48506-4033. 313/239-7677. Employs: 50-99.

SIGNS AND ADVERTISING SPECIALTIES

Design Fabrication Inc
1080 Naughton Rd, Troy MI 48083-1910. 313/689-8206.
Employs: 50-99.

Detroit Transp-Traffic Sig
1601 Modern St, Detroit MI 48203-2452. 313/876-0271.
Employs: 50-99.

Exhibit Works
13211 Merriman Rd, Livonia MI 48150-1826. 313/525-9010. Employs: 50-99.

Fairmont Sign Co
3750 E Outer Dr, Detroit MI 48234-2946. 313/368-4000.
Employs: 50-99.

Gannett Outdoor Co Of Mi
556 Custer St, Detroit MI 48202-3126. 313/872-6030.
Employs: 50-99.

George P Johnson Co
800 Tech Row, Madison Hts MI 48071-4678. 313/585-5888. Employs: 100-249.

H B Stubbs Co
27027 Mound Rd, Warren MI 48092-2615. 313/574-9700.
Employs: 100-249.

Hexon Corp
700 E Whitcomb, Madison Hts MI 48071-1416. 313/585-7585. Employs: 50-99.

Kux Manufacturing Co
12675 Burt Rd, Detroit MI 48223-3314. 313/255-6460.
Employs: 100-249.

O' Brien Agency Inc
924 Terminal Rd, Lansing MI 48906-3063. 517/321-0188.
Employs: 50-99.

Shaw & Slavsky Inc
13821 Elmira St, Detroit MI 48227-3016. 313/834-3990.
Employs: 100-249.

Vultron Inc
2600 Bond St, Rochester MI 48309-3509. 313/853-2200.
Employs: 100-249.

MISCELLANEOUS MANUFACTURING INDUSTRIES

Advanced Material Process Corp
3850 Howe Rd, Wayne MI 48184-1829. 313/729-1817.
Employs: 50-99.

Arc Inds
7775 18 1/2 Mile Rd #A, Sterling Hts MI 48314-3675.
313/254-8590. Employs: 50-99.

Astro-Netics Inc
1780 E 14 Mile Rd, Madison Hts MI 48071-1543. 313/585-4890. Employs: 100-249.

Creative Inds/Cars & Concepts
255 Rex Blvd, Auburn Hills MI 48326-2954. 313/853-2600. Employs: 50-99.

Irvin Automotive Products Inc
2444 Koppy Blvd, Auburn Hills MI 48326-2634. 313/377-1500. Employs: 100-249.

Irvin Inds
6560 Highland Rd, Waterford MI 48327-1607. 313/666-1133. Employs: 50-99.

T D M Technologies Inc
13000 Farmington Rd, Livonia MI 48150-4201. 313/458-9100. Employs: 50-99.

Walker Engineering Center
3901 Willis Rd, Grass Lake MI 49240-9007. 517/522-5500. Employs: 100-249.

Britt Manufacturing
1805 Cleveland Ave, Port Huron MI 48060-6722. 313/982-9720. Employs: 50-99.

Wolverine Metl Splty Suby
1013 Thorrez Rd, Jackson MI 49201-8903. 517/750-3414.
Employs: 50-99.

For more information on career opportunities in consumer manufacturing:

<u>Associations</u>

ASSOCIATION OF HOME APPLIANCE MANUFACTURERS
20 North Wacker Drive, Chicago IL 60606. 312/984-5800.

NATIONAL ASSOCIATION OF MANUFACTURERS
1331 Pennsylvania Avenue, NW, Suite 1500, Washington DC 20004. 202/637-3000.

NATIONAL HOUSEWARES MANUFACTURERS ASSOCIATION
6400 Schafer Court, Suite 650, Rosemont IL 60018.
708/292-4200.

ASSOCIATION FOR MANUFACTURING TECHNOLOGY
7901 Westpark Drive, McLean VA 22102. 703/893-2900.

SOAP AND DETERGENT ASSOCIATION
475 Park Avenue South, New York NY 10016. 212/725-1262.

<u>Directories</u>

APPLIANCE MANUFACTURER ANNUAL DIRECTORY
Corcoran Communications, Inc., 29100 Aurora Road, Suite 200, Solon OH 44139. 216/349-3060.

HOUSEHOLD AND PERSONAL PRODUCTS INDUSTRY BUYERS GUIDE
Rodman Publishing Group, 17 South Franklin Turnpike, Ramsey NJ 07446. 201/825-2552.

<u>Magazines</u>

APPLIANCE
1110 Jorie Boulevard, Oak Brook IL 60522-9019. 708/990-3484.

COSMETICS INSIDERS REPORT
Advanstar Communications, 7500 Old Oak Boulevard, Cleveland OH 44130. 216/243-8100.

HOUSEWARES
Harcourt Brace Jovanovich, 1 East First Street, Duluth MN 55802. 714/231-6616.

MANUFACTURING: MISCELLANEOUS INDUSTRIAL

Trend to watch for: In the machinery manufacturing segment, many of the biggest company names will continue to disappear due to mergers and buy outs. While hundreds of U.S. companies still make machine tools, materials handling equipment, and compressors for American factories, the fastest-growing machinery markets are now overseas. This means that U.S. firms will have to build overseas presences just to survive. In fact, foreign orders for a number of American-made tools remain strong.

Although mergers are often followed by layoffs, workers who survive these cuts should be better positioned for the long-term. Many manufacturers are giving workers a much greater degree of across-the-board involvement, with team-based product management allowing individual workers to gain training in a number of different job functions.

ATLAS TOOL INC.
29880 Groesbeck Highway, Roseville MI 48066. 313/778-3570. **Contact:** Markus Schmidt, Owner. **Description:** A leading area manufacturer of special dies and tools. **Employees:** 200.

BRASS-CRAFT MANUFACTURING COMPANY
100 Galleria Office Center, Suite 100, Southfield MI 48034. 313/827-1100. **Contact:** Don Vogler, Office Manager. **Description:** Engaged in the manufacture of plumbing supplies, including valves, drainage tubular, copper water inlet tubes, flexible appliance connectors, brass fittings, and accessories. **Employees:** 1,100. **Common positions:** Accountant; Advertising Worker; Computer Programmer; Credit Manager; Customer Service Representative; Industrial Engineer; Personnel and Labor Relations Specialist; Purchasing Agent; Quality Controller; Systems Analyst; Transportation and Traffic Specialist. **Educational backgrounds sought:** Accounting; Business Administration; Computer Science; Engineering; Finance; Marketing. **Benefits:** medical, dental, and life insurance; pension plan; tuition assistance; disability coverage; profit sharing; employee discounts; savings plan; stock options. **Other U.S. locations:** North Carolina, California, Texas. **Parent company:** Maco Corporation. **Operations at this facility:** Administration.

BUNDY CORPORATION
12345 East 9 Mile Road, Warren MI 48090. 313/758-6500. **Contact:** Mr. Lef Nursey, Personnel Director. **Description:** A manufacturer of steel pipe and small diameter steel tubing. **Employees:** 2,900

CMI INTERNATIONAL INC.
30333 Southfield Road, Southfield MI 48076. 313/642-9450. **Contact:** Personnel Department. **Description:** Engaged in the manufacture of aluminum foundries and cast metal.

CADILLAC PRODUCTS INC.
1650 Research Driveay, Suite 200, Troy MI 48083-2100. 313/740-4000. **Contact:** Bob Sughroue, Director of Human Resources. **Description:** Engaged in the manufacture of plastic, thermo-formed plastics, paper packaging materials, and automotive parts. **Employees:** 400. **Common positions:** Accountant; Administrator; Blue-Collar Worker Supervisor; Buyer; Computer Programmer; Customer Service Representative; Draftsperson; Chemical Engineer; Electrical Engineer; Industrial Engineer; Mechanical Engineer; Financial Analyst; Department Manager; Operations/Production Manager; Purchasing Agent; Quality Control Supervisor; Sales Representative. **Educational backgrounds sought:** Accounting; Business Administration; Chemistry; Computer Science; Engineering; Finance; Marketing. **Benefits:** medical, dental, and life insurance; pension plan; tuition assistance; disability coverage; profit sharing; savings plan. **Corporate headquarters:** This location. **Operations at this facility:** regional headquarters.

CARBIDEX WYANDOTTE CORPORATION
4459 Thirteenth Street, Wyandotte MI 48192. 313/283-3000. **Contact:** Katie Chambers, Personnel. **Description:** A precision metal stamping company serving the automotive, computer, hardware, and electronic industries. **Common positions:** Accountant; Buyer; Customer Service Representative; General Manager; Operations/Production Manager; Purchasing Agent; Sales Representative. **Educational backgrounds sought:** Engineering; Purchasing; Design Engineering. **Benefits:** medical and life insurance; profit sharing. **Corporate headquarters:** This location. Operations at this facility: divisional headquarters; manufacturing; research/development; administration; service; sales.

CARBOLOY, INC.
P.O. Box 330237, Detroit MI 48232-6237. 313/497-5000. **Contact:** Joseph J. Bontomasi, Jr., Director/Human Resources. **Description:** Engaged in the manufacture of carbide cutting tools. **Common positions:** Electrical Engineer; Mechanical Engineer; Metallurgical Engineer; Marketing Specialist; Quality Controller; Sales Representative. **Educational backgrounds sought:** Business Administration; Engineering; Marketing. **Benefits:** medical insurance; dental insurance; pension plan; life insurance; tuition assistance; disability coverage; savings plan. **Corporate headquarters:** This location. **Operations at this facility:** manufacturing; administration; service; sales. **Employees:** 675.

CARGILL DETROIT CORPORATION
1250 Crooks Road, Clawson MI 48017. 313/435-3500. **Contact:** Personnel Department. **Description:** A leading area company engaged in the design and manufacture of special machine tools.

CARRON & COMPANY INC.
26700 Princeton, Inkster MI 48141. 313/274-2300. **Contact:** John Marek, Personnel Manager. **Description:** A leading manufacturer of metal stampings and automotive prototypes. **Employees:** 600. **Common positions:** Draftsperson. Principal educational backgrounds include: Engineering. **Benefits:** medical, dental, and life insurance; pension plan; tuition assistance; disability coverage. **Corporate headquarters:** This location. Operations at this facility: manufacturing; research/development; administration; sales.

CENTRI-SPRAY CORPORATION
39001 Schoolcraft, Livonia MI 48150. 313/464-0100. **Contact:** Personnel Director. **Description:** A manufacturer of industrial heating and thermo-bonding equipment. **Employees:** 300.

CHRYSLER/TRENTON ENGINE DIVISION
2000 Van Horne Road, Trenton MI 48183. 313/671-4129. **Contact:** R.J. Horoky, Personnel Manager. **Description:** A major area manufacturer of industrial combustion engines. **Employees:** 3,000.

CONCORD TOOL AND MANUFACTURING
106 North Groesbeck, Mount Clemens MI 48043. 313/465-6537. **Contact:** Personnel Director. **Description:** Engaged in the manufacture of special dies and tools. **Employees:** 100.

CONTAINER PRODUCTS INC.
20245 12 Mile Road, Suite 200, Southfield MI 48076. 313/827-7720. **Contact:** Ms. Sue Paul, Personnel Director. **Description:** A leading area manufacturer of industrial steel drums and plastic containers. **Employees:** 500.

CONVEYOR-MATIC INC.
31475 Utica Road, Fraser MI 48026. 313/296-0200. **Contact:** Fred Kysia, General Manager. **Description:** An area company engaged in the manufacture and distribution of conveyor systems and equipment.

CREATIVE FOAM CORPORATION
300 North Alloy, Fenton MI 48430. . **Contact:** Salary Employment. **Description:** Foam fabricator and manufacturer of OEM foam products and foam packaging. **Common positions:** Customer Service Representative; Industrial Engineer; Mechanical Engineer; Operations/Production Manager; Quality Control Supervisor; Sales Representative. **Educational backgrounds sought:** Business Administration; Engineering. **Benefits:** medical and life insurance; tuition assistance; disability coverage; profit sharing; employee discounts; savings plan; 401K. **Corporate headquarters:** This location. **Operations at this facility:** manufacturing; research/development; administration; sales.

CROSS COMPANY
17801 14 Mile Road, Fraser MI 48026. 313/293-3000. **Contact:** Tom Trecker, Personnel Director. **Description:** A leading Detroit company engaged in the manufacture of machine tools.

D-M-E CORPORATION
29111 Stephenson Highway, Madison Heights MI 48071. 313/398-6000. **Contact:** Deb Ruwart, Manager of Employee Relations. A manufacturer of tooling products for the plastics industry. **Common positions:** Accountant; Advertising Worker; Blue-Collar Worker Supervisor; Buyer; Computer Programmer; Credit Manager; Customer Service Representative; Electrical Engineer; Industrial Engineer; Mechanical Engineer; Metallurgical Engineer; Financial Analyst; Operations/Production Manager; Marketing Specialist; Personnel and Labor Relations Specialist; Purchasing Agent; Quality Control Supervisor; Sales Representative; Systems Analyst; Transportation and Traffic Specialist. **Educational backgrounds sought:** Accounting; Business Administration; Computer Science; Engineering; Finance; Marketing. **Special programs:** training programs. **Benefits:** medical, dental and life insurance; pension plan; tuition assistance; disability coverage; savings plan. **Corporate headquarters:** This location. **Parent company:** Fairchild Corporation. **Operations at this facility:** manufacturing; research/development; administration; service; sales. **Employees:** 1,000.

DANA CORPORATION/FORMSPRAG-WARREN PLANT
INDUSTRIAL POWER TRANSMISSION DIVISION
Box 778, 23601 Hoover, Warren MI 48090. 313/758-5000, ext. 245. **Contact:** Kirby Smith, Human Resources Manager. **Description:** The Warren Plant manufactures precision sprag-clutches for machine tool and aerospace industries. **Employees:** approximately 150.

DEARBORN FABRICATING AND ENGINEERING
19440 Glendale, Detroit MI 48223. 313/273-2800. **Contact:** Personnel Department. **Description:** A company engaged in the manufacture of conveyor systems and equipment. **Employees:** 100.

DELTA TOOLING COMPANY
1360 East Big Beaver, Troy MI 48083. 313/689-4990. **Contact:** Personnel Department. **Description:** An area company engaged in the manufacture of industrial patterns. **Employees:** 200.

DETROIT DIESEL CORPORATION
13400 West Outer Drive, Detroit MI 48239-4001. 313/592-5101. **Contact:** Salaried Personnel Administration. **Description:** The Detroit Diesel Corporation (formerly Detroit Diesel Allison-General Motors Corporation) is 80% owned by Penske Corporation and 20% by General Motors. It is one of the leading U.S. manufacturers of heavy-duty diesel engines for use in the transportation, construction, industrial, marine, and stationary power markets. The world headquarters is located in Detroit MI; regional sales offices are located in San

Francisco, Atlanta, Detroit, Red Bank, and Dallas. **Common positions:** Customer Service Representative; Electrical Engineer; Industrial Engineer; Mechanical Engineer; Sales Representative; Quality Control Engineer; Manufacturing Engineer. **Educational backgrounds sought:** Business Administration; Engineering. **Benefits:** medical, dental, and life insurance; pension plan; tuition assistance; disability coverage; profit sharing; employee discounts; savings plan. **Operations at this facility:** research/development; administration; service; sales.

DOMINION TOOL AND DIE
15736 Sturgeon, Roseville MI 48066. 313/773-3303. **Contact:** Mary Trometer, Personnel Director. **Description:** Engaged in the manufacture of special dies and tools. **Employees:** 100.

DURR AUTOMATION, INC
10301 Enterprise Drive, Davisburg MI 48350. 313/625-5400. **Contact:** Personnel Director. **Description:** Manufacturer of Assembly Systems, Automation, and Industry Parts Washers. **Employees:** 100. **Common positions:** Electrical Engineer; Mechanical Engineer; Sales Representative. **Educational backgrounds sought:** Engineering. **Benefits:** medical, dental, and life insurance; tuition assistance; disability coverage. **Corporate headquarters:** This location. **Operations at this facility:** manufacturing; administration; service; sales.

DURR INDUSTRIES INC.
P.O. Box 2129, Plymouth MI 48170. 313/459-6800. **Contact:** Diana Thomas, Payroll Supervisor. **Description:** Areas of operation include: paint finishing systems, automation metal cleaning technology, robot systems, and related environmental equipment. Regional headquarters location. **Corporate headquarters:** Stuttgart, West Germany. **Common positions:** Accountant; Buyer; Computer Programmer; Draftsperson; Engineer; Electrical Engineer; Mechanical Engineer; Sales Representative. **Educational backgrounds sought:** Accounting; Computer Science; Engineering; Finance. **Benefits:** medical, dental, and life insurance; tuition assistance; disability coverage; profit sharing.

EVANS INDUSTRIES
200 Renaissance Center, Suite 3150, Detroit MI 48243. 313/259-2266. **Contact:** Barry Woodrow, President. **Description:** A private conglomerate engaged in the manufacture of various industrial products. **Educational backgrounds sought:** Business Administration. **Corporate headquarters:** This location.

FARNAM SEALING SYSTEMS
650 Stevenson Hwy, Troy MI 48083. 313/362-5457. **Contact:** Carolyn Kott, Human Resources. **Description:** An area manufacturer of gaskets. **Employees:** 400.

FEDERAL-MOGUL CORPORATION

P.O. Box 1966, Detroit MI 48235. 313/354-7700. **Contact:** Personnel Department. **Description:** A manufacturer of cylindrical and tapered roller bearings, bushings, sleeve bearings, ball bearings, thrust washers, and related products. **Corporate headquarters:** This location.

FISONS INSTRUMENTS/ARL

15300 Rotunda Drive, Suite 306, Dearborn MI 48120. 313/336-3900. **Contact:** Jim Faber, Service Manager. **Description:** A major area company which manufactures and installs measuring, controlling, and analytical instruments.

FORWARD INDUSTRIES INC.

25315 Kean Street, Dearborn MI 48124. 313/278-0200. **Contact:** Cindy Haslem, Personnel Director. **Description:** A manufacturer of special dies and tools. **Common positions:** Accountant; Administrator; Buyer; Computer Programmer; Draftsperson; Electrical Engineer Mechanical Engineer; Department Manager; General Manager; Purchasing Agent; Sales Representative. **Educational backgrounds sought:** Accounting; Computer Science; Engineering; Marketing.**Corporate headquarters:** This location. **Parent company:** Livernois Engineering Co. **Operations at this facility:** manufacturing.

GT PRODUCTS

P.O. Box 1404, Ann Arbor MI 48106. 313/761-7666. **Contact:** Fran Lobbestael, Personnel Manager. **Description:** A Southeastern Michigan company engaged in the manufacture of valves and screw machine parts.

GALLAGHER-KAISER CORPORATION

13710 Mt. Eliot, Detroit MI 48212. 313/368-3100. **Contact:** Personnel Department. **Description:** Manufacturer of paint finishing systems and air pollution control equipment.

GELMAN SCIENCES INC.

600 South Wagner Road, Ann Arbor MI 48106. 313/665-0651. **Contact:** Human Resources. **Description:** Engaged in the manufacture of micro-filtration devices. **Employees:** 625. **Common positions:** Biomedical Engineer; Chemical Engineer; Sales Representative; Quality Engineer. **Educational backgrounds sought:** Biology; Chemistry; Engineering. Special programs: Internships. **Benefits:** medical, dental, and life insurance; tuition assistance; disability coverage; profit sharing; savings plan. **Corporate headquarters:** This location. **Operations at this facility:** Manufacturing; Research and Development; Administration; Service. **Listed on:** American Stock Exchange. **Projected hires for the next 12 months:** 35.

GILCO INC.

16000 Common Road, Roseville MI 48066. 313/779-5850. **Contact:** Personnel. **Description:** Engaged in the manufacture of wire springs. **Employees:** 200.

HERCULES MACHINE TOOL AND DIE
13920 East 10 Mile Road, Warren MI 48089. 313/778-4120. **Contact:** Joseph Bering, Vice President/General Manager. **Description:** Engaged in the manufacture of special dies and tools. **Employees:** 200.

HOLNAM INC.
P.O. Box 122, Dundee MI 48131. 313/529-2411. **Contact:** Suzanne Prokup, Human Resource Development Manager. **Description:** An area manufacturer and distributor of hydraulic cement. **Employees:** 3,000.

ISI MANUFACTURING INC.
P.O. Box 220, Fraser MI 48026. 313/294-9500. **Contact:** Personnel Department. **Description:** Engaged in the manufacture of non-electrical machinery.

ITW WOODWORTH COMPANY
1300 East 9 Mile Road, Ferndale MI 48220. 313/541-7500. **Contact:** Bill Murray, Director of Personnel. **Description:** Engaged in the manufacture of metal working machinery. **Employees:** 200.

INDUCTOHEAT INC.
32251 North Avis Drive, Madison Heights MI 48071. 313/585-9393. **Contact:** Marge Piercey, Personnel Director. **Description:** Engaged in the manufacture of industrial furnaces. **Employees:** 500.

INDUSTRIAL TECTONICS INC.
P.O. Box 1128, Ann Arbor MI 48106. 313/426-4681. **Contact:** Aurora Dickson, Personnel Director. **Description:** Engaged in the manufacture of high precision spherical products. **Employees:** 95.

IROQUOIS DIE AND MANUFACTURING COMPANY
24400 Hoover Road, Warren MI 48089. 313/756-6920. **Contact:** Gary Laine, Controller. **Description:** Engaged in the manufacture of special dies and tools. **Employees:** 100.

GEORGE L. JOHNSTON COMPANY
1200 Holden Avenue, Detroit MI 48202. **Contact:** Thomas C. Perna, Personnel. **Description:** Wholesale trader of refrigeration, heating, and air conditioning parts and equipment. **Employees:** 100. E.O.E.

KASPER MACHINE COMPANY
29275 Stephenson Highway, Madison Heights MI 48071. 313/547-3150. **Contact:** Jack Accardo, Vice President of Human Resources. **Description:** A company engaged in the manufacture of machine tools. **Employees:** 100.

KENT-MOORE CORPORATION
28635 Mound Road, Warren MI 48092. 313/574-2332. **Contact:** Dave Mied, Personnel Director. **Description:** Engaged in the manufacture of special industrial machines. **Employees:** 1,000.

KEY MANUFACTURING GROUP
3200 West 14 Mile Road, Royal Oak MI 48073. 313/280-0880. **Contact:** Nancy Hill, Administrative Assistant. Manufacturers of automotive and industrial fasteners. **Common positions:** Accountant; Blue-Collar Worker Supervisor; Financial Analyst; Industrial Manager; Operations/Production Manager; Personnel and Labor Relations Specialist; Purchasing Agent; Quality Control Supervisor. **Educational backgrounds sought:** Accounting; Business Administration; Computer Science; Engineering; Finance. **Special programs:** training programs. **Benefits:** medical, dental and life insurance; pension plan; tuition assistance; disability coverage; savings plan. **Corporate headquarters:** This location. **Operations at this facility:** manufacturing; administration; sales.

KLOCKNER NAMASCO CORPORATION
P.O. Box 638, Roseville MI 48066-0638. 313/779-7950. **Contact:** Marie MacMillan, Corporate Human Resources Manager. **Description:** Sales, storage, and processing of steel products. **Common positions:** Accountant; Administrator; Blue-Collar Worker Supervisor; Computer Programmer; Credit Manager; Customer Service Representative; Electrical Engineer; Industrial Engineer; Mechanical Engineer; Metalurgical Engineer; Financial Analyst; Branch Manager; Department Manager; General Manager; Management Trainee; Operations/Production Manager; Marketing Specialist; Personnel and Labor Relations Specialist; Purchasing Agent; Quality Control Supervisor; Sales Representative; Systems Analyst. **Educational backgrounds sought:** Accounting; Business Administration; Communications; Computer Science; Engineering; Finance. **Special programs:** Training programs. **Benefits:** medical insurance; dental insurance; pension plan; life insurance; tuition assistance; disability coverage; employee discounts; savings plan. **Corporate headquarters:** This location.

KOLENE CORPORATION
12890 Westwood, Detroit MI 48223. 313/273-9220. **Contact:** Personnel. **Description:** A metropolitan Detroit company engaged in the sale of metal cleaning chemicals and related equipment. **Corporate headquarters:** This location. **Operations at this facility:** manufacturing; research and development; administration; service; sales.

LAMINA INC.
14925 West 11 Mile Road, Oak Park MI 48237. 313/542-8341. **Contact:** Bob Capoccia, Personnel Manager. **Description:** Engaged in the manufacture of special dies and tools. **Employees:** 300.

MPI INTERNATIONAL, INC.

2129 Austin Ave., Rochester Hills MI 48309. 313/853-9010. **Contact:** Robert R. Kurth, Director of Operations. **Description:** An international company with four operating divisions which manufacturers precision fineblanked stampings including finishing and assembly operations. Markets/applications include automotive, computer, scientific and medical. **Common positions:** Mechanical Engineer; Quality Engineer. **Educational backgrounds sought:** Engineering. **Special programs:** training programs; internships. **Benefits:** medical and life insurance; pension plan; tuition assistance; disability coverage; profit sharing. **Corporate headquarters:** This location. **Other U.S. locations:** Knox, Indiana; Deerfield, Wisconsin; Spartanburg, South Carolina. **Operations at this facility:** administration.

MALLOY MANUFACTURING

18450 15 Mile Road, Fraser MI 48026. 313/293-9000. **Contact:** Mario Bastianelli, Personnel Director. **Description:** Engaged in the manufacture of blast furnaces. **Employees:** 300.

MASCO CORPORATION

21001 Van Born, Taylor MI 48180. 313/274-7400. **Contact:** Personnel Department. **Description:** A major area manufacturer of plumbing fixtures and fittings. **Employees:** 800.

MATHER SEAL
A SUBSIDIARY OF FEDERAL MOGUL

525 Redman Road, Milan MI 48160-1222. 313/439-2481. **Contact:** Carol Schuler, Employee Relations Manager. **Description:** A major Southeastern Michigan manufacturer of teflon seals. **Employees:** 200.

McCLAIN INDUSTRIES INC.

6200 Elmridge, Sterling Heights MI 48310. 313/264-3611. **Contact:** Personnel Department. **Description:** Engaged in the manufacture of industrial machines. **Employees:** 100.

NSK CORPORATION

P.O. Box 1507, Ann Arbor MI 48106-1507. 313/761-9500. **Contact:** James Breen, Manager of Human Resources. **Description:** An area company engaged in the manufacture of ball bearings. **Employees:** 1030. **Common positions:** Accountant; Buyer; Computer Programmer; Customer Service Representative; Electrical Engineer; Mechanical Engineer; Financial Analyst; Operations/Production Manager; Marketing Specialist; Purchasing Agent; Quality Control Supervisor. **Educational backgrounds sought:** Accounting; Computer Science; Engineering; Marketing; Physics. **Benefits:** medical, dental, and life insurance; pension plan; tuition assistance; disability coverage; savings plan. **Corporate headquarters:** This location. **Parent company:** NSK-Tokyo. **Operations at this facility:** corporate headquarters; research/development; administration. **Listed on:** Tokyo Exchange.

NEWCOR INC.
1825 South Woodward, Suite 240, Bloomfield Hills MI 48302. 313/253-2400. **Contact:** Thomas Parker, Personnel Director. **Description:** Engaged in the manufacture of metalworking machinery. **Employees:** 700.

OVERHEAD CONVEYOR INC.
1330 Hilton Road, Ferndale MI 48220. 313/547-3800. **Contact:** Personnel. **Description:** Engaged in the manufacture of conveyor systems and related equipment. **Employees:** 100.

PBM INTERMET
50925 Richard W. Boulevard, Chesterfield MI 48051. 313/949-1433. **Contact:** Sandra Lauch, Personnel Director. **Description:** Engaged in the manufacture of non-electrical machinery. **Employees:** 200.

PASLIN COMPANY
25411 Ryan Road, Warren MI 48091. 313/758-0200. **Contact:** Personnel Department. **Description:** An area company engaged in the manufacture of special dies and tools. **Employees:** 100.

PEERLESS INDUSTRIES/YPSILANTI DIVISION
2800 Tyler Road, Ypsilanti MI 48197. 313/482-3900. **Contact:** Karen Beisch, Human Resources Manager. **Description:** A leading area manufacturer of screw machine products. **Employees:** 200.

PENINSULAR DIESEL INC.
P.O. Box 907, Dearborn MI 48121-0907. 313/584-5800. **Contact:** David Miller, Controller. **Description:** A leading area wholesale distributor of industrial machinery and equipment. **Employees:** 200.

PROGRESSIVE TOOL AND INDUSTRIAL
21000 Telegraph Road, Southfield MI 48034. 313/353-8888. **Contact:** Fred Beagle, Personnel. **Description:** A major Southeastern Michigan manufacturer of special dies and tools. **Employees:** 1,200.

R & B MACHINE TOOL COMPANY
P.O. Box 100, Saline MI 48176. 313/429-9421. **Contact:** T. Cornelius, Director of Operations and Training. **Description:** A Southeastern Michigan manufacturer of metal cutting machinery. **Employees:** 200. **Common positions:** Computer Programmer; Draftsperson; Electrical Engineer; Mechanical Engineer; Blue-Collar Worker Supervisor; Industrial Engineer; Metallurgical Engineer; Operations/Production Manager; Personnel and Labor Relations Specialist; Sales Representative. **Educational backgrounds sought:** Engineering; Mathematics; Business Administration. **Benefits:** medical, dental, and life insurance; pension plan; disability coverage; profit sharing; Tuition Assistance. **Corporate headquarters:** This location. **Operations at this facility:** manufacturing; sales. **Special programs:** Training programs. **Employees:** 235. **Projected hires for the next 12 months:** 5.

REPUBLIC DIE AND TOOL COMPANY
P.O. Box 339, Belleville MI 48112. 313/699-3400. **Contact:** Mark Prendeville, Personnel. **Description:** A leading area manufacturer of special dies and tools. **Employees:** 400.

RICHFIELD IRON WORKS INC.
3313 Richfield, Flint MI 48506. 313/736-2110. **Contact:** Dick McKenzie, Comptroller. **Description:** A manufacturer of shipping and storage racks. **Employees:** 200.

RITE-ON INDUSTRIES INC.
12540 Beech Daley Road, Redford MI 48239. 313/937-2000. **Contact:** Margaret Caron, Personnel. **Description:** A leading Southeastern Michigan manufacturer of metal cutting machinery.

ROSS OPERATING VALVE COMPANY
P.O. Box 7015, Troy MI 48007-7015. 313/362-1250. **Contact:** Susan L. Osborn, Personnel Assistant. Manufacturer of directional air control devices and related pneumatic products. **Corporate headquarters:** This location. **Operations include:** administration; service; sales. **Common positions:** Accountant; Administrator; Advertising Worker; Computer Programmer; Customer Service Representative; Industrial Engineer; Financial Analyst; Department Manager; Marketing Specialist; Personnel and Labor Relations Specialist; Sales Representative; Systems Analyst; Fluid Power Specialist. **Educational backgrounds sought:** Accounting; Business Administration; Communications; Computer Science; Finance; Marketing. **Benefits:** medical insurance; dental insurance; pension plan; life insurance; tuition assistance; disability coverage; profit sharing.

SCHWEITZER CORPORATION
P.O. Box 46, Madison Heights MI 48071. 313/583-1900. **Contact:** Bill Harry, Personnel Director. **Description:** Engaged in the manufacture of industrial furnaces. **Employees:** 400.

STAR CUTTER COMPANY
23461 Industrial Park Drive, Farmington Hills MI 48335. 313/474-8200. **Contact:** Howard Didier, Personnel Department. **Description:** A major area manufacturer of machine tools.

H.O. TRERICE COMPANY
12950 West 8 Mile Road, Oak Park MI 48237. 313/399-8000. **Contact:** Joe Zub, Personnel Director. **Description:** Engaged in the manufacture of industrial instruments. **Employees:** 300.

US GROUP INC.

20580 Hoover Road, Detroit MI 48205. 313/372-7900. **Contact:** General Manager. **Description:** A Detroit-based company which manufactures pumps and related equipment. **Employees:** 300.

VISIONEERING, INC.

P.O. Box 127, Fraser MI 48026. 313/293-1000. **Contact:** Angela Goudreau, Human Resources Director. **Description:** Producer of first class tooling for major automotive and aerospace manufacturers around the world. The company uses the latest CAD/CAM, machining and material technologies to remain at the leading edge of model and tooling techniques. **Common positions:** Computer Programmer; Aerospace Engineer; Industrial Engineer; Mechanical Engineer; Tool Builder. **Educational backgrounds sought:** Engineering. **Benefits:** medical insurance; dental insurance; life insurance; tuition assistance; disability coverage; 401K plan. **Corporate headquarters:** This location. **Operations at this facility:** manufacturing; administration; sales.

WALBRO AUTOMATIC CORPORATION

P.O. Box 291, Lambertville MI 48144. 313/856-4151. **Contact:** Robert Balger, Personnel Administrator. **Description:** Engaged in product design, brazed assemblies, precision stamping, refrigeration products, and auto parts. **Corporate headquarters:** This location. Send resumes to 925 North Main Street, Ligonier IN 46767. **Common positions:** Accountant; Administrator; Blue-Collar Worker Supervisor; Buyer; Computer Programmer; Credit Manager; Draftsperson; Engineer; Mechanical Engineer; Industrial Designer; Operations/Production Manager; Personnel and Labor Relations Specialist; Purchasing Agent; Quality Control Supervisor. **Benefits:** medical, dental, and life insurance; pension plan; tuition assistance; disability coverage.

JERVIS B. WEBB COMPANY

34375 West Twelve Mile Road, Farmington Hills MI 48331. 313/553-1000. **Contact:** Human Resources. **Description:** Engaged in the design, fabrication, and installation of material handling systems. Custom engineered products include conveyors, driverless vehicles, and automated storage and retrieval systems. Established in 1919, the firm maintains sales offices and plant locations throughout the United States, and through foreign licenses around the world. **Common positions:** Computer Programmer; Draftsperson; Civil Engineer; Electrical Engineer; Industrial Engineer; Mechanical Engineer. **Educational background sought:** Engineering. **Benefits:** medical, dental, and life insurance; pension plan; tuition assistance; disability coverage; savings plan.

WELDMATION

31720 Stephenson Highway, Madison Heights MI 48071. 313/585-0010. **Contact:** Personnel Department. **Description:** A leading area manufacturer of welding apparatus. **Employees:** 300.

WILLIAMS INTERNATIONAL CORPORATION

P.O. Box 200, Walled Lake MI 48390-0200. 313/624-5200. **Contact:** Manager of Personnel. **Description:** Engaged in the manufacture of gas turbine engines. Industry classifications: aerospace (primary), applied research, basic scientific research, defense. Established 1955. **Employees:** 2,000.

WILSON AUTOMATION COMPANY

27101 Groesbeck Highway, Warren MI 48089. 313/776-8000. **Contact:** Mike Anderson, Chief Controller. **Description:** Engaged in the manufacture of special industrial machines. **Employees:** 100.

WIRTZ MANUFACTURING COMPANY INC.

P.O. Box 5006, Port Huron MI 48061-5006. 313/987-4700. **Contact:** David Peshke, Personnel Director. **Description:** A major area manufacturer of special dies and tools. **Employees:** 200.

Additional large employers: 250+

INTERNAL COMBUSTION ENGINES, MISC.

Chrysler Corp
2000 Van Horn Rd, Trenton MI 48183-4204. 313/671-4129. Employs: 1000+.

Ford Romeo Engine Plant
701 E 32 Mile Rd, Romeo MI 48065. 313/752-8000. Employs: 500-999.

G M Corp/Powertrain Div
902 E Hamilton Ave, Flint MI 48550-0001. 313/236-5000. Employs: 1000+.

FARM MACHINERY AND EQUIPMENT

Morbark Industries Inc
P O Box 1000, Winn MI 48896-1000. 517/866-2381. Employs: 250-499.

CONSTRUCTION MACHINERY AND EQUIPMENT

Detroit Stoker Company
1510 E First St, Monroe MI 48161-1915. 313/241-9500. Employs: 250-499.

MACHINE TOOLS, METAL CUTTING TYPES

Creative Industries Group Inc
275 Rex Blvd, Auburn Hills MI 48326-2954. 313/852-5700. Employs: 500-999.

Devlieg Machine Co
Fair St, Royal Oak MI 48068. 313/280-1100. Employs: 500-999.

Efficient Engineering Co
130 Town Center Dr, Troy MI 48084-1773. 313/528-2888. Employs: 250-499.

Giddings & Lewis
17801 14 Mile Rd, Fraser MI 48026-2258. 313/293-3000. Employs: 250-499.

National Broach & Machine Co
17500 23 Mile Rd, Macomb MI 48044-1103. 313/263-0100. Employs: 250-499.

Valiant International
1180 E Big Beaver Rd, Troy MI 48083-1934. 313/541-1400. Employs: 250-499.

Veet Industries
25755 Gravesbeck Hwy, Warren MI 48089. 313/776-3000. Employs: 250-499.

Wyman-Gordon Co Jackson Div
2218 E High St, Jackson MI 49203-3420. 517/787-6022. Employs: 250-499.

SPECIAL DIES AND TOOLS, DIE SETS, JIGS AND FIXTURES

Allied Products Corp
235 E Bacon St, Hillsdale MI 49242-1703. 517/437-7371. Employs: 250-499.

Atlas Tool Inc
29880 Groesbeck Hwy, Roseville MQI 48066-1925. 313/778-3570. Employs: 250-499.

Delta Tooling Co
1350 Harmon Rd, Auburn Hills MI 48326-1540. 313/391-6800. Employs: 250-499.

Progressive Tool & Inds Co
21000 Telegraph Rd, Southfield MI 48034-4218. 313/353-8888. Employs: 500-999.

SPECIAL DIES AND TOOLS, DIE SETS, JIGS AND FIXTURES, AND INDUSTRIAL MOLDS

Aero-Detroit Inc
1100 E Mandoline, Madison Hts MI 48071-1403. 313/583-4900. Employs: 500-999.

Carboloy Inc
11177 E 8 Mile Rd, Warren MI 48089-3071. 313/497-5000. Employs: 1000+.

ELECTRIC AND GAS WELDING AND SOLDERING EQUIPMENT

Lamb Technicon/Welding Group
5663 E 9 Mile Rd, Warren MI 48091-2562. 313/497-6000. Employs: 250-499.

PUMPS AND PUMPING EQUIPMENT

Coltec Automotive Division
1748 Northwood Dr, Troy MI 48084-5521. 313/362-5300.
Employs: 250-499.

Vickers Inc
5445 Corporate Dr, Troy MI 48098-2683. 313/641-4200.
Employs: 500-999.

BALL AND ROLLER BEARINGS

Federal Mogul
310 E Steel St, Saint Johns MI 48879-1238. 517/224-3221.
Employs: 500-999.

MISC. MECHANICAL POWER TRANSMISSION EQUIPMENT

Allison Detroit Div Gm
13400 W Outer Dr, Redford MI 48239-1309. 317/242-5000. Employs: 500-999.

Borg Warner Auto Powdered Met
32059 Schoolcraft, Livonia MI 48150-1810. 313/261-5322.
Employs: 500-999.

N S K Corp/Bearing Div
5400 S State Rd, Ann Arbor MI 48108-9754. 313/996-4400. Employs: 250-499.

Detrex Corporation
P O Box 511, Southfield MI 48037-0511. 313/358-5800.
Employs: 500-999.

MISC. OFFICE MACHINES

Irwin Magnetic Systems Inc
2101 Commonwealth Blvd, Ann Arbor MI 48105-1561.
313/930-9000. Employs: 250-499.

Northern Telecom
100 Phoenix Dr, Ann Arbor MI 48108-2202. 313/973-4000. Employs: 250-499.

AIR-CONDITIONING AND WARM AIR HEATING EQUIPMENT AND COMMERCIAL AND INDUSTRIAL REFRIGERATION EQUIPMENT

Addison Products Co
215 Talbot St, Addison MI 49220. 517/547-6131. Employs: 500-999.

Ford Motor Co/Sheldon Rd Plant
14425 Sheldon Rd, Plymouth MI 48170-2407. 313/451-8750. Employs: 250-499.

Tecumseh Products Co
100 E Patterson St, Tecumseh MI 49286-2041. 517/423-8411. Employs: 1000+.

CARBURATORS, PISTONS, PISTON RINGS AND VALVES

Holley Replacement Parts Div
11955 E Nine Mile Rd, Warren MI 48089-3703. 313/497-4000. Employs: 250-499.

Wohlert Corp
700 E Grand River, Lansing MI 48906-5340. 517/485-3750. Employs: 250-499.

FLUID POWER CYLINDERS AND ACTUATORS

Auto Bend Corp
1800 W Maple Rd, Troy MI 48084-7104. 313/541-9030.
Employs: 250-499.

Core Industries Inc
500 N Woodward Ave, Bloomfield MI 48304-2961.
313/642-3400. Employs: 1000+.

Detroit Center Tool Inc
20101 Hoover St, Detroit MI 48205-1031. 313/839-9800.
Employs: 250-499.

Ingersoll-Rand Co
23400 Halstead Rd, Farmington MI 48335-2840. 313/477-0800. Employs: 250-499.

Johnson Controls Inc
10501 Hwy M-52, Manchester MI 48158. 313/428-8371.
Employs: 250-499.

Olofsson Corp
2727 Lyons Ave, Lansing MI 48910. 517/393-4700.
Employs: 250-499.

SEARCH, DETECTION, NAVIGATION, GUIDANCE, AERONAUTICAL AND NAUTICAL SYSTEMS AND INSTRUMENTS

Kelsey-Hayes Co
7300 Whitmore Lk Rd, Brighton MI 48116-8533. 313/229-9556. Employs: 250-499.

INSTRUMENTS FOR MEASURING AND TESTING OF ELECTRICITY AND ELECTRICAL SIGNALS

Chrysler Corp
12000 Chrysler Dr, Detroit MI 48288-1899. 313/956-5252.
Employs: 1000+.

Additional small to medium sized employers: 50-249

STEAM, GAS AND HYDRAULIC TURBINES AND TURBINE GENERATOR SET UNITS

Aeroquip Corp
614 Mill St, Leslie MI 49251-9462. 517/589-8203.
Employs: 50-99.

Morrell Inc
2333 Commercial Dr, Auburn Hills MI 48326-2408.
313/373-1600. Employs: 50-99.

MISCELLANEOUS INTERNAL COMBUSTION ENGINES

Crusader Engines
7100 E 15 Mile Rd, Sterling Hts MI 48312-4522. 313/264-1200. Employs: 50-99.

Deco-Grand Inc

1600 W Maple Rd, Troy MI 48084-7125. 313/643-0660.
Employs: 100-249.

Ford Motor Company
2500 Oakwood Bl, Melvindale MI 48122-1349. 313/594-1340. Employs: 100-249.

Mc Laren Engines Inc
32233 W 8 Mile Rd, Livonia MI 48152-1372. 313/477-6240. Employs: 50-99.

Peaker Services Inc
8080 Kensington Ct, Brighton MI 48116-8520. 313/437-4174. Employs: 50-99.

FARM MACHINERY AND EQUIPMENT

New Holland Inc
2500 E Maple Rd, Bloomfield MI 48301-2749. 313/637-7000. Employs: 50-99.

CONSTRUCTION MACHINERY AND EQUIPMENT

Evans Equipment Inc
G3283 S Dort Hwy, Burton MI 48529 1446. 313/744-4840. Employs: 50-99.

Hartman-Fabco Inc
1415 Lake Lansing Rd, Lansing MI 48912-3738. 517/485-9493. Employs: 50-99.

State Fabricators Inc
30550 W Eight Mile Rd, Farmington MI 48336-5301. 313/471-1500. Employs: 50-99.

Sweepster
2800 N Zeeb Rd, Dexter MI 48130-9714. 313/996-9116. Employs: 100-249.

OIL AND GAS FIELD MACHINERY AND EQUIPMENT

Nova Vista Industries Inc
2019 E High St, Jackson MI 49203. 517/787-1350. Employs: 100-249.

ELEVATORS AND MOVING STAIRWAYS

Detroit Elevator Co
1938 Franklin St, Detroit MI 48207-4008. 313/259-3710. Employs: 50-99.

Montgomery Elevator Co
336 W 1st St Rm 105, Flint MI 48502-1382. 313/232-8261. Employs: 50-99.

CONVEYORS AND CONVEYING EQUIPMENT

Acco Systs
12755 E 9 Mile Rd, Warren MI 48089-2621. 313/755-7500. Employs: 100-249.

Automatic Handling Inc
360 Lavoy Rd, Erie MI 48133-9638. 313/847-0633. Employs: 100-249.

Automation Service Eqpt/Plant 2
23220 Pinewood St, Warren MI 48091-4753. 313/754-5940. Employs: 100-249.

B T Systems Inc
2791 Research Dr, Rochester MI 48309-3575. 313/299-8825. Employs: 50-99.

Bond Robotics
6750 19 Mile Rd, Sterling Hts MI 48314-2112. 313/254-7600. Employs: 100-249.

Bristol Steel & Conveyor Corp
4144 Jimbo Dr, Burton MI 48529-1847. 313/743-8560. Employs: 50-99.

C E C Products Co
24650 Sherwood Ave, Center Line MI 48015-1046. 313/758-1111. Employs: 50-99.

Conveyor Products Inc
6906 Kingsley Ave, Dearborn MI 48126-1941. 313/846-6000. Employs: 100-249.

Excel Corp
1101 Copper Ave, Fenton MI 48430-1770. 313/629-5100. Employs: 100-249.

Fabricating Engrs Inc
2256 W Hill Rd, Flint MI 48507-4655. 313/257-2270. Employs: 50-99.

Idea Engineering & Fabricating Inc
13881 Elmira St, Detroit MI 48227-3016. 313/834-8000. Employs: 50-99.

Jervis B Webb Co
55500 Grand River Ave, New Hudson MI 48165-9717. 313/437-7900. Employs: 50-99.

Lockwood Manufacturing Co
31251 Indl Rd, Livonia MI 48150. 313/425-5330. Employs: 50-99.

Planet Corp
16641 Airport Service Dr, Lansing MI 48906. 517/321-0200. Employs: 50-99.

Roberts Sinto Corp
150 Orchard St, Grand Ledge MI 48837-1210. 517/627-1174. Employs: 50-99.

Robotic Transfer Corporation
810 Fowler St, Howell MI 48843-2319. 517/546-9300. Employs: 50-99.

Webb-Triax Co
34375 W 12 Mile St, Farmington MI 48331-3375. 313/553-1000. Employs: 100-249.

OVERHEAD TRAVELING CRANES, HOISTS AND MONORAIL SYSTEMS

D W Zimmerman Manufacturing Inc
29555 Stephenson Hwy, Madison Hts MI 48071-2332. 313/398-6200. Employs: 50-99.

Detroit Hoist & Crane Co
6650 Sterling Dr N, Sterling Hts MI 48312-4558. 313/268-2600. Employs: 50-99.

Verne Corp
50405 Patricia, Harrison Twp MI 48045. 313/949-5850. Employs: 100-249.

INDUSTRIAL TRUCKS, TRACTORS, TRAILERS AND STACKERS

Jesco Inds Inc
950 Anderson Rd, Litchfield MI 49252. 517/542-2903. Employs: 50-99.

Newcor Inc
3270 W Big Beaver Rd, Troy MI 48084-2901. 313/643-7730. Employs: 100-249.

Union Fork Lift Service
1211 S Monroe St Rear, Monroe MI 48161-3933. 313/242-2400. Employs: 50-99.

MACHINE TOOLS, METAL CUTTING TYPES

Crankshaft Machine Group
314 N Jackson St, Jackson MI 49201-1221. 517/787-3791. Employs: 50-99.

Detroit Broach & Mach Co
950 S Rochester Rd, Rochester MI 48307-2742. 313/651-9211. Employs: 50-99.

Ekman Machine Tool Co
12910 Westwood Ave, Detroit MI 48223-3436. 313/273-7600. Employs: 50-99.

Empire Tool Co
11500 Lambs Rd, Memphis MI 48041-3106. 313/392-2101. Employs: 100-249.

G T E Valenite Corp
750 Stephenson Hwy, Troy MI 48083-1124. 313/589-1000. Employs: 100-249.

G T E Valenite Corp
21100 Coolidge Hwy, Oak Park MI 48237-3203. 313/589-6744. Employs: 100-249.

Garr Tool Co
7800 N Alger Rd, Alma MI 48801-9783. 517/463-6171. Employs: 100-249.

Hueller Hille Corp
1740 E Maple Rd, Troy MI 48083-4209. 313/589-3000. Employs: 100-249.

Industrial Metal Products Corp
3417 W St Joseph St, Lansing MI 48917-3707. 517/484-9411. Employs: 100-249.

M K Chambers Co
2251 Johnson Mill Rd, North Branch MI 48461-9744. 313/688-3750. Employs: 50-99.

Parliament Design Inc
1945 Heide St Box 99009, Troy MI 48099-9009. 313/362-1650. Employs: 100-249.

Schenck Turner Inc
100 Kay Indl Dr, Lake Orion MI 48359. 313/377-2100. Employs: 100-249.

Tarus Products Inc
38100 Commerce Dr, Sterling Hts MI 48312-1006. 313/977-1400. Employs: 100-249.

Thermatool Alpha Inds Inc
22750 Heslip Dr, Novi MI 48375-4143. 313/348-0070. Employs: 50-99.

Three M Tool & Machine Inc
8155 Richardson Rd, Walled Lake MI 48390-4131. 313/363-1555. Employs: 50-99.

MACHINE TOOLS, METAL FORMING TYPES

Anderson-Cook Inc
17650 15 Mile Rd, Fraser MI 48026-3450. 313/293-0800. Employs: 50-99.

Pyles Business Unit
28990 Wixom Rd, Wixom MI 48393-3416. 313/349-5500. Employs: 50-99.

Tishken Products Co
13000 W Eight Mile Rd, Oak Park MI 48237-3214. 313/399-9200. Employs: 50-99.

Gampco Sales
200 E Main St, North Adams MI 49262-9754. 517/287-4201. Employs: 50-99.

H P R M Inc
2560 Wolcott St, Ferndale MI 48220-1447. 313/399-1660. Employs: 50-99.

Mueller-Weingarten Corp
1680 S Livernois Rd, Rochester MI 48307-3365. 313/652-0505. Employs: 50-99.

St Lawrence Press Co
12500 Wayne Rd, Romulus MI 48174-3776. 313/941-7577. Employs: 50-99.

Verson Division Of Allied Prod
25511 Southfield Rd, Southfield MI 48075-1830. 313/559-0170. Employs: 50-99.

INDUSTRIAL PATTERNS

American Model & Pattern Co
22926 Indl Dr W, St Clair Shrs MI 48080. 313/778-5450. Employs: 50-99.

Commerce Engineering & Pattern

3351 Oakley Pk, Walled Lake MI 48390-1651. 313/624-4514. Employs: 50-99.

Gibbins Pattern & Plastic Inc
12360 Beech Daly Rd, Redford MI 48239-2433. 313/937-8020. Employs: 50-99.

K-Barr Inds Inc
9440 Grinnell Ave, Detroit MI 48213-1151. 313/571-0110. Employs: 50-99.

Models & Tools Inc
1880 E Maple Rd, Troy MI 48083-4240. 313/585-4540. Employs: 50-99.

Sherwood Metal Products Inc
4670 Hatchery Rd, Waterford MI 48329-3633. 313/673-2303. Employs: 50-99.

Simco Inds Inc
16580 Industrial Dr, Roseville MI 48066-1931. 313/772-1910. Employs: 50-99.

Ring Pattern & Manufctring Co
12901 Stephens Rd, Warren MI 48089-4333. 313/759-3500. Employs: 50-99.

SPECIAL DIES AND TOOLS, DIE SETS, JIGS AND FIXTURES AND INDUSTRIAL MOLDS

A E P Technologies
33957 Riviera Dr, Fraser MI 48026-1614. 313/296-2100. Employs: 100-249.

Air Gage Co
12170 Globe, Livonia MI 48150-1143. 313/591-9220. Employs: 100-249.

Birmingham Benders Co
1271 W Maple Rd, Clawson MI 48017-1060. 313/435-0330. Employs: 50-99.

Blom Industries Inc
25551 Joy Blvd, Harrison Twp MI 48045-1323. 313/468-5600. Employs: 50-99.

Burton Industries Inc
6202 S State Rd, Goodrich MI 48438-9706. 313/636-2215. Employs: 50-99.

C K S Tool & Engineering Inc
700 Soper Rd, Bad Axe MI 48413. 517/269-9702. Employs: 50-99.

Cameron Tool Corp
1800 Bassett St, Lansing MI 48915-1568. 517/487-3671. Employs: 50-99.

Capitol Tool & Die Co
1492 W Grand River Ave, Williamston MI 48895-9772. 517/655-4304. Employs: 50-99.

Centerline Tool & Die Co
28661 Van Dyke Ave, Warren MI 48093-7135. 313/979-6580. Employs: 50-99.

Century Tool & Gage Co
200 Alloy Dr, Fenton MI 48430. 313/629-0784. Employs: 50-99.

Citation Tool Inc
16660 E 13 Mile Rd, Roseville MI 48066-1556. 313/773-4330. Employs: 100-249.

Cole Carbide Inds Inc
24703 Ryan Rd, Warren MI 48091-3388. 313/757-8700. Employs: 50-99.

Composite Forgings
2300 W Jefferson Ave, Detroit MI 48216-2055. 313/496-1226. Employs: 50-99.

Corban Inds Inc
169 W Clarkston Rd, Lake Orion MI 48362-2809. 313/693-0442. Employs: 50-99.

D & F Corporation
42455 Merrill Rd, Sterling Hts MI 48314-3239. 313/254-5300. Employs: 100-249.

Davalor Mold Corp
46480 Continental Dr, Harrison Twp MI 48045. 313/598-0100. Employs: 50-99.

Detroit Precision Tool Co
1505 W Hamlin Rd, Rochester MI 48309-3366. 313/853-5888. Employs: 50-99.

Distel Tool & Machine Co
12800 E 10 Mile Rd, Warren MI 48089-2046. 313/755-5505. Employs: 100-249.

Eldon Tool & Extrusions Inc
50350 E Russell Schmidt Blvd, Harrison Twp MI 48045. 313/949-7733. Employs: 100-249.

Formation Plastics Inc
15055 32 Mile Rd, Romeo MI 48065-4901. 313/752-3500. Employs: 100-249.

Franchino Mold & Engineering
5867 W Grand River Ave, Lansing MI 48906-9124. 517/321-5609. Employs: 100-249.

Futuramic Tool & Engineering Co
24680 Gibson Dr, Warren MI 48089-4313. 313/758-2200. Employs: 50-99.

Gathen Industries Inc
24133 Northwestern Hwy Ste 201, Southfield MI 48075-2576. 313/779-2300. Employs: 50-99.

Greenville Tool & Die Co
1215 S Lafayette Rd, Greenville MI 48838-9386. 616/754-5693. Employs: 100-249.

Harry Major Machine & Tool Co
17850 14 Mile Rd, Fraser MI 48026-2271. 313/294-0200. Employs: 50-99.

Henze Stamping & Manufacturing Co
31650 Stephenson Hwy, Madison Hts MI 48071-1642. 313/588-5620. Employs: 50-99.

Hi-Tech Mold & Engineering Inc
2775 Commerce Dr, Rochester MI 48309-3815. 313/852-6600. Employs: 50-99.

Hydro-Cam Engineering Co
1900 E Maple Rd, Troy MI 48083-4213. 313/588-2900. Employs: 50-99.

I E M
1111 E Main St, Ionia MI 48846-9715. 616/527-0210. Employs: 50-99.

Integral Engineerng & Manufacturing
42400 W 11 Mile Rd, Novi MI 48375-1751. 313/348-6000. Employs: 50-99.

Itm Inland Tool & Manufacturing
611 Hillger St, Detroit MI 48214-3428. 313/823-3900. Employs: 50-99.

Iverson Inds
580 Hillsdale, Wyandotte MI 48192-7124. 313/284-5301. Employs: 100-249.

Jolico/J B Tool Inc
4325 22 Mile Rd, Utica MI 48317-1507. 313/739-5555. Employs: 50-99.

Koppy Corp
199 Kay Indl Dr, Lake Orion MI 48359. 313/373-5200. Employs: 50-99.

Lunar Industries Inc
34335 Groesbeck Hwy, Fraser MI 48026. 313/792-0090. Employs: 50-99.

Manter Technologies
7177 Marine City Airport, Marine City MI 48039. 313/765-4041. Employs: 50-99.

Mc Kenna Inds Inc
2200 Stephenson Hwy # B, Troy MI 48083-2153. 313/689-4800. Employs: 50-99.

Miller Tool & Die Co
829 Belden Road, Jackson MI 49203-1908. 517/782-0347. Employs: 100-249.

Moeller Manufacturing Co Inc/Punch Div
12173 Market St, Livonia MI 48150-1124. 313/591-6222. Employs: 50-99.

Mold Masters Co
301 E 1st St, Imlay City MI 48444-1311. 313/724-6447. Employs: 50-99.

Mold-A-Matic Inc
2000 E Avis Dr, Madison Hts MI 48071-1551. 313/588-9600. Employs: 50-99.

Norbert Inds Inc
38111 Commerce Dr, Sterling Hts MI 48312-1007. 313/977-9200. Employs: 50-99.

North Tool & Manufacturing Co
17140 10 Mile Rd, East Detroit MI 48021-1283. 313/776-6680. Employs: 50-99.

O Keller Tool Engineering Co
12701 Inkster Rd, Livonia MI 48150-2216. 313/425-4500. Employs: 50-99.

One Way Inds Inc
845 E Mandoline, Madison Hts MI 48071-1472. 313/585-8550. Employs: 50-99.

Ort Tool & Die Inc
6555 S Dixie Hwy, Erie MI 48133-9637. 313/848-6845. Employs: 100-249.

Perfect Mold Co Inc
1919 Concept Dr, Warren MI 48091-6013. 313/756-5577. Employs: 50-99.

Proper Mold & Engineering Inc
13870 E 11 Mile Rd, Warren MI 48089-1471. 313/779-8787. Employs: 50-99.

Punchcraft Co
30500 Ryan Rd, Warren MI 48092-1902. 313/573-4840. Employs: 50-99.

R & B Manufacturing Co Inc
7495 M 36 Ste 36, Hamburg MI 48139. 313/961-6692. Employs: 100-249.

Rebmann Products Corp
12265 Dixie Ave, Redford MI 48239-2452. 313/538-6666. Employs: 50-99.

Reo Hydraulics & Manufacturing Inc
18495 Sherwood St, Detroit MI 48234-2832. 313/891-2244. Employs: 50-99.

Richard & Trute Tool & Die
23751 Hoover Rd, Warren MI 48089-1980. 313/758-3400. Employs: 50-99.

Ronart Inds Inc
19365 Sherwood St, Detroit MI 48234-2820. 313/893-4800. Employs: 50-99.

Schaller Tool & Die Co
49505 N Gratiot Ave, Clinton Twp MI 48035-4039.
313/949-5500. Employs: 50-99.

Smith Bros Tool
35430 Beattie Dr, Sterling Hts MI 48312-2612. 313/978-0800. Employs: 50-99.

Spearing Tool & Manufacturing
98 Glaspie Rd, Oxford MI 48371. 313/628-0680. Employs: 50-99.

Superior Cam Inc
31240 Stephenson Hwy, Madison Hts MI 48071-1620. 313/588-1100. Employs: 50-99.

T R W Inc
15226 Common Rd, Roseville MI 48066-1810. 313/778-7412. Employs: 100-249.

Teledyne Howell Penncraft
3333 W Grand River Av, Howell MI 48843-9601. 517/548-2250. Employs: 50-99.

Thomas Die & Stamping Inc
2170 E Walton Blvd, Auburn Hills MI 48326-1950. 313/373-0388. Employs: 50-99.

Thumb Tool & Engineering Co
354 Liberty St, Bad Axe MI 48413-9302. 517/269-9731. Employs: 100-249.

Tomco Tool & Die Inc
807 Edna St, Belding MI 48809-2431. 616/794-1640. Employs: 50-99.

Tonys Die & Machine Co
24358 Groesbeck Hwy, Warren MI 48089-4718. 313/773-7379. Employs: 50-99.

Troy Design & Manufacturing Co
12675 Berwyn, Redford MI 48239-2748. 313/537-4055. Employs: 100-249.

Troy Pattern & Model
1842 Rochester Indl Dr, Rochester MI 48309. 313/652-8600. Employs: 50-99.

V-Tech Inc
2555 Bishop Cir W, Dexter MI 48130-1563. 313/426-4774. Employs: 50-99.

W K Industries Inc
6120 Millett Ave, Sterling Hts MI 48312-2642. 313/268-4090. Employs: 50-99.

Wilhelm Engineering Co
755 W Big Beaver Rd, Troy MI 48084-4903. 313/362-2280. Employs: 100-249.

Yarema Die & Engineering Co
283 Minnesota Rd, Troy MI 48083-4674. 313/585-2830. Employs: 100-249.

Spartan International Inc
1845 Cedar St, Holt MI 48842-1701. 517/694-3911. Employs: 100-249.

Farathane Division C J Edwards
23514 Groesbeck Hwy, Warren MI 48089-4246. 313/774-7900. Employs: 50-99.

Spearhead Dev Techlgy Inc
2250 E West Maple Rd, Walled Lake MI 48390-3828. 313/624-1571. Employs: 50-99.

CUTTING TOOLS, MACHINE TOOL ACCESSORIES, AND MACHINISTS' PRECISION MEASURING DEVICES

A A Gage Inc
350 Fair St, Ferndale MI 48220-2647. 313/548-3810. Employs: 50-99.

Advanced Fastening Systs Inc
5500 18 Mile Rd, Sterling Hts MI 48314-4106. 313/268-7400. Employs: 50-99.

Barnes Inds Inc
1161 E 11 Mile Rd, Madison Hts MI 48071-3801. 313/541-2333. Employs: 50-99.

Brothers Inds Inc
32471 Indl Dr, Madison Hts MI 48071. 313/588-8090. Employs: 50-99.

Buckeye Die & Engineering Co Inc
19000 15 Mile Rd, Clinton Twp MI 48035-2506. 313/791-2400. Employs: 50-99.

C F T Co
1235 Holden Ave, Milford MI 48381-3137. 313/685-8850. Employs: 50-99.

Coe Press Eqpt Corp
40549 Brentwood Dr, Sterling Hts MI 48310-2210. 313/979-4400. Employs: 50-99.

Dearborn Gage Co
32330 Ford Rd, Garden City MI 48135-1507. 313/422-8300. Employs: 50-99.

Duramet Corp
11350 Stephens Rd, Warren MI 48089-1833. 313/759-2280. Employs: 50-99.

Eonic Inc
464 E Hollywood, Detroit MI 48203-2042. 313/893-8100. Employs: 100-249.

Giddings & Lewis Drillunit
11450 Stephens Rd, Warren MI 48089-3861. 313/756-3730. Employs: 50-99.

Haber Tool Operation
12850 Inkster Rd, Redford MI 48239-3003. 313/255-1750. Employs: 50-99.

Hanlo Gage & Engineering Co
41225 Plymouth Rd, Plymouth MI 48170-1855. 313/455-9650. Employs: 50-99.

Huron Tool & Engineering Co
635 Liberty St, Bad Axe MI 48413-9490. 517/269-9927. Employs: 50-99.

I T W Woodworth
1300 E 9 Mile Rd, Ferndale MI 48220-2018. 313/541-7500. Employs: 100-249.

J R Control Systems Corp
21133 Bridge St, Southfield MI 48034-4004. 313/358-1620. Employs: 50-99.

Jedav Inds
51400 Bellestri Ct, Shelby Twp MI 48315-2749. 313/726-0500. Employs: 100-249.

Marposs Corp
3300 Cross Creek Pkwy, Auburn Hills MI 48326-2758. 313/370-0404. Employs: 50-99.

Micro-Measurements
38905 Chase Rd, Romulus MI 48174-1302. 313/941-3900. Employs: 50-99.

Quinco Tool Products Co
23855 Telegraph Rd, Southfield MI 48034-3010. 313/353-1340. Employs: 50-99.

Raycon Corporation
2850 S Industrial Hwy, Ann Arbor MI 48104-6768. 313/677-2614. Employs: 100-249.

Rock Tool & Machine Co Inc
45145 5 Mile Rd, Plymouth MI 48170-2556. 313/455-9840. Employs: 50-99.

Sandvik Inc
2066 Franklin Rd, Bloomfield MI 48302-0326. 313/338-9655. Employs: 50-99.

Sidley Diamond Tool Co
32320 Ford Rd, Garden City MI 48135-1507. 313/261-7970. Employs: 50-99.

Suburban Tool/Taft-Peirce Inc
2295 E Lincoln St, Birmingham MI 48009-7123. 313/646-7900. Employs: 50-99.

T M Smith Tool International Corp
360 Hubbard St, Mount Clemens MI 48043-5403. 313/468-1465. Employs: 50-99.

Universal Beck
27588 Northline Rd, Romulus MI 48174-2826. 313/941-1300. Employs: 50-99.

Valenite Gaging Systs
31750 Sherman Dr, Madison Hts MI 48071-1423. 313/589-7421. Employs: 50-99.

POWER-DRIVEN HANDTOOLS

Ace Drill Corp
2600 E Maumee St, Adrian MI 49221-3533. 517/265-5184. Employs: 50-99.

U S Industrial Tool & Sply Co
15101 Cleat St, Plymouth MI 48170-6015. 313/455-3388. Employs: 50-99.

ROLLING HILL MACHINERY AND EQUIPMENT

Acutus Inds Inc
2800 Alliance Dr, Waterford MI 48328-1800. 313/674-4861. Employs: 100-249.

ELECTRIC AND GAS WELDING AND SOLDERING EQUIPMENT

Clear Inds Inc
450 Fair St, Ferndale MI 48220-2648. 313/548-0700. Employs: 50-99.

Grossel Tool Co
34190 Doreka, Fraser MI 48026-3434. 313/294-3660. Employs: 50-99.

Key Welder Corp
15686 Sturgeon, Roseville MI 48066-1817. 313/778-7700. Employs: 100-249.

Lamb Technicon
316 Hoffman St, Marysville MI 48040-1910. 313/364-4400. Employs: 50-99.

Medar Inc
38700 Grand River Ave, Farmington MI 48335-1521. 313/477-3900. Employs: 50-99.

Milco Manufacturing Co
2147 E 10 Mile Rd, Warren MI 48091-3784. 313/755-7320. Employs: 100-249.

Novi Inds
44000 Grand River Ave, Novi MI 48375-1119. 313/344-0100. Employs: 100-249.

Oakland Engineering Inc
915 Oakland Ave, Pontiac MI 48340-2374. 313/858-2718. Employs: 50-99.

Weld Mold Co
750 Rickett Rd, Brighton MI 48116-1825. 313/229-9521. Employs: 50-99.

Weldaloy Products Co
11551 Stephens Rd, Warren MI 48089-3848. 313/758-5550. Employs: 50-99.

MISCELLANEOUS METALWORKING MACHINERY

A B Myr Inds
39635 Detroit Indl Fwy, Belleville MI 48111. 313/941-2200. Employs: 100-249.

Apex Broach & Machine Co
6401 E Seven Mile Rd, Detroit MI 48234-2828. 313/891-8600. Employs: 100-249.

Cargill Detroit Corp
4475 Purks Dr, Auburn Hills MI 48326-1749. 313/377-0300. Employs: 100-249.

Continental Lap Co
19620 Sherwood St, Detroit MI 48234-2923. 313/368-3900. Employs: 50-99.

Hines Inds Inc
661 Airport Blvd, Ann Arbor MI 48108-1637. 313/769-2300. Employs: 100-249.

Industrial Welding Inc
2200 Olds Ave, Lansing MI 48915-1054. 517/372-0950. Employs: 50-99.

Sesco Inc
7800 Dix St, Detroit MI 48209-1106. 313/843-7710. Employs: 50-99.

Technical Tooling Specialties
1708 S Airline Dr Se, Jackson MI 49203-4417. 517/782-8898. Employs: 50-99.

Wright Tool Company
1738 Maplelawn Dr, Troy MI 48084-4604. 313/643-6666. Employs: 50-99.

PAPER INDUSTRIES MACHINERY

Future Box
12871 Westwood St, Detroit MI 48223-3435. 313/272-3388. Employs: 50-99.

PRINTING TRADES MACHINERY AND EQUIPMENT

A B Dick/Itek Graphix Corp
25330 Telegraph Rd #110, Southfield MI 48034-7455. 313/352-9860. Employs: 50-99.

FOOD PRODUCTS MACHINERY

I & H Conveying & Machine Co
10456 N Holly Rd, Grand Blanc MI 48439. 313/694-6900. Employs: 100-249.

Pure-Pak Inc
30000 S Hill, New Hudson MI 48165-9787. 313/486-4600. Employs: 100-249.

The Coffee Beanery
804 Briarwood Cir, Ann Arbor MI 48108-1616. 313/747-7166. Employs: 50-99.

MISCELLANEOUS SPECIAL INDUSTRY MACHINERY

Ann Arbor Assembly Corp
251 Airport Indl Dr, Ypsilanti MI 48198. 313/484-0380. Employs: 50-99.

Ann Arbor Machine Co
78 Jackson Plz, Ann Arbor MI 48103-1917. 313/769-7226.
Employs: 100-249.

Bekum America Corp
1140 W Grand River Ave, Williamston MI 48895-1214.
517/655-4331. Employs: 100-249.

Belco Inds Inc
9138 Belding Rd, Belding MI 48809-9201. 616/794-0410.
Employs: 50-99.

C C Mitchell Co
650 W 12 Mile Rd, Madison Hts MI 48071-2407. 313/547-
6770. Employs: 100-249.

Combine Tool & Die Co
17157 E 10 Mile Rd, East Detroit MI 48021-1284.
313/777-9720. Employs: 50-99.

Dedoes Inds Inc
1060 W Maple Rd, Walled Lake MI 48390. 313/624-7710.
Employs: 50-99.

Diamond Automation
23400 Haggerty Rd, Farmington MI 48335-2613. 313/476-
7100. Employs: 100-249.

Expert-Kuka Inc
40675 Mound Rd, Sterling Hts MI 48310-2263. 313/977-
0100. Employs: 50-99.

Fori Automation Inc
50955 Wing Dr, Shelby Twp MI 48315-3271. 313/247-
2336. Employs: 50-99.

Freedland Ind Corp
4200 Miller Rd, Dearborn MI 48126-3711. 313/584-3033.
Employs: 50-99.

Giddings/Lewis Intgrtd Autmtn
23655 Hoover Rd, Warren MI 48089-1986. 313/755-6000.
Employs: 100-249.

Grant-Durban
26600 Telegraph Rd, Southfield MI 48034-2438. 313/352-
7300. Employs: 50-99.

Haden Schweitzer Corp
32200 N Avis Dr, Madison Hts MI 48071-1503. 313/583-
1900. Employs: 100-249.

Lo Mar Machine & Tool
135 Main St, Horton MI 49246-9540. 517/563-8136.
Employs: 50-99.

Mac Dermid Inc
1221 Farrow St, Ferndale MI 48220-1959. 313/399-3553.
Employs: 50-99.

McClain Industries Inc
6200 Elmridge Rd, Sterling Hts MI 48313-3706. 313/264-
3611. Employs: 100-249.

Michigan Machine & Engineering
1100 Copper Ave, Fenton MI 48430-1771. 313/750-1811.
Employs: 50-99.

Parma Wire Assembly
345 S Union St, Parma MI 49269-9501. 517/531-3316.
Employs: 50-99.

Premier Inds Corp
513 N Dixie Hwy, Monroe MI 48161-2563. 313/241-8474.
Employs: 50-99.

Rapiturn Machining Co Inc
1200 Benstein Rd, Walled Lake MI 48390-2200. 313/669-
2660. Employs: 50-99.

Simplicity Engineering Inc

212 S Oak St, Durand MI 48429-1621. 517/288-3121.
Employs: 100-249.

Standard Machine & Tool Co
29900 Hayes Rd, Roseville MI 48066-1820. 313/773-6800.
Employs: 50-99.

Stellar Inds
1020 W 13 Mile Rd, Madison Hts MI 48071-1603.
313/585-1500. Employs: 50-99.

T A Systems
1873 Rochester Indl Ct, Rochester MI 48309. 313/656-
5150. Employs: 50-99.

Tarus Products
24443 John R Rd, Hazel Park MI 48030-1113. 313/977-
1400. Employs: 100-249.

Visi-Trol Engineering Co
12720 Burt Rd, Detroit MI 48223-3315. 313/535-4140.
Employs: 50-99.

PUMPS AND PUMPING EQUIPMENT

Great Lakes Filter
5151 Loraine St, Detroit MI 48208-1925. 313/894-1950.
Employs: 50-99.

M & M Pump Inc
G3491 Ann Dr, Flint MI 48504. 313/659-7567. Employs:
50-99.

M P Pumps Inc
34800 Bennett Dr, Fraser MI 48026-1694. 313/293-8240.
Employs: 50-99.

N L B Corp
29830 Beck Rd, Wixom MI 48393-2824. 313/624-5555.
Employs: 100-249.

Sherwood Pump
6331 E Jefferson Ave, Detroit MI 48207-4317. 313/259-
2095. Employs: 50-99.

BALL AND ROLLER BEARINGS

N S K Corporation Tech Center
3917 Research Park Dr, Ann Arbor MI 48108-2219.
313/668-0877. Employs: 50-99.

AIR AND GAS COMPRESSORS

Duerr Indl Eqpt Inc
1911 Northfield Dr, Rochester MI 48309-3824. 313/853-
2400. Employs: 100-249.

Karmazin Products Corp
3776 11th St, Wyandotte MI 48192-6436. 313/282-3776.
Employs: 100-249.

Saylor-Beall Manufacturing Co
401 N Kibbee St, Saint Johns MI 48879-1677. 517/524-
2371. Employs: 50-99.

**INDUSTRIAL AND COMMERCIAL FANS AND
BLOWERS AND AIR PURIFICATION EQUIPMENT**

Brundage Blowers
1300 Falahee Rd, Jackson MI 49203-3512. 517/787-4823.
Employs: 100-249.

General Filters Inc
43800 Grand River Ave, Novi MI 48375-1115. 313/349-
2481. Employs: 50-99.

Monnier Inc
Box 409, Algonac MI 48001-0409. 313/794-4935.
Employs: 50-99.

Rosedale Products Inc
3730 W Liberty Rd, Ann Arbor MI 48103-9706. 313/665-8201. Employs: 50-99.

Salem Inds Inc
245 S Mill St, South Lyon MI 48178-1486. 313/437-1400. Employs: 50-99.

Tri-Mer Corp
1400 Monroe St, Owosso MI 48867-3868. 517/723-7838. Employs: 50-99.

United Technologies Automotive
1641 Porter St, Detroit MI 48216-1935. 313/962-7311. Employs: 100-249.

SPEED CHANGERS, INDUSTRIAL HIGH-SPEED DRIVES AND GEARS

Jackson Gear Co Mi
221 Mill, Brooklyn MI 49230-9784. 517/592-6021. Employs: 50-99.

Mell Gear Inc
3506 Scheele Dr, Jackson MI 49202-1218. 517/787-8276. Employs: 50-99.

Veit Tool & Gage
1289 N Belsay Rd, Burton MI 48509-1601. 313/743-1170. Employs: 50-99.

Flow Engineering Inc
20630 Harper Ave, Harper Woods MI 48225-1429. 313/881-3600. Employs: 50-99.

Hub City
9859 Walfran Dr, Brighton MI 48116-9603. 313/227-4970. Employs: 50-99.

Cleveland Gear Co
31825 Mound Rd, Warren MI 48092-4785. 313/826-8585. Employs: 50-99.

Penngear Regional Office
6561 E Galway Cir, Dimondale MI 48821-9424. 517/646-0711. Employs: 50-99.

Schell Tool & Gear
435 S Livernois Rd Apt 104, Rochester MI 48307-2568. 313/335-2552. Employs: 50-99.

Sound Gear & Spline
123 Avery St, Clinton Twp MI 48036-3256. 313/465-0530. Employs: 50-99.

INDUSTRIAL PROCESS FURNACES AND OVENS

American Induction Heating
33842 James J Pompo Dr, Fraser MI 48026-3468. 313/294-1700. Employs: 50-99.

Envotech Management Svc Inc
1349 S Huron St, Ypsilanti MI 48197-9701. 313/485-6485. Employs: 50-99.

Gladd Inds Inc
15450 Dale St, Detroit MI 48223-1038. 313/537-2800. Employs: 50-99.

Holcroft/Loftus
12068 Market St, Livonia MI 48150-1125. 313/591-1000. Employs: 100-249.

Moco Thermal Inds
1st Oven Pl, Romulus MI 48174. 313/728-6800. Employs: 100-249.

Specialty Steel Treating Inc
34501 Commerce Rd, Fraser MI 48026-3419. 313/293-5355. Employs: 100-249.

MISCELLANEOUS MECHANICAL POWER TRANSMISSION EQUIPMENT

Daikin Clutch
8601 Haggerty Rd, Belleville MI 48111-1607. 313/397-3333. Employs: 100-249.

Great Lakes Industry Inc
1927 Wildwood Ave, Jackson MI 49202-4046. 517/784-3153. Employs: 50-99.

Hydramechanica Corp
6625 Cobb Dr, Sterling Hts MI 48312-2625. 313/939-0620. Employs: 50-99.

MISCELLANEOUS GENERAL INDUSTRIAL MACHINERY AND EQUIPMENT

B & H Machine Inc
2000 W Parnall Rd, Jackson MI 49201-8612. 517/782-9343. Employs: 50-99.

Finite Filter Co
500 Glaspie St, Oxford MI 48371-5132. 313/628-6400. Employs: 50-99.

Kleer Water
3272 Lake Dr, Fort Gratiot MI 48059-4202. 313/984-5630. Employs: 50-99.

Time Manufacturing Systs
1522 E Big Beaver Rd, Troy MI 48083-2008. 313/528-2650. Employs: 100-249.

CALCULATING AND ACCOUNTING MACHINES, EXCEPT ELECTRONIC COMPUTERS

National Cash Register
3775 Varsity Dr, Ann Arbor MI 48108-2223. 313/971-5185. Employs: 50-99.

MISCELLANEOUS OFFICE MACHINES

Arbor Image Corp
230 Collingwood Av Ste 250, Ann Arbor MI 48103-3898. 313/741-8700. Employs: 50-99.

Creative Solutions Inc
230 Collingwood Av Ste 250, Ann Arbor MI 48103-3898. 313/995-8811. Employs: 50-99.

Dempsey Data Serv
6007 Miller Rd, Swartz Creek MI 48473-1514. 313/635-4134. Employs: 50-99.

Eagle Data Products
400 Elm St, Holly MI 48442-1418. 313/634-0990. Employs: 50-99.

Gemeni Technology
1080 Creekwood Trl, Burton MI 48509-1580. 313/742-4804. Employs: 50-99.

I B M Corporation
G3235 Beecher Rd, Flint MI 48532. 313/733-9100. Employs: 50-99.

Interactions Incorporated
527 E Liberty St Ste 213, Ann Arbor MI 48104-2242. 313/761-6300. Employs: 50-99.

Pitney Bowes Inc Br
1545 Keystone Av, Lansing MI 48911. 517/393-4100. Employs: 50-99.

United Technologies
11850 Mayfield St, Livonia MI 48150-1708. 313/458-8830. Employs: 50-99.

United Technologies
26575 Northline Rd, Taylor MI 48180-4479. 313/946-1600. Employs: 50-99.

AIR-CONDITIONING AND WARM AIR HEATING EQUIPMENT AND COMMERCIAL AND INDUSTRIAL REFRIGERATION EQUIPMENT

Blissfield Manufacturing Co
626 Depot St, Blissfield MI 49228-1358. 517/486-2121. Employs: 100-249.

Mechanical Heat & Cold Inc
24535 Hallwood Ct, Farmington MI 48335-1667. 313/471-0600. Employs: 100-249.

Refrigeration Research Inc
525 N 5th St, Brighton MI 48116-1212. 313/227-1151. Employs: 100-249.

MISCELLANEOUS SERVICE INDUSTRY MACHINERY

Belanger Inc
1001 Doheny Ct Box 4, Northville MI 48167-1957. 313/349-7010. Employs: 100-249.

Michigan Softwater
2075 M-78 E, East Lansing MI 48823. 517/339-0722. Employs: 50-99.

Midwest Ultrasonics
15214 W Warren Ave, Dearborn MI 48126-1356. 313/584-5616. Employs: 50-99.

Mills Products Inc
33106 W 8 Mile Rd, Farmington MI 48336-5400. 313/476-4550. Employs: 100-249.

Proto-Vest Inc
600 Glaspie Rd, Oxford MI 48371-5017. 313/628-3600. Employs: 50-99.

CARBURETORS, PISTONS, PISTON RINGS AND VALVES

Bayport Manufacturing Co
27365 Mound Rd, Warren MI 48092-2626. 313/751-4040. Employs: 50-99.

Cold Extrusions Inc
34260 James J Pompo Dr, Fraser MI 48026-3411. 313/296-1877. Employs: 50-99.

FLUID POWER CYLINDERS AND ACTUATORS

C M Smillie & Co
1200 Woodward Hgts Blvd, Ferndale MI 48220-1427. 313/544-3100. Employs: 50-99.

Hennells Inc
1200 Woodward Hgts Blvd, Ferndale MI 48220-1427. 313/545-4120. Employs: 50-99.

Lynair Inc
3515 Scheele Dr, Jackson MI 49202-1217. 517/787-2240. Employs: 50-99.

Production Engineering Inc
2330 Brooklyn Rd, Jackson MI 49203-4750. 517/788-6800. Employs: 50-99.

Soramatic Industries Inc
5590 Enterprise Ct, Warren MI 48092-3460. 313/574-9770. Employs: 50-99.

FLUID POWER PUMPS AND MOTORS

Rhm Fluid Power Inc
375 Manufacturers Dr, Westland MI 48185-4038. 313/326-5400. Employs: 50-99.

MISCELLANEOUS INDUSTRIAL AND COMMERCIAL MACHINERY AND EQUIPMENT

A C R Industries Inc
15375 23 Mile Rd, Macomb MI 48042-4000. 313/781-2800. Employs: 100-249.

Ace Controls Inc
23435 Industrial Park Dr, Farmington MI 48335-2855. 313/476-0213. Employs: 50-99.

Advance Turning & Manufacturing Inc
2515 Precision St, Jackson MI 49202-3925. 517/783-2713. Employs: 50-99.

Aero Grinding Corp
28300 Groesbeck Hwy, Roseville MI 48066-2382. 313/774-6450. Employs: 50-99.

Air-Matic Products Co Inc
22218 Telegraph Rd, Southfield MI 48034-4211. 313/356-4200. Employs: 50-99.

Atlas Technologies Inc
201 S Alloy Dr, Fenton MI 48430-1703. 313/629-6663. Employs: 100-249.

Automated Systs Inc
2400 Commercial Dr, Auburn Hills MI 48326-2410. 313/373-5600. Employs: 50-99.

Bernal Rotary Systems Inc
2565 Industrial Row, Troy MI 48084-7037. 313/280-2500. Employs: 100-249.

Birch Machinery
11160 Dixie Hwy, Birch Run MI 48415-9760. 517/624-9373. Employs: 100-249.

Brown City Castings Corp
6892 Maple Valley Rd, Brown City MI 48416-9101. 313/346-2787. Employs: 50-99.

Comau Productivity Systs
754 W Maple Rd, Troy MI 48084-5315. 313/244-2200. Employs: 100-249.

Craft Inds Inc
13231 23 Mile Rd, Shelby Twp MI 48315-2713. 313/726-4300. Employs: 50-99.

Cyntell Tool Co
17950 Allen Rd, Melvindale MI 48122-1512. 313/383-1444. Employs: 50-99.

D-M-E Co
155 Madison Ave, Mount Clemens MI 48043-1629. 313/465-0406. Employs: 50-99.

Daisy Parts I
52 Willow St, Hillsdale MI 49242-1738. 517/439-1531. Employs: 50-99.

Danly Die Set
255 Industrial Pkwy, Ithaca MI 48847-9476. 517/875-5134. Employs: 50-99.

Derco Inc
10005 U S Rt 223 E, Blissfield MI 49228. 517/486-4337. Employs: 50-99.

Ex-Cell-0 N American Sls & Svc
22705 Heslip Dr, Novi MI 48375-4144. 313/344-4300. Employs: 50-99.

Fraser Grinding Co
34235 Riviera Dr, Fraser MI 48026-1624. 313/293-6060. Employs: 50-99.

Fraser Manufacturing Corp
7235 Boyington St, Lexington MI 48450. 313/359-5338. Employs: 50-99.

Galaxy Precision Machining Co
41150 Joy Rd, Plymouth MI 48170-4634. 313/459-5600.
Employs: 50-99.

Grant-Durban West
175 Rawsonville Rd, Belleville MI 48111-1051. 313/485-3111. Employs: 50-99.

Grippe Machine & Manufacturing Co
15642 Common Rd, Roseville MI 48066-1826. 313/778-3150. Employs: 50-99.

H T M
4691 Beck Rd, Jonesville MI 49250-9401. 517/849-9918.
Employs: 100-249.

Hy-Tek Systs Inc
30930 Indl Rd, Livonia MI 48150. 313/421-3910.
Employs: 50-99.

I S I Robotics
6100 Titan Dr, Anchorville MI 48004. 313/725-2500.
Employs: 100-249.

Inland Craft Products Co
32046 Edward Ave, Madison Hts MI 48071-1420.
313/583-7150. Employs: 50-99.

J Miller Co
29991 M-60 E, Homer MI 49245. 517/568-4398. Employs:
100-249.

Lans Corp
704 E Oakland Ave, Lansing MI 48906-5313. 517/372-8450. Employs: 50-99.

Loc Performance Products Inc
201 Indl Dr, Plymouth MI 48170. 313/453-2300. Employs:
50-99.

Machining Enterprises Inc
11400 Toepfer, Warren MI 48089-4031. 313/755-3180.
Employs: 100-249.

Mexican Inds In Michigan Inc
1600 Howard St, Detroit MI 48216-1921. 313/963-6114.
Employs: 100-249.

Miller Industrial Products Inc
801 Water St, Jackson MI 49203-1963. 517/783-2756.
Employs: 100-249.

Modern Engineering Tool Construction Inc
15990 Sturgeon St, Roseville MI 48066-1819. 313/772-1660. Employs: 50-99.

National Machine Repair Inc
1159 S Pennsylvania Ave, Lansing MI 48912-1657.
517/371-2940. Employs: 50-99.

Numerical Machining Co Inc
30 Corporate Dr, Auburn Hills MI 48326-2918. 313/335-8400. Employs: 50-99.

Parker-Hannifin/Cylinder Div
900 Plymouth Rd, Plymouth MI 48170-1855. 313/455-1700. Employs: 50-99.

Premier Engineering Co
28000 Dequindre Rd, Warren MI 48092-2468. 313/547-8153. Employs: 100-249.

Rapidfil Inc
12841 Stark Rd, Livonia MI 48150-1525. 313/522-1900.
Employs: 100-249.

Raycon Corp
1550 E South St, Owosso MI 48867-9779. 517/725-2129.
Employs: 50-99.

Royal Oak Boring

2625 Nakota, Royal Oak MI 48073-1816. 313/549-7061.
Employs: 50-99.

Saginaw Machine Systs Inc
301 Park St, Troy MI 48083-2778. 313/583-7200.
Employs: 100-249.

Sanyo Machine America Corp
950 Rochester Rd, Rochester MI 48307-2742. 313/651-5911. Employs: 50-99.

Sequoia Inds Inc
11813 Hubbard, Livonia MI 48150-1732. 313/261-4470.
Employs: 50-99.

Shiawasee Manufacturing Co
1470 S McMillan St, Owosso MI 48867-9702. 517/723-8891. Employs: 50-99.

Soramatic Precision Machining
2455 E 10 Mile Rd, Warren MI 48091-3704. 313/758-1100. Employs: 50-99.

T S M Corp
244 Rex Blvd, Auburn Hills MI 48326-2953. 313/853-7700. Employs: 50-99.

Trew-Craft Corp
24877 21 Mile Rd, Macomb MI 48042-5113. 313/949-7000. Employs: 50-99.

Turn Matic Inc
34657 Centaur Dr, Clinton Twp MI 48035-3702. 313/792-5500. Employs: 50-99.

Unison Corp
1601 Wanda Ave, Ferndale MI 48220-2022. 313/544-9500.
Employs: 100-249.

Vickers Incorporated
2425 W Michigan Av, Jackson MI 49202-3964. 517/787-7220. Employs: 100-249.

Wellington Manufacturing Inc
69620 Lowe Plank Rd, Richmond MI 48062. 313/727-3775. Employs: 100-249.

Wisne Automation & Engineering
42445 W 10 Mile Rd, Novi MI 48375-3211. 313/348-7070.
Employs: 100-249.

Acme Manufacturing Co
650 W 12 Mile Rd, Madison Hts MI 48071-2407. 313/547-6700. Employs: 100-249.

Neuman Engineering Products
32450 Industrial Dr, Madison Hts MI 48071-1527.
313/585-8085. Employs: 100-249.

C B S Boring & Machine Co Inc
33750 Riviera Dr, Fraser MI 48026-4806. 313/294-7540.
Employs: 100-249.

Spirit Industries Inc
1305 S Cedar St, Lansing MI 48910-1529. 517/371-7840.
Employs: 50-99.

Systrand
340 S Oakwood, Detroit MI 48217-1453. 313/841-9250.
Employs: 50-99.

**SEARCH, DETECTION, NAVIGATION,
GUIDANCE, AERONAUTICAL AND NAUTICAL
SYSTEMS AND INSTRUMENTS**

Eaton Corp
1728 Maplelawn Dr, Troy MI 48084-4604. 313/643-0220.
Employs: 100-249.

Radar S Custom Instln Svc
78 St James St, Marysville MI 48040-1121. 313/364-7943.
Employs: 50-99.

LABORATORY APPARATUS AND FURNITURE

Laser Enterprises Co
3820 Trade Center Dr, Ann Arbor MI 48108-2006.
313/971-1414. Employs: 50-99.

AUTOMATIC CONTROLS FOR REGULATING RESIDENTIAL AND COMMERCIAL ENVIRONMENTS AND APPLIANCES

A E G Westinghouse Indl
500 Stephenson Hwy, Troy MI 48083-1118. 313/597-5500.
Employs: 100-249.

Dimango Products Corp
7258 Kensington Rd, Brighton MI 48116-8513. 313/486-0770. Employs: 50-99.

INDUSTRIAL INSTRUMENTS FOR MEASUREMENT, DISPLAY AND CONTROL OF PROCESS VARIABLES; AND RELATED PRODUCTS

Acromag Inc
30765 Wixom Rd, Wixom MI 48393-2417. 313/624-1541.
Employs: 100-249.

Electro Mechanical Prod Inc
1900 S Livernois Rd, Rochester MI 48307-3368. 313/656-2722. Employs: 100-249.

Federal A P D
24700 Crestview Ct, Farmington MI 48335-1506. 313/477-2700. Employs: 100-249.

G S E Inc
23640 Research Dr, Farmington MI 48335-2621. 313/476-7875. Employs: 100-249.

Industrial Tectonics Inc
P O Box 1128, Ann Arbor MI 48106-1128. 313/426-4681.
Employs: 100-249.

K J Law Engrs Inc
42300 W 9 Mile Rd, Novi MI 48375-4103. 313/347-3300.
Employs: 50-99.

Nematron Corp
5840 Interface Dr, Ann Arbor MI 48103-9515. 313/994-0501. Employs: 100-249.

Promess Inc
11429 E Grand River, Brighton MI 48116-9547. 313/229-9334. Employs: 50-99.

Sterling Technologies Inc
23177 Commerce Dr, Farmington MI 48335-2723.
313/471-0990. Employs: 100-249.

TOTALIZING FLUID METERS AND COUNTING DEVICES

Freeland Gauge Co
11777 Grand River, Brighton MI 48116-8505. 313/227-5095. Employs: 50-99.

Link Engineering Co
13840 Elmira Ave, Detroit MI 48227-3017. 313/933-4900.
Employs: 50-99.

Universal Flow Monitors
1755 E 9 Mile Rd, Hazel Park MI 48030-1939. 313/542-9635. Employs: 50-99.

MISC. COMMERCIAL EQUIPMENT WHOLESALE

R M R Enterprises
11345 Mound Rd, Detroit MI 48212-2556. 313/893-6900.
Employs: 250-499.

INSTRUMENTS FOR MEASURING AND TESTING OF ELECTRICITY AND ELECTRICAL SIGNALS

Bindicator Co
1915 Dove Rd, Port Huron MI 48060-6767. 313/987-2700.
Employs: 50-99.

Comtel Instruments Co
21223 Hilltop St, Southfield MI 48034-4010. 313/358-2505. Employs: 50-99.

Digital Elexs Automation Inc
37100 Plymouth Rd, Livonia MI 48150-1132. 313/591-3800. Employs: 100-249.

Ram Meter Inc
1100 Hilton Rd, Ferndale MI 48220-2839. 313/398-6767.
Employs: 50-99.

Scans Associates Inc
13000 Farmington Rd, Livonia MI 48150-4201. 313/427-8800. Employs: 50-99.

For more information on career opportunities in industrial manufacturing:

Associations

APPLIANCE PARTS DISTRIBUTORS ASSOCIATION
228 East Baltimore Street, Detroit MI 48202. 313/875-8455.

NATIONAL ASSOCIATION OF MANUFACTURERS
1331 Pennsylvania Avenue, NW, Suite 1500, Washington DC 20004. 202/637-3000.

ASSOCIATION FOR MANUFACTURING TECHNOLOGY

7901/ Westpark Drive, McLean VA 22102. 703/893-2900.

NATIONAL SCREW MACHINE PRODUCTS ASSOCIATION
6700 West Snowville Road, Breckville OH 44141.
216/526-0300.

NATIONAL TOOLING AND MACHINING ASSOCIATION
9300 Livingston Road, Fort Washington MD 20744.
301/248-1250.

MISCELLANEOUS SERVICES

CENTRAL-QUALITY SERVICE
7043 East Palmer, Detroit MI 48211. 313/921-8180. **Contact:** Mrs. Moore, Personnel. **Description:** A Detroit industrial laundry cleaning service. **Employees:** 500.

COMP-U-CHECK INC.
24901 Northwestern Highway, Suite 700, Southfield MI 48075. 313/827-4300. **Contact:** Donna Feltner, Personnel Director. **Description:** Provides check authorization, manually or via automated device, to the retail and banking industries. Primary customers are large retail chains. **Common positions:** Accountant; Computer Programmer; Customer Service Representative; Department Manager; Sales Representative. **Educational backgrounds sought:** Accounting; Business Administration; Finance; Marketing. **Benefits:** medical insurance; dental insurance; life insurance. **Corporate headquarters:** This location. **Operations at this facility:** research/development; administration; service; sales. **Employees:** 96. **Projected new hires for the next 12 months:** 25.

DOMESTIC LINEN SUPPLY AND LAUNDRY
3800 18th Street, Detroit MI 48208. 313/831-6700. **Contact:** Office Manager. **Description:** A major metropolitan Detroit linen supply and laundry service. **Employees:** 600.

FACTORY MUTUAL ENGINEERING AND RESEARCH
30150 Telegraph Road, Suite 141, Bingham Hills MI 48025-4250. 313/540-0500. **Contact:** Mike Dekamp, Office Manager. **Description:** A loss-prevention service organization maintained by the Factory Mutual System (Norwood, MA). District offices are located throughout the United States and Canada. Loss Prevention Consultants, also known as field engineers, inspect insured properties on a periodic basis to help pinpoint hazards or conditions that could cause fires or explosions, or result in damage to property or lost production.

PSI
11900 Mayfield, Livonia MI 48150. 313/261-4160. **Contact:** Personnel Department. **Description:** A major Livonia area hydraulic and electronic repair service. **Employees:** 300.

Additional large employers: 250+

INDUSTRIAL LAUNDERERS

Ace-Tex Corporation
7601 Central Ave, Detroit MI 48210-1038. 313/834-4000.
Employs: 250-499.

J C Penney Co Inc
700 W 14 Mile Rd, Troy MI 48083-4236. 313/585-2960.
Employs: 500-999.

PHOTOGRAPHIC STUDIOS, PORTRAIT

BEAUTY SHOPS

Hudson's
35000 Warren Rd, Westland MI 48185-2021. 313/427-5261. Employs: 250-499.

EMPLOYMENT AGENCIES

Kelly Services Inc World Hqs
999 W Big Beaver Rd, Troy MI 48084-4730. 313/362-4444. Employs: 1000+.

COMPUTER INTEGRATED SYSTEMS DESIGN

Schlumberger Cad/Cam
4251 Plymouth Rd, Ann Arbor MI 48105-2734. 313/995-6000. Employs: 1000+.

INFORMATION RETRIEVAL SERVICES

3 Pm Inc
30881 Schoolcraft Rd, Livonia MI 48150-2010. 313/427-2000. Employs: 250-499.

NEWS SYNDICATES

Great Lakes Media Group
2929 Covington Ct, Lansing MI 48912-4911. 517/371-2142. Employs: 250-499.

BUSINESS SERVICES, NOT ELSEWHERE CLASSIFIED

Florist Transworld Dlvry Assn
29200 Northwestern Hwy, Southfield MI 48034-1013. 313/355-9300. Employs: 250-499.

Howard Ternes Packaging

808 Detroit Ave, Monroe MI 48161-2543. 313/242-8100. Employs: 250-499.

Howard Ternes Packaging Co
12285 Dixie St, Redford MI 48239-2452. 313/531-5867. Employs: 250-499.

Salvation Army
118 W Lawrence St, Pontiac MI 48341-1725. 313/338-9601. Employs: 500-999.

Anchor Motor Freight
2400 W Saint Joseph St, Lansing MI 48917-3876. 517/342-2600. Employs: 250-499.

ELECTRICAL AND ELECTRONIC REPAIR SHOPS, NOT ELSEWHERE CLASSIFIED

Hudson's
21500 Northwestern Hwy, Southfield MI 48075-5018. 313/443-6000. Employs: 1000+.

WATCH, CLOCK AND JEWELRY REPAIR

Hudson's
269 N Telegraph Rd, Waterford MI 48328-3315. 313/683-5872. Employs: 250-499.

E R I M
3300 Plymouth Rd, Ann Arbor MI 48105-2551. 313/994-1200. Employs: 500-999.

BUSINESS CONSULTING SERVICES, NOT ELSEWHERE CLASSIFIED

Rolm Co
30150 Telegraph Rd, Franklin MI 48025-4519. 313/540-9000. Employs: 250-499.

Additional small to medium sized employers: 50-249

VETERINARY SERVICES FOR ANIMAL SPECIALTIES

Professional Veterinary Hospital
15565 W 10 Rd, Southfield MI 48075. 313/569-5210. Employs: 100-249.

GARMENT PRESSING AND AGENTS FOR LAUNDRIES AND DRYCLEANERS

One Hour American Htchng Post
36843 Garfield Rd, Clinton Twp MI 48035-1137. 313/791-8850. Employs: 100-249.

LINEN SUPPLY

Central Quality Services Corp
7043 E Palmer, Detroit MI 48211-3417. 313/921-8180. Employs: 100-249.

DRYCLEANING PLANTS, EXCEPT RUG CLEANING

Troy Cleaners
12500 Saginaw Rd, Grand Blanc MI 48439-1481. 313/695-4860. Employs: 50-99.

M G M Cleaners Inc
2927 N Woodward Ave, Royal Oak MI 48073-6925. 313/288-5750. Employs: 50-99.

PHOTOGRAPHIC STUDIOS, PORTRAIT

Jc Penney Portrait Studio
Westland Mall, Westland MI 48185. 313/422-6330. Employs: 50-99.

K Mart

1396 S Main St, Adrian MI 49221-4307. 517/263-0234. Employs: 50-99.

K Mart Discount Dept Strs
20891 E 13 Mile Rd, Roseville MI 48066-4530. 313/296-1650. Employs: 100-249.

K-Mart Portrait Studio
19800 West Rd, Trenton MI 48183-3319. 313/692-1422. Employs: 100-249.

Kmart Corporation
37175 Grand River Ave, Farmington MI 48335-2821. 313/478-9650. Employs: 100-249.

Kmart Discount Department Str
37000 Van Dyke Ave, Sterling Hts MI 48312-1824. 313/264-6636. Employs: 50-99.

Kmart Discount Department Strs
30225 Plymouth Rd, Livonia MI 48150-2128. 313/427-8634. Employs: 50-99.

Sears Roebuck and Co
18950 Mack Ave, Grosse Pointe MI 48236-2926. 313/884-6000. Employs: 50-99.

BEAUTY SHOPS

J C Penney Co Inc
2231 S Mission St, Mount Pleasant MI 48858-4428. 517/772-3355. Employs: 50-99.

Jacobson's
1220 Walton Blvd, Rochester MI 48307-1857. 313/652-9337. Employs: 50-99.

Life Wear Inc
9530 Perry Rd, Goodrich MI 48438-9745. 313/636-7026.
Employs: 50-99.

Meijer Hairstyling Salon
2000 16 Mile Rd, Sterling Hts MI 48310. 313/977-7718.
Employs: 100-249.

FUNERAL SERVICE AND CREMATORIES

Harry J Will Funeral Home Inc
37000 6 Mile Rd, Livonia MI 48152-2752. 313/591-0838.
Employs: 50-99.

R G Harris & G R Fnrl Homes
4251 Cass Ave, Detroit MI 48201-1709. 313/831-1144.
Employs: 50-99.

Penn Funeral Home
3015 Inkster Rd, Inkster MI 48141-2321. 313/278-6300.
Employs: 50-99.

TAX RETURN PREPARATION SERVICES

H & R Block
235 N Leroy St, Fenton MI 48430-2788. 313/629-0707.
Employs: 50-99.

Nationwide Income Tax Service
14507 Warren Av, Dearborn MI 48126-1364. 313/584-7640. Employs: 50-99.

MISCELLANEOUS PERSONAL SERVICES

Hilton Northfield
5500 Crooks Rd, Troy MI 48098-2806. 313/879-2100.
Employs: 100-249.

Lord Fox
5400 Plymouth Rd, Ann Arbor MI 48105-9520. 313/662-1647. Employs: 50-99.

Red Lobster Restaurants
13800 Hall Rd, Sterling Hts MI 48313-1222. 313/247-6250. Employs: 50-99.

The Embers
1217 S Mission, Mount Pleasant MI 48858. 517/773-5007.
Employs: 100-249.

PHOTOCOPYING AND DUPLICATING SERVICES

Metro Blueprint Inc
24490 W 10 Mile Rd, Southfield MI 48034-4831. 313/961-5252. Employs: 50-99.

COMMERCIAL ART AND GRAPHIC DESIGN

Detroit Art Services Inc
1699 Stutz Dr, Troy MI 48084-4501. 313/643-0900.
Employs: 100-249.

Lighthouse Graphics
1422 Water St, Port Huron MI 48060-4213. 313/987-5087.
Employs: 50-99.

SECRETARIAL AND COURT REPORTING SERVICES

C R's Cat Services Inc
6354 Englewood Dr, Clarkston MI 48346-1105. 313/625-0007. Employs: 50-99.

DISINFECTING AND PEST CONTROL SERVICES

Eradico Pest Control Co
1030 Woodward Hts, Ferndale MI 48220-1457. 313/546-6200. Employs: 50-99.

MISCELLANEOUS BUILDING CLEANING AND MAINTENANCE SERVICES

Custom Maid Inc
30455 Greenfield Rd, Southfield MI 48076-1510. 313/258-6243. Employs: 50-99.

HEAVY CONSTRUCTION EQUIPMENT RENTAL AND LEASING

Fraza Equipment Inc
15725 Twelve Mile Rd, Roseville MI 48066-1844.
313/778-6111. Employs: 50-99.

Klochko Equipment Rental
2782 Corbin Av, Melvindale MI 48122-1806. 313/386-7220. Employs: 100-249.

Intrntl Ind Cntrctng Corp
35900 Mound Rd, Sterling Hts MI 48310-4730. 313/264-7070. Employs: 100-249.

MISCELLANEOUS EQUIPMENT RENTAL AND LEASING

Brockman Forklift Inc
15800 Tireman, Detroit MI 48228-3610. 313/584-4550.
Employs: 50-99.

Contract Interiors
10 Oak Hollow St, Southfield MI 48034-7405. 313/358-2000. Employs: 50-99.

EMPLOYMENT AGENCIES

K & J Associates Inc
109 W Washington St, Howell MI 48843-2232. 517/546-6570. Employs: 50-99.

Manpower Temporary Servs
2325 W Shiawassee St Ste 204, Fenton MI 48430-1792.
313/629-8571. Employs: 50-99.

Career Decision Strategies
15305 Windmill Pointe Dr, Grosse Pointe MI 48230-1743.
313/824-1911. Employs: 50-99.

HELP SUPPLY SERVICES

All Tech Management
2444 E Hill Rd, Flint MI 48507-3821. 313/695-1940.
Employs: 50-99.

Norrell Temporary Services
414 S Main St Ste 208, Rochester MI 48307-2070.
313/651-1500. Employs: 50-99.

Sentry Svc
218 S Main St, Milford MI 48381-1962. 313/685-8229.
Employs: 50-99.

COMPUTER INTEGRATED SYSTEMS DESIGN

Eds
30009 Van Dyke St, Warren MI 48093. 313/492-8453.
Employs: 50-99.

I B M Information Systems Gp
1 E Michigan Av 3dfl, Lansing MI 48933. 517/377-3700.
Employs: 100-249.

T & B Computing
1968 Green Rd, Ann Arbor MI 48105-2557. 313/973-1900.
Employs: 100-249.

INFORMATION RETRIEVAL SERVICES

Man Guard Systems Inc
25974 Novi Rd, Novi MI 48375-1671. 313/349-3830.
Employs: 50-99.

Wang Laboratories Inc
380 S Woodward Av, Farmington Hi MI 48018. 313/737-1000. Employs: 100-249.

COMPUTER FACILITIES MANAGEMENT SERVICES

National Techteam Inc
22000 Garrison, Dearborn MI 48124-2306. 313/277-2277.
Employs: 100-249.

COMPUTER RENTAL AND LEASING

Csp
30801 Barrington St Ste 100, Madison Hts MI 48071-5134.
313/689-8190. Employs: 50-99.

MISCELLANEOUS COMPUTER RELATED SERVICES

E G & G Structural Kinematics
950 Maplelawn, Troy MI 48084-5347. 313/643-4622.
Employs: 50-99.

Medstat Systems Inc
777 E Eisenhower Pkwy, Ann Arbor MI 48108-3258.
313/996-1180. Employs: 100-249.

Ciber Inc
4 Parklane Blvd, Dearborn MI 48126-2660. 313/271-1221.
Employs: 50-99.

DETECTIVE, GUARD AND ARMORED CAR SERVICES

Smith Security Corp
225 S Averill Av, Flint MI 48506-4003. 313/257-1000.
Employs: 50-99.

Wells Fargo Guard Services
2500 Packard Rd Ste 200, Ann Arbor MI 48104-6895.
313/971-6071. Employs: 50-99.

Chief Protective Agcy
4660 Cimmarron Dr, Bloomfield MI 48302-2216. 313/855-9510. Employs: 50-99.

Endress Detective Agency
3742 Rutherford Ct, Waterford MI 48329-2178. 313/673-7840. Employs: 50-99.

Merch Det Agcy & Sec Service Inc
1378 Dix Hwy, Lincoln Park MI 48146-1347. 313/383-3750. Employs: 50-99.

PHOTOFINISHING LABORATORIES

Jack's Camera
210 Washington Sq S, Lansing MI 48933-1808. 517/372-1155. Employs: 50-99.

Meteor Photo Co
1099 Chicago Rd, Troy MI 48083-4204. 313/583-3090.
Employs: 50-99.

MISCELLANEOUS BUSINESS SERVICES

Adistra Corp
101 Union St, Plymouth MI 48170. 313/425-2600.
Employs: 100-249.

Art Craft Display Inc
2920 W St Joseph St, Lansing MI 48917-3740. 517/485-2221. Employs: 50-99.

Blue Ribbon Demonstrator
22176 Bernard St, Taylor MI 48180-3653. 313/295-0088.
Employs: 50-99.

Brass Craft Manufacturing Co
20505 Sibley Rd, Wyandotte MI 48192-8429. 313/479-0410. Employs: 100-249.

C W A Manufacturing Co
G-7406 N Dort Hwy, Mount Morris MI 48458. 313/686-3030. Employs: 100-249.

Demmer Corporation
1010 Ballard St, Lansing MI 48906-5358. 517/321-3600.
Employs: 100-249.

Eagle Packaging Corp
12680 Burt Rd, Detroit MI 48223-3315. 313/535-6760.
Employs: 50-99.

Earl Dalip Signs Limited
6060 Birch Rd, Flint MI 48507-4648. 313/767-2020.
Employs: 100-249.

Feblo Inc
34450 Indl Rd, Livonia MI 48150. 313/525-9100.
Employs: 100-249.

Liberty Eng
1350 John R Rd, Troy MI 48083-4328. 313/588-5130.
Employs: 100-249.

Pickard & Associates
335 Pine Ridge Dr, Bloomfield MI 48304-2140. 313/258-6520. Employs: 50-99.

Quality Packaging Systs
24260 Mound Rd, Warren MI 48091-5324. 313/756-5330.
Employs: 50-99.

Rapid Design Service Br
624 Hupp Av, Jackson MI 49203-1930. 517/782-0429.
Employs: 50-99.

Tigon Corporation
1 Parklane Blvd Ite 1205E, Dearborn MI 48126-2402.
313/322-6000. Employs: 100-249.

Troy Design Services
2653 Industrial Row, Troy MI 48084-7038. 313/280-0500.
Employs: 100-249.

Tuar Company
G5365 Hill 23 Dr, Flint MI 48507. 313/239-5552.
Employs: 50-99.

Venchurs Packaging
800 Liberty St, Adrian MI 49221-3955. 517/263-8937.
Employs: 50-99.

Vu Com Data Services Inc
1120 Keystone Av, Lansing MI 48911. 517/393-8610.
Employs: 50-99.

Worthington Specialty Process
4905 S Meridian Rd, Jackson MI 49201-8752. 517/789-0200. Employs: 100-249.

Value Village
987 Manufacturers Dr, Westland MI 48185-4036. 313/728-4568. Employs: 100-249.

Complete Auto Transit Inc
2901 Tyler Rd, Ypsilanti MI 48198-6126. 313/483-5700.
Employs: 100-249.

Kabenung Industries Inc
2720 Saradan Dr, Jackson MI 49202-1216. 517/782-9407.
Employs: 50-99.

R G I S Inventory Specialists
805 Oakwood Dr, Rochester MI 48307-1359. 313/651-2511. Employs: 100-249.

Graphic Sciences Inc
4208 Normandy Ct, Royal Oak MI 48073-2263. 313/549-6600. Employs: 50-99.

Pioneer Micrographix Inc
228 S Mill St, South Lyon MI 48178-1455. 313/437-7677.
Employs: 50-99.

Technical Industries Inc
25631 Little Mack Ave, St Clair Shrs MI 48081-2175.
313/777-0160. Employs: 100-249.

Planterra Tropical GrnHouses Inc
7315 Drake Rd, W Bloomfield MI 48322-3164. 313/661-
1515. Employs: 50-99.

Robertson Bros Pool Svc
3190 Haggerty Hwy, W Bloomfield MI 48323-2010.
313/669-9070. Employs: 100-249.

**REFRIGERATION AND AIR-CONDITIONING
SERVICE AND REPAIR SHOPS**

Johnson Controls Inc
375 Robbins Dr, Troy MI 48083-4561. 313/585-6490.
Employs: 50-99.

**MISCELLANEOUS ELECTRICAL AND
ELECTRONIC REPAIR SHOPS**

P T Brad S
112 E Ellen St, Fenton MI 48430-2115. 313/750-9341.
Employs: 50-99.

WATCH, CLOCK AND JEWELRY REPAIR

Brennan Jewelry Inc
7627 Allen Rd, Allen Park MI 48101-1925. 313/388-1140.
Employs: 50-99.

WELDING REPAIR

C & H Industries Inc
1187 Souter St, Troy MI 48083-2821. 313/589-3696.
Employs: 100-249.

Michigan Railcar Repair Co
13101 Eckles Rd, Plymouth MI 48170-4201. 313/455-
6900. Employs: 50-99.

ARMATURE REWINDING SHOPS

GE Supply
684 Robbins Dr, Troy MI 48083-4563. 313/588-7300.
Employs: 50-99.

**MISCELLANEOUS REPAIR SHOPS AND RELATED
SERVICES**

Allied Inc
260 Metty Dr, Ann Arbor MI 48103-9444. 313/665-4419.
Employs: 50-99.

F P Miller Co

420 Ingham St, Jackson MI 49201-1251. 517/787-3100.
Employs: 50-99.

Wickman Corporation
10325 Capital Ave, Oak Park MI 48237-3103. 313/548-
3822. Employs: 50-99.

Grinders For Industry Inc
51300 Pontiac Trl, Wixom MI 48393-2045. 313/624-5755.
Employs: 100-249.

Raisin River Golf Club
1500 N Dixie Hwy, Monroe MI 48161-5205. 313/289-
3700. Employs: 50-99.

Dumont Taxidery Inc
2772 Leach Rd, Rochester MI 48309-3559. 313/852-0200.
Employs: 50-99.

MISCELLANEOUS SERVICES

Eastwood Community Services
19855 Outer Dr Ste 204-W, Dearborn MI 48124-2027.
313/561-2790. Employs: 50-99.

Gabriel Roeder Smith & Co
407 E Fort St, Detroit MI 48226-2940. 313/961-3346.
Employs: 50-99.

Hewitt Associates
100 Renaissance Center, Detroit MI 48243-1002. 313/567-
9100. Employs: 50-99.

William M Mercer Inc
400 Renaissance Center, Detroit MI 48243. 313/259-1000.
Employs: 50-99.

The Wyatt Co
200 First National Bg, Detroit MI 48226. 313/961-5485.
Employs: 50-99.

America Suzuki Motor Corp
1012 Pontiac Trail, Ann Arbor MI 48105-1715. 313/747-
9840. Employs: 50-99.

Center For Mach Intelligence
2001 Commonwealth Blvd Ste 102, Ann Arbor MI 48105-
1562. 313/995-0900. Employs: 50-99.

Coldwater Corporation
2001 Commonwealth Blvd Ste 202, Ann Arbor MI 48105-
1568. 313/668-2621. Employs: 50-99.

Genova Incorporated
7034 E Court St, Burton MI 48529. 313/744-4500.
Employs: 50-99.

NEWSPAPER PUBLISHING

Throughout the recession, the newspaper industry has been suffering from a severely shrinking share of advertising dollars. Classified advertising was especially hard hit, and recovery will depend on improvement in the retail, automotive, and real estate industries, as well as on a growing employment market. For the long-term, look for newspaper companies to target specific readers in order to attract advertisers.
Lifestyle, health care, and business sections will grow in importance.

DETROIT NEWSPAPER AGENCY
615 West Lafayette Boulevard, Detroit MI 48226. 313/222-2177. **Contact:** Linda Conroy, Human Resources. **Description:** A business operating unit for two major Detroit newspapers--The Detroit News and The Detroit Free Press. **Common positions:** Accountant; Advertising Worker; Advertising Sales Representative; Computer Programmer; Customer Service Representative; Reporter; Editor. **Educational backgrounds sought:** Business Administration. **Special programs:** Training programs. **Benefits:** medical, dental, and life insurance; pension plan; tuition assistance; disability coverage; employee discounts; savings plan. **Corporate headquarters:** This location. **Operations at this facility:** divisional headquarters; research/development; administration; service; sales.

OAKLAND PRESS COMPANY
48 West Huron, Pontiac MI 48342. 313/332-8181. **Contact:** Jan Allen, Personnel Director. **Description:** An area newspaper company which publishes the Oakland Press. **Employees:** 300.

OBSERVER & ECCENTRIC SUBURBAN COMMUNICATIONS
36251 Schoolcraft, Livonia MI 48150. 313/953-2253. **Contact:** Donna Roy, Personnel Coordinator. **Description:** A Southeastern Michigan company engaged in the publishing and printing of newspapers. **Employees:** 700.

Large employers: 250+

NEWSPAPERS: PUBLISHING AND PRINTING

Detroit News
6200 Metropolitan Pkwy, Sterling Hts MI 48312-1022. 313/826-7010. Employs: 1000+.

Flint Journal
200 E 1st St, Flint MI 48502-1911. 313/767-0660. Employs: 250-499.

Lansing State Journal
120 E Lenawee St, Lansing MI 48919-0001. 517/377-1000. Employs: 250-499.

The Ann Arbor News
340 E Huron St, Ann Arbor MI 48104-1909. 313/994-6989. Employs: 250-499.

The Flint Journal
200 East Rd, Holly MI 48442-1435. 313/766-6100. Employs: 250-499.

Small to medium sized employers: 50-249

NEWSPAPERS: PUBLISHING OR PUBLISHING AND PRINTING

Action Ad Newspapers Inc
504 Main St, Belleville MI 48111-2650. 313/697-8255.
Employs: 50-99.

Adams Publishing
67 Cass Ave, Mount Clemens MI 48043-2347. 313/296-0810. Employs: 100-249.

Argus-Press Co
201 E Exchange St, Owosso MI 48867-3009. 517/725-5136. Employs: 50-99.

Associated Newspapers Inc
35540 W Michigan Ave, Wayne MI 48184-1626. 313/729-4000. Employs: 50-99.

Brill Media Co
215 N Main St, Mount Pleasant MI 48858-2306. 517/772-2971. Employs: 100-249.

Building Tradesman
1640 Porter St, Detroit MI 48216-1936. 313/961-3800. Employs: 50-99.

Circulation
113 E Grand River Ave, Brighton MI 48116-1509. 313/685-7546. Employs: 50-99.

Community Newspapers
219 S Bridge St, Grand Ledge MI 48837-1526. 517/627-4001. Employs: 50-99.

Conques Newspaper
44844 Michigan Ave, Canton MI 48188-2431. 313/397-1170. Employs: 50-99.

Daily Telegram
133 N Winter St, Adrian MI 49221-2042. 517/265-5111. Employs: 50-99.

Detroit News Editorial Bureau
330 E Liberty St, Ann Arbor MI 48104-2206. 313/665-8902. Employs: 50-99.

Greenville Daily News
109 N Lafayette Rd, Greenville MI 48838-1853. 616/754-9301. Employs: 100-249.

Huron Publishing Co Inc
211 N Heisterman St, Bad Axe MI 48413-1239. 517/269-6461. Employs: 50-99.

Huron Valley News
3922-26trade Center Dr, Ann Arbor MI 48108. 313/973-0919. Employs: 50-99.

International Journalist
13530 Michigan Ave, Dearborn MI 48126-3555. 313/581-3344. Employs: 50-99.

Japan Detroit Press
47900 W Huron River Dr, Belleville MI 48111-4401. 313/697-4999. Employs: 50-99.

Livingston County Press Inc
323 E Grand River, Howell MI 48843-2322. 517/548-2000. Employs: 50-99.

Lynns Printing Service Inc
215 N Main St, Mount Pleasant MI 48858-2306. 517/773-3984. Employs: 50-99.

Macomb Daily
67 Cass Ave, Mount Clemens MI 48043-2347. 313/469-4510. Employs: 100-249.

Manchester Enterprise
150 E Main, Manchester MI 48158. 313/428-8173. Employs: 50-99.

Masonic World
5th Mezz Masonic Temple, Detroit MI 48201. 313/831-6250. Employs: 50-99.

Michigan Catholic
305 Michigan, Detroit MI 48226. 313/224-8000. Employs: 50-99.

Michigan Review
911 N University Ave, Ann Arbor MI 48109-1010. 313/662-1909. Employs: 50-99.

Monroe Evening News
26037 E Huron River Dr, Flat Rock MI 48134-1218. 313/782-9555. Employs: 50-99.

Monroe Publishing Co
20 W First St, Monroe MI 48161-2333. 313/242-1100. Employs: 100-249.

News-Herald Newspapers
1 Heritage Pl #100, Southgate MI 48195-3053. 313/246-0800. Employs: 100-249.

Observation Balloon News Ltr
1 Lafayette Plaisance St, Detroit MI 48207-2815. 313/393-0670. Employs: 50-99.

Oxford Leader & Advertiser
666 S Lapeer Rd, Oxford MI 48371-5034. 313/628-4801. Employs: 50-99.

Revelator
14660 Woodmont Rd, Detroit MI 48227-1469. 313/835-1212. Employs: 50-99.

S-G Publications Inc
140 E Ash St, Mason MI 48854-1646. 517/676-5100. Employs: 50-99.

State News
345 Student Services Building, East Lansing MI 48824. 517/355-3447. Employs: 100-249.

Stephen Kornacki
2130 Scio Church, Ann Arbor MI 48103. 313/662-0404. Employs: 50-99.

Suburban News
17205 Lahser Rd, Detroit MI 48219-3255. 313/535-2400. Employs: 50-99.

The Bedford Press
8336 Monroe Rd, Lambertville MI 48144-9645. 313/856-6680. Employs: 50-99.

The Detroit News
3920 Trade Center Dr, Ann Arbor MI 48108-2006. 313/973-7177. Employs: 50-99.

The Detroit Times
11000 W McNichols Rd, Detroit MI 48221-2357. 313/342-1717. Employs: 50-99.

The Fifth Estate
4632 2nd Ave, Detroit MI 48201-1224. 313/831-6800. Employs: 50-99.

The Michigan Daily
420 Maynard St, Ann Arbor MI 48109-1327. 313/764-0562. Employs: 50-99.

The New York Times
845 Free Press, Detroit MI 48226. 313/961-7858. Employs: 50-99.

The Peoples Weekly World Newspaper
908 Michigan, Detroit MI 48226. 313/961-2025. Employs:
50-99.

The Ypsilanti Press
20 E Michigan Av, Ypsilanti MI 48198-5610. 313/487-
8300. Employs: 100-249.

Times Herald Co
911 Military St, Port Huron MI 48060-5414. 313/985-7171.
Employs: 100-249.

Town & Country Gazette
106 Park Pl, Dundee MI 48131-1016. 313/529-3086.
Employs: 50-99.

United Press International

333 E Stadium Blvd, Ann Arbor MI 48104. 313/662-1102.
Employs: 50-99.

Washtenaw
2935 Birch Hollow Dr, Ann Arbor MI 48108-2301.
313/971-1800. Employs: 50-99.

Washtenaw County Child Care Journal
2245 Pittsfield Blvd, Ann Arbor MI 48104-5234. 313/971-
8778. Employs: 50-99.

West Valley News
10801 Saginaw Rd, Grand Blanc MI 48439-8126. 313/238-
5222. Employs: 50-99.

Wolverine Newspaper
777 Eisenhower Pkwy E Ste 323A, Ann Arbor MI 48108-
3267. 313/996-9092. Employs: 50-99.

For more information on career opportunities in newspaper publishing:

Associations

**AMERICAN NEWSPAPER PUBLISHERS
ASSOCIATION**
Newspaper Center, 11600 Sunrise Valley Drive, Reston
VA 22091. 703/648-1000.

AMERICAN SOCIETY OF NEWSPAPER EDITORS
P.O. Box 17004, Washington DC 20041. 703/648-1144.

THE DOW JONES NEWSPAPER FUND
P.O. Box 300, Princeton NJ 08543-0300. 609/520-4000.

**INTERNATIONAL CIRCULATION MANAGERS
ASSOCIATION**
P.O. Box 17420, Washington DC 20041. 703/620-9555.

NATIONAL NEWSPAPER ASSOCIATION
1627 K Street NW, Suite 400, Washington DC 20006.
202/466-7200.

NATIONAL PRESS CLUB
529 14th St. NW, 13th Floor, Washington DC 20045.
202/662-7500.

THE NEWSPAPER GUILD
Research and Information Department, 1125 15th Street
NW, Washington DC 20005. 301/585-2990.

Directories

**EDITOR & PUBLISHER INTERNATIONAL
YEARBOOK**
Editor & Publisher Co. Inc., 11 West 19th Street, New
York NY 10011. 212/675-4380.

**JOURNALISM CAREER AND SCHOLARSHIP
GUIDE**
The Dow Jones Newspaper Fund, P.O. Box 300, Princeton
NJ 08543-0300. 609/520-4000.

Magazines

EDITOR AND PUBLISHER
Editor & Publisher Co. Inc., 11 West 19th Street, New
York NY 10011. 212/675-4380.

NEWS, INC.
49 East 21st Street, New York NY 10010. 212/979-4600.

PAPER AND PACKAGING/GLASS AND FOREST PRODUCTS

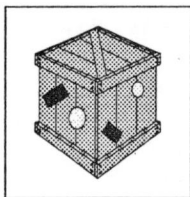

The next few years hold both promise and problems for the paper industry. If the economy strengthens and export markets regain the momentum lost during the last few years, the industry should see revenues grow about 10 percent by the end of 1996. Technological advances should strengthen the industry both at home and abroad. In addition, environmental concerns should give the paper packaging segment the upper hand over plastics.

BRAVER LUMBER AND SUPPLY
P.O. Box 3013, Birmingham MI 48012. 313/644-5300. **Contact:** Personnel. **Description:** A major area distributor of lumber, plywood, and building construction materials. **Employees:** 300.

CHRYSLER/McGRAW GLASS DIVISION
9400 McGraw, Detroit MI 48288. 313/943-4951. **Contact:** Bill McCullum, Compensation and Employment Supervisor. **Description:** Engaged in the manufacture of glass products and windshields for automobiles. **Employees:** 1,000. **Common positions:** Accountant; Administrator; Blue-Collar Worker Supervisor; Draftsperson; Electrical Engineer; Industrial Engineer; Mechanical Engineer; Financial Analyst; Industrial Manager; Personnel and Labor Relations Specialist. **Educational backgrounds sought:** Accounting; Engineering; Finance. **Benefits:** medical and dental Insurance. **Corporate headquarters:** Highland Park - Auburn Hills, MI. **Parent company:** Chrysler Corporation. **Operations at this facility:** manufacturing; research and development; administration. **Projected hires for the next 12 months:** 4.

CONTINENTAL PAPER AND SUPPLY
6400 East 8 Mile Road, Detroit MI 48234. 313/892-7600. **Contact:** Dave Marshall, Controller. Engaged in the wholesale trade of industrial and personal service paper products. **Employees:** 100.

H.A. DAVIDSON BOX COMPANY
P.O. Box 27066, 11435 Shaeffer, Detroit MI 48227. 313/834-6770. **Contact:** George Reneaud, General Manager. **Description:** A metropolitan Detroit company engaged in the manufacture of wood containers. **Employees:** 100.

DAVIDSON INTERIOR TRIM TEXTRON
1515 Newburgh Road, Westland MI 48185. 313/721-1000. **Contact:** Paul Collucci, Director of Human Resources. **Description:** A leading area manufacturer of vehicle parts. **Employees:** 1,200.

E.B. EDDY PAPER COMPANY
1700 Washington, Port Huron MI 48060. 313/982-0191. **Contact:** Allen Kutcher, Human Resources. **Description:** A leading manufacturer of paper rolls for printing, specialty, and packaging purposes. **Employees:** 700.

FAYGO BEVERAGES, INCORPORATED
3579 Gratiot Avenue, Detroit MI 48207. 313/925-1600. **Contact:** Personnel. **Description:** A major metropolitan bottler and cannery of soft drinks. **Employees:** 400.

FRYE COPY SYSTEMS
1210 Progress Street, Sturgis MI 49091. 616/651-3251. **Contact:** Ron Pacelli, General Manager, or Cory Wilbur for office work and Duane Schisser for production. **Description:** An area producer of carbon and carbonless papers, ribbons, and inks. Parent company, Allied Signal Corporation, serves a broad spectrum of industries through its more than 40 strategic businesses, which are grouped into five sectors: Aerospace; Automotive; Chemical; Industrial and Technology; and Oil and Gas. Allied Signal is one of the nation's largest industrial organizations, and has 115,000 employees in over 30 countries. **Corporate headquarters:** Morristown, NJ.

GRAPHIC DIRECT
1451 East Lincoln, P.O. Box 9632, Madison Heights MI 48071-9632. 313/399-3300. **Contact:** Nancy Pierce, Personnel. **Description:** An area company whose primary business is the manufacture of manifold business forms. **Employees:** 200.

GUARDIAN INDUSTRIES/CARLETON GLASS PLANT
14600 Romine Road, Carleton MI 48117. 313/962-2252. **Contact:** Craig B. Richardson, Human Resources Manager. **Description:** Engaged in the manufacture of flat glass. **Employees:** 550. **Common positions:** Ceramics Engineer; Chemical Engineer; Electrical Engineer. **Educational backgrounds sought:** Chemistry; Ceramic Engineering. **Benefits:** medical and dental insurance; various incentive and production bonus programs. **Corporate headquarters:** Northville, MI. **Operations at this facility:** manufacturing; sales.

HELM INC.
14310 Hamilton Avenue, Highland Park MI 48203. 313/865-5000. **Contact:** Debbie Holder, Personnel Director. **Description:** An area company engaged in the packing and distribution of literature. **Employees:** 300.

HEUBLEIN INC./MICHIGAN DIVISION
2500 Enterprise Drive, Allen Park MI 48101. 313/594-8900. **Contact:** Sheila Finney, Personnel Director. **Description:** A major Southeastern Michigan bottler and distributor of liquor. **Employees:** 400.

LIFETIME DOORS INC.
30700 Northwestern Highway, Farmington Hills MI 48334. 313/851-7700. **Contact:** Personnel Department. **Description:** A leading area manufacturer of wooden interior doors.

MIAMI SYSTEMS/SHELBY DIVISION
28120 Dequindre, Warren MI 48092. 313/573-6451. **Contact:** Personnel Department. **Description:** The sales office for a company which manufactures business forms. **Employees:** 500. **Common positions:** Sales Representative. **Special programs:** Training programs. **Corporate headquarters:** Cincinnati, OH. **Operations at this facility:** sales.

MICHIGAN LUMBER COMPANY
P.O. Box 766, Flint MI 48501. 313/232-4108. **Contact:** Personnel Department. **Description:** A major Flint area retailer of lumber and related materials. **Employees:** 100.

MICHIGAN TYPESETTING INC.
1959 East Jefferson, Detroit MI 48207. 313/567-8900. **Contact:** Personnel Department. **Description:** A metropolitan Detroit company engaged in typesetting. **Employees:** 200.

NATIONAL LUMBER COMPANY
24595 Groesbeck, P.O. Box 1003, Warren MI 48090-1003. 313/775-8200. **Contact:** Ms. Danielle Trybus, Personnel Director. **Description:** A leading area wholesale dealer of lumber and related materials. **Employees:** 100.

STONE CONTAINER CORPORATION
6400 Harper, Detroit MI 48211. 313/925-1804. **Contact:** Ms. Ronnie Cresentti, Personnel. **Description:** A manufacturer of corrugated boxes. **Corporate headquarters:** Chicago, IL. **Common positions:** Accountant; Customer Service Representative; Industrial Designer; Operations/Production Manager; Personnel and Labor Relations Specialist; Quality Control Supervisor; Sales Representative; Transportation And Traffic Specialist. **Educational backgrounds sought:** Accounting; Business Administration; Engineering; Liberal Arts; Marketing. **Benefits:** medical, dental, and life insurance; tuition assistance; disability coverage; profit sharing; savings plan; stock purchase plan. **Operations at this facility:** manufacturing. **Listed on:** New York Stock Exchange.

Additional large employers: 250+

MILLWORK

Lifetime Doors Inc
30700 Northwestern Hwy, Farmington MI 48334-2511.
313/851-7700. Employs: 500-999.

WOOD KITCHEN CABINETS

Merillat Inds Inc
2075 W Beecher St, Adrian MI 49221-9769. 517/263-8282.
Employs: 1000+.

CORRUGATED AND SOLID FIBER BOXES

Tecumseh Corrugated Box Co
707 S Evans, Tecumseh MI 49286-1919. 517/423-2126.
Employs: 250-499.

MISC. PACKAGING PAPER AND PLASTICS FILM

American Tape Co
317 Kendall Ave, Marysville MI 48040-1911. 313/364-9000. Employs: 250-499.

ENVELOPES

The John Henry Co
P O Box 17099, Lansing MI 48901-7099. 517/323-9000. Employs: 250-499.

MISC. CONVERTED PAPER AND PAPERBOARD PRODUCTS

G & L Industries Inc
48175 N Gratiot Ave, Clinton Twp MI 48035-4039. 313/949-9000. Employs: 500-999.

GLASS CONTAINERS

Owens-Brockway Glass Container
500 E Packard Hwy, Charlotte MI 48813-9701. 517/543-1400. Employs: 250-499.

GLASS PRODUCTS, MADE OF PURCHASED

Acorn Building Components Inc
12620 Westwood Ave, Detroit MI 48223-3434. 313/272-5700. Employs: 250-499.

Libbey-Owens-Ford Co
11700 Tecumseh-Clinton Rd, Clinton MI 49236-9541. 517/456-7451. Employs: 250-499.

Mc Graw Glass
9400 McGraw Ave, Detroit MI 48210-2078. 313/943-4905. Employs: 500-999.

INDUSTRIAL AND PERSONAL SERVICE PAPER: WHOLESALE

Mid-West Paper Prods Co
2250 W Grand Bl, Detroit MI 48208-1106. 313/539-1470. Employs: 250-499.

Additional small to medium sized employers: 50-249

SAWMILLS AND PLANING MILLS, GENERAL

L L Johnson Lumber Manufacturing Co
563 N Cochran St, Charlotte MI 48813-1178. 517/543-1660. Employs: 50-99.

HARDWOOD DIMENSION AND FLOORING MILLS

Hardwoods Of Michigan Inc
430 Division St, Clinton MI 49236-9702. 517/456-7431. Employs: 100-249.

MILLWORK

Michigan Birch Door Manufacturers
50450 E Russell Schmidt Blvd, Harrison Twp MI 48045. 313/949-2020. Employs: 100-249.

Plymouth Flush Door Inc
100 P F D Dr, Litchfield MI 49252. 517/542-2332. Employs: 100-249.

WOOD KITCHEN CABINETS

Kurtis Kitchen & Baths
12500 Merriman Rd, Livonia MI 48150-1923. 313/522-7600. Employs: 50-99.

La Fata Cabinet Shop
50905 Hayes Rd, Shelby Twp MI 48315-3237. 313/247-1140. Employs: 50-99.

Lemica Corp
19690 Filer St, Detroit MI 48234-2836. 313/892-8800. Employs: 50-99.

HARDWOOD VENEER AND PLYWOOD

Marco Wood Products Co
2000 Easy St, Walled Lake MI 48390-3222. 313/624-1010. Employs: 100-249.

MISCELLANEOUS STRUCTURAL WOOD MEMBERS

Allwood Building Components
35377 32 Mile Rd, Richmond MI 48062-1301. 313/727-2731. Employs: 50-99.

Bear Truss & Components Co
721 E Washington St, Saint Louis MI 48880-1986. 517/681-5774. Employs: 100-249.

Century Truss Co Of Mi
8085 Boardwalk Rd, Brighton MI 48116-8312. 313/486-4000. Employs: 100-249.

Heart Truss & Engineering Corp
1830 N Grand River Ave, Lansing MI 48906-3905. 517/372-0850. Employs: 50-99.

WOOD PALLETS AND SKIDS

Complete Packaging Inc Plant
601 Detroit Av, Monroe MI 48161-2540. 313/241-2900. Employs: 50-99.

MISCELLANEOUS WOOD CONTAINERS

Fontana Forest Products
7175 Clayton St, Detroit MI 48210-2751. 313/841-8950. Employs: 50-99.

PREFABRICATED WOOD BUILDINGS AND COMPONENTS

Active Homes Corp
7938 S Van Dyke, Marlette MI 48453-9131. 517/635-3532. Employs: 100-249.

Riverbend Timber Framing Inc
9012 U S Rt 23, Blissfield MI 49228. 517/486-4355. Employs: 50-99.

PAPER MILLS

Curtis Paper Division James River
1000 Huron St, Ypsilanti MI 48197-9701. 313/482-2600. Employs: 50-99.

Genesee Business Systems
8469 S Saginaw St, Grand Blanc MI 48439-2069. 313/695-5133. Employs: 50-99.

I P M C Inc
9125 W Jefferson Ave, Detroit MI 48209-2659. 313/842-0042. Employs: 100-249.

James River Corporation
218 Riverview St, Port Huron MI 48060-2976. 313/984-5523. Employs: 100-249.

Lakeview Distributors
815 24th St, Port Huron MI 48060-7310. 313/987-8008. Employs: 50-99.

Monroe Paper Co
1205 E Elm Av, Monroe MI 48161-2522. 313/241-7700.
Employs: 100-249.

Okaysions
156 W Michigan Av, Jackson MI 49201-1302. 517/784-2270. Employs: 50-99.

Owosso Paper & Sup Co
211 Corunna Av, Owosso MI 48867-3503. 517/725-2004.
Employs: 50-99.

Pro Paper Products
601 Clinton St, Owosso MI 48867-2669. 517/723-8639.
Employs: 50-99.

Steindler Paper Co
1514 Daniel Rd, Jackson MI 49202-4055. 517/787-6295.
Employs: 50-99.

PAPERBOARD MILLS

Jefferson Smurfit Corp
1151 W Elm St, Monroe MI 48161-2801. 313/241-7776.
Employs: 50-99.

Michigan Packaging Co
223 N Main St, Eaton Rapids MI 48827-1227. 517/663-8121. Employs: 100-249.

Simplex Products
3000 W Beecher St, Adrian MI 49221-9702. 517/263-8881.
Employs: 50-99.

Westcott Paper Products Co
450 Amsterdam St, Detroit MI 48202-3408. 313/872-1200.
Employs: 50-99.

CORRUGATED AND SOLID FIBER BOXES

Ace Paper Products Co
7986 N Telegraph Rd, Newport MI 48166-8901. 313/586-2111. Employs: 50-99.

All American Container Corp
22445 Groesbeck Hwy, Warren MI 48089-4232. 313/777-3700. Employs: 50-99.

Bay Corrugated Container Inc
1655 W 7th St, Monroe MI 48161-1686. 313/243-5400.
Employs: 100-249.

Compak Inc
8789 E Lansing, Durand MI 48429-1056. 517/288-3199.
Employs: 50-99.

Georgia-Pacific Corp
951 County St, Milan MI 48160-9701. 313/439-2441.
Employs: 100-249.

Georgia-Pacific Corp
465 S Delaney Rd, Owosso MI 48867-9114. 517/725-5191.
Employs: 100-249.

International Paper Co/Container Div
1450 McPherson Pk Dr, Howell MI 48843-1936. 517/546-1220. Employs: 100-249.

Packaging Corp Of America
936 N Sheldon Rd, Plymouth MI 48170-1016. 313/453-6262. Employs: 50-99.

Stone Corrugated Inc
25445 W Outer Dr, Melvindale MI 48122-1941. 313/386-5700. Employs: 100-249.

FIBER CANS, TUBES, DRUMS AND SIMILAR PRODUCTS

Advance Packaging Corp
2400 E High St, Jackson MI 49203-3422. 517/788-9800.
Employs: 50-99.

Consolidated Pkg Flint Div
1409 E Pierson Rd, Flint MI 48505-3081. 313/787-6503.
Employs: 100-249.

The Box Shoppe
2887 Krafft Rd Ste 1400, Port Huron MI 48060-1530.
313/985-8780. Employs: 50-99.

FOLDING PAPERBOARD BOXES, INCLUDING SANITARY

Eastern Box Co
19420 Mt Elliott St, Detroit MI 48234-2741. 313/893-9000.
Employs: 50-99.

Modern Packaging Corp
504 Huber Dr, Monroe MI 48161-3327. 313/242-4014.
Employs: 50-99.

PACKAGING PAPER AND PLASTIC FILM, COATED AND LAMINATED

Whitlam Label Co Inc
24800 Sherwood Ave, Center Line MI 48015-1059.
313/757-5100. Employs: 50-99.

3M Company
22100 Telegraph Rd, Southfield MI 48034-4213. 313/827-2450. Employs: 100-249.

UNCOATED PAPER AND MULTIWALL BAGS

Cadillac Products Inc
530 Stephenson Hwy, Troy MI 48083-1118. 313/583-1525.
Employs: 100-249.

Roblaw Inds Inc
21130 Trolley Indl Dr, Taylor MI 48180. 313/291-6500.
Employs: 50-99.

DIE-CUT PAPER AND PAPERBOARD AND CARDBOARD

K D G Finishers Corp
13121 Prospect St, Dearborn MI 48126-3603. 313/846-7870. Employs: 50-99.

Weyerhaeuser Paper Co
12850 E 9 Mile Rd, Warren MI 48089-2641. 313/771-7676. Employs: 100-249.

ENVELOPES

Husky Envelope Products Inc
1225 W Maple St, Walled Lake MI 48390. 313/624-7070.
Employs: 100-249.

Service Envelope Manufacturing Co Inc
1301 Harper Ave, Detroit MI 48211-2556. 313/872-6000.
Employs: 100-249.

Wolf Detroit Envelope Co
725 S Adams Rd Rm 275, Birmingham MI 48009-6928.
313/258-5700. Employs: 100-249.

MISCELLANEOUS CONVERTED PAPER AND PAPERBOARD PRODUCTS

James River-Rochester Inc
340 Mill St, Rochester MI 48307-2063. 313/651-8121.
Employs: 100-249.

S K S Industries
951 Jones St, Howell MI 48843-2631. 517/546-1117.
Employs: 50-99.

American Label Services
5750 Whethersfield Ln, Bloomfield MI 48301-1824.
313/644-3050. Employs: 50-99.

Delta Labels
16392 Harper Ave, Detroit MI 48224-2616. 313/882-6080.
Employs: 50-99.

Design Label
10810 Whittier St, Detroit MI 48224-1616. 313/839-6022.
Employs: 50-99.

Flamingo Label Co Inc
18110 E 14 Mile Rd, Fraser MI 48026-2295. 313/757-
5050. Employs: 50-99.

Fsi Label Co
95 Victor St, Detroit MI 48203-3129. 313/867-0909.
Employs: 50-99.

Label Tech Inc
6084 28 Mile, Washington MI 48094. 313/781-5650.
Employs: 50-99.

Rohm Graphics Inc
1629 W Lafayette Blvd, Detroit MI 48216-1927. 313/872-
2700. Employs: 50-99.

Style Rite Label Corp
2243 Starr Ct, Rochester MI 48309-3625. 313/853-7977.
Employs: 50-99.

Technicote
12480 Concord Ct, Plymouth MI 48170-3036. 313/459-
7888. Employs: 50-99.

Wildcat Label
23855 Cottrell St, Clinton Twp MI 48035-3811. 313/792-
5180. Employs: 50-99.

D R Smith Inc
20905 Greenfield Rd, Southfield MI 48075-5360. 313/569-
5149. Employs: 50-99.

FLAT GLASS

Glass & Mirror Craft Inc
2111 Haggerty Rd, Walled Lake MI 48390-2837. 313/624-
5050. Employs: 50-99.

Guardian Inds Corp
43043 W 9 Mile Rd, Northville MI 48167-8903. 313/347-
0100. Employs: 100-249.

Guardian Walled Lake Fabctn
3160 Ridgeway Ct, Walled Lake MI 48390-1670. 313/624-
0300. Employs: 50-99.

**MISCELLANEOUS PRESSED AND BLOWN GLASS
AND GLASSWARE**

Fahrenheit
4214 Packard St, Ann Arbor MI 48108-1508. 313/677-
1818. Employs: 50-99.

Fiber Tex Inc
220 Grover, Montrose MI 48457. 313/639-5353. Employs:
50-99.

Total Concepts Inc
18717 E 14 Mile Rd, Clinton Twp MI 48035-3900.
313/756-0202. Employs: 50-99.

Fairlane Manufacturing Co
616 Main, Fowler MI 48835. 517/593-2393. Employs: 50-
99.

Manco Enterprises
3152 Sheridan Rd, Lennon MI 48449. 313/6214533.
Employs: 50-99.

MISCELLANEOUS GLASS PRODUCTS

B & G Glass Co Inc
11866 Hubbard St, Livonia MI 48150-1733. 313/522-0300.
Employs: 50-99.

Britax Rainsfords Inc
1855 Busha, Marysville MI 48040-1892. 313/364-4141.
Employs: 50-99.

Double Seal Glass
43043- Mile Rd, Northville MI 48167. 616/349-6700.
Employs: 100-249.

Inalfa Hollandia Inc
1880 W West Maple Rd, Walled Lake MI 48390-2951.
313/553-3671. Employs: 50-99.

Reflections
1515 Michigan Ave, Marysville MI 48040-1791. 313/364-
3580. Employs: 50-99.

Undercover Window Tinting
3004 Lapeer Rd, Port Huron MI 48060-2550. 313/987-
8468. Employs: 50-99.

Weathervane Window Inc
5936 Ford Ct, Brighton MI 48116-8511. 313/227-4900.
Employs: 50-99.

Winter Seal Of Flint Inc
209 Elm St, Holly MI 48442-1404. 313/634-8261.
Employs: 50-99.

For more information on career opportunities in the paper, packaging, glass, and forest products industries:

Associations

AMERICAN FOREST COUNCIL
1250 Connecticut Avenue NW, Washington DC 20036.
202/463-2455.

AMERICAN PAPER INSTITUTE
260 Madison Avenue, New York NY 10016. 212/340-
0600.

FOREST PRODUCTS RESEARCH SOCIETY
2801 Marshall Court, Madison WI 53705. 608/231-1361.

NATIONAL FOREST PRODUCTS ASSOCIATION
1250 Connecticut Avenue NW, Washington DC 20036.
202/463-2700.

NATIONAL PAPER TRADE ASSOCIATION
111 Great Neck Road, Great Neck NY 11021. 516/829-
3070.

PAPERBOARD PACKAGING COUNCIL
1101 Vermont Avenue NW, Suite 411, Washington DC
20005. 202/289-4100.

**TECHNICAL ASSOCIATION OF THE PULP AND
PAPER INDUSTRY**
P.O. Box 105113, Atlanta GA 30348. 404/446-1400.

Directories

**DIRECTORY OF THE FOREST PRODUCTS
INDUSTRY**
Miller Freeman Publications, Inc., 600 Harrison Street, San
Francisco CA 94107. 415/905-2200.

**LOCKWOOD-POST'S DIRECTORY OF THE PAPER
AND ALLIED TRADES**
Miller Freeman Publications, Inc., 600 Harrison Street, San
Francisco CA 94107. 415/905-2200.

POST'S PULP AND PAPER DIRECTORY
Miller Freeman Publications, Inc., 600 Harrison Street, San Francisco CA 94107. 415/905-2200.

Magazines

FOREST INDUSTRIES
Miller Freeman Publications, Inc., 600 Harrison Street, San Francisco CA 94107. 415/905-2200.

PAPERBOARD PACKAGING
Advanstar Communications, 1 E. First Street, Duluth MN 55802. 218/723-9200.

PULP AND PAPER WEEK
Miller Freeman Publications, Inc., 600 Harrison Street, San Francisco CA 94107. 415/905-2200.

PRINTING/GRAPHIC ARTS

As the U.S. economy improves, accompanied by growth in print advertising, the printing industry should begin to rebound. The price of paper is expected to remain soft, with paper mill capacity outstripping demand. The printing industry's employment levels will rise.

DELUXE CHECK PRINTERS-MICHIGAN
24900 Capital Avenue, Detroit MI 48239. 313/538-5353. **Contact:** Francis Edgar, Personnel Director. **Description:** A major Detroit commercial letter printing and lithography company. **Employees:** 300.

FLINT INK CORPORATION
25111 Glendale, Detroit MI 48239-2689. 313/538-6800. **Contact:** Personnel Director. **Description:** Engaged in the manufacture of printing ink. **Employees:** 1,000.

MALLOY LITHOGRAPHING INC.
P.O. Box 1124, Ann Arbor MI 48106. 313/665-6113. **Contact:** Personnel Department. **Description:** An Ann Arbor lithographing company which specializes in the printing of books. **Common positions:** Blue-Collar Worker Supervisor; Computer Programmer; Customer Service Representative; Instructor/Trainer; Operations/Production Manager; Graphic Artist; Printing Press Operator. **Educational backgrounds sought:** Art/Design; Computer Science; Engineering. **Benefits:** medical insurance; dental insurance; life insurance; tuition assistance; disability coverage; profit sharing; savings plan. **Corporate headquarters:** This location. **Operations at this facility:** manufacturing; administration; sales. **Employees:** 330. **Projected number of new hires for the next 12 months:** 30.

NORTHWEST BLUEPRINT & SUPPLY COMPANY
13450 Farmington Road, Livonia MI 48150. 313/525-1990. **Contact:** Kathy Charest, Personnel Manager. **Description:** A company supplying printing and art supply services.

PANGBORN DESIGN LTD.
275 Iron Street, Detroit MI 48207. 313/259-3400. **Contact:** Dominic Pangborn, President. **Description:** A leading metropolitan Detroit graphic communications firm specializing in the design of brochures and pamphlets.

TAS GRAPHIC COMMUNICATIONS
11191 Lappin, Detroit MI 48234. 313/372-9770. **Contact:** Dave Laczynski, Controller. **Description:** A major metropolitan Detroit company engaged in commercial letter printing. **Employees:** 200.

VALASSIS INSERTS
36111 Schoolcraft Road, Livonia MI 48150. 313/591-3000. **Contact:** Christen Keller, Human Resources Supervisor. **Description:** A growth- oriented company specializing in the printing of four-color coupon inserts. Started in 1972, Valassis has grown to over 1000 employees and over $400 million in sales. **Common positions:** Accountant; Computer Programmer; Credit Manager; Customer Service Representative; Electrical Engineer; Industrial Engineer; Mechanical Engineer; Department Manager; Management Trainee; Operations/Production Manager; Marketing Specialist; Purchasing Agent; Quality Control Supervisor; Sales Representative; Systems Analyst; Transportation and Traffic Specialist; Human Resources Specialist; Supervisor; Artist; Industrial Supervisor; Manufacturing Supervisor. **Educational backgrounds sought:** Accounting; Art/Design; Business Administration; Communications; Computer Science; Engineering; Liberal Arts; Marketing; Printing Management and Technology; Operations/Manufacturing Management. **Benefits:** medical, dental, and life insurance; pension plan; tuition assistance; disability coverage; profit sharing; 401K. **Corporate headquarters:** This location. **Operations at this facility:** regional headquarters; divisional headquarters; manufacturing; administration; service; sales.

Large employers: 250+

BOOK PRINTING

Thomson-Shore
7300 W Joy Rd, Dexter MI 48130-9701. 313/426-3939. Employs: 250-499.

COMMERCIAL PRINTING: LITHOGRAPHIC

Braun-Brumfield Inc
100 N Staebler Rd, Ann Arbor MI 48103. 313/662-3291. Employs: 250-499.

Realtron Corp
24065 5 Mile Rd, Redford MI 48239-3552. 313/255-1200. Employs: 250-499.

Wintor Swan Assoc Inc
1614 Clay St, Detroit MI 48211-1914. 313/874-0015. Employs: 250-499.

MISC. COMMERCIAL PRINTING

Brian Unltd Dstbn Co
13131 Lyndon St, Detroit MI 48227-3947. 313/933-5100. Employs: 250-499.

BOOKBINDING AND RELATED WORK

Bookcrafters Inc
140 Buchanan St, Chelsea MI 48118-1250. 313/475-9145. Employs: 250-499.

Small to medium sized employers: 50-249

BOOK PRINTING

American Eagle Co Inc
1130 E Big Beaver Rd, Troy MI 48083-1934. 313/689-9458. Employs: 50-99.

Bates Roto-Press
3445 North Rd, Port Huron MI 48060. 313/985-7988. Employs: 50-99.

Cushing-Malloy Inc
1354 N Main St, Ann Arbor MI 48104-1045. 313/662-6238. Employs: 50-99.

Perry Printing Co
4710 W Saginaw St Ste 1B, Lansing MI 48917-2601.
517/323-7506. Employs: 50-99.

COMMERCIAL PRINTING, LITHOGRAPHIC

Adair Printing
18544 W 8 Mile Rd, Southfield MI 48075-4194. 313/569-
1122. Employs: 100-249.

Business Card Express
2708 American Dr, Troy MI 48083-4625. 313/583-7070.
Employs: 50-99.

Colortech Graphics Inc
28700 Hayes Rd, Roseville MI 48066-2316. 313/779-7800.
Employs: 50-99.

Continental Marketing Corp
15160 N Commerce Dr, Dearborn MI 48120-1225.
313/271-6800. Employs: 100-249.

Data Reproductions Corp
1480 N Rochester Rd, Rochester MI 48307-1117. 313/652-
7600. Employs: 100-249.

Detroit Legal News
2001 W Lafayette, Detroit MI 48216-1852. 313/961-3949.
Employs: 50-99.

Gaylord Printing Inc
15555 Woodrow Wilson, Detroit MI 48238-1586. 313/883-
7800. Employs: 100-249.

Graphic Enterprise Inc
11111 Lappin St, Detroit MI 48234-3542. 313/839-6800.
Employs: 50-99.

Inco Graphics
222 W Ash St, Mason MI 48854-1649. 517/676-5188.
Employs: 50-99.

Inland Press
2001 W Lafayette Blvd, Detroit MI 48216-1852. 313/961-
6000. Employs: 100-249.

J & M Reproduction Corp
1200 Rochester Rd, Troy MI 48083-2833. 313/588-8100.
Employs: 50-99.

Johnston Lithograph Inc
11334 Hunt St, Romulus MI 48174-3818. 313/941-3510.
Employs: 50-99.

National Reproductions Corp
29400 Stephenson Hwy, Madison Hts MI 48071-2337.
313/585-1330. Employs: 50-99.

Page Litho Inc
6445 E Vernor Hwy, Detroit MI 48207-3438. 313/921-
6880. Employs: 50-99.

Perry Printing Co
1025 E 4th Ave, Flint MI 48503-1737. 313/232-6162.
Employs: 50-99.

Printco Inc
1321 Van Diense, Greenville MI 48838-1472. 616/754-
3672. Employs: 100-249.

Printco Inc
109 N Lafayette St, Greenville MI 48838-1853. 616/754-
3673. Employs: 100-249.

Q & Q Printing Co Inc
40 Hague St, Detroit MI 48202-2119. 313/872-5151.
Employs: 50-99.

Speaker-Hines & Thomas Inc
3366 Remy Dr, Lansing MI 48906-2727. 517/321-0740.
Employs: 100-249.

Stylecraft Printing Co Inc
8472 Ronda Dr, Canton MI 48187-2002. 313/525-0001.
Employs: 100-249.

The Ypsilanti Press
20 E Michigan, Detroit MI 48226. 313/961-1141. Employs:
50-99.

Three-Sixty Services
12623 Newburgh Rd, Livonia MI 48150-1001. 313/591-
9360. Employs: 50-99.

Webco Press
588 McCormick Dr, Lapeer MI 48446-2518. 313/664-
7403. Employs: 50-99.

MISCELLANEOUS COMMERCIAL PRINTING

Ameritech Publ National Yellow
100 E Big Beaver Rd Ste 1200, Troy MI 48083-1253.
313/649-5555. Employs: 50-99.

Asu Printing Service
821 E Kalamazoo St, Lansing MI 48912-1327. 517/372-
9750. Employs: 50-99.

Consolidated Business Form Inc
18050 15 Mile Rd, Fraser MI 48026-1605. 313/293-8100.
Employs: 100-249.

Highlite Printers Inc
880 W Jefferson Ave, Trenton MI 48183-1221. 313/284-
8944. Employs: 50-99.

Industrial Printing Co
68834 S Main St, Richmond MI 48062-1265. 313/727-
3715. Employs: 50-99.

John H Harland Co
15150 Cleat St, Plymouth MI 48170-6014. 313/459-4780.
Employs: 50-99.

Pontiac Graphics Inc
605 Oakland Ave, Pontiac MI 48342-1056. 313/338-6467.
Employs: 50-99.

Printing Service Inc
1451 E Lincoln, Madison Hts MI 48071-4136. 313/399-
3300. Employs: 100-249.

Pyc-Davis Graphics Inc
19925 Hoover St, Detroit MI 48205-1641. 313/371-1012.
Employs: 50-99.

Servant Ministries
840 Airport Blvd, Ann Arbor MI 48108-1642. 313/761-
8505. Employs: 50-99.

MANIFOLD BUSINESS FORMS

Continuous Forms Inc
12238 Woodbine, Redford MI 48239-2420. 313/255-7600.
Employs: 50-99.

Harmony Business Forms
29563 Northwestern Hw, Southfield MI 48034-1021.
313/358-0818. Employs: 50-99.

Ray's Offset Inc
2860 Wiltshire Dr, Lambertville MI 48144-9536. 313/854-
5486. Employs: 50-99.

Rotary Multiforms Inc
3900 Beaufait St, Detroit MI 48207-1805. 313/923-4400.
Employs: 100-249.

Schober Printing Co
7550 Chrysler Dr, Detroit MI 48211-1974. 313/872-2508.
Employs: 100-249.

Total Business Systs Inc
1341 Wanda Ave, Ferndale MI 48220-2057. 313/547-6910.
Employs: 50-99.

Uarco Inc
1357 Division St, Adrian MI 49221-4204. 517/263-7811.
Employs: 100-249.

BLANKBOOKS, LOOSELEAF BINDERS AND DEVICES

McBee Binders
5436 S Waverly, Dimondale MI 48821. 517/646-9315.
Employs: 50-99.

BOOKBINDING AND RELATED WORK

McNaughton & Gunn Inc
960 Woodlawn Dr, Saline MI 48176-1203. 313/429-5411.
Employs: 100-249.

Bill's Bindery
527 E Liberty St, Ann Arbor MI 48104-2209. 313/995-1320. Employs: 50-99.

Dunn Bindery Inc

33 Temple, Detroit MI 48201. 313/831-5133. Employs: 50-99.

TYPESETTING

Pak Printers
One Heritage Pl, Southgate MI 48195-3047. 313/246-0130.
Employs: 50-99.

T P H Graphics Inc
1177 W Baltimore St, Detroit MI 48202-2905. 313/875-1950. Employs: 50-99.

Willens-Michigan Corp
1959 E Jefferson Ave, Detroit MI 48207-4125. 313/567-8900. Employs: 100-249.

PLATEMAKING AND RELATED SERVICES

Adgravers Inc
269 Walker St, Detroit MI 48207-4258. 313/259-3780.
Employs: 50-99.

Precision Color Plate Inc
9200 General Dr, Plymouth MI 48170-4626. 313/459-5640. Employs: 50-99.

For more information on career opportunities in printing and graphic arts:

Associations

AMERICAN INSTITUTE OF GRAPHIC ARTS
1059 3rd Avenue, New York NY 10021. 212/752-0813.

ASSOCIATION OF GRAPHIC ARTS
330 7th Avenue, 9th Floor, New York NY 10001-5010.
212/279-2100.

BINDING INDUSTRIES OF AMERICA
70 East Lake Street, Suite 300, Chicago IL 60601-5905.
312/372-7606.

GRAPHIC ARTISTS GUILD
11 West 20th Street, New York NY 10011. 212/463-7730.

INTERNATIONAL GRAPHIC ARTS EDUCATION ASSOCIATION
4615 Forbes Avenue, Pittsburgh PA 15213. 412/682-5170.

NATIONAL ASSOCIATION OF PRINTERS AND LITHOGRAPHERS
780 Pallisade Avenue, Teaneck NJ 07666. 201/342-0700.

PRINTING INDUSTRIES OF AMERICA
100 Dangerfield Road, Arlington VA 22314. 703/519-8100.

TECHNICAL ASSOCIATION OF THE GRAPHIC ARTS

Box 9887, Rochester NY 14623. 716/272-0557.

Directories

GRAPHIC ARTISTS GUILD DIRECTORY
Madison Square Press, Ten East 23rd Street, New York NY 10010. 212/505-0950.

GRAPHIC ARTS BLUE BOOK
A.F. Lewis & Co., 79 Madison Avenue, New York NY 10016. 212/679-0770.

Magazines

AIGA JOURNAL
American Institute of Graphic Arts, 1059 Third Avenue, New York NY 10021. 212/752-0813.

GRAPHIC ARTS MONTHLY
249 West 49th Street, New York NY 10011. 212/463-6836.

GRAPHIS
141 Lexington Avenue, New York NY 10016. 212/532-9387.

PRINT
104 Fifth Avenue, New York NY 10011. 212/463-0600.

RESEARCH AND DEVELOPMENT

Science technicians with good technical skills should experience excellent employment opportunities in the next decade, largely due to the increased emphasis on research and development of technical products.

AST INC.
7183 M-15, Clarkston MI 48346. 313/625-0191. **Contact:** Chuck Swanson, Personnel. **Description:** A major Michigan research and development firm specializing in the manufacture of hand-held data gathering terminals. Founded in 1980.

ENVIRONMENTAL RESEARCH INSTITUTE
OF MICHIGAN (ERIM)
Human Resources Department, P.O. Box 134001, Ann Arbor MI 48113-4001. 313/994-1200. **Contact:** James J. Miles, Human Resources Manager. **Description:** A private, not-for-profit research and development organization serving both the public and private sectors in sensor development and image processing. **Common positions:** Computer Programmer; Electrical Engineer; Physicist; Accountant; Buyer; Mechanical Engineer; Metallurgical Engineer; Geographer; Geologist; Writer/Editor; Technical Writer/Editor. **Educational backgrounds sought:** Computer Science; Engineering; Mathematics; Physics; Accounting; Art/Design; Business Administration; Communications; Geology. **Special programs:** Training programs; Internships. **Benefits:** medical, dental, and life insurance; pension plan; tuition assistance; disability coverage. **Corporate headquarters:** This location. **Operations at this facility:** research and development. **Other U.S. locations:** Washington, DC; Los Angeles, CA; Niceville, FL; Dayton, OH. **Employees:** 850.

Large employers: 250+

COMMERCIAL PHYSICAL AND BIOLOGICAL RESEARCH

Eaton Corp/Research & Dvlpt
26201 Northwestern Hwy, Southfield MI 48076-3926. 313/354-2700. Employs: 250-499.

Hawtal Whiting Inc
165 Kirts Blvd, Troy MI 48084-5244. 313/362-4466. Employs: 250-499.

Parke-Davis Pharmaceutical
2800 Plymouth Rd, Ann Arbor MI 48105-2430. 313/996-7000. Employs: 1000+.

Robert Bosch Corp
38000 Hills Tech Dr, Farmington MI 48331-3418. 313/553-9000. Employs: 250-499.

TESTING LABORATORIES

G M Corp
General Motors Rd, Milford MI 48380. 313/685-5000. Employs: 1000+.

Small to medium sized employers: 50-249

COMMERCIAL PHYSICAL AND BIOLOGICAL RESEARCH

Bendix Safety Restraint Group
1755 Maplelawn Dr, Troy MI 48084-4603. 313/649-8610.
Employs: 100-249.

Budd Co/Wheel & Brake Div
24755 Halsted Rd, Farmington MI 48335-1612. 313/473-9700. Employs: 50-99.

C M I Tech-Center Inc
1600 W 8 Mile Rd, Ferndale MI 48220-2202. 313/399-9600. Employs: 100-249.

Chivas Technology Center
6100 19 Mile Rd, Sterling Hts MI 48314-2102. 313/254-3233. Employs: 100-249.

Chrysler Engineering-Research
12800 Oakland Av, Detroit MI 48288. 313/956-3226.
Employs: 100-249.

Ciba-Geigy Corp
31601 Research Park Dr, Madison Hts MI 48071-4626.
313/585-7200. Employs: 50-99.

Dundee Research
100 Research Pkwy, Dundee MI 48131-9777. 313/529-2436. Employs: 50-99.

Engineering Research Div
Mich State Univ/10 Ste 106, East Lansing MI 48823.
517/353-7958. Employs: 100-249.

Hemco Machine Co
36200 Mound Rd, Sterling Hts MI 48310-4737. 313/264-8911. Employs: 100-249.

I C I Americas Inc
6555 E 15 Mile Rd, Sterling Hts MI 48312-4511. 313/826-7660. Employs: 100-249.

Industrial Technology Inst
2901 Hubbard St, Ann Arbor MI 48105-2435. 313/769-4000. Employs: 100-249.

Lindon Industries
17097 17 Mile, Macomb MI 48044. 313/263-7440.
Employs: 100-249.

National Steel Corp
1745 Fritz Dr, Trenton MI 48183-2100. 313/676-8080.
Employs: 50-99.

New Mack Viper Assembly Plant
11801 Mack Ave, Detroit MI 48214-3535. 313/956-7563.
Employs: 50-99.

Nissan Research & Dvlpt Inc
39001 Country Club Dr, Farmington MI 48331-3456.
313/488-4123. Employs: 100-249.

Ois Optical Imaging Syst Inc
1896 Barrett St, Troy MI 48084-5360. 313/362-2738.
Employs: 50-99.

Simpson Inds Inc
917 Anderson Rd, Litchfield MI 49252. 517/542-5555.
Employs: 100-249.

Toyota Technical Center USA Inc
1588 Woodridge Ave R R 7, Ann Arbor MI 48105-9748.
313/769-1350. Employs: 50-99.

Carlo Environ Techlgy Inc
21570 Hall Rd, Clinton Twp MI 48038-1540. 313/468-9580. Employs: 100-249.

Eart Alert Inc
26343 Audrey Ave, Warren MI 48091-4104. 313/754-0933. Employs: 100-249.

Herbie & Co
37545 Charter Oaks Blvd, Clinton Twp MI 48036-2414.
313/465-2410. Employs: 100-249.

Life Shield Air Testing Inc
28727 Waverly St, Roseville MI 48066-2446. 313/776-4620. Employs: 100-249.

Sierra Technical Services
27440 Hoover Rd, Warren MI 48093-7709. 313/759-6766.
Employs: 100-249.

B G M Engineering Inc
11145 25 Mile, Shelby Twp MI 48315. 313/781-6111.
Employs: 100-249.

Circuit-Stuff
41315 Belvidere St, Harrison Twp MI 48045-1406.
313/469-3977. Employs: 100-249.

Concept Electronic Systems Inc
40200 Brentwood Dr, Sterling Hts MI 48310-2274.
313/264-8810. Employs: 100-249.

Quartech Corporation
44479 Phoenix Dr, Sterling Hts MI 48314-1468. 313/739-3660. Employs: 100-249.

TESTING LABORATORIES

Detroit Testing Laboratory Inc
7111 E Eleven Mile Rd Box 0869, Warren MI 48090-0869.
313/754-9000. Employs: 100-249.

Mechanical Design & Engineering Co
G-4033 S Center Rd, Burton MI 48519. 313/743-5980.
Employs: 50-99.

Michigan Biotechnology Institute
3900 Collins Rd, Lansing MI 48910-8396. 517/337-3181.
Employs: 100-249.

Testing Engrs & Consultants
1333 Rochester Rd, Troy MI 48083-6015. 313/588-6200.
Employs: 100-249.

Valeo Clutches & Transmissions
37564 Amrhein Rd, Livonia MI 48150-1012. 313/591-6550. Employs: 50-99.

Herman Miller Research Corp
3970 Varsity Dr, Ann Arbor MI 48108-2226. 313/994-6665. Employs: 50-99.

Ind Sctfc Cyclical Researchers
2414 N Franklin Av, Flint MI 48506-4452. 313/239-0727.
Employs: 50-99.

Iron & Metals Research & Dev
450 N Woodward Av 1stfl, Birmingham MI 48009-5361.
313/646-0644. Employs: 50-99.

Kelsey Hayes Research & Development Center
2500 Green Rd, Ann Arbor MI 48105-1550. 313/769-5890.
Employs: 50-99.

Kimley Horn Research Institute Inc
1114 Beach St, Flint MI 48502-1407. 313/238-5305.
Employs: 50-99.

Market Research Associates Inc
777 Eisenhower Pkwy E Ste 316, Ann Arbor MI 48108-3288. 313/994-9500. Employs: 50-99.

Tactical Research & Cnsltg Inc
2500 Packard Rd Ste 211, Ann Arbor MI 48104-6827.
313/971-4142. Employs: 50-99.

U M Institute For Social Research
426 Thompson St, Ann Arbor MI 48104-2321. 313/764-8354. Employs: 50-99.

U M Kresge Hearing Research
1301 E Ann St, Ann Arbor MI 48104. 313/764-8110.
Employs: 50-99.

U S Renal Data System
315 W Huron St Rm 340, Ann Arbor MI 48103-4277.
313/998-7794. Employs: 50-99.

Vector Research Inc
2536 Packard Rd, Ann Arbor MI 48104-6802. 313/973-9210. Employs: 50-99.

RUBBER AND PLASTICS

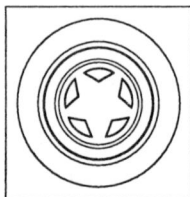

During the next five years, the demand for plastics is expected to be slow, and the U.S.' share of the world's plastics trade will continue to fall. The rubber industry, especially the synthetic rubber segment, will do much better. The highest growth rates will be for high-value, small-volume elastomers. In fabricated rubber, the big trend is toward customized production. Jobseekers with experience in Computer Aided Design and Manufacturing will reap the benefits of this trend.

AMERICAN PLASTIC TOYS INC.

799 Ladd Road, Walled Lake MI 48390. 313/624-4881. **Contact:** Jim Reid, Personnel Director. **Description:** Engaged in the manufacture of plastic injection molded toys. **Employees:** 500. **Common positions:** Blue-Collar Worker Supervisor; Industrial Engineer; Management Trainee; Operations/Production Manager; Quality Control Supervisor. **Benefits:** medical, dental, and life insurance; tuition assistance; disability coverage; profit sharing; employee discounts. **Corporate headquarters:** This location. **Operations at this facility:** manufacturing; administration; sales.

ATTWOOD CORPORATION

1016 North Monroe Street, Lowell MI 49331. 616/897-9241. **Contact:** Thomas Powell, Director/Human Resources. **Description:** A subsidiary of Steelcase Inc. Manufactures components of molded plastics for parent company. Involved in chrome plating. Also manufactures a proprietary product line for the pleasure marine industry. Manufacturing processes include diecast, injection molding, light assembly, and chrome plating. **Common positions:** Buyer; Computer Programmer; Draftsperson; Industrial Engineer; Mechanical Engineer. **Educational backgrounds sought:** Accounting; Computer Science; Engineering; Marketing. **Benefits:** medical insurance; dental insurance; pension plan; life insurance; tuition assistance; disability coverage; profit sharing; employee discounts. **Parent company:** Steelcase Inc. **Corporate headquarters:** Grand Rapids, MI.

H.L. BLACHFORD INC.
P.O. Box 397, Troy MI 48007-0397. 313/689-7800. **Contact:** Dee Rataj, Personnel Director. **Description:** Engaged in the manufacture of plastic noise reduction equipment and products. **Employees:** 200.

CADILLAC RUBBER & PLASTICS, INC.
805 West 13th Street, Cadillac MI 49601. 616/775-1345. **Contact:** Dale Rosser, Vice President/Industrial Relations. **Description:** Produces rubber extrusions and profiles. Other manufacturing facility in Manton, MI, produces plastic injection molded components and assembles vacuum emission harnesses for the automotive industry. **Corporate headquarters:** This location. **Operations include:** manufacturing; research/development; sales. **Common positions:** Blue-Collar Worker Supervisor; Buyer; Computer Programmer; Customer Service Representative; Draftsperson; Engineer; Chemical Engineer; Industrial Engineer; Mechanical Engineer; Financial Analyst; Industrial Designer; Department Manager; General Manager; Operations/Production Manager; Marketing Specialist; Personnel and Labor Relations Specialist; Purchasing Agent; Quality Control Supervisor; Systems Analyst; Technical Manager; Chemist; Product Engineer. **Educational backgrounds sought:** Business Administration; Chemistry; Computer Science; Engineering; Chemical Engineering. **Benefits:** medical, dental, and life insurance; pension plan; tuition assistance; disability coverage; profit sharing.

COLOR CUSTOM COMPOUNDING
24060 Hoover Road, Warren MI 48089. 313/755-1010. **Contact:** Personnel Department. **Description:** A company engaged in the manufacture of molded and extruded plastic materials for the automotive industry. **Employees:** 200.

EMHART CORPORATION/WARREN DIVISION
A BLACK & DECKER COMPANY
P.O. Box 868, Mount Clemens MI 48045. 313/949-0440. **Contact:** Royce Toffolo, Director of Human Resources. **Description:** A leading area manufacturer of plastic products. **Employees:** 500. **Common positions:** Mechanical Engineer. **Educational backgrounds sought:** Engineering. **Special programs:** Training programs; internships. **Benefits:** medical insurance; dental insurance; pension plan; life insurance; tuition assistance; disability coverage; employee discounts; savings plan. **Parent company:** Black & Decker (Towson, MD). **Operations at this facility:** divisional headquarters location; manufacturing; research and development; administration; service; sales. **Listed on:** New York Stock Exchange.

EXOTIC RUBBER & PLASTICS CORP.
P.O. Box 395, Farmington Hills MI 48332-0395. **Contact:** Carolyn Palmer, Human Resource Administrator. Engaged in the sales, manufacture, distribution, and fabrication of automotive, robotic, and business machinery; and rubber and plastic products. **Corporate headquarters:** This location. **Common positions:** Accountant; Administrator; Buyer; Computer Programmer; Credit Manager; Branch Manager; Department Manager; General Manager; Management

Trainee; Operations/Production Manager; Marketing Specialist; Purchasing Agent; Quality Control Supervisor; Production Worker. **Educational backgrounds sought:** Accounting; Business Administration; Computer Science; Economics; Engineering; Marketing; Physics; Liberal Arts. **Benefits:** medical and life insurance; tuition assistance; profit sharing; monthly bonus program. **Operations at this facility:** manufacturing; research and development; administration; sales. **Employees:** 120.

FLEET CARRIER CORPORATION
1450 West Long Lake Road, P.O. Box 7084, Troy MI 48007-7084. 313/952-2000. **Contact:** Personnel. **Description:** A leading Southeastern Michigan company engaged in non-local trucking. **Employees:** 300.

FORD MOTOR/MILAN PLASTICS DIVISION
800 County Street, Milan MI 48160. 313/481-9411. **Contact:** Personnel Director. **Description:** A major manufacturer of plastic products. **Employees:** 1,000.

GENOVA INC.
7034 East Court Street, Davison MI 48423. 313/744-4500. **Contact:** Barry Brang, Personnel Director. **Description:** A leading area manufacturer of plastic products. **Employees:** 400.

HURON PLASTICS INC.
P.O. Box 195, St. Clair MI 48079. 313/329-4711. **Contact:** Robert LaGrath, Controller. **Description:** Engaged in the manufacture of plastic products. **Employees:** 600.

LAPEER FABRICATORS INC.
1455 Imlay City Road, Lapeer MI 48446. 313/664-4524. **Contact:** John Brauner, Personnel Director. **Description:** A leading area manufacturer of plastic products. **Employees:** 600.

LINDSAY & PAVELICH MANUFACTURING
8595 Ronda Drive, Canton MI 48187. 313/451-1171. **Contact:** Personnel Department. **Description:** A leading manufacturer of plastic products for the automotic industry. **Common positions:** Accountant; Industrial Manager; Quality Control Supervisor; Plastics Professional. **Educational backgrounds sought:** Maintenance; Plastics. **Special programs:** internships. **Benefits:** medical, dental, and life insurance; tuition assistance; disability coverage; savings plan; 401 K. **Corporate headquarters:** Sterling Heights, MI. **Operations at this facility:** manufacturing.

MICHIGAN CHROME AND CHEMICAL
8615 Grinnell Avenue, Detroit MI 48213. 313/267-5200. **Contact:** Mary Torrey, Director of Personnel. **Description:** A Detroit based company engaged in the manufacture of plastic material. **Employees:** 200.

MIDWEST RUBBER COMPANY
3525 Rangeline, P.O. Box 98, Deckerville MI 48427. 313/376-2085. **Contact:** Hiring. **Description:** A major area manufacturer of fabricated rubber products. **Employees:** 300.

OLSONITE CORPORATION
8801 Conant Avenue, Detroit MI 48211-1403. 313/875-5831. **Contact:** Personnel Department. **Description:** A Detroit manufacturer of plastic products. **Employees:** 500.

PLASTOMER CORPORATION
37819 Schoolcraft Road, Livonia MI 48150. 313/464-0700. **Contact:** Tom Weis, Personnel. **Description:** A leading Southeastern Michigan manufacturer of plastic products. **Employees:** 400.

SIGNET INDUSTRIES INC.
17085 Masonic, Fraser MI 48026. 313/296-2000. **Contact:** Lisa Bellissimo, Personnel Manager. **Description:** A Southeastern Michigan company engaged in the manufacture of plastic products. **Common positions:** Accountant; Administrator; Buyer; Computer Programmer; Customer Service Representative; Industrial Engineer; Financial Analyst; Operations/Production Manager; Personnel and Labor Relations Specialist; Quality Control Supervisor. **Benefits:** medical insurance; dental insurance; life insurance; tuition assistance; disability coverage; savings plan. **Corporate headquarters:** This location. **Operations at this facility:** manufacturing.

UNIQUE FABRICATING INC
1601 West Hamlin Road, Rochester Hills MI 48309. 313/853-2333. **Contact:** Mary Szymanski, Personnel Director. **Description:** A company involved in the manufacture of sponge rubber and flexible plastic foams. **Employees:** 200.

F.B. WRIGHT COMPANY
P.O. Box 770, 9999 Mercier Avenue, Dearborn MI 48121. 313/843-8250. **Contact:** Jack Doerr, Personnel. **Description:** An area manufacturer of fabricated rubber products. **Employees:** 100.

YALE SOUTH HAVEN, INC.
180 North Dawson, Sandusky MI 48471. 313/648-2100. **Contact:** Dave Cox, Personnel Director. **Description:** A leading Southeastern Michigan manufacturer of fabricated rubber products. **Employees:** 500.

Additional large employers: 250+

PLASTICS MATERIALS, SYNTHETIC RESINS AND NONVULCANIZABLE ELASTOMERS

Du Pont Co
950 Stephenson Hwy, Troy MI 48083-1113. 313/583-8000. Employs: 500-999.

GE Co
25900 Telegraph Rd, Southfield MI 48034-5222. 313/356-3000. Employs: 250-499.

Monsanto Co
5045 W Jefferson Ave, Trenton MI 48183-4730. 313/676-4400. Employs: 500-999.

Wacker Silicones Corp
3301 Sutton Rd, Adrian MI 49221-9335. 517/264-8500.
Employs: 500-999.

RUBBER AND PLASTIC HOSE AND BELTING

Aeroquip Corp/Aerospace Div
300 S East Ave, Jackson MI 49203-1973. 517/787-8121.
Employs: 500-999.

GASKETS, PACKING, AND SEALING DEVICES

Farnam Sealing Systems Div
1707 Northwood Dr, Troy MI 48084-5524. 313/362-5457.
Employs: 250-499.

Mc Cord Gasket Corp Genl Ofc
191 Labadie St, Wyandotte MI 48192-2721. 313/284-3600.
Employs: 250-499.

Wolverine Gasket Co
2638 Princess St & M C R R, Inkster MI 48141-2350.
313/562-6400. Employs: 250-499.

MOLDED, EXTRUDED AND LATHE-CUT

Yale Rubber Manufacturing Co
180 N Dawson St, Sandusky MI 48471-1034. 313/648-
2100. Employs: 250-499.

MISC. FABRICATED RUBBER PRODUCTS

Borg Warner Auto Transmission
6700 18 1/2 Mile Rd Box 8022, Sterling Hts MI 48311-
8022. 313/726-4400. Employs: 1000+.

Wirtz Manufacturing Co Inc
1105 24th St, Port Huron MI 48060-4849. 313/987-4700.
Employs: 250-499.

PLASTIC FOAM PRODUCTS

Manchester Plastics Inc
300 Elm St, Homer MI 49245-1337. 517/568-4134.
Employs: 250-499.

Mobil Chemical Co
1511 1st St, Detroit MI 48226-1309. 313/965-2010.
Employs: 250-499.

Thetford Corp
7101 Jackson Rd, Ann Arbor MI 48103-9506. 313/769-
6000. Employs: 250-499.

MISC. PLASTIC PRODUCTS

A M P Industries
42050 Executive Dr, Harrison Twp MI 48045-1311.
313/469-4100. Employs: 250-499.

A-Line Plastics
40300 Plymouth Rd, Plymouth MI 48170-4210. 313/453-
0113. Employs: 500-999.

Aeroquip Corp
345 E Main St, Spring Arbor MI 49283-9617. 517/750-
1610. Employs: 250-499.

Albar Inds Inc
780 Whitney Dr, Lapeer MI 48446-2565. 313/667-0150.
Employs: 250-499.

Atron Inc Of Mi
460 E Main St, Saranac MI 48881-9750. 616/642-9321.
Employs: 500-999.

Auto Air Composites Inc
5640 Enterprise Dr, Lansing MI 48911. 517/393-4040.
Employs: 250-499.

Autodynamics Corp Of America
30900 Stephenson Hwy, Madison Hts MI 48071-1617.
313/585-8500. Employs: 250-499.

Automotive Plastic Tech Inc
6600 E 15 Mile Rd, Sterling Hts MI 48312-4512. 313/979-
5000. Employs: 500-999.

Becker Manufacturing
3800 Lapeer Rd, Auburn Hills MI 48326-1734. 313/377-
1110. Employs: 250-499.

Bundy Corporation
12345 E Nine Mile Rd, Warren MI 48089. 313/758-6500.
Employs: 1000+.

Cadillac Plastic & Chemical Co
143 Indusco Ct, Troy MI 48083-4644. 313/583-1200.
Employs: 500-999.

Cadillac Products Inc
7000 E 15 Mile Rd, Sterling Hts MI 48312-4520. 313/264-
2525. Employs: 250-499.

Dart Container Corp
500 Hogsback Rd, Mason MI 48854-9541. 517/676-3800.
Employs: 250-499.

Detroit Plastic Molding Co
18125 E 10 Mile Rd, Roseville MI 48066-3803. 313/774-
8620. Employs: 250-499.

Ford Motor Co
Regent Ct 16800 Executive Plaza, Dearborn MI 48126.
313/3909670. Employs: 500-999.

Ford Motor Co
7700 Michigan Ave, Saline MI 48176-1502. 313/429-4911.
Employs: 1000+.

Gencorp Automotive
119 S Dexter St, Ionia MI 48846-1547. 616/527-1000.
Employs: 500-999.

Inland Fisher Guide Division
6600 12 Mile Rd, Warren MI 48092. 313/578-3000.
Employs: 1000+.

JAC Products Inc
1901 E Ellsworth Rd, Ann Arbor MI 48108-2408. 313/973-
1120. Employs: 250-499.

Johnson Controls Inc
825 Victors Wa, Ann Arbor MI 48108-1767. 313/665-
1500. Employs: 500-999.

Johnson Controls Inc
435 W 8 Mile Rd, Whitmore Lake MI 48189-9626.
313/449-4411. Employs: 250-499.

Letica Corp
1700 W Hamlin Rd, Rochester MI 48309-3372. 313/652-
0557. Employs: 250-499.

Libralter Plastics Inc
3175 Martin Rd, Walled Lake MI 48390-1628. 313/669-
4900. Employs: 250-499.

Mayco Plastics Inc
42400 Merrill Rd, Sterling Hts MI 48314-3238. 313/254-
1550. Employs: 250-499.

Milford Fabricating Co
19200 Glendale Ave, Detroit MI 48223-3424. 313/272-
8400. Employs: 250-499.

Modular & Plastic Products
6300 Hughes Dr, Sterling Hts MI 48312-2634. 313/939-
3030. Employs: 250-499.

Pilot Industries Inc
7931 Grand St, Dexter MI 48130-1325. 313/426-4376.
Employs: 250-499.

Regal Plastics Co
15700 Common Rd, Roseville MI 48066-1893. 313/772-7120. Employs: 250-499.

Voplex Corp
1455 Imlay City Rd, Lapeer MI 48446-3142. 313/664-4524. Employs: 500-999.

Wolverine Technologies Inc
701 Liberty St, Jackson MI 49203-1935. 517/787-8665. Employs: 250-499.

Wolverine Technologies Inc
17199 Laurel Park Dr N, Livonia MI 48152-2679. 313/953-1100. Employs: 250-499.

Additional small to medium sized employers: 50-249

PLASTIC MATERIALS, SYNTHETIC RESINS AND NONVULCANIZABLE ELASTOMERS

Advanced Elastomer Systems Lp
2401 E Walton Blvd, Auburn Hills MI 48326-1957. 313/373-5544. Employs: 50-99.

Amoco Performance Products Inc
605 Apple Hill Ln, Rochester MI 48306-4206. 313/650-8360. Employs: 50-99.

Anderson Development Company
1415 E Michigan St, Adrian MI 49221-3445. 517/263-2121. Employs: 100-249.

Arise Productions
2909 2nd Ave, Detroit MI 48201-2629. 313/831-4788. Employs: 100-249.

B A S F Corp
3301 Bourke Ave, Detroit MI 48238-2167. 313/861-1000. Employs: 100-249.

Bruck Plastics Co
28300 Hayes Rd, Roseville MI 48066-2317. 313/777-2828. Employs: 50-99.

Ciba-Geigy Formulated Systs
4917 Dawn Ave, East Lansing MI 48823-5605. 517/351-5900. Employs: 50-99.

Container Recycling Inc
20902 Mack Ave, Grosse Pointe MI 48236-1315. 313/885-9360. Employs: 100-249.

Cyro Industrials
4406 Knightsbridge Ln, W Bloomfield MI 48323-1626. 313/682-1400. Employs: 50-99.

Delta Polymers Co
6685 Sterling Dr N, Sterling Hts MI 48312-4559. 313/795-2900. Employs: 50-99.

Eaton Associates
3210 Kernway Dr, Bloomfield MI 48304-2435. 313/646-9270. Employs: 50-99.

Foamade Industries
2550 Auburn Ct Box 4494, Auburn Hills MI 48326-3200. 313/852-6010. Employs: 100-249.

Genesis Polymers
2550 Busha Hwy, Marysville MI 48040-1904. 313/364-5555. Employs: 100-249.

Himont
900 Wilshire Dr, Troy MI 48084-1628. 313/244-8900. Employs: 50-99.

Hoechst Celanese Corp Engineering
1195 Centre Rd, Auburn Hills MI 48326-2603. 313/377-2700. Employs: 50-99.

J M Klein Co
455 S Livernois Rd, Rochester MI 48307-2578. 313/852-9210. Employs: 50-99.

Lewallen L Co
185 Malow St, Mount Clemens MI 48043-2114. 313/468-1038. Employs: 50-99.

Park Chemical Co
8074 Military Ave, Detroit MI 48204-3518. 313/895-7215. Employs: 50-99.

Plastic Plus Inc
1091 Centre Rd, Auburn Hills MI 48326-2665. 313/377-1670. Employs: 50-99.

Pms Consolidated
16014 Virgi Ct, Clinton Twp MI 48038-4181. 313/263-5810. Employs: 50-99.

Polymerland Divsn Gen Electric
1173 Highview Dr, Lapeer MI 48446-3363. 313/667-1533. Employs: 100-249.

Spectrum Colors Inc
30785 Red Maple Ln, Southfield MI 48076-5354. 313/258-8864. Employs: 50-99.

Texapol Corporation
16459 Truwood St, Trenton MI 48183-1668. 313/676-8819. Employs: 100-249.

Woodland Prime Alliance
1345 Rickett Rd, Brighton MI 48116-1879. 313/227-1780. Employs: 50-99.

SYNTHETIC RUBBER (VULCANIZABLE ELASTOMERS)

Marsh Industries Inc
49680 Leona Dr, Harrison Twp MI 48045. 313/949-9300. Employs: 50-99.

TIRES AND INNER TUBES

Halo Burger
3410 Corunna Rd, Flint MI 48503-3266. 313/767-0022. Employs: 50-99.

RUBBER AND PLASTIC HOSE AND BELTING

Flexible Products Co
2600 Auburn Ct, Auburn Hills MI 48326-3201. 313/353-5200. Employs: 50-99.

Molding Tooling Supplies
15055 32 Mile Rd, Romeo MI 48065-4901. 313/752-5053. Employs: 50-99.

GASKETS, PACKING AND SEALING DEVICES

Argent Corp
41131 Vincenti Ct, Novi MI 48375-1924. 313/473-0500. Employs: 50-99.

Dynamic Seals Inc
1966 Heide St, Troy MI 48084-5314. 313/362-0170. Employs: 50-99.

Hahn Elastomer Corp
14557 Keel St, Plymouth MI 48170-6002. 313/455-3300.
Employs: 50-99.

Mather Seal
525 Redman Rd, Milan MI 48160-9282. 313/439-2481.
Employs: 100-249.

R/O Manufacturing Corp
2735 Paldan Dr, Auburn Hills MI 48326-1827. 313/373-4700. Employs: 50-99.

Thunderline Corporation
8707 Samuel Barton Dr Box 309, Belleville MI 48112-0309. 313/397-5000. Employs: 100-249.

MOLDED, EXTRUDED AND LATHE-CUT
MECHANICALS RUBBER GOODS

Armada Rubber Manufacturing Co
24586 Armada Ridge Rd, Armada MI 48005. 313/784-9135. Employs: 50-99.

Wayne Ind Inc
138 N Groesbeck Hw, Mount Clemens MI 48043-1529.
313/498-0961. Employs: 100-249.

MISCELLANEOUS FABRICATED RUBBER
PRODUCTS

Production Rubber Prod Co Inc
12326 Stark Rd, Livonia MI 48150-1522. 313/422-5800.
Employs: 100-249.

Schlegel N American Auto Opers
900 Whitcomb, Madison Hts MI 48071-5612. 313/583-1122. Employs: 100-249.

Oon Corp International Inc
24035 Research Dr, Farmington MI 48335-2632. 313/477-3111. Employs: 50-99.

Radiant Dyes Chemie
27221 Karen Marie, Harrison Twp MI 48045. 313/598-0855. Employs: 50-99.

UNSUPPORTED PLASTIC FILM AND SHEET

Bilcor Plastics Inc
2450 Mechanic Rd, Hillsdale MI 49242-1072. 517/439-1462. Employs: 100-249.

Hercules Advanced Materials Co
4221 Meadow Pond Ln, Metamora MI 48455-9751.
313/797-5781. Employs: 50-99.

Imperial Graphics
2218 Phillips Rd, Auburn Hills MI 48326-2447. 313/377-4111. Employs: 50-99.

Vcf Films
1100 Sutton St, Howell MI 48843-1716. 517/546-2300.
Employs: 50-99.

Polycrest Co
3138 St, Detroit MI 48207. 313/832-4030. Employs: 50-99.

LAMINATED PLASTIC PLATES, SHEETS AND
PROFILE SHAPES

D & B Plastic Products
40715 Brentwood Dr, Sterling Hts MI 48310-2214.
313/268-1880. Employs: 50-99.

Arrow Laminates Inc
6520 Arrow Dr, Sterling Hts MI 48314-1412. 313/254-6700. Employs: 50-99.

H J Oldenkamp Co
4669 E 8 Mile Rd, Warren MI 48091-2709. 313/756-0600.
Employs: 50-99.

Pioneer Plastics
8114 Vanden Dr, White Lake MI 48386-2548. 313/698-1777. Employs: 50-99.

PLASTIC BOTTLES

Econo-Pak
1236 Watson Ave, Ypsilanti MI 48198-9114. 313/481-1373. Employs: 50-99.

Johnson Controls Inc
43700 Gen-Mar, Novi MI 48375-1667. 313/347-7777.
Employs: 50-99.

Plastipak Packaging
1351 Hix Rd, Westland MI 48185-3258. 313/326-6184.
Employs: 100-249.

PLASTIC FOAM PRODUCTS

Michigan Industrial Manufacturing
3250 Old Farm Rd, Walled Lake MI 48390-1656. 313/669-6400. Employs: 50-99.

CUSTOM COMPOUNDING OF PURCHASED
PLASTIC RESINS

Rhe-Tech Inc
1500 E N Territorial Rd, Whitmore Lake MI 48189-9548.
313/769-0585. Employs: 50-99.

PLASTIC PLUMBING FIXTURES

Genova Products Inc
7034 E Court St, Davison MI 48423-2546. 313/744-4500.
Employs: 100-249.

MISCELLANEOUS PLASTIC PRODUCTS

A T S Manufacturing
11791 Longsdorf St, Wyandotte MI 48192-4200. 313/284-9006. Employs: 50-99.

A-Line Plastics
27777 Franklin Rd, Southfield MI 48034-2337. 313/962-1530. Employs: 50-99.

Advanced Auto Trends Inc
2230 Metamora Rd, Oxford MI 48371-2347. 313/628-6111. Employs: 50-99.

Advanced Plastics Corp
24874 Groesbeck Hwy, Warren MI 48089-4726. 313/773-6920. Employs: 50-99.

Advanced Techl Innovations Inc
570 E Main, Potterville MI 48876. 517/645-2990.
Employs: 50-99.

Aeroquip Corp
40550 Brentwood Dr, Sterling Hts MI 48310-2208.
313/939-9590. Employs: 100-249.

Aeroquip Corp/Trinova Div
5972 Product Dr, Sterling Hts MI 48312-4560. 313/978-8040. Employs: 100-249.

Albion Industries Inc
800 N Clark St, Albion MI 49224-1456. 517/629-9441.
Employs: 100-249.

Alco Plastics Inc
160 E Pond Dr, Romeo MI 48065-4902. 313/752-4527.
Employs: 50-99.

Allmand Assocs Inc
12001 Levan Rd, Livonia MI 48150-1403. 313/591-1600.
Employs: 100-249.

American Plastic Fabr Inc
14275 Fordham St, Detroit MI 48205-2421. 313/365-6650.
Employs: 50-99.

Arden Corp
26899 N Western Hwy #201, Southfield MI 48034.
313/355-1101. Employs: 100-249.

Arrow Plastic Products Inc
14700 E 11 Mile Rd, Warren MI 48089-1555. 313/777-4640. Employs: 50-99.

Artjay Industries Inc
27250 Gloede Dr, Warren MI 48093-6033. 313/772-7860.
Employs: 50-99.

Avon
2776 Commerce Dr, Rochester MI 48309-3814. 313/853-3230. Employs: 50-99.

Avon Plastic Products
2890 Technology Dr, Rochester MI 48309-3586. 313/852-1000. Employs: 50-99.

B & H Plastic Company Inc
66725 S Forest Av, Richmond MI 48062. 313/727-7100.
Employs: 50-99.

Becker Manufacturing
401 S Chestnut St, Owosso MI 48867-3307. 517/723-5121.
Employs: 100-249.

Bentley Tool Inc
28214 Beck Rd, Wixom MI 48393-3623. 313/347-3400.
Employs: 50-99.

Black River Plastics Corp ,
2600 20th St, Port Huron MI 48060-6444. 313/985-9730.
Employs: 50-99.

Brooklyn Products Inc
171 Wamplers Lk, Brooklyn MI 49230-9585. 517/592-2185. Employs: 50-99.

Calahan Industries
37950 Commerce Dr, Sterling Hts MI 48312-1002.
313/978-0500. Employs: 100-249.

Carroll Packaging Co Inc
6340 Miller Rd, Dearborn MI 48126-2310. 313/584-0400.
Employs: 50-99.

Castino Corp
16777 Wahrman Rd, Romulus MI 48174-3633. 313/941-7200. Employs: 50-99.

Cavalier Tool & Manufacturing
6762 Balfour St, Allen Park MI 48101-2306. 313/961-4159. Employs: 50-99.

Champion Plastics
641 S Eton St, Troy MI 48008. 313/646-6778. Employs: 50-99.

Chemcast Corp
550 E Mandoline, Madison Hts MI 48071-1401. 313/583-9560. Employs: 50-99.

Combine Plastic Products
18720 Krause Av, Wyandotte MI 48192-4249. 313/283-0200. Employs: 50-99.

Consolidated Industrial Corp
430 N Woodward Av, Birmingham MI 48009-5359.
313/647-3337. Employs: 100-249.

Continental Plastics Co
33525 Groesbeck Hwy, Fraser MI 48026-4205. 313/294-4600. Employs: 100-249.

Continental Vinyl Windows
11705 Lennon Rd, Lennon MI 48449-9627. 313/6214660.
Employs: 50-99.

Contour Technologies

29 Superior St, Hillsdale MI 49242-1734. 517/439-1571.
Employs: 100-249.

Creative Techniques Inc
2441 N Opdyke Rd, Auburn Hills MI 48326-2442.
313/373-3050. Employs: 50-99.

Croswell Plastics Inc
100 Seltzer Rd, Croswell MI 48422-9179. 313/679-4200.
Employs: 50-99.

D & A Industries Inc
60 Seltzer Rd, Croswell MI 48422-9179. 313/679-4887.
Employs: 50-99.

D & L Plastics Inc
15075 32 Mile Rd, Romeo MI 48065-4901. 313/752-7910.
Employs: 50-99.

Dak Plastic Co Inc
15244 Martin Rd, Roseville MI 48066-2348. 313/772-9797. Employs: 100-249.

Deckerville Plastics
3729 Marquette St, Deckerville MI 48427-9385. 313/376-2285. Employs: 50-99.

Deco Trim I I
30150 S Hill Rd, New Hudson MI 48165-9787. 313/437-5080. Employs: 100-249.

Delta Product Engineering Co
1360 E Big Beaver Rd, Troy MI 48083-1936. 313/689-4990. Employs: 50-99.

Detroit Forming Inc
19100 W 8 Mile Rd, Southfield MI 48075-5726. 313/352-8108. Employs: 100-249.

Detroit Gasket
26899 Northwestern Hwy, Southfield MI 48034-2195.
313/353-8960. Employs: 100-249.

Drake Molding Corp
801 Fairplains St, Greenville MI 48838-2706. 616/754-4645. Employs: 100-249.

Dri-Print Foils Inc
29600 Northwestern Hw, Southfield MI 48034-1016.
313/961-3759. Employs: 50-99.

Duall Industries
700 Mc Millan Av, Owosso MI 48867-9776. 517/725-8184. Employs: 50-99.

Dunnage Engineering
721 Advance St, Brighton MI 48116-1238. 313/229-9501.
Employs: 50-99.

Dynaplast Corp
6305 Wall St, Sterling Hts MI 48312-1078. 313/978-1400.
Employs: 100-249.

E & M Industries
212 Elm St, Holly MI 48442-1403. 313/634-1366.
Employs: 50-99.

E-T-M Enterprises Inc
920 N Clinton St, Grand Ledge MI 48837-1106. 517/627-8461. Employs: 100-249.

Ferro Industries Inc
35200 Union Lake Rd, Harrison Twp MI 48045-3149.
313/792-6001. Employs: 50-99.

Formtech Plastics
250 W 8 Mile Rd, Ferndale MI 48220-2439. 313/544-8204.
Employs: 50-99.

G-P Plastics Inc
3910 Indl Dr, Rochester MI 48309. 313/852-5022.
Employs: 50-99.

Great Lakes Plastics Inc
7941 Salem Rd, Northville MI 48167-9423. 313/349-1180.
Employs: 50-99.

Greenfield Die & Manufacturing Corp
8301 Ronda Dr, Canton MI 48187-2079. 313/454-4000.
Employs: 50-99.

H & N Manufacturing Co
14487 Stowell Rd, Dundee MI 48131-9733. 313/529-3952.
Employs: 50-99.

Harbor Plastic Products
1701 Sinclair St, Saint Clair MI 48079-5512. 313/329-6646. Employs: 50-99.

Hi-Tech Plastic Inc
500 E 2nd St, Rochester MI 48307-2200. 313/652-4100.
Employs: 50-99.

Huron Plastics Group Inc
1219 Fred Moore Hwy, Saint Clair MI 48079. 313/329-9091. Employs: 50-99.

I T T Higbie Baylock
180 E Elmwood St, Leonard MI 48367-1801. 313/628-4899. Employs: 50-99.

J B Rath Co
6385 Wall St, Sterling Hts MI 48312-1079. 313/979-3044.
Employs: 50-99.

J K Assemblies Limited
1108 Smith St, Algonac MI 48001-1292. 313/794-1110.
Employs: 50-99.

Jazz Fabrications
19237 Conant St, Detroit MI 48234-1443. 313/366-2810.
Employs: 50-99.

Johnson Controls
290 McCormick Dr, Lapeer MI 48446-2518. 313/664-7212. Employs: 50-99.

Jordan Creek Plastics
2015 Range Rd, Saint Clair MI 48079. 313/329-2287.
Employs: 100-249.

Kalfact Plastics Co
864 Fairplains St, Greenville MI 48838-2478. 616/754-7118. Employs: 50-99.

Kenco Owosso Plastics
503 S Shiawassee St, Corunna MI 48817-1663. 517/743-6361. Employs: 100-249.

Kenco-Owosso Plastics Inc
1650 E South St, Owosso MI 48867-9779. 517/723-8991.
Employs: 50-99.

Kurtz Plastics
5300 N Dort Hwy, Flint MI 48505-3037. 313/787-6540.
Employs: 50-99.

Lacks Industries
6138 Riverside Dr, Saranac MI 48881-9779. 616/897-9288.
Employs: 100-249.

Laird Plastics Inc
26403 Groesbeck Hwy, Warren MI 48089-1539. 313/773-9050. Employs: 50-99.

Lawrence Plastic Inc
3250 Oakley Pk Rd, Walled Lake MI 48390-1648.
313/624-9292. Employs: 50-99.

Lexington Plastics Inc
5140 S Lakeshore Rd, Lexington MI 48450-9380. 313/359-7331. Employs: 50-99.

Libralter Plastics Inc

1000 Manufacturers Dr, Westland MI 48185-4037.
313/595-4900. Employs: 50-99.

Luckmarr Plastics Inc
35795 Stanley Dr, Sterling Hts MI 48312-2661. 313/978-8498. Employs: 50-99.

M & N Plastics Inc
1196 Souter St, Troy MI 48083-2820. 313/588-0150.
Employs: 50-99.

Mac Donald Molding Inc
36870 Green St, New Baltimore MI 48047-1608. 313/725-2111. Employs: 100-249.

Mac-Assemblys
1117 Badder St, Troy MI 48083-2861. 313/583-6960.
Employs: 50-99.

Manchester Plastics
500 W Madison St, Manchester MI 48158. 313/428-8383.
Employs: 100-249.

Mantex Corp
1800 Metamora Rd, Oxford MI 48371-2418. 313/628-8200. Employs: 100-249.

Mark I Molded Plastics Inc
U S 12 E, Jonesville MI 49250. 517/849-9911. Employs: 100-249.

Marysville Plastics Corp
315 Cuttle Rd, Marysville MI 48040-1804. 313/364-6688.
Employs: 50-99.

Mayfair Plastics Inc
2275 Cole St, Birmingham MI 48009-7073. 313/644-3316.
Employs: 50-99.

Met-Pro Corporation Duall Div
1550 E Industrial Dr, Durand MI 48429. 517/725-8184.
Employs: 50-99.

Metamora Products Corp
4057 S Oak St, Metamora MI 48455-9336. 313/6782295.
Employs: 100-249.

Mid-American Products Inc
1623 Wildwood Av, Jackson MI 49202-4041. 517/789-8116. Employs: 50-99.

Midwest Rubber
370 E Sanilac, Sandusky MI 48471-1151. 313/648-3014.
Employs: 50-99.

Modern Acrylic Designs
321314 Donnelly, Garden City MI 48135. 313/261-5770.
Employs: 50-99.

Modern Plastics & Abrasives
32439 Industrial Dr, Madison Hts MI 48071-1528.
313/585-7523. Employs: 50-99.

Molded Materials Inc
14555 Jib St, Plymouth MI 48170-6011. 313/459-5955.
Employs: 50-99.

Molmec Inc
2655 E Oakley Pk Rd, Walled Lake MI 48390-1640.
313/669-7840. Employs: 50-99.

N Y X Inc
30111 Schoolcraft Rd, Livonia MI 48150-2006. 313/421-3850. Employs: 100-249.

N Y X/Rebmann Plastic Molding
24555 Capitol Ave, Redford MI 48239-2447. 313/255-0800. Employs: 100-249.

Nero Plastics Inc
401 S Delaney Rd, Owosso MI 48867-9114. 517/725-2900.
Employs: 50-99.

Noecker Vinyl & Plastics
6535 E McNichols St, Detroit MI 48212-2027. 313/893-2000. Employs: 100-249.

Nova
7474 Van Riper Rd, Fowlerville MI 48836-9535. 517/223-9158. Employs: 50-99.

Omega Plastics Inc
21356 Carlo Dr, Clinton Twp MI 48038-1510. 313/465-1910. Employs: 50-99.

P & M Products Co
155-B Malow St, Mount Clemens MI 48043-2114. 313/463-3840. Employs: 50-99.

P S I Telecommunications Inc
565 S Cedar St, Imlay City MI 48444-1333. 313/724-6461. Employs: 50-99.

P T I Engineered Plastics Inc
44755 Centre Ct, Clinton Twp MI 48038-1317. 313/263-5100. Employs: 50-99.

Pinckney Molded Plastics Inc
3970 Parsons Rd, Howell MI 48843-9617. 517/546-9900. Employs: 50-99.

Pine River Plastics
1796 S Parker Ave, Marine City MI 48039-2337. 313/765-3517. Employs: 50-99.

Plastech Engineered Products Inc
33195 Harper Ave, St Clair Shrs MI 48082-1025. 313/294-9440. Employs: 100-249.

Plasti-Paint Inc
801 Woodside Av, Saint Louis MI 48880-1054. 517/681-5702. Employs: 50-99.

Plastic Specialties
2701 John R Rd, Troy MI 48083-2352. 313/689-0620. Employs: 50-99.

Plastics Research Corp
316 Lincoln St, Fenton MI 48430-1804. 313/629-1595. Employs: 50-99.

Plastigage Corporation
2917 Wildwood Rd, Jackson MI 49202-3936. 517/788-8000. Employs: 100-249.

Polymeric Processes Inc
414 S Maumee St, Tecumseh MI 49286-2055. 517/423-8318. Employs: 100-249.

Port Huron Molded Products Inc
1717 Beard St, Port Huron MI 48060-6420. 313/984-2621. Employs: 50-99.

Precision Standard Inc
721 E Saratoga St, Ferndale MI 48220-2824. 313/548-4700. Employs: 50-99.

Pride Plastics Inc
575 Glaspie Rd, Oxford MI 48371-5133. 313/628-2627. Employs: 50-99.

Pyramid Products Inc
33639 Riviera Dr, Fraser MI 48026-1622. 313/296-0500. Employs: 100-249.

Q D C Plastic Container
111 W Mt Hope Av, Lansing MI 48910-9051. 517/487-4612. Employs: 50-99.

Quick Industries Inc
3530 Wayland Dr, Jackson MI 49202-1234. 517/787-3131. Employs: 50-99.

R N Fink Manufacturing Co Inc

1530 Noble Rd, Williamston MI 48895-9749. 517/655-4351. Employs: 50-99.

Regal Plastics Co
655 Wabassee Dr, Owosso MI 48867-9766. 517/723-6717. Employs: 100-249.

Roto Plastics Corp
1001 Division St, Adrian MI 49221-4023. 517/263-8981. Employs: 50-99.

Sebro Plastics Inc
29200 Wall St, Wixom MI 48393-3526. 313/348-4121. Employs: 100-249.

Sebro Plastics Inc
6175 Trumbull St, Detroit MI 48208-1347. 313/871-0709. Employs: 100-249.

Shuert Industries Inc
6600 Dobry Dr, Sterling Hts MI 48314-1425. 313/254-4590. Employs: 50-99.

Special Plastic Products Inc
8720 Dixie Hwy, Fair Haven MI 48023. 313/725-1990. Employs: 100-249.

Spiratex Co
6333 Cogswell Rd, Romulus MI 48174-4039. 313/722-0100. Employs: 100-249.

Stemaco Products Inc
5139 Lapeer Rd, Port Huron MI 48060. 313/987-5151. Employs: 100-249.

Superior Plastic Inc
417 E 2nd St, Rochester MI 48307-2007. 313/651-9311. Employs: 50-99.

The Sturdevant Corp
271 1st St, Milan MI 48160-1005. 313/439-2401. Employs: 50-99.

Thermofil Inc
6150 Whitmore Lk Rd, Brighton MI 48116-1926. 313/227-3500. Employs: 100-249.

Thumb Plastics Inc
400 Liberty St, Bad Axe MI 48413-9490. 517/269-9791. Employs: 50-99.

Tri-State Hospital Sply Corp
301 Catrell Dr, Howell MI 48843-1703. 517/546-5400. Employs: 100-249.

Troy Co's Inc
7700 19 Mile Rd, Sterling Hts MI 48314-3224. 313/254-5370. Employs: 50-99.

U S Farathane Corp
11650 Park Ct, Shelby Twp MI 48315-3108. 313/726-1200. Employs: 100-249.

Venture Industries Corp
17400 Malyn Blvd, Fraser MI 48026-3482. 313/293-9060. Employs: 50-99.

Wellman Incorporated
1100 N Woodward Av Ste 222, Birmingham MI 48009-6739. 313/645-0032. Employs: 50-99.

White Lake Plastics Inc
5020 White Lake Rd, Clarkston MI 48346-2641. 313/625-8880. Employs: 50-99.

Wol Pac Inc
30233 Groesbeck Hwy, Roseville MI 48066-1548. 313/774-3380. Employs: 50-99.

Wolf Engineering
13201 Prospect St, Dearborn MI 48126-3605. 313/584-6811. Employs: 100-249.

Wright Plastic Products Inc
201 Condensery Rd, Sheridan MI 48884-9758. 517/291-3211. Employs: 100-249.

2 B System Corp
6575 Arrow Dr, Sterling Hts MI 48314-1413. 313/254-6900. Employs: 50-99.

A T C Nymold D
6 Parklane Blvd, Dearborn MI 48126-2618. 313/4412733. Employs: 50-99.

Accurate Molded Products
20521 Dwyer St, Detroit MI 48234-2613. 313/368-9333. Employs: 50-99.

Accurate Plastic Products Inc
6732 Transparent, Clarkston MI 48346-1651. 313/625-8377. Employs: 50-99.

Advanced Auto Trends Inc
3485 Metamora Rd, Oxford MI 48371-1619. 313/628-4850. Employs: 50-99.

Advanced Thermoforming
6210 Product Dr, Sterling Hts MI 48312-4566. 313/939-1720. Employs: 50-99.

Air Flex Corp
18666 Fitzpatrick, Detroit MI 48228. 313/836-3205. Employs: 50-99.

Altair International Inc
22800 Hall Rd, Clinton Twp MI 48036-1130. 313/466-1200. Employs: 100-249.

Amhurst Plastic Industries
777 Doheny Dr, Northville MI 48167-1957. 313/349-1525. Employs: 50-99.

Amhurst Plastic Industries
8659 W Haggerty Rd, Plymouth MI 48170. 313/451-0100. Employs: 50-99.

Apollo Molded Products Inc
195 Ajax, Madison Hts MI 48071. 313/547-8220. Employs: 50-99.

Armex Corp
1827 Northfield, Rochester MI 48309. 313/852-9330. Employs: 50-99.

Art Priebe Designing
6636 Neckel St, Dearborn MI 48126-1837. 313/581-0210. Employs: 50-99.

Bailey Corp
3250 W Big Beaver Rd, Troy MI 48084-2902. 313/643-7280. Employs: 50-99.

Barnum Brothers Fibre Co Inc
17321 Telegraph Rd, Detroit MI 48219-3143. 313/533-4500. Employs: 50-99.

Billy Whitelaw & Talented
2050 N Woodward Ave, Bloomfield MI 48304-2257. 313/645-6880. Employs: 50-99.

Blue Water Plastics Co
315 Whiting St, Saint Clair MI 48079-4981. 313/329-2271. Employs: 100-249.

Breitkreuz Plastics
26352 Lawrence Ave, Center Line MI 48015-1268. 313/758-2030. Employs: 50-99.

C A E Plastics Inc
6400 Product Dr, Sterling Hts MI 48312-4570. 313/978-8300. Employs: 50-99.

Castano Plastics

22839 Heslip Dr, Novi MI 48375-4146. 313/344-2585. Employs: 50-99.

Color Custom Livonia Inc
38700 Plymouth Rd, Livonia MI 48150-1055. 313/464-0800. Employs: 100-249.

Complax America
1650 Research Dr, Troy MI 48083-2100. 313/524-3001. Employs: 50-99.

Contour Technologies
850 Stephenson Hwy, Troy MI 48083-1152. 313/585-6800. Employs: 50-99.

Dawn Engineering
43683 Utica Rd, Sterling Hts MI 48314-2359. 313/726-1540. Employs: 50-99.

Delmet Detroit Sales
1471 S Woodward Ave, Bloomfield MI 48302-0553. 313/253-9700. Employs: 50-99.

Delta Molded Products
6650 Highland Rd, Waterford MI 48327-1660. 313/666-8924. Employs: 50-99.

Den-Tek Inc
5801 Concord St, Detroit MI 48211-3237. 313/923-8788. Employs: 50-99.

Dott Manufacturing Co
28333 Telegraph Rd, Southfield MI 48034-1948. 313/948-6980. Employs: 50-99.

Du-Val Industries
42019 Irwin Dr, Harrison Twp MI 48045-1337. 313/463-9711. Employs: 50-99.

Dunlop Automtv Composites Inc
7704 Ronda Dr, Canton MI 48187-2447. 313/453-9920. Employs: 50-99.

Duotec Product
1001 E Lincoln Ave, Royal Oak MI 48067-3361. 313/548-9500. Employs: 50-99.

Duotex Product Associates
5501 Enterprise Ct, Warren MI 48092-3497. 313/558-9838. Employs: 50-99.

Elite Plastics
7225 19 Mi, Sterling Hts MI 48314. 313/731-2055. Employs: 50-99.

Encore Sales
200 N Capitol Ave, Lansing MI 48933-1304. 517/484-5131. Employs: 50-99.

Four Phase Plastic Concepts Inc
21300 Carlo Dr, Clinton Twp MI 48038-1510. 313/468-8270. Employs: 50-99.

Geauga Co
850 Stephenson Hwy, Troy MI 48083-1152. 313/589-1312. Employs: 50-99.

General Mould Products
2903 Depot, Orleans MI 48865. 616/761-3106. Employs: 50-99.

Gilreath Manufacturing Inc
15565 Northland Dr, Southfield MI 48075. 313/443-1200. Employs: 50-99.

H & L Engineering Corp
19921 E 12 Mile Rd, Roseville MI 48066-2278. 313/777-4180. Employs: 50-99.

Hanson Group Lts
4 Parklane Blvd, Dearborn MI 48126-2660. 313/336-4550. Employs: 50-99.

Heritage Services Co
18582 Jefferson, Wyandotte MI 48192-4266. 313/282-4566. Employs: 50-99.

Hi-Craft Plant II
34632 Nova Dr, Clinton Twp MI 48035-3716. 313/7909390. Employs: 50-99.

Hicks Plastics
33739 Groesbeck Hwy, Fraser MI 48026-4207. 313/293-8970. Employs: 50-99.

High-Tech Plastics
125 W Michigan Av, Grass Lake MI 49240. 517/522-4369. Employs: 50-99.

Hill Machinery Co
8137 Grand River Rd, Brighton MI 48116-9346. 313/227-8323. Employs: 50-99.

Huppert Engineering
2852 Orchard, Keego Harbor MI 48320. 313/681-4300. Employs: 50-99.

Innovative Concepts Inc
1200 Holden Ave, Milford MI 48381-3134. 313/685-2707. Employs: 50-99.

J S Plastics
25791 Commerce Dr, Madison Hts MI 48071-4158. 313/543-6570. Employs: 50-99.

Jared Manufacturers Sales & Co
5030 Hardworks Dr, W Bloomfield MI 48323. 313/681-5538. Employs: 50-99.

Lexamar Corp
61 Mill St, Lapeer MI 48446-2311. 313/667-4090. Employs: 50-99.

M T R Associates
2655 S Woodward Ave, Bloomfield MI 48304-1667. 313/335-0444. Employs: 50-99.

Manchester Plastics
201 W Big Beaver Rd, Troy MI 48084-4152. 313/524-9650. Employs: 50-99.

Metaplast Inc
321 South St, Rochester MI 48307-2241. 313/651-6830. Employs: 50-99.

Modular Trim Industries
7425 Mayer Rd, Fair Haven MI 48023. 313/725-8610. Employs: 50-99.

Multidimensional Extrusion
450 Park St, Troy MI 48083-2774. 313/588-8885. Employs: 50-99.

Pilot Industries Inc
1911 Ring Dr, Troy MI 48083-4229. 313/583-3076. Employs: 50-99.

Pine River Plastics Inc
1111 Fred W Moore Hwy, Saint Clair MI 48079-4967. 313/329-9004. Employs: 100-249.

Plastic Engineering Corp
1281 Harmon Rd, Oakland MI 48363-1037. 313/693-2800. Employs: 50-99.

Plastico Industries Inc
320 W Main St, Carson City MI 48811-9642. 517/584-3985. Employs: 50-99.

Plastronics Plus
12763 Stark Rd, Livonia MI 48150-1551. 313/261-4210. Employs: 50-99.

Q I P Products Inc

44309 Macomb Industrial Dr, Clinton Twp MI 48036-1143. 313/468-7276. Employs: 50-99.

Seville Enterprises Inc
15055 32 Mi, Romeo MI 48065. 313/752-3500. Employs: 50-99.

Shoulders Benching & Polsg Co
7563 19 Mi, Sterling Hts MI 48314. 313/254-3488. Employs: 50-99.

Smt Polymers Inc Sls & Engrs
31333 Southfield Rd, Franklin MI 48025-5473. 313/642-8000. Employs: 50-99.

Special Plastic Products Inc
8720 Dixie Hwy, Clarkston MI 48348-4237. 313/725-1990. Employs: 50-99.

St Clair Plastics Corp
1295 S Parker St, Marine City MI 48039-2331. 313/765-8833. Employs: 100-249.

Sterling Plastics Inc
7225 19 Mi, Sterling Hts MI 48314. 313/739-2080. Employs: 50-99.

Subsidiary
9620 General Dr, Plymouth MI 48170. 313/451-0076. Employs: 50-99.

The Colonel's
490 S Chestnut St, Owosso MI 48867-3308. 517/723-8792. Employs: 100-249.

Three 60 Corporation
10823 Plaza Dr, Whitmore Lake MI 48189-9737. 313/449-0099. Employs: 50-99.

Tom Smith Industries
835 Mason St, Dearborn MI 48124-2221. 313/565-9060. Employs: 50-99.

Tuscarora Plastics Inc
4013 W Baldwin Rd, Grand Blanc MI 48439-9336. 313/694-8036. Employs: 50-99.

Venture Industries
33662 James J Pompo Dr, Fraser MI 48026-3466. 313/294-1500. Employs: 50-99.

Webster Plastic Detroit Sales Office
463 E 14 Mile Rd, Birmingham MI 48009-2023. 313/642-3676. Employs: 50-99.

Welco Products Inc
2165 Avon Industrial Dr, Rochester MI 48309-3611. 313/852-3710. Employs: 50-99.

Erico Plastic
22212 Dequindre Rd, Warren MI 48091-5131. 313/754-6602. Employs: 50-99.

Fabri-Form Of Michigan
2392 Columbia Rd, Berkley MI 48072-1715. 313/544-4152. Employs: 50-99.

Maige Industrial Supply
165 Arlington St, Inkster MI 48141-1246. 313/277-8350. Employs: 50-99.

U S Assembly
928 Minion St, Ypsilanti MI 48198-5814. 313/482-5244. Employs: 50-99.

Allen Extruders
1650 Kendale Blvd, East Lansing MI 48823-2076. 517/351-1210. Employs: 50-99.

Detroit Manufactured Prod Co
1605 E Avis Dr, Madison Hts MI 48071-1514. 313/583-9049. Employs: 50-99.

Eller Corp
41135 Irwin Dr, Harrison Twp MI 48045-1329. 313/468-6300. Employs: 50-99.

Lyntex Manufacturing Co
4385 Garfield, Ubly MI 48475. 517/6588557. Employs: 100-249.

Paul Murphy Plastics Co
15301 E 11 Mile Rd, Roseville MI 48066-2772. 313/774-4880. Employs: 50-99.

Truesdell Co
2840 Auburn Ct, Auburn Hills MI 48326-3203. 313/852-7344. Employs: 50-99.

For more information on career opportunities in the rubber and plastics industries:

<u>Associations</u>

SOCIETY OF PLASTICS ENGINEERS
14 Fairfield Drive, Brookfield CT 06804. 203/755-0471.

SOCIETY OF PLASTICS INDUSTRY
355 Lexington Avenue, New York NY 10017. 212/351-5410.

TRANSPORTATION

Aviation: The airlines are about as closely linked with the overall economy as any industry. Competition between airlines will remain brutal. Increasingly, the industry will be dominated by three companies - American, Delta, and United, with others at risk of falling by the wayside. With fewer major players, fewer jobs will be available. On a brighter note, according to the U.S. Labor Department, the hiring picture will improve over the long-term.

JOHN V. CARR AND SON, INC.
P.O. Box 33479, Detroit MI 48232-5479. 313/965-1540. **Contact:** Linda Mora, Personnel Assistant. **Description:** A customs broker and foreign freight forwarder. **Employees:** 550 nationwide. Corporate headquarters are in Detroit with subsidiaries in Los Angeles, Boston, New York, and Vermont. Branch offices coast to coast. **Common positions:** Computer Programmer; Credit Manager; Department Manager; Personnel and Labor Relations Specialist; Sales Representative; Systems Analyst; Transportation And Traffic Specialist. **Educational backgrounds sought:** Business Administration; Computer Science; Clerical. **Benefits:** medical, dental, and life insurance; tuition assistance; disability coverage; profit sharing; savings plan. **Corporate headquarters:** This location. **Operations at this facility:** administration; service; sales.

CENTRAL TRANSPORT INC.
12225 Stephens Road, Warren MI 48089. 313/939-7000. **Contact:** Mary Huegmer, Personnel Director. **Description:** Engaged in non-local trucking. **Employees:** 700.

DETROIT MARINE TERMINALS

P.O. Box 127, Detroit MI 48128-0127. 313/843-7575. **Contact:** Ms. Pearl McClain. A major metropolitan Detroit marine cargo handling company. **Employees:** 100.

E & L TRANSPORT

35005 Michigan Avenue, Wayne MI 48184. 313/729-9500. **Contact:** Shirley Sanislow, Personnel. **Description:** A major Detroit based non-location trucking company. **Employees:** 600. **Parent company:** Transco, Inc.

GRAND TRUNK WESTERN RAILROAD

1333 Brewery Park, Detroit MI 48207. 313/396-6120. **Contact:** James Smith, Jr., Manager of Human Resources. **Description:** A transportation industry company involved in railroad freight (no passengers). **Employees:** 4,000. **Common positions:** Accountant; Attorney; Computer Programmer; Customer Service Representative; Financial Analyst. **Educational backgrounds sought:** Accounting; Business Administration; Computer Science; Engineering; Finance; Marketing. **Special programs:** Training programs.

JONES TRANSFER COMPANY

300 Jones Avenue, Monroe MI 48161. 313/241-4120. **Contact:** Matt Hall, Payoll Supervisor. **Description:** An area company specializing in non-local trucking. **Employees:** 1,100.

EARL C. SMITH INC.

P.O. Box 610369, Port Huron MI 48060. 313/984-2626. **Contact:** Judy Moore, Payroll Clerk. **Description:** A leading Michigan-based interstate trucking company. **Employees:** 200.

SULZER PLASMA TECHNIK, INC.

1972 Meijer Drive, Troy MI 48084. 313/288-1200. **Contact:** Diane Spampinato, Human Resources Director. **Description:** Engaged in the manufacture of primary metal products. Specializes in the production of powders for coating and brazing jet engine parts. Founded in 1961.

Additional large employers: 250+

SHIP BUILDING AND REPAIRING

K-H Corporation
38481 Huron River Dr, Romulus MI 48174-1158. 313/941-2000. Employs: 1000+.

MISC. TRANSPORTATION EQUIPMENT

Durakon Industries Inc
2101 N Lapeer Rd, Lapeer MI 48446-8611. 313/664-0850. Employs: 250-499.

MISC. LOCAL PASSENGER TRANSPORTATION

Charlotte Area Ambulance Svc
321 E Harris St, Charlotte MI 48813-1629. 517/543-1050. Employs: 250-499.

TRUCKING, EXCEPT LOCAL

Centra Inc
34200 Mound Rd, Sterling Hts MI 48310-6613. 313/939-7000. Employs: 1000+.

E & L Transport Co
21000 Hayden Dr, Trenton MI 48183-4366. 313/675-9000. Employs: 500-999.

LOCAL TRUCKING WITH STORAGE

COURIER SERVICES, EXCEPT BY AIR

Jones Transfer Co
300 Jones Ave, Monroe MI 48161-1351. 313/241-4120.
Employs: 1000+.

AIR TRANSPORTATION, SCHEDULED

Delta Airlines Inc
26400 Lahser Rd, Southfield MI 48034-2624. 313/351-4230. Employs: 1000+.

Additional small to medium sized employers: 50-249

BOAT BUILDING AND REPAIRING

American Boat Manufacturing Inc
303 Valley Av, Alma MI 48801-2837. 517/463-1138.
Employs: 50-99.

Maurell Products Inc
2710 M-52 S, Owosso MI 48867. 517/725-5188. Employs: 50-99.

Playbuoy Pontoon Manufacturing Inc
903 Michigan Ave, Alma MI 48801-1933. 517/463-2112.
Employs: 50-99.

Waterway's Unlimited Inc
720 Michigan Ave, Alma MI 48801-1930. 517/463-2628.
Employs: 50-99.

RAILROAD EQUIPMENT

Northern Engineering Corp
210 Chene St, Detroit MI 48207-4429. 313/259-3280.
Employs: 50-99.

MOTORCYCLES, BICYCLES AND PARTS

Walt Industries Inc
12572 Delta Dr, Taylor MI 48180-4081. 313/946-2930.
Employs: 50-99.

TRAVEL TRAILERS AND CAMPERS

Xplorer Motor Homes
3950 Burnsline Rd, Brown City MI 48416-8658. 313/346-2771. Employs: 50-99.

RAILROAD SWITCHING AND TERMINAL ESTABLISHMENTS

Norfolk-Western Rail
19400 Prospect St, Melvindale MI 48122-1691. 313/246-1875. Employs: 50-99.

LOCAL AND SUBURBAN TRANSIT

Coast Refrigerated Trucking Co
1480 E Ferry St, Detroit MI 48211-2506. 313/872-7510.
Employs: 50-99.

Detroit Transportation Corp
150 Michigan Ave, Detroit MI 48226-2623. 313/962-7245.
Employs: 50-99.

Hyman Freightways
3936 Lonyo St, Detroit MI 48210-2103. 313/582-1830.
Employs: 50-99.

J E Transport Inc
Winsor, Detroit MI 48207. 313/961-5833. Employs: 50-99.

Morningwind Transportation
11265 College St, Detroit MI 48205-3203. 313/839-2664.
Employs: 50-99.

D H T Transportation
5150 12th St, Detroit MI 48208-1702. 313/895-1300.
Employs: 50-99.

Absolute Class Limousine Svc
23563 Powers Ave, Dearborn Hts MI 48125-2150.
313/295-4522. Employs: 50-99.

Anthony's Limousine Service Inc
31522 Rush St, Garden City MI 48135-1708. 313/425-2121. Employs: 50-99.

Centennial Limousine Inc
7423 Mohawk St, Westland MI 48185-6907. 313/422-2550. Employs: 50-99.

Gambino's Limousine Svc
35465 Avondale St, Westland MI 48185. 313/728-8736.
Employs: 50-99.

Let's Go Shuttle Express
20270 Middlebelt Rd, Livonia MI 48152-2000. 313/473-7010. Employs: 50-99.

Metro Cars Inc Detroit Metro
28900 Goddard Rd, Romulus MI 48174-2702. 313/946-5700. Employs: 50-99.

Michael's Limousine Service Inc
32825 8 Mile Rd, Livonia MI 48152-1337. 313/476-2550.
Employs: 50-99.

Pryor & Pryor Limousine Svc
6101 E Nevada St, Detroit MI 48234-2609. 313/368-0707.
Employs: 50-99.

Quality Air Freight
11701 Metro Airport Center Dr, Romulus MI 48174-1403.
313/942-0432. Employs: 50-99.

Ready Limousine Svc
18445 Wildemere St, Detroit MI 48221-2212. 313/861-7499. Employs: 50-99.

Robinson Bus Service Inc
8053 Military St, Detroit MI 48204-3517. 313/895-5507.
Employs: 50-99.

Special Touch Limo & Sedan Svc
21541 Cambridge Ave, Detroit MI 48219-1919. 313/531-6363. Employs: 50-99.

Summit Limousine Inc
13101 Eckles Rd, Plymouth MI 48170-4201. 313/454-7377. Employs: 50-99.

Superior Express Svc
7015 Merriman Rd, Romulus MI 48174-1913. 313/595-8288. Employs: 50-99.

MISCELLANEOUS LOCAL PASSENGER TRANSPORTATION

Kirby Tours
2451 S Telegraph Rd, Dearborn MI 48124-2520. 313/278-2224. Employs: 50-99.

A Gem Limousine Service Inc
19145 Pennington Dr, Detroit MI 48221-1620. 313/863-2120. Employs: 50-99.

A Luxurious Rose Limousine Svc
10006 Winthrop St, Detroit MI 48227-1622. 313/273-0012.
Employs: 50-99.

Archie's Limousine Service Inc
1351 Lenox-Detroit, Detroit MI 48215. 313/3311271.
Employs: 50-99.

Dan's Limousine Svc
30243 Mich Ink, Inkster MI 48141. 313/595-6156.
Employs: 50-99.

Five Star Limousine Service Inc
19789 Ashley Ct, Livonia MI 48152-4023. 313/464-7774.
Employs: 50-99.

Larry's Limousine Fleet Svc
9245 Ward St, Detroit MI 48228-2646. 313/834-1087.
Employs: 50-99.

Starfire Limousine Svc
12003 Kilbourne, Detroit MI 48213-1313. 313/839-0774.
Employs: 50-99.

Winfield Taylor Limousine Services
3632 Cass Ave, Detroit MI 48201-2310. 313/833-2266.
Employs: 50-99.

Zirker Limousine
5557 Farnum St, Westland MI 48185-5120. 313/595-2992.
Employs: 50-99.

A Air Ambulance America
1365 Cass Ave, Detroit MI 48226-1501. 313/963-3290.
Employs: 50-99.

INTERCITY AND RURAL BUS TRANSPORTATION

Capital Area Trans Auth
4615 Tranter St, Lansing MI 48910-3661. 517/394-1100.
Employs: 50-99.

Detroit & Canada Tunnel Corp
100 E Jefferson Ave, Detroit MI 48226-4327. 313/567-4422. Employs: 50-99.

Indian Trails Inc
109 E Comstock St, Owosso MI 48867-3152. 517/725-5105. Employs: 50-99.

Mass Transportation Authority
1401 S Dort Hwy, Flint MI 48503-2878. 313/767-0100.
Employs: 50-99.

BUS CHARTER SERVICE, EXCEPT LOCAL

Pressley Motor Coach
14350 Cloverdale St, Detroit MI 48238-2456. 313/342-4044. Employs: 50-99.

MOTOR FREIGHT TRANSPORTATION AND WAREHOUSING

St Clair Underground Stg Trmnl
2510 Busha Hwy, Marysville MI 48040-1904. 313/364-8100. Employs: 50-99.

LOCAL TRUCKING WITHOUT STORAGE

L J Beal & Son Inc
212 S Main St, Brooklyn MI 49230-9121. 517/592-2161.
Employs: 50-99.

Overnite Transportation
6150 Inkster Rd, Romulus MI 48174-2442. 313/295-1300.
Employs: 100-249.

Roadway Express Inc
22701 Van Born Rd, Taylor MI 48180-1310. 313/274-2222. Employs: 50-99.

Tandem Transport
1001 Michigan Ave, Saint Louis MI 48880-1019. 517/681-5754. Employs: 50-99.

Yellow Freight System Inc
1300 E Big Beaver Rd, Troy MI 48083-1936. 313/689-7171. Employs: 50-99.

Mgs Instant Courier Inc
9170 Thaddeus St, Detroit MI 48209-2670. 313/843-9547.
Employs: 50-99.

Outbound Express Inc
28478 Highland Rd, Romulus MI 48174-2507. 313/946-4000. Employs: 100-249.

United Parcel Svc
29855 Schoolcraft Rd, Livonia MI 48150-2004. 313/261-8500. Employs: 50-99.

TRUCKING, EXCEPT LOCAL

A B F Freight Systems Inc
9680 Eagle St, Dearborn MI 48120-1403. 313/849-1100.
Employs: 50-99.

Anchor Motor Freight Inc
30800 Telegraph Rd, Franklin MI 48025-4542. 313/647-5340. Employs: 100-249.

Liquid Transport Corp
130 S Green St, Detroit MI 48209-2845. 313/843-9460.
Employs: 50-99.

Manfredi Motor Transit
4007 Lonyo St, Detroit MI 48210-2102. 313/945-1800.
Employs: 50-99.

N K Parker Transport Inc
3501 Wyoming Av, Dearborn MI 48120-1424. 313/554-4700. Employs: 50-99.

Refiners Transport & Termina
3335 Greenfield Rd, Melvindale MI 48122-1241. 313/382-8500. Employs: 50-99.

Wolverine Allied
38000 Amrhein Rd, Livonia MI 48150-1016. 313/464-2550. Employs: 50-99.

Bridge Terminal Transport Co
12601 Southfield Fwy, Detroit MI 48223-3534. 313/837-3233. Employs: 50-99.

Freeman Trucking
13241 Gd River Av, Detroit MI 48227. 313/834-5070.
Employs: 50-99.

Isc Equipment
8610 Puritan St, Detroit MI 48238-1162. 313/862-9333.
Employs: 50-99.

Jan L Hemme Transport
3100 Lonyo St, Detroit MI 48209-1089. 313/841-9222.
Employs: 50-99.

K B S Leasing
11511 Shoemaker St, Detroit MI 48213-3418. 313/925-9170. Employs: 50-99.

K Webb Inc
2200 One Kennedy Sq Bg, Detroit MI 48226. 313/963-1511. Employs: 50-99.

Klavinger Transport
410 S Fordson St, Detroit MI 48217-1358. 313/842-4770.
Employs: 50-99.

Landrum and Sons Trucking
1544 Gray St, Detroit MI 48215-2741. 313/824-0902.
Employs: 50-99.

Richardson Trucking
17530 Sorrento St, Detroit MI 48235-1436. 313/342-6490.
Employs: 50-99.

S & G Group Inc
65 Cadillac Sq, Detroit MI 48226-2812. 313/961-2669.
Employs: 50-99.

Boardman Distribution Inc
280 S Ferdinand St, Detroit MI 48209-3263. 313/843-3990.
Employs: 50-99.

Bulkmatic Transport
9127 Hubbell St, Detroit MI 48228-2332. 313/273-5870.
Employs: 50-99.

Cast North America
12601 Southfield Fwy, Detroit MI 48223-3534. 313/837-2119. Employs: 50-99.

Clarence Jones Trucking
13180 Foley St, Detroit MI 48227-3555. 313/834-0616.
Employs: 50-99.

Coast Refrigerated Trucking Co
8350 Saint Aubin St, Detroit MI 48211-1331. 313/872-1140. Employs: 50-99.

D & G Hauling
16800 Plymouth Rd, Detroit MI 48227-1039. 313/836-6300. Employs: 50-99.

D T P Inc
11000 W McNichols Rd, Detroit MI 48221-2357. 313/864-4131. Employs: 50-99.

E Brown Trucking
12303 Cloverdale St, Detroit MI 48204-1148. 313/934-5090. Employs: 50-99.

Economy Transport
2290 24th St, Detroit MI 48216-1029. 313/843-7600.
Employs: 50-99.

Faith N Grance Transport Inc
4430 52nd St, Detroit MI 48210-2728. 313/841-9506.
Employs: 50-99.

Foreman Bros Inc
1799 14th St, Detroit MI 48216-1839. 313/961-5049.
Employs: 50-99.

H & W Trucking Co
3950 Lonyo St, Detroit MI 48210-2103. 313/581-0511.
Employs: 50-99.

H D Stepp Transportation Ltd
4815 Cabot St, Detroit MI 48210-2002. 313/843-9200.
Employs: 50-99.

Hansbro Corp
3535 Scotten St, Detroit MI 48210-3159. 313/895-2910.
Employs: 50-99.

Hawk Trucking Inc
8585 Dearborn St, Detroit MI 48209-2779. 313/849-1666.
Employs: 50-99.

Joe Jones Trucking
13180 Foley St, Detroit MI 48227-3555. 313/934-7463.
Employs: 50-99.

Luco Cartage Co Inc
7414 Clayton St, Detroit MI 48210-2752. 313/843-5600.
Employs: 50-99.

Magra Inc
4300 Saint James St, Detroit MI 48210-2044. 313/584-7088. Employs: 50-99.

Motor Carrier Specialist Inc
3503 Gaylord St, Detroit MI 48212-1081. 313/368-0522.
Employs: 50-99.

Ohio Fast Freight
4800 Wyomng, Detroit MI 48210. 313/584-6182. Employs:
50-99.

Rainbow Trucking Co Inc

11111 French Rd, Detroit MI 48234-4041. 313/922-6580.
Employs: 50-99.

Rex Transportation
1325 Atwater St, Detroit MI 48207-4015. 313/259-6060.
Employs: 50-99.

Roadrunner Trucking
4195 Central St, Detroit MI 48210-2705. 313/581-3910.
Employs: 50-99.

Roberts X-Press Carriers
176 Campbell River Rouge Mi, Detroit MI 48209.
313/843-6470. Employs: 50-99.

Rye Gentry Trucking
6134 W Jefferson Ave, Detroit MI 48209-3027. 313/843-2551. Employs: 50-99.

Sam's Trucking Corp
12209 W Jeffries Fwy, Detroit MI 48204-1144. 313/834-6600. Employs: 50-99.

Van De Hogen Group Inc
3800 Russell St, Detroit MI 48207-4714. 313/964-3945.
Employs: 50-99.

Wasserman Equipment
4890 E Nevada St, Detroit MI 48234-4215. 313/368-6100.
Employs: 50-99.

Wayne Hunt Inc
658 S Fordson St, Detroit MI 48217-1317. 313/842-0940.
Employs: 50-99.

Whiteford Truck Lines Flat Bed
4815 Cabot St, Detroit MI 48210-2002. 313/581-4114.
Employs: 50-99.

LOCAL TRUCKING WITH STORAGE

Corrigan Moving Systems
3600 E Ellsworth Rd, Ann Arbor MI 48108-2028. 313/973-9393. Employs: 50-99.

Neal's Express
15757 Murray Hill St, Detroit MI 48227-1909. 313/835-8469. Employs: 50-99.

COURIER SERVICES, EXCEPT BY AIR

United Parcel Service
241 E Saginaw St Ste 300, East Lansing MI 48823-2794.
517/351-8580. Employs: 100-249.

FARM PRODUCT WAREHOUSING AND STORAGE

Marlette Farmers Co Op Elev Co
3346 Main St, Marlette MI 48453-1263. 517/635-3578.
Employs: 50-99.

REFRIGERATED WAREHOUSING AND STORAGE

Boag Cold Storage WrHouse Inc
1448 Wabash St, Detroit MI 48216-1845. 313/964-3069.
Employs: 50-99.

GENERAL WAREHOUSING AND STORAGE

Central Detroit Warehouse Co
18765 Seaway Dr, Melvindale MI 48122-1954. 313/388-3200. Employs: 50-99.

Distron Detroit
36175 Herman St, Romulus MI 48174-3383. 313/941-4150. Employs: 50-99.

General Electric Co
2300 Meijer Dr, Troy MI 48084-7145. 313/280-4800.
Employs: 50-99.

Nicholson Terminal & Dock Co
P O Box 18066, River Rouge MI 48218-0066. 313/842-4300. Employs: 50-99.

M P G Transport Ltd
8750 Telegraph Rd, Taylor MI 48180-2368. 313/291-9100. Employs: 50-99.

Unit Ftt Inc
4002 James P Cole Blvd, Flint MI 48505-5501. 313/235-1500. Employs: 100-249.

MISCELLANEOUS SPECIAL WAREHOUSING AND STORAGE

Alexandra Enterprises
14301 W Chicago St, Detroit MI 48228-2314. 313/491-3060. Employs: 50-99.

Mann Steel Corp
9281 Freeland St, Detroit MI 48228-2308. 313/931-6266. Employs: 50-99.

Abrams Data Archives
13801 Schoolcraft St, Detroit MI 48227-3137. 313/837-1149. Employs: 50-99.

Box Records & Tapes
7701 E 7 Mile Rd, Detroit MI 48234-3149. 313/366-8742. Employs: 50-99.

Docustore Inc
12600 Greenfield Rd, Detroit MI 48227-2130. 313/838-8890. Employs: 50-99.

Tx Recording & Production Co
8832 Ashton Ave, Detroit MI 48228-1802. 313/838-8912. Employs: 50-99.

TERMINAL AND JOINT TERMINAL MAINTENANCE FACILITIES FOR MOTOR FREIGHT TRANSPORTATION

Auto Products Transport Inc
3767 Central St, Detroit MI 48210-2701. 313/843-8181. Employs: 50-99.

Jack Diamond River Tours
13000 Denmark St, Detroit MI 48217-1461. 313/843-7676. Employs: 50-99.

TOWING AND TUGBOAT SERVICES

Gaelic Tugboat Co
13000 Denmark St, Detroit MI 48217-1461. 313/841-9440. Employs: 50-99.

MARINAS

Toledo Beach Marina
11840 Toledo Beach Rd, La Salle MI 48145-9767. 313/243-3800. Employs: 50-99.

AIR TRANSPORTATION, SCHEDULED

American Airlines
200 Tandy Center Rm 203, Jackson MI 49202. 517/267-1151. Employs: 50-99.

British Airways
Detroit Metro Airport, Romulus MI 48174. 313/278-2200. Employs: 100-249.

British Airways
29265 Airport Dr, Rommlus MI 48174-2508. 313/946-9673. Employs: 100-249.

Comair Airlines
Det Metro Airpt, Romulus MI 48174. 313/941-1350. Employs: 100-249.

Continental Airlines

445 State St, Detroit MI 48226-1308. 313/963-4600. Employs: 100-249.

Continental Express
G3425 W Bristol Rd, Flint MI 48507. 313/239-1960. Employs: 50-99.

Delta Airlines Inc
535 Griswold St, Detroit MI 48226-3410. 313/355-3200. Employs: 100-249.

Five Way Airfreight
117011 Metro Airport Center Dr, Romulus MI 48174. 313/942-7010. Employs: 100-249.

Iberia Airlines
5600 W Maple Rd, W Bloomfield MI 48322-3704. 313/737-9060. Employs: 50-99.

K L M Royal Dutch Airlines
2000 Town Center, Southfield MI 48075. 313/350-0030. Employs: 50-99.

Mesaba-Northwest Air Link
G3425 W Bristol Rd, Flint MI 48507. 313/767-6011. Employs: 50-99.

Northwest Airlines
Capitol City Blvd, Lansing MI 48906. 517/323-2037. Employs: 50-99.

Pakistan International Airlines
24100 Southfield Rd, Southfield MI 48075-2819. 313/569-7790. Employs: 50-99.

Pan American World Airways
1365 Cass Ave, Detroit MI 48226-1501. 313/964-3800. Employs: 100-249.

Qantas Airways
25440 5 Mile Rd, Redford MI 48239-3837. 313/531-4914. Employs: 50-99.

Simmons Airlines
G3425 W Bristol Rd, Flint MI 48507. 313/233-4938. Employs: 50-99.

Skystar International Inc
29840 Muirland Dr, Farmington MI 48334-2047. 313/855-3302. Employs: 50-99.

Skyway Airlines
G3425 W Bristol Rd, Flint MI 48507. 313/767-2933. Employs: 50-99.

Trans Continental Airlines Inc
Willow Run Airpt, Ypsilanti MI 48198. 313/485-8770. Employs: 100-249.

U S Air
G3425 W Bristol Rd, Flint MI 48507. 313/234-6155. Employs: 50-99.

United Airlines
535 Griswold St, Detroit MI 48226-3410. 313/336-9000. Employs: 100-249.

United Airlines Reserv Ofc
17501 Michigan Av, Dearborn MI 48126-2732. 313/336-9000. Employs: 100-249.

Universal Airlines
1 Willow Run, Ypsilanti MI 48198. 313/481-1900. Employs: 100-249.

Usair
Detroit Metro Airport, Romulus MI 48174. 313/942-2456. Employs: 100-249.

Usair
3000 Town Center, Southfield MI 48075. 313/355-2299. Employs: 50-99.

Adcom Express
6684 Metro Plex Dr, Romulus MI 48174-2010. 313/595-0100. Employs: 100-249.

Air Canada Cargo
99000 Harrison, Romulus MI 48174. 313/946-5735. Employs: 100-249.

Airborne Express
110 E Ellsworth Rd, Ann Arbor MI 48108-2203. 313/677-2888. Employs: 100-249.

American Expediting
1850 2nd St, Westland MI 48185-4451. 313/728-0089. Employs: 100-249.

Burlington Air Express
7010 Middlebelt Rd, Romulus MI 48174-2043. 313/595-6100. Employs: 50-99.

Burlington Air Express
6710 Middlebelt Rd, Romulus MI 48174-2039. 313/728-2200. Employs: 100-249.

C T E
32500 Van Born Rd, Wayne MI 48184-2554. 313/326-5050. Employs: 50-99.

Cam'Am Logistics
11701 Metro Airport Center Dr, Romulus MI 48174-1403. 313/942-0070. Employs: 100-249.

Circle Freight International
46760 Metroplex, Romulus MI 48174. 313/729-4300. Employs: 100-249.

Computer Freight Brokers
27429 Highland, Romulus MI 48174. 313/946-9900. Employs: 100-249.

Data Air Courier
21649 Goddard Rd, Taylor MI 48180-4200. 313/287-3890. Employs: 100-249.

Dependable Transportation
12450 Universal Dr, Taylor MI 48180-4070. 313/946-9620. Employs: 100-249.

Elk Resource Express
35740 Booth St, Westland MI 48185-4281. 313/729-8317. Employs: 100-249.

Five Way Airfreight
11909 Beacon Hill Dr, Plymouth MI 48170-3603. 313/451-1026. Employs: 100-249.

Freight Force Inc
9328 Harrison St, Romulus MI 48174-2503. 313/946-4226. Employs: 100-249.

Galaxy Transport Inc
28510 Hildebrandt St, Romulus MI 48174-2706. 313/946-4404. Employs: 100-249.

Hanshin Air Cargo
28861 Highland Rd, Romulus MI 48174-2506. 313/946-4030. Employs: 100-249.

Japan Freight Consolidated
11700 Metro Airport Center Dr, Romulus MI 48174-1404. 313/942-1380. Employs: 100-249.

Jetstream Inc
9999 French Rd, Detroit MI 48213-1249. 313/921-3500. Employs: 100-249.

Kelly Air Express
9816 Harrison St, Romulus MI 48174-2505. 313/946-1430. Employs: 100-249.

Kintetsu World Express
28445 Highland Rd, Romulus MI 48174-2506. 313/946-9525. Employs: 100-249.

Kuehne & Nagel Inc
29107 Airport Dr, Romulus MI 48174-2508. 313/946-8180. Employs: 100-249.

Metro Direct Inc
11895 Wayne Rd # 100, Romulus MI 48174-1461. 313/946-9711. Employs: 100-249.

N N R Air Cargo
9330 Harrison St, Romulus MI 48174-2503. 313/946-8720. Employs: 100-249.

North American Airfreight
9328 Harrison St, Romulus MI 48174-2503. 313/946-4779. Employs: 100-249.

Northwest Airlines
Detroit Metro Airport, Romulus MI 48174. 313/562-3414. Employs: 100-249.

Northwest Cargo
Det Metro Airpt, Romulus MI 48174. 313/942-2508. Employs: 100-249.

Rivers Express
1971 Teaneck Cir, Wixom MI 48393-1856. 313/960-0050. Employs: 50-99.

Seko Air Freight
29060 Airport Dr, Romulus MI 48174-2509. 313/946-1466. Employs: 100-249.

Southwest Airlines Co
Detroit City Airport, Detroit MI 48213. 313/372-4370. Employs: 100-249.

Superior Aviation
2618 E Circle Dr, Lansing MI 48906-2165. 517/321-0224. Employs: 50-99.

Sureway Air Traffic
27470 Highland, Romulus MI 48174. 313/946-0060. Employs: 100-249.

Trans World Airlines Inc
Detroit Metro Airport, Romulus MI 48174. 313/565-4500. Employs: 100-249.

Twone Air Freight
29103 Airport Dr, Romulus MI 48174-2508. 313/946-1991. Employs: 100-249.

Unistar Air Cargo
11701 Metro Airport Center Dr, Romulus MI 48174-1403. 313/942-5959. Employs: 100-249.

United American Freight Co
29045 Airport Dr, Romulus MI 48174-2508. 313/946-8600. Employs: 100-249.

AIR COURIER SERVICES

D H L Worldwide Courier Express
1632 John A Papalas Dr, Lincoln Park MI 48146-1462. 313/388-6810. Employs: 50-99.

Flight Time
9358 Harrison St, Romulus MI 48174-2503. 313/946-7411. Employs: 50-99.

T N T Skypak
11700 Metro Airport Center Dr, Romulus MI 48174-1404. 313/941-8200. Employs: 50-99.

AIR TRANSPORTATION, NONSCHEDULED

Hansen Flying Svc
3999 W Seaman Rd, Alma MI 48801-9652. 517/463-5500. Employs: 50-99.

Triad Executive Services
11201 Conner St, Detroit MI 48213-1252. 313/839-3359.
Employs: 50-99.

AIRPORTS, FLYING FIELDS AND AIRPORT TERMINAL SERVICES

Cadillac Industries
12700 Marion, Redford MI 48239-2653. 313/537-0488.
Employs: 50-99.

Ground Service Inc
Detroit Metro Airport, Romulus MI 48174. 313/941-4141.
Employs: 50-99.

Miami Aircraft Support Inc
713 Detroit Metro Airpt, Romulus MI 48174. 313/941-7100. Employs: 50-99.

Page Avjet Corp
Det Metro Airpport, Romulus MI 48174. 313/941-7880.
Employs: 50-99.

Bird Dog Aviation Corporation
6080 Highland Rd, Waterford MI 48327-1831. 313/666-4800. Employs: 50-99.

H & S Propellor Shop
2151 Taxiway O, Waterford MI 48327. 313/666-3800.
Employs: 50-99.

Michigan Aviation Co Detroit
Detroit City Airport, Detroit MI 48213. 313/526-4650.
Employs: 50-99.

Top Flight Avionics Inc
1675 Airport Rd, Waterford MI 48327-1304. 313/666-1777. Employs: 50-99.

Davis Airport
Abbott, East Lansing MI 48823. 517/351-0224. Employs: 50-99.

TRAVEL AGENCIES

Embassy Travel Service Inc
23500 Michigan Av, Dearborn MI 48124-1909. 313/274-2720. Employs: 50-99.

Thomas Cook Travel

4 Parklane Bl Ste 500, Dearborn MI 48126-2685. 313/323-4300. Employs: 50-99.

MISCELLANEOUS ARRANGEMENT OF PASSENGER TRANSPORTATION

American Express
200 Renaissance Center, Detroit MI 48243-1209. 313/259-5030. Employs: 50-99.

ARRANGEMENT OF TRANSPORTATION OF FREIGHT AND CARGO

A N Deringer Inc
29320 Goddard Rd, Romulus MI 48174-2704. 313/946-4200. Employs: 100-249.

Annex Fast Freight
19330 Mount Elliott St, Detroit MI 48234-2725. 313/891-3300. Employs: 50-99.

E C Mc Afee Custom House Brkrs
1846 Penobscot Bg, Detroit MI 48226. 313/963-7225.
Employs: 100-249.

PACKING AND CRATING

Skilled Services
232 Sleeseman Dr, Corunna MI 48817-1076. 517/743-3396. Employs: 50-99.

Export Corporation
6060 Whitmore Lake Rd, Brighton MI 48116-1941.
313/227-6153. Employs: 50-99.

FIXED FACILITIES AND INSPECTION AND WEIGHING SERVICES FOR MOTOR VEHICLE TRANSPORTATION

McNilhols Scrap Iron & Metl Co
6500 E McNichols Rd, Detroit MI 48212-2028. 313/365-6100. Employs: 50-99.

O'Neill Weigh Station
4485 W Jefferson Ave, Detroit MI 48209-3233. 313/843-3553. Employs: 50-99.

Ambassador Bridge
1227 21st St, Detroit MI 48216-1714. 313/496-1166.
Employs: 100-249.

For more information on career opportunities in transportation:

<u>Associations</u>

AMERICAN BUREAU OF SHIPPING
2 World Trade Center, 106th Floor, New York NY 10048.
212/839-5000.

AMERICAN MARITIME ASSOCIATION
485 Madison Avenue, New York NY 10022. 212/319-9217.

AMERICAN SOCIETY OF TRAVEL AGENTS
1101 King Street, Alexandria VA 22314. 703/739-2782.

AMERICAN TRUCKING ASSOCIATION
2200 Mill Road, Alexandria VA 22314-4677. 703/838-1700.

ASSOCIATION OF AMERICAN RAILROADS
50 F Street NW, Washington DC 20001. 202/639-2100.

INSTITUTE OF TRANSPORTATION ENGINEERS
525 School Street SW, Suite 410, Washington DC 20024.
202/554-8050.

MARINE TECHNOLOGY SOCIETY

1828 L Street NW, Suite 906, Washington DC 20036.
202/755-5966.

NATIONAL ASSOCIATION OF MARINE SERVICES
5024-R Campbell Boulevard, Baltimore MD 21236.
410/931-8100.

NATIONAL MARINE MANUFACTURERS ASSOCIATION
401 North Michigan Avenue, Suite 1150, Chicago IL 60611. 312/836-4747.

NATIONAL MOTOR FREIGHT TRAFFIC ASSOCIATION
2200 Mill Road, Alexandria VA 22314. 703/838-1700.

NATIONAL TANK TRUCK CARRIERS
2200 Mill Road, Alexandria VA 22314. 703/838-1700.

SHIPBUILDERS COUNCIL OF AMERICA
4301 N. Fairfax Drive, Suite 330, Arlington VA 22203.
703/276-1700.

TRANSPORTATION INSTITUTE
5201 Authway Street, Camp Springs MD 20746. 301/423-3335.

Directories

MOODY'S TRANSPORTATION MANUAL
Moody's Investors Service, Inc., 99 Church Street, New York NY 10007. 212/553-0300.

NATIONAL TANK TRUCK CARRIER DIRECTORY
2200 Mill Road, Alexandria VA 22314. 703/838-1700.

OFFICIAL MOTOR FREIGHT GUIDE
1130 South Canal Street, Chicago IL 60607. 312/939-1434.

Magazines

AMERICAN SHIPPER
P.O. Box 4728, Jacksonville FL 32201. 904/355-2601.

DAILY TRAFFIC WORLD
The Traffic Service Corporation, 1325 G Street, Washington DC 20005. 202/626-4533.

FLEET OWNER
707 Westchester Avenue, White Plains NY 10604-3102. 914/949-8500.

HEAVY DUTY TRUCKING
Newport Communications, P.O. Box W, Newport Beach CA 92658. 714/261-1636.

MARINE DIGEST AND TRANSPORTATION NEWS
P.O. Box 3905, Seattle WA 98124. 206/682-3607.

OCEAN INDUSTRY
Gulf Publishing Co., P.O. Box 2608, Houston TX 77252. 713/529-4301.

SHIPPING DIGEST
51 Madison Avenue, New York NY 10010. 212/689-4411.

TRANSPORT TOPICS
2200 Mill Road, Alexandria VA 22314. 703/838-1772.

UTILITIES

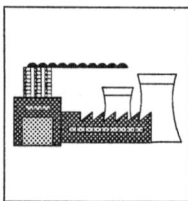

The major forces shaping the U.S. utilities industry are decreased regulation and competition from newly emerging alternative energy sources. Job prospects for those entering the utilities industry vary by sector; the best is electric, and at the bottom is the stagnant nuclear industry.

CONSUMERS POWER COMPANY
212 West Michigan Avenue, Jackson MI 49201. 517/788-1351. **Contact:** Professional Staffing Director. **Description:** A subsidiary of CMS Energy Corporation. The company is Michigan's largest public utility, and America's fourth-largest combination utility. The company provides electric and/or natural gas service in 67 of the 68 counties in Michigan's Lower Peninsula, and serves 6 million people (about two-thirds of Michigan's residents). **Common positions:** Accountant; Attorney; Computer Programmer; Chemical Engineer; Chemical Engineer; Civil Engineer; Electrical Engineer; Mechanical Engineer; Systems Analyst; Nuclear Engineer. **Educational backgrounds sought:** Engineering. **Benefits:** medical insurance; pension plan; life insurance; tuition assistance; disability coverage; savings plan. **Corporate headquarters:** This location. **Parent company:** CMS Energy. **Revenues (1991):** $700 million. **Employees:** 9,000.

Additional large employers: 250+

Cms Energy Corp
1100-330 Town Center Dr, Dearborn MI 48126. 313/436-9261. Employs: 1000+.

Detroit Edison Co
8301 Haggerty Rd, Belleville MI 48111-1601. 313/676-9300. Employs: 250-499.

Detroit Edison Co
4901 Pointe Dr, East China MI 48054-3504. 313/329-2207. Employs: 250-499.

Detroit Edison Co
2000 Second Ave, Detroit MI 48226-1203. 313/237-8000. Employs: 1000+.

Michigan Gas Utilites
899 S Telegraph Rd, Monroe MI 48161-4005. 313/242-4100. Employs: 250-499.

NATURAL GAS TRANSMISSION AND DISTRIBUTION

Great Lakes Gas Trnsmsn Co
One Woodward Ave, Detroit MI 48226-3402. 313/596-4400. Employs: 250-499.

NATURAL GAS DISTRIBUTION

American Natural Resources
500 Renaissance Center, Detroit MI 48243-1902. 313/965-1200. Employs: 500-999.

Anr Pipeline Co
500 Renaissance Center, Detroit MI 48243-1902. 313/496-0200. Employs: 1000+.

Michigan Consolidated Gas Co
500 Griswold St, Detroit MI 48226-3701. 313/965-2430. Employs: 1000+.

ELECTRIC AND OTHER SERVICES COMBINED

Consumers Power Co
530 W Willow St, Lansing MI 48937-0001. 517/373-6100. Employs: 500-999.

MISC. COMBINATION UTILITIES

Avf Resale
18114 Waltham St, Detroit MI 48205-2661. 313/527-5940. Employs: 250-499.

Additional small to medium sized employers: 50-249

ELECTRIC, GAS AND SANITARY SERVICES

Citizens Gas Fuel Co
127 N Main St, Adrian MI 49221-2711. 517/265-2144. Employs: 50-99.

Michigan Consolidated Gas Co
841 Broadway St, Ann Arbor MI 48105-1803. 313/663-8568. Employs: 50-99.

ELECTRIC SERVICES

Cameron Gas & Elec Co
4632 Smithville Rd, Eaton Rapids MI 48827-9729. 517/663-6181. Employs: 100-249.

Carsonville Fire Hall
3972 W Chandler, Carsonville MI 48419. 313/6579441. Employs: 50-99.

Clinton Village Offices
119 E Michigan Ave, Clinton MI 49236-9581. 517/456-4134. Employs: 50-99.

Consumers Power Co
2613 E Maumee St, Adrian MI 49221-3532. 517/265-6141. Employs: 50-99.

Consumers Power Co
212 W Michigan Av, Jackson MI 49201-2236. 517/788-0550. Employs: 100-249.

Consumers Power Co
1325 Wright Av, Alma MI 48801-1134. 517/463-1181. Employs: 100-249.

Consumers Power Co
1801 W Main St, Owosso MI 48867-1374. 517/723-5171. Employs: 100-249.

Croswell City Of
100 N Howard Ave, Croswell MI 48422-1224. 313/679-2299. Employs: 50-99.

D & B Electric Co
22703 Schoenherr Rd, Warren MI 48089-5039. 313/778-1420. Employs: 100-249.

Detroit Edison
425 S Main St, Ann Arbor MI 48104-2303. 313/761-8716. Employs: 100-249.

Detroit Edison Co
316 E Grand River, Howell MI 48843-2323. 517/548-1850. Employs: 50-99.

Enrico Fermi Nuclear Power
6400 Dixie Hw, Newport MI 48166-9726. 313/586-8030. Employs: 100-249.

Hilton Electronic Co
650 Livernois St, Ferndale MI 48220-2304. 313/542-6380. Employs: 100-249.

S & C Electric Co
3297 Orchard Lake Rd, Keego Harbor MI 48320-1305. 313/681-7544. Employs: 100-249.

Se Mi Rural Elec Co Op Inc
1610 E Maumee St, Adrian MI 49221-3584. 517/263-1808. Employs: 50-99.

Spane Electric Co
439 E Columbia St, Detroit MI 48201-3511. 313/739-7010. Employs: 100-249.

Spane Electric Co
12000 23 Mile, Shelby Twp MI 48315. 313/739-2030. Employs: 100-249.

The Detroit Edison Co
111 E 1st St, Monroe MI 48161-2114. 313/241-7000. Employs: 100-249.

The Detroit Edison Co
600 Grand River Av, Port Huron MI 48060-3817. 313/987-3520. Employs: 100-249.

White Pine Power
3245 Shawnee Ct, Waterford MI 48329-4335. 313/674-0099. Employs: 100-249.

NATURAL GAS DISTRIBUTION

Consolidated Fuel
20 S Gratiot Ave, Mount Clemens MI 48043-2370.
313/463-0311. Employs: 50-99.

Great Lakes Gas Transmission
5420 Puttygut Rd, Saint Clair MI 48079. 313/329-7138.
Employs: 50-99.

Transtate Gas Service Co
49919 Miller Ct, New Baltimore MI 48047-4329. 313/725-6482. Employs: 50-99.

REFUSE SYSTEMS

Browning-Ferris Ind Mich I
12546 Inkster Rd, Redford MI 48239-2562. 313/937-8670.
Employs: 50-99.

Painter & Ruthenberg Inc
2660 Beech Daly Rd, Inkster MI 48141-2449. 313/561-0303. Employs: 50-99.

Pollard Disposal Inc
11349 McKinley Rd, Montrose MI 48457-9007. 313/639-6000. Employs: 50-99.

Waste Management Of Michigan
19200 W 8 Mile Rd, Southfield MI 48075-5722. 313/357-0100. Employs: 50-99.

Waste Management Of Michigan
36850 Van Born Rd, Wayne MI 48184-1555. 313/729-0700. Employs: 50-99.

Browning-Ferris Industries
5380 Milford Rd, New Hudson MI 48165-9701. 313/437-4185. Employs: 50-99.

For more information on career opportunities in the utilities industry:

Associations

AMERICAN WATER WORKS ASSOCIATION
6666 West Quincy Avenue, Denver CO 80235. 303/794-7711.

EMPLOYMENT AGENCIES AND TEMPORARY SERVICES OF MICHIGAN

ACCENT ON ACHIEVEMENT
189 E. Big Beaver, Suite 202. Troy MI 48083. 313/528-1390. **Contact:** Charlene Brown, C.P.A., President. Employment agency. Temporary accounting help agency. Appointment required. Founded 1987. President has worked in executive recruiting since 1981. Over 30 affiliate offices. All candidates are personally interviewed. Credentials are verified. **Specializes in:** Accounting; Banking; Human Resources; Finance. **Common positions filled:** Financial Reporting; Controller; Financial Analyst; Management Consultant; Auditor; Actuary. Company pays fee. **Number of placements per year:** 50.

ACCOUNTANTS ONE INC.
24133 Northwestern Highway, Suite 202. Southfield MI 48075. 313/354-2410. **Contact:** Linda Hoffman, President. Employment agency; temporary help agency. Appointment required. Founded 1978. Started as temporary and expanded to permanent placement. **Specializes in:** Accounting; Banking and Finance. **Common positions filled:** Accountant; Accounting Clerk; Bookkeeper; Credit Manager; Data Entry Clerk; Financial Analyst. Company pays fee.

BPA ENTERPRISES, INC.
19967 James Couzens Highway. Detroit MI 48235. 313/345-5700. **Contact:** Will E. Atkins, President. Employment agency. Nonspecialized. **Common positions filled:** Accountant; Actuary; Administrative Assistant; Advertising Executive; Aerospace Engineer; Agricultural Engineer; Architect; Attorney; Bank Officer/Manager; Biochemist/Chemist; Biologist; Biomedical Engineer; Bookkeeper; Ceramics Engineer; Civil Engineer; Claims Representative; Computer Programmer; Customer Service Rep; EDP Specialist; Economist; Electrical Engineer; Executive Secretary; Financial Analyst; General Manager; Industrial Designer; Industrial Engineer; Insurance Agent/Broker; Interior Designer; Legal Secretary; Marketing Specialist; Mechanical Engineer; Medical Secretary; Metallurgical Engineer; Mining Engineer; Personnel Director; Petroleum Engineer; Physicist; Purchasing Agent, Receptionist; Sales Representative; Secretary; Statistician; Stenographer; Systems Analyst; Typist; Underwriter; Word Processor. Company pays fee. **Number of placements per year:** 51-100.

BARMAN PERSONNEL INC.
Post Office Box 121. Grandville MI 49468-0121. 616/531-4122. **Contact:** Bob Barman, President. Employment agency. Appointment required. Founded 1982. **Specializes in:** Accounting; Architecture; Computer Software and Hardware;

Engineering; Food Industry; Health and Medical; Industrial and Interior Design; Manufacturing; MIS/EDP. **Common positions filled:** Accountant; Aerospace Engineer; Agricultural Engineer; Architect; Ceramics Engineer; Electrical Engineer; Financial Analyst; General Manager; Industrial Designer; Industrial Engineer; Interior Designer; Mechanical Engineer; Metallurgical Engineer; Personnel Director; Purchasing Agent. Company pays fee. **Number of placements per year:** 0-50.

CALVERT ASSOCIATES, INC.
202 East Washington Street, Suite 304. Ann Arbor MI 48104. 313/769-5413. **Contact:** Peter Calvert Cokinos, President. Employment agency. Appointment requested. Founded 1983. **Specializes in:** Publishing; Sales and Marketing. **Common positions filled:** Architect; Editor; Marketing Specialist; Publisher; Sales Representative. Company pays fee. **Number of placements per year:** 50.

CONTRACT PROFESSIONALS
4141 West Walton Boulevard. Waterford, MI 48329. 313/673-3800. **Contact:** Rod Gillis, Director, Human Resources. Temporary help agency. Founded 1982. Provides temporary Technical personnel for limited durations. **Specializes in:** Architecture; Computer Hardware and Software; Engineering; Industrial and Interior Design; MIS/EDP; Technical and Scientific. **Common positions filled:** Aerospace Engineer; Agricultural Engineer; Architect; Biochemist/Chemist; Biomedical Engineer; Ceramics Engineer; Civil Engineer; Commercial Artist; Computer Programmer; Data Entry Clerk; EDP Specialist; Electrical Engineer; Financial Analyst; Industrial Designer; Industrial Engineer; Interior Designer; Mechanical Engineer; Metallurgical Engineer; Mining Engineer; Petroleum Engineer; Physicist; Purchasing Agent; Systems Analyst; Technical Writer/Editor; Technician; Word Processor. **Number of placements per year:** 501-1,000.

CORPORATE BUSINESS SERVICES, LTD.
913 West Holmes Road, Suite 100. Lansing MI 48910. 517/394-1800. **Contact:** Michael Keen, President/General Manager. Employment agency. Appointment requested. Founded 1974. **Specializes in:** Computer Hardware and Software; Engineering; Food Industry; Insurance; MIS/EDP; Manufacturing; Sales and Marketing. **Common positions filled:** Accountant; Advertising Worker; Chemical Engineer; Civil Engineer; Claim Representative; Computer Operator; Computer Programmer; Customer Service Representative; Data Entry Clerk; EDP Specialist; Electrical Engineer; Hotel Manager/Assistant Manager; Industrial Engineer; Insurance Agent/Broker; Marketing Specialist; Mechanical Engineer; Metallurgical Engineer; Public Relations Worker; Restaurant Manager; Sales Representative; Systems Analyst; Underwriter. Company pays fee; individual pays fee. **Number of placements per year:** 201-500.

DAVIS-SMITH MEDICAL EMPLOYMENT SERVICE INC.
24725 West Twelve Mile Road, Suite 302. Southfield MI 48034. 313/354-4100. **Contact:** Charles C. Corbert, C.P.C., Manager. Employment agency; temporary help service. Appointment requested. Founded 1946. **Specializes in:** Clerical;

Health and Medical. **Common positions filled:** Administrative Assistant; Bookkeeper; Clerk; Medical Secretary; Nurse; Office Worker; Receptionist; Secretary; Technician; Typist. Company pays fee; individual pays fee. **Number of placements per year:** 51-100.

DEPENDABLE HEALTH CARE, INC.
Post Office Box 2216. Dearborn MI 48123. 313/277-6887. **Contact:** Mercedes Watson, Director. Temporary help agency. Appointment required. Founded 1979. To provide the best Home Care possible without high cost. **Common positions filled:** LPN; Nurse, Nurses Aide; RN. Individual pays fee. **Number of placements per year:** 201-500.

DUNHILL OF ANN ARBOR
315 North Main, Suite 400. Ann Arbor MI 48104. 313/996-3100. **Contact:** Jim Irwin, President. Employment agency. Founded 1977. **Specializes in:** Computer Hardware and Software. **Common positions filled:** Computer Operator; Computer Programmer; Data Entry Clerk; Systems Analyst.

DUNHILL OF DETROIT
29350 Southfield Road, Suite 123. Southfield MI 48076. 313/557-1100. **Contact:** Don Dahlin, Owner. Employment agency. Founded 1964. **Specializes in:** Sales and Marketing; Engineering. **Common positions filled:** Electrical Engineer; Industrial Engineer; Mechanical Engineer; Sales Engineer.

DUNHILL PERSONNEL SERVICE OF KALAMAZOO
902 South Westnedge Avenue. Kalamazoo MI 49008. 616/381-3616. **Contact:** Ken Killman and Ron Hill, Owners. Employment agency. Founded 1978. **Specializes in:** Engineering; Manufacturing. **Common positions filled:** Electrical Engineer; Industrial Designer; Industrial Engineer; Light Industrial Worker; Mechanical Engineer.

DUNHILL PROFESSIONAL SEARCH
4406 Elmhurst. Saginaw MI 48603. 517/799-9300. **Contact:** Bill Post, President. Employment agency. Founded 1981. **Specializes in:** Health and Medical. **Common positions filled:** Administrative Assistant; Medical Secretary; Nurse; Pharmacist; Technician; Therapist.

EMPLOYMENT AND TRAINING OFFICE
16578 Enterprise Drive. Three Rivers MI 49093. 616/273-2717. **Contact:** Nancy Percival, Program Coordinator. Employment agency. No appointment required. Founded 1984. Works with federal and state employment programs Provides job placement and training services. **Common positions filled:** Accountant; Bookkeeper; Clerk; Driver; Factory Worker; Light Industrial Worker; Machine Tool Worker; Receptionist; Secretary; Typist; Welder. Individual pays fee. **Number of placements per year:** 51-100.

EXECTECH, INC.
2002 Hogback Road. Ann Arbor MI 48105. **Tel:** 313/483-8454; **Fax:** 313/483-0740. **Contact:** Don Fredrick, Chief Executive Officer. Employment agency. Founded 1978. **Specializes in:** Computer Hardware and Software; Engineering; MIS/EDP; Sales and Marketing; Technical and Scientific. **Common positions filled:** Ceramics Engineer; Computer Programmer; Customer Service Representative; EDP Specialist; Electrical Engineer; General Manager; MIS Specialist; Marketing Specialist; Physicist; Sales Representative; Systems Analyst; Technical Writer/Editor; Technician. Company pays fee. **Number of placements per year:** 50.

EXECUTIVE RECRUITERS
21751 West Nine Mile Road, Suite 202. Southfield MI 48075. 313/647-7400. Employment agency. Appointment requested. **Branch offices located in:** Annapolis, MD; Atlanta, GA; Baltimore, MD; Birmingham, AL; Boston, MA; Chicago, IL; Cincinnati, OH; Cleveland, OH; Dallas, TX; Ft. Worth, TX; Houston, TX; Jacksonville, FL; Los Angeles, CA; Miami, FL; Saddle Brook, NJ; King of Prussia, PA; Cherry Hill, NJ; St. Louis, MO; San Francisco, CA; McLean, VA. **Specializes in:** Sales and Marketing. **Common positions filled:** Application Engineer; Product Manager; Sales Manager; Sales Representative. Company pays fee. **Number of placements per year:** 1,001+.

JOE L. GILES AND ASSOCIATES, INC.
18105 Parkside Street, Suite 14. Detroit MI 48221. 313/864-0022. **Contact:** Joe L. Giles, Owner/President. Employment agency. Appointment requested. Founded 1979. **Specializes in:** Computer Hardware and Software; Engineering; MIS/EDP. **Common positions filled:** EDP Specialist; Electrical Engineer; MIS Specialist; Mechanical Engineer; Systems Analyst. Company pays fee. **Number of placements per year:** 50.

GROSSE POINTE EMPLOYMENT
18514 Mack Avenue. Grosse Pointe Farms MI 48236. 313/885-4576. **Contact:** Dolores Andreini, Manager. Employment agency. No appointment required. Founded 1930. We specialize in the placement of Domestic Help in private homes (Housekeepers, Cooks, Chefs, Nannies, Butlers, Housemen, Groundskeepers, Chauffeurs, Dayworkers, etc.). We also place some Clerical Workers and an occasional Professional or Technical Worker. There are two fees (as permitted by the Board of Licensing): one for the employer and one smaller one for the employee. **Number of placements per year:** 201-500.

HARPER ASSOCIATES
29870 Middlebelt. Farmington Hills MI 48334. 313/932-1170. No appointment required. Founded 1968. **Specializes in:** Architecture; Food Industry; Health and Medical. **Common positions filled:** Accountant; Architect; Biomedical Engineer; Dietician; Food Technologist; Hotel Manager/Assistant Manager; Medical Recorder; Nurse; Physical Therapist; Physician. Company pays fee. **Number of placements per year:** 101-200.

HART PERSONNEL
6340 Brookview Lane. West Bloomfield MI 48322. 313/960-3555. **Contact:** Stanley Hart, Owner. Employment agency. Founded 1976. **Specializes in:** Computer Hardware and Software. **Common positions filled:** Computer Operator; Computer Programmer; Data Entry Clerk; Systems Analyst.

HUMAN RESOURCES UNLIMITED, INC.
535 North Capital, Suite 1. P.O. Box 14306. Lansing MI 48901. 517/371-5220. **Contact:** Judy A. Daniels, President/Chief Executive Officer, or Sandra Lighthiser, Vice President/Secretary/Treasurer. · Employment agency. Appointment requested. Founded 1979. **Specializes in:** Computer Hardware and Software; Engineering; MIS/EDP. **Common positions filled:** Accountant; Aerospace Engineer; Chemical Engineer; Civil Engineer; Computer Programmer; EDP Specialist; Electrical Engineer; Financial Analyst; Industrial Designer; Industrial Engineer; Mechanical Engineer; Sales Representative; Systems Analyst. Company pays fee. **Number of placements per year:** 201-500.

INTERIM PERSONNEL
26241 Southfield Road. Lathrup MI 48076. 313/557-7444. Temporary help service. Appointment requested. Founded 1954. Interim Personnel has over 100 offices throughout the United States. Nonspecialized. **Common positions filled:** Bookkeeper; Clerk; Computer Operator; Customer Service Representative; Data Entry Clerk; Demonstrator; Draftsperson; Electronic Assembler; Factory Worker; General Laborer; Legal Secretary; Light Industrial Worker; Medical Secretary; Office Worker; Receptionist; Secretary; Stenographer; Technician; Typist; Word Processing Specialist. Company pays fee. **Number of placements per year:** 1,001+.

INTERIM PERSONNEL
2222 South Linden Road, Suite I. Flint MI 48532. 313/733-7180. Temporary help service. Appointment requested. Founded 1954. Interim Personnel has over 100 offices throughout the United States. Nonspecialized. **Common positions filled:** Bookkeeper; Clerk; Computer Operator; Customer Service Representative; Data Entry Clerk; Demonstrator; Draftsperson; Electronic Assembler; Factory Worker; General Laborer; Legal Secretary; Light Industrial Worker; Medical Secretary; Office Worker; Receptionist; Secretary; Stenographer; Technician; Typist; Word Processing Specialist. Company pays fee. **Number of placements per year:** 1,001+.

INTERIM PERSONNEL
2930 Shaffer Drive. Southeast Cantwood MI 49512. 616/942-2850. Temporary help service. Appointment requested. Founded 1954. Interim Personnel has over 100 offices throughout the United States. Nonspecialized. **Common positions filled:** Bookkeeper; Clerk; Computer Operator; Customer Service Representative; Data Entry Clerk; Demonstrator; Draftsperson; Electronic Assembler; Factory Worker; General Laborer; Legal Secretary; Light Industrial Worker; Medical Secretary; Office Worker; Receptionist; Secretary;

Stenographer; Technician; Typist; Word Processing Specialist. Company pays fee. **Number of placements per year:** 1,001+.

INTERIM PERSONNEL
One Jackson Square Building, Suite 113. Jackson MI 49201. 517/782-8231. Temporary help service. Appointment requested. Founded 1954. Interim Personnel has over 100 offices throughout the United States. Nonspecialized. **Common positions filled:** Bookkeeper; Clerk; Computer Operator; Customer Service Representative; Data Entry Clerk; Demonstrator; Draftsperson; Electronic Assembler; Factory Worker; General Laborer; Legal Secretary; Light Industrial Worker; Medical Secretary; Office Worker; Receptionist; Secretary; Stenographer; Technician; Typist; Word Processing Specialist. Company pays fee. **Number of placements per year:** 1,001+.

INTERIM PERSONNEL
3401 East Saginaw, Suite 109. Lansing MI 48912. 517/351-5553. Temporary help service. Appointment requested. Founded 1954. Interim Personnel has over 100 offices throughout the United States. Nonspecialized. **Common positions filled:** Bookkeeper; Clerk; Computer Operator; Customer Service Representative; Data Entry Clerk; Demonstrator; Draftsperson; Electronic Assembler; Factory Worker; General Laborer; Legal Secretary; Light Industrial Worker; Medical Secretary; Office Worker; Receptionist; Secretary; Stenographer; Technician; Typist; Word Processing Specialist. Company pays fee. **Number of placements per year:** 1,001+.

INTERIM PERSONNEL
15555 South Telegraph, Suite 2. Monroe MI 48161. 313/243-5067. Temporary help service. Appointment requested. Founded 1954. Interim Personnel has over 100 offices throughout the United States. Nonspecialized. **Common positions filled:** Bookkeeper; Clerk; Computer Operator; Customer Service Representative; Data Entry Clerk; Demonstrator; Draftsperson; Electronic Assembler; Factory Worker; General Laborer; Legal Secretary; Light Industrial Worker; Medical Secretary; Office Worker; Receptionist; Secretary; Stenographer; Technician; Typist; Word Processing Specialist. Company pays fee. **Number of placements per year:** 1,001+.

INTERIM PERSONNEL
4800 Fashion Square Boulevard, Suite 120. Saginaw MI 48604. 517/799-5960. Temporary help service. Appointment requested. Founded 1954. Interim Personnel has over 100 offices throughout the United States. Nonspecialized. **Common positions filled:** Bookkeeper; Clerk; Computer Operator; Customer Service Representative; Data Entry Clerk; Demonstrator; Draftsperson; Electronic Assembler; Factory Worker; General Laborer; Legal Secretary; Light Industrial Worker; Medical Secretary; Office Worker; Receptionist; Secretary; Stenographer; Technician; Typist; Word Processing Specialist. Company pays fee. **Number of placements per year:** 1,001+.

INTERIM PERSONNEL
33300 Five Mile, Suite 204. Livonia MI 48154. 313/261-3830. Temporary help service. Appointment requested. Founded 1954. Interim Personnel has over 100 offices throughout the United States. Nonspecialized. **Common positions filled:** Bookkeeper; Clerk; Computer Operator; Customer Service Representative; Data Entry Clerk; Demonstrator; Draftsperson; Electronic Assembler; Factory Worker; General Laborer; Legal Secretary; Light Industrial Worker; Medical Secretary; Office Worker; Receptionist; Secretary; Stenographer; Technician; Typist; Word Processing Specialist. Company pays fee. **Number of placements per year:** 1,001+.

HENRY LABUS PERSONNEL
820 Ford Building. Detroit MI 48226. 313/962-4461. **Contact:** Henry Labus, President. Employment agency. Founded 1971. **Specializes in:** Accounting and Finance; Banking; Legal. **Common positions filled:** Accountant; Attorney; Bank Officer/Manager. Company pays fee. **Number of placements per year:** 51-100.

LUDOT & ASSOCIATES
3000 Town Center. P.O. Box 208. Southfield MI 48037. 313/353-9720. **Contact:** Michael Morton, Vice President. Employment agency. Founded 1969. **Specializes in:** Automotive; Computer Hardware and Software; Engineering; Manufacturing; Minorities; MIS/EDP; Women. **Common positions filled:** Accountant; Aerospace Engineer; Economist; Electrical Engineer; Industrial Engineer; MIS Specialist; Mechanical Engineer; Metallurgical Engineer; Quality Control Supervisor; Systems Analyst. Company pays fee. **Number of placements per year:** 51-100.

MANPOWER TEMPORARY SERVICES OF JACKSON
333 Louis Glick Highway. Jackson MI 49201-1200. 517/789-7193. **Contact:** Nancy Konopacki, Branch Manager. Temporary help service. No appointment required. Founded 1948. Manpower Inc. has over 1,000 offices worldwide. **Specializes in:** Office Automation. **Common positions filled:** Bookkeeper; Clerk; Computer Operator; Computer Programmer; Construction Worker; Data Entry Clerk; Demonstrator; Draftsperson; Driver; Mechanical Engineer; Factory Worker; General Laborer; Industrial Designer; Legal Secretary; Light Industrial Worker; Medical Secretary; Office Worker; Receptionist; Sales Representative; Secretary; Stenographer; Technical Writer/Editor; Typist; Word Processing Specialist. **Number of placements per year:** 1,001+.

METRO STAFF
28500 Southfield Road. Lathrup Village MI 48076. 313/557-8700. Temporary help service. Appointment requested. Founded 1961. **Branch offices located in:** Arizona; California; Connecticut; District of Columbia; Florida; Georgia; Illinois; Indiana; Kansas; Louisiana; Maryland; Massachusetts; Minnesota; Missouri; Nevada; New Jersey; New Mexico; New York; Ohio; Oklahoma; Oregon; Pennsylvania; Rhode Island; Tennessee; Texas; Virginia; Washington. Nonspecialized. **Common positions filled:** Accountant; Administrativ‸

Assistant; Bookkeeper; Clerk; Companion; Computer Operator; Computer Programmer; Customer Service Representative; Data Entry Clerk; Demonstrator; Draftsperson; Drive; EDP Specialist; Factory Worker; General Laborer; Health Aide; Legal Secretary; Light Industrial Worker; Medical Secretary; Nurse; Office Worker; Public Relations Worker; Receptionist; Sales Representative; Secretary; Stenographer; Technician; Typist; Word Processing Specialist. Company pays fee. **Number of placements per year:** 1,001+.

MICHIGAN EMPLOYMENT SECURITY COMMISSION
2827 North Lincoln Road. P.O. Box 356. Escanaba MI 49829. 906/786-6841. **Contact:** Barbara Banvansickle, Manager. Employment agency. No appointment required. Founded 1937. There is no fee to either the applicant or to the employer. We service all worker and all company job orders no matter what the job is. **Specializes in:** Accounting; Advertising; Architecture; Banking and Finance; Computer Hardware and Software; Construction; Education; Engineering; Food Industry; Health and Medical; Industrial and Interior Design; Insurance; Legal; Manufacturing; MIS/EDP; Nonprofit; Printing and Publishing; Real Estate; Sales and Marketing; Secretarial and Clerical; Technical and Scientific; Transportation. **Common positions filled:** Accountant; Actuary; Administrative Assistant; Advertising Executive; Aerospace Engineer; Agricultural Engineer; Architect; Attorney; Bank Officer/Manager; Biochemist/Chemist; Biologist; Biomedical Engineer; Bookkeeper; Ceramics Engineer; Civil Engineer; Claims Representative; Clerk; Commercial Artist; Computer Programmer; Construction Worker; Credit Manager; Customer Service Rep; Data Entry Clerk; Dietician/Nutritionist; Draftsperson; Driver; EDP Specialist; Economist; Electrical Engineer; Executive Secretary; Factory Worker; Financial Analyst; General Laborer; General Manager; Hotel Manager; Industrial Designer; Industrial Engineer; Insurance Agent/Broker; Interior Designer; Legal Secretary; Light Industrial Worker; Management Consultant; Marketing Specialist; Mechanical Engineer; Medical Secretary; Metallurgical Engineer; Mining Engineer; Model; Nurse; Personnel Director; Petroleum Engineer; Physicist; Public Relations Worker; Purchasing Agent; Receptionist; Reporter Editor; Sales Representative; Secretary; Statistician; Stenographer; Systems Analyst; Technical Writer/Editor; Technician; Typist; Underwriter; Word Processor. **Number of placements per year:** 1,000+.

MICHIGAN INDIAN EMPLOYMENT AND TRAINING SERVICES, INC.
325 East Lake Street. Petoskey MI 49770. 616/347-9330. **Contact:** Quintin Walker, Employment Coordinator. Employment agency. No appointment required. Founded 1975. JTPA Program. **Specializes in:** Alaskan Indians; American Indians; Hawaiians; Nonprofit. **Common positions filled:** Assembly Line Worker; Bookkeeper; Carpenter; Clerk; Construction Worker; General Laborer; Light Industrial Worker; Office Worker; Receptionist; Reporter; Secretary; Typist. Company pays fee. **Number of placements per year:** 51-100.

ROTH YOUNG PERSONNEL SERVICE OF DETROIT, INC.
25505 West 12 Mile Road. Southfield MI 48034. 313/948-8800. **Contact:** Sam Skeegan, President. Employment agency. No appointment required. Founded 1970. **Specializes in:** Accounting and Finance; Advertising; Banking; Broadcasting; Engineering; Food Industry; Health and Medical; Manufacturing; MIS/EDP; Personnel and Human Resources; Sales and Marketing; Technical and Scientific. **Common positions filled:** Accountant; Advertising Worker; Agricultural Engineer; Bank Officer/Manager; Biologist; Biomedical Engineer; Buyer; Ceramics Engineer; Chemical Engineer; Chemist; Civil Engineer; Computer Programmer; Credit Manager; Dietician; EDP Specialist; Economist; Electrical Engineer; Financial Analyst; Food Technologist; General Manager; Hotel Manager/Assistant Manager; Industrial Engineer; MIS Specialist; Marketing Specialist; Mechanical Engineer; Metallurgical Engineer; Operations/Production Specialist; Personnel and Labor Relations Specialist; Physicist; Quality Control Supervisor; Sales Representative; Statistician; Systems Analyst; Technical Writer/Editor. Company pays fee. **Number of placements per year:** 101-200.

ROYAL OAK EMPLOYMENT SERVICE
27623 Jonn R. Madison Heights MI 48071. 313/542-6870. **Contact:** Edmund Tatarek, Owner. Temporary help service. No appointment required. Founded 1978. Nonspecialized. **Common positions filled:** Accountant; Bookkeeper; Clerk; Computer Operator; Computer Programmer; Data Entry Clerk; Draftsperson; Factory Worker; General Laborer; Light Industrial Worker; Office Worker; Receptionist; Secretary; Stenographer; Typist. **Number of placements per year:** 1,001+.

SALES EXECUTIVES INC.
755 West Big Beaver, Suite 2107. Troy MI 48084. 313/362-1900. **Contact:** Mr. Dale Statson, Vice President. Employment agency. Appointment requested. **Specializes in:** Chemicals; Computer Hardware and Software; Finance; Health and Medical; Management; Mechanical; Plastics; Sales and Marketing. **Common positions filled:** Marketing Specialist; Sales Manager; Sales Representative. Company pays fee. **Number of placements per year:** 201-500.

SHERMTECH ENGINEERING SERVICES
16647 Airport Service Drive. Lansing MI 48906. 517/626-6343. **Contact:** Robert L. Tvorik, Manager. Employment agency. Appointment required. Founded 1979. Functions as recruiter on assignment basis to fill positions from staff Engineers to mid-level Managers. **Specializes in:** Engineering. Concentrates in Consumer Products. **Common positions filled:** Industrial Designer; Mechanical Engineer. Company pays fee.

SOFTWARE SERVICES CORPORATIONS
20850 South Industrial, Suite 300. Ann Arbor MI 48108. 313/971-2300. **Contact:** Jack Reinelt, General Manager. Employment agency; temporary help agency. No appointment required. Founded 1976. Acknowledged as providing the highest quality human resources, specializing in Computer Software and

Engineering. **Specializes in:** Computer Hardware and Software; Engineering; Manufacturing; MIS/EDP; Technical and Scientific. **Common positions filled:** Ceramics Engineer; Computer Programmer; EDP Specialist; Electrical Engineer; Industrial Engineer; Mechanical Engineer; Systems Analyst; Technical Writer/Editor. Company pays fee. **Number of placements per year:** 201-500.

TEMP FORCE OF GRAND RAPIDS
122 Lyon Street. Grand Rapids MI 49503. 616/459-1111. **Contact:** Stephen Crociani, Manager. Temporary help service. No appointment required. Founded 1965. **Branch offices located in:** Alabama; Arkansas; California; Colorado; Connecticut; Florida; Illinois; Indiana; Kansas; Maryland; Massachusetts; Mississippi; Nevada; New Jersey; New Mexico; New York; Ohio; Oklahoma; Pennsylvania; Tennessee; Utah; Vermont; Virginia. Nonspecialized. **Common positions filled:** Accountant; Bookkeeper; Clerk; Computer Operator; Computer Programmer; Customer Service Representative; Data Entry Clerk; Demonstrator; Driver; Factory Worker; General Laborer; Legal Secretary; Light Industrial Worker; Medical Secretary; Office Worker; Purchasing Agent; Receptionist; Secretary; Statistician; Stenographer; Typist; Word Processing Specialist.

UNIFORCE TEMPORARY SERVICES
1000 South Woodward, Suite 301. Birmingham MI 48009. 313/646-7660. **Contact:** Manager. Temporary help service. Appointment requested. Founded 1980. Nonspecialized. **Common positions filled:** Bookkeeper; Data Entry Clerk; Light Industrial Clerk; Office Worker; Receptionist; Secretary; Stenographer; Typist; Word Processing Specialist. Company pays fee. **Number of placements per year:** 50.

WILLIAM HOWARD AGENCY
38701 Seven Mile Road, Suite 445. Livonia MI 48152. 313/464-6777. **Contact:** Howard Saum, Senior Partner. Employment service. No appointment required. **Specializes in:** Accounting; Advertising; Architecture; Banking and Finance; Computer Hardware and Software; Construction Management; Education; Engineering; Food Industry; Health and Medical; Industrial and Interior Design; Insurance; Legal; Manufacturing; MIS/EDP; Nonprofit; Printing and Publishing; Real Estate; Sales and Marketing; Secretarial/Clerical; Technical and Scientific; Transportation. **Common positions filled:** Accountant; Actuary; Administrative Assistant; Advertising Executive; Aerospace Engineer; Agricultural Engineer; Architect; Attorney; Bank Officer/Manager; Biochemist/Chemist; Biologist; Biomedical Engineer; Bookkeeper; Ceramics Engineer; Civil Engineer; Claims Representative; Clerk; Commercial Artist; Computer Programmer; Credit Manager; Customer Service Rep; Data Entry Clerk; Dietician/Nutritionist; Draftsperson; EDP Specialist; Economist; Electrical Engineer; Executive Secretary; Financial Analyst; General Manager; Hotel Manager; Industrial Designer; Industrial Engineer; Interior Designer; Insurance Agent/Broker; Legal Secretary; Management Consultant; Marketing Specialist; Mechanical Engineer; Medical Secretary; Metallurgical Engineer;

Mining Engineer; Model; Nurse; Personnel Director; Petroleum Engineer; Physicist; Public Relations Worker; Purchasing Agent; Receptionist; Secretary; Statistician; Stenographer; Systems Analyst; Technical Writer/Editor; Technician; Typist; Underwriter; Word Processor. Individual pays fee. **Number of placements per year:** 51-100.

WISE PERSONNEL SERVICES, INC.
1020 S. Westnedge Avenue. Kalamazoo MI 49008. 616/381-9400. **Contact:** Mrs. Rory Wise, Owner/President. Employment agency. Appointment required; unsolicited resumes accepted. Founded 1967. Wise Personnel Services, Inc., with four offices in Michigan -- Grand Rapids, St. Joseph, Muskegon and Kalamazoo -- is a full-service agency dedicated to the best possible service for our client companies and valued candidates. **Specializes in:** Accounting; Administration, MIS/EDP; Banking and Finance; Clerical (temporary and permanent); Computer Hardware and Software; Contract Engineering; Electrical; Engineering; General Management; Human Resources; Manufacturing; Operations Management; Sales and Marketing; Technical and Scientific.

INDEX TO PRIMARY EMPLOYERS

NOTE: Below is an alphabetical index of Detroit's primary employer listings included in this book. Those employers in each industry that fall under the headings "Additional large employers" or "Small to medium sized employers" are not indexed here.

A

ATOCHEM NORTH AMERICA INCORPORATED, 114
ATTWOOD CORPORATION, 302
AUSTIN COMPANY, 56
AUTOMATIC DATA PROCESSING, 136
AUTOMOTIVE MOULDING COMPANY, 68
AUTOMOTIVE PLASTIC TECHNOLOGY, 68
AWREY BAKERIES INC., 185

B

BASF CORPORATION, 114
BASF/COATINGS AND COLORANTS DIVISION, 114
H.L. BLACHFORD INC., 303
BOC BLANC PLANT, 68
BOC POWER TRAIN/LIVONIA PLANT, 68
BABY BLISS, INC., 53
BAKER BOOK HOUSE, 106
BARFIELD MANUFACTURING COMPANY, 155
BARRIS, SOTT, DENN, AND DRIKER, 250
BARRONCAST INC., 155
BARTON-MALOW COMPANY, 56
BEAVER PRECISION PRODUCTS, 155
BERMAN, BRAND, AND GOODMAN, 250
BERRY, MOORMAN, KING, COOK, AND HUDSON, 250
BLUE CROSS AND BLUE SHIELD, 247
BODMAN, LONGLEY, AND DAHLING, 250
BOOTH AMERICAN COMPANY, 109
BORG-WARNER AUTOMOTIVE, 155
BRASS-CRAFT MANUFACTURING COMPANY, 258
BRAUN ENGINEERING COMPANY, 68
BRAVER LUMBER AND SUPPLY, 290
BRECTEEN COMPANY, 185
BRENCAL CONTRACTORS INC., 57
BROAD, VOGT & CONANT, INC., 57
THE BUDD COMPANY, 68
BUESSER, BUESSER, BLANK,, 250
BUICK MOTOR DIVISION/GENERAL MOTORS, 196
BUNDY CORPORATION, 258
BUTZEL LONG, 250

C

CIS CORPORATION, 196
CMI INTERNATIONAL INC., 259
CADILLAC GAGE COMPANY, 68
CADILLAC MOTOR CAR DIVISION, 197
CADILLAC PRODUCTS INC., 259
CADILLAC RUBBER & PLASTICS, INC., 303
CAMPBELL MANIX COMPANY INC., 57
CAMPBELL, O'BRIEN, AND MISTELE P.C., 250
CARBIDEX WYANDOTTE CORPORATION, 259
CARBOLOY, INC., 259

J

JABIL CIRCUIT COMPANY, 140
JACKSON NATIONAL LIFE INSURANCE COMPANY, 247
JAY DEE CONTRACTORS INC., 59
JOHNSON CONTROLS, INC., 76
GEORGE L. JOHNSTON COMPANY, 264
JONES TRANSFER COMPANY, 315
JORGENSEN STEEL & ALUMINUM, 159

K

K-MART ENTERPRISES, 200
KMS ADVANCED PRODUCTS, INC., 137
KUX MANUFACTURING COMPANY, 45
KASLE STEEL CORPORATION, 159
KASPER MACHINE COMPANY, 264
KAUL GLOVE MANUFACTURING COMPANY, 53
KELLER, THOMA, DUBAY & KATZ PC, 252
KELLOGG COMPANY, 187
KELSEY-HAYES COMPANY, 76
KENT-MOORE CORPORATION, 265
KENWAL PRODUCTS CORPORATION, 159
KEY MANUFACTURING GROUP, 265
KLOCKNER NAMASCO CORPORATION, 265
KOEGEL MEATS INC., 187
KOENIG FUEL & SUPPLY, 59
KOLENE CORPORATION, 265
KOLTANBAR ENGINEERING, 151
THE KOREX COMPANY, 254
KOTZ & SANGSTER PC, 252
KOZAK DISTRIBUTORS INC., 187

L

L & L PRODUCTS, INC., 76
LAMB TECHNICON, 141
LAMINA INC., 265
LAPEER COUNTY CO-OP INC., 200
LAPEER FABRICATORS INC., 304
LAWRENCE TECHNOLOGY UNIVERSITY, 121
DON LEE DISTRIBUTORS INC., 186
LIFETIME DOORS INC., 292
LINCOLN BRASSWORKS INC., 159
LINDSAY & PAVELICH MANUFACTURING, 304
LINTAS
CAMPBELL-EWALD, 45
LONDON DAIRY, 187
LOPATIN, MILLER, FREEDMAN, BLUESTONE,, 252
LUDINGTON NEWS COMPANY INC., 107

M

Z

Knock 'em Dead

The Ultimate Job Seeker's Handbook

The all-new 1993 edition of Martin Yate's classic now covers the entire job search. The new edition features sections on: Where the jobs are now and where they will be tomorrow, how best to approach companies; keeping the financial boat afloat; how to recharge a stalled job hunt; "safety networking" to protect your job regardless of the economy; why corporate resume databases and electronic bulletin boards are the new wave for the career savvy; and bridging the gender gap in salary negotiations. Of course, the new addition also includes Yate's famous great answers to tough interview questions. When it comes to proven tactics that give readers the competitive advantage, Martin Yate is the authority to turn to. 6x9 inches, 312 pages, $7.95.

Resumes that Knock 'em Dead

Martin Yate reviews the marks of a great resume: what type of resume is right for each applicant, what always goes in, what always stays out, and why. Every single resume in *Resumes that Knock 'em Dead* was actually used by a job hunter to successfully obtain a job. No other book provides the hard facts for producing an exemplary resume. 8-1/2x11 inches, 216 pages, $7.95.

Cover Letters that Knock 'em Dead

The final word on not just how to write a "correct" cover letter, but how to write a cover letter that offers a powerful competitive advantage in today's tough job market. *Cover Letters that Knock 'em Dead* gives the essential information on composing a cover that wins attention, interest, and job offers. 8-1/2x11 inches, 184 pages, $7.95.

ALSO OF INTEREST...

The JobBank Series

There are now 20 *JobBank* books, each providing extensive, up-to-date employment information on hundreds of the largest employers in each job market. Recommended as an excellent place to begin your job search by *The New York Times, The Los Angeles Times, The Boston Globe, The Chicago Tribune,* and many other publications, *JobBank* books have been used by hundreds of thousands of people to find jobs.

Books available: *The Atlanta JobBank--The Boston JobBank--The Carolina JobBank--The Chicago JobBank--The Dallas-Ft. Worth JobBank--The Denver JobBank--The Detroit JobBank--The Florida JobBank--The Houston JobBank--The Los Angeles JobBank--The Minneapolis JobBank--The New York JobBank--The Ohio JobBank--The Philadelphia JobBank--The Phoenix JobBank--The St. Louis JobBank--The San Francisco JobBank--The Seattle JobBank--The Tennessee JobBank--The Washington DC JobBank.* Each book is 6x9 inches, over 300 pages, paperback, $15.95.

If you cannot find a book at your local bookstore, order it directly from the publisher. Please send payment including $3.75 for shipping and handling (for the entire order) to: Bob Adams, Inc., 260 Center Street, Holbrook, MA 02343. Credit card holders may call 1-800-USA-JOBS (in Massachusetts, 617-767-8100). Please check first at your local bookstore.